INTERNATIONAL TAX HAVENS GUIDE

2000 INTERNATIONAL TAX HAVENS GUIDE

THE PROFESSIONAL'S SOURCE FOR OFFSHORE INVESTMENT INFORMATION

BARRY SPITZ

Harcourt Professional Publishing

San Diego New York Chicago London

Portions of this work were published in previous editions.

Printed in the United States of America

ISBN: 0-15-607007-3

00 01 02 03 EBA 5 4 3 2

To Luther Andrews Henderson
with deep appreciation
—B. K. S.

Contents

Preface

I keep six honest serving-men
(They taught me all I knew)
Their names are What and Why and When
And How and Where and Who

—Rudyard Kipling

These six honest instructors have taught us how to win the offshore game by playing straight down the line and by taking advantage of the laws and practices of the high tax countries of the world, as well as of the international offshore financial centers (IOFCs) themselves, all of which have conspired to make the offshore game what it is.

The "What" of Offshore

Fully 60% of the world's money is offshore, and more than half of the world's financial transactions take place offshore. *Old* offshore money grows faster than onshore money because there is no tax "waste," and there is an ever expanding supply of *new* offshore money. Hence the exponential growth of offshore money.

The "Why" of Offshore

Corporations and high net wealth individuals are concerned with increased profits, freedom from restrictive regulations, and asset protection. If there were no taxation, restrictions, or problems onshore, there would be no funds deposited offshore and no activities carried on offshore.

International offshore financial centers (IOFCs) are in strong competition with one another to attract investors. It should never be forgotten that among the IOFCs there lurk a vast number of high tax countries—wolves in sheep's clothing.

High tax countries play a four-handed offshore game:

- as instigators, they make the rules, choose the playing field, tilt its level, and move the goal posts;
- as cops, they develop anti-evasion and anti-avoidance rules and procedures, thereby introducing elements of unimaginable complexity;
- as rivals they seek to attract offshore money in fair competition with the offshore countries;
- as wheeler-dealers, they also seek to attract offshore money unfairly through disloyal competition with other high tax countries, and in so doing they frequently cheat on the spirit and even the letter of treaty and other international obligations.

Because tax practitioners and financiers who handle offshore transactions and operations normally make more money than those who stay domestic, their professional activities provide ever more grist to the offshore mill.

The "When" of Offshore

The development and growth of offshore financial centers is an important chapter in the financial history of the 20th century. The flow of funds offshore has grown from a small stream before the 1930s into a cataclysmic deluge by the end of the century, a flow that the high tax countries have been unable or unwilling to stem.

At the present time, the newest development of all, in the form of electronic commerce on the Internet, lies at the furthest frontier of offshore.

The future of offshore will be marked by a collective attack by the OECD and other high tax countries, and the resistance to this attack by both offshore countries and onshore taxpayers.

The "How" of Offshore

The taxpayer can frequently win international and offshore tax games while respecting the letter and the spirit of the rules predicated by the inconsistent fiscal behavior of the high tax countries. In other words, best results frequently come through respect for substance as well as form. On the other hand, respect for form but not for substance is not safe because it invites the operation of anti-avoidance provisions.

Many of the offshore planning techniques used by the unsophisticated add up to little more than fancy dress, cosmetics, and plastic surgery. However, even if you use blue food coloring on your T-bone steak, you are still eating red meat.

Much more to the point, since it is possible to achieve most offshore objectives by playing straight down the line and taking advantage of the opportunities created by the high tax countries, and since the high tax countries are mounting a concerted attack on harmful tax practices, it makes sense to keep clear of unnecessary problems.

The "Where" of Offshore

The line between onshore and offshore is blurred by the tax haven possibilities and incentives offered by the high tax countries.

Nearly any country can be offshore for certain taxpayers and certain transactions. In the result, the world's tax systems make an untidy and incomplete mosaic, partly intended and partly unintended.

It may be anticipated that the introduction world-wide of measures to combat harmful tax practices will have a major impact on the "where" of offshore.

The "Who" of Offshore

The offshore players are thus countries (both onshore and offshore), the taxpayers themselves (e.g. individuals, corporations, trusts, and estates), professionals and financial institutions, and lawyers, accountants, bankers, and other members of the offshore services industry.

The "What" and "Why" of Offshore are dealt with in Part One of this work, "The Structure of Offshore." The "When" and "How" of Offshore are dealt with in Part Two, "Offshore Tax Planning." The "Where" and "Who" of Offshore are dealt with in Part Three, "International Offshore Financial Centers (IOFCs)."

Barry Kuper Spitz
1601 Elm Street
Suite 3000
Dallas, TX 75201

Acknowledgments

My profound gratitude goes to Paula Bouwer for researching and editing the material used in Part Four; to Piers Coke-Wallis, John Crowley, Barry Engel, Cym Lowell, and Michael Maskall for providing material; to the Financial Action Task Force on Money Laundering, the Maastricht Economic Research Institute of Innovation and Technology, the Task Force of Interactive Services Association, the OECD, and the Institute of Advanced Studies for permission to use their copyrighted material; and to Daniel Saksenberg, Jason Spriggs, Mark van Blommestein, Philippa Davies, and St. John Dunn for editorial support.

About the Author

Professor Barry Spitz taught the world's first course on International Tax Planning at the Jesse Jones Graduate School of Administration, Rice University, Houston Texas. He is a member of the London Bar and a Doctor of the University of Paris School of Law.

He is the author and editor of many works, including *International Tax Planning*, *Spitz Tax Havens Encyclopedia* (50 issues), and the *Offshore Service* (with Clarke) (now in its 54th issue), both published by Butterworths of London. He is currently a Visiting Professor at the HEC School of Management in Paris.

Professor Spitz has advised many of the world's largest companies, particularly in the United States and Europe, as well as a number of governments and government agencies, including the Oversight Subcommittee of the Ways and Means Committee of the U.S. Congress and the IRS.

Abbreviations

AEC	Aruba exempt corporation
AG	*Aktiengesellschaft*
AIBT	Association of International Banks and Trust Companies
APT	asset protection trust
AVV	*Aruba Vrijgestelde Vennootschap*
BRK	*Belastingregeling voor het Koninkrijk*
BV	*Besloten Vennootschap met beperkte aansprakelijkheid*
BVI	British Virgin Islands
Cap.	chapter
CARICOM	Caribbean Common Market and Community
CBI	Caribbean Basin Initiative
CGT	capital gains tax
CI	Cayman Islands
Co.	company
Corp.	corporation
CPF	combined publications folder
ECI	effectively connected income
ECM	foreign exchange of Malaysia
ELP	exempted limited partnerships
ETVE	*Entidad de Tenencia de Valores Extranjeros*
EU	European Union
FDAP	fixed or determinable or annual or periodic (income)
FLP	foreign limited partnership
FSC	foreign sales corporation
GDP	gross domestic product

GmbH	*Gesellschaft mit beschränkter Haftung*
GMT	Greenwich Mean Time
GRT	Gross registered tons
GSP	General System of Preference
HM	His/Her Majesty
IBC	international business company
IC	international company
Inc.	incorporated
IOFC	international offshore financial center
LDC	limited duration companies
LLC / LC	limited liability company
LP	limited partnership
Ltd.	Limited
MMC	Multi-currency management center
N/A	Not applicable
NV	*Naamloze Vennootschap*
NWP	Net written premium
OAS	Organization of American States
OECD	Organization for Economic Cooperation & Development
OFLR	Offshore Financial Law Reports
PGR	*Personen-und Gesellschaftsrecht*
PIC	public investment company
SA	*Societat per accions*
SA	*Société anonyme*
SAM	*Société anonyme Monégasque*
SAR	Special Administrative Region
SARL	*Société à responsabilité limitée*
SL	*Societat de responsabilitat limitada*

SP	Segregated portfolio
SPC	Segregated portfolio company
SRC	*Societat colectiva*
TRE	Temporary residence and employment
UCITS	Undertakings for Collective Investments in Transferable Securities
v.	*versus*
VAT	Value added tax

Currencies

A$	Australian dollar
B Fr	Belgian franc
BAH/B$	Bahamian dollar
Bds$	Barbados dollar
CHF	Swiss franc
CI$	Cayman Islands dollar
Dfl	Netherlands guilder / florin
EC$	Eastern Caribbean dollar
FF	French franc
HK$	Hong Kong dollar
J$	Jamaican dollar
Lm	Maltese pound
LUF	Luxembourg franc
NAF	Netherlands Antilles Florin
NZ$	New Zealand dollar
Pta.	Peseta
US$	United States dollar
VT	Vatu (Vanuatu currency)

About the CD-ROM

The CD-ROM provided with the 2000 edition of International Tax Havens Guide provides incisive tools to aid the professional advisor. Specifically the CD-ROM includes the ITH Interview Wizard, a decision aid that alerts the advisor to issues crucial to the recommendation. The Wizard can be used to document important issues to discuss with the client and keep track of hours spent on a particular project.

Also included are a wide range of practice aids in major word processing formats, with sample client letters and proposals as well as precedents and protocols for the engagement.

Subject to the conditions in the license agreement and the limited warranty, which is displayed on screen when the disc is installed and is reproduced at the end of the book, you may duplicate the files on this disc, modify them as necessary, and create your own customized versions. Installing the disc contents and/or using the disc in any way indicates that you accept the terms of the license agreement.

The data disc is intended to be used in conjunction with your word processing software. There are versions of each document in WordPerfect® 6.0 and Microsoft Word® 6.0, both for Windows™. If you do not own either of these programs, your word processing package may be able to convert the documents into a usable format. Check your owner's manual for information on the conversion of documents.

Installing the Templates

To install the files on the disc using Windows 95 or above, select the Control Panel from the Start menu. Then choose Add/Remove Programs and select Install. If you are using Windows 3.1, choose File, Run from the Windows Program Manager and type D:/INSTALL in the command line or type D:/INSTALL at the DOS prompt. You will be asked a series of questions. Read each question carefully and answer as indicated.

First, the installation program will ask you to specify which drive you want to install to. You will then be instructed to specify the complete path where you would like the files installed. The installation program will suggest a directory for you, but you can name the directory anything you like. If the directory does not exist, the program will create it for you.

You can choose to install the entire system (both Word and WordPerfect files) or just the files for one application. The program will automatically install the files in Word and/or WordPerfect subdirectories.

Opening the Files

Open your word processing program. If you are using Microsoft Word or WordPerfect 6.0, choose Open from the File menu. Select the subdirectory that contains the loaded files to list the names of the files. Highlight the name of the file you want to open and click OK or press ENTER. You can also open a document in the Windows Explorer (in Windows 95 or above) or from the File Manager (in Windows 3.1) by highlighting the name of the file you want to use and double-clicking your left mouse button.

Refer to the Disc Contents to find the filename of the document you want to use. The Disc Contents is also available on your disc in a file called "TOC." You can open this file and view it on your screen or print a hard copy to use for reference.

Word Processing Tips

Microsoft Word and WordPerfect are equipped with search capabilities to help you locate specific words or phrases within a document. The Find option listed under the Edit menu performs a search in both Microsoft Word and in WordPerfect 6.0.

Important: When you are finished using a file you will be asked to save it. If you have modified the file, you may want to save the modified file under a different name rather than the name of the original file. (Your word processing program will prompt you for a file name.) This will enable you to reuse the original file without your modifications. If you want to replace the original file with your modified file, save but do not change the name of the file.

Print Troubleshooting

If you are having difficulty printing your document, the following suggestions may correct the problem:

Microsoft Word

- Select Print from the Microsoft Word File menu. Then choose the Printer function.
- Ensure that the correct printer is selected.
- From this window, choose Options.
- In the media box, make sure that the paper size is correct and that the proper paper tray is selected.
- Check your network connections if applicable.
- If you still have trouble printing successfully, it may be because your printer does not recognize the font Times New Roman. At this point, you should change the font of the document to your default font by selecting the document (CTRL + A) and then choosing Font from the Format menu and highlighting the name of the font you normally use. Changing the font of the document may require additional adjustments to the document format, such as margins, tab stops, and table cell height and width. Select Page Layout

from the View menu to view the appearance of the pages before you try to print again.

WordPerfect

- Select Print from the WordPerfect 6.0 File menu. Then choose Select.
- Make sure the correct printer is selected.
- From this menu, press Setup.
- Ensure the correct paper size and paper source are selected.
- You may be having difficulty because your printer does not recognize the selected font. You can correct this problem by changing the base font of the document to your default font. From the Edit menu choose Select All (or press CTRL+A). The entire text of the document should be highlighted. Then choose Font from the Layout menu and highlight the font you normally use. Changing the font of the document may require additional adjustments to the document format, such as margins, tab stops, and table cell height and width. Select Two Page from the View menu to view the appearance of the pages before you try to print again.

Disc Contents

File Name	*Document Title*
App-I	Examples of Offshore Discretionary Trust Deeds and Letters of Wishes
App-II	Hague Convention on the Law Applicable to Trusts and on Their Recognition
App-III	Statute of Elizabeth
App-IV	Exchange of Information under Article 26 of the OECD Model Convention
App-V	OECD Report on Harmful Tax Competition—An Emerging Global Issue
App-VI	Financial Action Task Force 1998–1999 Report on Money-Laundering Typologies
App-VII	White Paper: Logging on to Cyberspace Tax Policy
WithLet	Sample Client Letter on the Question of Withholding Tax on International Dividends
WithPro	Sample Client Proposal on the Question of Withholding Tax on International Dividends
IntLet	Sample Client Letter on the Question of Withholding Tax on International Interest Payments
IntPro	Sample Client Proposal on the Question of Withholding Tax on International Interest Payments
RoyLet	Sample Client Letter on the Question of Withholding Tax on International Royalties
RoyPro	Sample Client Proposal on the Question of Withholding Tax on International Royalties
TrustLet	Sample Client Letter on the Question of Offshore Trusts
TrustPro	Sample Client Proposal on the Question of Offshore Trusts
CompLet	Sample Client Letter on the Question of Setting up an Offshore Company
CompPro	Sample Client Proposal on the Question of Setting up an Offshore Company
IOFC-Let	Sample Client Letter on the Question of Choosing Between Different Possible International Offshore Financial Centers (IOFCs)
IOFC-Pro	Sample Client Proposal on the Question of Choosing Between Different Possible International Offshore Financial Centers (IOFCs)

File Name	*Document Title*
ShipLet	Sample Client Letter and Proposal on the Question of International Shipping
ShipPro	Sample Client Letter and Proposal on the Question of International Shipping
ServLet	Sample Client Letter and Proposal on the Question of the Provision of Offshore Services
ServPro	Sample Client Letter and Proposal on the Question of the Provision of Offshore Services
AdminLet	Sample Client Letter on the Question of Offshore Administrative Office, Headquarters, or Management Company
AdminPro	Sample Client Proposal on the Question of Offshore Administrative Office, Headquarters, or Management Company
CoordLet	Sample Client Letter on the Question of Coordination Centers
CoordPro	Sample Client Proposal on the Question of Coordination Centers
InsLet	Sample Client Letter on the Question of Offshore Insurance
InsPro	Sample Client Proposal on the Question of Offshore Insurance
FundLet	Sample Client Letter on the Question of an Offshore Unit Trust or Mutual Fund
FundPro	Sample Client Proposal on the Question of an Offshore Unit Trust or Mutual Fund
FinLet	Sample Client Letter on the Question of Offshore Finance or Business
FinPro	Sample Client Proposal on the Question of Offshore Finance or Business
EmployLet	Sample Client Letter on the Question of the Offshore Remuneration of Employees
EmployPro	Sample Client Proposal on the Question of the Offshore Remuneration of Employees
IncentLet	Sample Client Letter on the Question of Incentives
IncentPro	Sample Client Proposal on the Question of Incentives
BankLet	Sample Client Letter on the Question of Offshore Banking
BankPro	Sample Client Proposal on the Question of Offshore Banking
GenPro1	Tax Structuring of Multinational Activities in General: Sample Client Proposal #1
GenPro2	Tax Structuring of Multinational Activities in General: Sample Client Proposal #2

OFFSHORE TAX GAMES

1. The Players

Offshore tax games are played by some taxpayers and by nearly all governments. The offshore games played by taxpayers are a direct extension of those games that have been played by taxpayers everywhere since the introduction of taxation, and remain generically what they always were. The principal differences are (a) geographic, and (b) technical.

On the other hand, the offshore tax games played by governments bring in totally new dimensions. Countries deliberately provide sanctuary to taxpayers coming mainly from other countries. They do so as part of national policy to increase treasury earnings, to develop certain areas or activities, or simply to achieve social change. This inevitably brings them into direct competition with one another.

It follows that while the offshore tax games played by taxpayers are generically what they always were, the rules of the game and the playing fields are now a direct function of the offshore games played by governments. In this Introduction, we seek to situate the taxpayer's offshore tax games in a context that is limited neither in time nor in space.

The body of this work, on the other hand, is a compendium of offshore tax games played by countries with the explanation as to how taxpayers can best benefit from the offshore tax games played by the countries themselves.

2. The Confrontation Between Tax Collector and Taxpayer in History

The confrontation between tax collector and taxpayer is as old as taxation itself, and many of our present-day attitudes are products of history. In ancient—and not so ancient—times, the power of conquest brought with it the right to tax. So too did the enforced "protection" of weaker neighbors. The great empires of Egypt, Babylon, and Assyria went further and even levied direct taxes on their own peoples. To the Greeks this seemed to epitomize despotism and tyranny. To the ancient Greeks, direct taxation was considered degrading and constituted a deprivation of the essential rights of freedom enjoyed by the citizens. Only noncitizens and the "members of despised professions" (prostitutes, soothsayers, and doctors) were subject to direct taxation.

Every Roman schoolboy knew that Cicero considered excessive taxes to be "crimes," and that when the Roman Senate voted to collect unjust taxes, Cicero pronounced that even pirates had a higher sense of honor than the Senate. In the feudal system, from vassalage down to serfdom, the dominated members of the social structure or hierarchy were commonly obliged to pay tax or perform services for the benefit of their superiors.

Hence the past has engraved on our collective psyche the notion that direct taxation is linked to subjugation, whether as a defeated or "protected" nation, or as a dominated social group. Free men paid direct taxes only in time of emergencies.

The British introduced income tax during the Napoleonic wars. Although it was an emergency measure and was quickly repealed in 1815, it returned to Britain in 1842. After a rather hand-to-mouth existence during the 19th century, it gradually became a permanent and flourishing institution—so flourishing, in fact, that it has even broken through the notional ceiling of 100 percent. Small wonder that tax evasion and tax avoidance games have become a national sport!

Income tax took a little longer to take a firm hold on the United States. The direct taxes imposed during the Civil War were abolished soon after its end. In 1894, Congress enacted an income tax law, which was held by a Supreme Court decision to be unconstitutional, and it was not until 1913 that the sixteenth amendment gave Congress the power "to lay and collect taxes on incomes, from whatever source derived."

It is interesting to recall[1] that during the 1913 debates, a number of opponents expressed the fear that the proposed law, even with its low rates, was the camel's nose under the tent, and that once a tax on income was enacted, rates would tend to rise. One senator is reported to have derided any suggestion that the rate might eventually climb as high as 20 percent, and is quoted as having said: "Who could impose such socialistic, confiscatory rates? Only Congress. And how could Congress—the representative of the American people—be so lacking in fairness, justice and patriotism?"

And so the camel got its nose under the tent. In fact, it got its nose under the tent everywhere in the West, liked what it smelled, and decided to stay. Rates went up and up—the curtain raiser to the fiscal prodigality games.

By no means a 20th century exclusive, overtaxing and overspending games were played by Egypt, Babylon, Assyria, Rome, Spain—and contributed in part to the demise of their empires. An insatiable appetite for taxes and profligate spending are as characteristic of great empires of the past as they are of our modern world. Ibn Khaldun, the 14th century Arabic philosopher, wrote that "It should be known that at the beginning of the dynasty, taxation yields a large revenue from small assessments. At the end of dynasty, taxation yields a small revenue from large assessments . . ."

Unfair and unequal tax treatment dates from earliest times and has always been fiercely resented. Sounding every bit like an editorial from the *Wall Street Journal*, Salvian complained in the 5th century: "Taxation, however harsh and brutal, would be less severe if shared equally in the common lot. But the situation is made more shameful and disastrous by the fact that we do not bear the burden together."

Increasing taxes through inflation was a well-known game in the ancient world, as were other games whereby resources are surreptitiously transferred from the private to the public sector. Calling taxes by other names to disguise their true character is a very old trick; nor is there anything new about corrupt tax collection games.

Most of the old tax games are still very much in play, but there are also some brand new games—as well as new variants of the old ones. The most important new game is to use the raising of taxes, and also spending of the revenue raised, as levers for social change. Because this new game is played along with the old game of targeting on tax saturation, the new rules of play produce overwhelmingly complex fiscal systems. The scope for tax games is at least as wide as the rules themselves. The play between tax collector and taxpayer has never known such strange turns and unexpected moves.

Tax evasion games may have started even before the first taxpayer hid his oil and corn from the collector. Tax avoidance games too have a long and continuous incidence. Tax revolt games are the stuff of which bloody history is made, while tax protest games are familiar political ploys.

3. Tax Games

3.1 Thesis

Tax games are adversary fiscal transactions where, for one or more of the parties, there is an ulterior dimension. By definition, such games have the distinctive attribute of dishonesty, dissimulation, or artificiality and thus invariably go beyond what is openly revealed or proper.

Case Studies

- Lady Godiva's husband, Leofric Earl of Mercia, promises to remit the oppressive taxes that he has imposed on the inhabitants of Coventry if she will ride naked through the streets at noon. Lady Godiva duly directs the people to keep within doors and shut their windows. Then, accompanied by two stalwart soldiers, she undertakes the ride with only her hair covering her body. On her return Leofric issues a charter freeing the city of Coventry "from servitude." Leofric's payoff does not lie in indulging a penchant for vicarious exhibitionism. On the contrary, he uses the incident to head off a dangerous tax revolt led by his own good lady.
- A few centuries later the inhabitants, not merely of Coventry, but of most of the British Isles proceed to brick up their windows altogether. The object of

this exercise is not to keep out the noonday sight of naked ladies roaming the streets on white horses, but simply to avoid having to pay the window tax.

- Ivan Ivanovich and his neighbor Boris remove the dividing wall between their houses. This is not an expression of friendship as Ivan and Boris detest one another. Rather they are involved in a tax game, since by having a common front door they will only be liable to make one joint payment of the Czar's new household tax.
- President Jimmy Carter makes a voluntary payment of tax that is not due at all. It is unlikely that in so doing he is giving in to an irrepressible impulse of public-spiritedness. The fact is that in the years before his election as president, he had played the tax break game so well that it had become politically embarrassing. He may even have taken note of the case of the wealthy French Prime Minister, Jacques Chaban-Delmas, who not only contrived to pay no tax at all but even managed to get a tax refund, thus evoking an extremely hostile response from the French taxpayers and contributing to the ruin of his political ambitions.
- Switzerland encourages foreigners to make use of the special tax advantages under its tax treaties, thereby building up a major tax haven industry. The other treaty partners, like the United States, France, and Germany suffer such losses in tax revenue that they eventually threaten to terminate the treaties. In response Switzerland enacts measures purporting to stop the abuse. However, a careful reading of the regulations reveals that the Swiss have deliberately left wide loopholes—and business remains brisk.

What all of these diverse cases have in common is that the fiscal transactions are colored by an ulterior quality. Thus they are all tax games.

3.2 Antithesis

Where there is no ulterior factor, there is no tax game. The following idealized situations serve to exemplify tax relationships where no game is being played.

Case Studies

- Take a small city state at the birth of democracy in Greece some time before 400 BC. In the ancient Greek view, direct taxation was degrading and constituted a deprivation of the essential rights of freedom enjoyed by the citizens.[2] Only noncitizens and the "members of the despised professions" (such as prostitutes, soothsayers, and doctors) were subject to direct taxation. Insofar as it manages to survive on revenues arising from indirect taxation levied at rates acceptable to the people, but nevertheless manages to provide the services expected of it, such a city state is not involved in a tax game.

- Consider Oliver Wendell Holmes and his much-quoted epigram to the effect that "taxes are what we pay for civilized society."[3] Let us assume that this statement of Justice Holmes reflects both his personal philosophy and his fiscal conduct. We may presume a willingness to pay tax and no attempt at minimizing the burden, since by reducing his contribution he would presumably also reduce the amount of civilization for which he is paying and which he clearly values highly. The ulterior quality that is an essential characteristic of the tax game would thus be completely absent. Also Holmes's seeming approbation of the fiscal process would appear to eliminate (at least as far as he is concerned) an adversary position. Justice Holmes is therefore not involved in a tax game.[4]

3.3 Tax Games Played by Taxpayers

A paradigm is an outstandingly clear or typical example or archetype. The role of a paradigm in the elucidation of a tax game is to bring into sharp focus the ulterior quality that is the *sine qua non* of a game.

Consider the following transactions, which are paradigms of three of the most common taxpayer games:

- Tax avoidance
- Tax evasion
- Lobbying for favored tax treatment

(a) Tax avoidance

Tax avoidance is the result of a transaction or series of transactions whereby one so arranges one's affairs that one is liable to pay less tax than one would have paid but for the arrangement. Thus, the situation that one achieves may, in the absence of anti-avoidance provisions, be legally correct. U.S. judges have always been outspoken in their views that there is no patriotic duty to increase one's taxes.

Case Study

A while back the 236 residents of Hardenburgh found to their considerable displeasure that more and more land in their Catskill Mountain town was being bought by religious and educational organizations and thereby being removed from the tax roll. As their own taxes had thus crept up by three and four times in the preceding six years, the long-time residents at first tried to have the property law changed. But having failed to get the results they wanted, they recalled the old saying: "If you can't beat 'em, join 'em!" And they did. The neighborhood plumber duly became a bishop of the Universal Life Church, a California-based organization that bestows degrees by mail, then called a big meeting in the Hardenburgh community hall and "ordained" all comers. Now the residents of

Hardenburgh address other residents as "reverend" and ask one another half-jestingly: "Brother, have you seen the light?"

The ordainment of the residents of Hardenburgh represented an ulterior transaction par excellence. Mammon simply turned the Church on its ear. But the transaction was lawful, and the many new reverends of Hardenburgh are entitled to the fiscal fruits of their tax game unless and until some new rule is introduced that puts them in the wrong.

(b) Tax evasion

As distinct from tax avoidance, which may remain lawful no matter how devious the transactions involved, tax evasion or dodging always involves a breach of the law.

Case Study

Al Capone, the most notorious gangster in the annals of organized crime, was nailed for what was certainly the least heinous of his crimes—tax evasion. At a time when the other law-enforcement agencies were losing the battle against the underworld, the only card that the U.S. government was able to play effectively in its game to beat Al Capone, turned out to be his fiscal delinquency.[5]

By 1930 the Special Intelligence Unit of the Treasury had obtained enough evidence to prove that Al Capone was evading tax and invited him in for some intense grilling. Remembering that his brother Ralph had been sentenced to three years for tax evasion, Al Capone accepted the invitations and made several visits, suitably escorted by a Washington lawyer who answered all questions for him. Al Capone was understandably somewhat sensitive about the source of his income, and his lawyer explained to the Commissioner that he was a member of an organization that kept no books. Consequently, it was difficult for him to reach any accurate figure of his share of the profits. Finally, his lawyer did admit that Capone had some income, though never in excess of $100,000 in any single year. The Commissioner asked for this in writing and Capone wrote confirming it, but drawing the Commissioner's attention to the fact that he was the sole support of his widowed mother, that his house was mortgaged to the hilt, and that he had a sister and son to support. It was very touching. Nevertheless it was this letter that helped to tie up his conviction.

An exposé of the ulterior motives inherent in these transactions shows that both Al Capone and the government were involved in tax games. From Capone's point of view, it is possible that at first he regarded the duty to pay tax as being as of little relevance to his operations as was the damage done to the walls at the St. Valentine's Day massacre. His business was organized crime on a big scale. Nonetheless, he was also evading tax, and it was this unlawful transaction that proved to be his undoing. The Supreme Court had already held in an earlier case,[6] where a bootlegger from Carolina was arrested and charged with income tax evasion, that all gains, legal and illegal, were taxable. In the judgment of the court, the government was entitled to cut itself in on the gains from bootlegging.

From the government's point of view, prosecuting Capone for tax evasion was colored by an ulterior motive throughout. The government was not primarily after a share in the income deriving from Al Capone's criminal operations. It was after Al Capone himself. Because the normal law-enforcement agencies were powerless, the government turned to the Treasury Intelligence Unit as its last resort. Capone was unable to deflect the Unit by intimidation or bribery. He tried both—but the Unit was not the FBI. The government was thus able to have the Big Guy convicted and put away safely for—of all things—tax dodging.

(c) Tax Lobbying

The term *lobby* refers to those who influence members of the legislature. Tax lobbying is the use of the corridors of power to influence the drafting of tax laws, regulations, and rulings. Dominant groups are normally the direct or indirect beneficiaries of the emphasis for the tax system.

Case Study

Louis B. Mayer of MGM was a spectacularly successful cinema tycoon—so successful that his lump-sum retirement payment would have been taxable at the rate of 91 percent. His plight was brought to the attention of the Senate Finance Committee in the form of a proposed amendment vaguely titled "Taxability to Employees of Termination Payments." Mr. Mayer's lawyer appeared in his capacity as the official spokesman of the United States Chamber of Commerce and gently eased through the passage of the special provisions. Under the amendment, Mr. Mayer's golden handshake qualified for tax treatment as a capital gain at the substantially more favorable effective rate of 25 percent.

The letter of the law was observed, since it met the "uniform" test, in that it applied to "all persons similarly situated"—but it is doubtful whether any other person ever qualified or could have qualified under it. Clearly, the amendment would not have passed so smoothly if it had been called "A special tax break for Louis B. Mayer and any other retiring tycoon who happens to be situated in precisely the same position."

Again the ulterior factor in the tax game did not involve a breach of the rules. The lobbying transactions remained within the letter, if not precisely within the spirit, of the law.

4. Dynamics of Tax Games

4.1 Moves and Counter Moves

The moves in a tax game may be few and isolated or many and diverse. They may straddle a lengthy period of time.

Case Study: The Trust

The trust furnishes us with a strikingly good example of move and countermove *in moto perpetuo*. Since its earliest origins in Medieval England, the trust has been used to get around inconvenient rules of law. Its forerunner, the so-called *use,* was a frequently employed device to overcome feudal dues.

Take the case of the knight dying and leaving his estate to his minor son. The lord of the manor would be entitled to use the heir's land for his own benefit until the youngster turned 21. The lord could even select a bride for the heir and, if the heir had different ideas about conjugal bliss and refused to marry her, the lord could exact a fine. On turning 21 the heir was obliged to pay over to the lord an additional sum amounting to a half-year's profits of the land before he could receive outright transfer.

Enter the *use*. On his deathbed a knight would convey the land to his friends to hold *to the use* of his son. In this way, his heir would not become the legal owner and the lord would be deprived of his feudal rights. This old-fashioned bit of tax avoidance worked so effectively that in the 16th century a law was passed[7] abolishing the advantages of the use.

By the end of the 19th century the trust was well and truly in position to fulfill its prime vocation of income tax and estate duty avoidance. It has steadily maintained its place as the favored tax game of the rich.

As a logical countermove, the trust became a target of British anti-avoidance measures. Because the moves to restrict the free operation of the tax avoidance games were domestic, however, the wealthy had an easy riposte. They duly set up their trusts offshore: in the Channel Islands, Bermuda, and the Caribbean islands, where the British Empire had carried the English law of trusts but not the British tax system. The United Kingdom then retaliated by enacting far-reaching legislation to prevent avoidance through the transfer of assets by U.K. residents to foreign trusts. At this point the tax game took a strange turn. Some sharp English lawyers spotted a flaw in the U.K. law and persuaded the Cayman Islands (ever eager to grab a tax-fugitive buck) to introduce a new Trusts Law. This law was specifically designed to open a loophole in the U.K. anti-avoidance measures. British trustors exploited this new opportunity enthusiastically. The British government again counterattacked with a new amendment, finally slamming the bolt on the use of Cayman Islands trusts for U.K. residents.

Of course, this did not end a game that has been going strong for a millennium. The trust game took on different forms, and Britons continued to express their inventive genius with new moves at home and abroad, while the English Revenue continued to evolve new counter moves.

The Tom and Jerry of the world's great tax games!

4.2 Levers for Social Change

Tax games are used to realize political objectives, to redistribute wealth, and to influence our investment policies, our trade patterns, our recreational preferences, our smoking and drinking habits, and in fact to promote all sorts of goals that one would expect to find on the expenditure side of the budget or in the criminal law.

Case Study

The French tax code gives powerful inducements to marry and have many children, but penalizes those who have a taste for X-rated movies or adult magazines. In other countries, the tax system encourages taxpayers to live in sin and does little for those who breed—but there is absolutely no fiscal discrimination against pornography.

The scope for playing with social change through tax measures is limitless.

4.3 Exposé of Tax Games

The exposé of any tax game reveals

- The parties
- Its structure
- The sociodynamics of the ulterior factor in the transaction
- The payoff, if the game succeeds
- The downside, if the game is lost or misfires

Where a participant feels called upon to defend the ulterior factor in the game, there may be a rationalization or justification.

5. The International Factor

The major development that interests us here lies in the internationalization of tax games. Countries compete with one another as never before to draw in various kinds of investments and to offer attractive bases for international enterprises. How better to seduce foreign investors than by cutting taxes through favorable provisions in tax law and treaties? So for corporate and individual taxpayers, the choice between and the interaction of different fiscal systems opens a whole new world of fiscal play.

Where governments are play tax games against one another, the taxpayer who takes advantage of this situation engages in a triangular game. The three parties to the game could be, for instance, the Netherlands, the United States, and the investor.

There is of course no limit to the possible number of players, particularly where an ongoing series of transactions straddles several countries.

Much of international tax planning consists of a series of tax games where the taxpayer plays or should play according to the letter of the law, but where the taxing jurisdictions themselves engage in competition with one another in order to attract certain types of investors or activities, and, in so doing, permit their own tax systems and tax treaties to be used to the detriment of other countries, in particular their treaty partners.

Offshore tax planning is the direct follow-through of traditional taxpayer games according to new rules and in new territories as dictated by the onshore and offshore tax games of the different countries of the globe.

The complexity of these offshore games is now being compounded by the new initiative by the high tax countries to develop measures to counter the effects of what is now perceived by them to have resulted in harmful tax competition. (See Chapter 14, "International Measures to Combat Harmful Tax Practices.")

Notes

1. Olson W E, "A Birthday You May Want to Forget," *Wall Street Journal*, October 5, 1973.
2. Thomsen R, *Tisphora*: *Direct Taxation in Ancient Athens*, Gyldendahl, 1964.
3. *Compania General de Tobacos de Filipinas v Collector*, 175 US 87,100 (1927), formerly quoted in the instruction to federal income tax forms (Form 1040) as encouragement to taxpayers to do their annual duty.
4. In 1927 when Holmes wrote, he and his fellow taxpayers were getting a pretty good deal: the rates of tax at that time did not exceed 8 percent.
5. J. Kobler, *Capone*, Putman, 1971; E. L. Irey and W.J. Slocum, *The Tax Dodgers*, Garden City Publishing Co., 1949.
6. In the 1927 case of *Manley Sullivan*, 47 S Ct 607.
7. Statute of Uses 1535 (27 Hen. 8 c.10).

PART ONE

THE STRUCTURE OF OFFSHORE

CHAPTER ONE

INTRODUCTION TO OFFSHORE

1. What Is Offshore?

The term *offshore* was used originally to refer to the tax havens off the shores of the United Kingdom and the United States, and by extension to any company or trust located in a tax haven or a country where tax can be kept low. It is being used more and more in connection with financial transactions.

The offshore scene is currently undergoing some important changes.

The main new development is the amount of money offshore (estimated at 60% of the world's money). Another very significant feature is the vast increase in the number of persons participating in offshore activities. Never before have so many offshore companies and trusts been set up or have so many expatriates changed residence for purely fiscal reasons.

Then there is the increase in the number of countries offering tax haven or finance center possibilities. In particular, the seeming high tax jurisdictions are actively seeking new "offshore" business.

Another important recent development in the offshore area is to be found in the widened scope of offshore transactions and operations. The esoteric is becoming more and more commonplace, and there is an ongoing merging of onshore and offshore.

2. Scope of Offshore

It is now, more than ever, necessary to understand the laws and regulations, the procedures, the markets, and available services of the offshore world. It is considered that half the world's financial transactions measured in money take place offshore.

One reason is that "offshore" goes well beyond tropical islands. There are now almost sixty offshore financial centers in the world, many within the jurisdiction of major economic powers with ostensibly high levels of taxation. The sums involved are huge. The most recent estimates are that US$5 trillion is held offshore. To gain a feel for the relative scale of offshore operations, it should be remembered that all central bank reserves at December 31, 1991, were estimated at approximately US$1 trillion.

The makeup of this vast horde of offshore wealth is estimated as

- US$2 trillion in offshore trusts,
- US$1 trillion in shipping,
- US$1 trillion in bank deposits,
- US$0.75 trillion in captive insurance companies, and
- US$0.25 trillion in mutual funds.

Wealth, like any other commodity, tends to gravitate to where it will earn its greatest return (in economic terms, of course, after-tax return is the only really relevant statistic). As a result of this phenomenon, huge amounts of funds have been transferred to offshore locations over the last thirty years.

In addition, parallel with the development of offshore, fiscal and parafiscal pressure on individuals and businesses has increased considerably. The move toward reducing high marginal tax rates in the 1980s has, in the aggregate, merely stabilized the trend rather than reversed it, since more subtle changes, such as rising social contributions and other nonwage costs, have generally compensated for declining "headline" tax rates. The fiscal crisis emerging in most Organization for Economic Cooperation and Development countries as a result of unfavorable demographics makes the medium-term outlook bleak. The point is not primarily that governments remove wealth from taxpayers, since government spending is equally for the benefit of taxpayers. However, governments have proved almost uniformly inefficient in their social-insurance and redistributive functions, and the inefficiency represents an economic loss for society generally. The difference between tax-efficient offshore and high tax jurisdictions is therefore likely to grow, making competitive pressures stronger on all businesses.

Persons who have not worked with offshore financial centers frequently think that cross-border transactions are difficult, time-consuming, and unsafe. However, establishing a corporation or a trust in an offshore jurisdiction as part of an international tax plan can be accomplished painlessly and quickly. Advances in communications technology, such as the fax machine and the Internet, considerably simplify the mechanics, and legal issues raise fewer problems than is generally recognized.

Many of the legal systems of offshore islands are based on English common law. Transferring money from an offshore fund to a domestic account is accomplished in a few minutes with an instruction transmitted to the bank and the costs of the wire fee. Setting up a company or trust could even be executed in an afternoon by filling out fewer forms than a domestic jurisdiction requires.

3. Terminology: *Offshore* and *Tax Havens*

The term *international offshore financial center,* or *IOFC*, is now the more "politically correct" term for what used to be called a "tax haven." However, the difference in vocabulary does make the important point that a jurisdiction may provide specific facilities for offshore financial centers without being in any general sense a tax haven.

Countries like Switzerland and Luxembourg, though landlocked, are often referred to as offshore jurisdictions. The differences between offshore countries and home countries have also become blurred. In the struggle between states to attract investment in the face of high business costs (whether the costs be associated with expensive labor in developed countries or with lack of infrastructure in developing countries), many high tax jurisdictions act like tax havens, offering low tax burdens as an incentive to business. For instance, after lower tax or incentive countries attracted a substantial share of the world's shipbuilding (and all the jobs associated with shipbuilding) away from home countries, many home countries began offering tax incentives in an attempt to lure the shipbuilders back.

At best, a tax haven can be described as a place where you pay no tax at all or much less tax than you would pay somewhere else. With such confusion, such inconsistencies, so many exceptions and special rules in the world of tax, it is little wonder that so many companies and individuals are seeking to turn onshore into offshore.

The classical tax havens generally have a common denominator of no taxes on income and capital, bank and commercial secrecy, no exchange controls (at least for offshore), an active banking sector, good communications, an appearance of political and economic stability, a favorable disposition toward foreign capital, and adequate professional advisors. The classical havens of this type are the Bahamas, Bermuda, and the Cayman Islands. More recently the Turks and Caicos and the Cook Islands have started to make their presence felt.

Hong Kong's special position has been a result of the territorial tax system (no taxes on foreign source income) and an incomparable infrastructure.

Another group of little countries, such as Gibraltar, Guernsey, the Isle of Man, Jersey, Liechtenstein, and the Netherlands Antilles, has captured a large slice of the tax haven industry by offering reduced rates, special tax exemptions, incentives, and privileges, as well as excellent financial and professional infrastructures. The insecurities that threatened Panama caused a major move of offshore companies in favor of the British Virgin Islands, which is now developing into a major new financial center with more new company incorporations than any other tax haven.

You can add to these groups half of the islands in the Caribbean and a good representation of tropical paradises from the South Pacific and the Indian Ocean, all with tax haven pretensions of one kind or another.

The number of tax havens and the variety of types of tax havens and offshore situations are multiplying all the time. This is a fascinating and proliferating species. Just the past few years have seen the arrival of active newcomers such as Mauritius, Western Samoa, Nevis, and Aruba, which recently seceded from the Netherlands Antilles.

There is so much offshore business around that it is not particularly surprising that the major countries don't want to waste it all on the palm-tree economies, and they are making a strong bid for their share of the action. Many of them offer very tempting packages.

There are probably nearly as many offshore possibilities as there are countries. High in the tax haven league you will find some very improbable candidates, like the United States, the United Kingdom, the Netherlands, Singapore, and Switzerland. Their offshore products have unusual features, and they are usually styled financial centers rather than tax havens.

Take a look at the excellent tax deal you can get by putting your shipping operations in the United States, where the combination of credits and allowances can give you below zero tax. The United States has beaten Panama and Liberia at their own game, because if there is one thing better than paying no tax, it's paying negative tax: The government actually pays you. You may recall the British government providing Delorean with a grant of some £80 million to set up his gull-wing car factory in Northern Ireland.

In the 1960s, financial institutions and banks were interchangeable words for the same entity. The term *financial institution* began to pull away from the traditional legal entity of the bank as international finance projects and international tax planning strategies became more sophisticated. Yet the single most important factor in the development of offshore centers was the development of communications technology.

The ability to communicate with foreign subsidiaries quickly and effectively opened up the real possibility of firms maintaining funds offshore in relatively unsophisticated consumer market surroundings, such as on an island. Financial institutions on the (comparatively) unregulated islands were free to enter different types of business forbidden to banks in high tax jurisdictions. These types of business included provision of insurance, equity ownership in companies, organization of new structures to protect corporate income from taxation, and the creation of new financial vehicles and methods tailored to the customers' needs.

Newly semi-independent jurisdictions, mainly former British colonies, in pursuit of potential financial center fees and jobs, emerged as competitors for the business of financial institution incorporations. The islands used the new fee revenue to set up communications infrastructures and build financial districts. The islands' parliaments passed modern corporate legislation based on their common law traditions, enacted laws insuring capitalist stability based on the English heritage, promised little government interference, and enacted privacy laws. The Bahamas, the Cayman Islands, Bermuda, Turks and Caicos, the Isle of Man, Jersey, Guernsey, and the Cook Islands are good examples of this trend.

Offshore jurisdictions also include seemingly high tax jurisdictions that allow their tax treaties to be used for treaty conduit purposes.

(See Chapter 8, "Double Taxation in Offshore Tax Planning.")

4. Terminology: *International Financial Centers* and *Offshore Financial Centers*

The term *international financial center* is *not* a synonym for *offshore financial center*, even though many offshore financial centers are also the world's largest international financial centers.

International financial centers are in the home countries of multinational businesses, which are generally high tax jurisdictions, such as London, New York, and Tokyo. However, international financial centers may also be in offshore jurisdictions, such as the Cayman Islands, Bermuda, and Hong Kong. The differences between high tax financial centers and low tax financial centers are becoming blurred. For example, high tax financial centers, like London and Geneva/Zurich, may act as tax havens, offering very low taxes, with regard to international finance or the setting up of a company's headquarters.

5. Offshore *versus* Onshore Institutions

International tax planning has matured past a point of the mere establishment of holding structures and private accounts in offshore jurisdictions. International tax planning now includes such choices as where to operate the production plant, where to locate technology development, where to base the multinational information center, and where to place service centers. Alongside established participants such as the Netherlands, Luxembourg, and Switzerland, countries like Ireland, Belgium, and Portugal have become aggressive players in offshore/international tax planning procedures.

The emergence of multitasked financial institutions located in tax havens, as opposed to traditional bank organizations located in home jurisdictions, has expanded and diversified international finance. Multinationals, through years of shifting their funds offshore to escape uncompetitive tax burdens, now operate their own financial companies in competition with home jurisdiction banks. Companies can often provide, at a reduced cost, their own project financing, their own insurance, and just about any other service that used to be sourced from home institutions.

The move toward bringing functions such as finance, insurance, etc., "in-house" is in some respects paradoxical, and it is not without risks. It is paradoxical to the extent that it conflicts with a growing tendency toward "unbundling" excessively large organizations. The hypothetical "synergies" and "economies of scale" that size and diversification were intended to produce generally failed to materialize. In particular, the belief that something called "management" provides universal solutions has now largely been abandoned. On the one hand, the larger an organization, the more management can become burdensome rather than productive. On the other hand, the ability of managers with (say) industrial experience to be effectively in control of (say) insurance cannot be taken for granted. The commonly accepted view that many things are best left to specialists applies to offshore as much as to anything.

Going offshore, especially to perform functions normally outsourced, is a decision that goes far beyond tax and may carry hidden risks alongside the obvious financial benefits. The tax tail shouldn't wag the business dog.

The financing potential of the offshore institutions now outweighs that of the institutions in the home jurisdictions. Offshore financial centers constitute half of the world's twelve largest banking centers. For example, the combined foreign deposits of six offshore jurisdictions (the Cayman Islands, the Bahamas, Hong Kong, Singapore, Switzerland, and Luxembourg) almost equal the combined foreign deposits in the three home economies of the United States, Japan, and the United Kingdom. The Cayman Islands has well over five hundred registered banks, including 80% of the world's top one hundred.

The project financier cannot ignore the offshore possibility if more than half of international financing takes place offshore. Furthermore, in some circumstances, financial deals cannot be implemented because of the tax and regulatory consequences associated with high tax jurisdictions.

A multinational acquisition or development of a mineral exploration project may need hundreds of millions of dollars of finance. A half percentage point of interest for such a finance structure may be make or break. The half percentage point may turn on whether the financial institution must pay withholding tax or profits tax on the income from the interest payments.

Offshore offers the potential for tailored financing, which has led to the development of financial instruments offering an array of variations in types of interest, maturity dates, advance refunding, and conversion possibilities. Offshore offers the potential for structured insurance and reinsurance. Many high-risk insurance policies (such as political risk or environmental casualty) could not be written onshore because of government regulation and taxation, and many insurance companies would be forced to significantly increase premiums if they were not allowed to reinsure groups of risk.

Offshore jurisdictions are not without regulation. Offshore centers must answer to the companies and the boards that choose to use them, just as those companies in turn must answer to their shareholders. Generally, the little old lady down the street is not involved with offshore finance. But she may be an investor in an offshore fund through her advisor.

Offshore is normally the domain of the sophisticated businessperson, the corporate counselor, and the entrepreneur who understand the risks associated with investment and finance and therefore do not need government interference in their decision processes.

If an offshore center attracts a poor reputation, corporate work shifts elsewhere. For an offshore jurisdiction, reputation means everything.

6. Offshore *versus* Onshore Tax Planning

Many international tax plans include offshore techniques, offshore structures, and offshore vehicles located in high tax countries. Thus, a multinational company might diversify its operations into the following sectors:

- an offshore foreign exchange loss conversion company in Ireland,
- a production plant in a tax-free zone in France,
- an offshore financing company in the Netherlands,
- an offshore international management office in the United Kingdom, in combination with
- a European coordination center in Belgium,
- an offshore wholesale purchase company in the Isle of Man,
- a distribution company in Singapore, and
- an offshore marketing company in Hong Kong.

The availability of offshore structures in ostensibly high tax jurisdictions also minimizes risk with respect to anti-avoidance legislation in the home country.

(See Chapter 2, Section 2, "High Tax Jurisdictions with IOFC Features.")

7. What Do the Offshore Centers Offer?

The principal products stocked by the offshore supermarkets are companies and trusts. *Offshore companies* usually hold investments and may get involved in trading. *Offshore trusts* protect the ownership of assets and frequently of the companies themselves. The true beneficiaries are usually individuals residing in high tax countries.

Offshore companies and *trusts* hold every imaginable kind of asset: real estate, art collections, jewelry, stocks and bonds, insurance policies, contingent claims, in fact anything at all. And offshore is not only for the very wealthy and the multinationals. Depending on what you want and which haven you use, an offshore company and trust don't need to cost all that much. A few thousand dollars initial outlay can usually take care of both.

No one can count the number of *offshore companies,* and the number is expanding exponentially. They are put there for a very good reason: An offshore company can be used for any purpose for which a company in a high tax country can be used, and it mostly does not have to pay tax in the offshore jurisdiction. The bulk of offshore companies simply collect income consisting of dividends, loan interest or patent royalties, and license fees. But many are also used for business purposes. Handled correctly, the offshore company plays a turntable role using tax-exempt income to make more tax-exempt income. Apart from tax, an offshore company can be used for other purposes such as privacy and freedom from exchange control, or protection of assets against future developments in the home country. Though companies in most offshore jurisdictions offer basic similarities, there are useful differences. For example, what information must be contained in the bylaws? Can the true promoters and beneficial owners be kept entirely out of the picture? What are the costs of incorporation? How much time is involved, and can it be accelerated? Are there limits on the powers of the company? Is there any limitation of liability? Can there be bearer shares, no par value shares, preference shares, redeemable shares, shares with special rights?

The wonder product is the *offshore trust*. The trust concept is over six hundred years old, older than company law. Trusts play a unique role in offshore tax planning as they do in common law. The trust vehicle, from the tax planning perspective, may allow a taxpayer to break the connecting factor between the trust assets, the taxpayer, and the taxing jurisdiction. The trust vehicle can provide ultimate privacy. It can provide protection from fraudulent lawsuits. It can give residents of civilian law jurisdictions the opportunity to escape forced heirship laws. However, the trust is not recognized in many jurisdictions, nor is it always recognized for tax purposes in common law jurisdictions. Therefore, careful planning is necessary. The way the trust works is for the settlor to transfer assets to trustees who control the fund. The trustees may decide on the way in which the trust assets are invested and also on how the trust assets should be made available to the beneficiaries. There are different types of trusts, and it is perfectly possible to have a settlement in which all the income is paid as of right to the settlor and the trustees also have the power to give him the capital. It is equally possible to have trusts in which the settlor has no rights at all to any income and no rights at all to the capital. This type of "nongrantor" trust may be useful for anyone planning to emigrate to the United States.

A huge and increasing volume of *international banking* takes place offshore. Indeed it is extremely easy for an individual or a company with acceptable references to open a bank account offshore, and even numbered accounts are possible. In most countries, one of the terms of the relationship between banker and customer is that the banker will keep the customer's affairs secret. In some tax havens this rule is now being widened and made a marketing feature, for instance, the elaborate bank secrecy regulations in the Bahamas and the Cayman Islands. The ironic side of these regulations is that they are so complicated that a lot of banks and trust companies require all clients to sign form waivers.

On the other hand, Switzerland, which has traditionally been the world's guardian of bank secrecy, is moving toward greater openness. This has been good for banking business in Austria, where secret savings accounts, available without any proof of identity, are the house special. Although theoretically restricted to Austrian citizens, there are an estimated 26 million savings accounts and an Austrian population of 8 million. This practice is considered by the European Union as "a flagrant breach of the principle of identification." This is outlined in an EU anti-money laundering directive 91/308/EEC, which requires banks to know the identity of their customers. Severe pressure is currently being brought to bear on onshore and offshore jurisdictions to fight money laundering. (See Chapter 15, "International Measures to Combat Money Laundering.")

Other products on the shelves of the offshore supermarkets are finance subsidiaries, captive banks, captive insurance companies, shipping and transshipment companies, licensing companies, headquarters companies, management services companies, manufacturing and export bases, and tax shelters.

A *captive bank* is a banking subsidiary set up in a tax haven or financial center that operates principally for the benefit of the members of a multinational group and their customers and suppliers. Such captive banks may also operate as merchant banks and offer commercial banking as well as financing services.

Similarly, a *captive insurance company* is an insurance company that is fully owned (directly or indirectly) by a noninsurance commercial company and exclusively insures or reinsures the risks of the parent company and/or its affiliated companies. The function is thus one of self-insurance from the group point of view. Captives are now becoming more and more commonplace.

Owing to the innate mobility of the *shipping* industry, it has always been normal practice for shipowners and operators to have recourse to tax havens. Frequently, the ownership, operation, administration, and registration are situated in fiscally favorable (and often different) jurisdictions in order to keep global tax burdens at a low level. The list of flags of convenience countries gets longer every year.

Technology that can be the subject matter of *licensing* covers all forms of industrial enterprises. It embraces industrial property that may be protected by patents, trademarks, etc., as well as technology that cannot be patented. The Netherlands is the grand master of the international royalties game, owing to its wide networks of treaties and the special concessions at home. And an increasing number of cinema and television companies are joining the ranks of the technology companies in exploiting these opportunities.

Headquarters offices are offices situated abroad to exercise certain management, coordination, and control functions for the sole or principal benefit of an enterprise or group. Headquarters offices may benefit from a favorable tax regime even in an otherwise high tax jurisdiction like Belgium, France, or Germany. The competition between these countries is resulting in the de facto introduction of more and more favorable tax regimes through what may amount to a partial system of unpublished revenue rulings.

One of the main features of high tax systems with offshore potential is the *tax shelter*, which is really an investment with a flow-through of tax benefits. Artificial losses may be offset not only against income from the investment out of which they arise, but also against the taxpayer's other income, usually from his regular business or professional activity. Skilled players are able to sit tight onshore and simply let tax shelters transform their *onshore* earnings into *offshore* earnings.

8. Anti-Avoidance

The term *tax evasion* denotes those activities deliberately undertaken by a taxpayer to attempt to free himself in an illegal manner from the tax to which he is subject. Tax evasion embraces such activities as sham transactions and the falsification of tax returns or of books and accounts. The element of illegality distinguishes tax evasion from tax avoidance.

The term *tax avoidance* implies that a taxpayer has arranged his affairs in such a way that either his tax burden is less than it would otherwise have been or no tax is payable as a result of such arrangement. The term is generally employed to indicate that the taxpayer has acted in a lawful manner, and it differs fundamentally in this regard from the concept of tax evasion, which is illegal.

The object of anti-avoidance measures, insofar as they relate to tax havens, is to prevent the avoidance or reduction of tax through the displacement of one or more connecting factors (i.e., the basis of tax liability) from the taxing jurisdiction concerned to a tax haven jurisdiction.

Anti-avoidance measures may be of general application or may refer to specific tax havens. Such measures usually appear in domestic tax systems; they may, however, be imposed by tax treaties.

If a multinational's manufacturing plant could sell, at cost, to its offshore trading company, and then the offshore trading company could sell, at the third party market price, to the distribution company that sits in a high tax jurisdiction, then why should any company pay tax?

Revenues of the world must provide tax dollars in order to enable government to perform its functions. Thus, the revenue departments seek to combat this type of offshore tax planning. However, high effective tax rates can kill the goose that lays the golden egg. Hence the symbiotic relationship between the revenue, the multinational, and the offshore tax planner.

If the revenue shuts down a multinational's ability to use offshore, the revenue shuts down the engine that allows multinationals to build up the capital and funds needed to produce cheap products and services. If, on the other hand, the revenue allows a multinational unfettered use of offshore, then the multinational's tax base may feasibly be reduced to nil.

For the above reason, anti-avoidance legislation and anti-abuse principles of law are directed against some forms of offshore tax planning but not against others. Different countries seek to encourage or discourage different classes of offshore activities. Some national legislation attempts to pull certain classes of offshore income back into the national tax base but allows other classes of income to remain in tax-free status until the multinational repatriates it.

Tax mitigation is a concept introduced by the English courts. The essential differentiation from *tax avoidance* is that tax avoidance procedures can be attacked while tax mitigation is accepted by the courts as the exercise of a taxpayer's right to adopt whatever course was more advantageous, even if there is a tax purpose influencing the choice.

9. Exchange of Information

See Chapter 7, Section 10, "Exchange of Information."

10. Offshore's Furthest Shore—Electronic Commerce on the Internet

10.1 An Eroding Tax Base

Jean-Baptiste Colbert, treasurer to King Louis XIV of France, advised that "The art of taxation consists in so plucking the goose to obtain the largest amounts of feathers, with the least possible amount of hissing." In the world of electronic commerce, the tax collector's problem lies not in obtaining the most feathers but in getting hold of any at all. In fact, the real problem is getting hold of the goose; geese have gone virtual.

The Internet simply eliminates borders between countries and furthermore makes businesses virtually invisible.

At the consumer end, electronic commerce makes the tracing of transactions and thus the taxing of goods and services sold and distributed via the Internet almost impossible. As a result, state and national governments' tax bases are, or are at risk of, being eroded.

10.2 The Lack of Traceability

One problem with tracing "intangible goods" sold via the Internet, such as an electronic newspaper or a software program, is that the marginal cost of providing an extra unit is close to zero. Since no additional inputs are required, tax authorities can no longer cross-check a firm's units of input with its claimed units of output.

The development of electronic cash as opposed to credit card systems will probably further facilitate both electronic commerce and tax evasion since payment no longer leaves a paper trail but is rather anonymous and untraceable. Today tax inspectors can check reported income and spending against bank and credit card statements. At present, 90%, by volume, of all financial transactions with respect to consumption take place using cash, checks, and credit cards. These systems usually involve intermediaries such as banks, credit card companies, or other financial institutions that leave an audit trail of payment. In the world of the Internet, such an audit trail may not exist.

The Internet may also reduce the role of these intermediaries—important to tax authorities as they report financial transactions.

Such intermediaries allow tax inspectors to compare interest income declared by the individual with that paid out by banks. The Internet removes, to some extent, this middleman and thus the source for cross-checking. Furthermore, it will be increasingly easy for the average citizen to access offshore financial centers in cyberspace. These virtual tax havens are likely to further paralyze the tax collector.

Though Internet commerce is in its earliest stages, rapid growth is anticipated. As cryptology programs are developed that protect all forms of transmitted digital data, electronic commerce will certainly expand. Consumers will become confident that their payment information is protected, and businesses will be able to insure payment for the use of their products and services. The number of companies and individuals offering products and services on the Internet will also increase with the development of legal principle and enforcement systems worldwide in the areas of trademark infringement and domain names, copyright infringement, the application of traditional intellectual property principles to cyberspace, and problems relating to jurisdiction. Some estimates are that, in thirty years' time, consumer activity on-line could represent 30% of total consumer activity, and probably a very much higher percentage as measured in value.

10.3 White Paper on Cyberspace Tax Policy

Many of the problems inherent in the taxation of electronic commerce are considered in the White Paper of the Task Force of Interactive Service Association (ISA) entitled *Logging on to Cyberspace Tax Policy*. The full text of this White Paper is set out in Appendix VII.

11. International Drive to Stamp Out Tax Havens and Harmful Tax Competition

See Chapter 14, "International Measures to Combat Harmful Tax Practices."

12. The Common Denominator of Offshore

The growth of offshore financial centers was the result of transnational corporations and investors needing to offset tax on foreign profits in their home countries. Otherwise, they would be at a competitive disadvantage by being burdened with additional costs and inequitable economic hurdles.

Financial centers have emerged to facilitate competitive business expansion abroad, exploit available capital, or gain access to investment opportunities. Together these further encouraged the growth of the offshore services industries dealing with shipping, banking, insurance, licensing of intellectual property, marketing, accounting, and legal services. Established jurisdictions and newly emerging centers developed their own particular fiscal and legal environment as they came to realize that international commerce and investment provided local growth and prosperity as well as local political power.

No single jurisdiction meets all the necessary requirements for an effective international structure. However, by using a combination of base companies (being in a low tax offshore center) and conduit companies (being in a treaty jurisdiction), the goals of tax minimization, freedom from unnecessary regulation, and access to capital can be achieved. Trusts play a major role as investment vehicles and corporate ownership entities, and serve as investors' estate or asset protection plans.

Offshore commercial and investment planning is the art of structuring the proper combination of base and conduit companies and their ownership entities in coordination with the routing and characterization of the income and capital flows themselves.

More and more it becomes apparent that the only common denominator of the term *offshore*, as variously employed, is that it indicates the possibility of lower taxation and/or of a less strictly regulated administrative or legal system governing particular entities or classes of transactions or operations than would otherwise be the case if no alternative arrangements or structures were sought.

CHAPTER TWO

ANATOMY OF INTERNATIONAL OFFSHORE FINANCIAL CENTERS

1. Types of IOFCs

There are five basic types of IOFCs, many of which are known as tax havens:

1. Countries that have no income tax or that grant extensive tax exemptions;
2. Countries that only tax locally arising income (territorial basis of taxation that exempts foreign income);
3. Countries that combine features of (i) or (ii) with a treaty network;
4. Low tax financial centers in countries offering special incentives and privileges, including international business company legislation; and
5. High tax countries offering special incentives for offshore companies and qualifying holding companies.

Examples of IOFCs by category are set out below in a nonexhaustive list:

1. Countries that have no income tax or that grant extensive tax exemptions: Andorra, Anguilla, the Bahamas, Bahrain, Bermuda, Brunei (individuals), Campione, the Cayman Islands, the Cook Islands, French Polynesia, Grenada, Kuwait, Maldives, Monaco, Nauru, Oman (individuals only), the Turks and Caicos Islands, United Arab Emirates, Uruguay, Vanuatu
2. Countries that impose no income tax on foreign source income: Costa Rica, Djibouti, Dominican Republic, Ecuador, France (special rules), Guatemala, Hong Kong, Ireland (nonresident company), Jordan, Kenya, Lebanon, Liberia, Macau, Panama, South Africa, Uruguay, Venezuela
3. Countries that can be used as low tax areas but also have certain tax treaty benefits: Cyprus, the Netherlands, the Netherlands Antilles, Switzerland
4. Low tax financial centers and countries offering special incentives and privileges: Angola, Anguilla, Antigua, Barbados, the British Virgin

Islands, Brunei, Cyprus, Gibraltar, Grenada, Guernsey, Hong Kong, Ireland, the Isle of Man, Jamaica, Jersey, Liechtenstein, Luxembourg, Macau, Madeira, Malta, the Marshall Islands, Mauritius, Montserrat, the Netherlands, Nevis, Philippines, Puerto Rico, San Marino, Seychelles, Solomon Islands, Sri Lanka, St. Helena, St. Vincent, Switzerland, Tuvalu, Western Samoa

Note: Certain countries above also offer tax treaty benefits.

5. High tax countries offering special incentives and privileges for offshore companies and qualifying holding companies: Belgium, Cyprus, Denmark, France, Germany, Luxembourg, the Netherlands, the Netherlands Antilles, Singapore, Spain, Switzerland, the United Kingdom

2. High Tax Jurisdictions with IOFC Features

An extremely large percentage of otherwise high tax countries have special regions or regimes where offshore activities can be conducted.

Ireland is probably the high tax country with the widest range of offshore features, from manufacturing and exports to computer and financial services. (See Chapter 30, "Ireland.") However, the 10% tax regime for financial services companies ends on December 31, 2005, and for manufacturing companies on December 31, 2010, and there has been a clear indication for some time that the EU will not permit an extension of the 10% rate. Irish Government proposals to address this dilemma have been accepted by the European Commission. The proposals entail introducing a single low rate of corporation tax of 12.5% for financial service companies.

The *United Kingdom* is the world's prime residential haven. The particular provisions of the tax law that make it possible for wealthy persons to live in the United Kingdom without paying tax are considered in chapter 5, section 1.6, *The United Kingdom as the World's Prime Residential Tax Haven.*

Belgium has the typical structure of a high tax jurisdiction. However, in its attempt to become one of the major financial centers of the European Union, the government introduced a system favoring the establishment in Belgium of headquarters companies and coordination centers where international corporations pay tax on a nominal basis only.

Similarly, *France*, *Germany*, the *Netherlands* (see Chapter 44, "Netherlands"), *Singapore*, and the *United Kingdom*, all high tax countries too, offer management company, administrative, headquarters company, and/or coordination center facilities that can effectively be used as tax haven entities.

Cyprus, *Denmark*, the *Netherlands*, and *Switzerland* allow their tax treaties with other countries to be used in combination with special domestic tax concessions so as to produce an extremely low effective tax burden.

Switzerland gives favored tax treatment to holding companies. For purposes of qualification, a holding company is defined as a Swiss corporation that owns at least 20% of the capital of another company or a participation valued at more than 2 million Swiss francs, to include capital gains. The ownership threshold for relief is limited to 20% of the capital in another company provided the participation has been held for more than one year.

Spain has introduced a special tax regime for a new type of holding company, the Entidad de Tenencia de Valores Extranjeros (ETVE), which follows the pattern of the Netherlands holding company participation privilege. The ETVE is an ordinary Spanish company whose primary purpose is the administration and management of participations in equity of nonresident companies. The principal benefits are as follows:

- Total participation exemption for dividends and capital gains is realized on the disposal of shares in a nonresident company, provided the ETVE holds at least 5% of the share capital for at least one uninterrupted year before distribution;
- Distribution of non-Spanish source dividends is exempt from any withholding tax;
- Interest payments are fully deductible;
- No capital duty is payable on issue of share capital for entities established in certain provinces and on share-for-share contributions;
- Overseas branch income is exempt; and
- Advance rulings on transactions are available.

Following along these lines, *Denmark* is moving towards the abolition of withholding taxes on overseas dividends in a move that could create serious competition for existing European low-tax holding company regimes in the Netherlands, Luxembourg, Belgium, Switzerland, Spain, and Austria. This would promote the participation exemption regime that enables Danish companies repatriating profits to receive dividends tax-free from foreign subsidiaries. The only requirements are that the Danish company must own at least 25% of the foreign company and that the foreign company must be active. This abolition of withholding taxes on overseas dividends could make Denmark the most direct route for investing from offshore to onshore.

Singapore has recently widened its existing range of offshore facilities to include the following:

- Full tax exemption for fund managers managing a minimum S$5bn in offshore money (those managing less than S$5bn can qualify on a case-by-case basis);
- No tax on disposal gains from unit trusts with immediate effect;
- Two-year suspension of the tax deduction limits for general provisions made by banks from year of assessment 1998;

- No tax on fee income from arranging debt securities in Singapore;
- 10% tax on bond interest and bond trading income with immediate effect;
- Extension of the tax exemption for syndicated offshore credit and underwriting for five years from April 1, 1998;
- Five-year extension on the tax holiday for the Singapore International Monetary Exchange (SIMEX);
- Up to a five-year extension on the tax concession for venture capital; and
- Tax concession for offshore income from Internet transactions for five years from year of assessment 1999.

(For further examples of high tax jurisdictions with IOFC features, see Chapter 3, "Offshore Operations and Transactions," Chapter 4, "Offshore Incentives," and Chapter 8, "Double Taxation in Offshore Tax Planning.")

3. Key Activities Carried on in IOFCs

3.1 General and Corporate Activities

- Holding companies
- Finance companies and partnerships
- International headquarters and administration
- International shipping and air transport vehicles
- Insurance, life insurance, and reinsurance companies
- International pension funds
- Trust corporations and related activities
- Banking, finance, and treasury management
- Brokerage and arbitrage activities
- Venture capital funds and offshore funds
- Countertrade activities
- Joint ventures
- Funds for leveraged buyouts
- Location for ownership of intangible rights and licensing companies
- Assembly and manufacturing
- Professional services
- International and wholesale trading with third parties
- Joint ventures and partnerships in construction, mining, onshore and offshore drilling, and exploration activities
- Leisure industry activities

- Hotels and resorts
- Property and investment and international real estate ownership
- Time sharing and holiday homes

3.2 Services for Individuals

- Offshore trusts and trust management
- Employment trusts and employee share ownership plans
- Offshore employment companies
- Investment holding companies and private group holding companies
- Property and portfolio investments
- Insulation vehicles for estate and capital taxes
- Exchange control vehicles and planning
- Investment services and asset administration
- Offshore ownership of intellectual property rights
- Offshore roll-up funds and investment trusts
- Life insurance free of withholding taxes
- Offshore banking activities and brokerage advice
- Venture capital planning
- Retirement location
- Vacation resorts and time-sharing
- Location for producing works of artistic and cultural merit
- Pension planning
- Location for tax residence and tax shelter
- Tax deferment and secondary sheltering opportunities

4. Structures and Objectives of a Typical IOFC

4.1 Background

Many offshore financial center operations and transactions traditionally take place in the entirely tax-exempt environments characteristic of tax havens such as the Cayman Islands or the Bahamas.

Offshore financial center operations and transactions may also take place within a high tax system (technically onshore) but benefit from certain special features that enable them to function outside of the normal tax and exchange control restraints; these features are to be found typically in such onshore financial centers as London, Amsterdam, Zurich, or Singapore.

In many otherwise high tax jurisdictions, the creation of an offshore environment for certain forms of activity has proved valuable in attracting international capital and associated employment. Conversely, countries that have not done so may find their international competitiveness impaired. Developing countries with convenient geographical access to major markets can derive particular benefits from the development of an offshore sector.

4.2 Typical IOFC Structures

The typical IOFC may be structured to achieve many, and sometimes all, of the following:

- to provide for
  - — offshore companies
  - — offshore trusts
  - — offshore banking
  - — offshore insurance
  - — offshore shipping
  - — offshore funds
  - — coordination centers
  - — headquarters companies
  - — management and administrative offices;
- to create a new source of invisible earnings for the country;
- to increase the inflow of foreign currency and attract foreign qualifying companies;
- to generate employment;
- to create training and educational opportunities;
- to enhance the financial strength and status of the country;
- to foster the introduction and increased use of modern technology;
- to develop exports and associated activities; and
- to develop tax and/or nontax incentive programs.

4.3 Benefits of an IOFC Program

Inflow of New Revenue—Tax and Nontax

The potential revenue sources from a thriving IOFC include a wide range of income items, such as

- incorporation and annual fees for companies;
- stamp duties on companies and trusts, registration of deeds, and certain transactions;
- increased use of facilities, such as transport communications, postal services, hotels, etc.;
- indirect benefits from transactions in the banking, insurance, and other financial sectors;
- indirect benefits from transactions in the legal, accounting, and other professional services sectors; and
- indirect benefits from the property and construction sectors.

Generation of Employment and Creation of Training Opportunities

At the time of granting permission to companies to set up in an IOFC, rules and procedures sometimes attach conditions of employment and training of local staff. This is common in the incentive programs of many high tax jurisdictions.

Similarly, in order to qualify for favored treatment, an applicant company may be obliged to create new training opportunities. For example, the Irish incentives have as an important objective that the new generation should be given financial skills and be trained in processing, programming, computer software development, telecommunications, and other related skills.

Enhancing the Financial Strength and Status of the Country

The offshore industry inevitably benefits the economy, and it may lead to an improvement in the status of the country as a financial and business center. One need only make reference to a financial center such as Luxembourg or Singapore for an example of the role that financial center activities have played in the strengthening of the national economies.

Introduction and Increased Use of Modern Technology; Transfers of Technology

It may be made a condition for the grant of special tax and nontax treatment that a qualifying company be obliged to effect certain technology transfers.

4.4 Costs and Related Considerations

Costs of setting up and maintaining financial center structures are relatively low in relation to the benefits. Such costs may include the following:

Setting Up and Administration

A number of new laws and procedures would be required in order to create the necessary infrastructure for a financial center.

A special agency or "authority" is normally created for the entire offshore project. Efficient administration will maximize benefits to the economy by both reducing the cost of the offshore program and increasing its attractiveness. Multinational operators are particularly sensitive to streamlined, fast, and inexpensive procedures.

Infrastructure and Facilities

It is essential that there should be an adequate infrastructure with comprehensive facilities. It may be taken as an essential feature of an IOFC that there be state-of-the-art communications technology and facilities. The existence of professional firms of attorneys and accountants, as well as banks and other financial service companies, is vital. The opportunity will create the need, and, conversely, the need will create the opportunity. Existing hotel and related accommodations may have to expand. Additionally, it is of the greatest importance that adequate office accommodations should be available.

Promotion

Many IOFCs engage in a major promotion of their offshore facilities. In view of the large number of IOFCs and their broad similarities, certain IOFCs seek to develop innovative features and focus on these in addition to the favorable characteristics of the country itself.

"Leakage"

The possibility cannot be excluded that offshore incentives, even if designed not to be available to domestic taxpayers, might leak across and produce lower tax revenues from any given level of domestic activity than in the absence of the IOFC facilities. Conversely, the offshore sector is likely to have knockout effects on the whole domestic economy. There is no general rule by which this "trickle down" effect could be evaluated. Detailed practical analysis is required, based in particular on existing economic structures.

5. Selection Factors of an IOFC Location

In addition to tax considerations, many of the factors that determine the choice of one IOFC over another are of a nontax character.

Key selection factors for an IOFC are as follows:

- Political and economic stability
- Guarantees against future taxation
- Guarantees against expropriation or nationalization
- Freedom from exchange controls
- Good professional and banking facilities
- Favorable long-term government policies
- Favorable attitude to offshore activities
- Confidentiality
- Strength of banking and commercial secrecy
- Freedom from banking controls and availability of local capital
- Location of offshore banking activities
- Effective legal, accounting, and administrative systems
- Favorable company law requirements
- Ability to use IOFC for central distribution activity
- Availability of duty-free zones
- Minimum import duty scales
- Good communications and transportation facilities
- Ability to conduct substantial business activities
- No withholding taxes
- Liberality of corporation legislation
- Low or no direct or indirect taxes on all or certain types of income and capital
- No inheritance taxes
- Flexibility to move out of tax haven location
- Minimum governmental controls
- Minimal currency risks
- Opportunity to obtain local tax rulings
- Acceptable level of fees and legal costs
- Availability of tax treaties
- Availability of investment concessions
- Freedom to import necessary raw materials and obtain work permits
- Security of property rights

- Minimal filing requirements (tax and corporate)
- Ability to take advantage of redomiciliation provisions
- Bearer shares availability
- Availability of share warrants to bearer or no par value shares
- Legislation permitting exempt companies and trusts
- Acceptance of trust legislation
- Ability to use nominee shareholders
- Good local directors
- Availability of qualified local staff

6. Forms of Offshore Entities

Different legal systems contain a variety of companies, trusts, partnerships, and other legal entities.

The selection of the form to be given to the proposed entity is often made as a function of the whole body of rules (both tax and nontax) governing formation, administration, and dissolution.

6.1 Corporations

A corporation (company) is an association of persons formed for the purpose of an undertaking or a business carried on in the name of the association.

The corporation laws of different offshore jurisdictions may show considerable variations of structure and detail.

The general requirements and conditions governing incorporation are important, and it is helpful to know what information must be contained in the memorandum and articles of association, bylaws, statutes, or other incorporation documents; whether a Table A[1] system is employed; which persons are authorized to handle incorporation; and who usually do.

Limits on the powers of the corporation may be important, particularly where borrowing rights are concerned, and it is sometimes useful to know in advance to what extent the powers of the company may be circumscribed in the incorporation documents or subsequently and whether there is an ultra vires doctrine. Limitation of liability should be checked.

Certain provisions governing the share capital of the corporation may have to be taken into account (i.e., the minimum issued and paid-up capital and the types or classes of shares that may be issued), in particular, whether bearer shares, no par value shares, preference shares, redeemable shares, shares with special (or no) voting rights, or classes of shares with different rights as to income or capital are permitted.

EXAMPLE

Assume that an Anglo-American type of company has a share capital consisting of 100 A shares and 1,000 B shares. The A shares carry 10 votes for each B share. In all other respects the two classes of shares are equal.

As part of an international corporation reorganization, it is proposed to establish a Swiss company, the share capital of which will be divided into two classes having the same rights as the existing A and B shares.

For the purpose of the proposed arrangement, it is considered that a branch of the existing company would not be appropriate and that a partnership would be an unsuitable type of entity.

The choice is thus between a joint stock company[2] or a limited liability company.[3]

The joint stock company[4] is the usual form of company used for business operations in Switzerland. It approaches most closely to the Anglo-American type of company. There are no nationality requirements for shareholders, but the majority of the directors must be both nationals of and resident in Switzerland. This requirement can, however, be overcome by the appointment of nominees.

The limited liability company[5] is similar to the joint stock company in many respects. However, members participate in the capital with a fixed amount that does not correspond to a share in a company. There are no nationality or residence requirements for members or directors. However, a manager who is resident in, but not necessarily a national of, Switzerland must be appointed and registered as such. Though establishment and operating costs of a joint stock company are slightly higher than those of a limited liability company, the amount of money involved in the proposed arrangement is such that this difference in expenditure is considered to be irrelevant.

The crucial difference between the two types of companies from the point of view of the shareholders in the existing company is that there are no shares in the limited liability company and the transfer of participations would be much more difficult than in the case of the shares of a joint stock company.

For this reason, the type of entity chosen is the joint stock company. The next difficulty to be overcome is the differentiation between the A and B shares, since it is not possible to issue shares with increased voting rights, as in the case of an Anglo-American type of company.[6]

However, it is possible to create a class of shares enjoying increased rights as to dividend and liquidation distributions but with the same voting rights as other classes of shares.[7]

The solution to this problem is as follows:

100 A shares and 100 B shares are issued in the Swiss company. Each B share has a nominal value of 10 times that of each A share and entitles the holder to receive 10 units in respect of all distributions, whether in the form of dividends, liquidation dividends, or otherwise.

	A Shares	*B Shares*
Existing company		
Share capital	100:	1,000
Nominal value, in the ratio of	1:	10
Voting rights, in the ratio of	1:	1
Distribution rights, in the ratio of	1:	10
Swiss company		
Share capital	100:	100
Nominal value, in the ratio of	1:	10
Voting rights, in the ratio of	1:	1
Distribution rights, in the ratio of	1:	10

The rules applying to the organs and officers of the company are often material from the point of view of the nationality or residence of shareholders and directors, the requirement of and the place of the holding of meetings, and the disclosure of names. The fees of local officers or nominees where these are required or desired should usually be ascertained in advance.

Requirements with regard to the maintenance of a local registered office and of statutory records, and the duty to file information returns, in particular financial statements, should be noted.

Requirements with regard to auditors vary considerably. Sometimes the auditors (or *commissaires aux comptes*) constitute an organ of the corporation.

In certain cases the ease with which a corporation can be wound up is valuable. Winding-up rules should generally be checked for possible problems.

Government and professional/banking fees payable not merely on incorporation but annually and on winding-up usually merit scrutiny.

In some cases regard should be had to the rules governing increases or reductions of capital, reconstructions, invitations to the public to subscribe, and the public raising of loan capital.

Depending on the proposed operations, it may be important to examine whether the type of corporation contemplated may receive favored treatment or be subject to any special requirements or restrictions.

It is sometimes advantageous to make use of a corporation incorporated elsewhere, and in such cases it is necessary to know whether there are any special requirements in order to carry on business or to have a branch or permanent establishment of such foreign corporation.

Special treatment is often accorded to holding companies. The definitional content of the term *holding company* may vary from one legal system to another.

In certain legal systems it implies the holding of a majority or the whole of the equity capital of one or more other companies. In other systems the criterion may be the holding of as little as 5% of the equity capital of the subsidiary, or simply the holding of shares in other companies. The shareholding qualification may result in the reduction of tax or other consequences either by virtue of the provisions of the domestic system or by virtue of a tax treaty.

The term *holding companies* is sometimes employed more loosely to refer to companies that are used to control industrial or commercial companies; to act as investment funds; to finance the other companies in their group by supplying them with funds that they may obtain through the floating of bond issues; or to collect income in the form of dividends, loan interest or patent royalties, and licensing fees.

Often holding companies are intermediary companies in a group structure and hence are also subsidiaries of their parent companies.

A financial holding company is generally established as a wholly owned subsidiary of a foreign parent company for the purpose of channeling financial transactions such as the issue of debentures or notes in the Eurocurrency market and the taking up of bank loans under the guarantee of the parent.

6.2 Segregated Portfolio Companies (Protected Cell Companies)

This concept applies primarily to offshore insurance companies, but also has a natural application in the mutual fund industry.

A segregated portfolio company may create segrated portfolios to segregate the company's assets and liabilities held in that portfolio from:

- company assets and liabilities held in other segregated portfolios; or
- assets and liabilities of different lines of business to protect the assets supporting these lines.

6.3 Partnerships

A partnership is an association of two or more persons (individuals or companies) normally formed for the purpose of making a profit. Such an association may be based on an oral or written agreement. A partnership can be a *general partnership* or a *limited partnership*, depending on the extent of each party's liability. A general partnership is characterized by the unlimited liability of the general partners for partnership debts. A limited partnership comprises at least one general partner who has unlimited liability for partnership debts, and one or more limited partners who are liable only to the extent of their capital contributions; limited partners, however, may not participate in the management of the business. The characterization of a partnership is normally a function of the domestic law. At times, however, it may be that this question falls to be determined by a foreign legal system.

EXAMPLE

In characterizing business entities, U.S. Treasury Regulations[8] invoke the six corporate characteristics identified by the Supreme Court:[9]

(i) associates;
(ii) objective to carry on business and divide the profits;

(iii) continuity of life;
(iv) centralized management;
(v) free transferability of ownership interests; and
(vi) limited liability.

Since the existence of (i) and (ii) are common to both the corporation and the partnership, in differentiating between these business forms, only the remaining four corporate characteristics are considered, and a highly mechanical test is adopted:

"An unincorporated organization shall not be classified as an association (taxable under the Code as a corporation) unless such organization has more corporate characteristics than non-corporate characteristics."[10]

Thus, under existing law, if a business organization has no more than two of the corporate characteristics (iii) through (vi), it will be characterized as a partnership for U.S. tax purposes.

In certain jurisdictions, a partnership may have a corporate form, and in such a case a checklist would resemble a checklist for a corporation. However, even if a partnership does not have a corporate form, requirements relating to formation and registration, the citizenship and/or residence of parties, limited liability, and restrictions on activities should be examined in the context of the general law governing partnerships.

It may be necessary to take into account whether or not a partnership constitutes a taxable person from the point of view of each of the legal systems involved.

The legal and tax position not merely of foreign partners but of the foreign partnership itself may require consideration.

In a 1998 case, the United Kingdom Court of Appeal clarified the question of the legal personality of a foreign partnership. The Court held that either the individual partners of a foreign partnership or the partnership itself could be sued in the English courts even if the partnership did not carry on business within the jurisdiction and was not a corporation. The reasoning given by the Court is that the partnership had a legal personality, enabling it to enter into contracts.

In this case,[11] the plaintiffs' payment claim was for the balance of the share purchase price from a Swiss banking partnership in which the four defendants were partners. Under Swiss Law, a general partner is an entity distinct from individual partners; it could make contracts in its name, could sue or be sued in its name, and could own property. Individual partners were liable for the partnership's debts but could only be sued if a partner became bankrupt or if the partnership were dissolved.

It was held that it was permissible under English law to sue the Swiss banking partnership in England by naming as defendants the individual natural persons who were partners in it, who traded under that name, and who were sued in that capacity as partners. In the judgment of the Court, the claim was against the bank, while the individuals were being sued only in their capacity as partners in the foreign entity. It was the foreign general partnership that was being sued by joining the individual partners. Thus, they were being sued in the capacity of partners with respect to the contract made by the partnership. It followed that the foreign entity could be sued by reference to either the partners or the Swiss banking partnership.

6.4 Trusts

The word *trust* refers to the duty or aggregate accumulation of obligations that rest upon a person described as a trustee.

The responsibilities are in relation to property held by the trustee or under the trustee's control. The trustee is obliged to administer the trust property in the manner lawfully prescribed by the trust instrument (trust deed or settlement) or, in the absence of specific provision, in accordance with equitable principles or statute law. The administration will thus be in such a manner that the consequential benefits and advantages accrue not to the trustee but to the beneficiaries.

The Anglo-Saxon trust is merely a bundle of rights and obligations in equity and is thus not strictly speaking a legal entity. Though the law of trust varies from system to system, those patterned on the English law of trusts resemble one another closely, differences usually being of statutory origin. In the case of civil law systems in which the trust is to be found, it is invariably a creature of statute and may take the form of a legal entity.

Trust deeds and ancillary or related documents should always be drafted or checked by a local expert. It is obvious that a trust or settlement must be valid from the point of view of the domestic law; however, in certain cases it is important to consider its validity and characterization from the point of view of any other legal system the courts or administrative tribunals of which may be called upon to construe it.

The rules governing the rights and duties of settlors, trustees, beneficiaries, and third parties; the legal effect of discretionary trusts; the possible role of protectors; perpetuity periods; registration requirements; and the ability to transfer the situs of a trust from one jurisdiction to another are factors that should be taken into account.

The trust is often the key element of an arrangement seeking to sever or to prevent the formation of a connecting factor with a high tax jurisdiction. Certain legislation has been drafted with this objective, such as the Cayman Islands Trusts Law,[12] from the tax point of view, and Gibraltar and Turks and Caicos Trust Laws, from the asset protection point of view.

Certain offshore jurisdictions that do not enjoy the Anglo-American trust traditions have introduced domestic equivalents by legislative procedures (e.g., Liechtenstein, Monaco, and Panama).

(See Chapter 6, "Offshore Trusts and Asset Protection.")

6.5 Sole Proprietorships

The sole proprietorship is not a common offshore vehicle. However, it may sometimes be convenient to operate in an individual capacity, and here the principal points to watch for usually relate to work permits and business licenses.

6.6 Other Legal Entities

A certain number of other legal entities that are *sui generis* to a given legal system may merit consideration as they have features that may be particularly appropriate for the purposes of a proposed arrangement.

Liechtenstein, for example, has the following entities (in addition to the company[13] and two types of trusts[14]): the establishment, or *Anstalt*, and the foundation, or *Stiftung*.

The establishment, or *Anstalt,* is an extremely flexible form of legal association that is very suitable for international setups. Such an entity may be set up by one or more founders who need not have Liechtenstein nationality or residence.

The establishment is governed by the founder or by any one or more persons to whom the founder's rights have been assigned. The founder appoints the beneficiaries to whom the net profits are to be allotted. In the absence of such designation, the founder is the beneficiary.

The foundation, or *Stiftung,* of Luxembourg law is used primarily for the management and investment of family property or for charitable purposes, though it may also have a commercial object. The transfer of property to the foundation may be made irrevocably or with the right of revocation reserved. The foundation is managed by one or more managers appointed by the founder.

A new type of offshore entity is the private foundation recently introduced by Netherlands Antilles law. The *stichting*, or foundation, has been recognized for many years in the Netherlands and the Netherlands Antilles. It has always been used as a vehicle for charitable, social or non-profit-making purposes. Realizing that there is a need for a vehicle such as the foundation for private purposes, the Netherlands Antilles legislators introduced the concept of a "private foundation."

The private foundation is a foundation that is established as such in accordance with its articles. The determining factor is the purpose clause. The private foundation may have any purpose that is legal under the laws of the Netherlands Antilles that is not against public order to pursue. The private foundation can make any distribution that is appropriate under its purpose clause. The purpose clause may not, however, include the running of a business or enterprise, but this prohibition does not extend to the active management of the funds of the foundation. The foundation is allowed to old shares in a company which, in turn, runs a business. The private foundation is a suitable vehicle to separate the legal and economic ownership of assets. Unlike a corporation, a foundation does not have shares that entitle the shareholders to the underlying assets in the company or to its income.

The beneficiaries of a foundation are appointed by the board, subject to the prior approval and direction of the founder, if the articles so provide. A beneficiary of a foundation is entitled to distributions of income and/or capital from the foundation only after his or her appointment as such by the board, in accordance with the articles of the foundation. Until such an appointment is made, a contingent or future beneficiary does not have any claim against the assets or the income of the foundation.

The most important difference between a private foundation and a common law trust is that the foundation is a legal entity, while the trust is not. On formation, the founder transfers full ownership of the assets to the foundation as a separate legal entity. The affairs of the foundation are then manage by its board. There are no specific residency rules for private foundations. There are no statutory accounting or audit requirements other than those stipulated in the articles of the foundation.

7. Nontax Features of IOFCs

Nontax factors that may have to be taken into account obviously vary from case to case. The following indications are thus only of a general nature.

Legal and Administrative Systems

The legal and administrative systems of a given country may be relevant from the point of view of practice and procedure.

Political and Economic Stability

The political and economic stability of the countries involved in a proposed arrangement and likely future developments should always be considered. This is an essential precaution where it is proposed to invest capital in a foreign country or where any funds or other assets are exposed to the risk of nationalization, expropriation, or outright confiscation. Cuba left the kind of memories that threatened for a moment to destroy the offshore financial center operations of Panama under Manuel Noriega.

Professional, Commercial, and Banking Facilities

The availability of good lawyers, accountants, and secretarial and other staff, and of commercial and banking facilities, may be of considerable importance in deciding whether to locate a subsidiary, branch, or trust in a particular country.

Business Climate

Note should also be taken of the business climate in any country included in an international arrangement, since considerably different standards may be encountered with respect to business ethics.

Incentives

See Chapter 4, "Offshore Incentives."

Position of Foreigners

It is advisable to know in advance whether foreign individuals and entities are subject to legal or factual disabilities as compared with residents and, if so, whether there is any simple method of overcoming them (e.g., by the use of nominees).

Communications

In addition to the essential requirement of good telecommunications, another factor that may be of some importance is the availability of good air and sea links and of good postal and telecommunications services. Transportation facilities are particularly relevant in the case of manufacturing subsidiaries.

Markets

It may be material in certain cases also to take into account the natural markets of a given country as well as any agreements giving it preferential treatment. Such agreements may be bilateral or multilateral and may be institutional (i.e., creating international customs or economic unions or communities).

Labor

The availability of skilled and unskilled labor and rates of pay may be important with regard to operations in a given country.

Accountancy Laws, Procedure, and Customs

Accountancy laws, procedure, and customs may also have to be taken into consideration for the purposes of an international setup. Problems may arise in connection with consolidated accounts and with the computation of depreciation allowances, which may have a direct effect on the tax position.

Languages

Difficulties may be encountered in handling and presenting material in foreign languages. It is important to establish contact with lawyers, accountants, and banks operating in foreign countries with whom it is possible to communicate in a language understood by the parties.

Exchange Control

Offshore money normally seeks to keep clear of exchange controls and restrictions.

In IOFCs that have exchange restrictions, special provisions normally govern nonresident or external accounts (i.e., the accounts of account holders not regarded as resident or carrying on business in that country) and the facilities and limitations attached to such accounts.

However, offshore operations do very often start onshore where they may be subject to domestic exchange controls and restrictions.

The exchange control system of a country is a body of statutory and administrative regulations and rules the principal objects of which are to control that country's liquid resources abroad and the international movement of currency owned by its residents. The main heads of classification employed by the International Monetary Fund in its Annual Report on Exchange Restrictions are the administration of control; the prescription of currency; nonresident accounts; imports and import payments; payments for invisibles; exports and export proceeds; proceeds from invisibles; capital; and gold.

Exchange control is an essential factor to be taken into account in the creation of an international tax plan, since restrictions on convertibility and transferability of funds may have the effect of making a contract unenforceable or of rendering any international transaction, operation, or relationship unworkable.

The problems attendant upon the appreciation of this factor are considerable, as it is necessary to take into account not only existing restrictions but also likely future developments. This kind of prediction is often difficult in the case of short-term developments and is nearly always impossible in the case of long-term developments. It is therefore advisable to seek undertakings from the appropriate authorities *prior* to investing in a foreign country, with a view to insuring the right to transfer and convert current profits and (on the realization of the investment) the capital proceeds.

In certain cases, import and export restrictions may affect a project, and it may thus also be advisable to obtain undertakings from the appropriate authorities with respect to future rights to import and export.

Currency and Exchange Rates

The currency and exchange rates may act as deterrents to using certain countries as IOFCs (for example, South Africa, which would otherwise be an excellent tax treaty conduit country).

An exchange rate is the price at which one currency can be exchanged for another, expressed in units of such currencies. Like all other prices, exchange rates tend to vary from time to time, however slightly.

Far more extensive and sudden rate variations result from the devaluation and revaluation of currencies. In periods of monetary instability, the greatest possible care must be exercised in determining the currencies to be employed with respect to the various elements of a proposed international structure. Changes in international monetary markets may result in substantial losses to the one party and corresponding gains to the other.

In the case of contracts for imports, exports, licenses, and many other international business agreements, possible changes in exchange rates require careful consideration for the selection of a currency for stipulating prices. Fluctuations in the exchange rates are of particular importance in the case of loans.

This is well illustrated in the choice of currencies for Eurobond issues. In the early days of this market, most Eurobonds were expressed in U.S. dollars, as this was considered to be the most stable currency. However, as other currencies strengthened, it became more common to find issues in deutsche marks, Swiss francs, and Dutch guilders.

The use of forward markets may constitute a useful hedge against adverse currency changes. To protect the value of future receipts in a foreign currency, a company may sell forward the foreign currency, though only effecting delivery of such foreign currency at the time provided for in the contract. Prices vary according to the currencies involved but are normally related to current interest rates.

The forward market may also be used as a protection against the devaluation of the currency of a country where a foreign subsidiary is located. In such a case, a parent company may sell forward in the amount required for the operations of the subsidiary. Sometimes it is necessary for a borrower or an importer to use forward markets as a protection against the devaluation of a particular currency.

Notes

1. Table A is a model of bylaws (articles) that may be adopted by any company if it wishes and usually applies unless the company makes provision to the contrary. Table A is to be found in U.K. companies legislation and in other systems that are patterned thereon.
2. *Société anonyme* (SA) or *Aktiengesellschaft* (AG).
3. *Société à responsabilité limitée* (SARL) or *Gesellschaft mit beschränkter Haftung* (GmbH).

4. *Code des Obligations* or *Obligationsrechts*, arts. 620 to 763.
5. *Code des Obligations* or *Obligationsrechts*, arts. 772 to 827.
6. Ibid., arts. 692 and 693.
7. Ibid., arts. 656 and 693.
8. Treasury Regulations issued pursuant to sec. 7701 of the Internal Revenue Code, Regulations § 301.7701–1 to 301.7701–4.
9. *TA Morrisey, Trustee,* 36–1 USTC 9020, 296 U.S. 344, 56 S. Ct. 289 (1953).
10. Regulations § 301.7701–2(a)(3).
11. *Oxnard Financing SA v. Rabn & Others* (CHANI 96/1298 CMS3).
12. Law No. 6 of 1967, as amended.
13. That is, the joint stock company *(Aktiengesellschaft),* which corresponds to the Anglo-American type of company.
14. That is, the trust organization *(Treuunternehmen),* which is a separate legal entity managed by one or more trustees, and the private trust, which can be set up by private agreement between a settlor and a trustee.

CHAPTER THREE

OFFSHORE OPERATIONS AND TRANSACTIONS

Many of the operations and transactions that can be performed onshore can potentially also be performed offshore. Every day, new technology reduces the number of business, commercial, financial, and professional activities that are entrapped onshore.

The following are some of the more common offshore operations and transactions.

1. Offshore Banking Operations

1.1 Offshore Banking

A considerable volume of international banking takes place offshore, and many of the world's major banks have banking and trust company operations in one or more IOFCs.

Most IOFC jurisdictions have enacted legislative provisions and set up administrative authorities whose function is to control banking and trust company activities.

Banking services offered in the tax havens are of different types:

The commercial banks offer full commercial and retail facilities to both residents and nonresidents of the jurisdictions where they are located. These banks usually provide an extremely wide range of services through their network of branches, their ability to move funds swiftly, and their expertise in handling international transactions.

Representative offices in IOFC jurisdictions offer a more limited range of services than do the commercial banks; however, they do normally handle currency transactions, deposits, and the issue of letters of credit. Representative offices of banks located elsewhere are usually licensed as nonresident banks.

Nonresident banks are licensed to serve only those clients who reside outside the tax haven jurisdiction or to transact business of a nonlocal character. The precise terminology and the limitations may vary according to the jurisdiction in question.

Offshore banking operations include the following:

- Taking deposits
- Nonbank lending and syndicated loans, including related off-balance-sheet transactions
- Buying and selling foreign currencies, both spot and forward
- Interest rate and currency swaps
- Future rate agreements
- Interbank deposits
- Fund management
- Trading bonds and other financial instruments
- Credit sales
- Factoring
- Hire purchase of goods and equipment
- Leasing
- Credit card operations

1.2 Captive Banks

The term *captive bank* is sometimes used to refer to a banking subsidiary set up in an IOFC tax haven or financial center that operates principally for the benefit of the members of a multinational group and their customers and suppliers. Such captive banks may also operate as merchant banks and offer commercial banking as well as financing services.

1.3 Bank Secrecy

In most countries, one of the terms of the relationship between banker and customer is that the banker will keep the customer's affairs secret. Staff members are normally required to sign a declaration of secrecy concerning the business of the banks. If numbered accounts are used, their purpose is to limit the number of persons who know the identity of the client.

In certain countries (e.g., the Bahamas and the Cayman Islands), specific legislation makes breaches of bank secrecy subject to criminal law sanctions. However, in all legal systems (including Switzerland), there are specific cases in which the duty of secrecy of a banker is discharged. Furthermore, the current attacks being waged worldwide against money laundering have resulted in significant restrictions and controls on bank secrecy.

The exchange of information clause contained in most tax treaties may enable the tax administration of one treaty country to obtain information concerning bank accounts that its residents have in the other country. (See Chapter 7, Section 10, "Exchange of Information" and Appendix IV, "Exchange of Information under Article 26 of the OECD Model Convention.")

1.4 Back-to-Back Loans

Back-to-back loans are matching deposit arrangements. They may be used to solve a financing or exchange control problem. However, in the case of certain IOFCs, the function of back-to-back loans is to reduce the taxable base subject to withholding taxes on interest payments, by interposing an intermediary subsidiary company between the source of the income and the recipient. For example, an intermediary company located in the Netherlands or the Netherlands Antilles may be interposed to take advantage of a favorable tax treaty. In such cases, the authorities usually require a certain spread or "turn" on the rates to create a small profit that is subject to tax locally.

This type of transaction involves the prospective lender placing funds or securities on deposit with a bank operating in the lender's own country or elsewhere, while an associate of that bank (or the same bank) operating locally or in that other country lends an equivalent amount to an associate of the lender in another country. It is an arrangement for the avoidance of withholding tax on interest paid to a foreign country and of exchange controls on the remittance of funds outside the borrower's country.

The advantage of using an IOFC as a location for the initial deposit is that the interest received on the bank deposit will be paid free of tax. In the country of the back-to-back loan, the loan interest should be designed to be an allowable tax deduction. This structure may be utilized in financing structures for the purchase of property in high tax jurisdictions. It is also used to route money from IOFC jurisdictions to high tax countries, without the use of conduit vehicles using tax treaty structures.

1.5 Eurocurrencies and Eurobonds

Eurocurrencies are currencies other than the domestic currency of the country in which the bank taking the deposit or lending the funds is located. Originally, the U.S. dollar was deposited and lent by West European banks, hence the term Eurodollars, which may be defined as an entry denominated in U.S. dollars on the books of a non-U.S. bank. All major currencies are now dealt in Eurocurrencies, so the prefix *Euro* is now a misnomer because the term applies outside Europe. The market is not subject to exchange controls or like restrictions, although investors and borrowers may be subject to them in their own countries.

Eurobonds are long-term loans issued in terms of U.S. dollars or other currencies or in terms of composite units of account. They may take the forms of loans, debentures, or convertible debentures.

When the Eurobond market started in 1963, the borrowers were mainly governments, nationalized industries, and public utilities. These were soon joined by large companies, particularly as a result of the restrictions imposed during the 1960s on U.S. enterprises with regard to their investments abroad. The market has since enjoyed considerable growth.

Eurobonds are usually issued in countries where interest payments are not subject to withholding tax. Major issues are normally handled by international underwriting syndicates, including major world banking and financial institutions.

2. Offshore Financial and Business Operations

2.1 Multicurrency Management Center

Specific objectives of such a multicurrency management center (MMC) will normally include the following:

- to exercise strict control over international payments in order to plan and effectively control the liquidity of an international group (the center should be able to channel funds to those companies that need them most or where borrowing costs are highest);
- to pool exchange risks in one location;
- to execute foreign exchange transactions at the lowest costs;
- to reduce foreign exchange risks through
  - —matching income and outgoing payments in the same currency
  - —leading and lagging of payments
  - —hedging operations (e.g., forward contracts, borrowing, depositing in domestic and/or European markets);
- to decrease overall borrowing costs;
- to house medium- and long-term intercompany and other loans; and
- to provide intercompany loans.

These activities can of course be combined with those of an international financing company.

In addition, the center must be capable of transferring funds freely without exchange control restrictions.

The MMC would be remunerated on an arm's-length basis and would charge a fee for its services to recover its costs plus a reasonable markup.

2.2 Brokerage and Securities Operations

It is possible to use a tax haven or an IOFC for these activities since it is quite feasible, with electronic mail and information systems, for the whole operation to be carried on at the IOFC location.

2.3 Dealing in Commodities or Financial Futures

The above comments relating to brokerage and securities operations apply equally to commodity dealing and financial futures. As long as there is no need to take physical delivery of the commodities traded, the geographic location of the business is unimportant, provided that the tax haven or IOFC chosen is fully equipped with the most up-to-date methods of communicating with the outside world, as well as a suitable commercial and financial environment.

2.4 Debt Factoring

This is another example of a genuine trading operation that can be wholly carried on in a tax haven or an IOFC. The debt factoring company purchases the debts of group trading companies at an arm's-length valuation. The tax liabilities of the group trading companies will be reduced by the difference between the face value of the debts and the amount actually received. The debt factoring company collects the debts, and any profits it makes may be free of tax.

2.5 Leasing Company and Plant Rentals Company

A company could be established in an IOFC to purchase business assets and lease them to the user. The user may obtain a tax deduction for the lease rent, which would be tax-free in the hands of the lessor or taxable at a low rate.

2.6 Trading Operations

There is much scope for conducting trading operations through a tax haven or an IOFC. The type of business or trade selected should be suitable for being carried on in that jurisdiction.

Some offshore companies specialize in activities such as advertising, marketing, architecture, electronics, audio and video services, computerized information, printing and publishing, engineering, and consultancy services, as well as administration, invoicing, and reinvoicing services.

Many IOFCs offer incentives for warehousing as well as duty-free zones.

Sales, distribution, and agency companies trading internationally often have flexibility as to where the dealing profit or agency commission can be taken, and it may be advantageous to establish an offshore sales or distribution company. The key to effective planning in this area is to insure the offshore vehicle is trading *with* and not *within* high tax countries. To this end, it is very important to avoid creating an onshore permanent establishment of the offshore vehicle. It is also necessary to show substance (i.e., real commercial activity at arm's-length prices) and to write sales contracts from within the offshore location.

2.7 Intangibles

Intangibles are intellectual property rights that may be owned by a vehicle (company or trust) located in a tax haven or suitable IOFC. It is important to determine the structure correctly at the outset and to insure that the rights that are to be licensed arise in the tax haven or IOFC, or are at least acquired at market price by the tax haven or IOFC vehicle before they have any real value. This is to insure that only minimal tax problems are encountered in transferring the rights from the country where the property (which is the subject matter of the rights) has been developed.

Tax-deductible arm's-length royalties, fees, etc., are then paid by the licensees in high tax countries. Similar structures may apply for other intangibles including franchising.

2.8 Joint Ventures and Partnerships

Joint ventures and partnerships, including professional service partnerships, are sometimes formed and operated in an IOFC.

2.9 International Construction Company

A construction company located in an IOFC could recruit a team of engineers and other specialists and hire its personnel to work on construction projects in high tax jurisdictions. Profits, and in many cases the employees' salaries, may be tax-free, or only subject to a low rate of tax.

2.10 Mail Order Trading Center

Mail order is a good example of the type of business that may be carried on genuinely and legitimately in an IOFC since the business does not always need to take delivery of the goods that it buys and sells. Business newsletters can also be written, edited, and mailed from these locations.

2.11 Purchase and Sale of Special Items and Bulk Purchase Companies

Where opportunities arise to purchase a single item for resale at a substantial profit, an IOFC company could be used to take the profit (e.g., purchase of liquidation goods, etc.). A similar structure could be used for a bulk purchase of goods for subsequent on-sale in smaller lots. Substantial discounts may be obtained by purchasing in bulk from third parties for onward sale to group companies or third parties.

2.12 Assembly and Testing Operations

An IOFC can be used to carry out such operations for a group. Payment for its services or goods on an arm's length basis should be tax deductible to the companies in a high tax jurisdiction using the products and tax-free or taxed at low rates in the tax haven.

2.13 Research and Development

An IOFC may be a suitable location for carrying on a particular type of research or development work.

3. Offshore Shipping and Aircraft Operations

3.1 Offshore Shipping

Owing to the innate mobility of the shipping industry, it is common for shipowners and operators to have recourse to tax havens. Frequently, the ownership, operation, administration, and registration are situated in fiscally favorable (and often different) jurisdictions to keep global tax burdens at a low level.

International shipping companies are often incorporated for commercial reasons under flags of convenience in countries that either are IOFCs or offer special tax treatment. It is common to have only one ship owned by each company for insulation purposes.

Shipping companies have used IOFCs to shelter income from chartering and other activities. Container leasing is also sometimes operated from IOFCs.

Even a landlocked IOFC can have a maritime flag.

3.2 Flags of Convenience

The flag of a ship is the flag of the country of its registration. The term *flag of convenience* refers to the flag of a country that is chosen for ship registration in order to achieve fiscal benefits (no income tax being levied by such countries on international shipping operations) and other nontax advantages relating to lower labor costs and manning scales, officer and crew requirements, trade union practices, etc. In the past there used to be considerable differences with regard to international safety standards; however, satisfactory standards are now generally being applied by most convenience flag countries.

Ownership of the ship is frequently vested in a company incorporated in the country of the flag.

In addition to Liberia and Panama, the following countries offer or are preparing incentives to offer flag of convenience facilities: the Cayman Islands, Costa Rica, Cyprus, Gibraltar, Haiti, Honduras, Hong Kong, Malta, Morocco, the Netherlands Antilles, Sierra Leone, Singapore, Somalia, and Vanuatu.

3.3 International Aircraft Operations

Some private groups own their aircraft via an IOFC vehicle. The aircraft is then hired out to operating companies on an arm's length basis in order to make a profit on operations in an IOFC.

4. Offshore Provision of International Services

4.1 Trust Services

A large number of banks located in IOFCs offer trust services. In addition, there are trust companies specifically offering trust services.

Services offered by banks and trust companies normally include a fairly wide range of trusteeship, management, and related services. The trusteeship services involve not merely acting as trustee of settlements but many other services such as acting as trustee for debenture holders or as custodian trustee for pension funds, acting as the executor or administrator of estates, including acting as the attorney for foreign executors, etc. Management services are not limited to investment and holding companies and, in appropriate cases, are extended to the activities of trading companies. The management services usually include attending to statutory requirements and the maintenance of financial records. Often, nominee shareholders, directors, and other officers are furnished. Investment management services are normally provided; in certain cases, the management of specific assets is undertaken. Services may also extend to such activities as the preparation of share issues and participation in the registration and transfer work.

Fee scales tend to vary from country to country and from institution to institution. However, there is often a fixed schedule of acceptance fees, annual fees, and withdrawal fees for acting as trustee, executor, or administrator or for providing the headquarters and nominee shareholders, directors, etc., of a company. In addition, there may be special fees for unduly onerous or prolonged administration; dealing with a business; administering real property, mortgages, or foreign assets; litigation; the preparation of investment valuations or tax returns and claims; etc.

4.2 Employment of International Staff

IOFC locations are often utilized to employ international staff.

Offshore employment companies are also utilized to give effect to a separate contract of employment for offshore employment duties to minimize home country tax.

Professional partnerships often employ staff in low tax jurisdictions for international consultancy projects.

(See also Chapter 5, Section 3, "Remuneration of Offshore Employees.")

4.3 Management Advisory Services

This type of company may be used, for example, in the hotel industry, where a hotel is situated in a high tax jurisdiction. The service company located in an IOFC could provide coordination and advisory services to the hotel located in a high tax jurisdiction, for which a tax-deductible fee would be paid. The service company should have substance, personnel, and premises if it is sought to deduct such service fees for tax purposes in the high tax jurisdiction.

(See also next section.)

5. Headquarters, Administrative Offices, Management Companies

Headquarters offices may be defined as offices that belong to an enterprise or an international group of enterprises that are situated abroad and that exercise certain management, coordination, and control functions for the sole or principal benefit of the enterprise or group. Headquarters offices may benefit from a favorable tax regime even in an otherwise high tax jurisdiction. Such an office may take any legal form; in particular, it may be a subsidiary company or a branch of a foreign company.

An administrative office is frequently located in a country other than that of the headquarters office, the parent company, or a country of operation. The role of such an administrative office may be to coordinate international or regional activities, to provide particular services (such as management analysis, financial, or other related services), or to perform a given function (such as marketing). A number of otherwise high tax jurisdictions grant special tax treatment to attract the administrative offices of multinationals.

Belgium, France, Germany, Malaysia, Monaco, Singapore, the United Kingdom, and many other countries are in active competition to attract these kinds of centers and offices. In many of these countries, there are government departments actively soliciting multinationals to base operations in their countries. The benefits, in terms of prestige, white-collar employment, and general economic development, are universally considered sufficiently attractive for a variety of specific incentives to be introduced. It is particularly valuable that large, reputable companies with bona fide multinational activities should be associated with an IOFC to offset the impact in terms of image and credibility of the inevitable abuses of offshore structures by certain less-scrupulous operators.

The two key features of headquarters, administrative offices, and management companies are as follows:

(a) *Tax at standard rates is levied on a tax base calculated on a cost-plus basis.*

For example, if the office spends $100,000 and if the cost-plus basis negotiated with the tax administration is 5%, then the deemed tax base will be $5,000.

(b) *The company must not be engaged in trade or certain other activities that are not of an administrative or management nature.*

The example of a U.K. management company illustrates this point, since a management company is on a deemed tax basis not otherwise within the charge to corporation tax unless it trades in the United Kingdom. The question whether a company is exercising a trade within the United Kingdom is a question of fact. Most important is the place where the contracts for the sale of the goods or the rendering of the services in question are made. If the contracts are made in the United Kingdom, a trade is being carried on within that country, but if the contracts are made abroad, it may be possible to show that no trade is being carried on within the United Kingdom. However, the contract test may not be decisive in all circumstances. There can be cases in which, although the contract with the customer is made abroad, nevertheless the negotiations for the sale and even the complete carrying out of the contract may take place in the United Kingdom in such circumstances as to show that the trade was exercised in the United Kingdom. As a practical matter, such a company should not send its invoices out of the United Kingdom; payments by customers should not be received in the United Kingdom; and, similarly, payments should not be effected from the United Kingdom.

Many of the features of headquarters and administrative offices and management companies are replicated in coordination centers. (See also next section.)

6. Coordination Centers

Coordination centers were originally developed in Belgium and are now found in other jurisdictions such as the Netherlands and Luxembourg.

Operating through a coordination center allows multinational groups to carry out a large variety of financial and management services on a virtually tax-free basis.

6.1 Requirements for Recognition as a Coordination Center

To qualify for coordination center status, a number of conditions must usually be satisfied.

International Group

The coordination center must form part of an international group of affiliated companies with a very substantial aggregate capital and annual turnover. A group is normally defined to include all companies in which the common shareholdings, direct or indirect, represent a certain minimum percentage of capital.

Exclusion of Financial Institutions

Banks, insurance companies, and certain other financial institutions may be excluded from establishing a coordination center.

Qualifying Activities

The activities that may be carried out in a coordination center are normally restricted to activities that are specifically authorized.

Employment Requirements

It is normally a condition for coordination center status that the coordination center have a specified number of full-time employees.

There is normally no condition as to the citizenship or rank of the employees. Generally, personnel transferred from an affiliated company may be counted toward fulfillment of the employee requirement.

6.2 Tax Concessions for Coordination Centers

Corporation Income Taxes

Coordination centers are typically subject to tax on a notional base only. The tax base is determined as a percentage of certain operating costs borne by the coordination center. However, personnel costs and financing costs may be excluded from the calculation of the notional tax base.

The percentage to be applied to the remaining costs depends upon the markup applied by the coordination center itself in charging affiliated companies for its services. This leaves the discretion to the center itself, within certain parameters, to determine the formula for the notional tax system. Corporation tax will be calculated according to the normal rate on the tax base computed in this manner.

The arm's-length character of internal group payments forming part of the taxable base should be determined by comparing them to similar operations carried out between unrelated parties. Provided that the terms offered by the coordination center to group members are no less favorable than those applied between independent parties, there would be no problem.

Exemption from Withholding Taxes

Coordination centers are normally not subject to withholding taxes.

In application of this principle, all payments of dividends, interest, and royalties by a coordination center are excluded from application of the normal withholding tax.

It is also recognized that coordination centers may receive investment income. For this reason, payments of interest on deposits made by coordination centers with banks and other financial institutions may be exempt from withholding tax.

6.3 Concessions for Expatriate Employees of Coordination Centers

Foreign executives and researchers are normally exempted from the requirement to obtain a work permit.

Foreign executives, researchers, and other specialists who meet the requirements for nonresident status are normally entitled to substantial concessions for personal income taxes.

These concessions consist principally in the exclusion from personal income tax of a variety of expatriate allowances representing the special cost of living allowances, housing allowances, tuition, and home leave grants, as well as tax equalization payments.

6.4 Procedure for Coordination Center Recognition

Coordination center concessions are not normally automatic but are granted only on the basis of a written request followed by a favorable decision by the relevant department.

The request for recognition should contain a detailed description of all the activities of coordination and centralization that are intended for the center. Applicants are usually also encouraged to include activities that are not planned for the initial stages of operations but might be added later on.

Once the department is satisfied that all conditions are met, formal recognition will be granted for the coordination center during a fixed period.

6.5 Broad Range of Uses for Coordination Centers

The principal attraction of the coordination center system is that it allows, besides support services to group members, a broad range of sophisticated intragroup financing to be carried out in a virtually tax-free environment. These latter operations include leasing, reinvoicing, and factoring as well as more traditional group lending activities.

Multinationals have found a great variety of uses for coordination centers. The system permits each multinational to construct a "tailor-made" coordination center as a function of its present and future needs, provided that services are performed solely for the benefit of group members.

As a general rule, a coordination center may centralize specific activities for affiliated companies, charge affiliates for such services, and even recover a profit margin on a "cost-plus" formula. However, the center may not perform services for other companies that are not members of the group.

The activities that can be carried out by coordination centers generally fall into two principal categories:

1. support services rendered directly to other members of the group; and
2. financial services provided indirectly through intercompany transactions.

Support Services Rendered Directly to Group Members

The first category comprises a variety of support services provided directly to other group members. Such centralized services make unnecessary the duplication of the same activities in a variety of different locations. This increases efficiency and can result in important cost savings.

Services in this category are normally charged directly by the coordination center to the affiliated companies that receive them. Generally, such charges are based on the costs incurred by the center in carrying out the services, often with a small profit margin calculated according to a cost-plus formula. Activities that fall into this category include the following:

- Advertising and sales promotion
- Collection and dissemination of information
- Insurance and reinsurance
- Scientific research
- Accounting, administrative, and electronic data processing activities
- Preparatory and auxiliary activities

Financial Services Provided Indirectly Through Intercompany Transactions

The second major category of activities carried out in coordination centers consists of intercompany transactions with the objective to centralize financial management and the hedging of foreign exchange risks.

A common feature of these activities is that they are not rendered directly by the coordination center and invoiced as management services to the affiliated companies of the group. Instead these services are carried out in the form of intercompany transactions, such as leasing and factoring. The coordination center covers its costs with revenues from the transactions themselves. Such revenues take a variety of forms (interest, lease payments, etc.) depending on the nature of the particular transactions.

This category of activities enables multinational companies to carry out a variety of centralized financing operations in a favorable tax climate and to take advantage of the country's network of tax treaties.

Activities that fall into this category include the following:

- Reinvoicing
- Factoring
- Leasing
- Financing

The advantages of a group using a coordination center are, above all,

- to provide centralized support services to other members of the group, thus taking advantage of "economies of scale,"
- to meet the various financing needs of group members by taking advantage of the absence of withholding taxes, of double taxation treaties, and of a virtually tax-free environment, and
- to provide foreign-exchange risk hedging to group members and indeed to reduce the risk itself, with no exchange control restrictions, by aggregating a variety of sources of fluctuations.

7. Offshore Licensing

7.1 In General

Technology that can be the subject matter of licensing covers all forms of industrial enterprise. It embraces industrial property that may be protected by patents, trademarks, etc., as well as technology that cannot be patented.

Industrial enterprises frequently exploit their technology by transferring it to licensing companies in tax havens so that royalties and other sums may be received by the licensing company from related companies or third parties, thus reducing the total tax burden.

The anti-avoidance provisions of certain developed countries have limited the use of tax havens for this purpose.

When it comes to international licensing, a suitable country for sublicensing arrangements would require the following elements:

(a) a usable tax treaty or network of treaties;

(b) the reduction in withholding taxes that are normally levied abroad on royalties paid to a licensing company, pursuant to the tax treaty or treaties negotiated by that country;

(c) the concessions given to group or other licensing companies by the tax administration in that country on the spread of taxable income receivable; and

(d) the absence of any withholding tax on the onward payment of royalties to any nonresident.

7.2 The Netherlands Licensing Structure

The benefits of using a Netherlands licensing company lie, above all, in the reduced rates of withholding in treaty countries. The withholding rates for royalty payments under many of the treaties concluded with the Netherlands are either zero or very low. There is no withholding tax in the Netherlands on payments of royalties.

A choice that would normally have to be made would be between

(a) obtaining a ruling that is issued in appropriate cases by the Netherlands Tax Administration, or

(b) simply using a third party bona fide resident company or individual in the Netherlands for this purpose.

In the usual structure, a related Netherlands licensing company would sublicense the rights.

The Netherlands Tax Administration usually gives a ruling fixing the taxable base of a licensing company that is a related party to the principal licensor. The administration normally requires, as the taxable base, a minimum spread between royalties received and royalties paid as follows:

On income of up to Dfl 2 million pa: 7%

Between Dfl 2 million pa and Dfl 4 million pa: 6%

Between Dfl 4 million pa and Dfl 6 million pa: 5%

Between Dfl 6 million pa and Dfl 8 million pa: 4%

Between Dfl 8 million pa and Dfl 10 million pa: 3%

On income of Dfl 10 million pa upward: 2%

The required spread is calculated on the incoming royalties (net of foreign withholding taxes), and the Netherlands tax is then imposed at the rate of 35% on the spread.

In the case of such a ruling, the tax base is fixed and no deductions for expenditure would be allowed.

In an alternative structure in which the Netherlands licensing vehicle is not related to the royalty payer or the ultimate recipient, then the royalties paid and received can be those commercially acceptable in the case of any other company in the same type of business, however small the tax base.

In such a case, the normal tax law applies, and the commercial profits of the Netherlands recipient would be taxed at the usual rate of 35%. The tax base would be the reality of the profits. The spread could then be a fraction of a percent (instead of according to the formula of 7% decreasing by slices to 2%). This would be the gross tax base from which could be deducted any normal business expenditure relating to the running of the company.

The overall Netherlands tax burden in such a case could be very small indeed. However, no advance ruling could be obtained.

8. Offshore Insurance

8.1 Offshore Captive Insurance Companies

The term *captive insurance company* is used to refer to an insurance company that is owned (directly or indirectly) by a noninsurance commercial company and exclusively insures or reinsures the risks of the parent company and/or its affiliated companies. The function is thus one of self-insurance from the group point of view. The underlying reasons for the formation of foreign captive insurance companies are usually of an insurance and business nature quite apart from any fiscal benefits that may accrue.

Foreign captive insurance companies are located in a certain number of tax havens, in particular, in Bermuda, and to a lesser extent in the Bahamas, the Cayman Islands, Guernsey, Hong Kong, the Isle of Man, Jersey, Panama, and Vanuatu. A major reason for using one of these jurisdictions is to obtain freedom from the onerous requirements and restrictions of insurance legislation in the principal countries where the group operates.

A foreign captive insurance company may be used to insure against certain risks that the normal insurance market will not accept or to obtain broader types of insurance that the commercial insurance companies do not have the flexibility to provide.

Money savings can be achieved through the use of reinsurance as opposed to direct insurance. Also, as distinct from direct insurance where premiums are paid in advance, payments by a captive insurance company to a reinsurance company are generally made at the close of a predetermined period.

Furthermore, captive insurance companies located in IOFC jurisdictions are often not subject to the same controls as insurance companies located in the country of the parent company and can invest surplus accumulations relatively freely, including investments for the direct or indirect benefit of the parent company or other affiliated companies.

An offshore captive insurance company is thus a limited-purpose, wholly owned insurance subsidiary, which has as its primary function the insuring of some of the exposures and risks of its parent and the parent's affiliates. A protected cell company or segregated portfolio company may also be used. (See Chapter 2, Section 6.2, "Segregated Portfolio Companies.")

A captive thus usually takes the form of a wholly owned foreign subsidiary incorporated in a jurisdiction that levies little or no foreign tax on premiums or investment income from the insurance of the worldwide risks of the captive's parent and related domestic or foreign subsidiaries. Thus tax advantages may be obtained through the deductibility of premiums.

Apart from any fiscal benefits that may accrue, the objectives of setting up a foreign captive insurance company are of an insurance and business nature, such as meeting insurance needs, providing a funding mechanism, reducing the price cycle, obtaining an acceptable rating, obtaining cover in certain particularly difficult cases, and obtaining adequate service.

8.2 Tax Considerations

Tax legislation in most jurisdictions makes a sharp distinction between insurance premiums (which are tax deductible) and risk-related provisions (which are not).

From a business point of view, there is no material difference (although provisions can provide the equivalent of insurance only for large companies with highly diversified risks). Yet the rule makes a company's risk-management strategy entirely dependent on the vagaries of an insurance market that is unable to provide adequate cover for a whole series of significant risks.

Captive insurance is a powerful tool to solve, at least partly, this problem. The tax benefit is obvious: Paying premiums to an offshore subsidiary in effect makes provisions tax deductible. However, this in itself makes no contribution to improved insurance cover (leading some jurisdictions to disallow premiums paid to captive subsidiaries that do not spread and transfer risk). The decision to set up an offshore captive insurance company, while ostensibly a tax planning tool, should in fact be primarily driven by insurance considerations.

Most high tax countries seek to limit the tax advantages, but even on an arm's-length basis these can be significant. Generally, a company can deduct insurance premiums as expenses to reduce its taxable income if the premiums are ordinary and necessary to the conduct of its business.

One major attack the courts have aimed at companies attempting to convert nondeductible self-insurance reserves into deductible self-funding arrangements with bona fide insurance companies is that the premium payments made to the insurer are not, in fact, premium payments for insurance, but payments into a self-insurance reserve merely held by the insurer as agent of the insured and thus not deductible.

Before an insurance payment can be classified as a premium, two essential factors must be present: *risk shifting* and *risk distribution*. To shift the risk, the insured must transfer it to another who has the financial capacity to make good the losses. Distribution of the risk is a device by which the insurer combines large numbers of unrelated risks and thus reduces the risk through the law of probability.

8.3 The Reinsurance Market

The reinsurance market usually enables the buyer to obtain a more attractive discount or credit for his self-retention than would be possible from the direct insurance market. The main reason for the differential between these two parts of the insurance industry is that the direct insurer has very considerable expenses, most of which are funded by the premium he receives from the low-level loss area. On the other hand, the reinsurer has minimum expenses, since the services it provides are not as comprehensive as those that the direct insurer has to provide to its customers, and particularly to its private customers, who need much greater attention and service than the major industrial buyer.

Companies considering the establishment of captive insurance companies recognize that one of the major advantages is access to the reinsurance market.

8.4 The Management Decision

There is a limit to the extent to which risks can be shifted and diluted. Ultimately, there is one reinsurance market with a finite number of operators and a finite amount of capital. As shown by the Lloyd's debacle of the early 1990s, that market can collapse if its cover is incorrectly priced or if it is dealing with risks that do not obey the law of large numbers. Captives may be more efficient than outside insurance, but they cannot escape the market altogether.

The option of setting up a captive insurance company should be screened by reference to the following considerations:

(a) the savings, both short- and long-term, in insurance premiums, and their impact on cash flow, taking account of investment income on the savings;
(b) future developments in the insurance market, to the extent they can be anticipated;
(c) the impact the captive will have on loss control in the company;
(d) whether the captive will improve the insurance cover available to the company; and
(e) whether the captive will improve the company's overall risk financing strategy. In this context, account should be taken of any problems of local implementation throughout the world, opportunities to optimize the funding mechanism, the tax position, and the implementation of an overall risk retention program.

8.5 Implementation

Implementation of an offshore captive insurance strategy requires a clear decision concerning

(a) the most suitable location of the captive, taking into account the most important factors, such as convenience, government attitude, and taxation;
(b) whether the multinational company should manage the captive itself or use outside services;
(c) the tax implications of the decision in relation to both the captive location that is being considered and the attitude of the country's domestic revenue authorities;
(d) whether the fronting companies will require parental guarantees or letters of credit;
(e) whether there are any international problems in the form of insurance legislative difficulties, exchange control, or political problems that need to be taken into account;
(f) the political considerations to be taken into account both domestically and elsewhere in the world;

(g) in relation to the risks that the captive will be retaining and its overall exposure, the needs for capitalization and the attitudes of the company to solvency margin (i.e., the ratio between total assets—weighted for differential liquidity where appropriate—and total insured risk—net of reinsurance where appropriate); and

(h) whether there are any exchange control restrictions that need to be taken into account in relation to capitalizing the captive both from the company's domicile and to the location that is being chosen.

8.6 Choice of Location of the Captive (Domestic or Offshore)

In principle there is no reason why a captive insurance company cannot be established in any country where insurance legislation permits insurance companies to operate. From a practical point of view, domestic captives, located in the country of origin of the parent, are usually subject to additional legislation, high capitalization, high taxation, and the onerous data requirements of the authorities. There may, however, be cases in which, for political reasons, it is necessary to form the captive domestically, particularly if the parent company is government owned or the government has a substantial shareholding.

One of the benefits of the domestic captive is that it is convenient from an operational point of view and can be managed within the operations of the parent corporation. A possible disadvantage, however, is that in some parts of the world the domestic captive may not be able to select the risks that would be most beneficial, since there may be some pressure from the authorities for it to participate in other classes. This is a particular problem in countries where there is a method of sharing substandard risks for compulsory insurances through the whole insurance community. The captive in this environment might be involved automatically in underwriting outside business of an undesirable underwriting nature.

Most captives are located offshore in an environment that is reasonably free of legislative restraints and has a low taxation position. This offers clear benefits in relation to the buildup of reserves, reduction of management time, and the cost and speed of establishment. In many of these offshore locations it would be possible to form a captive within thirty days and to render information to the authorities on a very limited basis and in total confidence. However, even in IOFCs insurance legislation is a factor that needs to be taken into account when deciding on the best location so far as the parent company is concerned.

9. Offshore Funds and International Investment Trusts

9.1 Offshore Funds

An offshore fund is generally an investment company, unit trust (a trust in which the investing public are the beneficiaries), mutual fund, or other entity usually incorporated and resident in an IOFC. The fund may be open-ended or closed.

The majority of offshore funds are open-ended investment companies; however, funds may take any of the forms permitted by the legal system or systems concerned. The more popular locations for offshore funds are Bermuda, the Cayman Islands, Guernsey, Hong Kong, the Isle of Man, Jersey, and Luxembourg.

Offshore funds generally enjoy greater investment flexibility than do funds located in high tax countries. However, there is a growing tendency to require greater disclosure and, generally, to tighten the regulations governing offshore funds.

The bulk of investors in offshore funds are residents or citizens of high tax countries, many of which severely restrict the local marketing activities of funds.

The fund will be designed to be free of income tax in its chosen location, and it may be able to make bank deposits and other investments without suffering withholding taxes in the source country. The fund will also be designed to be exempt from tax on any capital gains arising from the sale of investments.

Funds located in suitable IOFCs have been used to raise low cost finance (e.g., by way of preference shares in bearer form); to invest in zero coupon bonds, as well as growth stocks and securities on behalf of foreign investors; to raise venture capital finance; to raise funds for use in leveraged and management buyouts; to act as offshore multicurrency roll-up funds; and to invest in gilt-edged stocks. Other activities include equity funds, bond funds, and funds specializing in particular sectors.

Umbrella offshore funds have been introduced to offer investors the possibility of investing in different portfolios. These may offer a variety of investment strategies incorporated in a single investment vehicle.

An offshore fund located in a suitable IOFC will generally be "managed" by a management company owned by the fund's promoters. Such a management company may also be located in the same IOFC as the offshore fund or possibly in another favorable IOFC location.

Alternatively, or in addition, the fund may enter into a professional services agreement with an independent broker, advisor, or merchant bank located in another international financial center for the provision of investment advice at a fee based on market rates.

9.2 International Investment Trusts

Since mutual funds and unit trusts are to be found in high tax jurisdictions and since investors too are to be found onshore as well as offshore, the laws governing the onshore taxation and regulation of onshore investment trusts will, of necessity, seek to accommodate the requirements of the onshore investor.

Minimizing the tax burden on the international transactions of an onshore investment fund (as distinct from genuine inflows from, and outflows to, investors) will typically be a key objective.

Collective investment is a huge, highly technical, and fast-developing sector. It is a useful indicator of the way in which business issues, including tax, should be seen within a wider economic and even political context. Recent developments have been driven primarily by two objectives:

1. to stimulate saving and investment in order to promote economic growth and job creation, and
2. to reduce the demographic pressure on unfunded entitlement schemes by encouraging collective investment-based provision for retirement benefits.

Favorable treatment for schemes such as pension funds is explained by their perceived ability to contribute simultaneously to both these objectives. Conversely, their failure to do so would certainly trigger significant changes in the rules.

The use of specific incentives for tax-planning purposes is inseparable from anti-avoidance issues. Any scheme promoting investment funds could also, prima facie, provide an opportunity for money laundering, even without any genuine saving element. Many of the complications in the regulations of high tax jurisdictions derive specifically from attempts to prevent such "nonsaving" use.

CHAPTER FOUR

OFFSHORE INCENTIVES

1. Tax Incentives in Offshore Tax Planning

Tax incentives may convert otherwise high tax countries into limited purpose tax havens.

Tax incentives are tax concessions that are granted to attract local or foreign investment capital to particular activities or areas. Nearly all countries grant tax incentives of some kind as part of their general or regional economic development programs.

As the legal and tax systems of different countries and the economic exigencies that lie behind the tax incentives vary inter se, so too do the form and the scope of the incentives. The benefits that may be derived from tax incentives must be judged against their total background.

Since *offshore* does by definition imply that there is a tax (or other) deal available elsewhere that is better than if one stayed within the confines of the normal tax or regulatory system, tax incentives do by their very nature introduce an offshore factor into the planning equation.

The attacks by the OECD and the European Union on what are becoming known as "harmful preferential tax regimes" are likely to curtail the proliferation and operation of tax incentives. (See Chapter 14, "International Measures to Combat Harmful Tax Practices.")

2. Categories of Tax Incentives

Most tax incentive measures fall into one or more of the following categories:

- Tax exemption (tax holiday)
- Deduction from the taxable base
- Reduction in the rate of tax
- Tax deferral

2.1 Tax Exemption

The tax exemption, or tax holiday, is the most valuable form of tax incentive. However, it may be subject to important conditions. Furthermore, in the absence of official undertakings or guarantees against future taxes for a specified period, an exemption may fail to attract long-term investment capital.

2.2 Deduction from the Taxable Base

A deduction from the taxable base is the most frequently encountered form of tax incentive. It is granted with respect to expenditure and losses that would not normally be deductible under the general principles of the tax system.

Common examples of such deductions are allowances granted in cases of expenditure on industrial buildings and structures, machinery and plant, hotels, foreign market development, industrial and intellectual rights, scientific research, and training of staff.

Many of these allowances are depreciation allowances. They may be in the form of

- an *initial allowance,* which is a type of accelerated depreciation whereby a larger than normal deduction is obtained upon the acquisition or construction of certain assets;
- an *investment allowance,* which is an exceptional additional deduction that does not reduce the full cost of the asset, which may thus still be written off in full; or
- *annual allowances,* which are deducted annually until the deductible value of the asset is exhausted.

In some cases, the incentive is the right to carry forward certain expenditure, losses, and unabsorbed depreciation for more years than would normally be permitted under the general principles of the tax system.

2.3 Reduction in the Rate of Tax

A large number of systems impose tax on certain types of entities or particular activities at a lower rate than is normally applicable.

Sometimes the reduction in the tax rate takes the form of a refund of a percentage of the tax paid in respect of the particular item of income.

2.4 Tax Deferral

A tax deferral may operate either to postpone the inclusion of the income or gain in the taxable base or to postpone the date upon which the tax itself becomes due or payable.

For example, in the case of a merger or similar operation, the gain may not be subject to tax until a later year.

3. Scope of Tax Incentives

Tax incentives may be of general or regional application. At the international level, the sphere of application of a tax incentive may be extended by way of a tax sparing clause in a tax treaty between a capital importing country and a capital exporting country. (See Section 6 below, "Tax Sparing.")

Tax incentives frequently favor specific activities such as farming, prospecting for minerals and mining, shipping, and air transport.

Many countries provide either an exemption or some type of special tax treatment with regard to certain categories of interest income, such as, in particular, national or local government-sponsored bonds. Nonresidents will most often benefit little, if at all, from such concessions, since they will generally be subject to tax on the interest in question in the country of residence. The few tax treaties that do contain tax sparing clauses usually limit their operation to concessions applying within the framework of a development program.

A concession may apply in respect of national taxes or only in respect of taxes imposed at a lower level in the constitutional hierarchy (e.g., provincial taxes, cantonal taxes, etc.). In countries where there are schedular taxes, the incentive may well relate to only certain types of tax.

Sometimes concessions are granted in favor of indirect taxes only, such as reductions of the rate of, or exemptions from, turnover taxes or import and export duties.

Often a tax concession is available without regard being had to the person benefiting. In other cases, however, the concession may be available only to residents or to nonresidents, or only to individuals or to companies (or to certain special types of companies).

Tax incentives may be limited in time. This is usually so in the case of tax holidays, and particularly where government guarantees are granted.

In certain cases, there is a ceiling on the amount of a tax benefit. Sometimes the ceiling affects only the tax year in question with the right to carry over any excess into subsequent tax years. In other cases, the ceiling is absolute, and any amount in excess of such ceiling will be included in the taxable base.

The grant of favored tax treatment may be subject to conditions that are able to be fulfilled only by a limited clientele. An example is the Belgian Law on Coordination Centers.

(See Chapter 2, Section 2, "High Tax Jurisdictions with IOFC Features.")

4. Common Domains for Tax and Nontax Incentives

Nontax incentives are frequently included in incentive packages. These may include subsidized factory sites, training of local staff, transportation facilities, soft loans, and other benefits.

Common incentive domains include the following:

- Exports
- Export-related services
- Technical services including construction, distribution, design, and engineering services

- Consultancy, management, supervisory, or advisory services relating to any technical matter or to any trade or business
- Fabrication of machinery and equipment and procurement of materials, components, and equipment
- Data processing, programming, computer software development, telecommunications, and other computer services
- Professional services including accounting, legal, medical, and architectural services
- Educational and training services
- Technopark
- Freeport
- Warehousing and servicing incentives
- Operational headquarters
- Management companies
- Administrative offices
- The exporting of manufactured goods by a special trading house where the goods are sold by wholesale
- Repair and maintenance of aircraft and aircraft engines or components
- Film production
- Meat processing
- Remanufacture and repair of computer equipment of subassemblies
- Defined processes or series of defined processes applied to material acquired in bulk
- The alteration of articles without changing their character
- Refurbishment of articles

5. Special Incentives and Grants

5.1 Financial and Banking Facilities

In addition to the credit facilities of private banks, government-sponsored finance houses operating on a commercial basis may make capital available to industry by way of medium- and long-term loans, direct share investment, and hire-purchase and equipment leasing finance. They may also act as underwriters for public issues of shares. Special arrangements may be made for the provision of finance for undercapitalized concerns.

Such finance houses may also initiate and facilitate mergers by providing financial advice, undertaking share valuations, advising on terms for mergers, and assisting in the carrying through of negotiations and formalities. In cases where finance is required in connection with a merger operation, they may provide facilities.

Commercial banks often establish subsidiary organizations to provide an extended range of financial services and to facilitate increased investment in the industrial and commercial sectors.

5.2 Reductions in Corporation Tax

Companies providing certain financial services may also benefit from reduced rates. A special license may be required. The activities that may qualify may include the following:

- foreign currency transactions normally provided by banks;
- international financial activities including global money management, insurance, and related activities and dealings in foreign currencies, options, and similar financial assets;
- services or facilities for processing, control, accounting, communication, clearing, settlement, or information storage in relation to financial activities;
- the development and supply of computer software for use in the provision of the services or facilities referred to above or for reprocessing and analyzing information on financial activities;
- dealing in commodity futures or commodity options on behalf of unconnected persons who are not themselves involved in commodity trading;
- trading operations similar or ancillary to any of the above and that contribute to the use of the area as an international financial services center;
- life assurance business with policyholders and annuitants abroad; and
- the management of the investments of unit trusts.

Reductions in corporation tax are frequently granted to manufacturing companies from the sale of manufactured goods. The term *manufacturing* may be extended to include commodities or materials belonging to another person that are subjected to a process of manufacturing.

A reduction in corporation tax may also be extended to certain trading operations of a qualified company carried on within specified zones.

The classes of trading operations may be extended to the repair or maintenance of aircraft and to trading operations that contribute to the use or development of an airport.

5.3 Cash Grants and Other Incentives for Industrial Development

Development authorities may provide nonrefundable cash grants toward the cost of the fixed assets of new industries that are considered to have good prospects of success and permanence in free trade conditions and are likely to contribute to the growth of the economy. For the purposes of cash grants, "fixed assets" may include the factory site, site development, factory buildings, and new machinery, plant, and equipment. Higher grants are usually available in the designated areas (i.e., certain underdeveloped areas).

Specially arranged packages of incentives, embracing industrial grants, interest subsidies, loan guarantees, and training grants, may be provided for approved subjects. Industrial and commercial facilities and important financial incentives may also be made available in the airport or other customs-free zones.

Incentive programs may permit the carrying on of trade, business, or manufacture under license within the airport or other zones and may grant exemptions from payment of tax on profits from certain business operations.

Such programs may also assist the establishment of new projects through the payment of cash grants, the amount of any such grant usually being subject to negotiation.

5.4 Machinery and Plant

An initial allowance may be granted in respect of capital expenditure incurred on the provision of new machinery or plant.

An annual allowance is usually available in respect of reasonable wear and tear of machinery and plant.

A form of free depreciation may also be available in the case of new machinery or plant acquired for use in a development area. The system of free depreciation allows the writing off of machinery or plant to be accelerated according to the specifications of the taxpayer.

A balancing allowance or charge may be made where machinery or plant ceases to belong to the trader or permanently ceases to be used for the purposes of his trade.

5.5 Industrial Buildings and Structures

Initial allowances of capital expenditure incurred on the construction of an industrial building or structure are usually granted.

An annual allowance may also be available in respect of capital expenditure incurred on the construction of industrial buildings or structures.

If an industrial building or structure is purchased prior to the exhaustion of the annual allowance, an adjustment may be made with regard to the allowance that may be claimed by the new owner.

A balancing allowance or charge may be made where an industrial building or structure is sold, destroyed, or ceases to be used and the residue of the expenditure on construction that has not been allowed for tax purposes exceeds or falls short of the amount of sale, insurance, salvage, or compensation moneys received.

5.6 Training of Local Staff

A trader proposing to manufacture goods for sale, or in the case of certain other qualifying activities, may claim an allowance for the full amount of certain expenditure incurred, before the commencement of trading, on recruitment and training of personnel.

5.7 Regional Development Grants

Regional development grants on buildings and equipment may be granted in the form of cash grants to encourage investment in industry in development areas. Training grants may also be granted on the cost of internal and external training programs for work in new industries.

5.8 Export Sales Relief

Companies that export manufactured goods frequently benefit from a reduction in corporation tax.

The definition of *manufacture* may be extended to include a wide range of items, such as the following:

- goods processed by a company and then returned to the foreign owner;
- design and planning services carried out on behalf of nonresident persons in connection with a variety of projects such as chemical, civil, electrical, or mechanical engineering works, carried on abroad; and
- shipping profits, gold transactions, and financial futures transactions.

5.9 Export Credit Guarantees

There may be provision for exporters to insure with an official insurance corporation the credit they give their overseas customers. The basic export credit insurance policy provides cover against the main risks of nonpayment, whether this arises from insolvency, default, or political causes.

5.10 Pioneer Industries

Pioneer industries may be entitled to complete freedom from income tax on the basis of the product investment levels, skills, and advanced technology, and dividends paid out of the exempt income may also be free of tax.

Pioneer status may be extended to companies providing engineering, technical, and computer-based industrial design services.

Post-pioneer companies may also be taxed at a concessionary rate.

5.11 Investment Allowances

Investment allowances may be granted as an alternative to the pioneer and export incentive holidays.

5.12 Expansion of Established Enterprises

Existing businesses may be entitled to a tax holiday if the enterprise incurs, or intends to incur, capital expenditure on productive equipment, and dividends paid out of the exempt income may also be free of tax.

5.13 Free Zones and Free Ports

Free zones are designated areas that receive special treatment through their exclusion from the area to which the country's normal customs rules apply. A free port is one at which imports may be landed without paying customs duties. The system of free zones or free ports favors export processing, transshipment, and the entrepôt trade since there is no need to pay and then reclaim customs duties.

Warehousing and servicing companies may receive favored treatment in respect of these services generally or in respect of certain designated products only.

Though free zones are often part of a tax incentive package in what would otherwise be a high tax jurisdiction, they may also be found in tax havens, such as Freeport in the Bahamas.

5.14 Venture Capital Incentives

An investor investing in an approved venture company that is developing or using a new technology that is of economic or technical benefit may be allowed to deduct up to the full amount of the investment, or any loss arising from the sale of shares or from the liquidation of the approved venture company.

5.15 Research and Development

The entire amount of capital expenditure incurred on scientific research may, subject to certain conditions, be written off.

Research and development activities may benefit from incentives in the form of accelerated depreciation, investment allowances, etc.

A product development assistance scheme may also be set up to make grants to manufacturing companies developing certain new products.

5.16 Patents

Income from registered patents could receive favored treatment and may be tax-free.

If a trader incurs capital expenditure for the purpose of acquiring certain patent rights, he may be allowed an annual allowance amortized or spread over a period of years or over the remaining life of the patent.

A balancing allowance or charge may be made where patent rights terminate or are sold for less or for more, as the case may be, than the residue of the expenditure that has not yet been allowed.

5.17 Urban Renewal Incentives

Urban renewal incentives may be granted for buildings that would not otherwise qualify once the premises are in use for the purposes of a trade. Similarly, a lessee of an industrial building who is engaged in a trade or profession may be entitled to claim a special additional deduction in respect of the amount of rent actually paid.

5.18 Joint Ventures

Favored treatment may be accorded to companies engaged in certain joint ventures where they carry on such activities through the medium of tax-efficient partnerships or limited partnerships.

5.19 Film Production

Favored treatment, normally including at least a tax deduction, may be accorded to companies in respect of investments in film production companies.

5.20 Capital Assistance Scheme

Capital insurance schemes may provide funding for projects that are considered to be of benefit to the economy.

5.21 Operational Headquarters

Operational headquarters providing management, technical, or other supporting services to subsidiaries and/or associated companies in other countries may benefit from favored tax treatment.

5.22 Tax Shelters

A *tax shelter* or *tax sheltered investment* may be defined as an investment with a flow-through of tax benefits, generally having some or all of the following characteristics: deferral of taxes, conversion of ordinary deductions for future capital gains, and leverage.

The flow-through of tax benefits is a material factor, whether the entity is organized as a limited partnership, joint venture, trust, or company and whether it is offered to investors as a private or public program.

The term is applied generally to a variety of devices that allow taxpayers to deduct certain artificial losses (i.e., losses that are not really economic losses but represent losses that are available as deductions under the current tax laws). These artificial losses may be offset not only against income from the investment out of which they arise, but also against the taxpayer's other income, usually from his regular business or professional activity.

6. Tax Sparing

The sphere of application of a tax incentive may be extended by way of a tax sparing clause in a tax treaty between a capital importing country and a capital exporting country.

Such clauses allow residents of the capital exporting country a credit against their domestic tax for profits or gains derived in the developing country in respect of which all or specified taxes are subject to exemption or reduction in the latter country.

The failure of a capital exporting country to provide for tax sparing or some similar arrangement leads to a distortion of competition at the international level, since investors who are taxed on foreign income in their country of residence are at a disadvantage as compared with investors who are resident in countries giving full or partial exemptions for foreign source income, and also as compared with investors resident in the developing country itself.

A tax sparing arrangement is thus a concession offered by a capital exporting or investing country to insure that an incentive offered by a developing country is effective. Without it, the incentive offered by the developing country may be nullified because it merely results in more tax being payable in the investing country.

EXAMPLE

Assume that the taxpayer is a company resident in a developed country that is operating a branch in a developing country that has granted it a five-year tax holiday on all income and withholding taxes. A comprehensive tax sparing provision is in the tax treaty between the two countries. In year three of the holiday, the taxpayer earns $1 million in the developing country. It pays no foreign tax because of the tax holiday.

Assume further that such companies are taxable on foreign earnings, subject to a tax credit. Thus the taxpayer would normally be subject to full tax in its country of residence on the $1 million of earnings. Moreover, it would normally not be able to credit any foreign tax because it paid none.

The tax sparing article provides that the company may take a tax credit against taxes in its country of residence (subject to normal limitations) in the amount of the taxes it would have paid to the developing country if there had been no tax holiday.

7. Examples of Incentives in European Union Countries

The extent to which any country may offer offshore potential to investors is exemplified by the types of incentives available in European Union countries that are normally high tax jurisdictions.

Belgium

Coordination centers

Special regional incentives

Companies located in the reconversion zones

Innovation companies

Job-creating incentives

Denmark

Incentives in certain regions (particularly in Jutland, the island of Bornholm, and other smaller islands)

France

Underdeveloped and depressed areas

Newly created companies

Germany

Premiums for investments in certain regions

Investments premiums

State government grants

Greece

Direct cash grants

Cash grants for special investments

Incentives granted to foreign investments in Greece

Large-scale investments

Export incentives

Ireland

International Financial and Service Center (located in the Custom House Docks area in Dublin)

Tax incentives in certain regions (e.g., Shannon)

Tax incentives for software development

Capital grants

10% rate of corporation tax

Export credit guarantees

Patents

Film production

Undertakings for collective investments in transferable securities (UCITS)

Italy

Capital expenditure subsidies

Incentives in certain regions (e.g., Southern Italy, Sardinia, Sicily)

Luxembourg

1929 holding company regime

Special regime in favor of financial holding companies (*sociétés de participation financiére* or SOPARFI).

Partial tax holiday for new industrial activities

The Netherlands

Substantial participation (*"deelneming"*) regime

Distribution center regime

Regime in favor of finance companies (*"concern financieringsmaatschappij"*)

Investment incentives

Portugal

Incentives for investments in certain regions

Financial incentives

The SIBR scheme (regionally based incentive scheme)

Employment incentives

Incentive scheme for industrial restructuring

Madeira/Azores free zones

Madeira IOFC facilities

Spain

Special holding company regime (*Entitad de Tenencia de Valores Extranjeros* or ETVE)

Incentives for investment in certain regions (i.e., the Canary Islands, Ceuta, and Melilla)

Industries of preferential interest

Tax benefits for urgent reindustrialization zones and technological innovation

United Kingdom

Development areas

Intermediate areas

Northern Ireland

8. Caveat

It will be seen from the above that many otherwise high tax countries offer significant *offshore* features through the creation of tax and nontax incentives.

Investment incentive programs, together with, or in the absence of, tax incentives, may well prove decisive in the choice of location of a project. Such programs are particularly attractive where substantial grants, interest-free or low-interest loans, factory sites, etc., are available in addition to tax incentives.

There are two areas where care should be exercised:

(1) the international measures to contain preferential tax regimes and tax havens (see Chapter 14, "International Measures to Combat Harmful Tax Practices."); and

(2) the question as to whether the incentive is really beneficial.

In examining whether use should be made of a given incentive, at least the following general considerations should be taken into account:

- Are the reasons that influenced the government to introduce the concessions (usually the underdevelopment of the area) likely to constitute a disadvantage with regard to the proposed investment?
- If the absence of good communications was the principal reason why the region became backward in the first place, has there been an improvement in the situation, or, if not, would this constitute a disadvantage if the incentive were to be used for the purposes of the project under consideration?
- Is there any likelihood of nationalization or other political or economic risk attendant upon investment in the incentive area?
- Are there any exchange controls, and, if so, are there any guarantees with regard to the repatriation of profits and investment capital under the incentive scheme?
- Are there any special difficulties affecting foreign controlled enterprises?

- Are there any strings attached to the grant of the concession that may subsequently prove to be a disadvantage?

Caveat emptor—let the buyer beware!

CHAPTER FIVE

THE OFFSHORE PERSON

1. The International Person

Inevitably, offshore tax planning extends to the world of the "international person" every bit as much as it does to the corporation. Indeed, much offshore business involves the affairs of entrepreneurs who have effective control over their activities.

While many similar tax considerations come into operation, the combination of tax and nontax factors applying to individuals focuses essentially on residence, domicile, and citizenship. Offshore solutions to individual tax planning problems can be achieved only if the offshore component succeeds in breaking or modifying connecting factors between the individual and the relevant high tax jurisdictions.

1.1 Residence

One's residence is where one lives. But more important from some points of view is where one has the right to live.

As a general rule one can live in a country where one is a citizen. But one can normally also live in many other countries as well—sometimes casually, sometimes by virtue of a residence permit or merely a visa.

In most countries resident individuals are subject to income and other taxes on worldwide income and assets, wherever situated. In some countries, like the United States, Denmark, and Germany, tax can follow an emigrant for a number of years after he or she leaves the territory.

Despite its importance, the meaning of *residence* is not comprehensively defined in most countries for either legal or tax purposes. Criteria for determining residence are generally based on practical considerations and derived largely from court cases, although many countries use as a test the number of days of presence in the country in some stipulated period. In the case of the United States, days in the current year as well as days in the previous two years are taken into account for determining residence for tax purposes.

If there is a double taxation treaty between two countries, there will usually be "tie-breaker" rules under which a dually resident individual's residence status is resolved.

1.2 Emigration

Emigration to a tax haven or to a country offering special retirement incentives may serve to break totally or in part the link between a taxpayer and the high tax jurisdiction from which he or she is emigrating. Normally, it is the change in the place of residence that is material; however, in other cases a change in domicile or even citizenship (in the case of the United States) may be necessary. Anti-avoidance provisions or exchange controls may delay or render extremely difficult the coming into effect of the fiscal advantages of emigration.

In addition to countries where no relevant taxes are levied or where taxation is levied at very low rates, certain countries offer favorable tax treatment to all or certain categories of immigrants in respect of their foreign source income. Special exchange control treatment may also be granted to qualifying immigrants.

The obvious way of giving up one's residence is to emigrate. However, while the right of any person to leave any country is generally recognized, the right to *immigrate*—to choose a new country of residence—is not. Immigration is therefore the main practical issue in emigration.

All European Union (EU) citizens can choose any of the member countries, but those countries can and do tax.

Monaco, which is not an EU country, is fairly liberal with new residents of adequate means, although the procedure can be slow. Jersey and Guernsey are very difficult to get into, while the Isle of Man is more welcoming. Switzerland is theoretically qiote difficult, although the right budget can usually do the trick.

Then there are specials like Austria, Costa Rica, Israel, Malta, the Philippines, and Sri Lanka that are keen to attract retirees with a bit of loose cash to invest and seek to tempt them with tax exemptions.

Many expatriates, of course, want to work in their new homes, and this requires the correct visa and/or work authorization. An expatriate leaving home usually has a long checklist:

- buying or renting property in a new country
- overseas removal
- pre-retirement savings and investment
- the pension position
- social security benefits
- private medical treatment and health care
- exchange control
- and of course, tax.

If the expatriate returns home—and many do—the checklist is shorter. Mainly it is tax and, particularly, estate tax. Becoming a full-scale non-resident creates a very special opportunity. In matters of estate planning and probate, remember the two folk adages: "Have a little trust" and "Where there's a will, there's a way."

1.3 Artists and Athletes

Bjorn Borg and Anthony Burgess weren't the first, and Boris Becker and Ringo Starr aren't the last. Monaco is full of musical, literary, and sporting stars—many of them earning big bucks. And so are the other residential havens. The influx seems to be gathering momentum.

Some stars may decide to emigrate, but many don't. They just stay right where they are and treat their own countries as tax havens, often by turning their income into a capital appreciation in their own companies. This technique can work so well that companies have even been floated on the stock exchange on the basis of book earnings generated from the performances of the stars. Tom Jones and the Beatles were masters of this game.

Many big earners use an offshore company to employ them. The company makes the profits and pays them a salary spread over a number of years. Of course, this ploy doesn't always work. Take what happened to Ingemar Johannson, the Swedish prize fighter. He had incorporated a Swiss company of which he was the sole employee and source of revenue; he was entitled to receive 70% of the company's gross income plus a pension fund. He then fought in the United States for the heavyweight boxing championship of the world and was hit for taxes on his prize winnings by the IRS. He claimed tax exemption under the Switzerland–United States Tax Treaty on the grounds that he and the company were really Swiss residents. That was one time the "Hammer of Thor" well and truly got hammered. The IRS rejected his argument and so did the U.S. tax court.

For every loser, however, there are many winners. There are people living for more than 10 months of the year in high tax countries where they are legally designated as nonresidents for tax purposes; others who are deemed residents in havens of convenience and who barely spend more than a couple of days there from time to time. Sometimes one spouse is a resident and the other is not; though technically separated, they manage to live together happily ever after.

1.4 What About Taxes Abroad?

The offshore person has usually left old tax (and sometimes other) problems behind. But what about tax in the country of adoption? Is the expatriate off the tax hook in France, Italy, Spain, or Greece? No, indeed. The taxes in most of the countries on the Mediterranean shore are quite high indeed, and their systems contain a full barrage of income taxes, inheritance taxes, gift taxes, and wealth taxes.

In the past, expatriates benefited from Mediterranean neglect. The local tax administration simply didn't bother with them. But that has changed. Not only is the expatriate an easy target of the computer and a welcome source of additional tax revenue, but European Union pressures are leading to a tightening of tax systems generally.

Having no tax address at all can sometimes work, but it could be more difficult to prove a clean break with the previous country of residence, particularly if the would-be expatriate still visits there.

1.5 Domicile

Domicile may have considerable practical significance for foreigners coming from abroad to visit or live in Anglo-American countries—also for those who leave those countries to make a new home in another country. Unlike residence, domicile has ramifications beyond the sphere of taxation. It determines which system of law is to govern one's personal position in situations such as succession, marriage and divorce, legitimacy, and questions of legal capacity.

It is a fundamental principle of Anglo-American legal systems that every individual must at all times have a domicile. Domicile of origin is a domicile automatically acquired by all individuals at birth and is determined solely on the basis of parentage, without reference to the place of birth. So an individual need never have set foot in the country of his domicile of origin.

An individual's domicile of origin continues indefinitely to be his domicile unless and until he acquires a new domicile. Children usually follow their parents' domicile. Otherwise, for a domicile of choice to be effective, two essential requirements must be met. First, the individual must take up residence in the country concerned; and secondly there must be an intention to remain indefinitely, or without time limit, in the adopted country. Married women can usually establish an independent domicile.

In determining domicile, the courts look at material factors such as the residence in the country concerned of members of the individual's family, cultural connections such as the ability to speak the local language, making a will and appointing locally resident executors, financial or business interests, and involvement in social activities such as membership in clubs, societies, and churches. Even expressing a desire to be buried in a particular country after death may be relevant, especially if a burial plot is actually acquired.

An individual may also be deemed to be domiciled in a particular country for tax purposes even though he is not domiciled there in general law.

1.6 The United Kingdom as the World's Prime Residential Tax Haven

The United Kingdom is the favorite residential tax haven of the world's rich and famous expatriates.

Basis for U.K. Tax Liability of Foreign Domiciliaries

Liability to U.K. tax on both income and capital is dependent on the two concepts of residence and domicile.

The U.K. tax regime is currently particularly favorable to individuals who are resident in the United Kingdom but are not U.K. domiciled. To benefit from such a position, it is necessary for non-U.K. domiciled individuals to insure that they retain some connection with, or desire to return to, their domicile of origin.

Residence. An individual is deemed to be resident in the United Kingdom if he is physically in the United Kingdom for more than 183 days, excluding days of arrival and departure in any tax year (April 6 to April 5).

If the individual is able to remain outside the United Kingdom for more than half the year but still spends a considerable amount of time in the United Kingdom, there is a further test that the Inland Revenue will apply in determining whether the individual is resident for tax purposes. If the individual averages, over a 4-year period, more than 90 days physically in the United Kingdom in each tax year, then the Revenue will deem the individual to be resident from the beginning of the 5th tax year. If, however, it becomes apparent before the end of the 4th year that the 90-day test will be exceeded, then the Revenue will deem residence from an earlier date. Indeed, if it is clear that it was the individual's intention always to exceed the 90-day test as from the beginning, the Revenue will deem the individual to be U.K. resident for tax purposes from the moment of arrival in the United Kingdom.

Domicile. The other factor that affects an individual's liability to U.K. tax is the concept of *domicile.* Under U.K. law an individual has one (and only one) domicile. This concept is not to be confused with the idea of accommodation, since it is more closely linked to the concept of a "permanent home."

A person is born with a domicile of origin, which will generally be his father's domicile at the date of his birth. This can be changed when the individual is still a minor by the father changing his domicile. Upon reaching the age of majority, an individual can acquire a domicile of choice by making a positive decision to abandon his domicile of origin and to settle in a new country.

Income tax

Where it is established that an individual is a U.K.-resident nondomiciliary, income tax is chargeable on all income arising in the United Kingdom and on any income arising outside the United Kingdom that is remitted to the United Kingdom.

The concept of remittance covers not only the physical importation of money but also deemed remittance, whereby the individual has the use of, or enjoyment of, money in the United Kingdom that has arisen outside.

As a U.K. resident, an individual is entitled to certain allowances and is taxed on the total of his income on a sliding scale. All U.K. individuals are entitled to a personal allowance, and in addition there are other allowances, such as a married couples' allowance, as well as extra allowances for age and disability for which various conditions must be satisfied.

Capital gains tax

Gains on the disposal of assets are taxable in the hands of individuals who are resident or ordinarily resident in the United Kingdom.

However, if the individual is not domiciled in the United Kingdom, in the case of a sale of an asset situated outside the United Kingdom, only proceeds that are actually or constructively remitted to the United Kingdom will be subject to capital gains tax. Capital gains are deemed to be remitted where they are in some form or other enjoyed or used in the United Kingdom.

A nondomiciled U.K. resident individual is therefore taxable on the difference between the sales proceeds and the cost of purchase of any relevant assets.

Inheritance tax

Liability to inheritance tax for a nondomiciled individual arises only on assets physically situated in the United Kingdom at the time of death. However, it should be noted that as well as the normal meaning of domicile discussed above, the Inheritance Tax Act also deems as a U.K. domiciliary, for inheritance tax purposes, any person who has been resident in the United Kingdom in 17 out of the past 20 years.

Inheritance tax applies to the transfer of any asset from one person to another, whether or not on the event of a death. Most lifetime gifts, however, are treated as exempt if the transferor survives for 7 years.

Income Accounts and Capital Accounts

Any earned income that is paid for services conducted outside the United Kingdom can, by the use of separate employment contracts, be paid outside the United Kingdom and, as long as not remitted, will be free of U.K. tax.

It is possible to avoid the U.K. tax on non-U.K.-source income. The U.K. Revenue does, however, deem remittances to the United Kingdom to be income first, capital gains second, and capital last, unless proved otherwise.

In order to differentiate between these, an individual should set up, outside the United Kingdom, three separate accounts before arrival in the United Kingdom.

(a) The first will be all the available cash before arrival in the United Kingdom. This will be a "clean" capital account, and as such moneys can be remitted to the United Kingdom from this account without any U.K. tax consequences. This account should, however, not receive any injections other than the proceeds of sale of assets that are exempt from capital gains tax in the United Kingdom (e.g. your principal private residence, motor vehicles, etc.)

(b) The second account should be the income account. This will receive all non-U.K. source income, both from non-U.K. employment and from non-

U.K. investments. Moneys from this account should never be remitted to the United Kingdom, as they would be immediately liable to U.K. tax.

(c) The third account should be used for the proceeds of sale of any non-U.K. assets concluded while the individual is resident in the United Kingdom. As with the income account, any remittance from this third account will be immediately liable to U.K. tax.

By the setting up of these accounts it will therefore be possible for the foreigner to prove to the U.K. Revenue, by the production of bank statements, that any remittances to the United Kingdom are from tax-free capital.

If it is necessary to bring any assets into the United Kingdom at the time of establishing residence here, it would be advisable to consider "bed and breakfasting" (selling an asset and immediately repurchasing it) any assets that would be subject to U.K. capital gains tax. This would therefore raise the base cost of the assets, so lowering any ultimate gain and reducing any tax liability on eventual sale. This, of course, should be done before actually establishing residence in the United Kingdom. It follows that the consideration of future needs is advisable.

The foreigner should retain his membership in his church, business, and social club in the foreign country and continue to emphasize in all documents (such as his will) that he considers his place of permanent residence and domicile to be in the foreign country.

When the foreigner completes his future U.K. tax returns, he should indicate that he is still domiciled in the foreign country.

See also Chapter 13, "Case Study: Estate Tax Implications of Domicile."

2. Citizenship and Passports

2.1 Acquiring a New Citizenship

Many offshore persons need more than just residence. Citizenship can be the critical problem—and usually a more difficult one—to resolve. The United States, for example, taxes on the basis of citizenship, and shedding U.S. citizenship may be a painful procedure.

The other side of the coin is the acquisition of citizenship. Frequently the problem is solved by producing an Irish grandparent as the passport to Irish citizenship. An Italian ancestor can do the same for Italy, and a Jewish ancestor for Israel. But for many the wrong citizenship can be a greater hardship than just tax liability; and the search for a new citizenship is generally quite arduous.

France is a relatively hospitable country, particularly for people who have three or more children or who have a degree from a French university. Austria may accept you if you give a huge and well placed donation and show a special love for all that is Austrian (which means rather more than Mozart and Strauss). For most countries, however, you need 3–5 years residence to qualify for citizenship.

Flaky passports from Latin America are mostly little more than travel documents of doubtful validity. Perhaps some forty years ago, your parents were traveling through an isolated village in Bolivia when your mother unexpectedly gave birth to you. It was a bumpy llama ride that triggered her labor. Fortunately, some old villagers still remember the incident well and will sign a document certifying that you were born there. The rest is easy: citizenship, passport, driver's license, exemption from military service. How about a change of name for the same trouble? Or anything else you fancy? You can even come out of the procedure 12 years younger.

A second passport, providing proof of citizenship and (usually although not invariably) access to the benefits associated with citizenship, may require one or more of the following:

Conditions to be met

- place of birth
- parent's or grandparent's nationality
- remoter ancestry
- religion
- military service
- spouse, concubine, or similar relationship
- meritorious service (very)
- special arrangements (very)

Evidence to be produced

- valid current passport
- birth certificate
- police good-conduct certificate
- medical certificates
- financial statements
- evidence of languages
- character references
- religious certificates
- a compliant spouse
- patronage
- money

2.2 Types of Passports

In addition to the simple passports based on citizenship, there are also a number of other classes that may meet the needs of an individual seeking to move offshore.

Marriage of convenience passports

A number of countries, including many European countries, grant immediate citizenship to persons who marry citizens. It may even be enough to have a "serious relationship." Female spouses often receive preferential treatment. Males usually have to have a period of residence as well as a marriage of convenience before getting their passports.

Noncitizenship passports

Although passports are usually only issued to citizens, sometimes passport-like documents are issued that are little more than travel permits. Sometimes, too, passports are issued that look identical to normal passports notwithstanding that the bearer is a noncitizen.

Provisional passports

Some Latin American countries grant citizenship to property owners. During the waiting period for such citizenship a *cedula,* or national identity card, may be granted and even a provisional passport if the property owner needs to travel. These documents may appear to be identical to regular passports.

Honorary diplomatic passports

Honorary consul diplomatic passports are sometimes awarded to friends of the country or to international business people who are considered useful. These diplomatic passports are usually treated seriously throughout the world.

Service passports

Service passports are of limited application but may be granted to certain classes of government employees.

Refugee passports

Stateless or persecuted persons may be granted refugee passports to enable them to travel beyond the country of asylum.

2.3 Countries Offering Favored Treatment

A large number of countries offer various kinds of opportunities to the offshore person seeking the citizenship of a new country. See Table 5-1.

Table 5-1 Citizenship Requirements for Various Countries

Australia, Canada, New Zealand	Three years, but this period may be shortened for special categories of immigrants.
Austria	Can be almost instant in the case of persons with the right patronage and attitudes, and certain classes of refugees.
Belize	A nonrefundable economic contribution to the country of US$50,000 can earn you both citizenship and a passport.
Bolivia	Special formulas exist.
Brazil	The right contacts can get you a passport in as little as 3 weeks.
Dominican Republic	Can be very quick if you buy a home and some bonds as well.
France	Military service or three or more children or a university degree; plus a measure of permanence in France.
Germany	Some classes of refugees receive immediate citizenship and passports. Descent from a proven German citizen (especially from a passport-holder) can also work.
Honduras	A matter of price.
Ireland	See paragraph 2.4 below.
Israel	The Law of Return makes an instant passport available to anyone of Jewish descent.
Italy	Citizenship is easy in the case of "ethnic Italians" or public benefactors.
Paraguay	Special formulas exist.
Portugal	Ownership of a property in Portugal for 7 years may be deemed to meet the residence requirements for naturalization purposes.
St. Kitts and Nevis	The purchase of approved real estate to the value of a minimum of US$50,000; or making an investment in an approved enterprise may earn you both citizenship and a passport.
Spain	Two years residence only if you are from a former Spanish colony, i.e., most of Latin America except Brazil.
Switzerland	Start with 12 consecutive years of residence and money (remember *"pas d'argent, pas de Suisse"*).

2.4 Ireland

Ireland offers immediate citizenship through proof of an Irish grandparent. The fact that many Irish birth records were destroyed by a fire at the Dublin Births Registry Office can hamper proof but has conversely created the opportunity for certain postulants to fake Irish ancestry.

In addition, Ireland offers citizenship, pursuant to the Irish Nationality and Citizenship Act of 1956, as amended by the 1986 Act, for a qualifying applicant who either makes a job-creating or job-maintaining investment or makes a long-term loan of 1 million Irish pounds.

Ireland is a full member of the European Union, so that having its nationality and passport is particularly valuable for visa-free travel or for residing, working, or establishing a business anywhere within the European Union.

Applications for naturalization can be made on the basis of investment in Ireland, and any such applications received by the Minister are referred to an Advisory Group that will make recommendations to the Minister based on the Advisory Group's assessment of the job-creating and job-maintenance capacity of the investment. After successful application the applicant must travel to Ireland to make a simple Declaration in Court swearing his allegiance to the Irish State, following which naturalization papers are issued. The naturalization papers can be presented to the Irish Passport Office, which will then issue an Irish passport to the applicant. The whole application process from start to finish will usually take between 3 and 6 months.

Because of the complexity of the Irish Citizenship Scheme, a full business plan will be called for in the case of viable investment proposals, which may entail professional and legal fees of 25,000 Irish pounds upwards, depending on the work involved.

3. Remuneration of Offshore Employees

3.1 Objectives

It is necessary to find a way to remunerate employees for the contributions they make to a multinational group's international activities. A second important need is for international mobility, with employees rendering services wherever the changing needs of the Group take them. Linked to the above needs is the need to provide flexibility regarding the provision of retirement benefits for employees.

In structuring the proposed arrangements, it is important to focus on the provision of internationally competitive rewards with specific attention being paid to:

- salaries and similar cash entitlements,
- bonuses,

- share participation, and
- retirement benefits

by means of tax-efficient simple, dual or multiple contractual arrangements.

Attention should also be directed at the establishment of an employment structure that is consistent with other benefits and which provides for:

- contractual relationships with standard conditions;
- a reward and benefit framework;
- primary conditions of employment;
- flexibility in employment benefits;
- competitiveness.

3.2 Tax Considerations

Payments that are effected offshore for services performed offshore will normally escape tax. However, it is always necessary to take into account the domestic and treaty rules governing each specific situation. In particular, persons resident (or in some cases domiciled, in the strict Anglo-American sense of the word) in countries that tax worldwide income will be liable in respect of offshore income.

In each of the countries concerned there are specific tax rules determining the incidence of tax liability of residents working abroad.

In addition, a tax treaty between the country of residence of an employee and the country where the services are performed may contain specific rules governing the apportionship of earnings.

3.3 Nontax Considerations

Nontax issues will, however, in most cases have a greater impact on the overall position of the employees. All of the rules and general considerations governing the remuneration of employees, their conditions of employment, and their benefit packages, have to be taken into account, every bit as much as tax factors, in the design of an international employment structure.

3.4 Exchange Control

Wherever employees are resident in a country that imposes exchange control restrictions, they are normally limited in their freedom to keep their funds abroad. In such cases, it is usual for the employer to be faced with a request that an offshore trust of some kind be set up by the employer in such a way that a portion of the remuneration may be received abroad without this constituting a breach of the exchange control regulations concerned.

3.5 Employment Structure

Contractual relationship between the employer company/ies and employees

Employees could be employed solely by one of the companies in the Group, with all provisions relating to their employment embodied in one sole contract. Alternatively, employees could be retained or employed under dual or multiple contracts as follows:

- in respect of home duties, by the home company; and
- in respect of foreign duties, by the offshore headquarters company.

The rationale for using the headquarters company in respect of international duties would be to allow them to build up a tax-free retirement fund in hard currency in respect of international duties and to ensure that they will not be taxed at home in respect of income derived from international duties.

Administration

It is important that the activities of the headquarters company should not be regarded by the local tax authorities as actually being part of local activities. In order to ensure this, the following practical aspects should, *inter alia*, be attended to:

- central management and control;
- retainer and employment contracts should be initiated at the headquarters of the headquarters company and signed by the headquarters company;
- accounting and administration should physically be done by and at the headquarters of the headquarters company;
- cost recoveries and invoicing should be handled by the headquarters company.

Contractual relationship between the headquarters company and local companies

The headquarters company could enter into formal agreements with the local companies in terms of which the headquarters company will provide certain services (including secondment services) to a the local company at an agreed fee. These agreements should be correctly drafted to ensure that this is clearly a service provided by the headquarters company and not a contractual relationship between the employee and the local company.

Each time an employee is sent to work for a new local company for the first time, he or she should receive an appropriate letter of direction from the headquarters company.

3.6 Conditions of Employment

General

It may not be possible to harmonize all of the conditions of employment applicable at the headquarters company level, with the prevailing conditions of employment in the many local companies.

The conditions of employment that should be focused on are:

- remuneration (salary package);
- bonuses;
- benefits;
- tax equalization; and
- terms of employment, which should be addressed fully before the conclusion of the employment contract.

Remuneration (salary package)

Employees of multinational companies who have dual contracts generally receive packages that are apportioned in accordance with actual services rendered in the various jurisdictions.

The apportionment of remuneration between the respective employment companies under dual contracts should be justifiable in terms of actual time spent in the home country and in other jurisdictions.

However, marginal flexibility exists in terms of apportionment of remuneration, for example, a ratio of 1.5:1 in favor of offshore remuneration, on the basis of annual calculations, can usually be justified by the need to travel, the nature of offshore duties, and so on. This ratio is generally acceptable to the tax authorities in most countries. Higher weightings could be regarded as a diversion of local remuneration to other jurisdictions by the local tax authorities, thus triggering their intervention. Regular reviews of the weightings used versus actual time spent on duties, should be undertaken.

The international portion of the remuneration may be adjusted to offshore market conditions to accommodate the cost of living differentials and to secure services. In appropriate circumstances, special allowances may be paid to compensate for lifestyle adjustments (e.g. hardship allowances).

In the case of some countries, it may be worthwhile noting the concept of a flexible salary package, in terms of which employees may (within certain limits) structure tax efficient packages on a cafeteria basis by means of a salary sacrifice. This kind of arrangement may be more difficult to implement in some countries because of adverse tax legislation. Package structuring will be implemented only in appropriate circumstances (where it is practical and manageable). Insofar as the headquarters company will apply a policy of tax equalization, employees will largely be discouraged from package structuring.

By applying a policy of tax equalization, the employer bears the cost of additional taxes or reaps the reduction in taxes that applies in the various jurisdictions where the services are rendered. The employee's net salary (after-tax salary) therefore remains unchanged.

Bonuses

Annual and other bonuses for international services should be attached exclusively to the work of the employees and their successes in connection with such work, outside of the home country. In this regard, it is important to note that if there is any fudging of the lines, all or a part of the bonuses in question could be attached by the local Revenue to a local source.

Benefits

(a) Retirement benefits. To ensure that contractual arrangements are legitimate, retirement benefits (including the funding thereof) should mirror the distribution of earnings—which in turn should be aligned with the actual and physical rendering of services in the various jurisdictions.

A defined-contribution provident fund could also be set up offshore and benefits could be aligned with the most favorable of the local funds.

(b) Exchange control. In the case of exchange control, regulations affecting certain persons who render services on a noncontinuous basis to an offshore company, consideration might perhaps be given to the provision of retirement benefits via a discretionary trust. The discretionary trust will be funded by the headquarters company, and employees will sacrifice income equal to their own contributions. The trust will invest the funds and pay the proceeds to the beneficiaries on retirement or resignation. It is recommended that the beneficiaries should have no legal entitlement to the benefits. A protector should be appointed to ensure through a letter of wishes that beneficiaries will ultimately receive benefits (i.e. their portion of the investments of the trust).

(c) Tax treatment. The deductibility of contributions for tax purposes will be determined in accordance with relevant local tax laws in the jurisdiction where services are rendered, since contributions will be funded from such earnings. The growth in the fund will be exempt from tax, and the benefits will normally also be free of tax. Withholding taxes on dividends received by the trust will not be recoverable. Planning may furthermore ensure that benefits can be taken in lump-sum form free from tax anywhere.

(d) Share incentive schemes. Different types of share incentive schemes are possible, depending on whether shares are granted outright or distributed as options and whether the incentive scheme has immediate or deferred effect.

The issue of shares to employees in terms of a bonus is straightforward, as the bonus is taxable as normal remuneration—on payment.

The issue of shares in terms of a deferred sale scheme may have more complex tax implications in some countries where the difference between the issue price and market value of the shares on the date of exercise of the option is taxable. Usually this difference becomes tax-free if certain conditions are met, typically that a specified period lapses between exercising the option and selling the shares.

If the issue of shares is related to services rendered locally, the local tax legislation would normally apply. If the issue of shares is related to services rendered offshore, local tax legislation will not necessarily apply.

(e) Insurance. Life cover premiums qualify for tax deduction, the proceeds form part of taxable income in the hands of the employee, but the employer qualifies for a tax deduction on payment of the proceeds to the estate of the deceased employee. The employer is therefore tax neutral, the premiums are tax deductible, and the proceeds are taxable in the hands of the employee.

Accident cover premiums qualify for a tax deduction, and employees are taxed on the proceeds.

Care must be taken to examine all issues, for example, whether premiums may qualify for deductions, the position of the estates of deceased employees, whether the employer would be tax neutral, and whether the proceeds would be taxable in the hands of the employee.

The deductibility of the cost of the premiums would generally depend on the tax legislation of the jurisdiction in which the services are rendered.

Cash could be offered in lieu of life cover, as the tax treatment normally does not differ from cash payments unless a discount on the premiums can be achieved through economies of scale. Employees could then be permitted to decide whether they wish to self-insure.

(f) Medical coverage. The funding of medical schemes is, in most countries, tax deductible in the hands of the employer, and employees are not taxed on the funding or the benefits.

It may not be practical to provide medical benefits at the headquarters company level, as the employees will be rendering services in other jurisdictions; so it may be preferable to simply extend the local scheme internationally.

Ancillary Issues

The following ancillary issues may also need to be addressed:

- confidentiality,
- nonsolicitation clauses,
- agreements on conflicts of interest,
- legal jurisdiction matters etc.

3.7 Overall Considerations

The organization of a multinational operation requires a high level of employee mobility. From the employee's perspective, mobility is generally expensive and disruptive. A degree of additional remuneration is therefore necessary.

Where mobility leads to discontinuous employment, it may have detrimental consequences as far as employees' social-insurance and retirement benefits are concerned. Providing a remuneration and benefits package that gives employees appropriate incentives can be extremely expensive for the employer if its tax implications are not correctly accounted for.

It will almost invariably be preferable for employees to remain under contract to one participating company for the duration of their service. However, split contracts involving payment partly in the country of employment and partly offshore enable mobility, relocation, and tax-equalization allowances to avoid tax altogether. The last is of particular importance, as many countries require taxable tax-equalization allowances to be grossed up, producing a burden that increases exponentially with the marginal rate of tax. The most convenient solution is therefore that the offshore portion of the payment should be covered by a specific contract with the headquarters company.

Gross-up Principle

Assume an employee currently earning X pre-tax and paying tax at rate $t1$. Assume the employee is relocated, and as a consequence is taxable at the (higher) rate $t2$. He (reasonably) insists that his after-tax income be maintained. The employer therefore pays him an allowance of ($t2$ minus $t1$)X. But this allowance is taxable, which requires a further equalization allowance of $t2(t2\text{-}t1)X$, and so on…

The problem has a simple algebraic solution. If A is the taxable tax equalization allowance, then:

$$(1 - t_2)(X + A) = (1 - t_1)X$$

from which it follows:

$$A = \frac{t_2 - t_1}{1 - t_2} X$$

One needs only to assume that $t1 = 30\%$ and $t2 = 60\%$ (say), for A to be equal to 75% of X. If A could be paid tax-free, however, it would be only 30% of X, i.e. less than half the otherwise required tax-equalization allowance.

The conversion of expatriate allowances (wholly or partly) into enhanced retirement benefits held in trust offshore will often permit complete deferral of tax, or even complete avoidance of tax in the case of relocation on retirement to a tax haven.

A wide variety of ad hoc solutions can be considered, depending on the specific legislation of the jurisdiction involved. However, there are obvious advantages, in terms of administration and of equity among employees, in implementing a standardized company-wide scheme (assuming, of course, a significant number of expatriates in a variety of different jurisdictions). Such a scheme must meet the relevant requirements. The most efficient option may involve the use of an offshore trust providing deferred benefits.

CHAPTER SIX

OFFSHORE TRUSTS AND ASSET PROTECTION

1. Legal Nature of the Trust[1]

The word "trust" refers to the duty or aggregate accumulation of obligations that rest upon a person described as a trustee. The responsibilities are in relation to property held by him or under his control. The trustee is obliged to administer the trust property in the manner lawfully prescribed by the trust instrument (trust deed or settlement), or in the absence of specific provision, in accordance with equitable principles or statute law. The administration will thus be in such a manner that the consequential benefits and advantages accrue, not to the trustee, but to the beneficiaries.

The Anglo-Saxon trust is merely a bundle of rights and obligations in equity and is thus not strictly speaking a legal entity. Though the law of trusts varies from system to system, those patterned on the English law of trusts resemble one another closely, differences usually being of statutory origin. In the case of civil law systems where the trust is to be found it is invariably a creature of statute.

According to *The Oxford Companion to Law*, a trust is an arrangement for the holding and administration of property under which property or legal rights are vested by the owner of the property or rights (truster) in a person or persons (trustees) which they are then to hold or to exercise for or on behalf of another (*cestui que trust* or beneficiary), or others, or for the accomplishment of a particular purpose or purposes. The essence of the concept is the separation of legal and beneficial ownership, the property being legally vested in one or more trustees but in equity held for and belonging to others. The concept of trust is the most important contribution of English equity to jurisprudence. It is not derived from Roman law, from such institutions as *fidei commissa*, and its origin is doubtful. Significance in its development attaches to the idea of conscience, which was treated as important by the early chancellors, who were ecclesiastics. Statutes have only to a small extent affected English trust law, though the few statutes are important.

The trustees stand in a fiduciary relation and must hold the property or exercise the rights in a fiduciary capacity. In many relationships, e.g. partnership, a person stands towards another or others in a fiduciary relationship and may be deemed a trustee for some purposes.

A trust may be created expressly, by statute, by *inter vivos* declaration, or by will, or arise by operation of law, which includes constructive trusts and resulting trusts. It may be a private trust, for the benefit of individuals, or a public trust for charitable or public purposes. It may extend to any property or interest in property which a person can transfer, or assign, or dispose of. It may be in favor of any person, or for charitable or other lawful purposes. The objects of the trust must be declared with sufficient certainty to permit the court to enforce it.

Where a trust is created expressly there must be an adequate declaration of trust and certainty of intention, as to subject matter, and as to objects or persons to be benefited.

Among trusts arising by operation of law a constructive trust attaches to property which a person holding property in trust has acquired by means of his ownership of or dealings with that trust. A resulting trust arises where an intention to create a trust is indicated but the trust is not fully declared or fails in whole or in part, or where property is put in the possession of a person ostensibly for his own use but truly to effect a purpose which fails, or where property is put in the possession without intimation that he is to hold in trust but retention of the beneficial interest by the purchaser is presumed intended and is held to be equitable.

The courts have over the centuries greatly elaborated principles laying down the rights, powers, and duties of trustees. In particular, high standards have always been demanded of trustees in respect of care for the trust estate, careful investment, strict accounting, fair apportionment between income and capital, duty to pay the right beneficiaries, and absence of personal profit or self-interest and trustees have frequently been held liable to repay to the trust losses caused by lack of care or other breach of trust. Trust property can be recovered from a third party who has obtained it unless he obtained a legal title, for valuable consideration, and without notice that his acquisition was in breach of trust.

Equity has always shown great favor to charitable trusts, which comprise trusts for the relief of poverty, for the advancement of education, for the advancement of religion, and for other purposes beneficial to the community, and the court will not allow a charitable trust to fail because the purpose is uncertain but will give effect to the truster's intention by settling a scheme for administration of the trust to give effect as nearly as possible to the truster's intentions.

A trustee must accept or disclaim office, and persons may be authorized to appoint new trustees, or the court may do so. A trustee may retire but remains liable for things done while he was a trustee, or may be removed by the court. A trustee must not make use of trust property for his private advantage and must account for profit made out of his trust. He is not entitled to any remuneration, may not acquire trust property, and dealings with beneficiaries are voidable.

The trustees' duties are to take possession of and preserve the trust property, be diligent and prudent in administering it, act personally, be impartial as between beneficiaries, keep accounts and give information to the beneficiaries as required, and invest the trust funds in the manner permitted by statute. If in doubt, trustees are entitled to obtain the opinion of the court as to the right course of action, and they may have specific questions determined by the court.

The court now has wide powers to approve arrangements varying or revoking the trusts or enlarging the powers of the trustees.

Breach of trust is any act in contravention or excess of the duties imposed on the trustees by the trust, including neglects, omissions, and dishonesty, and trustees are liable in so far as loss has resulted to the trust estate. They may be relieved from liability by provision in the trust deed, or by the court under statutory power. Beneficiaries can obtain no relief against trustees if they concurred or acquiesced in the breach of trust.

There is no generally accepted definition of the word "settlement" but it may be defined as any disposition of property, of whatever nature, by any instrument or number of instruments, whereby trusts are constituted for the purpose of regulating the enjoyment of the settled property successively among the persons or classes of persons nominated by the settlor. However, for certain tax purposes the word "settlement" is given a much wider meaning.

The trust concept has analogies with, but is distinct from, the *fidei commissa* of civil law systems, which is really a different concept altogether. For this reason, certain countries, such as Panama, Liechtenstein, and Monaco, have introduced trusts by statute. However, these creatures of statute lack the body of equitable principles that characterize the Anglo-Saxon trust.

2. Tax Treatment of Trusts

In many countries, the income of the trust bears tax in the hands of the trustees, either by deduction at source or by direct assessment.

Trustees stand, broadly speaking, in the shoes both of the creator of the trust, who may be living or dead, and of the beneficiaries. Their powers of dealing with the property entrusted to them are to be gathered from the true construction of the trust instrument, if any, as supplemented or restricted by the principles of equity and by statutory provisions. In most countries, the court exercises ultimate control over all trusts.

The following generally form part of the total income of the beneficiary (though there are significant differences in the various tax systems):

(a) income in which the beneficiary has a vested interest, whether this is paid to him or accumulated;

(b) sums in the nature of income applied for the benefit of the beneficiary under the terms of the trust;

(c) sums in the nature of income paid to or applied for the benefit of the beneficiary in exercise of a discretion.

Income in which the beneficiary has a contingent interest, and which is accumulated, does not generally form part of the beneficiary's income as it arises.

The income from certain types of settlement may in certain countries be deemed for tax purposes to be income of the settlor; sometimes there are provisions that require the settlor to pass on to the trustees or beneficiaries the benefit of any reliefs he may receive in respect of the trust income concerned, and empower the settlor to recover from the trustees or beneficiaries the amount of any additional tax liability he incurs in respect of such trust income.

To determine whether a sum forms part of a beneficiary's total income, it may be necessary to ascertain, not whether the sum arises from capital or income of the trust, but whether it is received by the beneficiary in the quality of income.

3. Origins of Offshore Trusts

The Medieval trust became a tax avoidance technique which worked so effectively that by the end of the last century the trust was well and truly in position to fulfil its prime vocation of income tax and estate tax avoidance.

Inevitably, the trust became a target of U.K. and U.S. anti-avoidance measures. But since the first moves to restrict the free operation of tax avoidance were domestic, the wealthy simply moved their trusts offshore. Anti-avoidance measures gradually came to be directed also at the offshore trust.

A prime example of a far-reaching anti-avoidance measure is the U.K. imposition of tax liability on a U.K. resident who has power to enjoy income of any person (a term which includes companies and trusts) outside the United Kingdom. Although there must be a "transfer of assets" to bring the provision into play, this can be a transfer between two non-residents and it is practically impossible to conceive of a situation where an offshore entity could be set up without there being a transfer of assets within the meaning of the section.

For the most part, it is the Anglo-Americans that have the monopoly of the offshore trust business. But there is one contender that has done extraordinarily well with its own inventivity and marketing skills — Liechtenstein. The most common and best known of the Liechtenstein entities is the *Anstalt* or establishment. The *Anstalt* is the duck-billed platypus of offshore creatures. A curious mixture of a company and a trust, it is formed in much the same way as a regular company, but has beneficiaries as well.

The most unusual feature is that the supreme authority of the *Anstalt* vests in the current holder of the founder's rights. For this reason, the certificate evidencing the founder's rights is often transferred or assigned from one person to another in blank without any name filled in — thus making the certificate the approximate equivalent of a bearer share document for all the shares of a corporation. The current holder of the founder's rights has the power to amend the articles of incorporation and to appoint or remove directors. He can also appoint beneficiaries and determine their rights. If beneficiaries are not designated, the founder's rights constitute an asset in the estate of the holder upon his death.

Because of these oddities the *Anstalt* does not find a ready niche in the legal systems of other countries. Some courts refuse to accept that an *Anstalt* is a separate legal entity at all. Sometimes they treat the *Anstalt* as a company and sometimes as a trust, their choice seeming to turn on little more than the way they can raise more tax. To make things worse, most European tax administrators assume that a taxpayer who has dealings with an *Anstalt* is hiding assets and income.

The *Stiftung* or foundation has many of the features of a trust. It has been described as a charitable foundation with non-charitable beneficiaries, a sort of equivalent of a family Red Cross. If an eligible family member asks the *Stiftung's* board for money he is likely to get it; an outsider will not. There are no founder's rights. The board administers the assets and may even have the power to designate beneficiaries and determine their rights.

Again, it is far from obvious whether a foreign court would classify a *Stiftung* as a trust or as an association; and in some systems it might even be taxed as if it were a company.

All of these factors conspire to make the Liechtenstein *Anstalt* and *Stiftung* somewhat less than the ideal entities for most purposes.

4. International Aspects of Offshore Trusts

4.1 Foreign Elements

The tax status of trustees may be affected by various foreign elements. The settlor of a trust may himself be a nondomiciled or nonresident individual; the trustees, individual or corporate, may be nonresident; and some or all of the beneficiaries may be resident in different countries. In addition, the law applicable may be that of a foreign country, since there is no obligation to select the legal system of a country in which the settlor, the beneficiaries, or the trustees are resident.

Again, the income and capital gains arising to trustees may have foreign sources, and the management of trust investments may be carried on in a country different from that in which the trustees or any of the other parties are resident.

Another complicating factor is that the tax status of trustees is determined according to different rules depending upon whether the liability is to income tax or to capital gains tax. Thus it is possible for trustees to be liable to one tax and exempt from the other. Special treatment may be accorded to professional trustees, those carrying on the business of managing trusts.

Frequently trust deeds contain the so-called "Cuba Clause" allowing the trustees to be changed and the situs and proper law of the trust to be transferred from one jurisdiction to another.

The retirement of trustees and the appointment of new trustees with a different residence status may produce a situation in which the residence status of the trust changes within one tax year. The question then arises as to whether there will be different liability for parts of a year; or whether the status before or after the change will apply throughout.

4.2 Effect of Foreign Law

The question may arise as to what are the particular effects of the proper law of a nonresident settlement on the tax liabilities of a resident beneficiary.

In *Lord Inchyra v Jennings*[1] the question was whether certain periodical payments out of the capital of a will trust made under the law of the District of Columbia in the USA constituted income in the hands of a U.K. resident beneficiary. It was accepted that the nature of the right to the income must be determined in accordance with the law of the District of Columbia. However, it was held that whether the receipts represented capital or income in the hands of the beneficiary must be determined in accordance with English law. In this case, there was a right to receive annual payments for 20 years, so that these payments constituted income.

In *Lawson v Rolfe*[2] the appellant, who was at all times resident and domiciled in England, held a life interest in a share of the residue under a will trust, the proper law of which was the law of California; and she was thereby entitled to receive the income of specific stocks in U.S. companies. For the relevant years, certain companies distributed stock dividends (i.e., bonus shares), a proportion of which was passed over to the life tenant under a rule of Californian law. It was contended by the Revenue that because the appellant received the stock dividends in her capacity as life tenant, they therefore assumed the quality of income in her hands. It was held, however, that although it was correct to ascertain the nature of the life-tenant's interest under the relevant foreign law, the nature and quality of the receipt then fell to be determined under English law, so that the stock dividends (i.e., bonus shares) retained the quality of capital not income in the hands of the recipient[3].

4.3 Form of Offshore Trusts

The concept of the trust originated in English law and the idea has been exported from England to all those territories which adopted and embraced the common law system.

However, there is no universal trust law. Each territory has adapted English trust law as necessary for its own purposes. For example, under English trust law, a trust must be for a natural person or established for charitable purposes only. Some common law jurisdictions allow for a "purpose" trust to be established. This is a trust established for a particular purpose which may or may not be charitable.

The application of the tax rules is problematical in relation to civil law jurisdictions which do not recognize trusts. Such jurisdictions often have their own civil law concepts which may in some ways resemble trusts but which may be characterized under local law as contract or agency. The *Hague Convention on the Law Applicable to Trusts and on their Recognition* has been signed by certain of the civil law countries. See Appendix II.

4.4 Protector in a Foreign Trust

Many offshore trust deeds include the appointment of a protector, who has the power to remove and appoint trustees. Similarly, a protector may have the power to change the residence of the trust, and generally to represent the interests of a class of beneficiaries.

A protector can be given the power of veto over the exercise of powers by trustees. The office of protector is of a fiduciary nature not for personal benefit.

EXAMPLE

In the U.K. case of IRC v Schroder[4] the settlor of a settlement was a member of a committee of protection with power to remove and appoint trustees. A committee member could be removed by a majority of the committee and in the event of a vacancy occurring, the settlor himself had power to fill the vacancy and appoint additional members. The Revenue claimed that the settlor, as a result of his power to appoint members of the committee of protection and therefore trustees, was able to insure that the dispositive powers of the trustees were exercised in accordance with his directions. He was thus able to control the application of the trust income and he therefore had power to enjoy that income within the meaning of Taxes Act 1988 s 742.

However, the court held that the settlor did not have the power to enjoy the trust income for the following reasons:

(a) the settlor's powers as protector were fiduciary powers which could not be properly used to insure he had a majority of the committee which would follow his directions;

(b) the question was not whether he was able to influence the exercise by the trustees of their fiduciary powers but whether he was able to control the application of the trust income.

Despite this decision, a settlor is normally advised not to become the protector in relation to an offshore trust, and not to appoint a resident individual as a protector. This is to insure that the residence of the trust is not influenced by the residence status of the protector.

Similarly, it is important that the protector's powers are not so wide as to imply that he is, for example, carrying on the general administration of the trust, or he is himself a trustee.

5. General Administration of a Trust

In many Anglo-American tax systems a trust would be held to be a resident unless two conditions are both satisfied:

(a) all or a majority of the trustees are neither resident nor ordinarily resident in the country concerned; and

(b) the general administration of the trust is ordinarily carried on outside the country concerned.

It may therefore be necessary to determine what constitutes the general administration of a trust. However, there is no clear authority to interpret this difficult expression.

Normally, the general administration of a trust would include the trustees' management of trust investment portfolios, trust bookkeeping and accounting, and the operations of the trustees' bank accounts. There is a view that general administration would not include decisions to appoint income or capital to beneficiaries and the general exercise of fiduciary powers. However, the function of the trustees is to administer the trust assets for the benefit of the beneficiaries. Therefore, in order to determine where the general administration is carried on one must look to where the real work of the trust is carried on.

For example, a distinction may be drawn between the general administration of an offshore trust and the management of particular assets, say, a portfolio of securities in the country concerned which constitutes the whole or part of the trust fund. However, such arrangements should be established with care and the trustees should retain control over how, and when, investment decisions are made, monitor portfolio performance and make any distributions of income and capital themselves.

See Chapter 12, "Case Study: U.S. Tax Implications of a U.S. Person Supervising an Offshore Trust."

6. Asset Protection Trusts

The term *asset protection trust* (APT) is a term of art referring to the trusts that are specifically designed to address the limits to the uses of standard trusts. It is of course arguable that the term is a misnomer since nearly every trust may be considered to have asset protection as one of its objectives.

Asset protection, as its name indicates, is aimed at protecting companies and individuals from creditors, real and phony, from spouses and children, from partners and employees.

Aside from protecting assets, a number of other estate and financial planning objectives can be achieved through the use of a foreign situs APT. Generally, the APT is considered to be the most effective asset protection planning tool available.

6.1. Superiority of Offshore Trusts Over Domestic Trusts

As an asset protecting planning device, foreign situs trusts are generally considered to be superior to domestic trusts for the following reasons:

(a) *Enhanced Ability to Retain Benefit and Control*

Domestic trust law generally restricts the extent of benefit and control that a settlor can retain following establishment of the trust. A maxim of domestic law is that one does not place property out of a creditor's reach if the property has not been placed out of the transferor's reach. Accordingly, a domestic trust settled when the settlor's seas are calm may nevertheless remain vulnerable to the reach of creditors during the settlor's lifetime to the extent benefit or control is retained by the settlor.

(b) *Offshore Trusts not Automatic Targets*

Because a domestic trust remains subject to local jurisdiction, it can be expected to be a target in litigation against the settlor if the trust corpus is substantial. Due to geographical, jurisdictional, and other factors (such as whether the judgments and orders of a domestic court will be recognized by a foreign court ("comity"), an APT is not nearly as likely to be the same automatic defendant as a domestic trust.

(c) *Offshore Trusts Create Practical Barriers*

The mere fact that an APT is a foreign entity will have a definite impact on a creditor's decision either regarding instituting suit in the first instance or concerning how far the creditor is willing to go to pursue assets. Factors such as:

- the psychological barrier of dealing with foreigners and foreign legal systems,
- the costs of pursuing litigation overseas (particularly if a new, non-contingency-based suit must be brought against the defendant in the foreign court),
- the added uncertainty of prevailing under foreign law, and

  the increased time required to litigate abroad,
- substantially enhance the protection the trust assets will enjoy should a problem develop in the future.

(d) *Offshore Trusts Ultimately more Protective*

The trust law of certain offshore jurisdictions is usually more specific and protective than is the trust law of the domestic jurisdiction. See Section 7 below.

It should be noted that certain states (e.g., South Dakota, Alaska, and Delaware) have adopted ATP legislation, which offers many of the features to be found in the IOFCs themselves.

6.2 Selecting the Appropriate Offshore Jurisdiction

There are a number of considerations that should be analyzed in choosing the offshore jurisdiction whose laws will govern an APT, including, *inter alia:*

- whether the jurisdiction's trust law is favorable, well defined, and protective,
- the political, economic, and social stability of the jurisdiction,
- the jurisdiction's reputation in the world business community,
- the tax laws of the jurisdiction,
- whether language barriers exist,
- whether the jurisdiction has modern telecommunications facilities,
- whether the jurisdiction offers adequate legal, accounting, and financial services.

A number of offshore financial centers, such as the Bahamas, Belize, the Cayman Islands, the Cook Islands, Cyprus, Gibraltar, and the Turks & Caicos Islands, satisfy these conditions to varying degrees. Though recently enacted legislation clarifies to some extent the myriad of issues relating to when and under what circumstances a creditor of a settlor can reach assets of the settlor's trust, a great deal of uncertainty in this area exists under domestic as well as English common law.

The laws of the Bahamas, the Cayman Islands, Cyprus, the Cook Islands, and certain other jurisdictions provide a fixed period of time following a transfer within which a creditor must commence a suit against the trust or its settlor or both.

Other important provisions to look for in APT legislation include the following:

- the standard of proof that a creditor must meet in attempting to show fraudulent intent on the part of the transferor,
- the extent to which a transferor may retain benefit in, and control over, an APT without exposing the APT to the transferor's creditors,
- the relevance of the settlor's solvency following transfers to the APT,
- the recognition to be given to judgments and orders of foreign courts that may affect an APT, its trustees, and its assets,
- what conditions must be satisfied in order to freeze trust assets.

The asset protection trust law of Gibraltar, Turks & Caicos, and the Cook Islands cover these points.

Moreover, a number of other offshore financial centers, such as the Bahamas, the British Virgin Islands, Bermuda, Guernsey, Jersey, and the Isle of Man, are enhancing their asset protection trust legislation.

The United Kingdom is able to bring pressure to bear on its Overseas Territories (notably Bermuda and the Cayman Islands) to open their financial records to official investigators; this has led Belize to introduce new mutual funds and other financial services legislation.

6.3 Location of Trust Assets

The choice of location of the trust assets is not the same issue as the choice of location of the trust itself. A properly drafted foreign situs APT allows the trustees to invest trust assets in any part of the world.

Through the concurrent use of other planning techniques, such as a foreign limited partnership ("FLP"), the settlor can be given direct control and management over the protected assets without being a trustee and without compromising the protection afforded.

6.4 Deterrent Effect of APTs

Although a domestic court should recognize the settlor's choice of law and bona fide purposes for the APT planning, a safety valve is necessary to protect against the possibility that a court will disregard the settlor's decision as to choice of law and will apply domestic law in an effort to reach the trust assets.

The ultimate safety valve is the ability of the APT, as an international instrument, to invest and reinvest assets in any part of the world. The option exists for the trustees to best exercise their fiduciary duty to protect trust assets by diversifying investment of the assets outside any jurisdiction in which a problem may be foreseen, thereby forcing the battle over the assets into one or more foreign courts.

6.5 Foreign Tax Considerations

A correctly drafted APT provides neither tax benefits (other than tax benefits that one can achieve through a living or testamentary trust) nor tax detriments. Because an APT is not a tax-motivated structure, it should not saddle the settlor with any additional domestic or foreign tax burden.

An APT that is structured correctly and governed by an appropriate foreign jurisdiction is not subject to any income, gift, estate, transfer, excise, or like tax in the selected jurisdiction. The foreign jurisdictions that have enacted APT legislation generally treat APTs as "exempt trusts" as long as none of the beneficiaries is resident in the jurisdictions.

6.6 Fraudulent Conveyance Considerations

If there is an identifiable creditor problem — whether pending, threatened, or expected — the scope of planning opportunities is narrowed. For this reason, asset protection planning is best implemented when the legal seas are calm. Attempting to protect assets when the legal seas turn choppy may be like trying to buy fire insurance during a fire.

The issue arises as to whether one is free to plan for potential problems with creditors when one has no pending or threatened litigation and has not otherwise been involved in a situation that could reasonably be expected to develop into a problem with a creditor in the future.

The common law system favors the free alienability of property. If there is no creditor entitled to protection under applicable fraudulent conveyance law, one is generally free to do with property as one deems fit. One is free to consume, destroy, sell, or make gifts of assets. Assets may be sold or given to an entity or a trust, whether domestic or foreign. The issue as to whether a transfer is fraudulent or not, does not in general turn on the identity of the transferee.

Although most fraudulent conveyance law seeks to protect present as well as subsequent creditors, the definition of "subsequent" creditor is not so broad as to include all the nameless, faceless persons whom the transferor has yet to meet or give cause to complain (i.e., future potential creditors). The class of subsequent creditors is a relatively narrow one and includes those persons against whom the transferor harbored an actual intent to injure or defraud as of the date of the transfer, or persons who are injured as a result of the transferor conducting his affairs with reckless disregard for the rights of others following a transfer of property.

However, it has been held that while subsequent creditors are entitled to protection under fraudulent conveyance law, future potential creditors are not. The "no harm, no foul" approach is expressed as follows: "If there were no creditors, the conveyance could not be fraudulent to them."

6.7 Avoiding Risks

A properly structured APT should contain all necessary checks and balances in a carefully drafted trust deed. Moreover, as an international vehicle, the APT can hold assets in any part of the world; the assets need not be physically held in the jurisdiction the laws of which govern the APT's administration, interpretation, or validity. For so long as, and to the extent that, assets are held in an FLP, the general partner (not the trustees) has direct control over, and management of, the protected assets.

Another material issue is whether a party may some day be in the awkward position of either having to repatriate assets or else be held in contempt of court.

A well-drafted APT would, under such a circumstance, make it impossible for the assets held by the trust to be repatriated. Impossibility of performance is usually a complete defense to a civil contempt charge. An exception exists if the party claiming impossibility of performance is responsible for the creation of the impossibility. For this exception to apply, however, there must be a nexus in time between the order in question and the creation of the impossibility. This nexus would be lacking if the APT were established and funded at a proper time.

Another material issue is whether a domestic court can be expected to recognize the foreign-based planning when assets remain physically at home.

In the context of an APT, the danger would be that a court would disregard the choice of law made by the settlor and determine that trust assets are indeed available to satisfy a creditor's claim.

For this reason, it frequently makes sense for the foreign trustee, in exercising its fiduciary duty to protect trust assets, to diversify those assets out of the jurisdiction in which the settlor's problem may be developing. Through this protective step, the battle over the assets can be forced into the foreign court, which would apply its protective legislation.

An effective offshore tax plan is one that anticipates the worst case foreseeable at the time it is designed and implemented.

7. Asset Protection and the Statute of Elizabeth (See Appendix III)

7.1 The Problem

Since the creation of a trust involves the settlor transferring legal ownership of property to trustees who hold that property upon terms outlined by the trust deed, on the face of it, from the moment the trust is properly constituted the property comprised within the trust is no longer the property of the settlor and ceases to be available to discharge a liability owed by the settlor to a creditor or otherwise. The trust, and particularly the offshore trust, would seem to be the obvious asset protection mechanism. In a sense, this premise is legally correct. But the mechanism may nonetheless not work, owing to an important provision in a 1571 English law, known as the Statute of Elizabeth, which has also been introduced into the law of a number of legal systems based on English law, and this includes many of the states in the United States and most of the tax havens of the world.

Under such legislation it is sometimes possible to set aside transfers into trust even if the settlor transferred the property many years before the debt arose and, at the time of making the transfer, had no indication that the particular debt would arise in the future.

For example, in U.K. law the provisions under which a disposition into trust may be challenged are contained in the Insolvency Act 1986, dealing with transfers made at an undervalue and preferences.

Under U.S. Federal Law the equivalent provisions are contained within section 548 of the Bankruptcy Reform Act of 1978, as amended, and in state law within the Uniform Fraudulent Conveyance Act of 1918, which currently applies in 18 states including New York, and the Uniform Fraudulent Transfer Act which currently applies in 17 states including California.

Most other developed countries have laws which have a similar effect to those noted above and in many common law jurisdictions it is difficult to determine whether, and to what extent, the Statute of Elizabeth applies.

With the above in mind, laws governing asset protection trusts have been developed by certain jurisdictions to provide an extra degree of protection to that afforded by a normal trust and to remove the doubts over whether a trust arrangement does completely protect the trust assets. This has been achieved by enacting legislation which specifically overrides the Statute of Elizabeth type legislation and states that, subject to certain conditions being fulfilled, no application for the return of trust property will be entertained irrespective of judgments obtained outside the offshore jurisdiction.

In a wave of recent developments, one offshore base after another is changing its laws to accommodate asset protection trusts. Three jurisdictions (among others) which are commonly used to shelter asset protection trusts from the application of the Statute of Elizabeth are Gibraltar, the Turks & Caicos Islands, and the Cook Islands.

7.2 Gibraltar Asset Protection Trusts

Trust law in Gibraltar is based on English Common Law, and Gibraltar recognizes and gives full effect to the concept of trusts.

The legislation creating the concept of the asset protection trust is the *Bankruptcy (Amendment) Ordinance* 1990 and the *Bankruptcy (Register of Dispositions) Regulations* 1990.

The *Bankruptcy (Amendment) Ordinance* 1990 amends the *Bankruptcy Ordinance* to the effect that a disposition of assets by a settlor into a Trust will not be voidable at the instance of a creditor provided the following conditions are met:

- the settlor is an individual,
- the settlor is not insolvent at the date of the disposition,
- the settlor does not become insolvent in consequence of the disposition,
- the settlement is registered in accordance with the Regulations.

The disposition must be registered in order to gain the protection allowed for under the law. The requirements of registration are specified in section 5 of the *Bankruptcy (Register of Dispositions) Regulations* 1990. A disposition may be simply registered by providing the Registrar with the following minimal information:

- the name and address of the trustee,
- the name of the disposition,
- the date of making the disposition and the duration thereof, i.e. the perpetuity of the trust,
- the country of ordinary residence of the settlor.

The application is accompanied by undertakings from the trustee making the application for registration to the effect that:

- the settlor has satisfactorily completed forms of inquiry establishing the financial position of the settlor and inquiring as to any claims which are being made against the settlor or which will or might be made in the future,
- the trustee has taken all reasonable steps to substantiate the information within the forms of inquiry mentioned above,

- the trustee has obtained an affidavit of solvency from the settlor.

A fee of £300 is payable upon registration of the trust and a renewal fee of £100 annually thereafter.

The details contained on the Register are available only to the Financial & Development Secretariat and are specifically not available for public inspection. The law contains secrecy provisions which make it a criminal offence for any person to reveal these details.

Gibraltar has attempted to insure that asset protection trusts are not used by those seeking to avoid a current or contingent liability which is within their knowledge at the time of making the disposition and have imposed very high standards on those administering and setting up trusts.

7.3 Turks & Caicos Islands Asset Protection Trusts

Section 61 of the Turks & Caicos Islands *Trust Ordinance* 1990 specifically refers to asset protection trusts and estates:

1. If by virtue of a disposition made by or on behalf of a settlor his property becomes trust property which is the subject of a Turks & Caicos trust, and:
   (a) the settlor is an individual;
   (b) the settlor is not insolvent when the disposition is made; and
   (c) the settlor does not become insolvent by reason of the disposition, that disposition shall not be voidable at the instance of any creditor of the settlor.
2. In any proceedings in which the provisions of this section are to be applied the burden of proof of the fact that a settlor is or has been insolvent shall be upon the person asserting that fact.

It is not necessary to register the trust in order to gain the protection of the Ordinance and the effect of the law is that applications through the Courts of the Turks & Caicos made by a creditor of the settlor for the return of the trust property would be bound to fail as long as the provisions of the Ordinance have been adhered to.

Any trust which is set up and administered within the Turks & Caicos automatically gains the added protection of the asset protection legislation without further formality or registration.

The legislation abolishes all rules regarding perpetuity and accumulation periods. A Turks & Caicos trust may therefore last indefinitely and there is no requirement to distribute income.

Protectors are given statutory recognition as being persons whose consent the trustees must obtain before exercising a power or discretion. The legislation specifically provides that the Protector shall not be deemed to be a trustee.

A trustee is not required to disclose information to any person except for accounting information which need only be revealed to the beneficiaries.

The legislation provides that the interest of a beneficiary may be reduced or terminated in the event of that beneficiary becoming insolvent or any of his property becoming liable to sequestration by a creditor.

The legislation stipulates that a trust may be revocable either wholly or in part. There is a modern trend of creating revocable trusts and there has been some doubt in other jurisdictions as to whether such trusts are initially valid, so this provision lends great clarity to the law in this area.

Provision is made that the terms of the trust may allow for changing the law from that of the Turks & Caicos to the law of another jurisdiction provided that the trust deed stipulates that the change cannot invalidate any other terms of the trust and that the change is consistent with the intention of the settlor.

7.4 Cook Islands International Trusts

The 1995 amendments to the International Trusts Act 1984 are designed to reinforce the element of certainty in the Cook Islands trust law. The following are the most significant elements.

An amendment removes the requirement for an international trust to be limited to a period no longer than 100 years, and applies automatically to all new international trusts. Provision is made for existing international trusts to adopt the new law. The validity of existing trusts and their flexibility are preserved because a settlement may provide for bequests to vest on the occurrence of an event or within a time limit. A "safety-net" provision counters the danger that a trust without a perpetuity period might be void for uncertainty.

The exercise of a power contained in a trust instrument to change the governing law of the trust is conclusive of that change. Provision is made for continuity of trust relationships and trust validity of transfers of property to or from the trustee to continue, in spite of a change in the governing law. A trust may be governed by different laws in respect of different aspects of its management and administration, and the trust instrument may also provide for a change in the governing law of a trust in the event of a specified event or state of affairs, permitting the urgent removal of a trust from one jurisdiction to another.

The trustee may delegate any or all of the trustee's powers, functions or discretions, including management of trust property (but excluding powers of disposal concerning distributions to beneficiaries). In so doing, the trustee is required to exercise the standard of care of a "reasonable and prudent man of business".

A trust instrument may provide a trustee with a general power to undertake any kind of investment in any property, equivalent to that of a natural person.

Any person or group may be appointed a custodian trustee, and any action concerning the trust property must be brought or defended in the name of the custodian trustee. Upon termination of a custodian trustee's appointment, any restriction upon the powers of a managing trustee lapse and the managing trustee assumes all trustee functions, unless the trust instrument provides otherwise.

A trust instrument may effectively be executed in counterpart in different places and times within or without the Cook Islands. The period allowed for registration of an international trust is 45 days from the date of establishment of the trust, which period may be extended at the Registrar's discretion.

It is possible for a trust to adopt a name for the purpose of identification and for the trust instrument to authorize the trustees to have trust property registered in that name rather than in the name of the trustees. Legal title remains in the trustees. The trustees may delegate the function of holding title to trust property as between themselves.

There is segregation of trust property from that of a trustee's own property in the event of the trustee's insolvency. A trustee must exercise the care, diligence and skill that a prudent person would exercise in managing the affairs of others.

The trust instrument may provide for one or more persons to be a "nominated person" to represent all or any beneficiaries who are minors or yet to be ascertained.

A trustee's contractual liability to third parties may be effectively limited to an amount no greater than the value of the trustee's right to be indemnified out of the assets of the trust.

There is a provision expressly permitting majority decision-making by the trustees.

A "protector" means a person who has the power to appoint or remove a trustee, or who controls whether by vote or otherwise, the trustee's exercise of powers.

There is specific recognition of both purpose trusts (in favor of an object) and trading trusts (where third party rights may be prescribed and thus controlled).

Notes

1. See Appendix I, "Example of Offshore Discretionary Trust Deed and Letter of Wishes."
2. 1 [1966] Ch 37; [1965] 2 All ER 714; 42 TC 388.

   [1970] Ch 612; [1970] 1 All ER 761; 46 TC 199.
3. Since this case was decided certain stock dividends have become taxable in the U.K.: TA 1988 s 249 (formerly F(No 2)A 1975 s 34).
4. [1983] STC 480.

PART TWO

OFFSHORE TAX PLANNING

CHAPTER SEVEN

METHOD OF OFFSHORE TAX PLANNING

1. Tax Planning in General

It is both lawful and sensible to arrange business and personal affairs in such a way as to attract the lowest possible incidence of tax. The widening scope of tax laws, the complexity of their provisions, and high tax rates make it more necessary than ever for business enterprises and individuals alike to plan their taxable events with considerable care.

For a commercial or industrial enterprise, an unnecessarily increased tax burden represents a business waste that not only reduces its distributable profits but may well make it uncompetitive.

In the case of an individual, the net return from personal endeavor and the investment of capital is in most countries so severely reduced by the Revenue that the failure to take advantage of potential tax minimization benefits may have a considerable effect on his spending power and accumulated wealth. The omission to anticipate death duties and inheritance taxes will frequently cut an unnecessarily deep wedge into his estate.

Tax planning is the process of taking into consideration all relevant tax factors, in the light of the material nontax factors, for the purpose of determining

- whether (and if so),
- when,
- how, and
- with whom

to enter into and conduct transactions, operations, and relationships, with the object of keeping the tax burden falling on taxable events and persons as low as possible while attaining the desired business, personal, and other objectives.

2. Offshore Tax Planning

The term *offshore* applies to countries or transactions

(a) where there are no relevant taxes;

(b) where taxes are levied only on internal taxable events, but not at all, or at low rates, on profits from foreign sources; or

(c) where special tax privileges are granted to certain types of taxable persons or events (such special tax privileges may be accorded by the domestic internal tax system or may derive from a combination of domestic and treaty provisions).

Offshore tax planning is tax planning in which factors involving more than one country are included in the original database and an offshore element is introduced as an extension of domestic tax planning.

The different ways in which two or more systems may be linked offer considerable scope for tax minimization or deferral, particularly where at least one of the countries is offshore, since offshore does, by its very nature, generally refer to a better tax deal in a foreign country.

On the other hand, where a project crosses frontiers, there are far more tax and nontax factors to be taken into account than in a purely domestic case. It follows that offshore tax planning may often be exceedingly complex.

3. The Offshore Database

With the expansion of international trade and private foreign investment, it has become increasingly necessary to have access to a database containing general information regarding tax and business laws and practices in foreign countries. This need is catered to by a number of publications and on-line services, which are of varying degrees of accuracy, completeness, and speed of updating.

However, most of the available information is far from comprehensive, and it therefore follows that one is dependent to a greater or lesser extent on secondhand information.

The difficulty of obtaining adequate information is aggravated in the case of countries where administrative rulings (and even judicial decisions) are not published fully and quickly, where the ultimate tax bill is subject to negotiation (especially where such negotiation is open to graft), and generally where there is a contrast between the printed word and actual practice.

One is thus frequently obliged to obtain advice from experts in foreign countries involved in a proposed arrangement. Depending on the available documentation, it may be desirable to seek such advice at the outset, during the course of the research, or only at a much later stage for the purpose of controlling whether a possible benefit or pitfall may not have been overlooked.

The database required for the design of an offshore tax plan consists of

(a) the facts,

(b) tax factors, and

(c) nontax factors.

The Facts

The particular situation of a taxpayer and the business and other objectives vary from case to case. It is obviously not possible to draw up a correct offshore tax plan without a comprehensive and accurate briefing on the facts.

Bad briefing results partly from the lack of awareness that it is possible to take into account all possible solutions to a problem and avoid pitfalls only with access to the full and accurate database containing all the material facts.

Tax Factors

In analyzing the tax factors of an offshore tax plan, it is necessary to examine

(a) the domestic internal tax systems of the countries involved in the project; and

(b) the manner in which the general rules embodied in such systems are affected by the introduction of the offshore factor.

Nontax Factors

Nontax factors may also have to be taken into consideration for the purposes of a proposed offshore tax plan. These can be every bit as important as the tax factors since the tax tail must never be allowed to wag the business dog.

4. Types of Tax Encountered in Offshore Countries

It should not be assumed that taxes in offshore countries may be ignored. On the contrary, there are a number of classes of direct and indirect taxes and duties that may be encountered offshore, such as the following:

- Individual and corporate income taxes
- Capital gains taxes
- Special taxes on dividends, interest, and royalties
- Withholding taxes on salaries, dividends, interest, royalties, etc.
- Capital taxes (e.g., property, patrimony, net worth taxes, etc.) imposed on individuals and companies
- Payroll taxes
- Company duties
- Business taxes
- Business license and other trade taxes
- Stamp duties
- Transfer duties

- Registration duties
- Customs duties and other import and export duties
- Sales and use taxes
- Turnover taxes on value added
- Capital transfer taxes
- Estate and inheritance taxes
- Gift taxes

When dealing with foreign countries, it may be important to understand the precise nature of a foreign tax or duty. Similar terms frequently have quite different connotations in other systems. The particular taxes and duties that are imposed and the extent to which they overlap may vary considerably from one system to another.

5. Definitional Content of Terms

Problems may arise in determining the definitional content of terms, either within the context of the legal system or in relation to another onshore or offshore system or a tax treaty. The meaning of terms that are constantly employed in treaties and domestic laws (such as *income tax, total income, residence, domicile, immovable property,* and *permanent establishment*) may vary considerably according to the context.

The presence of different languages may lie at the root of the difficulty. The literal translation of terms may prove treacherous. Treaties are frequently concluded in more than one language. In such cases, it is specifically provided whether such texts are equally authentic or whether one text is to prevail in case of doubt.

A major part of tax planning involves the use of tax treaties. Treaties normally define certain terms that are employed. Recent treaties show a tendency toward the unification of these definitions. An important number of such treaties have been modeled on the draft conventions of the Fiscal Committee of the Organization for Economic Cooperation and Development (OECD) for the Avoidance of Double Taxation on Income and Capital, and on Estates and Inheritances.

In the absence of a definition, reference is made to the domestic law of the countries concerned. A standard clause contained in many treaties runs along the following lines:

> As regards the application of the Convention by a Contracting State any term not otherwise defined shall, unless the context otherwise required, have the meaning which it has under the laws of that Contracting State relating to the taxes which are the subject of the Convention.

Sometimes interpretative rulings are issued for the purpose of determining whether a foreign tax falls within the scope of a treaty or legislative provision. It may also occur that the tax authorities of the countries concerned enter into an agreement to settle such questions.

EXAMPLE[1]

The U.S. Internal Revenue Code, sec. 901, allows a credit against U.S. tax for foreign income, war profits, and excess profits taxes. For a tax paid to a foreign country to qualify as an income tax, it must be shown that the tax imposed by the foreign country is a tax on income within the U.S. concept thereof,[2] or is a tax in lieu of an income tax within the meaning of sec. 903.[3]

The question arose as to whether the Italian tax bonds (*imposta sulle obbligazioni*)[4] qualified as an "income tax" for the purposes of the foreign tax credit provisions of sec. 901.

The tax on bonds and like securities issued in Italy is payable by the issuers who are entitled to recover it from the bondholders. The tax is imposed at a rate based on the taxable value of the bonds. The value of the bonds is determined on the basis of the latest stock exchange settlement price prior to the closing of the taxpayer's balance sheet, or in the case of unlisted bonds or bonds that are listed but have no settlement price, the nominal value. In defining taxable value, it is provided that the tax is payable on the aggregate value of the bonds as shown in the issuer's balance sheet, reduced by one-half for the bonds issued in the second half of the fiscal year.

The IRS issued a ruling holding that the Italian tax on bonds bears no relation to the income or profits of the issuer or to the interest payable with respect to the bonds. It is therefore not an "income tax" within the meaning of sec. 901, nor a tax paid in lieu of an income tax within the meaning of sec. 903. It is therefore not a creditable tax under sec. 901.

Even where a term is defined for the purposes of the tax treaty, a dispute with the tax authorities may nevertheless arise on the question as to whether the particular facts fall within the definition.

A number of reported cases deal with the question of the existence of a *permanent establishment*. This term is frequently used in tax treaties as a basis for the apportionment of taxable income (particularly with regard to industrial and commercial profits). The term is usually defined for the purposes of such treaties owing to variations in its precise definitional content.

EXAMPLE[5]

The Italian branch office of a French corporation was involved in buying wine in Italy for the French corporation. The goods acquired by the branch office were regularly invoiced to the head office in France.

The question arose as to whether the branch office was a "permanent establishment" for the purposes of the France-Italy Tax Treaty[6] and therefore subject to Italian tax. Article 3(4)(1) of the treaty states that offices shall be deemed to be permanent establishments and that their profits are subject to tax in the state in which the office is located.

The tax commission in Milan decided that, as the branch office charged its head office the same prices as it had paid for the goods, it was not engaged in commercial activities but merely provided the head office with merchandise. The branch office was not, therefore, a permanent establishment and was not subject to Italian tax.

However, it may happen that a particular treaty does not define a term that it employs. In such a case, the courts or the revenue authorities may be called upon to furnish the definition. Frequently, reference is made to the provisions of the OECD Model Conventions.

EXAMPLE[7]

The taxpayer was a French citizen resident in France who had contracted with an unrelated U.S. corporation to be his representative in connection with concert appearances in the United States. The corporation was under a contractual duty to promote the taxpayer's career in the United States and had exclusive power to execute contracts for his services; the corporation received a percentage of the taxpayer's earnings for performing these functions. Inquiries concerning the taxpayer's concert tour in the United States could be made only to the corporation's offices.

Article 14(2) of the France–United States Tax Treaty provides that income derived by a resident of one of the treaty countries in respect of independent activities performed in the other country is not taxable in that other country if

(a) the recipient of the income is present there for a period not exceeding 183 days; and

(b) the recipient does not maintain a fixed base in the other country for a period not exceeding 183 days.

Fixed base is not defined by the convention, and the meaning of the term is derived from article 14 of the OECD Model Convention. Article 14 equates "fixed base" with "permanent establishment," which means a center of industrial or commercial activities of a fixed or permanent character. Under article 4(5) of the France–United States Tax Treaty, a resident of one of the treaty countries is not deemed to have a permanent establishment in the other country merely because he carries on business there through an independent agent acting in the ordinary course of business.

The taxpayer's concert tour in the year in issue required him to spend a total of 36 days in the United States. He was thus not liable for tax in the United States as neither of the necessary conditions was fulfilled.

6. Nexus and Offshore Tax Planning

The most effective offshore tax plans derive from the ability to sever the nexus or connecting factor with a taxing country in favor of an offshore country or to rearrange the connecting factors in such a way that a lower overall tax burden is suffered. Liability to tax is dependent upon the existence of a connecting factor between a taxing jurisdiction on the one hand and a taxpayer or taxable event on the other.

In the case of an individual taxpayer, the principal connecting factors are residence, ordinary residence, domicile, and citizenship (nationality). In the case of a company, they are management and control, beneficial ownership, place of incorporation, and location of the registered office. In the case of a trust, they are the place of creation, the applicable law, the place of administration or trusteeship, and the residence, domicile, or citizenship of the beneficiaries or trustees.

Other important connecting factors may be the center of economic interests, the presence of a permanent establishment, and effectively connected income.

The principal connecting factor with regard to a taxable event is the real or deemed source. For example, in the case of profits deriving from the sale of goods, the source might be the place of the execution of the contract, the place where a trader or manufacturer employs his capital or where activities are exercised, while in the case of a real property tax or a capital gains tax on the sale of real property, geographic source or situs would normally constitute the connecting factor.

Many parameters relating to the taxpayer, the source, or the nature of the taxable event may affect (a) the liability to tax, (b) the computation of the tax burden, and (c) whether the connecting factor has indeed been severed with the taxing country in favor of an offshore country.

The definitional content and criteria affecting the existence or otherwise of a connecting factor and its characterization must be determined from within any given legal system or treaty.

6.1 Residence, Domicile, and Citizenship

Residence is normally a critical factor in determining the content of the taxable base. However, setting up a residence offshore will seldom on its own terminate residency status in another taxing country.

It is important to bear in mind that an individual may be resident for tax purposes in more than one country. In most cases, he will be treated in each country as if it were his only place of residence. In certain countries, however, an individual may acquire a secondary residence, thus incurring what will usually be a lesser tax burden in such country.

For example, an alien having a secondary residence in France is subject to income tax on a base computed at three times the estimated rental value of his home or on his income from French sources, whichever is the higher.[8]

Domicile and citizenship may also be material considerations.

For example, an individual who is resident and domiciled in the United Kingdom is subject to income tax on his total income from sources within and outside the United Kingdom.[9] However, an individual who is resident but not domiciled in the United Kingdom, or who is a British subject or a citizen of the Republic of Ireland and not ordinarily resident in the United Kingdom, is in general taxable only on income that is derived from U.K. sources, or on foreign source income that is remitted to the United Kingdom.[10]

In the United States, on the other hand, citizenship is a material factor in determining tax liability, while in most other countries citizenship is merely of marginal relevance for tax purposes.

EXAMPLE[11]

The taxpayer, who had renounced his citizenship of the United States and established a bona fide residence in the Bahamas, was held to be a nonresident alien and was not taxable as a U.S. citizen. He was, however, in receipt of income, earned while he was still a citizen, from sources within the United States, and it was held that this income was to be included under sec. 872(a) of the Internal Revenue Code.

His wife, who had not renounced her citizenship, was chargeable with reporting one-half of the income as community property.

In certain legal systems that follow U.K. law in this regard, a corporation is treated as being resident in the country in which its central management and control is exercised, and not necessarily in the country of its place of registration or incorporation.

Since connecting factors, such as residence, domicile, citizenship, source of income, or situs of property, are not necessarily mutually exclusive, double taxation of the same taxable event may ensue.

Furthermore, anti-avoidance provisions may have the effect of maintaining or creating a connecting factor with a taxing jurisdiction or of preventing the reduction of the potential tax burden through the alteration of one or more connecting factors.

EXAMPLE[12]

The Danish Department of Finance was called upon to give a ruling as to whether Danish emigrants who established residence in Monaco would continue to be subject to Danish income tax.

According to Danish tax law, liability to tax on the basis of residence normally terminates if proof is submitted to the effect that the taxpayer is subject to income tax in a foreign country according to the rules for residents of that country.

The issue that arose for consideration by the department was whether this rule was applicable to a taxpayer who is subject to tax in Monaco. There is no individual income taxation in Monaco; the only taxes levied on individuals there are indirect taxes and duties, principally consumption and turnover taxes.

The department ruled that these taxes do not have any resemblance to Danish income taxation, and Danish emigrants to Monaco would hence still be subject to resident tax liability in Denmark.

Similar anti-avoidance measures in the U.S. Internal Revenue Code[13] lay down that a nonresident individual who has given up his U.S. citizenship will continue to be taxable as a U.S. taxpayer if he lost his citizenship within ten years preceding the taxable year.

6.2 The Legal Status of the Taxpayer

In most tax systems, the legal personality of the taxpayer has a direct effect on liability to tax.[14]

Individuals, companies, trusts, partnerships, and other types of legal entities may be subject to different tax burdens or may benefit from different deductions or credits. Frequently, too, they suffer tax at different rates.

Other notions may also be relevant, such as "close company," "private company," "dealer," "trader," "profit-making institution," "importer," "married person," "head of the household," etc.

Sometimes legal status is determined by rulings of the tax administration.

EXAMPLE[15]

Under article 11(3)(c) of the Belgium-Switzerland Tax Treaty,[16] interest paid on any loan guaranteed by a Swiss bank (which is not embodied in a bearer instrument) is exempt from tax in the country of source. Article 11(3) of the Spain-Switzerland Tax Treaty[17] provides that interest arising in Spain and paid to a Swiss bank over five years or more may not be taxed in Spain.

The question arose as to which kinds of financial institutions should be regarded as "Swiss banks" for the purposes of these treaties. It has been agreed among Switzerland, Spain, and Belgium that a "Swiss bank" is either (a) a normal bank or savings institution or (b) a financial institution or private enterprise that has the characteristics of a bank and that solicits deposits from the general public; therefore it fulfills all the conditions imposed by the Federal Law on Banks and Savings Institutions[18] and submits to the Federal Bank Commission's control.

If a Swiss financial institution has been wrongly granted exemption under the treaties, because it does not come within the requirements of a "Swiss bank," the Swiss tax administration has the right to inform the foreign tax administration, collect the relevant tax, and remit it to the appropriate country.

6.3 The Source of the Income or Gain

Source is normally the most significant connecting factor in determining the tax liability of the income or gain.

The typical offshore tax plan locates the source of the taxable event well and truly offshore. This is because geographic source is frequently the sole or the principal connecting factor between a taxing jurisdiction and a taxable event.

EXAMPLE[19]

A French reinsurance broking company had its registered office (*siège*) and its regular offices (*bureaux*) in France. It carried on business in France and abroad, but foreign operations were exclusively carried out by correspondence or through subbrokers established abroad.

The *Conseil d'Etat* held that in such a case the income derived through foreign contracts is in fact derived through activities carried on in France and must therefore be considered as domestic source income. The company was thus liable to corporate income tax with respect to contracts concluded abroad.

EXAMPLE[20]

A nonresident alien sold and conveyed motion picture rights in a literary work to a U.S. corporation. The contract for the deal was negotiated in New York, executed in Hungary, and paid for in New York.

Gross income from sources within the United States includes payments of royalties derived from intangible property such as patents, copyrights, secret processes and formulas, goodwill, trademarks, trade brands, and franchises.

It was held that the payment was gross income from U.S. sources and subject to tax, in spite of the fact that the contract gave worldwide rights.

More than one country may consider income or a gain as deriving from a source within its jurisdiction. Furthermore, there may be a conflict between this and another connecting factor. These situations may result in cases of double taxation. Sometimes provision is made with regard to the tax position in cases where sources are partly in and partly out of the country concerned.

6.4 The Nature of the Transaction or Operation

The nature of the transaction or operation may determine whether it is subject to tax at all and, if so, whether expenditure incurred in connection with it is deductible from the taxable base.

In many tax systems, the crucial distinction is between income and capital. These notions are often not defined in the tax legislation, and their precise meanings must be obtained from judicial and administrative decisions and rulings.

EXAMPLE[21]

The taxpayer was a New Zealand company that entered into an agreement with a U.S. company under which the latter agreed to supply it for a period of fifteen years with technical knowledge, plans and facilities, new developments, etc. The consideration was in the form of royalty payments.

After the agreement had been running for five years, the taxpayer negotiated the cancellation of the agreement in consideration of a lump-sum payment.

This payment was effected in order to achieve an economy in working expenses and left the capital structure of the taxpayer unaffected.

The taxpayer treated this expenditure as being on revenue account and deducted this sum from its assessable income.

The New Zealand commissioner of Inland Revenue disallowed the deduction claimed.

On appeal, the New Zealand Supreme Court held that the royalties represented expenditure incurred by the taxpayer in operating its manufacturing process to best advantage.

Since the expenditure was on revenue account, it was deductible from the taxpayer's assessable income.

Income arising from mergers or similar types of operations may receive favored tax treatment or may suffer from various kinds of economic double taxation. The tax position may also vary according to whether the operation crosses frontiers or is purely domestic.

6.5 The Relationship of the Taxpayer to Other Persons

The relationship of the parties may determine whether an item is included in the taxable base. It may also affect the rate of tax.

In most tax systems and tax treaties, special provisions govern parent and subsidiary or otherwise associated companies, as variously defined. There are considerable differences encountered in the definitional content of the term *holding company*.

Sometimes special tax benefits favor certain relationships, for example, in the cases where subvention payments are allowed or where the losses of an associated company may be deducted.

In certain countries, provision is made for the profits and losses of a group of companies to be consolidated and taxed as if the various companies were one company. The existence of the consolidated subsidiary or subsidiaries is to a large extent ignored for corporation tax purposes.

Fiscal unity can be advantageous as it can help in avoiding the payment of tax in one group company where the other group company suffers loss. Without fiscal unity a group cannot easily transfer losses from one company to another, nor can assets easily be transferred at book value if the real value is higher.

In other cases, the fact that companies are related may attract the operation of anti-avoidance provisions, particularly where transactions are not at arm's length.

The amount of a share participation may also have a material effect on the determination of the tax burden, for example, in the case of a Netherlands holding company or a Swiss substantial participation holding company.

The amount of a share participation is also relevant for the purposes of a number of tax treaties. Dividends may benefit from a reduction in the withholding tax where a company of one contracting state controls more than a certain percentage of the voting power of a company of the other contracting state. In certain cases, a qualifying percentage may entitle the shareholder to an indirect credit in respect of taxes paid by the company in the other country.

For example, many of the tax treaties contain a provision to the effect that the country of which the company paying the dividends is resident may tax such dividends in most cases at a maximum rate, such maximum rate being reduced to 5% or 10% if the recipient company that is resident in the other country controls a certain minimum percentage of the voting power of the company paying the dividends. In certain of these treaties, there is also an indirect credit available to a company controlling 10% of the voting power of the distributing company for the tax payable in the other country by the distributing company in respect of the profits out of which the dividend is paid.

In the case of individuals, kinship may also be material. Often gifts between spouses, and the income deriving therefrom, are not subject to tax. On the other hand, income deriving from gifts to children may be treated as income in the hands of the donor parent. This is to prevent the avoidance of tax through the splitting of income among members of the family.

In many cases, estate, inheritance, and gift tax laws reduce the rate of tax or the taxable base in the case of heirs, legatees, and donees who are close relatives.

7. Tax Incentives in Offshore Tax Planning

Tax incentives may convert otherwise high tax countries into limited purpose tax havens. Tax incentives are tax concessions that are granted to attract local or foreign investment capital to particular activities or areas. Nearly all countries grant tax incentives of some kind as part of their general or regional economic development programs.

At the international level, the sphere of application of a tax incentive may be extended by way of a tax sparing clause in a tax treaty between a capital importing country and a capital exporting country. Tax sparing clauses allow residents of the capital exporting country a credit against their domestic tax for profits or gains derived in the developing country in respect of which all or specified taxes are subject to exemption or reduction in the latter country.

(See also Chapter 4, "Offshore Incentives.")

8. Anti-Avoidance

As a general principle, there is no obligation, either morally or legally, to suffer a heavier tax burden than is necessarily attendant upon a given taxable event. (See also Chapter 14, "International Measures to Combat Harmful Tax Practices.")

However, even though a taxpayer may stay within the letter of the law, there is usually a limit to the tax minimization steps that he may take. Most tax systems contain some general or specific anti-avoidance provisions. The substance *versus* form rule enables the revenue to disregard appearances and to rewrite transactions so as to reflect the true situation.

Sometimes loopholes in anti-avoidance provisions offer comparatively simple solutions to tax problems. These loopholes are frequently plugged as soon as the tax authorities become aware of their potential for abuse, and most anti-avoidance provisions become progressively more comprehensive as taxpayers grow more ingenious. The anti-avoidance techniques that have been adopted by various countries have been classified by the Carter Commission[22] into four groups:

1. The *sniper approach* contemplates the enactment of specific provisions that identify with precision the type of transaction to be dealt with and prescribes with precision the tax consequences of such a transaction.

2. The *shotgun approach* contemplates the enactment of some general provision that imposes tax on transactions that are defined in a general way. The difference from the sniper approach lies in its conscious rejection of certainty.

3. The *transaction not at arm's-length approach* provides that the tax consequences shall be different from what they would be by treating the transaction as if it had taken place between parties at arm's length. Typical examples are the rules substituting market value for the price, if any, actually received for disposal of capital assets and sales between associated persons for income tax purposes. Technically, this is a means of carrying out one of the other approaches rather than a separate approach

since the circumstances in which the technique is to be applied can be described with more or less precision.

4. The *administrative control approach* contemplates the grant of wide powers to an official or administrative tribunal in order to counteract tax avoidance transactions.

Offshore counters to anti-avoidance provisions are setups whereby the taxpayer's affairs are arranged in such a way that, as far as possible, they do not fall within the taxing net.

Though most offshore tax plans are conceived by taxpayers, it does occasionally happen that the game is played by governments themselves.

An example of this is the legislative repartee between the United Kingdom and the Cayman Islands.

EXAMPLE

The U.K. Income Tax Act 1952, sec. 412[23] was designed to prevent the practice of transferring stocks and shares and other assets by U.K. residents to foreign companies and trusts in such a way that the U.K. transferor would be able to enjoy the income yielded by the assets while only being subject to U.K. tax on the amount of income remitted to that country. One of the requirements of this anti-avoidance provision was that an individual should have "rights" to the income in question.

It was clearly with sec. 412 and analogous provisions in other countries in sight that the Cayman Islands Trust Law 1967[24] laid down that

"where any right or remedy in respect of a Caymanian exempted trust would vest in one or more of the beneficiaries under any such trust, the right or remedy in question would instead vest in and be exercisable by the Registrar of Trusts; and

"no beneficiary would enjoy in relation to the trust fund or its income any right or remedy at law or in equity."

Offshore tax planners were immediately enthusiastic and assiduous in exploiting the divesting techniques offered by such exempted trusts.

To counter the Caymanian counter–anti-avoidance measures, the U.K. Finance Act 1969, sec. 33, amended sec. 412 in such a way that it was no longer a requirement that an individual should have "rights" to enjoy the income in question, and the Caymanian divesting provision thus lost much of its relevance for offshore planning arrangements of U.K. residents.

Many systems contain anti-avoidance provisions that hit at dividend stripping and bondwashing arrangements.

Dividend stripping is a device whereby a favorably placed person from the tax point of view purchases shares prior to a declaration of a large dividend and thereafter resells the shares to the original purchaser at a lower price.

Bondwashing is a device similar to dividend stripping whereby a high-rate taxpayer owning securities in respect of which interest is due shortly thereafter agrees to sell such securities to a low-rate or exempt taxpayer with the right to repurchase the securities after the accrual of the interest.

In the case of a gift by a corporation or trust, the anti-avoidance provision may be directed at the individual at whose instance the gift is made.

A tax court often penetrates the memorandum and articles of association or the bylaws of a company and looks to the real situation. This is particularly so for the purposes of determining the residence of a corporation.

EXAMPLE[25]

Three wholly owned subsidiaries of a U.K. company were companies registered in Kenya. The meetings of the directors of these subsidiaries, in whom the powers of management were vested by the subsidiary companies' articles of association, could not validly be held in the United Kingdom.

Initially, the management of the Kenyan subsidiaries was carried on in Kenya. Subsequently, the control and management of the Kenyan subsidiaries was taken over by the parent company, and de facto control of the Kenyan subsidiaries was exercised by the directors of the parent company in London (though this was contrary to the articles of association of the Kenyan subsidiaries). The local directors of the Kenyan subsidiaries stood aside and did not exercise their powers of management.

A U.K. subsidiary of the parent company sought to deduct, in a computation of its profits for income tax purposes (under the law as it then was),[26] payments made to the Kenyan subsidiaries as being subvention payments to associated companies. A company could not be an "associated company" unless it was resident in the United Kingdom.

The House of Lords held that the place where the central management and control of a company was situated in fact determined the place of residence of the company, even though their being situated there was irregular and contrary to the constitution of the company.

Accordingly, the Kenyan subsidiaries were considered to be resident in the United Kingdom, and the subvention payments were deductible in computing the profits of the U.K. subsidiary.

Where a corporation is merely a conduit or a dummy that does not carry on substantial activity, courts frequently refuse to treat it as having legal personality for tax purposes.

EXAMPLE[27]

A Swedish prizefighter incorporated a Swiss corporation of which he was the sole employee and source of revenue. He entered into an agreement with this corporation, under which he was entitled to receive 70% of the company's gross income plus a pension fund.

He thereafter fought in the United States for the heavyweight boxing championship of the world and was assessed by the U.S. tax authorities on the income earned in the United States from his boxing and certain related activities.

He claimed tax exemption under the Switzerland–United States Tax Treaty on the grounds that he was a Swiss resident.[28]

The U.S. Tax Court, however, held that the taxpayer was not a resident of Switzerland for the purposes of the treaty and that the Swiss corporation had no legitimate business purpose but was a device used by the taxpayer as a controlled depository and conduit by which he attempted to divert temporarily his personal income, earned in the United States, so as to escape U.S. tax. The taxpayer was held liable for the taxes assessed against him.

In most tax systems, there are transfer pricing provisions giving the tax authorities the power to reallocate profits and losses where the parties are related and/or the transactions in question are not at arm's length or for a legitimate business purpose.

EXAMPLE[29]

Corporation A and Corporation B had at least one common shareholder. A granted interest-free loans to B and also bought goods from B at an inflated price.

Under the French General Tax Code,[30] taxpayers are only allowed to deduct expenses incurred with a view of furthering their own business interests.

The French tax administration reallocated the profits of both corporations, on the grounds that, despite the fact that they had a common shareholder, they were in fact two distinct legal entities and therefore the expenses incurred by A in making the loans and purchasing the goods were not in furtherance of their own business interests. Therefore A's income was increased by the amount of the charges incurred to grant the advantages to B.

EXAMPLE[31]

The taxpayer, a Belgian corporation, allowed overdrafts on current accounts to two subsidiaries in Panama. No interest was payable on the

> overdrafts. The tax authorities considered that the nonpayment of interest amounted to "advantages granted to related enterprises" and added a fictitious interest charge to the profits of the Belgian corporation for the purpose of computing tax.
>
> The court agreed with the view of the tax authorities and held that the subsidiaries, which were separate legal entities, had benefited from interest-free loans and that the advantages so obtained were to be added to the profits of the Belgian corporation. Because of the distinct legal personalities of the taxpayer and its subsidiaries, no double taxation relief could be sought for the alleged double taxation of the fictitious interest added to the profits and dividends actually received.

In many tax systems, the main anti-avoidance provisions relating to arm's-length transactions refer specifically to international situations. Tax havens are often used for the purpose of transfer pricing or reinvoicing.

In the first place, a manufacturing company located in a high tax jurisdiction could effect sales to a related company in a tax haven jurisdiction at cost or at prices involving a very small profit margin; the tax haven company could then in turn sell the goods to one or more related marketing companies in high tax jurisdictions at high prices, which would produce a low profit in the hands of the latter company or companies. A variation of this technique would involve selling to unrelated marketing companies at arm's-length prices, the primary object of the exercise still being achieved since the manufacturing company would have avoided taxation on the real profits that would otherwise have accrued to it.

Secondly, raw materials or goods or components manufactured at a very low cost abroad could be purchased by a tax haven company and then sold to a related company in a high tax jurisdiction at high prices, which would give the latter company a substantially lower profit than if purchases had been effected directly.

Often transfer pricing takes place by companies merely passing invoices without the subject matter of the sale actually being transferred to or by the intermediary company.

Most developed tax systems have anti-avoidance provisions aimed directly at counteracting the tax saving effects of transfer pricing; transfer pricing issues currently account for more major tax cases world-wide than all other tax issues put together.

Following first the United States guidelines and then the OECD guidelines, an important development world-wide is now for countries to issue transfer pricing guidelines. U.S. law now provides that the following transfer pricing methods may be used to determine an arm's-length price in a controlled transaction involving intangible property:

1. the comparable uncontrolled price method ("CUP");
2. the resale price method;
3. the cost-plus method;

4. the comparable profits method;
5. the profit split method; and
6. certain other unspecified methods.

The methods permitted with respect to transfers of intangibles are:

1) the comparable uncontrolled transactions method ("CUT");
2) the comparable profits method;
3) the profit split method; and
4) certain other unspecified methods.

9. Enforcement of Foreign Revenue Judgments

As a traditional rule, the courts of most countries did not entertain a claim by a foreign government for its taxes or recognize or enforce a foreign revenue law judgment. This rule did not necessarily mean that courts would countenance transactions that are knowingly designed to violate the revenue laws (such as fraudulent tax evasion schemes) of a foreign and friendly state. For example, in *Re Emery's Investment Trusts, Emery v. Emery* (1959) Ch. 410 (1959), 1 All E.R. 577, an English court refused to recognize a transaction carried out in contravention of a U.S. revenue law. (While the meaning of the term *revenue law* may vary from one legal system to another, it generally includes income taxes, capital gains taxes, capital taxes, succession and estate duties, customs duties, stamp duties, and profit levies.)

EXAMPLE[32]

A company that was registered in the United Kingdom but carried on business in India sold its undertaking to the Indian government for a sum of money that was immediately remitted to the United Kingdom. After the company had gone into voluntary liquidation, the Indian commissioner of income tax claimed payment of a large sum of income tax in respect of the capital gain derived from the sale of business.

The House of Lords followed the generally accepted rule that no action lies in the United Kingdom for the enforcement of a foreign revenue law. It made no difference that the country in question was a Commonwealth country.

A narrowing of the traditional rule of non-enforcement of foreign revenue judgments is currently accompanying the international regulation of offshore activities. (See Chapter 14, "International Measures to Combat Harmful Tax Practices" and Chapter 15, "International Measures to Combat Money Laundering.")

10. Exchange of Information

10.1 Treaty Provisions for Formal Exchanges of Information

The principal formal exchange of information mechanism is the tax treaty. Most tax treaties contain an article providing for the exchange of information between the competent authorities. Frequently, too, provision is made for the contracting states to render to each other administrative and legal assistance in connection with the assessment and collection of taxes.

EXAMPLE[33]

Under the Austrian Federal Fiscal Code,[34] the Austrian tax authorities are entitled to request that information that is relevant for the imposition of taxes be disclosed. Every person is obliged to pass on such information, even if his own tax liability is not affected thereby.

The Law on Fiscal Penalties[35] provides that no such information should be disclosed by the authorities unless the disclosure

- supports the enforcement of tax proceedings;
- is required in the public interest or by law; and
- does not violate any legitimate interest of the taxpayer.

The Austria-France Tax Treaty[36] authorizes the full exchange of all information between the two countries relevant to the proper collection of taxes, unless such information, because of its nature, cannot be obtained under the laws of the country; would disclose a manufacturing process, industrial, commercial, or professional secret; or would endanger law and order.

The French tax authorities sought information regarding an Austrian corporation from the Austrian tax authorities. The corporation refused to give the information to the Austrian authorities on the grounds that disclosing it to the French authorities would constitute a violation of its rights under the Law on Fiscal Penalties.

The Austrian Administrative Court[37] ruled that the corporation had to provide the information and that the Austrian authorities could furnish it to the French authorities without violating the corporation's rights. The court held that, as the Law on Fiscal Penalties prohibits only the unauthorized disclosure of information, and since the Austria-France Tax Treaty authorized the Austrian authorities to disclose the information to the French authorities, such disclosure would not constitute a violation of the Law on Fiscal Penalties.

It follows that the much-vaunted Austrian banking secrecy regulations would take second place to an exchange of information provision in a tax treaty.

Although the exact wording of the exchange of information article may differ from treaty to treaty, the article will typically be based on article 26 of the 1963 OECD Model Convention as amended in 1992 and 1997. There is also a detailed commentary on each article in the Model Convention that is intended to illustrate or interpret its provisions. (See Appendix IV, "Exchange of Information under Article 26 of the OECD Model Convention.")

In general terms, article 26 comprises three elements:

- the information that can be exchanged;
- the secrecy of such information; and
- the steps a treaty country must take to comply with its obligations.

It is likely that information relating to offshore operations and transactions may be the subject of exchanges of information between high tax jurisdictions.

The Information That Can Be Exchanged

The first principle is that the only information that can be exchanged is that which is necessary to secure the correct application of the treaty, and the domestic laws of the treaty countries concerning taxes covered by the treaty.

This means, for example, that a request for information concerning sales tax need not be complied with as it is not covered by the treaty. Conversely, in the context of granting an exemption from withholding tax pursuant to the royalty article, a request by one country to the other treaty country as to whether the recipient of the royalty is in fact a resident of that country and the beneficial owner of the royalties is within the scope of the provisions. Furthermore, in the context of applying domestic transfer pricing provisions, a request by one treaty country to the other concerning the price a company in the other country paid for goods bought from a company in the requesting country would be within the scope of information that can be exchanged.

Secrecy of Information

The second principle is that any information that is exchanged must be kept secret, taking into account a country's domestic laws on this point. Therefore information communicated under the provisions of a treaty must be treated as secret in the receiving country in the same manner as information obtained under the domestic laws of that country. Similarly and logically, sanctions for the violation of such secrecy are to be governed by the administrative and penal laws of that country. If the information appears to be of value to the receiving country for purposes outside the scope of the treaty, the country may not use the information for such other purposes. Rather, it must resort to means specially designed for those purposes (e.g., in the case of a nonfiscal crime, to a treaty concerning judicial assistance).

Compliance Steps

Subject to the above qualifications, however, the competent authority of State A is obliged to collect the information that State B requires "in the same way as if its [State A's] own taxation was involved" (see para. 16 of the observations in the commentary concerning article 26). As pointed out in *United States v. AL Burbank & Co.* 525 F2d 9, the avowed intent of a tax treaty is to prevent fiscal evasion. It follows "that if [State A] is investigating the tax liability of [a taxpayer] who is potentially delinquent to it, the [State B] may utilize the same investigative techniques that it would employ if that [taxpayer] were under investigation [in State B] for a domestic tax liability. To do otherwise would be to negate the very purpose of the Treaty" (p. 13).

Another principle is that a country is not bound to go beyond its own internal laws and administrative practice in putting information at the disposal of the other treaty country. Subject to this rule, the OECD commentary illustrates the different ways in which information is likely to be exchanged (i.e., when there is a specific request by a tax authority for information or, if none, then either automatically or spontaneously). Insofar as the latter is concerned, no doubt many advisors among the readers will have come across the situation in which they have been negotiating with their own tax authorities and, as part of the "give and take," the tax authorities have innocuously referred to the possibility of spontaneously exchanging information with their counterparts in other relevant countries.

10.2 Informal Exchanges of Information

Though no statistics are available, it may be assumed that informal exchanges of information between the administrations are on the increase.

Also the leverage of the major powers on the small tax haven jurisdictions may be considerable. In the case of any confrontation between the United States and a Caribbean haven, the United States would be able to destroy the latter's offshore economy overnight by a refusal to process dollar transfers.

The recent U.K. case of *Regina v. Allcock* (unreported) has shed much light on informal exchange of information and has caused much concern among certain taxpayers.

10.3 Mutual Assistance Directive of the European Union (77/799)

The directive provides that information may be exchanged to enable a correct assessment of taxes on income and capital. In comparison, article 26 refers to the correct application of a treaty and the domestic laws of a treaty country concerning taxes covered by a treaty. The scope of the directive would appear in certain instances to be wider.

11. Choice of Law

Choice of law is a conflict of laws (private international law) issue, and the rules are part of the domestic law of each country. Choice of law problems frequently arise with respect to entities that are known to, or do not enjoy legal personality in, a foreign system. The determination of the applicable law for the purpose of characterizing such entities varies from one legal system to another. For example, an unusual type of entity, such as the Liechtenstein *Anstalt*, might be treated as a company in one country and as a trust in another country.

EXAMPLE[38]

A Netherlands partnership carried out the demolition of one of the pavilions at the Brussels World Fair.

The Belgian tax authorities thereafter sought to assess one of the partners individually for the full amount of income tax due on the total income derived from the partnership in Belgium.

Under Belgian law,[39] a partnership is a legal entity, and its distributed profits are subject to tax as if they were dividends distributed by a company.

Under Netherlands law,[40] on the other hand, a partnership is not a legal entity, and the members are taxed individually on their share of the partnership profits.

The Brussels Court of Appeal held that the Netherlands partnership could not be considered a legal entity for the purposes of Belgian taxation and, consequently, that each of the partners should have been assessed individually for his respective share of the profits.

The effect of this decision is that, under Belgian law, the tax status of foreign entities is to be determined according to the law of the country of their establishment.

The precise meaning of terms may vary from one context to another, and it may be necessary for a court to decide which law is applicable for the purpose of characterizing one or more of the elements of the taxable event.

EXAMPLE[41]

The taxpayer, a U.K. company, had a minority shareholding in an Italian corporation that issued a substantial amount of shares at a premium. From these issues, a certain sum was entered in the Italian corporation's share premium reserve, and a distribution was thereafter effected out of this reserve.

Under Italian law, 5% of the net annual profits of a corporation must be placed in a legal reserve until such reserve reaches 20% of the share capital. Sums received in consideration for the issue of shares at a premium cannot be distributed until the legal reserve reaches 20% of the share capital, the excess being normally transferred to the share premium reserve, which may then be distributed by resolution at a general meeting.[42]

The receipt by the taxpayer of its corresponding share of the dividend, the source of which was the share premium reserve, was assessed to U.K. tax as an "income receipt" (i.e., as a dividend).

Under Italian law, such a distribution is a return of capital, and thus no Italian withholding tax was due on the distribution.

The issue between the U.K. company and the Board of Inland Revenue was whether the distribution was a return of capital (Italian law) or an income distribution (English law). It was thus necessary for the court to decide which was the applicable law for the purpose of characterization.

The High Court of Justice (Chancery Division) held that Italian law decided the characterization issue, and the amount distributed from the Italian corporation's share premium reserve was a return of capital.

12. Foreign Currency Gains and Losses in Offshore Transactions

Frequently, offshore transactions are conducted in whole or in part in foreign currency. Problems therefore arise involving changes in exchange rates. Are the gains and losses attributable to changes in rates to be treated as capital or as income? At what date are such gains or losses to be taken into account for tax purposes? What exchange rates should be used for translating foreign branch profits into the domestic currency?

The tax laws of different countries must therefore be applied against the background of foreign exchange markets.

The translation of foreign currency into the domestic currency may follow various methods (e.g., the profit and loss method, the net worth method, or the transaction method).

In the case of an intermittent user of foreign currency, the transaction method deals with each foreign transaction separately and computes the domestic income at the appropriate exchange rate for that transaction.

EXAMPLE[43]

The taxpayer, a U.S. corporation, and its wholly owned foreign subsidiary entered into business transactions with each other. The transactions were recorded on the taxpayer's books as accounts payable or accounts receivable, depending on the nature of the transactions. In assessing its taxable income, the taxpayer adjusted the accounts to give effect to fluctuations in the foreign exchange prevailing at the end of the taxable year; for the year in question, this adjustment resulted in an overall loss. The question was whether a foreign exchange loss is allowable under sec. 164 of the Internal Revenue Code.

Section 165(a) provides that any loss sustained during the taxable year should be allowed as a deduction if it is not compensated for by insurance or other method. Section 1.165-1(b) of the Income Tax Regulations provides, however, that, if a loss is to be allowed as a deduction under sec. 165, it must be the result of closed and completed transactions, fixed by identifiable events.

In the present case, it was held that, as the accounts payable to and receivable from the subsidiary remained on the taxpayer's books for subsequent payment and collection, the loss suffered by the taxpayer was not the result of completed transactions. The taxpayer was not, therefore, entitled to a deduction under sec. 165.

13. Procedural and Related Matters

Matters of procedure are regulated by the law and practice of the taxing state.

Local law governs all matters relating to the collection of taxes (in particular, the form and time of presentation of tax returns).

Provision is often made for the withholding of tax at source and the prepayment of provisional payment of tax. Such withholding may have an effect on offshore tax planning.

The duty to make payment may in certain cases fall not on the taxpayer himself but on the company paying him dividends, the debtor paying him interest, the employer paying his salary, the trustee or the administrator handling a trust, or an estate of which he is beneficiary.

Objection to assessments and administrative and judicial appeals also follow the procedure laid down in the country concerned.

Notes

1. This example is based on U.S. Revenue Ruling 69–82, 1969–1 Cumulative Bulletins (hereinafter cited as "Cum Bull") 193.
2. *Mary D Biddle v. Commissioner* 302 U.S. 523 (1938) Ct. D 1303, C.B. 1938–1, 309.
3. Sec. 903 provides that the phrase "income, war profits, and excess profits taxes" includes "a tax paid in lieu of a tax on income, war profits, or excess profits otherwise generally imposed by any foreign country."

4. *Testo Unico Delle Leggi Sulle Imposte Dirette* (approved by Presidential Decree No. 645 of January 29, 1958, as supplemented and amended) Title VIII, arts. 156 to 158.
5. This example is based on a case ruling of the Milan Tax Commission of January 26, 1980. See *Bollettino Tributario d'Informazioni* of May 30, 1980, at p. 944 and 20 *European Taxation* 306 (October 1980).
6. Treaty of October 29, 1958, as amended.
7. This example is based on U.S. Revenue Ruling 75–131, 1975–1 Cum Bull 389.
8. *Code général des Impôts,* art. 164–C.
9. Income and Corporation Taxes Act 1970 (hereinafter cited as "TA 1970"), in particular Part IV, secs. 108 ff.
10. TA 1970, sec. 122.
11. This example is based on the U.S. case of *W N Dillin*, 56 T.C. 228.
12. This example is based on the Letter of the Department of Finance No. Skd 62/1971. See *Skattepolitisk Oversigt* No. 7–1972 and 13 *European Taxation* 71 (February 1973).
13. Secs. 877 and 2107. The purpose of Section 877 is to protect the U.S. income tax base through imposition of U.S. tax on U.S. citizens or certain long-term residents who expatriate from the United States. In its pre-1995 form, Section 877(a) was largely ineffectual because it imposed on the IRS an obligation to prove that an expatriation was undertaken for the principal purpose of avoiding U.S. tax. For expatriations after February 6, 1995, however, the situation is reversed. Section 877(a) subjects certain individuals to an expatriation tax without inquiry as to their motive for losing their citizenship or residency, but allows certain categories of persons to demonstrate to the IRS though a ruling process. The provisions of Section 877 do not provide any exclusion for assets or income acquired before the 10-year period, as in the case of residents who expatriate, or for property or income received via gift within the 10-year period.

    As was the case with Section 877 prior to the amendment, its essential tax counterpart, Section 2107, was applicable in the case of expatriations found to involve a principal purpose to avoid U.S. estate tax. Section 2107 was also amended in 1996 to replace this subjective test with an objective test in the absence of the individual obtaining an appropriate ruling from the IRS. In the case of individuals losing their U.S. citizenship after February 6, 1995, Section 2107(a) provides that a tax computed in accordance with the table contained in Section 2001 is imposed on the transfer of the taxable estate (determined as provided in Section 2106) of every decedent nonresidential U.S. citizen if, within the 10-year period ending with the date of the death, such decedent lost U.S. citizenship, unless such loss did not have for one of its principal purposes the avoidance of taxes. For this purpose, an individual is treated as having a principal purpose to avoid such taxes if such individual is so treated under Section 877(a)(2), unless one of the exceptions in Section 877(c)(1) is applicable. In addition, the tax so imposed is credited with the amount of any estate, inheritance, legacy, or succession taxes actually paid to any foreign country.

As is the case with Section 877, if the IRS establishes that it is reasonable to believe that an individual's loss of U.S. citizenship would, but for Section 2107, result in a substantial reduction in the estate, inheritance, legacy, and succession taxes in respect of the transfer of his estate, the burden of proving that such loss of citizenship did not have for one of its principal purposes the avoidance of taxes is on the executor of such individual's estate.

14. For example, the Irish tax holiday concessions that are available only to companies.
15. This example is based on the letter from the Swiss Federal Tax Administration to the Cantonal Tax Administrations dated December 9, 1981 (3.B/E.62–MG/Bam/Ae). See 21 *European Taxation* 408 (December 1981).
16. Treaty of April 28, 1978.
17. Treaty of April 26, 1966.
18. Law of November 8, 1934.
19. This example is based on the decision of the French *Conseil d'Etat* of June 18, 1969 (ref. no. 68,042). See *Bulletin Officiel des Contributions Directes et du Cadastre* no. 38, at II–492 (October 8, 1969) and 10 *European Taxation* II/13 (January 1970).
20. This example is based on *Marton Est* 47 BTA 184, Dec. 12, 567 and *Molnar v. Com* (CA–2) 46–1 U.S.T.C. 9303, 156 F. 2d 924.
21. This example is based on the New Zealand case of *J Gadsden & Co. Ltd. v. Commissioner of Inland Revenue*, 1964 Australasian Tax Decisions 18.
22. Carter Report (Canada) col. 3 Appendix A at p. 552.
23. Now TA 1970, sec. 478.
24. Law No. 6 of 1967, as amended, sec. 79.
25. This example is based on the U.K. case of *Unit Construction Co. Ltd. v. Bullock (Inspector of Taxes)* (1960) A.C. 351, (1959) 3 All E.R. 831 HL.
26. Finance Act 1953, sec. 20.
27. This example is based on the U.S. case of *Ingemar Johannson v. USA* 336 F.2d 809, 64–2 U.S. Tax Cases 9743.
28. The Switzerland–United States Tax Treaty, art. X(1), provides that "An individual resident of Switzerland shall be exempted from United States tax … if he is temporarily present in the United States for a period or

periods not exceeding a total of 183 days during the taxable year and … his compensation is received for such labor or personal services performed as an employee of, or under contract with, a resident or corporation or other entity of Switzerland."

29. This example is based on a decision of the French Supreme Court *(Conseil d'Etat)* No. 92,009 of December 4, 1974. See 27 *Droit Fiscal* 264 (March 10, 1975) and 15 *European Taxation* 144 (April 1975).
30. *Code Général des Impôts,* secs. 38 and 209.
31. This example is based on a decision of the Court of Appeal of Brussels of January 13, 1975. See *Algemeen Fiscaal Tijdschift* 1975, No. 10 at 319, and 16 *European Taxation* 394 (November 1976).
32. This example is based on the U.K. case of *Government of India v. Taylor* (1955) A.C. 491 (1955), 1 All E.R. 292.
33. This example is based on a decision of the Austrian Administrative Court *(Verwaltungsgerichthof)* of May 30, 1978, No. 594/78. See *Die Finanzrechtliche Erkenntnisse des VWGH und VFGH* No. 5 at 54 (March 1, 1979) and 19 *European Taxation* 65 (February 1979).
34. *Bundesabgabenordnung,* sec. 143(1).
35. *Finanzstrafgesetz,* sec. 251.
36. Treaty of October 8, 1959.
37. *Verwaltungsgerichthof.*
38. This example is based on the decision of the Brussels Court of Appeal of January 30, 1967, No. 1788. See *Bulletin des Contributions* No. 449 at 262 (February 1968) and 8 *European Taxation* 50 (February 1968).
39. *Code des Impôts sur les Revenus*, art. 11.
40. *Wet op de Inkomstenbelasting,* art. 6(1).
41. This example is based on the U.K. case of *Courtauld's Investments Ltd. v. Fleming* (1969) 3 All E.R. 1281, 46 T.C. 111.
42. *Codice Civile,* arts. 2428 and 2430.
43. This example is based on the U.S. Revenue Ruling 75–108, 1975–1 Cum Bull 69.

CHAPTER EIGHT

DOUBLE TAXATION IN OFFSHORE TAX PLANNING

1. Tax Treaty Conduit Havens

Offshore jurisdictions also include countries that allow foreign corporations to borrow their tax treaties.

Tax treaties are primarily contracts between countries regarding the countries' respective rights to tax the income or capital attributable to corporations or individuals when that income or capital may attract tax in both countries if there were no tax treaty.

1.1 Tax Treaties and Withholding Rates

Treaties normally also reduce the amount of tax a country is allowed to withhold on income being repatriated to another treaty partner country. For example, a subsidiary transferring a $1,000,000 dividend to its parent in a foreign country may have to withhold say 30%, or $300,000, of tax from the dividend. That tax is paid over to the revenue. If the country of the parent has a tax treaty with the subsidiary's country, then the withholding may be only 5%, or $50,000 (an up-front saving of $250,000). Where the withholding tax is not a final payment, the difference may eventually cancel out, but when one takes account of the time value of money, it may still be a material factor.

If the parent's country does not have a treaty with the subsidiary's country, then the parent may establish an intermediary company in a country that does have tax treaties with both the subsidiary's country and that of the parent. The withholding tax burden using the intermediary structure may be reduced to $100,000, not as good as $50,000 but better than $300,000. If the intermediary company costs $10,000 yearly, then the parent realizes a $190,000 savings.

In the above example, the intermediary jurisdiction gains the extra 5% of tax plus the $10,000 cost of the company. The intermediary jurisdiction that allows a foreign corporation to borrow its treaties, as per the above example, is thus also an offshore jurisdiction.

1.2 Offshore Trading Companies and Tax Treaties

In situations in which offshore companies wish to take advantage of the certainty and better provisions of double tax treaties, the possibility of structuring trade with a high tax country through a third country with which it has a tax treaty should be investigated in the diagnostic. For this type of structure to prove efficient, the costs of the structure plus the aggregate tax burden suffered in the third country by the conduit company should not exceed the high tax country's tax burden.

The objective of an offshore trading company is to trade within the offshore jurisdiction so that the diverted profits only occur in the offshore jurisdiction. Alternatively, one may want profits to be taxed in a foreign jurisdiction if the effective tax rate there is lower than that at home. Also, if there are accumulated losses abroad with the time limit of carry forward provisions, it may be possible to place the trading profits in that country to absorb the losses.

An alternative to establishing a conduit company in a country that has both a tax treaty with the high tax country and a nominal rate of tax lower than the high tax country's rate may be to choose a conduit country where, although the nominal rate of tax is in excess of the high tax country, the effective rate of tax can be reduced by extraction and diversion techniques to below that of the high tax country.

For this technique to be efficient, the rates of withholding tax on the diverted and extracted tax profits will need to be low. For example, both the Netherlands and Switzerland offer this possibility because of their domestic tax provisions concerning the exemption of foreign branch income.

When a company considers having commercial presence in a foreign country, but wants to avoid unnecessary foreign tax exposure, it may be allowed to set up either a nontaxable representative office that does not undertake activities that constitute a permanent establishment or a headquarters office. On the other hand, it may establish a service subsidiary and take care that its tax base is kept as low as possible by paying the subsidiary or headquarters office on a cost-plus basis. The cost represents the expenses of maintaining the subsidiary, while the plus represents a percentage of the costs. That percentage will be the taxable base.

To avoid foreign tax on "trading" operations, you should first analyze exactly those tax laws of the foreign country that subject trading transactions to tax. It is a general principle of most countries' tax laws that a tax treaty cannot impose a liability where none existed before. If one is not trading in a country according to its domestic law, then a tax treaty provision cannot impose tax.

Domestic tax laws imposing tax on trading transactions (source-based connecting factor) can vary significantly in detail. In general, they approximate to the definition of a permanent establishment found in the OECD Model Tax Treaty and bilateral tax treaties. In many cases, domestic tax laws imposing tax are wider than the permanent establishment provisions in tax treaties. In this situation, it is very advantageous to be able to rely on permanent establishment provisions in a tax treaty to limit the local source rule.

The local government will aim to increase a country's tax base, especially concerning international income. If a country finds that foreign companies make many sales to its residents, it may decide to base local taxability on the place where the sales are performed. Similarly, where services are frequently rendered locally or production is carried out locally, the location of those rendering the services, or the place where production is carried out, may determine whether a trade is being conducted within the country.

Even with clear domestic legislation concerning source rules, it is difficult to analyze precisely when a company is trading "within," as opposed to trading "with," another country. Much has to do with the revenue's attitude on a given day. Some civil law jurisdictions do not adhere to previous court decisions. Countries that do have adherence to previous decisions allow the revenue to overrule those decisions with newer notices. Whether a trade is being conducted in a particular country will be a question of fact, thus at the revenue's discretion. Therefore, it is usually better to rely on the terms of double tax treaties, which are often tighter than domestic law.

1.3 Treaty Shopping

Treaty shopping is the use of a tax treaty by a person resident in a country that is not a party to the treaty.

Both the OECD Model Income Tax Convention on Income and Capital (article 10) and the U.S. Treasury Model Income Tax Treaty (article 16) contain provisions limiting the use of treaty shopping.

Additionally, a provision is being considered for the OECD's Model Tax Convention to deny entities operating under harmful tax regimes access to certain or all of the Convention's benefits. (See Chapter 14, "International Measures to Combat Harmful Tax Practices.")

2. Domestic Double Taxation

Domestic double taxation occurs where one tax jurisdiction imposes tax twice in respect of the same taxable event and person.

In most countries, there are equitable provisions to prevent or alleviate such cases. For example, many taxing statutes define *gross income* as "the total amount received by or accruing to…a taxpayer." If income were to accrue in one year and suffer tax, but payment were only to be effected in the following year, the taxpayer would not in most cases be subjected to tax twice on the same amount.

The term *domestic double taxation* does not normally refer to cases where jurisdictions that are at different levels in a country's constitutional structure (e.g., federal, provincial, and municipal authorities) enjoy concurrent or overlapping taxing powers. Nor does it refer to cases in which an item is subject to two different types of taxes (e.g., income tax and value-added tax [VAT]).

Where the divisions of federal states enjoy parallel taxing powers, incidents of double taxation may well occur that are technically closer to international than domestic double taxation.

3. International Double Taxation

3.1 Definition

International double (or multiple) taxation occurs when the tax authorities of two or more countries concurrently impose taxes having the same bases and incidence, in such a way that a person incurs a heavier tax burden than if he were subject to one tax jurisdiction only.

Note: The term *double taxation* is normally used as referring only to cases of international double or multiple taxation.

3.2 Causes of Double Taxation

The cause of double taxation lies in the fact that the various possible connecting factors between taxing jurisdictions on the one hand and taxpayers on the other are not mutually exclusive.

These connecting factors may relate to a quality of the taxpayer (e.g., citizenship, residence, domicile, place of incorporation, etc.), of the income (real or deemed source usually constituting the relevant link), or of the property (usually situs, but sometimes source, being material).

One of the most common cases of overlapping tax jurisdictions is the combination of residence taxation and source taxation. This would occur, for example, where a taxpayer who is resident in a country that taxes on worldwide income derives income from a foreign country that imposes tax on the basis of source. If there were no tax treaty between the two countries nor any unilateral measures in either country to protect him from having to pay tax twice in respect of the same income, he would be subject to a double tax burden, which could conceivably even exceed the total amount of the income in question.

However, it may also occur that more than one jurisdiction regards an individual or a company as resident for tax purposes.

For example, it would be possible for a taxpayer to be considered resident in Ireland by the Irish tax authorities on the grounds of his renting an apartment in Dublin that he visits from time to time and considered resident in Belgium by the Belgium tax authorities on the grounds of his center of economic activities being located there, even though he was ordinarily resident in some third country for all practical purposes.

He could thus be taxed as a resident in all three countries. If he were also a citizen of a country that taxed on the basis of citizenship (e.g., the United States), he could also be subject to tax in that country, even though he never set foot there from one year to another and did not derive any income from sources in that country or own any property situated there.

Similarly, a company may be considered resident in Sweden by the Swedish tax authorities on the grounds of its being incorporated there and considered resident in the United Kingdom by the U.K. tax authorities on the grounds of its central management and control being located in the United Kingdom.

Just as criteria of residence are not mutually exclusive, so too with criteria of source. Even in the case of countries where the notion of "source" receives substantially similar treatment and judicial decisions of the one country are persuasive authority in the other (e.g., Singapore and South Africa), the respective tax authorities and even the appeal courts may well come to different conclusions in a given case.

For example, this situation could easily arise with regard to the source of income deriving from a contract concluded in one country but providing for performance in the other (or partially in one and partially in the other).

3.3 Relief Provisions

Many tax systems provide a measure of unilateral tax relief in cases of double taxation. These provisions present considerable differences in form as well as scope.

Furthermore, a number of countries have entered into bilateral double taxation treaties. Treaty provisions regulating bilateral tax situations often differ in material respects from the unilateral provisions normally applied by the contracting parties. Unfortunately, however, treaty networks are very far from being comprehensive, and the existing treaties show a considerable lack of harmony with regard to their provisions.

Unilateral and treaty provisions normally provide for one of the following types of relief:

- *tax exemption*, whereby all or part of the taxpayer's foreign source income or foreign situs property is excluded from the taxable base (it is frequently a condition that such income or property should have been subjected to tax in the foreign country);
- *tax credit,* whereby foreign tax, paid or payable, is credited against the taxpayer's domestic tax bill;
- *tax reduction,* whereby foreign tax, paid or payable, is deductible from the domestic taxable base; and
- *reduction in the rate of tax,* whereby foreign income or assets are taxed domestically at a lower rate.

Different national systems and tax treaties offer a wide variety of formulas for the computation of the amount of relief available.

For a foreign tax to be eligible for a tax credit or other relief treatment, it is normally required that it should be of the same generic type as the tax normally imposed by the domestic country (e.g., the United States).

Similarly, reciprocity may be required for tax relief to be granted.

EXAMPLE[1]

Under the German Net Worth Tax Law,[2] individuals with a domicile or customary place of abode in Germany and legal entities with their place of management in Germany are subject to German net worth tax on their worldwide property. German net worth tax liability does not, however, apply to certain fixed assets situated in a foreign state with which Germany has not concluded a double taxation treaty.[3]

The Ministry of Finance of Bavaria issued a ruling stating that this relief would be granted but only on the basis of reciprocity. The relief does not apply where the foreign country does not impose a net worth tax, as no double taxation occurs. Therefore immovable property and fixed assets belonging to a permanent establishment in those countries, owned by taxpayers who are German residents, would normally be subject to net worth tax in Germany.

The ruling has been approved by the Federal Ministry of Finance.

In certain cases, there are territorial extensions of a tax treaty, for example, U.K. or Netherlands tax treaties that have been extended to its colonies and former colonies. Where the extension of treaties is to an IOFC such as the Netherlands Antilles or Barbados, this may open interesting planning opportunities.

The presence of a tax sparing clause in a tax treaty may also be relevant. A tax sparing clause allows residents of a capital exporting country a credit against domestic tax for profits or gains in a developing country in respect of which foreign taxes benefit from an exemption or reduction.

Care should be taken to note whether a tax treaty is applicable to the taxes of the divisions of federal states as well as to the federal taxes.

EXAMPLE[4]

The deceased died resident in Texas. Among the assets of his estate were mortgages on real estate located in Canada.

These mortgages were omitted from the state inheritance tax return by the attorney for the estate on the grounds that Texas did not have jurisdiction, under Texas inheritance tax law, over mortgage on real property situated in Canada.

The argument of the attorney for the estate was based on the situs rules contained in the United States–Canada Estate Tax Treaty,[5] article II, and his case was that the treaty precluded the State of Texas from including in the estate the indebtedness and mortgage securing the payment thereof.

> However, article I provides that the tax referred to in the treaty with regard to the United States is the "federal estate tax."
>
> In the opinion of the attorney general, the legal ownership of intangibles by a person in Texas gives such intangibles a business situs in Texas and makes them "property without the jurisdiction of this State."
>
> It therefore followed that the value of an indebtedness secured by mortgages against real estate located in Canada and held by a resident deceased of Texas was to be included in the estate when computing the amount of inheritance taxes due.

Special unilateral provisions may govern the application of the provisions of a tax treaty in the domestic law.

Of particular interest are the Swiss measures for the prevention of the improper use of tax treaties. The Federal Decree of December 14, 1962,[6] provides that reduction of tax withheld at source granted by the other contracting state in accordance with the provisions of a tax treaty concluded by Switzerland may not benefit persons claiming abusively by an individual, a company, a partnership, or other legal entity resident in Switzerland if, through such claim, a substantial part of the tax relief would benefit, directly or indirectly, persons not entitled to the benefits of a Swiss tax treaty. Such claims will be refused.

Tax relief would be considered to be claimed abusively in the following four cases:

Case (i)

Treaty relief will be refused if the claim relates to income of which a substantial part is used, directly or indirectly, to satisfy the rights or claims of persons not entitled to the benefits of a Swiss tax treaty. As a rule, income used to write off assets, the value of which accrues or has accrued, directly or indirectly, to persons not entitled to the benefits of a Swiss tax treaty is deemed to be income used to satisfy rights or claims of such persons.

This limitation applies especially to foreign-owned licensing (patent-holding) and investment companies through which such income is merely channeled (i.e., conduit companies).

Tax relief will not be granted where more than 50% of the income for which such relief is claimed is used to satisfy the rights or claims of persons not entitled to the benefits of a Swiss tax treaty. Only administrative expenses and taxes allocable to the income in question are deductible from profits for the purposes of determining whether or not more than 50% of the income in question has been distributed.

Case (ii)

Treaty relief will also be refused if the claim relates to income that benefits a legal person resident in Switzerland, in which persons not entitled to the benefits of a

Swiss tax treaty have, directly or indirectly, a substantial interest by way of a participation in the financial structure, or otherwise, and which does not make appropriate profit distributions.

The amount that is considered to constitute an appropriate profit distribution for each annual accounting period is at least 25% of the gross income to which a tax treaty applies. If such distributions go first to one or more interrelated companies in Switzerland, such companies must redistribute them in the same amount, after deduction of taxes, if any. It should be noted, however, that a reserve is made for the covering of losses arising in the normal course of business.

Since unusual methods of financing an enterprise can lead to an abuse of tax relief, this limitation also applies in the case of companies in which persons not entitled to the benefits of a Swiss tax treaty are interested, where their interest-bearing loan accounts total more than six times the company's capital plus apparent reserves or where such loans bear interest at unacceptable rates.

Cases (iii) and (iv)

Treaty relief will similarly be refused if the claim relates to income

> that benefits, by virtue of a fiduciary relationship, a person not entitled to the benefits of a Swiss tax treaty; or
>
> that benefits a family foundation resident in Switzerland or a partnership resident but not carrying on business in Switzerland in which persons not entitled to the benefits of a Swiss tax treaty are substantially interested.

3.4 Tax Treaties

Tax treaties are international agreements or conventions concluded with the object of eliminating double taxation by the contracting states. International double taxation may be loosely defined as the imposition of comparable taxes in two (or more) states on the same taxpayer in respect of the same subject matter and for identical or overlapping periods. The most harmful effects of double taxation are on the exchange of goods and services and on the movement of capital and persons.

Tax treaties frequently contain provisions reducing the rates of withholding taxes. It is the existence of these provisions in a wide network of treaties that enables countries such as Switzerland (notwithstanding its measures against the abuse of tax treaties) and the Netherlands to be used as conduits.

Normally tax treaties are not concluded between high tax jurisdictions and tax havens. In line with this approach, certain tax treaties specifically exclude from their scope entities that benefit from specially favored tax treatment (e.g., the exclusion of Luxembourg holding companies from the provisions of tax treaties concluded with Luxembourg).

When relying on a tax treaty, care should always be taken to insure that it is applicable. It is important to check whether there are any amending treaties or protocols and whether there are any interpretative rulings or official statements concerning the scope of the treaty.

3.5 Withholding Taxes

Withholding taxes are taxes that are part of a country's income tax system and that the payer of a dividend, royalty, interest payment, etc., must withhold from each such payment and must pay over to his own tax authorities. In the case of nonresidents, a withholding tax may be a final tax or it may only constitute the advance payment of tax.

The rates of withholding taxes are frequently reduced by tax treaties. Indeed, certain jurisdictions qualify as tax havens by virtue of the exemptions or the reductions in the rates of withholding taxes to which their residents become entitled in accordance with the provisions of one or more (sometimes a network of) tax treaties. The use of such tax treaties may thus permit the creation of a conduit whereby profits are transferred from one country to another via a third country, thus suffering the smallest possible total tax burden.

The cost of withholding taxes may not be immediately apparent. However, it may be costly to ignore the time value of money. Receiving a dollar tomorrow is not the same as receiving a dollar today. The dollar received today will enable you to pay back debt (thereby avoiding interest charges) or to make an investment (thereby producing a stream of income). The difference in value between a dollar tomorrow and a dollar today is precisely the return earned by today's dollar between now and tomorrow.

In technical terms, this is known as the "discount rate." It is a key element in planning that has to be determined by each decision maker on the basis of an assumption about what an extra dollar today would earn in the future. The lowest reasonable discount rate is the current interest rate on risk-free securities such as treasury bonds. Most businesses, however, can expect to earn more than this (otherwise they would quite rapidly go out of business), and their discount rate should take account of the average return on their available investment opportunities. Typical rates of return for large corporations are in the region of 6% to 10% per annum. Small businesses may have much higher rates, especially when they have investment opportunities they regard as attractive for which they are unable to borrow money or raise equity.

Using a discount rate of x%, the value of a future dollar declines exponentially at a rate of x% per year. A few simple calculations show how dramatic the effect of discounting can be on deferred income. After ten years, a sum of money has lost 44% of its value at 6% p.a., 54% at 8%, 61% at 10%, and 75% at 15%.

Tax effects are typically over shorter periods, but they can still be significant. Overlapping connecting factors can lead to economically disadvantageous multiple taxation. Taxing authorities are subject to conflicting pressures: They have a vested interest in maintaining and stimulating taxable income, but they are also playing a "tax game" with other taxing authorities, the rules of which they do not control.

It follows that, while most tax systems contain unilateral mechanisms mitigating double taxation, these are generally both inadequate and uncoordinated—they may even aggravate the problem they purport to solve. Bilateral (or multilateral) treaties can be viewed as imposing stricter and more effective rules on the tax game that countries play.

3.6 OECD Model Convention

In July 1958, the Council of the Organization for European Economic Cooperation (OEEC) instructed its Fiscal Committee to submit a draft convention for the avoidance of double taxation with respect to taxes on income and capital, together with concrete proposals for the implementation of such a convention. In September 1961, the Organization for Economic Cooperation and Development (OECD) was established to succeed the OEEC, and the mandate of the Fiscal Committee was confirmed.

On July 6, 1963, the Fiscal Committee submitted a draft convention in a report to the council. In April 1972, and at subsequent sessions, the Committee on Fiscal Affairs (the former Fiscal Committee) adopted revised texts of various articles. The revised wording has been incorporated in the text of that 1963 draft convention.

In 1977, an updated model convention was published in a report to the Council of the OECD by the Committee on Fiscal Affairs. The 1977 model convention incorporated, with further amendments, the revisions mentioned above.

In 1992, a similar updating process culminated in the release of the present OECD Model Convention.

The members of the OECD are Australia, Austria, Belgium, Canada, Denmark, Finland, France, Germany, Greece, Iceland, Ireland, Italy, Japan, Luxembourg, the Netherlands, New Zealand, Norway, Portugal, Spain, Sweden, Switzerland, Turkey, the United Kingdom, and the United States.

The draft conventions have exercised a considerable influence on most tax treaties, including treaties between countries that are not members of the OECD, as well as on the U.S. Treasury Model. *(See next section.)*

3.7 U.S. Treasury Model Income Tax Treaty

The U.S. Treasury uses its own model income tax treaty as a starting point in its negotiation of tax treaties with other countries.

On September 20, 1996, the U.S. Treasury Department released a revised Model Income Tax Convention ("the 1996 Model") to serve as its basic negotiating document. The 1996 Model draws on the previous 1981 Model, which was withdrawn on July 17, 1992, as well as on the current OECD Model Tax Convention on Income and Capital, existing U.S. tax treaties, recent negotiating experience, current U.S. tax laws and policies, and the comments of interested parties.

The 1996 Model is designed to provide a basic explanation of U.S. treaty policy and to facilitate negotiations by identifying differences between income tax policies in the two countries. But it does not represent an ideal U.S. income tax treaty. Particular income tax treaties may depart from the 1996 Model on account of a variety of factors related to the tax laws and policies of the other country, their interaction with the treaty and U.S. tax law, treaty precedents, and the relative economic positions of the treaty parties.

4. Economic Double Taxation

4.1 Definition

The term *economic double taxation* is used to indicate, by analogy, the case in which the same profits are subject to tax at more than one level.

The most important example is the case in which corporate profits are first taxed in the hands of a company and then, upon distribution, are once again taxed in the hands of shareholders.

Economic double taxation is not strictly speaking a case of double taxation since the taxpayers are different legal personae and the quality of the income changes upon distribution. However, the practical effect is often similar to that of double taxation *stricto sensu*.

4.2 Relief Provisions

In many countries, intercorporate distributions are not taxed or they receive favorable treatment in the hands of a recipient company.

For example, the imputation system is a system under which at least part of the tax paid by a company on its profits is credited against the tax liability of shareholders in receipt of distributions paid by the company out of those profits. Imputation reduces or eliminates the double taxation of distributed profits that arises under the classical system of taxation. Under an imputation system, all taxable corporate profits, whether or not distributed, are subject to corporate income tax at statutory rates. When the corporate profits are distributed, an individual or corporate shareholder is entitled to a full or partial credit for the underlying corporation tax that can be attributed to the dividends.

The problem usually arises in cases in which the shareholder is an individual. At the one end of the spectrum are the countries that make no provision at all for the avoidance or mitigation of this form of double taxation.

At the other end are those countries that aim to eliminate entirely the double taxation burden. In between are the systems offering different types of relief, the most common being

(a) systems in which the distributed and undistributed profits are taxed at different rates;

(b) systems in which the shareholder pays tax on his dividend income at a lower rate than he would normally pay on the slice of income in question; and

(c) systems in which all corporate profits are taxed at substantially the same rate but a refund is granted at the shareholder level.

The problem of economic double taxation is most acute in the case of distributions from a company in one country to shareholders in another country where the relief measures do not dovetail in a satisfactory manner.

This would, for example, be the case of a company that is resident and makes profits in a country that taxes companies at a uniform rate in respect of both distributed and undistributed profits (even though it granted a tax credit to resident shareholders in respect of tax suffered at the corporate level) but the shareholders are resident in a country that taxes distributed corporate profits at a reduced rate and does not in consequence grant any tax credit at the shareholder level. If there were no unilateral or treaty provision for relief, the profits of a company would be taxed in full in its hands, and its distributions would be taxed once more in full in the hands of the shareholders. Certain treaty provisions deal specifically with this problem, for example, the extension of the French *avoir fiscal* to certain foreign shareholders.

5. The Permanent Establishment Concept

5.1 Taxation of Business Profits

Basis for Taxation

The treaties lay down which state will be entitled to tax business profits that an enterprise of one state makes in the other state. In most cases, this is by reference to whether there is a permanent establishment in such other state.

The relevant provision relating to business profits is contained in article 7(1) of the OECD Model Convention, which states:

> The profits of an enterprise of a Contracting State shall be taxable only in that State unless the enterprise carries on business in the other Contracting State through a permanent establishment situated therein. If the enterprise carries on business as aforesaid, the profits of the enterprise may be taxed in the other State but only so much of them as is attributable to that permanent establishment.

The rest of article 7 explains how the profits of a permanent establishment are determined.

The main use of the concept of a permanent establishment is thus to determine the right of a contracting state to tax the profits of an enterprise of the other contracting state.

It follows that the key to preventing exposure to tax on business profits arising in foreign treaty countries lies in avoiding the creation of a permanent establishment in such countries.

In effect, provided that a Swiss or a Netherlands company is not considered to have a permanent establishment in a treaty country, it will not be liable to tax on its business profits there. It could carry on business transactions and operations freely without tax implications.

Definition of a Permanent Establishment

The definition of *permanent establishment* may be found in article 5 of the OECD Model Convention.

The term *permanent establishment* means a fixed place of business in which the business of the enterprise is wholly or partly conducted. Permanent establishment includes especially

- a place of management;
- a branch;
- a factory;
- a workshop;
- a mine, quarry, or other place of extraction of natural resources; and
- a building site or construction or assembly project that exists for more than twelve months.

Under the OECD Model Tax Treaty, a permanent establishment will generally be deemed to exist if a "fixed place of business" is maintained in a country.

An alternative feature of the OECD Model Tax Treaty is the negative definition of permanent establishment.

The term *permanent establishment* does not include the following:

- the use of facilities solely for the purpose of storage, display, or delivery of goods or merchandise belonging to the enterprise;
- the maintenance of a stock of goods or merchandise belonging to the enterprise solely for the purpose of storage, display, or delivery;
- the maintenance of a stock of goods or merchandise belonging to the enterprise solely for the purpose of processing by another enterprise; or
- the maintenance of a fixed place of business solely for the purpose of purchasing goods or merchandise, or for collecting information, for the enterprise.

The OECD Model Tax Treaty further provides that the term *permanent establishment* shall not be deemed to include "the maintenance of a fixed place of business solely for the purpose of advertising, for the supply and collection of information, for scientific research or for similar activities which have a preparatory or auxiliary character." The official OECD commentary on the model treaty explains that these words extend the exemption by stating that all activities that fall within the spirit of the provisions above should be exempted, thus avoiding an exhaustive list of exceptions. These negative provisions may be useful in enlarging the scope of activities that companies will be permitted to carry out without incurring local tax liability.

To avoid mingling income from a business activity that of itself would not constitute a permanent establishment with income from other business activities that fall within the permanent establishment definition, it may be useful to form a subsidiary. The subsidiary could undertake the activities that would constitute a permanent establishment. The nontaxable activities pursuant to the permanent establishment article could then be conducted by the nonresident parent and these activities would be insulated from the subsidiary's taxable activities.

The Case of an Independent Agent

Under all treaties, where an enterprise carries on business dealings through a broker, general commission agent, or any other agent of an independent status in a treaty country, it cannot be taxed by such country in respect of those dealings if the agent is acting in the ordinary course of his business.

A person will not constitute a permanent establishment of the enterprise on whose behalf he acts provided that

- he is independent of the enterprise both legally and economically, and
- he acts in the ordinary course of his business when acting on behalf of the enterprise.

Whether a person is independent of the enterprise represented depends on the extent of the obligations that such person has vis-à-vis the enterprise. Where the person's commercial activities for the enterprise are subject to detailed instructions or to comprehensive control by it, such person cannot be regarded as independent of the enterprise. Another important criterion will be whether the entrepreneurial risk has to be borne by the person or by the enterprise the person represents. A subsidiary is not to be considered dependent on its parent company solely because of the parent's ownership of the share capital. Persons cannot be said to act in the ordinary course of their own business if, in place of the enterprise, such persons perform activities that, economically, belong to the enterprise rather than to that of their own business operations.

It is generally accepted that the existence of a subsidiary company does not, of itself, constitute that subsidiary company a permanent establishment of its parent company. This follows from the principle that, for the purpose of taxation, such a subsidiary company constitutes an independent legal entity. Even the fact that the trade or business carried on by the subsidiary company is managed by the parent company does not constitute the subsidiary company a permanent establishment of the parent company.

However, a subsidiary company will constitute a permanent establishment for its parent company under the same conditions stipulated above, as are valid for any other unrelated company (i.e., if it cannot be regarded as an independent agent and if it has and habitually exercises an authority to conclude contracts in the name of the company).

The same rules would apply to activities that one subsidiary carries on for any other subsidiary of the same company.

The Case of a Dependent Agent

Persons whose activities may create a permanent establishment for the enterprise are so-called dependent agents (i.e., persons, whether employees or not, who are not independent agents). Persons having the authority to conclude contracts can lead to permanent establishment for the enterprise maintaining them. In such a case, the person has sufficient authority to bind the enterprise's participation in the business activity in the country in question. The use of the term *permanent establishment* in this context presupposes, of course, that the person makes use of this authority repeatedly and not merely in isolated cases.

The authority to conclude contracts must cover contracts relating to operations that constitute the business proper of the enterprise. Moreover, the authority has to be habitually exercised in the other country; whether or not this is the case should be determined on the basis of the commercial realities of the situation. A person who is authorized to negotiate all elements and details of a contract in a way binding on the enterprise can be said to exercise this authority in the other country, even if the contract is signed by another person in the country in which the enterprise is situated.

It should be borne in mind, however, that a dependent agent simply provides an alternative test of whether an enterprise has a permanent establishment in a state. If it can be shown that the enterprise has a permanent establishment within the meaning of another provision of the permanent establishment article of the relevant tax treaty, it will not be necessary to show that the person in charge is a dependent agent pursuant to the treaty.

It follows that either an independent or a dependent agent of the operating company could carry on international operations without attracting tax in the countries of operation, provided that care is taken not to create a permanent establishment in such countries.

5.2 Tax Treaty Protection

It would be possible for an offshore company located in a country that does not have tax treaties to take advantage of the vast network of tax treaties of other countries (such as Switzerland and the Netherlands) in the following way: A Swiss or Netherlands company is set up with the profit center in a foreign permanent establishment. This would attract very little corporate tax in either Switzerland or the Netherlands. The company could take advantage of all the treaty advantages since it would be a bona fide Swiss or Netherlands company, notwithstanding the fact that there is little Swiss or Netherlands tax to be paid and the operations would take place in the IOFC.

The advantage of using a company incorporated in a country with tax treaties, such as a Swiss or a Netherlands company, is the possibility offered by the treaties to reduce worldwide taxes on business profits. This is as a function of the provisions of tax treaties that make it possible to avoid tax on business profits in a foreign treaty country even where the Swiss or the Netherlands company has profits in the other country. The critical point is to avoid the creation of an office or a branch (permanent establishment) in the country concerned.

5.3 Switzerland as an Illustration of the Planning Process

Switzerland is normally a high tax jurisdiction like any other. However, there are certain provisions that can make a Swiss company a suitable vehicle for the proposed structure.

Swiss taxes are frequently settled by negotiation with the tax administration before setting up. The effective tax may be substantially less than the amounts provided in Federal Direct Taxes Law or in the various cantonal tax codes.

At the federal level, corporation income tax is imposed on annual worldwide income, after deduction of business expenses.

However, an important exception should be noted: This is a proportional reduction of tax due on business income earned through a permanent establishment outside Switzerland (e.g., an offshore company). The income is included in the company's taxable income; a reduction of the resulting tax is then granted in the proportion that the qualifying foreign net income bears to the company's total net income.

Domiciliary Company

Important tax savings can also be achieved by operating through a domiciliary company. The distinguishing feature of the domiciliary company is that it conducts no business activities in Switzerland. There is no limitation as to its business activities worldwide, but it will generally have little more than a registered office (a nameplate) in Switzerland.

A domiciliary company is granted no federal tax relief. Its income will primarily be from foreign sources. Most cantons give extremely favorable cantonal tax treatment to domiciliary companies. It should be noted that the exact tax status of each domiciliary company is normally a matter of negotiation with the cantonal authorities.

Permanent Establishment Exemption

A valuable planning possibility lies in the rule contained in paragraph 1 of article 55 of the Direct Taxes Law (IDN). According to this rule, all income from foreign sources is included in Swiss taxable income with the exception of income attributable to a foreign permanent establishment and income from foreign immovable property. The tax rate, however, is determined on the basis of total income.

The following points should be noted:

(a) The Swiss tax authorities may require the company to prove the existence of a foreign permanent establishment, which in the absence of an applicable treaty is defined in domestic law as being a "fixed place of business where a qualitatively or quantitatively essential part (partie notable) of the business of the enterprise is carried on" (art. 6 IDN).

(b) The income attributable to the foreign permanent establishment is included with the other income of the company (if any) for the purposes of calculating the rate of tax applicable, but a reduction of the resulting tax is then granted in the proportion that the qualified foreign income bears to the net income.

(c) The Swiss tax authorities have issued comprehensive guidelines for the purpose of determining the amount of income that may be allocated to the foreign permanent establishment, but they are generally willing to accept the book profit or loss of the permanent establishment as a basis of the computation.

(d) At first sight it might seem that a Swiss company whose entire income was attributable to its overseas establishment would avoid payment of any federal or cantonal direct income taxes on its profits, but this will not necessarily be the case because of a rule that allows the tax authorities to attribute a percentage of net profits (between 10% and 30%) to the Swiss head office on the basis that the Swiss head office exercises some managerial function that contributes to the profit-generating activity of the overseas branch. The amount so attributed is known as the "preciput" and is taxable in Switzerland at the rate determined under the above rules.

(e) Most cantonal tax codes follow the principles of federal taxation outlined above, but the question may be an academic one if the Swiss company is incorporated in a canton that grants a full exemption for cantonal tax purposes for all overseas income (the domiciliary company exemption).

It follows that if the Swiss company were to attach all or some of its business profits to a foreign permanent establishment (say in an offshore jurisdiction), this could lead to substantial savings at the federal level.

Effective Swiss Tax Burden

It follows that there would be little corporate tax in either country provided that the income is earned by qualifying a foreign branch.

However, there are withholding taxes in Switzerland. For this reason, it would be advisable to reduce the taxable base in Switzerland by making deductible payments to other group companies. Such deductions should be in respect of items and in amounts acceptable to the revenue in the country concerned. This could leave a relatively small tax base.

Caveat

Given the proposed international measures to curb harmful preferential tax regimes, it is questionable for how long this type of tax structure will be practical. (See Chapter 14, "International Measures to Combat Harmful Tax Practices.")

Notes

1. This example is based on the ruling of the Bavarian Ministry of Finance of June 20, 1978, No. 34–S 35 32–2/16-37767. See *Finanz Rundschau*, No. 3 of February 8, 1979, at 69, and 19 *European Taxation* 67 (February 1979).
2. *Vermogensteuergesetz,* sec. 1(1).
3. Ibid., sec. 12(3).
4. This example is based on the Opinion of the Texas Attorney General No. M–92 (dated June 16, 1967) to the Comptroller of Public Accounts.
5. Treaty of February 17, 1961.
6. *Arrêté du Conseil fédéral instituant des mesures contre l'utilisation sans cause légitime des conventions conclues par la Confédération en vue d'éviter les doubles impositions; du 14 décembre 1962; Bundestratsbeschluss betreffend Massnahmen gegen die ungerechtfertige Inanspruchnahme von Doppelbesteuerungsabkommen des Bundes vom 14 Dezember 1962.* See *Swiss Measures against Abuse of Tax Conventions*, International Bureau of Fiscal Documentation, Amsterdam 1963; and Circular D3. Allg. 67/a of the Swiss Federal Tax Administration, dated December 31, 1962, as amended.

CHAPTER NINE

STRUCTURING THE OFFSHORE TAX PLAN

1. General

1.1 Object of Offshore Tax Planning

The object of offshore tax planning is

- to determine, from the tax point of view, whether or not to embark on a project,
- and, if so, or if the project has already been commenced,
- to minimize or defer the imposition of the tax burden falling on taxable persons and events,
- lawfully,
- in the attainment of the desired business and other objectives,
- taking into consideration all relevant tax factors with particular regard to the advantages that may be derived from the interrelationship of two or more tax systems, and in the light of the material offshore factors.

A wide range of possible structures may be employed for the purpose of attaining this object. Effective offshore tax planning depends on the accurate selection from a large number of possible transactions, operations, and relationships, those elements or combinations of elements that are likely to produce the most satisfactory overall solution to a given problem.

1.2 Timing in Offshore Tax Planning

It is a basic imperative of tax planning that it should be timely.

At the outset, a taxpayer is free to select the time and method of carrying out a project, and the parties, and is thus in a position to control, in important respects, the tax consequences of the project. Once concluded, however, the tax consequences are not in most cases easily altered.

Offshore tax planning is therefore all the more effective if the material factors are taken into consideration prior to the carrying into effect of any transaction, or operation, or relationship. An ounce of prevention may be worth many pounds of cure.

An international tax situation is in most cases more flexible than a purely national tax situation. It may therefore be possible to introduce a measure of offshore tax planning into an international project even after its commencement. However, every international tax situation consists of a number of domestic elements, and considerable difficulty is frequently encountered in varying such elements for the purposes of a new offshore tax plan.

EXAMPLE[1]

A settlor created two trusts in 1964 in favor of his sons and their descendants. The assets of the trusts consisted principally of a large number of valuable shares in a U.K. family company.

When the U.K. capital gains tax was introduced in 1965, it was apparent that any profits made on the future sale of the shares would, if the trustees and beneficiaries remained resident in the United Kingdom, be liable to a very substantial tax bill. Estate duty[2] was also likely to prove very high if the assets of the trust were not transferred and if the settlor remained domiciled in Great Britain.

The family purported to take up residence in Jersey and thereafter made application to transfer the trust funds to two new trustees in Jersey.[3]

The object of the scheme was to avoid capital gains tax and estate duty in the following way:

re: capital gains tax

Since trustees are a continuing body of persons, the transfer of trust funds on the appointment of new trustees does not constitute a "disposal" for the purpose of capital gains tax.[4]

By the time the funds were transferred out of the existing trusts, they would be assets owned by trustees who were neither resident nor ordinarily resident in the United Kingdom, and such transfer would thus not attract capital gains tax in their hands.[5]

If the beneficiaries were neither resident nor ordinarily resident in the United Kingdom, they would not be liable to tax on any capital gains arising to the trusts.[6]

re: estate duty

If the trustees were to transfer the trust funds to a Jersey company in exchange for shares (which would be property situated outside Great Britain), such property would not be subject to estate duty, since it would pass under a law that is neither the law of England nor of Scotland; and *either*

the deceased would not die domiciled in Great Britain, *or*

the property would pass by reason of a disposition made by a person not domiciled in Great Britain at the date at which the disposition took effect, such disposition not being made on behalf of, or at the expense of, or out of funds provided by, a person who was at that date domiciled in Great Britain.[7]

Upholding a decision[8] of the high court (Chancery Division) refusing the application of the transfer of the trusts to Jersey, the high court dismissed the appeal on the following grounds:

(a) While there was nothing improper nor contrary to public policy in approving the variation of trusts for the purpose of avoiding or reducing tax liability, where that was the sole purpose of such an application, the court ought to enquire into all the circumstances and to consider the interests of the infant and unborn beneficiaries and whether the appointment of new trustees was convenient or necessary for reasons connected with the trusts themselves; and

(b) since the beneficiaries' connection with Jersey was recent and tenuous and the appointment of the new trustees was mere machinery in the scheme to avoid tax, the court was entitled in the exercise of its statutory discretion not to consider it "fit" to approve the proposed scheme nor "expedient" to appoint new trustees.

1.3 Stages in the Offshore Tax Planning Process

The following are the successive stages in the planning process:

- analyzing the existing database;
- designing one or more possible offshore tax plans;
- evaluating the offshore tax plan;
- debugging the offshore tax plan; and
- updating the offshore tax plan.

2. Analysis of the Existing Database

The first stage in the tax planning process is to analyze the different items of tax involved in the project and to compute as accurately as possible the likely total tax burden.

It is only by considering each of the tax elements both separately and as a whole that it is possible to formulate an efficient tax plan.

It may also be necessary to take into account the likely gross return of the project and the nontax expenditure involved.

Caveat: Where there is relatively little money in issue, care should be taken not to incur expenditure in connection with the preparation and implementation of an offshore tax plan that is out of proportion to the possible savings.

3. Design of One or More Possible Tax Plans

The design of an international arrangement may involve one or more of the following:

- the selection of the form of an international transaction, operation, or relationship;
- the selection of a foreign investment country or new country of residence;
- the introduction of one or more additional offshore jurisdictions; and joint ventures.

3.1 Selection of the Form of an International Transaction, Operation, or Relationship

In most international tax situations, at least two of the countries are determined in advance. In such cases, the planning process may not go beyond the stage of selecting the most favorable form of a transaction, operation, or relationship from the tax point of view.

Dividends, interest, royalty receipts, and capital gains frequently receive quite different tax treatment at the domestic level and at the treaty level. It would thus be necessary to take such differences into account in deciding, for example, whether an investment should take the form of a dividend-producing share participation or an interest-producing loan. In the case of industrial and intellectual property, it might be necessary to decide whether the rights should be sold or be exploited by way of royalty arrangement.

EXAMPLE [9]

The taxpayer was a U.K. company that manufactured electric power tools and had evolved various secret production methods and drawings. It was faced with difficulties in connection with its established export trade to India, owing to the Indian government's policy of encouraging local factories.

The taxpayer decided to set up a new company in India to manufacture its tools and to provide the new Indian company with the necessary know-how and goodwill, the consideration therefore being in the form of shares in the Indian company.

A comprehensive arrangement was thus entered into between the two companies in accordance with which the taxpayer was to provide the Indian company for a fixed number of years with all present and future drawings, designs, schedules, and technical knowledge and data necessary for the establishment of a factory for the production of certain portable electric tools, and to assign to the Indian company all the Indian patents and the benefit of all future inventions relating to the selected tools. The taxpayer undertook further not to provide the above facilities to any other party in India nor to compete with the Indian company in India.

The United Kingdom had not yet introduced the tax on long-term capital gains, and it would obviously make a substantial difference to the taxpayer if such consideration were treated as being on capital and not on revenue account.[10]

If the transaction represented a method of trading by which the taxpayer acquired the shares as part of the gains of its trade, this income gain would have been taxable. If, however, the transaction represented the receipt of shares in return for the transfer to the Indian company of capital assets, the consideration would not have been subject to tax.

On appeal from the decision of the special commissioners, the court held that the effect of the arrangement was that the taxpayer transferred to the Indian company two capital assets comprising

(i) a fund of confidential material in relation to its manufacture of tools, and

(ii) its preexisting goodwill with exclusive rights precluding it from competing with the Indian company in India.

The consideration received by it was therefore on capital account and not on revenue account, and was therefore not subject to tax.

In certain countries, dividends arising from substantial share participations (as variously determined) receive favored tax treatment in the hands of corporate shareholders, for example, the Netherlands substantial participation (*deelneming*) exemption, where, subject to certain conditions, a 5% or greater shareholding can produce a 0% corporate tax base. This can prove an important consideration in fixing the amount of a proposed shareholding.

The tax consequences of operating through a subsidiary, through a branch office, or through an independent agent are frequently quite different. These differences may be crucial in determining the manner in which a proposed operation is to be conducted.

In many countries, the notion of "permanent establishment" is employed for the purpose of determining the tax liability of nonresident taxpayers carrying on business within such countries. In addition, this notion is frequently used in tax treaties as a basis for the apportionment of taxable income (particularly in the case of industrial and commercial profits).

This feature in tax treaties can be particularly valuable where there is no tax at home since it can be used to turn a high tax jurisdiction into a virtual tax haven for the purposes of a particular transaction or operation.

EXAMPLE [11]

An Australian company that carried on theatrical enterprises in Australia and abroad planned to promote a number of touring shows in New Zealand.

Under the former Australia–New Zealand Tax Treaty,[12] article III(1), an Australian enterprise is not subject to tax in respect of its New Zealand source industrial or commercial profits, unless these are derived through a permanent establishment in New Zealand, in which case they may be subject to New Zealand tax.

Article II(1) defines "industrial or commercial profits" as including "the profits of an industrial or commercial enterprise but does not include...income arising from, or in relation to, contracts or obligations to provide the services of public entertainers, such as stage, motion picture, television or radio artistes, musicians, and athletes."

Article II(1)(m) defines a "permanent establishment" as "a branch agency or other place of business," including a "management." It is further provided in article III(1)(m)(ix) that "where an enterprise of one of the Contracting States...has an agent in that other State other than an agent who has, and habitually exercises, a general authority to negotiate and conclude contracts on behalf of that enterprise...that enterprise shall not, merely by reason thereof, be deemed to have a permanent establishment in that other Contracting State."

The Australian company did not wish to pay New Zealand tax on the commercial profits that would accrue to it as a result of its New Zealand promotions. It therefore aimed to carry on its theatrical enterprises in such a way that it would not be considered to be engaged in trade or business in New Zealand through a permanent establishment in that country.

With regard to the definition of the term *permanent establishment* in the treaty, the Australian company organized its operations in New Zealand in the following way:

- Its executives and artistes were brought from overseas on tour;
- the Australian company did not open an office in New Zealand;
- the duties of the touring manager who accompanied each show did not go beyond the performance of the small tasks arising out of the day-to-day production of a show on tour;
- in respect of any major decision, the touring manager was required to refer to his principals in Australia who were alone empowered to make such decisions; and
- the only New Zealand staff engaged was casual staff in the nature of ushers, stage staff, etc.

There was thus no branch, agency, other place of business, management, or agent who had, and habitually exercised, a general authority to negotiate and conclude contracts on behalf of the Australian company in New Zealand. It was therefore held that the Australian company was not engaged in trade or business in New Zealand through a permanent establishment, and consequently it was not subject to New Zealand tax in respect of the commercial profits derived by it from its theatrical productions.

EXAMPLE [13]

The taxpayer was a Canadian company that entered into a number of transactions in the United States. For the purposes of its negotiation, it used certain U.S. resident individuals in a representative capacity.

The taxpayer did not wish to have a permanent establishment in the United States since it is provided under the former United States–Canada Tax Treaty,[14] article I, that

> An enterprise of one of the Contracting States is not subject to taxation by the other Contracting State in respect of its industrial and commercial profits except in respect of such profits allocable in accordance with the Articles of this Convention to its permanent establishment in the latter State.

The protocol[15] to the treaty, paragraph 3, defines the term *permanent establishment* as including branches, fixed places of business, etc., and goes on to state:

> When an enterprise of one of the Contracting States carries on business in the other Contracting State through an employee or agent established there, who has general authority to contract for his employer or principal, or has a stock of merchandise from which he regularly fills orders which he receives, such enterprise shall be deemed to have a permanent establishment in the latter State.
>
> The fact that an enterprise of one of the Contracting States has business dealings in the other Contracting State through a commission agent, broker or other independent agent or maintains therein an office used solely for the purchase of merchandise shall not be held to mean that such enterprise has a permanent establishment in the latter State.

Therefore to insure that it did not have such a permanent establishment, the taxpayer arranged its affairs in such a way that it did not have, in the United States,

- a real office;
- officers, directors, or employees;
- a bank account or books of account;
- a telephone listing;
- its name on any door or office; or
- an employee or agent with general authority to contract for it.

The taxpayer was thus not subject to U.S. tax on its industrial and commercial profits.

The method to be employed in analyzing and comparing the relative tax burdens and other expenditure attendant upon the project

- if no tax minimization plan is adopted; and
- if a tax minimization plan is adopted, and it (a) succeeds or (b) fails,

is considered below.

3.2 Selection of a Foreign Investment Country or New Country of Residence

Offshore tax planning may be occasioned by a choice between two or more possible investments in different countries. In examining their relative merits, it is important to regard not only business considerations but also comparative tax burdens.

For example, in deciding between offers to take up shares in companies in different countries, the following considerations should, *inter alia*, be taken into account:

1. the rate of tax imposed on corporate profits in the investment countries under examination;
2. whether dividend distributions are subject to withholding taxes, and if so, at what rates; and
3. whether any tax credits or deductions are available in the country of residence of the shareholder in respect of taxes paid in the investment countries under examination.

In the case of the setting up of a manufacturing subsidiary, the tax and nontax factors to be compared will be somewhat more complex. It may also be necessary to take into account the turnover tax on value added.

Value-added tax (VAT) is a general tax on consumption expenditure incurred in respect of

1. deliveries of goods,
2. the rendering of services, and
3. imports.

In the case of deliveries and services, the total tax is collected in fractional payments from the various persons involved, on the basis of the value added by them. In the case of imports, the tax is imposed on the value of the goods imported.

There is usually an exemption on exported goods and services or a refund of any VAT already paid on the exported goods or services.

The business effect of VAT is that export enterprises enjoy a distinct pricing advantage in both their own countries and foreign countries vis-à-vis enterprises located in countries that employ direct, rather than this form of indirect, taxation.

The following example illustrates this effect in a somewhat oversimplified way, deliberately ignoring the complex business considerations governing the fixing of prices.

EXAMPLE

Assume that company A is located in country A, which has introduced VAT, while company B is located in country B, which has not introduced VAT and relies instead on direct taxation. Assume further that a product manufactured by each such company costs 70 units to manufacture. VAT imposed by country A on this project is at the rate of 10%.

Taking into account the domestic tax structure, company B sets the domestic retail price of its product at 110.

The domestic retail selling price of company A's product is similarly 110, i.e., a basic price of 100 plus the 10% VAT.

When company B exports its product to country A, the addition of the 10% VAT will produce a retail selling price of 121, i.e., 11 units more expensive than company A's product.

In country B, on the other hand, the position will be the reverse. Country A will take off the 10% VAT on exportation and the product will therefore be priced in country B at 100, while the product of company B will be priced there at 110, again allowing company A's product to be marketed at a lower price in country B than company B's product.

Individuals frequently emigrate for business, pleasure, and health reasons.

International and particularly offshore planning may thus be required by a proposed change in residence, domicile, or nationality.[16]

In such cases, it is necessary to take into account the tax (including especially estate and inheritance taxes) and the exchange control implications of the change.

Switzerland is considered to be one of the most desirable countries by many emigrants. As a general policy, Switzerland rigidly controls the influx of new residents and admits only a limited number of applicants who (apart from the employees of international organizations and certain companies) are usually individuals who have retired for reasons of age or sickness. Those who are fortunate enough to obtain residence permits in Switzerland may, under certain conditions, benefit from favored tax treatment at federal level. Similar tax treatment is also available in certain cantons to resident aliens not carrying on trade or business in the canton in question.

Frequently the preferred country of residence imposes a high rate of income tax, net worth tax, and estate duty on the worldwide income and property of residents.

In such cases, the emigrant may find it advisable to resort to an offshore setup that could result in the divestment of certain assets prior to establishing residence in the new country.

Of considerable importance is the question of whether the connecting links with a former country of residence have been effectively severed from the tax point of view.

EXAMPLE [17]

The taxpayer was a Belgian citizen who had lived abroad for a long period of time. He had, however, maintained a home and a bank account in Belgium and had acquired some real property there.

The question at issue was whether the taxpayer maintained a *domicile*[18] or seat of fortune in Belgium and therefore was to be considered a Belgian resident taxpayer.

The Belgian Tax Code does not define *domicile*, but the courts take two factors into account, physical presence in Belgium and the intention to establish the main residence in Belgium on a permanent basis. A seat of fortune is considered to be the place where the fortune was administered, and not the place where the properties of the individual were situated.

The Supreme Court held that the taxpayer was not a Belgian resident. In reaching this decision, the Court took into account the fact that the taxpayer did not and had no intention of returning to his former home, which was occupied by his wife and children from whom he lived separately. It also noted that the real property was held to provide his child with income and that the Belgian bank account was used only to hold funds during his visits to Belgium.

EXAMPLE [19]

The taxpayer was resident in Germany and also had the center of his vital interests there. He was a partner in a German limited partnership. He stayed in Austria for eight to ten days per month for the management of a permanent establishment there owned by the partnership, and he had a customary place of abode there. The taxpayer sought to deduct losses incurred by the Austrian permanent establishment from his personal tax liability in Austria.

The Austrian Administrative Court[20] ruled that a taxpayer can have only one customary place of abode and that since his residence and the center of his vital interests were in Germany, that was where he was resident for tax purposes.

Tax liability in a previous country of residence or citizenship may cling for many years after a change (e.g., in the United States, Germany, or Denmark). This is especially to be weighted for in the use of a move to an offshore country.

3.3 Introduction of Additional Offshore Jurisdictions

In many cases, considerable tax savings may be effected not only by the careful selection of the form of an international transaction, operation, or relationship, but by the introduction of one or more IOFCs in addition to those countries that are already included in the database.

International tax planning may be merely a simple extension of national tax planning through the introduction of a foreign element, such as the creation of a trust or holding company in a tax haven or other country where low tax rates prevail.

EXAMPLE [21]

A U.S. resident was the owner of certain oil and gas leases in the United States.

With a view to minimizing the tax burden arising therefrom, he set up a Swiss company and transferred to it the major part of his interest in the leases in exchange for a 100% share participation in the Swiss company.

Under the Switzerland–United States Tax Treaty,[22] article III(1)(a), a Swiss enterprise is not subject to tax in the United States in respect of its industrial and commercial profits unless it is engaged in trade or business in the United States through a permanent establishment situated therein.

Care was taken to insure that the Swiss company carried on substantial business activity and was managed as a going concern so that it would be recognized as a separate taxable entity under U.S. tax law.

To this effect, it did all the necessary things to act like a viable company. It purchased and held title to working interests in oil and gas leaseholds; assumed and paid its proportionate share of the obligations under the operating agreement covering such leaseholds; executed division order for the disposition of production income; signed contracts to the management of its producing properties; collected income and deposited it in a bank account; paid expenses incurred in connection with its activities; and invested excess funds in securities.

The U.S. Tax Court held that the Swiss company was a separate entity for U.S. tax purposes and that its undistributed income was not subject to tax in the taxpayer's hands.

If there is already at least one foreign element in a project, the inclusion of an additional tax jurisdiction for the purposes of a tax minimization arrangement may be both obvious and simple to achieve.

EXAMPLE [23]

An Italian engineering company was engaged to undertake certain works in Switzerland, principally in the canton of Valais.

The Swiss Federal Constitution, article 46(2), prohibits the double imposition of tax on income and net worth by the cantons. In the absence of further legislative provisions, the rule has been consistently applied by the Swiss courts to the effect that if an enterprise that is established in one canton derives income from sources in another canton through a permanent establishment located in the latter canton, such income is subject to tax only in the canton where the permanent establishment is situated.

> The Swiss cantons constitute different tax jurisdictions and in this respect resemble different countries.
>
> On an examination of the tax rates applying in the various Swiss cantons, it was observed that the canton of Zug would produce the lowest tax burden on the proposed operation, and for this reason it was decided to set up a permanent establishment in Zug with the function of directing the project.
>
> A major tax saving could have been effected if the intercantonal rule had applied to a foreign company in the position of the taxpayer.
>
> However, the federal court held that this rule does not apply where foreign countries are involved. Nevertheless, the allocation between cantons, with respect to both income and net worth taxation, did result in the reduction of the total Swiss tax burden.

In more complicated cases in which it is decided that it is appropriate to investigate the potential advantages of introducing one or more additional countries into the existing international database, a preliminary examination should be made of combinations of bilateral tax situations, with special regard to the following:

- any particularly favorable provisions contained in the tax treaties concluded with other countries by each of the countries already involved (it is frequently here that the key to the most favorable setup is to be found); and
- the potential benefits of using a tax haven or some other country offering tax incentives or other special tax or nontax benefits.

Thereafter, a number of different possible schemes should be improvised, using various combinations of countries, transactions, operations, and relationships. There is scope for considerable imagination and ingenuity. It will usually be found that at least a few different arrangements would be suitable for the purposes of a tax minimization plan.

The number of possible parameters may in certain cases be extremely large. Each additional IOFC that it is proposed to include in the tax plan should be examined in the light of the existing database and all new tax and nontax factors that are material to such inclusion.

In designing the most appropriate arrangement, it is above all important to consider the following:

- whether ownership of the various rights, securities, etc., should be vested in one or more companies, individuals, trusts, or a combination of these;
- what should be the relationship *inter se* of the various individuals and entities; and
- insofar as this is not already predetermined, where each such entity should be located, since the characteristics of IOFCs may differ considerably.

3.4 Joint Ventures

When examining the setting up of joint ventures from scratch, it is useful to begin with a close analysis of what each of the parties is required to contribute to the venture, how the profits (if any) are to be divided between them, and how losses are to be borne. It is also helpful to consider how the venture can be unscrambled. Joint ventures go wrong far more often than is expected by the parties when they are first put together.

There are four broad ways by which profits from a venture can be moved offshore. These may be subject to difficult business considerations, which could in turn have an effect on tax considerations, in the case of joint ventures, and particularly so in the case of joint ventures where there are minority holdings.

(a) *Management charges, technical assistance fees, or royalties.* These will, subject to transfer pricing constraints, be allowed as a deduction against taxable profits in the country of source. They will be taxed in the country of destination, which may or may not be the parent company. Double tax agreements may be relevant.

(b) *Payment for supplies or raw materials bought from, or product supplied to, other members of the group.* This affords some scope for the transfer of taxable profits but is severely limited by transfer pricing rules. Related to this is the possibility of factoring where one company in the group purchases the receivables of another company at a substantial discount and proceeds to collect the full amount of the receivables itself.

(c) *Interest.* This may be interest on loans within the group. It may be arm's length interest. The group has a choice between borrowing and claiming a deduction at parent level (injecting funds into the subsidiaries' paid-up capital) or operating and claiming the deduction at subsidiary level. This may be constrained by "thin capitalization" or, in the case of the United States, "interest stripping" rules. Double tax agreements will often be relevant.

(d) *Profits.* Profits may be taxed in the country of source and then distributed as dividends either to the parent or to an intermediate company. There will then normally be a credit for the underlying tax paid. Again, double tax agreements will be relevant.

In the cases of (a), (b), and (c) above, a management charge (for instance) will typically be at the expense of all the shareholders. This can create intractable problems unless the intention to make such payments is built into the terms of the original agreements and compensated for by adjustments in the percentage shareholdings, the prices paid for the shares, or by payments made to the other parties via different routes. This problem should always be considered.

In the case of (d) above, it is important to make sure either that all parties have the same strategy as to the proportion of profits distributed or retained or that more complex provisions are made in the statutes of the company to permit the different parties to each pursue its optimum tax strategy. There is sometimes scope for using "dividend access shares," and problems can sometimes (but not always) be solved by interposing a local, 100%-owned "dividend trap" subsidiary between the parent and the minority shareholding. One problem is how to obtain any relief for any losses. Most countries have provisions by which losses suffered in one group company can be offset against profits in another, but these are subject to two restrictions:

- a common degree of ownership is required, and
- loss relief may not apply across frontiers. Typically, a parent company can offset the losses of a foreign branch, but this does not extend to foreign subsidiaries and does not work in reverse.

The greatest and most cost-effective value can be obtained by setting up onshore and offshore structures from the beginning. In those cases, it is better for all of the parties to be involved at an early stage of negotiation of any joint venture, once agreement in principle has been reached. The best starting point is a draft letter of intent. It is then possible to indicate what further information is likely to be needed.

All onshore and offshore factors can thus be taken into account in designing a tax plan that will accommodate the interests of all parties.

4. Evaluating the Offshore Tax Plan

4.1 Method

Tax planning is only a part of business planning as a whole. It is therefore necessary to take into account, in addition to the tax burden, any differences in gross profits and nontax expenditure that may result from the introduction of a tax plan.

These variables must be computed as accurately as possible for each of the following hypotheses:

1. if the plan is not adopted;
2. if the plan is adopted and succeeds; and
3. if the plan is adopted and fails.

EXAMPLE

Assume that A is the director and sole shareholder of a foreign company that is showing substantial profits.

The investment country imposes a withholding tax of 15% on dividend distributions to nonresidents but taxes directors on their fees at the marginal rate applying to the income concerned.

A's country of residence imposes tax at the marginal rate applying to income received by resident individuals, irrespective of whether such income is foreign or domestic, but grants a tax credit in respect of foreign taxes paid.

A is considering increasing the amount of directors' fees payable to him by 100,000 units.

This increase would be for the purposes of reducing the economic double taxation burden falling on the income in the hands of the company and in A's hands. It bears no relation to the value of the work done by him.

The tax authorities of the country of residence of the company have a discretion under which they may disallow the deduction in the hands of the company of fees and emoluments paid to directors that they consider to be excessive and not actually incurred in the production of income.

On the basis of the proposed increase in directors' fees of 100,000, the global tax burden (i.e., at the corporate level in the country of residence of the company and at the shareholder/director level in both countries) *with respect to this sum* is calculated in the following way:

If the tax plan is not adopted:

Company's tax (40% of 100,000)	40,000
Tax on dividends of 60,000 (dividend withholding tax = 15%)	9,000
Income tax in A's country of residence (at his marginal rate, taking into account the foreign tax credit)	21,000
	70,000

If the tax plan succeeds:

Company's tax	–
A's tax on the additional directors' fees (at the marginal rates applying in both countries, but taking into account the foreign tax credit in the country of residence)	50,000
	50,000

If the tax plan fails:

Company's tax	40,000
A's tax on the additional directors' fees (at the marginal rates applying in both countries, but taking into account the foreign tax credit in the country of residence)	50,000
	90,000

The total saving of tax (taking into account tax in the company's hands and in A's hands) would thus be 20,000 if the tax plan were to succeed; the increased tax burden in the case of failure would also be 20,000.

Other calculations could be made on the same basis for different hypotheses with respect to the amount of the increase in directors' fees and the highest estimated deduction that the tax authorities would be likely to allow as deductible in the company's hands. These figures would provide an indication as to whether, and if so, which, modifications should be made.

It would of course be necessary for the purposes of the above example to take into account legal and other expenses attendant upon an objection and appeal if the tax authorities were to disallow the deduction in the hands of the company. The inclusion of these items would increase the total possible tax and nontax expenditure and reduce the possible saving.

The purpose of a tax plan is in many cases the postponement of tax as well as or instead of any reduction in the aggregate tax burden. Where, therefore, tax would be chargeable at a different time as a result of the implementation of a tax plan, it is necessary to discount the tax burden back to the basic year (usually either the current tax year or the year of commencement of the project) for each year that is considered relevant for the purposes of comparison.

As in the case of the tax burden, the time at which income is received or expenditure incurred may make a considerable difference in calculating real savings or additional costs. It may thus also be necessary to discount each term that would be affected by the implementation of a tax plan back to the basic year.

Of course, it is not always necessary to discount each of these terms separately.

Where all the terms would change as a result of introducing a tax plan, the figure to be discounted is *gross profits less tax and nontax expenditure*.

Where only tax and nontax expenditure would change, the figure to be discounted is *the total of such expenditure*.

Where only gross profits and the tax burden would change, the figure to be discounted is *gross profits less the tax burden.*

Where only the tax burden would change, *only this figure need be discounted.*

In this way, constant terms are ignored.

4.2 The Formula for Computing the Win or Lose Odds

For the purpose of computing the win or lose odds of a tax plan,

let A = the estimated gross profits of the project if a tax plan is not adopted;

let B = the estimated gross profits of the project if the tax plan is adopted;

let C = the estimated tax burden if the tax plan is not adopted;

let D = the estimated tax burden if the tax plan is adopted and succeeds;

let E = the estimated tax burden if the tax plan is adopted and fails;

let F = the estimated cost (other than tax) of setting up and running the project if the tax plan is not adopted; and

let G = the estimated cost (other than tax) of setting up and running the project if the tax plan is adopted.

Certain items (e.g., future earnings, future taxable base, and tax rates) used for the purposes of calculating these terms can only be estimated. Since, however, the same figures are used to compare alternative arrangements, they nevertheless constitute a sound basis for comparison.

It is essential to be aware of any assumptions made in the database used for computing the various items and also of any nonquantifiable elements that have been left out of account.

Where identical items appear, respectively, in terms A and B; C, D, and E; or F and G, they may be ignored, as it is only comparative and not absolute figures that are required.

Where terms A and B, or F and G, are identical, they may be left out of account altogether.

Where additional expenditure is incurred as a result of introducing a tax plan, it is necessary to take into account any tax deduction that may be available in respect of such expenditure, otherwise a distortion may creep in regarding the comparison of the various alternatives.

In calculating term E, particular note should be taken of any applicable tax penalties.

4.3 Applying the Formula in Evaluating an Offshore Tax Plan

Obviously no tax plan should be adopted unless the tax saving, if the plan were to succeed, is substantially greater than the sum of any reduction in gross profits and any increase in expenditure resulting from its implementation.

> That is, if (A – F) is greater than (B – G), the plan should not be adopted unless the difference is smaller than (C – D).

Where the estimated tax burden if the plan is adopted and fails is materially greater than the estimated tax burden if the plan were not adopted at all (i.e., where E is materially greater than C), the decision as to whether or not to adopt a tax plan depends

(a) on the likelihood of the plan succeeding, and

(b) (i) in the case where there is no material difference between gross profits less nontax expenditure whether or not the plan is adopted, then:

on a comparison between the total discounted tax burden if the plan is not adopted, and the total discounted tax burden if

— the plan is adopted and succeeds; and

— the plan is adopted and fails;

That is, if there is no material difference between (A – F) and (B – G), then: on a comparison between (C – D) and (E – C)

or

(ii) in the case where there is a material difference between the gross profits less nontax expenditure according to whether or not the plan is adopted, then:

on a comparison between the total discounted gross profits less the total discounted tax and nontax expenditure if the plan is not adopted, and the total discounted profits less the total discounted tax and nontax expenditure if

— the plan is adopted and succeeds; and

— the plan is adopted and fails.

That is, if there is a material difference between (A – F) and (B – G), then:

on a comparison between

[B – (D + G)] – [A – (C + F)]

and

[A – (C + F)] – [B – (E + G)]

By calculating and comparing in this way the relative gross profits and tax and nontax expenditure applying to the different hypotheses, it is possible to determine to what extent the implementation of a given tax plan will place the taxpayer in a better position if it succeeds, or in a worse position if it fails.

The taxpayer will not necessarily choose the most favorable solution on the basis of the above formula, since nonquantifiable factors (such as difficulties of changing over, exchange control restrictions, etc.) may persuade him to choose the more expensive solution as calculated in this way.

EXAMPLE

Assume that a taxpayer is considering acquiring shares in a foreign company. The current market value of the shares is 100,000 units. The annual dividend is currently 2,500.

The taxpayer estimates (though he has strong reservations in this respect) that the value of the shares in 2001 will be approximately 150,000. He does not anticipate that the amount of the annual dividend will change during the relevant period (1998–2002).

The taxpayer is subject to tax in his country of residence at the top marginal rate of 66.7%. Though his foreign dividends are subject to domestic tax, he benefits from a tax credit in respect of income tax paid abroad on such dividends. The foreign country's nonresident shareholder's tax is levied at the rate of 15%. Thus his total annual tax burden in respect of the dividend would be as follows:

foreign tax (15% of 2,500)	375
domestic tax (66.7% of 2,500) – 375	1,2

In accordance with the present policy of the foreign country, the taxpayer would be entitled to have remitted any income as it falls due. On the realization of the shares, however, the proceeds would be blocked, and he would only be able to remit such proceeds by way of arbitrage dealings. It is estimated that he would lose approximately 5% in value of the capital sum in this way.

The taxpayer examines the pros and cons of an alternative arrangement whereby instead of becoming a shareholder he would lend the 100,000 to the company at the rate of 10% under a five-year mortgage bond. The country of residence does not impose tax on foreign interest receipts. The foreign country's nonresidents tax on interest is levied at the rate of 10%. His annual return would thus be 10,000; his annual tax burden, 1,000.

The estimated nontax expenditure (other than the arbitrage dealings) connected with the two alternative arrangements is sufficiently close to be able to be left out of account for the purposes of comparison.

The value of money to the investor is taken as 10% per annum.

The alternative arrangements are compared in the following way:

		Shareholding Arrangement	*Interest Arrangement*
1998			
Gross Profits		2,500	10,000
Tax		1,667	1,000
Net		833	9,000
1999			
Net		833	9,000
Discounted back to 1998		757	8,182
2000			
Net		833	9,000
Discounted back to 1998		688	7,438
2001			
Net		833	9,000
Discounted back to 1998		626	6,762
2002			
Gross Profits	2,500		
	50,000	52,500	10,000
Tax	1,667		1,000
Loss at 5% on arbitrage dealings on 50,000 (i.e., difference between two arrangements)	2,500	4,167	
Net		48,333	9,000
Discounted back to 1998		33,012	6,147

Total discounted gross profits less tax		
1998	833	9,000
1999	757	8,182
2000	688	7,438
2001	626	6,762
2002	33,012	6,147
	35,916	37,529

The aggregate return under the arrangement whereby the taxpayer holds shares in the company, receives dividends, and makes (hopefully) a substantial capital gain on the realization of the shares would seem at first glance to be greater than that produced by the interest arrangement.

However, the difference in the tax burdens and the time at which profits accrue, when discounted back to the basic year (1998), indicate clearly that the interest arrangement is the more advantageous.

Furthermore, the taxpayer is aware that the increase in value of the shares by 50% is merely an estimated figure and is dependent on market developments. His reservations in this regard are a nonquantifiable factor that strengthen his decision to enter into the interest arrangement rather than to acquire shares in the company.

4.4 Comparing Alternative Tax Plans

The method described above is equally appropriate for the purpose of determining the most favorable form of a proposed transaction, operation, or relationship; deciding whether it is appropriate to include an additional country in the existing database, and if so, which; and comparing with one another the advantages of two or more possible plans.

4.5 Estimating the Chances of a Tax Plan Succeeding

While the win or lose odds of a tax plan can to a certain extent be calculated, the chances of a plan succeeding can only be estimated.

One often hears estimates being given in percentages. Such figures cannot be taken too literally. "A 50-50 chance of success" really means little more than that it is considered to have an even chance of succeeding; "a 90% chance of success," that there is a strong likelihood of succeeding.

Such percentage estimates may, however, assist counsel in explaining to his client the interrelationship between the estimated chances of success, on the one hand, and the win or lose odds (i.e., the calculated potential savings if the tax plan were to succeed or the additional costs if it were to fail) on the other.

A taxpayer might be tempted to take a chance on a plan, even if the odds of success were very small, provided that the estimated savings would be considerable if he succeeded, while the additional cost would be minimal if he lost. Say, for example, his only additional expenditure would be the cost of taking the matter on appeal, whereas taxwise he would be placed in the same position as if he had never adopted the plan at all or were merely liable for interest on the difference in tax for the relevant period.

Conversely, he would be most reluctant to adopt a tax plan where he stood to lose a substantial amount if it failed (e.g., as a result of penalties) in relation to his potential gain if it succeeded, unless the chances of success were overwhelmingly in his favor.

It may thus be helpful to be able to express the risk as a percentage chance of succeeding, the other term of the equation being the potential benefit resulting from success against the potential loss resulting from failure.

EXAMPLE

Assume the facts of the example in section 4.1 above.

A is advised that there is a high probability that the tax authorities of the country of residence of the company will disallow the deduction of such increased fees in the hands of the company as being excessive and not actually incurred in the production of income. A thus has a relatively small chance of making a 28.6% tax savings, as against the likelihood of his tax burden being increased by 28.6%.

Legal and other expenses of an objection and appeal would amount to 5,000.

If, therefore, he were to resort to litigation with the tax authorities, A might find that he has only a small chance of making a saving of 21.4% against a high risk of incurring increased tax and related expenditure of 35.7%.

A is further advised that the chances of success would be considerably stronger if his increase in directors' fees were rather lower, thus of course reducing the potential tax saving but not inviting the attention of the tax authorities to a manifestly unrealistic deduction on the part of the company.

Considerable care must be taken in preparing a technical analysis in cases where the tax authorities have the power to allocate deemed income or losses.

EXAMPLE [24]

The taxpayer was a Belgian company. Its statutory director owned 96% of the shares. The director was also president of a Liechtenstein company, with which the Belgian company made an agreement not to conclude any transaction on its own account but to place all its organization and personnel at the disposal of the Liechtenstein company. The latter company would reimburse all costs and expenses but would not provide any remuneration for the service.

Under Belgian law, if a business enterprise established in Belgium has, directly or indirectly, an interdependent relationship with an enterprise established abroad, all abnormal benefits granted to a foreign enterprise as a result of that relationship will be added to the Belgian enterprise's profits.

The Belgian tax administration added a deemed 5% brokerage fee to the taxable profits of the taxpayer. This was contested. However, the Brussels Court of Appeal upheld the assessment. In the first place, it was decided that there was a link of dependency between the two companies. Furthermore, the court considered it abnormal that a business company created with a view to making profits should have acted free of charge as a cashier for a foreign sister company, thus forgoing the usual minimum broker's fee.

5. Debugging the Tax Plan

5.1 Local Advice

It is impossible for an outsider to be aware of all the pitfalls that lie in foreign legal, tax, and exchange control systems or of the special difficulties that may be encountered in operating in a foreign country.

The following example illustrates the danger that an individual who never sets foot in a particular country may, through his investing there, be taxed by such country as a resident.

EXAMPLE [25]

A resident of Monaco acquired immovable property in Belgium and share participations in several companies that were registered and established in Belgium, of which he became a director.

Under Belgian law, residents are subject to tax on their worldwide income, while nonresidents are subject to tax only on their Belgian source income. An individual is considered to be a Belgian resident if his domicile or the center of his economic interests is in Belgium.

Though he was a Monegasque resident and had no home whatsoever in Belgium, and despite the fact that he had substantial other business interests outside of Belgium, the taxpayer was deemed to have the center of his economic interests in Belgium and hence to be a Belgian resident for tax purposes.

He was thus taxed in Belgium on his worldwide income, not merely on his Belgian source income. He was consequently subject to a tax burden considerably higher than if he had made the same investments in a country where, in identical circumstances, he would have been taxed as a nonresident.

When a decision has been taken as to what seems to be the most favorable arrangement on the basis of

- the objectives;

- the total tax burden, in relation to gross profits and nontax expenditure, as discounted back to the basic year; and
- all other relevant considerations,

it is usually advisable to submit the proposed plan, for debugging, to a local expert in each of the foreign countries involved.

Where appropriate, foreign counsel should be asked to approach the necessary tax, exchange control, and other authorities to obtain rulings and, if possible, official commitments on matters that are essential to carrying out successfully a proposed arrangement.

EXAMPLE

Assume that a foreign property investment company proposes to invest in a township development scheme in a country that restricts the total borrowing rights of nonresidents.

For the purposes of the scheme, 30% of the capital is to be provided by the foreign company. The remaining 70% is to be raised locally by the way of mortgage finance.

It is considered essential by the foreign company that the profits resulting from the scheme should be freely remittable.

Prior to the conclusion of the scheme, the proposed arrangement is submitted to local counsel for debugging. He thereupon draws the attention of the foreign company to the local exchange control regulations that provide that no person may, without Treasury consent, make a loan or grant credit to any nonresident individual or to any company in which 25% or more of its voting securities, capital or earning, is held or controlled, directly or indirectly, by nonresidents.

To avoid the problem created by this provision, the following solution is adopted:

A local development company is formed, with its share capital consisting of ordinary shares and redeemable preference shares;

the foreign parent company takes up the ordinary shares; and

the redeemable preference shares, carrying cumulative rights as to dividends and certain other guaranteed rights, are taken up by local investors, the effect of which is to place the local investors in the same position as if they were receiving interest payments on a mortgage bond.

This arrangement does not fall within the scope of the regulations, since preference share capital does not constitute either a loan or credit; even if the development company were to find itself in a position where it needed to borrow, a gearing based on a holding by local investors of at least 76% of the share capital would in any case place the development company outside the scope of the regulations.

The development company would thus be in the same position as any other local company with regard to the right to raise capital locally.

5.2 Substance *versus* Form

The rule that the substance of a transaction, rather than its mere form, controls tax liability is one of very wide application. It can affect the amount of taxable income arising from practically any type of transaction. It is also applied frequently to settle questions of who is taxable on certain income.

The U.S. Supreme Court[26] has stated: "We cannot too often reiterate that taxation is not so much concerned with the refinements of title as it is with actual command over the property taxed—the actual benefit for which the tax is paid. And it makes no difference that such 'command' may be exercised through specific retention of legal title or the creation of a new equitable but controlled interest, or the maintenance of effective benefit through the interposition of a subservient agency."

Though many of the decisions that involve the principle of substance *versus* form arise because the tax authorities have detected a tax avoidance motive, it must be stressed that such a motive will not normally establish liability if the transaction does not do so without it.

One of the circumstances that may cause the test of substance *v* form to be applied is that the transaction involved was not an arm's-length transaction.

Application of the rule of substance *v* form is often called for when several separate steps are taken to reach the final result.

In a number of varied types of cases, the courts have applied the "business purpose" test. In most cases where the test is applied, the parties involved do not have adverse economic interests. They have consequently been held in many cases not to be dealing at arm's length.

Artificial avoidance schemes are particularly vulnerable to attack.

EXAMPLE [27]

The taxpayer had made a substantial capital gain and "purchased" a scheme to avoid paying tax. The effect of the scheme was, by a series of transactions, to create a deductible capital loss equivalent to the gain. A "real" loss was not suffered by the taxpayer because another effect of the scheme was to give rise to a tax-exempted capital gain to compensate for the loss. The taxpayer's only purpose in resorting to the scheme was to avoid tax. He relied on the fact that the form of transaction had often been held by the English courts to be more important than its overall effect, so that any loss or gain produced by the transaction would be upheld.

It has always been a principle of English law that the taxpayer is entitled to arrange his affairs so as to minimize his liability to tax, and, provided any steps taken were legal, the courts do not look behind a genuine document to seek the underlying substance of the transaction.

However, the House of Lords put a limit on this principle. The court looked at the scheme as a whole, instead of step by step as in previous cases, and said that the tax losses created were artificial losses and therefore were not deductible.

EXAMPLE [28]

The taxpayer was a Netherlands corporation, X. It had no offices in the Netherlands. In 1976, X held a 100% interest in four Swiss companies, none of which had offices or were staffed in Switzerland. The group also consisted of a holding company in the Netherlands Antilles, X Curaçao, which fully controlled X and which was, in turn, fully controlled by another corporation in Panama, X Panama. This corporation was owned by an individual resident in Germany, Mr. N. X purchased the Swiss companies from X Curaçao by means of a loan from X Curaçao. X Curaçao had originally bought the four companies from X Panama, and X Panama had financed the necessary loan. All loan contracts provided that the debts would be repaid only out of dividend income. The Swiss companies withheld the 35% "anticipatory tax" on the distributions of dividends to X. X then applied, in accordance with the Netherlands-Switzerland Tax Treaty,[29] for a full refund of the tax withheld on its dividends.

The issue in question was whether X was entitled to a full refund because it was resident in the Netherlands or only to a partial refund of 20%.

Under Swiss law, income from dividends, *inter alia*, is subject to a 35% withholding tax. Nonresident individuals and nonresident corporations having no permanent establishment in Switzerland are not entitled to receive a refund of withholding tax. Any refund of withholding tax must be claimed via the tax authorities of the country in which the claimant taxpayer is resident. The Netherlands-Switzerland Tax Treaty provides that the refund is available provided that insuring receipt of the total refund is not the main reason for the relationship between the two companies.

The Swiss Federal Tax Administration denied X the full refund of withholding tax on the grounds that the relationship between X and the four Swiss companies had been established primarily to receive the full refund and not for any sound business reasons.

X appealed against this ruling. The Federal Tax Administration held that, on the facts of this case, the issue raised was whether the transfer of control of the Swiss companies from X Panama to X Curaçao and then to X was primarily effected to avoid the "anticipatory tax." As an individual resident in Germany, Mr. N was not entitled to receive a full refund of the withholding tax, only to a refund equal to 20% of the dividends, and the administration noted that through the scheme of transferring shares to X against a debt claim equal to the purchase price, Mr. N was trying to have the reserves distributed to him without having to pay the withholding tax. The original decision of the Federal Tax Administration was thus upheld: X was not entitled to receive a full refund of the withholding tax paid in Switzerland, only to a refund equal to 20% of the dividends.

5.3 Applicability of Tax Treaties

When relying on a tax treaty, care should always be taken to insure that it is applicable. It is important to check whether there are any amending treaties or protocols and whether there are any interpretative rulings or official statements concerning the scope of the treaty.

EXAMPLE [30]

The taxpayer was a bank incorporated under Swiss law but with its central management and control in the United Kingdom. The Swiss branch of the bank had granted a loan to a bank in the United States and was in receipt of interest from sources in the United States.

The taxpayer fell within the provisions of the Switzerland–United States Tax Treaty,[31] article II (f), which defines a Swiss corporation as a corporation created or organized under Swiss law. Under article VII of the treaty, interest derived from sources in the United States by a Swiss corporation is subject to a tax of 5%, which is deducted at source.

On the other hand, the taxpayer also qualified as a resident of the United Kingdom under the former United Kingdom–United States Tax Treaty, which provides that a corporation is resident in the United Kingdom if its business is managed and controlled there. Interest from the United States to a U.K. resident is exempt from withholding tax (except where more than 50% of the debtor corporation is owned by the recipient corporation, which is not the present case).

A revenue ruling was issued that permits the taxpayer bank to choose the application of either the Swiss Treaty or the U.K. Treaty with the United States.

EXAMPLE [32]

In 1978, an affiliation privilege was introduced into the internal tax legislation of Luxembourg. This insured the relief from double taxation in respect of dividends paid between affiliated enterprises. The Belgium-Luxembourg Tax Treaty[33] provides for a reduction to 15% of the Belgian withholding tax on dividends. If a Luxembourg company directly holds at least 25% of the shares of the distributing Belgian company or if the direct holding was acquired for at least 250 million B Frs, the Belgian withholding tax is reduced to 10%. This means that Luxembourg companies entitled to an affiliation privilege can reduce or be exempt from Belgian withholding tax by using the provisions in the Belgium-Luxembourg Tax Treaty.

The Belgian Minister of Finance stated that no special measures need be enacted by Belgium to stop this practice, as the Luxembourg legislation was inspired by the *non bis in idem* principle, which is incorporated to a different degree in most countries, including Belgium.

5.4 Validity of Entities

Entities that are valid in one system of law may not be regarded as valid in the courts of other countries.

The following example illustrates a problem that arose in connection with the status of an *Anstalt.*

EXAMPLE [34]

Under Belgian civil law, the legal status of companies incorporated abroad is governed by their national law. They can therefore act in Belgium within the limits prescribed by that law but not in violation of the fundamental rules of Belgian law.

One of those fundamental rules is that all companies are based on a contract concluded between two or more partners. Therefore, "one-man companies" are not recognized by the Belgian courts, although they are not actually void under the Belgian law.

This means that such an entity (an *Anstalt*) does not have a separate legal personality, and thus the sole founder is personally liable for any debts incurred by the entity.

5.5 Substantial Risks or Disadvantages

Where there are substantial risks or disadvantages attendant upon the proposed setup and these cannot be easily avoided by the modification of the plan, it may be necessary to abandon the project altogether or to adopt the next most satisfactory of the alternative possible solutions considered.

Any such alternative solution must in turn be examined for weaknesses and pitfalls.

6. Updating the Tax Plan

Even after a plan has been adopted and the project has been embarked upon, it remains necessary to take into account any changes in the law or practice of any of the countries involved, which may have an effect on any of the elements of the arrangement.

This is comparatively easy with respect to one's own country. However, the financial press and various tax and business services usually provide only limited information with regard to changes in foreign countries.

It is therefore sound policy when briefing a foreign expert in connection with a proposed arrangement not only to ask specifically for information with regard to any impending or likely future changes in the existing law or practice of the country in question, but also to request him to report on any subsequent changes that may affect the arrangement.

Updating is the necessary corollary to the modifications that are concomitant with a dynamic society. By paying attention to future developments as well as to the present situation, it may be possible to lessen the harmful effects of some changes and to take full advantage of the potential benefits of others.

7. Caveat

For the purpose of evaluating the offshore tax plan (Section 4 above), debugging the tax plan (Section 5 above), updating the tax plan (Section 6 above), it is necessary also to keep abreast of the international regulation offshore activities. (See Chapter 14, "International Measures to Combat Harmful Tax Practices" and Chapter 15, "International Measures to Combat Money Laundering.")

Notes

1. This example is based on the U.K. case of *Re Weston's Settlements* (1969) 1 Ch. 223, (1968) 3 All E.R. 338.
2. Estate duty was abolished by the Finance Act 1975, which introduced capital transfer tax.
3. Under the Trustee Act 1925, sec. 41, and the Variation of Trusts Act 1958, sec. 1.
4. Finance Act 1965, sec. 25(1), provides that trustees of a settlement are treated as being a single and continuing body of persons that is distinct from the persons who may be the trustees from time to time. That body of persons is treated as being resident and ordinarily resident in the United Kingdom unless the general administration of the trust is ordinarily carried on outside the United Kingdom and the trustees or the majority of them for the time being are not resident or not ordinarily resident in the United Kingdom.
5. Finance Act 1965, sec. 20(1), provides that a person is subject to capital gains tax in respect of chargeable gains accruing to him in a year of assessment during any part of which he is resident in the United Kingdom, or during which he is ordinarily resident in the United Kingdom.
6. Finance Act 1965, sec. 42(1) and (2), provides that where a nonresident trust makes a gain and the settlor was domiciled and either resident or ordinarily resident in the United Kingdom when the gain was made or when the settlement was made, a proportion of the capital gain arising to the trust is attributed to any beneficiary resident or ordinarily resident in

the United Kingdom, the proportion being determined by reference to the interest of the beneficiary under the settlement.

7. Finance Act 1949, sec. 28(2), provides that property subject to estate duty does not include any property passing on death that is situate outside Great Britain if it is shown that the proper law regulating the devolution of the property, or the disposition under or by reason of which it passes, is the law neither of England nor of Scotland, and that at least one of the following conditions is satisfied:
   (a) that the deceased did not die domiciled in any part of Great Britain;
   (b) that the property so situate passes under or by reason of a disposition:
      (i) made by a person who, at the date at which the disposition took effect, was domiciled elsewhere than in some part of Great Britain; and
      (ii) not made, directly or indirectly, on behalf of, or at the expense of, or out of funds provided by, a person who at that date was domiciled in some part of Great Britain.
8. (1969) 1 Ch. 223, (1968) 1 All E.R. 720.
9. This example is based on the English case of *Wolf Electric Tools Ltd. v. Wilson* (1969) 2 All E.R. 724 (Ch. D).
10. Though the United Kingdom no longer exempts capital gains from tax, this distinction is still crucial in a number of jurisdictions that were inspired by the earlier U.K. legislation and that continue only to tax gains that are revenue gains or that tax capital gains at a substantially lower rate.
11. This example is based on 3 New Zealand Taxation Board of Review Decisions 49 (Case 5).
12. Treaty of May 12, 1960.
13. This example is based on the U.S. case of *Commissioner of Internal Revenue v. Consolidated Premium Iron Ores Ltd.* 265 F. 2d 320, 59 – 1 U.S. Tax Cases §9387.
14. Treaty of March 4, 1942, as amended.
15. Protocol of March 4, 1942.
16. The danger of being subject to tax in more than one country on the grounds of residence, domicile, or nationality is considered above.
17. This example is based on a decision of the Belgian *Cour de Cassation*. See *Recueil Général de l'Enregistrement et du Notariat*, February 1980, No. 22470 at 70, and 20 *European Taxation* 90 (March 1980).
18. The connotation of the French word *domicile* is closer to the English notion of dwelling place or home rather than to the English concept of domicile.

19. This example is based on the decision of the Administrative Court *(Verwaltungsgerichtschof)* of March 23, 1977, No. 308/75. See *Die Finanzrechtliche Erkenntnisse des VWGH und VFGH* No. 21/22 at 226 (November 1977), and 17 *European Taxation* 396 (November 1977).
20. *Verwaltungsgerichtshof.*
21. This example is based on the U.S. case of *Perry R. Bass and Nancy Lee Bass v. Commissioner of Internal Revenue* 50 T.C. 595.
22. Treaty of May 24, 1951.
23. This example is based on the decision of the Swiss Federal Court of April 3, 1968, CBGE 94 I. 328. See *Entscheidungen des Schweizerischen Bundesgerichts, Band* 94, 1, Teil, and 9 *European Taxation* 80 (April 1969).
24. This example is based on a decision of the Court of Appeal of Brussels of June 17, 1974. See *Journal de Droit Fiscal*, March/April 1975 at 90, and 15 *European Taxation* 357 (October 1975).
25. This example is based on the decision of the Belgian *Cour de Cassation* of September 7, 1965, *Pasicrisie* 1965, 1, 34, and 8 *European Taxation* 212 (September 1968).
26. *Griffiths v. Helvering* (1939) 308 U.S. 355 and *Corliss v. Bowers* 281 U.S. 376.
27. This example is based on the English case of *W T Ramsay Ltd. v. IRC, Eilbeck (Insp. of Taxes) v. Rawling* (1981) S.T.C. 174.
28. This example is based on a decision of the Swiss Federal Tax Administration of April 25, 1979. See *Archiv für Schweizerishes Abgaberecht/ Archives de droit fiscal suisse* Vol. 48, No. 5 (November 1979) and 20 *European Taxation* 91 (March 1980).
29. Treaty of June 22, 1966.
30. This example is taken from the Revenue Ruling No. 73–354, 1974 – 2 Cum Bull 326.
31. Treaty of May 24, 1951.
32. This example is based on the answer of the Belgian Minister of Finance to Parliamentary Question No. 90 of Mr. Declerq of January 14, 1981. See Bulletin of Questions and Answers of the House of Representatives at 1533, and 21 *European Taxation* 136 (April 1981).
33. Treaty of September 17, 1970.
34. This example is based on the decision of the Brussels Court of Appeal of January 29, 1975. See 29 *Tijdschrift* at 119 (May 1975), and 15 *European Taxation* 216 (June 1975).

CHAPTER 10

CASE STUDY: OFFSHORE TREASURY MANAGEMENT

1. The Issues

The skillful treasury management of a multinational company can produce significant tax savings through arm's length deductions being paid by members of the group to an administrative office, headquarters company, or coordination center.

The following are examples of tax-efficient structures that a multinational group might employ to accumulate income, and manage the income on the income, in an international offshore financial center (IOFC):

- Overseas purchases and sales
- Multicurrency management
- Interest received/Interest paid
- Debt factoring
- Advertising
- Transport/Distribution/Handling
- Travel
- Communications
- Captive Insurance/Reinsurance
- Royalties
- Computer charges
- Professional services
- Training
- Staff recruitment
- Printing and stationery

2. Proposed Structures

2.1 Overseas Purchases and Sales

Assume the following structure:

A centralized overseas purchase and sales office is set up in an IOFC to handle buying and selling of certain products for the group.

The overseas purchase and sales office is paid commissions by group members, on an arm's length basis, for performing such functions.

Tax Benefit The payment of commissions, on an arm's-length basis, would constitute an allowable deduction in the hands of the various group members.

Since less tax or no tax would be paid in the country where the overseas purchase and sales office is based, this differential would constitute an easily calculable tax saving.

Caveat All payments between related parties should be at arm's length. It would in principle be easier for the revenue, as well as for the group, to obtain information on comparable uncontrolled percentages payable as commissions in cases of payments to third parties than in most other cases of international pricing. Charging more than the arm's-length price would be risky, while charging less could be wasteful.

Transactions must be bona fide.

Care should be taken to insure that the profits of the overseas purchase and sales office do not fall within the tax nets of the countries of operation.

2.2 Multicurrency Management

Assume the following structure:

A multicurrency management center (MMC) is set up in an IOFC for the benefit of the group.

Specific objectives of the MMC will include some or all of the following:

- to exercise strict control over international payments in order to plan and effectively control the liquidity of an international group;
- to pool exchange risks in one location;
- to execute foreign exchange transactions at the lowest costs;
- to reduce foreign exchange risks through
  - —matching income and outgoing payments in the same currency,
  - —leading and lagging of payments, and
  - —hedging operations (e.g., forward contracts, borrowing, depositing in domestic and/or European markets);
- to decrease overall borrowing costs;
- to house medium- and long-term intercompany and other loans; and
- to provide intercompany loans.

The MMC can also be used as an international financing company.

The MMC would be remunerated on an arm's-length basis and would charge a fee for its services to recover its costs plus a reasonable markup.

Note: This could amount, at the very least, to 0.4% of all amounts owed or owing at any time in any foreign currency.

Business Benefits See above assumptions.

Tax Benefit Arm's-length fees payable by the various group members to the MMC would be deductible in their hands. At the very least, this would be 0.4% of any foreign currency owed or owing. These fees would be unconnected with any profits.

Caveat All payments between related parties should be at arm's length.

Transactions must be bona fide.

Care should be taken to insure that the profits of the MMC do not fall within the tax nets of the countries of operation.

2.3 Interest Received/Interest Paid

Assume the following structure:

An offshore finance company is used for certain lending and borrowing transactions of the group. The finance company participates in commissions and spreads.

Business Benefits The profits do not get altogether wasted on the banks.

It is possible to control the transactions.

Tax Benefit All of the above profits can be taken tax-free.

Caveat All payments between related parties should be at arm's length.

Transactions must be bona fide.

Care should be taken to insure that the profits of the finance company do not fall within the tax nets of the countries of operation.

2.4 Debt Factoring

Assume the following structure:

An offshore debt factoring company purchases the debts of the various group members at arm's-length prices in relation to those prices charged by unrelated debt factoring companies.

Tax Benefits The tax liabilities of the group members would be reduced by the difference between the face value of the debts and the amount actually received by them.

Any profits of the debt factoring company from the successful collection of the debts would be made free of tax.

Caveat All payments between related parties should be at arm's length.

Transactions must be bona fide.

Care should be taken to insure that the profits of the debt factoring company do not fall within the tax nets of the countries of operation.

2.5 Advertising

Assume the following structure:

A related offshore advertising agency handles advertising for all group members (the principals). The advertising agency receives a 15% commission from the media (newspapers, journals, TV, radio stations) for the placing of these advertisements.

Note: The average commission paid by the media internationally is 15%; the advertising agency uses subagents in the countries where the advertisements are placed; and the advertising agency splits the commission with the subagents 50–50.

Business Benefit Saving of 15%, or such percentage that has not already been granted to the subagents (assumed for these purposes to be 7.5%).

Tax Benefit Tax rate multiplied by 7.5% (assumed saving), say tax rate of 40% = 3%.

Caveat Normally, the domestic tax authorities will not question this transaction since

- the payment by the principal consists of a standard payment of the normal advertising fee, and
- the commission is paid by a third party (the media) to the advertising agency (i.e., the principals are not included).

It follows that there should not be any transfer pricing issues involved even though the advertising agency and the principals are related parties.

Care should be taken to insure that the profits of the advertising agency do not fall within the tax nets of the countries of operation.

2.6 Transport/Distribution/Handling

Assume the following structure:

A related overseas transportation and distribution office is set up in an IOFC.

This transportation and distribution office is responsible for transportation, distribution, freight, railage, shipping, handling, etc., required by the group members, and dealing with agents.

The transportation and distribution office is paid arm's-length commissions in line with those payable to any third party for the performance of these services.

Tax Benefit The payment of the transportation, etc., charges, on an arm's length basis, would constitute allowable deductions in the hands of the paying company.

Since less tax or no tax would be paid in the country where the transportation and distribution office is based, this differential would constitute an easily calculable tax saving.

Caveat All payments between related parties should be at arm's length. It would in principle be easier for the revenue, as well as for the group, to obtain information on comparable uncontrolled percentages payable as commissions in cases of payments to third parties than in most other cases of international pricing. Charging more than the arm's-length price would be risky, while charging less could be wasteful.

Transactions must be bona fide.

Care should be taken to insure that the profits of the transportation and distribution office do not fall within the tax nets of the countries of operation.

2.7 Travel

Assume the following structure:

An offshore travel agency is set up to handle all travel arrangements. The travel agency receives the usual agency commissions from the airlines, hotels, etc. (for example, in the case of most airlines, this is 9%).

Where the travel agency uses subagents, there would normally be a commission split, as in the case of advertising agencies. (See Section 2.5.)

Business Benefit Saving of full or partial commissions that would otherwise be wasted.

Tax Benefit Tax rate multiplied by 5% (assumed saving), say tax rate at 40% = 2%.

Caveat Normally, the domestic tax authorities will allow this deduction since the deduction consists of a standard payment of the normal travel commission paid by third parties.

The commission must be paid by third parties to the travel agency and not by the principals.

It follows that there should not be any transfer pricing issues involved, even though the travel agency is a related party to the principals.

Care should be taken to insure that the profits of the travel agency do not fall within the tax nets of the countries of operation.

2.8 Communications

Assume the following structure:

A centralized overseas communications office is set up in an IOFC to handle communications for group members. The communications office is paid an arm's length fee for performing such functions.

Tax Benefit The payment of communications charges, on an arm's-length basis, would constitute an allowable deduction in the hands of the various group members.

Since less tax or no tax would be paid in the country where the communications office is based, this differential would constitute an easily calculable tax saving.

Caveat All payments between related parties should be at arm's length.

Transactions must be bona fide.

Care should be taken to insure that the profits of the communications office do not fall within the tax nets of the countries of operation.

2.9 Captive Insurance/Reinsurance

Assume the following structure:

An offshore captive insurance company is set up to handle all insurance costs for the group.

The captive insurance company accepts for itself a lower slice on certain risks (technically known as "deductibles").

The captive insurance company reinsures all the rest through a reinsurance company.

Business Benefits It is possible to use a captive insurance company to obtain cover that the normal insurance market does not easily provide for, or does so only at very great expense.

It is possible to pay for reinsurance at the end of the stated term, whereas normal insurance premiums are paid at the beginning of the stated term.

If the members of the group are more careful than the average in the industry, it would be possible to achieve economies on insurance premiums that would not be possible in the normal course.

It is possible to obtain freedom from the onerous requirements and restrictions of insurance legislation in the principal countries where the group operates.

Tax Benefit It may be possible to charge premiums representing greater deductions than are reflected in the actual insurance and reinsurance costs of the captive insurance company, with the deductibility of such "inflated" premiums being accepted by the revenue as being in line with industry standards.

Caveat There must be both *distribution* of risk and *spreading* of risk to insure that deductions for the payment of premiums will be allowed.

All payments between related parties should be at arm's length.

Transactions must be bona fide.

Care should be taken to insure that the profits of the captive insurance company do not fall within the tax nets of the countries of operation.

2.10 Royalties

Assume the following structure:

Certain technology would be owned by an offshore licensing company.

The licensing company would use a sublicensing company in the Netherlands. (See also Chapter 3, Section 7, "Offshore Licensing.")

Tax Benefit In tax treaties between the Netherlands and many other countries, withholding taxes on royalties are normally reduced to 0%.

Netherlands taxes on a flow-through of royalties can also be extremely low.

There is no withholding tax on payments of royalties by a Netherlands company.

Caveat Payments of royalties are normally deductible subject to the following:

- All payments between related parties should be at arm's length. It would in principle be relatively easy for the revenue, as well as for the group, to obtain information on comparable uncontrolled royalty percentages.
- Transactions must be bona fide.

The United States–Netherlands Treaty cannot be used to benefit persons in third countries.

Care should be taken to insure that the profits of the licensing company do not fall within the tax nets of the countries of operation.

The source of the right must be situated in the correct profit center (see also above).

2.11 Computer Charges

Assume the following structure:

A related computer services office located in an IOFC performs certain computer functions that can be performed abroad, taking into account the practicalities of the performance.

The computer services office is paid an arm's-length fee for performing such functions.

The reasonable amount payable for such services, if paid to a third party, would be greater than the real cost to the group.

Tax Benefit The payment of the computer charges, on an arm's-length basis, would constitute an allowable deduction in the hands of the various group members.

Since less tax or no tax would be paid in the country where the computer services office is based, this differential would constitute an easily calculable tax saving.

Caveat The tax saving on an assumed tax rate of 40% would have to produce a significantly greater benefit than the additional costs attached to having these computer-related services performed abroad—otherwise it would not be worth the cost and the inconvenience.

All payments between related parties should be at arm's length.

Transactions must be bona fide.

Care should be taken to insure that the profits of the offshore computer services office do not fall within the tax nets of the countries of operation.

2.12 Professional Services

Assume the following structure:

Certain accounting, legal, engineering, etc., services are performed by one or more services companies overseas.

The billing for these services is in line with billing by comparable third parties.

Tax Benefit Payments by the various group members would be deductible.

Profits in the hands of the services companies would not be subject to tax.

Caveat All payments between related parties should be at arm's length.

Transactions must be bona fide.

Care should be taken to insure that the profits of the services companies do not fall within the tax nets of the countries of operation.

2.13 Training

Assume the following structure:

A specialized training company is set up overseas in an IOFC for the purpose of providing training to employees of the various group members.

Certain aspects of the training provided by this company would be effected abroad and other aspects would be on a distance learning basis.

The reasonable amount that would be payable to a third party for similar services would be greater than the real cost to the group.

Tax Benefit The training costs would be deductible in the hands of the various group members whose employees receive training from the training company.

The profits of the training company would suffer little or no tax in the other countries.

Caveat All payments between related parties should be at arm's length.

Transactions must be bona fide.

Care should be taken to insure that the profits of the training company do not fall within the tax nets of the countries of operation.

2.14 Staff Recruitment

Assume the following structure:

An offshore recruitment company is entrusted with recruitment of certain classes of employees for the various group members.

The billing for these services is in line with billing by comparable third parties.

Where the recruitment company uses subagents, there would normally be a commission split, as in the case of advertising agencies.

Business Benefit Saving of full or partial commissions that would otherwise be wasted.

Tax Benefit Tax differential multiplied by saving.

Caveat Normally, the domestic tax authorities will allow this deduction since the deduction consists of a standard payment of commissions normally paid by principals to third party employment agencies.

All payments between related parties should be at arm's length.

Transactions must be bona fide.

Care should be taken to insure that the profits of the recruitment company do not fall within the tax nets of the countries of operation.

2.15 Printing and Stationery

Assume the following structure:

A printing and stationery company located in an IOFC handles any appropriate printing, stationery, and related requirements of the group members.

There is a justifiable profit margin.

Business Benefit Potential cash earnings.

Tax Benefit Payments by the various members would be deductible.

Profits in the hands of the printing and stationery company would not be subject to tax.

Caveat The figures must take into account all material costs, including transport, to insure that the operation makes business sense.

All payments between related parties should be at arm's length.

Transactions must be bona fide.

Care should be taken to insure that the profits of the printing and stationery company do not fall within the tax nets of the countries of operation.

3. Conclusion

Deductions (particularly commissions) relate to gross income, thus making for a much higher percentage saving on net income. In some cases, a significant percentage of a group's net earnings may be paid out in the form of deductions.

On the assumption that the deductions are made to a related party in a lower tax or tax-free country, significant tax savings may be achieved.

Payments between related parties must be arm's length. This could be on a cost-plus or any other basis, provided the arm's length quality of the payments can be substantiated. (See also Chapter 7, section 8, "Anti-Avoidance.")

Care should always be taken to insure that any structure involving a preferential tax regime does not fall within the scope of any measures directed at the curtailing of such operations. (See Chapter 14, "International Measures to Combat Harmful Tax Practices.")

CHAPTER ELEVEN

CASE STUDY: U.S. TAX IMPLICATIONS OF AN OFFSHORE MANUFACTURING COMPANY

1. The Issues

An offshore manufacturing company ("the Company") is wholly owned by a U.S. shareholder.

It is possible for a U.S. person to form a foreign corporation to conduct an active business in a foreign, tax-efficient jurisdiction. The U.S. tax law has, however, been structured over the years to prevent U.S. tax benefits except in situations where the economic activities of the business in question are conducted by the foreign corporation outside the United States.

The following analysis deals with the U.S. tax considerations under which it would be possible for the Company to operate

(a) without attracting U.S. tax itself; and

(b) without causing the U.S. shareholder to suffer U.S. tax on the profits of the Company.

2. U.S. Taxation of Foreign Corporations

2.1 General Rule

The basic rule is laid out in code sec. 882(b), which provides that,

> In case of a foreign corporation, gross income includes only
> (1) gross income which is derived from sources within the United States and which is not effectively connected with the conduct of a trade or business within the United States, and

(2) gross income which is effectively connected with the conduct of a trade or business within the United States.

A foreign corporation engaged in business in the United States is taxed in the same manner as a domestic corporation on all U.S. source income that is effectively connected with its conduct of a trade or business in the United States. There is a flat rate of tax on U.S. source fixed or determinable periodical income (interest, dividends, rents, royalties, etc.) that is not effectively connected with the conduct of a U.S. trade or business. This rate is normally 30%, but may be reduced by treaty.

Of course, if a foreign corporation has income that is neither U.S. source nor effectively connected, it will not be included in its gross income for U.S. tax purposes [sec. 882(b)]. Otherwise, the usual statutory and case law rules for determining includability in gross income apply in most cases to foreign corporations just as much as to U.S. corporations. Thus, if an item would not be included in a U.S. corporation's gross income, it would generally not be included in a foreign corporation's effectively connected income either.

2.2 Source of Income

Secs. 861 and 862 and the regulations thereunder lay down the general rules for the determination of whether income is from sources within the United States.

(a) In the case of a sale of personal property, the rule contained in sec. 865(b) generally provides that income from the sale of personal property that is inventory is sourced under the general sourcing rules of secs. 861 and 862. In essence, these provisions provide that income from the sale of inventory is U.S. source if, for example, inventory is purchased from outside the United States and sold within the United States [sec. 861(a)(6)].

(b) Where the taxpayer produces and sells personal property abroad, none of the income is from sources within the United States [reg. secs. 1.861-7(a) and 1.862-1(a)(3)]. However, sec. 863(b)(2) provides that if the taxpayer produces goods in either the United States or a foreign country and then sells them in the other country, then the income from that sale is from sources partly within and partly outside the United States. The regulations set forth the method by which the income is to be allocated. Nevertheless, when the commissioner has challenged the taxpayer's methods of allocation of income or deductions, he has historically done so through the use of sec. 482 rather than the regulations under sec. 863(b).

(c) In the case of personal services, secs. 861(a)(3) and 862(a)(3) lay down that the place where the services are performed is the source of the compensation paid for those services. If services are performed partly within and partly outside the United States and no specific amount was paid for the services rendered in the United States, or no accurate allocation can be made, the compensation for those services is to be allocated "on the basis that most correctly reflects the proper source of the income on the facts and circumstances of the particular case" [reg. sec. 1.861-4(b)(1)].

(d) In the case of rents and royalties, secs. 861(a)(4) and 862(a)(4) provide that income received for the use or privilege of using property, tangible or intangible, real property or personal property, has its source in the place where the property is used or usable. The sections apply to payments received for the use of all forms of property, including rents or royalties for the use or the privilege of using in the United States patents, copyrights, secret processes and formulas, goodwill, trademarks, trade brands, franchises, and other like property.

2.3 Effectively Connected Income

In analyzing the definition of income that is effectively connected with the conduct of a trade or business within the United States, there are four questions, of which (a) is the key question:

(a) Is the income from U.S. sources? If not, the income can be effectively connected only if the sourcing rules discussed below come into operation. If the income is from U.S. sources, the three other questions that arise are as follows:

(b) In which tax year is the income to be taken into account for tax purposes?

(c) During that year, did the foreign corporation conduct trade or business activity in the United States?

(d) Does the necessary connection exist between the income and a U.S. trade or business activity?

Income can be effectively connected only if it is taken into account for tax purposes in the year during which the foreign corporation engaged in trade or business within the United States [sec. 864(c)(1)(B)]. Subject to the exceptions considered below, if there is no trade or business activity in the United States during the year, there will be no effectively connected income.

In the case of U.S. source income, if there is a trade or business in the United States during the year, the income is taxable as effectively connected income.

Note (i): Any U.S. business activity in the year will do the damage, even if it is unrelated to the income. This is so notwithstanding the use of the term *effectively connected.*

Note (ii): Any substantial U.S. business contacts of a foreign corporation may expose it to its being taxed as if it were carrying on a U.S. trade or business activity, including, for example, use of offices of an affiliate.

The crucial point in this whole question from the point of view of a foreign corporation is that *foreign source income* can be effectively connected only if two requirements are met in accordance with code sec. 864(c)(4). These are that the foreign corporation has an office or fixed place of business in the United States *and* that the income is attributable to that place of business.

Even if these conditions are present, the effectively connected rules are directed at only three categories of foreign source income in certain situations in which definite U.S. economic connections are present.

These three types of income are as follows:

(a) rents and royalties derived from the active conduct of a licensing business;

(b) dividends, interest, or gain from securities or debt obligations derived in the active conduct of a banking, financing, or similar business; and

(c) income from sales or exchanges of personal property outside the United States through a U.S. office [code sec. 864(c)(4)].

With regard to rents, royalties, and gains on sales of intangible property—i.e., (i) above—reg. sec. 1.864-5(b)(1) provides that income from sources outside the United States shall only be taken into account if it consists of

> (i) rents or royalties for the use of, or for the privilege of using, intangible personal property located outside the United States or from any interest in such property, including rents or royalties for the use, or for the privilege of using, outside the United States, patents, copyright, secret processes and formulas, good will, trademarks, trade brands, franchises, and other like properties, if such rents or royalties are derived in the active conduct of the trade or business in the United States.
>
> (ii) Gains or losses on the sale or exchange of intangible personal property located outside the United States or from any interest in such property, including gains or losses on the sale or exchange of the privilege of using, outside the United States, patents, copyrights, secret processes and formulas, good will, trademarks, trade brands, franchises, and other like properties, if such gains or losses are derived in the active conduct of the trade or business in the United States.
>
> (iii) Whether or not such an item of income, gain, or loss is derived in the active conduct of trade or business in the United States shall be determined from the facts and circumstances of each case. The frequency with which a foreign corporation enters into transactions of the type from which the income, gain, or loss is derived shall not of itself determine that the income, gain, or loss is derived in the active conduct of a trade or business.

With regard to sales of personal property, reg. sec. 1.864-5(b)(3) provides that

> the income from sources outside the United States shall be taken into account only if it consists of income from the sale of property held

> primarily for sale to customers in the ordinary course of business, where the sale is outside the United States but through the office or other fixed place of business which the foreign corporation has in the United States.

Reg. sec. 1.864-6 provides that

> such income shall be treated as effectively connected income only if the income is attributable to an office or other fixed place of business of the foreign corporation, and furthermore that such office is a *material factor* in the realization of the income. The office is only considered a material factor if it actively participates in soliciting the order, negotiating the contract of sale, or performing other significant services necessary for the consummation of the sale which are not the subject of a separate agreement between the seller and the buyer. The office or other fixed place of business in the United States shall be considered a material factor in the realization of income from a sale made as a result of a sales order received in such office or other fixed place of business except where the sales order is received unsolicited and that office or other fixed place of business is not held out to potential customers as the place to which such sales orders should be sent. The income must be realized in the ordinary course of the trade or business carried on through the office or other fixed place of business in the United States.

Notwithstanding the above provisions, an important limitation applies where the foreign office is a material factor in the realization of the income. It is further provided that

> an office or other fixed place of business which a foreign corporation has in the United States shall not be considered to be a material factor in the realization of income from sales of goods or merchandise if the property is sold for use, consumption, or disposition outside the United States and an office or other fixed place of business, as defined in reg. sec. 1.864-7, which such foreign corporation has outside the United States participates materially in the sale. For this purpose an office or other fixed place of business which the taxpayer has outside the United States shall be considered to have participated materially in a sale made through the office or other fixed place of business in the United States if the office or other fixed place of business outside the United States actively participates in soliciting the order resulting in the sale, negotiating the contract of sale, or performing other significant services necessary for the consummation of the sale which are not the subject of a separate agreement between the seller and buyer. An office or other fixed place of business which the taxpayer has outside the United States shall not be considered to have participated materially in the sale

> merely because of one or more of the following activities: (a) the sale is made subject to the final approval of such office or other fixed place of business, (b) the property sold is held in, and distributed from, such office or other fixed place of business, (c) samples of the property sold are displayed (but not otherwise promoted or sold) in such office or other fixed place of business, (d) such office or other place of business is used for purposes of having title to the property pass outside the United States, or (e) such office or other fixed place of business performs merely clerical functions incident to the sale.

It is therefore necessary to consult reg. sec. 1.864-7 for the definition of an office or other fixed place of business:

> The general rule is that an office or other fixed place of business is a fixed facility that is a place through which the foreign corporation engages in a trade or business.
>
> Due regard is given to the facts and circumstances of each case. A foreign corporation shall not be considered to have an office or other fixed place of business merely because it uses another person's office or other fixed place of business, whether or not the office or place of business of a related person, through which to transact a trade or business if the trade or business activities of the foreign corporation in that office or other fixed place of business are relatively sporadic or infrequent, taking into account the overall needs and conduct of that trade or business. A foreign corporation shall not be considered to have an office or other fixed place of business merely because a person controlling that corporation has an office or other fixed place of business from which general supervision and control over the policies of the foreign corporation are exercised. The fact that top management decisions affecting the foreign corporation are made in a country shall not of itself mean that the foreign corporation has an office or other fixed place of business in that country.
>
> For the present purposes a dependent agent is disregarded unless such agent (a) has the authority to negotiate and conclude contracts in the name of the foreign corporation, and regularly exercises such authority, or (b) has a stock of merchandise belonging to the foreign corporation from which orders are regularly filled on behalf of such foreign corporation.
>
> The office of an independent agent is *not* treated as the office or other fixed place of business of a principal that is a foreign corporation, irrespective of whether such agent has authority to negotiate and conclude contracts in the name of his principal, and regularly exercises that authority, or maintains a stock of goods from which he regularly fills orders on behalf of his principal. The determination of whether an agent is an independent agent for purposes of this paragraph shall be made without regard to facts indicating that either the agent or the principal

owns or controls directly or indirectly the other or that a third person or persons own or control directly or indirectly both.

Obviously, an employee of a foreign corporation is treated as a dependent agent. However, where the employee, in the ordinary course of his duties, carries on the trade or business of his employer in or through a fixed facility of such employer which is regularly used by the employee in the course of carrying out such duties, such fixed facility shall be considered the office or other fixed place of business of the employer.

The fact that a foreign corporation is related in some manner to another person who has an office or other fixed place of business shall not of itself mean that such office or other fixed place of business of the other person is the office or other fixed place of business of the foreign corporation.

Foreign base company sales income can also result if the foreign corporation is deemed to have a branch office in the United States and the effective tax rate in the United States is sufficiently higher than that of the foreign corporation in its country of incorporation [sec. 954(d)(2)].

In a situation where there is any danger of a U.S. trade or business, it is important to consider the possibility of having the foreign corporation file a protective U.S. income tax return. If a U.S. trade or business is found to exist, and such a return has not been filed, the foreign corporation may not be entitled to any deductions [sec. 882(c)(2)].

It is most important that there should be the reality of a fixed facility offshore through which the activities of the foreign company are effectively conducted. It is also important that evidence should be built on an ongoing basis that would leave no doubts as to the fact that the activities in question do indeed take place outside the United States.

3. U.S. Taxation of the Stockholders of Foreign Corporations

There are two hypotheses under which a U.S. stockholder of a foreign corporation may be taxable on a share of its undistributed earnings:

(a) if the foreign corporation is a "controlled foreign corporation"; or

(b) if the foreign corporation is a "foreign personal holding company."

3.1 Controlled Foreign Corporation (Subpart F)

General Rule

A foreign corporation in which U.S. shareholders own more than 50% of the combined voting power of all classes of stock entitled to vote is a controlled foreign corporation.

A U.S. shareholder is any U.S. person who owns or is considered to own, by applying the attribution rules of sec. 958(b), 10% or more of the total combined voting power of all classes of stock entitled to vote in the foreign corporation [sec. 951(b)].

A U.S. person means a citizen or resident of the United States, a domestic partnership, a domestic corporation, or any nonforeign estate or trust.

Any arrangement to shift formal voting power away from U.S. shareholders of a foreign corporation will not be given effect if in reality voting power is retained.

If a particular foreign corporation were a controlled foreign corporation as defined, only certain categories of income would be taxable. For present purposes, these are

(a) foreign base company income (i.e., foreign personal holding company income, foreign base company sales income, and foreign base company services income); and
(b) increase in earnings invested in U.S. property.

Sec. 951 requires that U.S. shareholders of a controlled foreign corporation include in their income their pro rata share of subpart F income (referred to also as "tainted income")—in this instance, the foreign base company income. Sec. 956 further provides that U.S. shareholders of a controlled foreign corporation are taxed currently on their pro rata share of the earnings of the corporation that are invested in U.S. property.

Foreign Personal Holding Company Income

By reference to the definition in sec. 553, the following are the categories of foreign personal holding company income: dividends; interest; royalties; annuities; gains from the sales of stocks and securities; commodity transactions; estates and trusts; personal service contracts; rents; and use of corporate property by a shareholder.

All of these categories essentially represent the same elements of passive income that apply in the case of the definition of a foreign personal holding company.

Foreign Base Company Sales Income

In general, foreign base company sales income is income (whether in the form of profits, commissions, fees, or otherwise) derived from the sale or purchase of personal property to (or from or on behalf of) a related person where the property is manufactured, produced, or extracted and sold outside the country of incorporation. More specifically, the purchases and sales included are as follows:

(a) the purchase of personal property from a related person and its sale to any person;

(b) the purchase of personal property from any person and its sale to a related person;

(c) the sale of personal property to any person on behalf of a related person; and

(d) the purchase of personal property from any person on behalf of a related person [sec. 954(d)].

For purposes of determining if a controlled foreign corporation is dealing with a related person, a related person is defined in the following ways:

(a) an individual partnership, trust, or estate that controls the controlled foreign corporation,

(b) a corporation that controls, or is controlled by, the controlled foreign corporation (parent-subsidiary relationship), or

(c) a corporation that is controlled by the same person or persons that control the controlled foreign corporation (brother-sister relationship) [sec. 954(d)(3)].

It follows that any income derived from purchases or sales between a controlled foreign corporation and a related U.S. corporation or by a foreign corporation on behalf of a related U.S. corporation would constitute subpart F income.

However, completely third party transactions would not be "foreign base company sales income" and would therefore not be taxable in the hands of a U.S. shareholder of the foreign corporation unless and until distributed to him.

Reg. sec. 1.954-3(a)(4) deals with the case of property manufactured or produced by a controlled foreign corporation:

(a) Foreign base company sales income does not include income of a controlled foreign corporation derived in connection with the sale of personal property manufactured, produced, or constructed by such corporation in whole or in part from personal property that it has purchased. A foreign corporation will be considered to have manufactured, produced, or constructed personal property that it sells if the property sold is in effect not the property that it purchased.

(b) If purchased personal property is substantially transformed prior to sale, the property sold will be treated as having been manufactured, produced, or constructed by the selling corporation.

(c) If purchased property is used as a component part of personal property that is sold, the sale of property will be treated as the sale of a manufactured product, rather than the sale of component parts, if the operations conducted by the selling corporation in connection with the property purchased and sold are substantial in nature and are generally considered to constitute the manufacture, production, or construction of property. Without limiting this substantive test, which is dependent on the facts and circumstances of each case, the operations of the selling corporation in connection with the use of the purchased property as a component part of the personal property that is sold will be considered to constitute the manufacture of a product if in connection with such property conversion costs (direct labor and factory burden) of such corporation account for 20% or more of the total cost of goods sold.

Foreign Base Company Services Income

Foreign base company services income is a term that encompasses the performance by a controlled foreign corporation of personal services for or on behalf of a related person outside the country in which the controlled foreign corporation is organized. Personal services include technical, managerial, engineering, scientific, industrial, commercial, and like services. The income from these services can be in the form of compensation, commissions, fees, or otherwise.

The regulations state that the place where services will be considered to be performed will depend on the facts and circumstances of each case. The general rule is that services are performed where the persons performing the services are physically located when they perform their duties [reg. sec. 1.954-4(c)].

If the controlled foreign corporation is not performing services for a related person and later requires the assistance of a related person, the income from a contract can be considered foreign base company services income. The regulations state that certain assistance by a related person will taint the income. Assistance for these purposes is defined as follows:

(a) Assistance in the form of know-how, supervision, direction, and services will not be considered assistance on the contract unless it is substantial and directly assists in the performance of the contract. *Substantial* is defined as being a principal element in producing the income—the costs equaling 50% or more of the total costs of the controlled foreign corporation on the job.

(b) Assistance in the form of financial help, equipment, material, or supplies will be considered assistance on the contract only if it is substantial as defined above. For purposes of the 50% test for substantial, the amounts to be included are only the excess of the arm's-length charges for these items, less the consideration actually paid by the controlled foreign corporation for them [reg. sec. 1.954-4(b)(ii)].

When the related person does nothing more than act as guarantor on the contract and does not perform any services, the income from the services is excluded from foreign base company services income [reg. sec. 1.954-4(b)(2) and (c)].

The performance of services that are directly related to the sale or exchange by a controlled foreign corporation of property manufactured by it and that are performed prior to the time of the sale or exchange, or of services directly related to an offer or effort to sell or exchange, is not foreign base company services income [sec. 954(e)].

Thus the treatment of foreign base company services income as subpart F income is intended to deny tax deferral where service activities are separated from manufacturing or selling activities primarily to obtain a low rate of tax for the services income. The policy is similar to that for foreign base company sales income. Subject to the above mentioned provisions, it follows that if any of the foreign corporations were to perform service activities on behalf of any other related corporation, income deriving therefrom would be subpart F income. However, any service activities performed for and on behalf of third parties would not be taxable in the hands of a U.S. shareholder of the foreign corporation unless and until distributed to such shareholder.

Increase in Earnings Invested in U.S. Property

To prevent tax avoidance through indirect repatriation of foreign earnings, code sec. 956 provides that U.S. shareholders are taxed currently on earnings of the controlled foreign corporation that are invested in U.S. property. In essence, earnings brought back to the United States are taxed to shareholders on the grounds that this investment is substantially equivalent to payment of a dividend. It is to be noted that the amount of the constructive dividend is dependent on how earnings are invested, not how they are earned. Thus *any* earnings of a controlled foreign corporation are subject to inclusion in income by U.S. shareholders under sec. 956.

3.2 Foreign Personal Holding Company

A U.S. shareholder is subject to tax on undistributed income, as well as on distributed income, of a "foreign personal holding company" as defined (code sec. 551; reg. sec. 1.551-1).

A foreign corporation is a foreign personal holding company if

(a) at least 60% (50% after the first taxable year) of its gross income (not gross receipts) is from certain specified types of essentially passive income (these are set out below);

(b) more than 50% in value of its outstanding stock is owned directly or indirectly by five or fewer U.S. citizens or residents (code secs. 552 and 553; reg. secs. 1.552-3 and 1.553-1).

The criterion of ownership in the case of a foreign personal holding company is "value" and not "control."

Sec. 553 sets out the categories of income that constitute foreign personal holding company income as follows:

Dividends. Distributions from a corporation that are considered dividends under the normal meaning of sec. 316. The term also includes constructive dividends from the corporation's ownership in other foreign personal holding companies.

Interest. Amounts received and/or imputed from the lending of money.

Royalties. A term that includes amounts received for the privilege of using patents, copyrights, secret processes and formulas, goodwill, trademarks, trade brands, franchises, and other like property. Also included are amounts received as royalties from minerals, oil, and gas.

Annuities. Include only the taxable portions of the annuities that are determined under sec. 72.

Stocks and securities. The excess of the gains over the losses from such transactions are to be included. However, to be excluded are transactions by regular dealers (corporations with an established place of business that is regularly engaged in the purchase and resale of stocks and securities). A regular dealer, however, must include the transactions from stock and securities that are held for investment purposes only.

Commodity transactions. The excess of gains over losses from certain designated transactions are to be included. The designated transactions are futures transactions in any commodity subject to the rules of the board of trade or commodity exchange, but not to include transactions by a producer, processor, merchant, or handler of the commodity that arise from bona fide hedging transactions necessary and customary to such business.

Estates and trusts. Income that must be included by a corporation from an estate or trust and gains from the sale or disposition of any interest in an estate or trust constitute foreign personal holding company income.

Personal service contracts. Amounts received by a foreign corporation for personal services rendered constitute foreign personal holding company income if some person other than the corporation can designate the individual who is to perform such services, or if the person who is to perform the services is designated in a contract, and if the person who has performed such services has owned, directly or indirectly, at any time during the taxable year 25% or more in value of the outstanding stock of the corporation.

Rents. Amounts received from the use of or right to use property. Rents are foreign personal holding company income unless they constitute

> 50% or more of a foreign corporation's gross income. However, rents do not include income from the category immediately below.
>
> *Use of corporate property by a shareholder.* Rents received from any shareholder who at any time during the taxable year owns 25% or more in value of the outstanding stock of a corporation will constitute foreign personal holding company income and will not be included in the 50% rental income test mentioned above. This separate treatment of such rents is not applicable unless a corporation's foreign personal holding company income, without the rents from these shareholders, exceeds 10% of its total gross income.

Gross income includes income from worldwide sources (sec. 555).

If any proposed foreign corporation were to meet the stock ownership test, it would only be possible to avoid the classification of a foreign personal holding company by avoiding the gross income test as set out above.

4. Anti-Avoidance

4.1 Allocation of Income and Deductions among Taxpayers

In the case of a multinational structure involving related parties, care should always be taken to keep intercorporate pricing on an arm's-length basis.

Code sec. 482 provides that,

> In any case of two or more organizations, trades, or businesses (whether or not incorporated, whether or not organized in the United States, and whether or not affiliated) owned or controlled directly or indirectly by the same interests, the Secretary may distribute, apportion, or allocate gross income, deductions, credits, or allowances between or among such organizations, trades, or businesses, if he determines that such distribution, apportionment, or allocation is necessary in order to prevent evasion of taxes or clearly to reflect the income of any of such organizations, trades, or businesses. In the case of any transfer (or license) of intangible property (within the meaning of section 936(h)(3)(B)), the income with respect to such transfer or license shall be commensurate with the income attributable to the intangible.

The purpose of sec. 482 is to place a controlled taxpayer on a tax parity with an uncontrolled taxpayer, by determining, according to the standard of an uncontrolled taxpayer, the true taxable income from the property and business of a controlled taxpayer. The interests controlling a group of controlled taxpayers are assumed to have complete power to cause each controlled taxpayer to conduct its affairs so that its transactions and accounting records truly reflect the taxable income from the property and business of each of the controlled taxpayers. If, however, this has not been done, and the taxable incomes are thereby understated, the district director shall intervene and, by making such distributions, apportionments, or allocations as he may deem necessary of gross income, deductions, credits, or allowances, or of any item or element affecting taxable income, between or among the controlled taxpayers constituting the group, shall determine the true taxable income of each controlled taxpayer. The standard to be applied in every case is that of an uncontrolled taxpayer dealing at arm's length with another uncontrolled taxpayer.

The transfer pricing provisions of sec. 482 are implemented by a series of information reporting requirements in the case of any transactions between U.S. persons and foreign affiliated corporations (form 5471; sec. 6038). There is also a rather draconian transfer pricing penalty that can be 20% or 40% depending on the level of adjustment [secs. 6662(e) and (h)]. There is a reasonable documentation exception in the penalty in which the taxpayer has compiled "contemporaneous documentation" at the time its return is filed and turns such information over to the IRS within thirty days of request.

In the present situation, the principal issue posed by these rules would concern the compensation for services rendered by U.S. persons to the foreign corporation and, possibly, sales of goods by a U.S. person purchased from a foreign person, provided that the U.S. person is under common control with the foreign corporation.

4.2 Substance *versus* Form

The rule that the substance of a transaction, rather than its mere form, controls tax liability is one of very wide application. It can affect the amount of taxable income from practically any type of transaction. It is also applied frequently to settle questions of who is taxable on certain income.

Bookkeeping entries are significant only as evidence or records of transactions, and the legal effect of such transactions and the method employed in keeping the books must be determined from the transactions themselves and not merely from book entries affecting them.

5. Conclusion

5.1 U.S. Tax Liability of the Company

The company will not be liable for U.S. tax on income that is not from a U.S. source and that is not effectively connected with the conduct of a trade or business within the United States.

5.2 U.S. Tax Liability of the U.S. Shareholder

Under the Controlled Foreign Corporation Provisions

Since the Company is wholly owned by a U.S. shareholder, it would be a controlled foreign corporation.

Its income that is not *foreign base company income* (as defined) and that is not an increase in earnings invested in U.S. property (i.e., not brought back to the United States) would not be subject to tax in the hands of the U.S. shareholder, until it is distributed to him.

In brief, income that would escape the definition of *foreign base company income* would be sales income derived from transactions with third parties and services income derived from transactions with third parties. Royalties income would be tainted income and would thus not escape.

Under the Foreign Personal Holding Company Provisions

Provided that 60% (50% after the first taxable year) is not from certain specified types of essentially passive income, the Company would not be a *foreign personal holding company* (as defined), and the income of the Company would not lead to tax liability in the hands of the U.S. shareholder prior to distribution to him.

The types of income to avoid are dealt with more fully below. In particular, these include royalties, personal service contracts, and the use of corporate property by a shareholder.

5.3 Caveat

Under IRC, section 482, controlled taxpayers can be subjected to the standards of uncontrolled taxpayers with respect to the intercompany transfer pricing matters. For example, if a U.S. company under common control with the foreign company provided services to the foreign company, the U.S. service provided would need to be compensated on an arm's length basis. The intercompany relationships must be reported and the economic relationships documented each year, subject to severe penalties (20%–40% penalty for failure to maintain and turn over to the IRS documentation).

The substance *versus* form rule can be used by the IRS to determine the amount of taxable income.

CHAPTER TWELVE

CASE STUDY: U.S. TAX IMPLICATIONS OF A U.S. PERSON SUPERVISING AN OFFSHORE TRUST

1. The Issues

A nonresident trust for U.S. tax purposes has been set up by a nonresident alien.

The trustee is a trust company that is a nonresident corporation for U.S. tax purposes. The trust company has no activities other than the administration of the trust and the investment of the trust assets.

The trust company employs a U.S. person as a supervisory executive to provide services such as the furnishing of investment advice, as well as general advice on the way in which the trust should be administered, and supervisory services.

The principal concern is the danger of the trust company or the trust itself becoming liable to U.S. tax, on the grounds of carrying on a trade or business in the United States, through the activities in the United States of the supervisory executive.

The following structure would permit the supervisory services to be carried on in the United States without attracting U.S. tax liability.

2. U.S. Trade or Business

2.1 General

In any situation where a U.S. person or company provides services to a foreign corporation, there is inevitably an issue as to whether the foreign corporation actually has a U.S. office, so it could be subject to tax in the United States.

As will be discussed more fully below, a foreign corporation would have a "U.S. trade or business" only if its operational activities are conducted by a U.S.

affiliate as opposed to being conducted offshore, since presumably the foreign corporation would have no other persons who perform such tasks. The situs could then be in the United States by default.[1]

Income earned by foreign corporations is taxed in the United States by one of two methods. Under the first method, if a foreign corporation is engaged in a U.S. trade or business, it will be taxed on its income effectively connected with the U.S. trade or business. Under this method, both foreign source and U.S. source income are taxed at the corporate income tax rates, so long as the income is effectively connected income (ECI). In some cases, the branch profits tax may impose a second level 30% tax (unless reduced by treaty) on the so-called dividend equivalent amount.[2] Under the second method, fixed or determinable or annual or periodic (FDAP) income of a foreign corporation is subject to U.S. withholding tax at a flat rate of 30%, unless reduced by treaty.

Whether the income from a foreign corporation's activities in the United States is subject to the graduated corporate income tax and the branch profits tax depends on whether the activities in the United States are considered a trade or business of the foreign corporation. The code and regulations give little guidance on the trade or business issue, and the courts and the IRS have addressed the issue infrequently. As the following discussion will demonstrate, the determination of whether a foreign corporation is engaged in a U.S. trade or business is based on the particular facts and circumstances. Moreover, the determination must be made for each tax year, and the IRS will not give an advance ruling on whether a foreign corporation is engaged in a U.S. trade or business.

2.2 Cases, Published Revenue Rulings, and Private Letter Rulings

Under the IRS's view, very few activities are necessary to constitute a trade or business. General Counsel Memorandum (GCM) 18835, 1937 C.B. 141, 144, stated that

> any activities beyond the mere receipt of income from property, and the payment or organization and administration expenses incidental to the receipt and distribution thereof...constitute engaging in trade or business.

Cases and rulings indicate that the trade or business status depends on a number of factors, including whether (i) there is an exclusive agency and (ii) the foreign corporation has employees in the United States who have authority to contractually bind the foreign company.

2.3 To Be Engaged in a Trade or Business, the Activities Must Be "Considerable, Continuous, and Regular"

The key issue is whether activities performed in the United States are ministerial or insignificant, as opposed to the exercise of discretion or business judgment that generates the income of the foreign corporation.[3]

If the U.S. office of a foreign corporation merely handles administrative duties and has no discretionary authority over business decisions, the foreign corporation should not be treated as being engaged in a U.S. trade or business.[4] If a foreign corporation's U.S. activity is not considerable and continuous, the foreign corporation may not be treated as being engaged in a U.S. trade or business.[5]

In *Pichot v. Commissioner*, 113 F. 2d 718 (2d Cir. 1940), the court held that the nonresident alien had been engaged in a trade or business within the United States through the management activities of her agent. In reaching its decision, the court relied on the conclusion that the amount of transactions involved "must have been considerable in both [amount and number] as well as continuous and regular."[6]

In *Spermacet Whaling and Shipping Co. v. Commissioner*,[7] the tax court considered whether Spermacet, a Panamanian corporation, was engaged in a trade or business within the United States, and stated the test as follows:

> We have consistently held that before a taxpayer can be found to be "engaged in trade or business within the United States" it must, during some substantial portion of the taxable year, have been regularly and continuously transacting a substantial portion of its ordinary business in this country.[8]

2.4 Trade or Business Activities of an Agent May Be Attributed to the Foreign Corporation

An agency relationship alone may cause a foreign corporation to be engaged in a U.S. trade or business.

In Rev. Rul. 70-424, 1970-2 C.B. 150, the IRS held that the agreement was an ordinary principal and agent relationship through which M carried on its activities in the United States and that M was thereby engaged in a trade or business within the United States.

2.5 Office or Fixed Place of Business

Income from sources outside the United States will be treated as ECI only if the foreign corporation has in the United States at some time during the year, but not necessarily at the same time the income is realized, an office or other fixed place of business. The facts and circumstances of each case will determine whether a foreign corporation that engages in a U.S. trade or business has an office or other fixed place of business in the United States.[9] In general, an office or other fixed place of business is a fixed facility.

An office of employees is more readily attributed to a foreign corporation than is an office of independent agents.

Foreign source income will be attributed to a U.S. office only if that office was a material factor in producing the income and it regularly carries on the activities that created the income.[10] It is not necessary, however, that the U.S. office be a major factor in the realization of foreign source income.[11]

2.6 Supervisory–Operating Activity Distinction

The regulations and cases have traditionally distinguished between activities conducted in the United States that are in the nature of supervisory functions and those that are actual operating functions. In other words, the conduct of supervisory activities within the United States may not rise to the level of a U.S. trade or business where the actual operating activities are conducted outside the United States.

This distinction is specifically stated in the section 864 regulations with respect to management activity:[12]

> A foreign corporation shall not be considered to have an office or other fixed place of business merely because a person controlling that corporation has an office or other fixed place of business from which general supervision and control over the policies of the foreign corporation are exercised. The fact that top management decisions affecting the foreign corporation are made in a country shall not of itself mean that the foreign corporation has an office or other fixed place of business in that country.

The mere supervision of long-term investments in subsidiaries, even where conducted in large part in the United States, is not considered to give rise to a U.S. trade or business, so long as the services are in the nature of stewardship. This statement is consistent with prior case law principles that maintained the distinction between active business operations and the mere receipt of passive income. (See, for example, *Chaing Hsiao Liang v. Commissioner*, 23 T.C. 1040 [1955] citing the section 162 distinction enunciated in *Higgens v. Commissioner*, 312 U.S. 212 [1941]; *Continental Trading, Inc. v. Commissioner*, 265 F. 2d 40 [9th Cir. 1959]; *Commissioner v. Consolidated Premium Iron Ores, Ltd.*, 265 F. 2d 320 [6th Cir. 1959].)

In short, the conduct of supervisory activities in the United States (such as by the U.S. related person) will not, standing alone, create a U.S. trade or business, so long as the foreign corporation has operational executives outside the United States to actually conduct the business activities.

2.7 *InverWorld* Case

These principles were recently addressed in a situation that has an important degree of relevance to the present situation:

In *InverWorld v. Commissioner*, T.C. Memo. 1996-301, WL 352998 (June 27, 1996), the tax court held that a Cayman Islands financial services corporation was engaged in a trade or business within the United States; its commissions and fees were effectively connected income; a section 482 allocation to a U.S. service subsidiary was appropriate; no deductions were allowable to the offshore entity (including the correlative adjustment that ordinarily results from a section 482 allocation); withholding taxes were due on dividends paid (from U.S. source income); and penalties were appropriately imposed. The net effect of the decision was to cause the Cayman Islands corporation and its U.S. subsidiary to incur multiple levels of U.S. taxation and penalties.

The case is significant for a variety of reasons. At the very least, it serves as a beacon for the U.S. tax disaster that can befall a company deemed to have a U.S. trade or business where protective action is not taken. It is also one of the few recent cases addressing U.S. trade or business issues in the context of a tax haven company.

InverWorld Ltd. (INLTD) was an investment management and financial services company organized under the laws of the Cayman Islands. INLTD owned all the outstanding stock of InverWorld Holdings Inc., a domestic corporation that owned all the outstanding stock of InverWorld Inc. (INC), also a domestic corporation. INLTD did not file any U.S. tax returns or foreign returns for the years in issue.

INC maintained INLTD's client account files in Texas, furnished INLTD with investment advice under a consulting agreement, and provided bookkeeping for INLTD. INC also acquired certain investments on behalf of INLTD clients and performed daily accounting of each client's investments. Under an agreement with INLTD, INC had the authority to invest the cash, securities, and other properties of INLTD's clients as instructed by INLTD.

The main issue presented to the tax court was whether INLTD was engaged in a trade or business within the United States pursuant to section 864(B) for the tax years in question.

After reviewing the pertinent provisions in the code and negotiations, the tax court held that INLTD was engaged in "trade or business within the United States." Specifically, the court held that the facts and circumstances show that INLTD was engaged in trade or business in the United States through INC's office in San Antonio. INLTD's involvement and activities in the San Antonio office were extensive, continuous, and regular. Moreover, INLTD has not shown that it maintained any other office or fixed place of business.

The court stated that "trade or business within the United States" generally includes the performance of personal services within the United States. Section 1.864-4(c)(5)(l) of the Treasury Regulations determines whether a foreign corporation is engaged in the active conduct of a banking, financing, or similar business in the United States. The court stated that INLTD had a fixed facility in the sense that it used the San Antonio office to engage in its trade or business.

Moreover, INLTD had not shown that it maintained any "other fixed facility through which it engaged in its activities."

INLTD argued that, notwithstanding a determination that its activities amounted to being engaged in a U.S. trade or business under the regulations, the exceptions contained in section 864(b) excluded the majority of INLTD's activities from the services that could lead to INLTD being found to be engaged in a trade or business within the United States. Section 864(b) states that the term *trade or business within the United States* does not include (i) trading in stocks or securities through a resident broker, commission agent, custodian, or other independent agent, or (ii) trading in stocks or securities for one's own account but only if the taxpayer's principal office is outside of the United States.

The court rejected INLTD's claim that the exclusions in section 864(b)(2)(A)(l) applied to its trading in stocks or securities, ruling that INLTD engaged in the above activities through INC as its agent but that INC was not an independent agent. The court found that INC was not an independent agent because it acted almost exclusively for one principal, INLTD.

The court also rejected INLTD's argument with respect to the exception for trading in stocks and securities for the taxpayer's own account. The exception does not apply to a dealer in stocks or securities, nor does it apply if the foreign corporation has an office or other fixed place of business in the United States through which, or by the direction of which, the transactions in stocks or securities are effected. The court found INLTD had a fixed place of business in the United States, namely, the San Antonio office, through which such transactions were effected.[13] Thus, the court held that none of the transactions in INLTD's financial services business qualified for the exclusion.

Once the court concluded that INLTD was engaged in a trade or business within the United States, it then examined the issue of which portion of INLTD's income was effectively connected with that trade or business. The court also held that nearly every item of INLTD income was "effectively connected with the conduct of trade or business within the United States," under section 882(a)(1).

With regard to the amount of income due to be reported by INLTD, the court held that INLTD was not entitled to any deductions to offset its effectively connected income because INLTD had not filed any U.S. tax returns.

The court also considered whether INLTD and INC were liable for section 1441 withholding tax.

Finally, the court sustained additions to tax for failure to file, negligence, failure to make timely deposits of tax, and substantial understatement.[14] Exceptions of reasonable reliance on advice from professional advisors could not be sustained since the advice did not deal with critical issues in question (filing U.S. return).

The implications of the court's decision are stark. On the facts of *InverWorld*, the offshore company had no facilities or personnel offshore.

The court's critical finding in *InverWorld* was the existence of an "office or other fixed place of business of a related person," for purposes of the U.S. trade or business provisions of the code. This finding appeared to, in part, have been drawn from the court's observation that the Cayman Islands company had not "maintained any other fixed facility through which it engaged in its activities." This issue could be material.

3. Conclusion

3.1 Consequences of U.S. Trade or Business Determination

If the trust company were to be determined to be engaged in U.S. trade or business, only income that is ECI will be taxed under section 11.[15]

Section 864 provides different rules for determining ECI, depending on whether the income is foreign source or U.S. source income. Generally, foreign source income is not ECI. Certain kinds of U.S. source income (e.g., capital gains income) are treated as ECI under certain force of attraction rules. All other income gain or loss from sources within the United States is treated as ECI.

If it were held that there was any U.S. tax liability at all, this could open the full tax can of worms.

3.2 Recommendations

(a) Fixed Facility Abroad

Absolutely necessary.

(b) U.S. Office, U.S. Business Activities, U.S. Supervisory Executive

— There should not be an office or fixed place of business in the United States.

— U.S. business activities should not be "considerable, continuous, or regular."

— The supervisory executive should not be an "agent" of the trust company.

— There should be an appropriate services agreement stating the services to be provided by the supervisor executive, his authority, method of compensation, and related matters.

(c) Board Meetings

Should be held in the country of incorporation or at the headquarters of the trust company.

(d) General Manager

A general manager should be appointed for the trust company. Ideally, this would be a manager with a residence outside the United States.

(e) Maintenance of Books and Records

— Procedures regarding the accounting books and records should be established and supervised outside of the United States, possibly at the headquarters of the trust company.

— The books and records should be maintained and kept by the trust company at its headquarters, or at the very least at a clearly defined place outside of the United States.

— Audited financial statements can be handled by and issued to the supervisory executive in the United States, since this is a supervisor function.

(f) Bank Accounts and Investments

— Should actually be handled from the country of incorporation of the trust company, or at the very least at a clearly defined place outside of the United States, even if pursuant to the policies formulated by the supervisory executive in the United States.

— There is no technical problem with having U.S. bank accounts.

Notes

1. See, e.g., D.M. Garelik, "What Constitutes Doing Business Within the United States by a Non-Resident Alien Individual or a Foreign Corporation," 18 *Tax Law Review* 423 at 451 and 457.
2. The branch profits tax under section 884 imposes up to a 30% tax on the "divided equivalent amount." The branch profits tax can be reduced by treaty, but, in this case, there is no treaty that would appear to reduce the branch profits tax rate below 30%. See section 884(e).
3. See also *United States v. Balanovski*, 236 F. 2d 298 (2d Cir. 1956), *cert. denied*, 352 U.S. 968 (1957) (a partnership engaged in U.S. trade or business when 80% partner was making important business decisions and exercising policy-making judgments for the trade or business while he was in the United States). The IRS can be aggressive in this area, as is indicated by *Taisei Fire and Marine Ins. Co., Ltd. v. Commissioner*, 104 T.C. 535 (1995) (a case involving whether certain Japanese companies had a permanent establishment in the United States as a result of a relationship with certain companies in the United States). The IRS did not prevail in *Taisei.*
4. See also *The Scottish American Investment Co., Ltd. v. Commissioner*, 12 T.C. 49 (1949), which held that a foreign investment corporation that made all decisions as to the purchase and sale of securities and investment policies in the home office in Scotland, handled all transactions in securities directly by the home office through resident brokers, and maintained a U.S. office only to maintain records, collect dividends, file reports to the home office, and perform other clerical and routine services for the home office was not engaged in a trade or business within the United States.
5. *The Linen Thread Co., Ltd. v. Commissioner*, 14 T.C. 725, 736 (1950) ("Moreover, even if...petitioner had a business purpose in involving its American office in these two sales, it would still be our conclusion that these two isolated transactions, profits from which constituted such a minute part of petitioner's total income from American sources in 1943, did not constitute engaging in trade or business in the United States.").

6. Id., at 719; see also, Rev. Rul. 55-282, 1955-1 C.B. 634 (Canadian corporation organized as an investment company, which had an agent in the United States with a discretionary power of attorney to purchase and sell U.S. securities and to keep records of the Canadian corporation in the United States, was engaged in a U.S. trade or business); Rev. Rul. 56-165, 1956-1 C.B. 849 (Swedish resident who was in United States with specially trained Swedish employees to demonstrate and sell logging equipment was held to be engaged in a U.S. trade or business).
7. 30 T.C. 618 (158), *aff'd*, 281 F. 2d 646 (6th Cir. 1960).
8. 30 T.C. 618 at 634.
9. Treas. Reg. § 1.864-7 (a)(2).
10. Secs. 864(c)(4)(B) and (c)(5)(B).
11. Treas. Reg. § 1.864-6(b)
12. Treas. Reg. § 1.864-7(c) (emphasis supplied).
13. Id., at 82-84.
14. Id., at 140-144.
15. Section 882(a)(1).

CHAPTER THIRTEEN

CASE STUDY: ESTATE TAX IMPLICATIONS OF DOMICILE

1. The Issues

Estate and gift planning should take place when the parties are in good health and outside of any emergency situation, and it should be updated from time to time as circumstances change and relationships evolve.

The purpose of this analysis is to demonstrate the role of a key connecting factor—domicile—in cases of Anglo-Saxon estate taxation.

Estate taxation is primarily governed by the law of domicile, which grants to one jurisdiction the exclusive right to tax. Domicile for estate purposes is quite distinct from residence with respect to taxation of income. In principle, rules are laid down in case law and in treaty provisions that enable domicile to be determined unambiguously even in cases of multiple residence.

This determination turns on what may be very detailed issues of fact (down to the minutiae of one's arrangement of one's social intercourse) yet may have major consequences for the heirs of an estate. A key issue in planning is to try to meet the major criteria rather than relying on the unpredictable interpretation of details. As the case study indicates, a key factor will generally be the status of one's domestic arrangements in both the jurisdiction in which one wishes to maintain a domicile and the one in which one wishes merely to reside temporarily.

The decedent was an Australian woman married to a U.S. citizen.

The decedent and her husband jointly owned homes in Australia (New South Wales); her husband owned a home in the United States; and they spent varying proportions of the year in each of the two homes. The decedent's estate also included stock in foreign corporations.

The determination of the decedent's domicile/residence will have an effect on estate tax and probate in U.S. and Australian law.

2. Domicile

It is a general principle of private international law that the state of domicile has the widest jurisdiction in the imposition of inheritance and estate taxes. It is in theory the state of domicile that can impose taxes on the transfer of the decedent's intangibles. The taxing power of the domiciliary state covers substantially all property of a decedent except real or tangible personal property located outside of its jurisdiction.

2.1 U.S. Law of Domicile

The American Law Institute Restatement of the Law defines domicile as follows:

> Domicile is the place with which a person has settled connection for certain legal purposes; either because his home is there, or because that place is assigned to him by law.

U.S. cases tend to define domicile as the

> place where one has his true fixed, permanent home and principal establishment and to which, whenever he is absent, he has the intention of returning.

In determining the decedent's place of domicile for U.S. estate tax purposes, a series of additional criteria has been laid down by case law.

(a) Every person has a domicile at all times, and, at least for the same purposes, no person has more than one domicile at a time.

(b) Home is the place where a person dwells and that is the center of his domestic, social, and civil life.

(c) The domicile of origin is the domicile that a person has at birth.

(d) A domicile of choice may be acquired by a person who is legally capable of changing his domicile.

(e) In addition to legal capacity, acquisition of a domicile of choice requires both physical presence and an attitude of mind.

(f) To acquire a domicile of choice in a place, a person must be physically present there.

(g) To acquire a domicile of choice in a place, a person must intend to make that place his home for the time at least.

(h) A domicile once established continues until it is superseded by a new domicile.

The real problems that arise are in respect of the provisions concerning the domicile of a person having two dwelling places and the position of a married woman. Generally speaking, when a person with capacity to acquire a domicile of choice has more than one dwelling place, his domicile is in the earlier dwelling place unless the second dwelling place is his principal home. A wife who lives with her husband has the same domicile as his unless the special circumstances of the wife make such a result unreasonable.

The actual home of a decedent, and, if he has several homes, his principal home—the one with which he has been associated most intimately—is thus his domicile.

A change of domicile may be made for any reason whatever, provided that there is an intention to abandon one domicile and acquire another and that the acts of the person affected confirm the intention. But mere intention to effect a shift of domicile is not sufficient, and the motive prompting the change (whether tax avoidance or not) is immaterial. Facts alone are determinative as to the reality of a purported domiciliary shift. However, the burden of showing a change from a former domicile is upon the party asserting the change.

Because of the presumption against change of domicile, despite material facts pointing to such a change, the question of a possible double domicile may arise.

Courts in two different states may each find that the decedent's domicile was located there. The decedent could not have had two domiciles, but there may be conflicting findings as to where the domicile was when the property owner died. In such case, there seems no escape from the imposition of two domiciliary taxes upon the succession to the estate, aside from the practical difficulties of collection.

It would seem entirely possible that courts of different jurisdictions may have occasion to adjudicate differently as to domicile with the practical result that a person may have several domiciles when it comes to payment of inheritance taxes, and his heirs may be compelled to pay the full amount of tax in the several states on his whole intangible personal estate, providing there be found sufficient property in the states decreeing domicile differently to satisfy the tax on the whole estate.

2.2 Australian Law of Domicile

A person will be a resident of Australia for the purposes of the Income Tax Assessment Act 1936, as amended, if that person is either a resident in the ordinary sense of the word or is a person who satisfies certain tests set out in the definition, of which the two relevant for this study are

(a) a person whose domicile is in Australia, unless the commissioner is satisfied that his permanent place of abode is outside Australia; or

(b) a person who has actually been in Australia continuously or intermittently during more than one half of the year of income, unless the commissioner is satisfied that his usual place of abode is outside Australia and that he does not intend to take up residence in Australia.

Residence in the ordinary sense is a question of fact. A person resides where he lives. However, as an exception to this general rule, test (a) creates a presumption of residence with regard to anyone within Australian domicile. The presumption is rebuttable by reference to certain facts.

Australia accepts the English common law tests of domicile, which, stated shortly, are as follows. The law ascribes to all persons a domicile and only one domicile. At birth all persons acquire a domicile of origin, which, in the case of a legitimate child, is the domicile of his father. This domicile continues until a new domicile is established, either, in the case of the infant, by a change in the domicile of the appropriate parent or, in the case of an adult, by the acquisition of a domicile of choice. To acquire a domicile of choice, the law requires not only that residence has in fact been set up in a new country or state but also that the person whose domicile is in question intends remaining in this new place of residence permanently. The onus of proving a change of domicile is upon the person alleging it.

The decedent could be regarded as having lost her Australian residence if the tax authorities were satisfied that she had a permanent place of abode outside Australia. Here the word *permanent* means "indefinite," so a person who had a home in the United Kingdom and who was working on an indefinite basis in Australia or the United States might cease to be a resident of Australia notwithstanding that ultimately that person intended to return home at the end of a tour of duty or for the purposes of retirement.

Loss of Australian domicile would furthermore require the severance of links with Australia and the absence of any intention to return there, neither of which is necessarily implied by the possession of a permanent place of abode outside Australia.

2.3 Applicable Taxes

In the United States, there are both federal and state estate and inheritance taxes. In Australia and the State of New South Wales, there are none.

It is therefore very important to determine whether the decedent was domiciled in Australia or in the United States.

3. The Domicile/Residence of the Decedent from an Australian Perspective

Residence is defined by the tests quoted above. These tests are independent of each other. Thus, a person need satisfy only one test to be a resident of Australia.

Although the question of residence is a conclusion of fact, the courts, when considering this question, take into account various factors. In determining whether a person resides in a particular country for a year of income, it is necessary to consider the following:

(a) whether the individual is physically present in the country at some time during the year of income;
(b) the nationality of the person;
(c) the history of his residence and movements;
(d) his mode of life;
(e) the frequency, regularity, and duration of his visits to the country;
(f) the purpose of any visits;
(g) the reason for any absences from the country during the year;
(h) family and/or business ties with the country; and
(i) whether a place of abode is maintained by the person in the relevant country or is available for his use while he is there.

The expression "place of abode" means, for these purposes, the house in which a person lived or the country, city, or town in which he was for the time being to be found. Further, it was considered that "permanent" was used in the sense of something that was to be contrasted with that which was temporary or transitory but that it did not mean everlasting.

It appears that the decedent did not have her permanent place of abode outside Australia since her stays outside Australia were of a temporary nature and no intention to remain outside the country was formed.

4. The Domicile/Residence of the Decedent from a U.S. Perspective

The imposition of U.S. federal estate tax upon the estate of the decedent will depend upon two factors:

1. whether the decedent was a citizen or resident of the United States at the time of her death, or
2. whether the decedent held any assets with a U.S. situs at the time of her death.

The decedent remained an Australian citizen throughout her life. Thus, the first issue is whether the decedent was a "resident" of the United States at the time of her death.

4.1 Residency Determined by "Domicile"

Although the U.S. Internal Revenue Code of 1986, as amended, contains a statutory definition of the term *resident*, by its terms that definition does not apply for estate tax purposes. Instead, for U.S. federal estate tax purposes, a decedent is a resident only if she was "domiciled" in the United States at the time of her death.

The decedent spent a significant amount of time in the United States. This satisfies the physical presence test. Thus, the question of domicile turns on whether the decedent had an intention to remain there permanently. Reported cases indicate that the courts will look to a variety of objective factors to test the ties of the decedent to Australia:

(a) the frequency with which the decedent returned to Australia and the length of her stays there;
(b) whether she owned and maintained a home in Australia;
(c) whether her home in the United States was maintained primarily for pleasure;
(d) the location of her family and friends;
(e) whether she maintained club, church, or social memberships in Australia;
(f) whether there were any written declarations of intention in wills, applications for visas, or other such documents; and
(g) various other items that may be applicable solely in the decedent's situation.

On the basis of the facts, it appears that the majority of the foregoing factors would support the decedent's intention to retain her Australian domicile. For example, the decedent returned to Australia at least once a year and remained there for at least three months out of every year, and usually for more than six months. Furthermore, she owned and maintained a home in Australia but only rented her home in the United States. Her home in Australia was in Sydney, but her home in the United States was in Aspen, Colorado. Some cases have discounted the importance of a residence if it is maintained at or near a resort area for pleasure purposes.

The fact that the decedent possessed a permanent U.S. visa (a "green card") will certainly provide some evidence that she intended to become a U.S. resident. In addition, her marriage to a U.S. citizen and resident will also provide some evidence that she intended to become a U.S. resident. It is important to note, however, that no cases were identified in which either of these factors was determinative. The fact that the decedent filed a U.S. federal income tax return should carry no weight whatsoever in determining her residency status for estate tax purposes.

Accordingly, based on the facts assumed herein, it appears that the objective indicia of intent support the decedent's intention to remain domiciled in Australia.

4.2 Status of Assets

Since the decedent remained both a citizen and a resident of Australia at her death, only those assets with a situs in the United States can be included in her estate for U.S. federal estate tax purposes. For U.S. federal estate tax purposes, stock of a foreign corporation is deemed to have a foreign situs, regardless of the location of the stock certificate, the stock transfer offices, or the sources of income.

4.3 U.S.–Australia Estate Tax Treaty

The estate tax treaty between Australia and the United States does not address either of the issues analyzed above. The treaty leaves the question of domicile to be determined by the local law of Australia and the United States. In addition, the treaty has no situs rules as to corporate stock; thus, the situs determination is again left to local law. As a result, the treaty does not alter the conclusions that the decedent should be treated as an Australian resident.

5. Conclusion

On the facts of the case, and in view of the applicable U.S. and Australian law, the decedent had an Australian domicile at the time of her death.

Therefore, there was no estate tax liability in the United States and no requirement to make any report for the purposes of estate tax.

In the absence of any applicable Australian federal or state taxes, no liability arises in respect of the estate.

PART THREE

INTERNATIONAL REGULATION OF OFFSHORE ACTIVITIES

CHAPTER FOURTEEN

INTERNATIONAL MEASURES TO COMBAT HARMFUL TAX PRACTICES

1. The Effects of Globalization and Liberalization on Harmful Tax Practices

The past decades have seen a rapid spread of preferential tax regimes in high tax countries as well as in the tax havens themselves. Liberalization and globalization have led a number of governments to introduce special tax structures; today virtually every high tax country has adopted some type of preferential tax regime. Over recent years, the number of tax havens has more than doubled, while the value of investments into low tax jurisdictions has expanded exponentially. (See Part One, "The Structure of Offshore.")

Because these tax policies may result in the siphoning off of parts of countries' tax bases, this proliferation of what are considered harmful preferential tax regimes and tax havens has become a growing concern for governments.

Globalization is a major economic process that breaks down economic barriers between nations and leads enterprises to develop global strategies. It was the liberalization of national economies that opened the way for globalization, just as the emergence of new technologies made that globalization happen.

Liberalization is at the core of the OECD's work and is aimed at facilitating cross-border flows of trade and investment. The OECD has made considerable efforts to eliminate double taxation, which is an obstacle to cross-border activities. Furthermore, the OECD is now undertaking similar efforts to curb harmful tax practices that are considered to have detrimental effects on world economic growth.

The perception of the OECD is that, if this situation is not redressed, governments may increasingly be forced to engage in competitive tax bidding in order to attract or retain mobile activities, thus leading to a "race to the bottom," in which location and financing decisions become primarily tax driven.

Developments within the G7, the European Union (EU), the OECD, and beyond are leading to a common approach against what is considered harmful tax practices. Similarly, countries in the Asian-Pacific region, Latin America, Africa, and in the former Soviet bloc are addressing these issues. In some ways, these countries are more exposed to tax havens and competitive bidding for financial and service activities since many of them lack the administrative capacity to implement sophisticated counteracting measures.

The work of the OECD is considered in sections 2 through 5 of this chapter; the work of the EU is considered in Section 6 of this chapter.

2. The Harmful Tax Competition Report of the OECD

2.1 The Report and the Recommendation to Member Governments

In May 1996 the ministers called upon the OECD to "develop measures to counter the distorting effects of harmful tax competition on investment and financing decisions and the consequences for national tax bases, and report back in 1998." The G7 heads of state endorsed this request at their 1996 summit, urging the OECD to "vigorously pursue its work in this field, aimed at establishing a multilateral approach under which countries could operate individually and collectively to limit the extent of these practices."

The OECD's Committee on Fiscal Affairs launched its project on harmful tax competition, and its report was presented to the ministers. The report addresses harmful tax practices in the form of tax havens and harmful preferential tax regimes in OECD countries and their dependencies and in non-member countries. It focuses above all on geographically mobile activities, such as financial and other service activities.

In approving the report on April 9, 1998, the OECD Council adopted a recommendation to the governments of member countries and instructed the committee to pursue its work in this area and to develop a dialogue with non-member countries. Luxembourg and Switzerland abstained in Council on the approval of the report and the adoption of the recommendation.

2.2 The OECD's Position

The OECD´s position on preferential taxes is stated clearly. The existence of low or no income taxes is not in itself enough to constitute harmful tax competition. Rather, when low or no taxes are combined with other legislative or administrative features, such as "ring-fencing," a lack of transparency, or the absence of exchange of information, then harmful tax competition may arise. The OECD report provides a framework for identifying harmful regimes and suggests counter-measures for them. Accordingly, harmonizing tax rates across countries or installing minimum tax levels is not the aim. Countries will remain free to decide their own tax rates, with checks and balances coming from competitive forces of the global marketplace. This will encourage countries to adopt "best practice" policies on taxation.

The report makes a distinction among three situations in which the tax levied on income from geographically mobile financial and other service activities in one country is lower than the tax that would be levied on the same income in another country:

1. the first country is a tax haven and, as such, generally imposes no or only nominal tax on that income;
2. the first country collects significant revenues from tax imposed on income at the individual or corporate level but its tax system has preferential features that allow the relevant income to be subject to low or no taxation; or
3. the first country collects significant revenues from tax imposed on income at the individual or corporate level, but the effective tax rate that is generally applicable at that level is lower than the tax rate levied in the other country.

Each of these situations may have undesirable effects when seen from the perspective of the other country. However, the report is careful not to suggest that there is some general minimum effective tax rate on income below which a country would be considered to be engaging in harmful tax practices.

2.3 Focus on Financial Services

The main focus of the OECD's work is on financial and other service activities because these are the activities that are the most geographically mobile and therefore the most sensitive to tax differentials. Tax havens located outside the OECD area and harmful preferential tax regimes in OECD countries are particularly involved in these activities.

2.4 The OECD's Concept of "Tax Haven"

The OECD report focuses on the following factors to determine whether a jurisdiction is a tax haven:

1. the jurisdiction imposes no or only nominal taxes and offers itself, or is perceived to offer itself, as a place to be used by nonresidents to escape tax in their country of residence;
2. practices of the jurisdiction prevent the effective exchange of relevant information with other governments on taxpayers benefiting from the low or no tax jurisdiction;
3. a lack of transparency exists;
4. there is an absence of a requirement that the activity be substantial, since this would suggest that a jurisdiction may be attempting to attract investment or transactions that are purely tax driven; and
5. there is no or only nominal taxation within the jurisdiction.

If combined with a situation in which the jurisdiction offers itself as a place where nonresidents can escape tax in their country of residence, any of the above factors may be sufficient to identify a tax haven.

The OECD's concept of "tax haven" thus refers to tax jurisdictions that offer themselves as a place that nonresidents can use to escape tax obligations in their countries of residence. A number of factors identify these jurisdictions, in particular the virtual absence of taxes (combined with minimum business presence requirements) and a lack of legislative and administrative transparency. Bank secrecy and other features that prevent effective exchange of information are also discernible. Using these definitions, a list of jurisdictions identified as tax havens is expected to be published in October 1999. This list is intended to help form the basis for unilateral or collective countermeasures.

2.5 The Concept of "Harmful" Preferential Tax Regimes

Similarly, four key factors assist in identifying harmful preferential tax regimes:

1. the regime imposes a low or zero effective tax rate on the relevant income;
2. the regime is "ring-fenced";
3. the operation of the regime is non-transparent; and
4. the jurisdiction operating the regime does not effectively exchange information with other countries.

A low or zero effective tax rate is the necessary starting point for an examination of a preferential tax regime.

The concept of "harmful" preferential tax regimes thus refers to low tax regimes—provided for either in the general tax legislation or as administrative measures—that are primarily tailored to tap into the tax bases of other countries. Characteristics of such regimes are their low effective taxes combined with "ring-fencing," whereby they are partly or fully insulated from the domestic economy. Furthermore, there is often a lack of legislative and administrative transparency, as well as difficulties in accessing information. The potentially harmful regimes in the OECD area tend to target banking, financing, insurance, location of headquarters, and distribution and similar services, although of themselves these are legitimate commercial activities.

2.6 Collective Action

Recognizing the positive aspects of the new global environment in which tax systems operate, member countries have concluded that they need to act collectively as well as individually to curb harmful tax competition and to counter the spread of harmful preferential tax regimes directed at financial and service activities. Since it is difficult for individual countries to combat effectively the spread of harmful preferential tax regimes, a coordinated approach and international cooperation are being be intensified to avoid competitive bidding by countries for geographically mobile activities. Consequently, a strong case is made for reinforcing existing measures and for intensifying international cooperation when formulating a response to the problem of harmful tax practices.

The Committee on Fiscal Affairs has already engaged in a dialogue with countries in the Asian-Pacific region, Latin America, Africa and in the former Soviet Bloc. Ministers have asked the OECD to explore further how contacts with non-member countries can be intensified.

3. The Recommendations and the Guidelines

(See Appendix V, "OECD Report on Harmful Tax Competition—An Emerging Global Issue")

In order to deal with harmful preferential tax regimes, OECD countries agreed to non-binding Guidelines for Dealing with Harmful Preferential Tax Regimes. They have undertaken to eliminate within five years of the adoption of the OECD´s report on harmful tax competition (or, if a particular "grandfather clause" applies, no later than December 31, 2005) the features of those preferential tax regimes identified as harmful under the guidelines.

In addition to the tax haven list and the guidelines, both of which are of a multilateral character, recommendations are made on how the OECD countries might strengthen their domestic and bilateral measures against harmful tax practices. At the national level, OECD countries are encouraged to adopt controlled foreign corporation (CFC) or equivalent legislation. This generally enables the home country of the parent to exercise taxing rights over lowly taxed foreign subsidiaries that the parent controls. The OECD countries are also encouraged to adhere to certain defined standards in providing tax rulings and to apply strictly the 1995 OECD Transfer Pricing Guidelines, which provide for internationally agreed-upon standards for establishing prices on intragroup transactions.

Bilaterally, OECD countries are encouraged to intensify their exchange of information on tax havens and preferential tax regimes. A provision is being considered for the OECD's Model Tax Convention that would deny entities operating under harmful tax regimes access to certain or all of the Convention's benefits. Furthermore, the OECD report asks countries to consider terminating any treaties they might have with tax havens.

After defining the factors to be used in identifying harmful tax practices, the report goes on to make 19 wide-ranging recommendations to counteract such practices. The recommendations set out in the report and the accompanying guidelines address the problem of harmful tax practices from different angles. Taken together, the recommendations with the guidelines represent a comprehensive approach by member countries for dealing with the problems of harmful tax competition created by tax havens and harmful preferential tax regimes. Some of the recommendations encourage countries to refrain from adopting harmful tax competition or to eliminate measures constituting harmful tax competition. Others are aimed at offsetting the benefits for taxpayers of certain forms of harmful tax practices. Still others address the issue indirectly by focusing on tax evasion and avoidance, because many forms of harmful tax competition are aimed at taxpayers willing to engage in tax evasion and tax avoidance.

The effectiveness of many of the recommendations concerning domestic legislation and tax treaties depends in part upon whether they can be implemented in a coordinated way. Consequently, one of the main recommendations is for the establishment of a forum on harmful tax practices (see next section) in order to monitor the application of the guidelines and to undertake an ongoing evaluation of existing and proposed regimes. The forum would assess the effectiveness of countermeasures and to propose ways to improve their effectiveness. It would also be responsible for monitoring the implementation of the other recommendations.

The guidelines are:

1. Refrain from adopting new measures, or extending the scope of or strengthening existing measures (in the form of legislative provisions or administrative practices related to taxation) that constitute harmful tax practices.
2. Review existing measures for the purpose of identifying those measures, in the form of legislative provisions or administrative practices related to taxation, that constitute harmful tax practices. These measures should be reported to the Forum on Harmful Tax Practices and should be included in a list within two years from the date on which these guidelines are approved by the OECD Council.
3. Remove, before the end of five years (starting from the date on which the guidelines are approved by the OECD Council), the harmful features of preferential tax regimes. However, in respect of taxpayers who are benefiting from such regimes on December 31, 2000, the benefits that they derive will be removed at the latest on December 31, 2005. This will ensure that such particular tax benefits have been entirely removed after that date. The list of harmful tax practices will be reviewed annually to delete those regimes that no longer constitute harmful preferential tax regimes.
4. Make certain requests. Each member country may request that a measure be examined by the member countries, through the Forum on Harmful Tax Practices, when it believes that an existing measure not already included in the list (or a proposed or new measure of itself or of another country) constitutes a measure that might qualify as a harmful tax practice. The purpose of this examination is to include the measure in the list. The measure may be in the form of a legislative provision or administrative practice related to taxation. The Forum may issue a non-binding opinion on that question.

5. Coordinate, through the Forum, national and treaty responses to harmful tax practices adopted by other countries.
6. Use the Forum to encourage actively non-member countries to associate themselves with these guidelines.

4. Forum on Harmful Tax Practices

The OECD established the Forum on Harmful Tax Practices in order to provide a framework for implementation of the 19 recommendations contained in the report. The Forum's role is to oversee the implementation and development of the recommendations and engage in a dialogue with non-member countries that share the concerns of OECD members. In addition to these recommendations, the report identifies a series of areas where further study could result in new recommendations. The Forum will be used to examine these areas (see next section).

5. Topics for Further Examination and Report by the Forum on Harmful Tax Practices

The OECD report contains proposals for the examination of issues of harmful tax competition to be explored, apart from the issue of geographically mobile financial and other service activities. It is proposed that, in the context of the Forum, member countries and interested non-member countries will continue to examine these issues with the aim of developing new recommendations.

1. Restriction of deduction for payments to tax haven entities

   A number of countries have rules imposing restrictions on the deduction of payments made to tax haven countries or rules imposing a reversal of the onus of proof in case of such payments.

2. Imposition of withholding taxes on certain payments to residents of countries that engage in harmful tax competition

   Many countries currently have legislation that imposes withholding taxes on various types of payments to nonresidents but substantially reduces or eliminates the rate of withholding tax on payments made to residents of treaty countries.

   It is considered by the OECD that the imposition of withholding taxes at a substantial rate on certain payments to countries that engage in harmful tax competition, if associated with measures aimed at preventing the use of conduit arrangements, would act as a deterrent for countries to engage in harmful tax competition and for taxpayers to use entities located in these countries.

3. Residence rules

   Revising the definition of corporate residence might be considered a possible measure to counteract the use of foreign corporations to avoid domestic tax. Accordingly, one option is to extend the domestic tax definitions of corporate residence so that a foreign corporation controlled by residents would be considered to be resident. Control for this purpose could be limited to the control of the affairs of a corporation as exercised by its board of directors or management. Alternatively, control could be determined by reference to the ownership of its shares. As noted earlier, several countries already treat corporations as residents if the corporation's management and control are located in the country. However, this concept of control is easily manipulated by taxpayers, in contrast to the share ownership concept of control.

   On the treaty side, the definition of "resident of a Contracting State" could be restricted to expressly exclude certain entities subject to no or little tax. One possibility is to narrow the scope of the definition of resident in the OECD Model Tax Convention to exclude other taxpayers who are liable to tax in a country but do not in fact pay tax on all of their income like ordinary residents. Moreover, a specific rule might be adopted to deny certain treaty benefits to corporations resident in countries that exempt foreign branch income. For example, the benefit of reduced withholding taxes might be denied to such a corporation with respect to amounts attributable to a foreign branch located in a tax haven. Furthermore, the definition of resident could be revised to exclude legal entities that take advantage of specified regimes that constitute harmful tax competition.

4. Application of transfer pricing rules and guidelines

   The application of transfer pricing rules may constitute a useful counteracting measure to the situation in which significant income may be attributed to a foreign entity that performs few, if any, real activities. (Transfer pricing rules typically start from an analysis of the true functions performed by each part of a group of associated enterprises.) It is suggested that rules affecting a reversal of onus of proof in certain cases might help to address the specific circumstances of tax havens and regimes that constitute harmful tax practices.

5. Thin Capitalization

   A large number of OECD countries apply general or specific legislative rules to address cases of base erosion that are attributable to the thin capitalization of resident companies by nonresidents. Such rules can act as a block against the tax-free repatriation of domestic profits to entities that may be located in tax havens or in countries that provide, directly or indirectly, favorable taxation of interest income from foreign subsidiaries. Some domestic rules, however, such as the setting of safe harbor debt/equity ratios, can, conversely, be used to facilitate harmful tax competition. The Committee intends to explore whether it should recommend to member countries lacking such rules that they consider their introduction, especially with respect to safe harbors. The committee also intends to review existing domestic rules.

6. Financial innovation

   Financial markets are constantly evolving, and innovative financial products are continually being created. Such instruments have the potential to be used to assist harmful tax competition, as well as being used for legitimate business purposes. For example, derivative products, in addition to hedging interest rate risk, can be used to create synthetic loans. Such "loans" give the taxpayer the same economic effect as if a loan had been made but with the potential to avoid withholding tax and thin capitalization rules. The Committee intends to keep monitoring this area to ensure financial innovation is not used to assist harmful tax competition.

7. Non-tax measures

   The Committee also intends to explore the possibility of addressing harmful tax competition using a wide range of non-tax measures.

6. European Union

Work on harmful tax competition has also been carried out in the European Union (EU). The EU Council agreed on December 1, 1997 to a package of measures that will tackle harmful tax competition in order to help to (1) reduce distortions in the single market, (2) prevent excessive losses of tax revenue, and (3) develop tax structures in a more employment-friendly way. The package includes a Code of Conduct on business taxation, taxation of savings income, and the issue of withholding taxes on cross-border interest and royalty payments between companies. The Code of Conduct identifies potentially harmful regimes in the field of business taxation and gives factors for the assessment of harmful regimes. It includes a commitment not to introduce new harmful tax regimes and to roll back existing regimes.

Under the Code, a standstill on unfair tax competition came into operation on January 1, 1998; the Commission is now conducting a review of tax practices in each member state. Member states have at least five years to dismantle unfair tax regimes—the EU Commission had proposed a two-year phase-out period—but some exceptions, such as an unspecified roll-back period for Ireland's 10% corporation tax rate for manufacturers, have been negotiated.

The Code is flanked by a package of measures, including a commitment to deal with taxes on savings (including withholding taxes on bank interest payments and share dividends) as well as a commitment to draft a directive on interest and royalty payments between companies.

Particular attention is being paid to peripheral parts of the EU such as the Canary Islands and Madeira. Member states are also called upon to promote the Code in their own dependencies, such as the United Kingdom for the Channel Islands and Gibraltar, and the Netherlands for the Netherlands Antilles.

Several favorable corporate tax regimes for foreign and domestic companies, such as those in the Netherlands, Belgium, and, more recently, Denmark also fall under scrutiny. Under the Code, all unfair tax regimes are to be withdrawn by January 1, 2003.

The Irish government has signaled that it will oppose EU interference in domestic tax policy by announcing plans to enshrine future corporation tax cuts in its legislation. It is concerned that other member states opposed to tax competition will seek to dismantle the bilateral tax deal struck with the European Commission.

The EU Competition Commission has drawn up draft guidelines to end discriminatory tax treatment that governments might exploit to protect domestic companies or attract foreign companies. The new rulebook states that all forms of exceptional tax treatment—special deductions or accelerated depreciation of assets, credits, exemptions or deferment of tax debt—can be prohibited under the Treaty of Rome's rules against the granting of illegal state aid. General measures that apply throughout the economy and do not give preference to certain sectors or regions will still be allowed, but regional aid schemes will have to be submitted to the Commission for prior approval on the basis of the new guidelines. If a scheme is found to be unlawful, the Directorate-General for Competition will instruct the government concerned to claw back the value of the illegal tax break plus interest.

While the EU Code and the OECD Guidelines are broadly compatible, particularly regarding the criteria used to identify harmful preferential tax regimes, and mutually reinforcing, the scope and operation of the two differ. The OECD Guidelines are clearly limited to financial and other service activities, whereas the Code looks at business activities in general, although with an emphasis on mobile activities. The review procedure reflects the different institutional frameworks within which each organization operates, and the OECD Guidelines are explicitly aimed at a much broader geographic grouping. The OECD work goes beyond harmful preferential tax regimes to encompass tax havens; it also focuses on exchange of information. In addition, as noted above, the EU Code is part of a package of measures, whereas the OECD Guidelines are accompanied by the 19 detailed recommendations relating to the specific issues of harmful tax competition.

CHAPTER FIFTEEN

INTERNATIONAL MEASURES TO COMBAT MONEY LAUNDERING

Money laundering knows no frontiers. Money laundering is ubiquitous. Money laundering is an evolving activity. It follows that, in order to be effective, any action to combat money laundering must rely on effective cooperation between experts from a wide range of disciplines: legal and judicial, financial and regulatory, and law enforcement.

1. Financial Action Task Force on Money Laundering (FATF)

The Financial Action Task Force (FATF) was established by the G7 Summit in Paris in 1989 in order to examine measures to combat money laundering. The FATF is not a permanent international organization. Its mandate has to be renewed periodically, usually for five-year stretches.

In 1990, the FATF issued forty recommendations for action against money laundering. These recommendations were revised in 1996 to reflect changes in money laundering trends. Membership of the FATF comprises 27 governments[1] and two regional organizations[2]; major financial centers of North America, Europe and Asia are all represented. The delegations of the task force's members are drawn from a wide range of disciplines, including experts from the ministries of finance, justice, interior and external affairs, financial regulatory authorities, and law enforcement agencies.

In 1998, FATF Ministers and the European Commissioner for Financial Services endorsed the report prepared by the FATF that defines a five year plan—1999–2004—to spread the anti-money laundering message to all continents and regions of the globe. To this end, ministers urged FATF to foster the establishment of a worldwide anti-money laundering network. The network would be based on adequate expansion of the FATF membership, the development of FATF-style regional bodies (such as the Caribbean FATF and the Asia/Pacific Group on Money Laundering), and close cooperation with all relevant international organizations, in particular the United Nations Office for Drug Control and Crime Prevention (UNODCCP) and the International Financial Institutions.

The FATF annual survey of money laundering typologies[3] clearly noted the emergence of new areas of money laundering, such as electronic money, new payment technologies, remittance businesses, non-financial professions, the insurance sector, and stock exchange dealers.

The success of the FATF's work so far demonstrates that there is no alternative international organization, body, or group, that has the necessary expertise of a multidisciplinary nature with the experience and ability to assume the responsibilities of the FATF in a flexible and efficient way.

2. FATF Collaboration with International Organizations and Non-Members

The FATF collaborates with the relevant international organizations and bodies rather than launching new initiatives. In particular, the FATF participates in anti-money laundering events organized by other bodies so that it can observe the developments taking place in non-members, particularly the adoption of money laundering countermeasures. The United Nations Global Program on Money Laundering will contribute significantly to the implementation of these measures through the provision of training and technical assistance.

To increase the effectiveness of international anti-money laundering efforts, the FATF and other organizations and bodies endeavor to coordinate their activities. Regional and international bodies concerned with combating money laundering have regular coordination meetings. As part of this mission, the FATF cooperates closely with international and regional organizations concerned with combating money laundering, including the following:

- Asia/Pacific Group on Money Laundering (APG);
- Caribbean Financial Action Task Force (CFATF);
- Council of Europe;
- Commonwealth Secretariat;
- European Bank for Reconstruction and Development;
- International Monetary Fund (IMF);
- Inter-American Development Bank (IDB);
- Inter-American Drug Abuse Control Commission (CICAD)
- Interpol;
- International Organization of Securities Commissions (IOSCO);
- Offshore Group of Banking Supervisors (OGBS);
- United Nations Office for Drug Control and Crime Prevention (UNODCCP); and
- World Bank and the World Customs Organization (WCO).

The FATF's strategy for relations with non-members is directed toward supporting the various activities of other regional and international bodies involved in the fight against money laundering. A select committee of the Council of Europe and the Offshore Group of Banking Supervisors has commenced mutual evaluations of the anti-money laundering measures taken by their members.

In September 1997, the FATF carried out a mission to Cyprus; in October 1997, it organized, with the Bank of Russia, an international money laundering conference in St. Petersburg. This conference was followed by the first meeting of the Asia/Pacific Group on Money Laundering, which was held in March 1998 and which was attended by 23 countries and territories throughout the region.

The FATF has adopted a policy for assessing the implementation of anti-money laundering measures in non-member governments. The rationale for this policy is that the implementation of a mutual evaluation procedure will encourage countries and territories not only to get on with implementing anti-money laundering laws but also to improve the counter-measures already in place. The task force has already validated and supported the mutual evaluation processes of other bodies that have agreed to carry out mutual evaluations of their members. In this respect, the FATF determined that the CFATF, the Council of Europe, and the OGBS's mutual evaluation procedures conformed with its own principles. The FATF has sought formal political endorsement of the procedures and the forty recommendations from those governments of the members of the OGBS that are not represented in either the CFATF or the FATF.

The FATF has furthered its cooperation with these bodies. First, it stands ready to provide assistance in the training of mutual evaluators of non-FATF bodies. Secondly, FATF member countries will supply observer examiners, if requested by one of the three bodies mentioned above.

3. Key Areas of Activity

The FATF has concentrated above all on the following key areas of activity:

- establishing standards;
- reviewing money laundering methods and countermeasures;
- monitoring the implementation of anti-money laundering measures by member governments; and
- promoting the widest possible international action against money laundering and the adoption of countermeasures by non-member countries.

Considerable progress has been made by FATF members in implementing anti-money laundering measures. By mid-1999, every member had undergone two evaluations of its anti-money laundering system. The first round of evaluations dealt with the question of whether all members had adequately implemented the forty recommendations, while the second round dealt with the effectiveness of the anti-money laundering system for each member.

Over the past decade, the FATF has played a key role in building an international consensus on the measures that need to be taken to combat money laundering. It has also helped to persuade many countries to implement these measures. In the process, it has helped to create a "network" of money laundering experts in each of the FATF members, improving cooperation and the flow of information, both at the domestic level and internationally. However, although the FATF's forty recommendations have gained some international prominence, a large number of countries around the world have not implemented anti-money laundering systems.

4. Objectives

The medium- to long-term objectives of the FATF are (1) to develop credible and effective FATF-style regional bodies and (2) to expand its membership to include strategically important new members. At the beginning of 2005, the FATF should ideally have achieved its objective of promoting the establishment of a worldwide anti-money laundering network. It is proposed that an assessment of the FATF's achievements and strategy between 1999 and 2004 and future should be carried out in 2003–2004.

Objective 1: Establish a worldwide anti-money laundering network in all continents and regions of the globe

This worldwide anti-money laundering network is to be based on:

- an adequate expansion of the FATF membership to strategically important countries that already have certain key anti-money laundering measures in place, that is, criminalization of money laundering, mandatory customer identification, and suspicious/unusual transactions reporting by financial institutions;
- the development of FATF-style regional bodies, especially in areas where FATF is not sufficiently represented and strengthening of the work of bodies that already exist (CFATF, Asia/Pacific Group on Money Laundering, Council of Europe, OAS/CICAD, and OGBS); and
- close cooperation with relevant international organizations, in particular the United Nations bodies and the International Financial Institutions.

Objective 2: Improve the implementation of the forty recommendations in FATF members

This objective involves the following elements:

- an enhanced self-assessment process, and
- a third round of simplified mutual evaluations for all FATF members starting in 2001, focusing exclusively on compliance with the revised parts of the

recommendations, areas of significant deficiencies identified in the second round, and the general effectiveness of the countermeasures.

Objective 3: Strengthen the review of money laundering trends and countermeasures

Because money laundering is an evolving activity, it is considered crucial for FATF members to acquire the best possible experience with and knowledge of money laundering trends and techniques. It is similarly considered to be of great importance to assess the effectiveness of the FATF recommendations and to extend the geographical scope of the future typologies exercises, with the possible need for new countermeasures.

On May 17, 1998, the G-8 Heads of State and Government "welcomed the FATF decision to continue and enlarge its work to combat money laundering in partnership with regional groupings" and "placed special emphasis on the issues of money laundering and financial crime, including issues raised by offshore financial centers."

5. Monitoring the Implementation of Anti-Money Laundering Measures

A considerable part of the FATF's work focuses on monitoring the implementation by its members of the forty recommendations. FATF members are clearly committed to the discipline of multilateral surveillance and peer review. All members have their implementation of the Recommendations monitored through a two-pronged approach:

- an annual self-assessment exercise; and,
- the more detailed mutual evaluation process under which each member is subject to an on-site examination.

5.1 The Self-Assessment Exercise

Legal Issues

Almost all members are in compliance with a large majority of the recommendations. All members have enacted laws to make drug money laundering a criminal offense, and all but three members have enacted an law that prohibits the laundering of the proceeds of a range of crimes in addition to drug trafficking.

Financial Issues

Almost all members comply fully with customer identification and record-keeping requirements for banks, but there are some persistent gaps in coverage with respect to certain categories of non-bank financial institutions. The serious concerns regarding the anonymous passbooks for residents in Austria have not been resolved, however, and are being pursued through the FATF noncompliance procedures.

In relation to the requirement for financial institutions to report suspicious transactions and related measures, the position is generally regarded as quite satisfactory in relation to banks and almost as good for non-bank financial institutions. However, there is still room for improvement regarding (1) non-bank financial institutions, (2) the need to pay attention to large, unusual transactions, and (3) the obligation to develop internal controls. Almost all bank members have now established anti-money laundering guidelines and taken steps to guard their banks against control or acquisition by criminals. Though there have been improvements, a number of countries still need to take similar measures for all categories of non-bank financial institutions.

The FATF has stated that there is also a pressing need in the United States to finalize and implement the proposed regulations to significantly enhance anti-money laundering controls over many categories of non-bank financial institutions. These are particularly *bureaux de change*, money remitters, check cashiers, issuers and sellers of money orders and travelers checks, casinos, and securities brokers and dealers. The United States has also been urged to place additional money laundering controls on insurance companies.

5.2 The Mutual Evaluation Process

The second and major element for monitoring the implementation of the FATF recommendations is the mutual evaluation process. Each member is examined in turn by the FATF on the basis of a report drawn up by a team of three or four selected experts drawn from the legal, financial, and law enforcement fields of other members. The purpose of this exercise is to provide a comprehensive and objective assessment of the extent to which the country in question has moved forward in implementing effective measures to counter money laundering and to highlight areas in which further progress may still be required.

Examples of mutual evaluation reports appear from Sections 6.1 through 6.8 below.

6. Measures to Combat Money Laundering

6.1 Canada

Canada's money laundering control scheme is based on a strong penal response involving the prosecution of money launderers and the confiscation of the proceeds of crime. The penal legislation appears to be working well, though it is generally thought that the extension of the more serious money laundering offense to all serious crimes, together with some minor changes to the forfeiture legislation, would make the system even more effective. However, the suspicious transaction reporting regime does not appear to be working effectively.

6.2 Switzerland

There are three main facets to Swiss anti-laundering policy: (1) a very broad definition of laundering offenses involving assets derived from any crime; (2) a system of self-regulation in the financial sector (banking and non-banking) accompanied by state monitoring; and (3) a "reporting right," which since 1994 has authorized financial intermediaries to convey their suspicions and which was replaced in April 1998 with a "reporting obligation."

For some years, the Swiss authorities have been endeavoring to toughen the penal law in order to step up the fight against new forms of crime, particularly economic offenses and organized crime. As a result, on August 1, 1990, Articles 305 bis and 305 ter of the Penal Code, on the offenses of money laundering and lack of due vigilance in financial transactions, respectively, entered into force. This arsenal of criminal law was supplemented on August 1,1994, by a second round of measures against organized crime that strengthened powers of confiscation and authorized financial intermediaries to report suspicious transactions (CP: Article 305 ter, paragraph 2). In addition, the Federal Act of October 7, 1994, on the Central Offices of the Federal Criminal Police, set up an organization vital to improved prosecution of persons involved in organized crime.

In the financial sector, the Federal Banking Commission (CFB) issued a circular on December 18, 1991, to all licensed banks and auditing firms, that contained guidelines for preventing and combating money laundering. Concerning the obligation to identify, CFB circular 91/3 mirrors the agreement on the Banks' Obligation of Diligence (CDB).

A law on counter-laundering in the financial sector ("The Money Laundering Act," or LBA) was adopted by the Parliament on October 10, 1997. Under this legislation, all physical and legal persons active in the financial sector would be subject to special obligations of diligence (to ascertain the identity of customers and beneficial owners, to clarify certain transactions, and to establish and keep certain documents.) These persons must also take organizational measures to prevent money laundering. The LBA calls for the creation of a Money Laundering Control Authority, which would be responsible for monitoring the compliance of financial intermediaries with anti-laundering obligations. Intermediaries will also be required to file reports with the Money Laundering Reporting Office and to freeze suspicious assets if they have reason to suspect that money is being laundered. The Money Laundering Act entered into force on April 1, 1998.

6.3 Netherlands

The principal aims of the anti-money laundering system in the Netherlands are to protect and maintain the integrity of the financial system, and to detect and prosecute activities concerning money laundering. The heart of the system is the mandatory reporting of unusual transactions on the basis of objective and subjective indicators. The investigation and prosecution of financial crimes are high priorities for the government, as is the exchange of information and cooperation, both nationally and internationally. Some of the more significant changes have been the enactment of the Identification (Financial Services) Act (the Identification Act) and the Disclosure of Unusual Transactions Act (the Disclosure Act); the licensing and supervision of *bureaux de change*; and the expansion of the reporting obligation to credit card companies, *bureaux de change,* and casinos.

The anti-money laundering system in the Netherlands is comprehensive and progressive and is subject to a continual process of review and improvement. The penal offense has a broad scope as it covers all predicate offenses, and the *mens rea* ("guilty mind") extends to reasonable suspicion.

Measures taken in the financial sector regarding such matters as customer identification and the supervision of institutions such as *bureaux de change* seem to be functioning exceptionally effectively. Through government committees and working groups, major financial institutions and their associations have shown a high level of commitment, and this has resulted in strong interaction between the government and the private sector and a constant examination and review of potential sources of weakness. The system of reporting unusual transactions to the financial intelligence unit (MOT), which then reports the suspicious transactions to law enforcement, appears to be working effectively in most respects.

The Netherlands is party to a wide range of international instruments that allow it to provide and make requests for all types of assistance.

6.4 Germany

In Germany, a twofold approach has been adopted to counter money laundering. Measures within the financial sector are intended to have a preventive effect, while criminal provisions such as the money laundering offense and confiscation laws will punish the offender for the criminal activity as well as deprivie the offender of any illegal benefits.

6.5 Italy

Law No. 197 of July of 1991 instituted measures to curtail the use of cash and bearer instruments in financial transactions as well as measures to prevent the criminal use of the financial system for money laundering purposes. Its key provision is the prohibition of transfers of cash and bearer instruments in amounts greater than L 20 million (about $12,000 in United States dollars), except when such transfers are carried out by means of authorized intermediaries who are required to identify customers and register transactions. Other main provisions deal with the reporting of suspicious transactions and the monitoring of financial intermediaries' compliance with the law.

The provisions establishing money laundering as an offense were amended in 1993, to widen the original scope of predicate offenses to "all intentional criminal offenses." Recently, a Legislative Decree (No. 153/97 of May 26, 1997) amended the laws in force by three important measures: (1) enhance compliance with the obligation to report suspicious transactions, ensuring that the identity of any person reporting such information be kept absolutely confidential; (2) centralize the reporting of suspicious transactions to the Ufficio Italiano dei Cambi (UIC), a public institution chaired by the Governor of the Bank of Italy; and (3) establish operational links for money laundering between financial, investigative, and judicial authorities as far as organized crime is concerned. In the near future, the government is planning to extend the scope of specific categories of non-financial businesses to anti-money laundering measures. Moreover, a review of the anti-money laundering legislation has already started in order to strengthen it by introducing new provisions or eliminating redundancies.

Legislative Decree No. 153/97 provides for the designation of the *Ufficio Italiano dei Cambi* as the single recipient for suspicious transaction reports, thus in effect becoming Italy's Financial Intelligence Unit (FIU). Previously, reports from financial institutions were reported to the local police.

6.6 Norway

Norwegian control policy on money laundering is based on international initiatives, and an old preventive principle of Norwegian law that crime shall not pay. Measures that are considered important in meeting Norway's anti-money laundering objectives are: (a) increasing the risk of detection and prosecution; (b) improving the tracing and confiscating of illegal proceeds; and (c) facilitating international cooperation.

The money laundering offense, which covers both money laundering and general receiving offenses, is broadly worded and provides a firm basis for prosecution. In general, the anti-money laundering system in Norway meets almost all the requirements of the FATF forty recommendations.

6.7 Japan

Until recently, the Japanese government focused its attention on combating drug money laundering.

The Japanese government has stated its intention to step up action against money laundering and to reinforce the legal measures at its disposal, by taking the following steps:

- the catalogue of predicate offenses for money laundering is to be substantially enlarged to include all criminal offenses of fundamental significance, which will make it easier for financial institutions to report suspicious transactions and the provisions for freezing and confiscating assets are to be extended; and

- a financial intelligence unit (FIU) is to be established in the Financial Supervisory Agency, in conjunction with a new STR system, in which the FIU evaluates the suspicious transaction reports and passes them on through official channels to the law enforcement agencies.

6.8 Greece

Greece has an effective legislative framework and organizational structure to insure compliance and enforcement. Law 2331 of August 24, 1995, establishes the money laundering offense, deals with confiscation and provisional measures, and makes provision for cooperation between law enforcement authorities and financial institutions, and suspicious transaction reporting (STR). It also laid the groundwork for the establishment of a central authority (the "Competent Committee"), the functioning of which was completed by Presidential Decree 401/10 December 1996. There is also a Financial and Economic Crimes Office with powers to investigate economic crimes, including money laundering. The money laundering offense extends to 20 predicate offenses, and makes it an offense if the defendant knew that the property was derived from criminal activity.

The Greek anti-money laundering system meets most of the forty recommendations.

6.9 Austria

In accordance with the request made at the June 1997 FATF meeting, Austria reported back to the FATF in February 1998 on the anti-money laundering measures it had taken and the plan of action that it proposed to remove the problems identified in the report.

Austria has advised the FATF that it has:

- amended the common note of interpretation to require identification of trust settlors by lawyers, notaries and certified public accountants;
- acted to clarify other identification requirements;
- created guidelines concerning the protection of employees of credit and financial institutions that act as witnesses;
- set up procedures to obtain extra statistics; and
- published a draft Bill regarding the removal of the monetary threshold under Article 165 of the Penal Code.

However, the problem of the anonymous passbook for Austrian residents remains.

6.10 Cyprus

The 1996 Law on the Prevention and Suppression of Money Laundering Activities contains, among other measures, a definition of a serious crimes money laundering offense and a requirement to report suspicious transactions to the Unit for Combating Money Laundering. Cyprus has also ratified the United Nations Convention Against Illicit Traffic in Narcotic Drugs and Psychotropic Substances and the Council of Europe Convention on Laundering, Search, Seizure and Confiscation of the Proceeds of Crime.

6.11 Russia

A joint FATF/Bank of Russia Money Laundering Conference took place in 1997. Participants included the nine FATF countries, the Russian Federation (represented by numerous delegates from the Bank of Russia), the Ministry of Finance, the Ministry of Justice, the Customs Committee, the Federal Service on Foreign Exchange and Export Control, the Ministry of the Interior, the Federal Security Service, the State Tax Service, the Tax Police, the General Prosecutor, and the Association of Russian Banks. The conference discussed the role of the financial and credit institutions in the combat of money laundering with particular emphasis on the regulatory bodies.

The Bank of Russia has taken a major anti-money laundering step by creating a national system of preventive measures aimed at safeguarding the banking community against dirty money. In July 1997, the Bank of Russia issued (1) recommendations to prevent illegal funds from passing through banks and credit institutions, and (2) a directive on organizing internal banking controls and a guideline on how to organize internal controls in credit institutions that participate in financial markets. Because of a lack of legislation, these texts will assist banks and credit institutions to undertake anti-money laundering work. For the elaboration of these texts, the Bank of Russia used as a basis the Forty FATF Recommendations.

6.12 Caribbean FATF (CFATF)

The Caribbean Financial Action Task Force (CFATF) endorsed the original Forty FATF Recommendations in the Kingston Declaration of November 1992.[4]

Since its inception, participation in the CFATF has grown to 24 states of the Caribbean basin. The current CFATF members[5] are: Antigua and Barbuda, Anguilla, Aruba, the Bahamas, Barbados, Belize, Bermuda, the British Virgin Islands, the Cayman Islands, Costa Rica, Dominica, Dominican Republic, Grenada, Jamaica, Montserrat, the Netherlands Antilles, Nicaragua, Panama, St. Kitts and Nevis, St. Lucia, St. Vincent and the Grenadines, Turks and Caicos Islands, Trinidad and Tobago and Venezuela.

The CFATF has instituted measures to ensure the effective implementation of, and compliance with, the recommendations. The CFATF Secretariat monitors members' implementation of the Kingston Ministerial Declaration through the following activities:

- self-assessment of the implementation of the recommendations;

- ongoing program of mutual evaluation of members;
- coordination of, and participation in, training and technical assistance programs;
- bi-annual plenary meetings for technical representatives; and
- annual Ministerial meetings.

To further its mandate to identify and act as a clearinghouse for facilitating training and technical assistance needs of members, the Secretariat works closely with regional Mini-Dublin Groups, the diplomatic representatives of countries with interest in the region. Prominent here are Canada, France, the Netherlands, the United Kingdom and the United States. There is also close liaison with CARICOM, the Caribbean Customs Law Enforcement Council (CCLEC), the Center Interministériel de Formation Anti Drogue (CIFAD) in Martinique, the Association of Caribbean Chiefs of Police (ACCP), the Commonwealth Secretariat, and the International United Nations Drug Control Program (UNDCP).

Supported by, and in collaboration with, UNDCP, the CFATF Secretariat has developed a regional strategy for technical assistance and training to aid effective investigation and prosecution of money laundering and related asset forfeiture cases. The development of this regional strategy parallels and closely coordinates with similar initiatives by the European Commission and with efforts arising from the Summit of the Americas Ministerial in Buenos Aires.

6.13 Asia/Pacific

A Working Party meeting of the Asia/Pacific Group on Money Laundering (APG) was held in Beijing in July 1997. Countries in the region have started to exchange information and examine the strengths and weaknesses of their systems through the mechanism of jurisdiction reports. Measures are also proposed for improving technical assistance and training, enhancing mutual legal assistance, and improving cooperation with the financial sector. The Working Party also recognized that, although regional differences need to be taken into account, the FATF forty recommendations provide guiding principles for action in establishing an effective anti-money-laundering system. The FATF stands ready to assist the APG in its consideration of how international standards such as the forty recommendations can best be implemented in the region.

The Asia/Pacific Group currently consists of 16 members in the Asia/Pacific region, including members from South Asia, Southeast and East Asia, and the South Pacific. The members of the APG are Australia, Bangladesh, China, Fiji, Hong Kong, India, Japan, New Zealand, Taiwan, Republic of Korea, Republic of the Philippines, Singapore, Sri Lanka, Thailand, United States of America, and Vanuatu. In March 1998, the first annual meeting of the APG was held in Tokyo and was attended by 25 jurisdictions from the region.

The revised Terms of Reference for the APG, adopted in Tokyo on March 10–12, 1998, recognized that the FATF's forty recommendations are accepted international standards. The Tokyo meeting represented the full establishment of the APG as a cohesive regional group following on from the earlier awareness-raising efforts.

6.14 Council of Europe

The Council of Europe Select Committee of Experts on the Evaluation of Anti-Money Laundering Measures takes into account, as one of the relevant international standards, the forty recommendations of the FATF.

The membership of the Committee consists of the Council of Europe member States that are not members of the FATF: Albania, Andorra, Bulgaria, Croatia, Cyprus, the Czech Republic, Estonia, Hungary, Latvia, Liechtenstein, Lithuania, Macedonia, Malta, Moldova, Poland, Romania, the Russian Federation, San Marino, Slovakia, Slovenia, and the Ukraine.

6.15 Offshore Group of Banking Supervisors (OGBS)

The conditions for membership of the Offshore Group of Banking Supervisors (OGBS) include a clear commitment to the FATF's forty recommendations. In addition, the following members of the OGBS, not members of the FATF or the CFATF, are formally committed to the forty recommendations through individual ministerial letters sent to the FATF president during 1997–1998: Bahrain, Cyprus, Gibraltar, Guernsey, Isle of Man, Jersey, Malta, Mauritius, and Vanuatu.

FATF has received ministerial letters indicating political endorsement of the forty recommendations and the mutual evaluation procedure from all but one member of the Offshore Group of Banking Supervisors (Lebanon). The Task Force has therefore endorsed the commencement of the OGBS mutual evaluation process, except for Lebanon, which, as a result, has been changed from full membership in OGBS to observer status.

6.16 United Nations

The Global Program against Money Laundering (GPML), a research and technical cooperation program, implemented by the United Nations Office for Drug Control and Crime Prevention (ODCCP), is now in operation. Its aim is to increase the effectiveness of international action against money laundering through comprehensive technical cooperation services offered to governments. The program is carried out in cooperation with other international and regional organizations. In the context of the GPML, the UNODCCP organized several important international anti-money laundering events in 1997–1998, including two awareness-raising seminars for West Africa in Ivory Coast on December 1–3, 1997, and for South Asian countries, plus Myanmar and Thailand, in New Delhi on March 2–4, 1998.

In December 1997, participants in the United Nations Workshop on Money Laundering recommended that states adopt or take into account the Recommendations of the Financial Action Task Force on Money Laundering.

In March 1998, a United Nations Conference on Money Laundering recommended that "in drafting their legislation, States should have regard to the standards set out in the forty recommendations of the Financial Action Task Force on Money Laundering."

The United Nations General Assembly met on June 8–10, 1998, in New York for a special session devoted to the fight against the illicit production, sale, demand, traffic, and distribution of narcotic drugs and psychotropic substances and related activities, including money laundering. In a declaration of June 10, 1998, the United Nations General Assembly in Special Session on the world drug problem recalled that the 1996 Resolution 5 of the United Nations Commission on Narcotic Drugs noted that "the forty recommendations of the Financial Action Task Force . . . remain the standard by which anti-money laundering measures adopted by concerned States should be judged. . . ."

The General Assembly adopted a Political Declaration in which the Member States of the United Nations:

- undertake to make special efforts against the laundering of money linked to drug trafficking, and
- recommend that states that have not yet done so adopt by the year 2003 national anti-money laundering legislation and programs in accordance with relevant provisions of the Vienna Convention and a package of measures for countering money laundering, adopted at the same session.

6.17 Commonwealth

In October 1997, the Commonwealth Heads of Government (CHOGM) welcomed the endorsement by Finance Ministers of the updated forty recommendations of the FATF.

The Commonwealth members that are not members of FATF[6] are: Antigua and Barbuda, the Bahamas, Bangladesh, Barbados, Belize, Botswana, Brunei Darussalam, Cameroon, Cyprus, Dominica, Gambia, Ghana, Grenada, Guyana, India, Jamaica, Kenya, Kiribati, Lesotho, Malawi, Malaysia, Maldives, Malta, Mauritius, Mozambique, Namibia, Nauru, Nigeria, Pakistan, Papua New Guinea, St. Kitts and Nevis, St. Lucia, St. Vincent and the Grenadines, Samoa, Seychelles, Sierra Leone, Solomon Islands, South Africa, Sri Lanka, Swaziland, Tonga, Trinidad and Tobago, Tuvalu, Uganda, the United Republic of Tanzania, Vanuatu, Zambia, and Zimbabwe.

Commonwealth Heads of Government have repeatedly called for concerted action to combat money laundering. A joint meeting of finance and law officials has been set up to develop a coordinated approach aimed at:

- improving domestic coordination through national interdisciplinary coordinating structure;
- dealing with the special problems concerning money laundering in countries with large parallel economies;
- strengthening regional initiatives for more effective implementation of anti-money laundering measures; and
- self-evaluating the progress made in implementing anti-money laundering measures in the financial sector.

6.18 Inter-American Development Bank

The Inter-American Development Bank (IDB), in conjunction with the Banking Superintendent of Colombia and the Andean Development Corporation, sponsored a seminar on the subject of asset laundering during the 1998 annual meeting of the Board of Governors in Cartagena de Indias, Colombia. The session addressed the multifaceted aspects of asset laundering activities, as well as international approaches to combat money laundering on the basis of presentations made by the United Nations, the OAS/CICAD, the IDB, the IMF, the Federation of Latin American Bankers Association, and the FATF. The seminar ended with certain common goals, focusing on a multilateral approach to combating asset laundering in Latin America and the Caribbean, as well as current and future activities in the region.

The IDB was encouraged to:

- use its own funds and seek additional funding for programs, including the training of supervisors, regulators, and financial institutions, particularly on the detection and prevention of new laundering techniques on a regional and/or national basis;
- serve as a clearinghouse for such proposed programs, sources of funding, and potential executing entities;
- strengthen the dialogue between private banking sectors and government regulators; and
- use its good offices to encourage implementation of effective laws and regulatory frameworks to address the issue of asset laundering.

6.19 Gulf Cooperation Council

In May 1997, the Gulf Cooperation Council (GCC) agreed to carry out, in conjunction with the FATF, an evaluation of the anti-money laundering measures that had been taken by its six member states—Bahrain, Kuwait, Oman, Qatar, Saudi Arabia, and the United Arab Emirates (UAE).

As a first step, self-assessment questionnaires were sent in August 1997. However, there have been only partial and incomplete replies to date from some GCC members.

6.20 OAS/CICAD

The CICAD Group of Experts to Control Money Laundering has continued to put into effect the Buenos Aires Plan of Action.[7] At its last meeting in May 1998, the CICAD Group of Experts, which meets twice a year, approved a training program for judges, prosecutors, FIU personnel, and law enforcement. It also undertook to amend the model regulations to expand the predicate offense for money laundering and to provide for the creation of national forfeiture funds. In addition, the group finalized a directory of contact points for the purpose of effecting information exchange and mutual legal assistance, which would be accessible through the OAS's web-page.

6.21 Asia-Europe Meeting (ASEM)

The Communiqué of the Asia-Europe meeting (ASEM2), held in London on April 3–4, 1998, stated that "[t]he development of policies against money laundering has been helped by the FATF's forty recommendations which are now the internationally accepted standard."

6.22 Riga Declaration

In a declaration signed at Riga in November 1996 by their Prime Ministers, Estonia, Latvia, and Lithuania committed their governments to the fight against money laundering. The preamble of the declaration states, *inter alia*, that these governments are committed to implementing anti-money laundering measures based on the forty recommendations of the FATF.

Notes

1. Australia; Austria; Belgium; Canada; Denmark; Finland; France; Germany; Greece; Hong Kong, China; Iceland; Ireland; Italy; Japan; Luxembourg; the Netherlands; New Zealand; Norway; Portugal; Singapore; Spain; Sweden; Switzerland; Turkey; the United Kingdom; and the United States.
2. European Commission and Gulf Cooperation Council.
3. See Appendix VI for the text of the Annual Report on Money Laundering Typologies dated February 10, 1999.
4. In the Kingston Declaration, the governments of the CFATF members also made a commitment to implement the 19 additional CFATF Recommendations. The CFATF has been conducting a typologies exercise to evaluate and determine whether any interpretative notes and/or amendments to the FATF revised Recommendations and the CFATF 19 recommendations are appropriate.
5. Aruba and the Netherlands Antilles are part of the Kingdom of the Netherlands, which is a member of FATF.
6. The Commonwealth members that are members of the FATF are: Australia, Canada, New Zealand, Singapore, and the United Kingdom.
7. In December 1995, the ministers responsible for addressing money laundering in the States of the Western Hemisphere met in Buenos Aires, where they endorsed a

Statement of Principles to combat money laundering and agreed to recommend to their Governments a Plan of Action reflecting this Statement of Principles for adoption and implementation. The Plan of Action specifically provided that the Governments intended to institute ongoing assessments of the implementation of the Plan of Action within the framework of the OAS. This and other activities identified in this Plan were remitted to the CICAD for action.

PART FOUR

INTERNATIONAL OFFSHORE FINANCIAL CENTERS

CHAPTER SIXTEEN

ANDORRA

Background Information

Geographic and Demographic Data

Location	Andorra is situated in the Eastern Pyrenees, between France and Spain. In winter, it is one hour ahead of Greenwich mean time (GMT); in summer, it is two hours ahead.
Capital	Andorra la Vella.
Area	174 square miles.
Population	64,000.
Languages	Catalan is the official language; French and Castilian are widely used.
Access	There is easy access to Andorra by air, train, and road.
Telecommunications	Excellent.

Government

Andorra is an independent European state. It is a democratic parliamentary coprincipality. The princes of Andorra are co-heads of state.

Political and Economic Stability

Andorra has no army and is a declared neutral territory. It has a high degree of political and economic stability, with 0% unemployment.

Business Environment

Andorra has a liberal business climate. The principality is a growing commercial and financial center that encourages foreign investment in the commercial and service sectors provided it is associated with Andorran interests.

Tourism, the mainstay of Andorra's economy, accounts for about 80% of gross domestic product (GDP). An estimated 10 million tourists visit annually, attracted by Andorra's duty-free status and by its summer and winter resorts. Andorra's comparative advantage has recently been eroded as the economies of neighboring France and Spain have opened up, providing broader availability of goods and lower tariffs. The banking sector, with its tax haven status, also contributes substantially to the economy. Agricultural production is limited by a scarcity of arable land, and most food has to be imported. The principal livestock activity is sheep raising. Manufacturing consists mainly of cigarettes, cigars, and furniture. Andorra is a member of the European Union (EU) Customs Union and is treated as an EU member for trade in manufactured goods (no tariffs) and as a non-EU member for agricultural products.

Currency and Exchange Control

There is no Andorran currency and no exchange control. Any internationally quoted currency may be used, but within Andorra the French franc and Spanish peseta are commonly used.

Disclosure of Information

Banking secrecy is specifically protected under Andorran finance legislation and the Penal Code. Banks are required to maintain secrecy and to protect against money laundering.

Legal System

Andorra is a civil law jurisdiction. The legal system is based on Roman, Catalonian, and traditional law. The court of justice has three instances, and there are criminal, civil, and administrative jurisdictions. The independence of the judiciary is assured under the 1993 constitution. Recent legislation of significance to offshore operations and transactions includes the Passive Residence Law 1996 and regulations.

Taxation (Direct and Indirect)

Corporations

Andorran companies and individuals are not subject to any direct or income tax.

Andorran resident companies are not subject to profit taxes on their worldwide or national income.

There is an annual fixed tax on the following corporations:

Sls[1] ptas[2] 100,000
Sas[3] ptas 110,000

The annual tax is reduced to ptas 25,000 if the corporation pays municipal taxes.

Capital Gains Tax

There is no tax on capital gains in Andorra.

Withholding Taxes

There are no withholding taxes imposed in Andorra.

Annual Registry Charge

An annual charge is levied on commercial and service activities. SLs are charged ptas 50,000; SAs are charged ptas 75,000.

Import Duties

Import duties are imposed under the customs union with European Union countries, allowing free circulation of goods originating from EU countries. The same customs duty is applied on goods originating from a third source, as is applied by the EU.

Indirect Goods Tax

This tax is similar to VAT and is levied on the internal production and import of goods at rates between 4% and 7%. Petrol, liquor, and tobacco are taxed at higher rates.

Utilities Tax

Electricity supply and telephone services are taxed at 10%.

Social Security Tax

Social security tax is paid at a rate of 18% of salaries: 5% by the employee and 13% by the employer.

Other Taxes

Residents of Andorra are not subject to inheritance or gift tax. There is no limitation or tax on the transfer of income to persons living abroad.

Tax Treaties and Double Taxation

Andorra has no tax treaties with other countries. Information concerning transactions carried out in Andorra is not divulged to foreign fiscal authorities. Foreign tax credits and double tax relief do not apply.

Other Treaties

Andorra has established a trade agreement and customs union with the European Union.

Incentives (Tax and Nontax)

Hotel developments can obtain credit from banking institutions at a reduced rate.

Corporations

Types of Corporations

A corporation may be incorporated under the Corporations Act 1983 as a *societat per accions* (SA), with capital divided into shares with limited responsibility; a *societat de responsabilitat limitada* (SL), with capital shared between partners with limited responsibility; or a *societat colectiva* (SRC), with capital shared between partners with unlimited responsibility.

Checklist for Corporations

- The corporate name is protected by registration.
- Two-thirds of the capital must be owned by Andorran citizens, except for companies of public or social interest.
- A draft of the articles of association must be submitted to the government prior to incorporation for approval of the foreign participation.
- Incorporation usually takes thirty days. Incorporation is registered in the register of companies. Once registered, a corporation can operate in Andorra or internationally. The cost of incorporation is the same for all types of companies, but the annual management costs vary.
- SAs require a minimum capital of ptas 5 million and three partners. There is no minimum capital requirement for SLs. The maximum capital is ptas 5 million, and there must be between two and ten partners. There is no minimum established capital requirement for SRCs.
- Shares must be registered. No share may carry more than one vote. Shareholders have the right to participate in the distribution of profits, the right to vote in the general meetings of shareholders, and preferred subscription in the event of an increase of capital. Although two-thirds of a corporation's capital must be owned by Andorran citizens, a notarial deed of promise of sale can be produced on behalf of the beneficial owner.
- The directors must keep proper books of accounts and prepare financial statements within five months of the year-end. Such statements must be

presented to the shareholders for approval. The statements are not required to be filed or audited, unless they are the statements of banks, financial companies, and insurance companies.

- The president, general manager, or sole director must be an Andorran citizen.

Other Forms of Business Organization

Sole Proprietorships

A citizen or resident of more than ten years may carry on business as a sole trader.

Partnerships

There are no limited partnerships. Civil companies may be established by two or more persons to incorporate a partnership with unlimited liability as reflected in a private contract or notarial deed.

Foreign Corporations

Branches may be established in Andorra only by insurance companies. A resident delegate must be designated. Such branches are not subject to direct tax.

Nonresidents and nonresident offshore companies have no legally defined status in Andorran law.

Banking

The banking system is regulated by the Finance Law 1993. It is controlled by the Insitut Nacional Andorra de Finances. Deposits may be made in any convertible currency, and the interest and principal are not subject to tax.

Trusts

There is no specific Andorran legislation concerning trusts.

Notes

1. See definition under *Corporations*.
2. Pesetas (ptas).
3. See definition under *Corporations*.

CHAPTER SEVENTEEN

ARUBA

Background Information

Geographic and Demographic Data

Location	Aruba is an island about twelve miles off the coast of Venezuela in South America; it is six hours behind GMT.
Capital	Oranjestad.
Area	75 square miles.
Population	68,031.
Languages	Dutch is the official language; Papiamento is the native dialect. English is widely spoken, and Spanish is also in use.
Access	There are daily flights to major cities in Europe, the United States, and Latin America.
Telecommunications	Excellent.

Government

Until 1986, Aruba formed part of the Netherlands Antilles. It has since acquired a separate status and has full autonomy in internal affairs. However, Aruba is not independent but is part of the Kingdom of the Netherlands. As such, it is an associate member of the European Union.

Political and Economic Stability

Aruba is politically and economically stable. It is a parliamentary democracy, and the queen of the Netherlands is represented by a governor. It has successful tourism and construction industries and has commenced oil refinement. Unemployment is below 1%.

Business Environment

Government attitude to offshore activities: Until 1988, tax haven activities in Aruba were treaty based. As a result of the termination of several tax treaties, the government has introduced legislation to encourage its zero-tax haven status. Aruba's well-developed legal and commercial infrastructure makes it an attractive Caribbean tax haven.

Employment: The low unemployment rate means that there are job vacancies in Aruba. Foreigners practicing a profession must have a work permit, which will usually be granted only if no suitably qualified local is available. Applications for work permits should be filed through a local employer, who will bear the cost of any government expenses in relation to the application.

Local business requirements: A business license is required for carrying on business in Aruba. Registration with the Chamber of Commerce is also required. Special licenses for holding corporations and finance and royalty corporations are not necessary.

Currency

The local currency is the Aruban florin. Since 1986, the florin has been tied to the U.S. dollar at a fixed rate of Af 1.79 to the dollar.

Disclosure of Information

Secrecy of information: All natural and legal persons carrying on business in Aruba are obliged to provide information to the tax inspector's office. However, tax advisors, law firms, trust corporations, banks, and auditors strive to maintain secrecy on behalf of their clients.

Banking secrecy: Numbered bank accounts are not permitted. A natural person must show identity to open an account, and a corporation must lodge a certificate from the Chamber of Commerce. There are no specific bank secrecy laws, although banks are required to report unusual transactions and to properly identify their clients when providing financial services. The Anti–Money Laundering Ordinances 1996 cover "all-crimes" money laundering.

Disclosure in company formation: Disclosure to a public authority of the beneficial owner of an offshore corporation is required in Aruba. Such disclosure must be made to the respective trust companies. The good standing of the beneficial owner must be documented. There are official guidelines relating to such documentation. The audit of Aruba exempt corporations and offshore NVs[1] is not required.

A local registered agent is required for Aruba exempt corporations. The information to be lodged with the agent concerns the beneficial owners and their good standing. The agent will disclose beneficial ownership if requested by the high commissioner's office.

International cooperation measures: Aruba is party to treaties for cooperation with foreign states and investigators. The procedure involved depends on the treaty. There is also a procedure in the new Code of Criminal Procedure. The code provides for an appeal against cooperation, and an appeal can also be discussed in summary proceedings.

The Tax Regulation, or *Belastingregeling voor het Koninkrijk* (BRK), governs fiscal relations among the three partners of the kingdom of the Netherlands in order to avoid double taxation. It contains an exchange of information agreement, which provides rules for the exchange of information among the three countries. Aruba has also entered into mutual legal assistance treaties with the United States, among others. These contain exchange of information agreements concerning fiscal delicts.

A request for assistance in an investigation into tax evasion will be treated favorably by the Aruban authorities if it is not in breach of Aruban law.

Legal System

General

The legal system is based on the Dutch civilian system, with a civil and a commercial code. The English common law has also influenced Aruban law. All laws are in Dutch, and the highest court is the Dutch Supreme Court at the Hague. A constitution has been in operation since January 1, 1986.

Treaties

See "Tax Treaties and Double Taxation."

Tax Treaties and Double Taxation

The United States–Netherlands Antilles and Aruban Tax Treaty and the U.K. Tax Treaty were terminated in 1988. The BRK governs fiscal relations among the three partners of the kingdom of the Netherlands in order to avoid double taxation.

Corporations

Types of Corporations

There are two groups of limited corporations in Aruba: the *Naamloze Vennootschap* (NV) and the *Aruba Vrijgestelde Vennootschap* (AVV), or Aruba exempt corporation (AEC). The latter has a more modern corporate structure than the Aruban NV. It provides an attractive vehicle for international tax planning because of the absence of taxes, the relatively low cost of formation and maintenance, the flexibility of its corporate structure, and the absence of red tape and regulatory restrictions.

The Aruba Exempt Corporation

The Aruba exempt corporation, or Aruban zero-tax corporation, is a limited liability corporation with a capital divided into shares. Shareholders are not bound to contribute to the corporation's losses over and above the amount that has been contributed to the share capital. There are fewer regulatory restrictions and licensing requirements for the AEC than for the NV corporation. There are also fewer corporate formalities to be observed. These features, together with the absence of taxation, make the AEC a suitable vehicle for international transactions.

An AEC may not conduct business activities in Aruba other than those activities that are necessary in connection with the maintenance of its office in Aruba. AECs may also not conduct banking activities, insurance company activities, or other activities that would make them creditors of financial institutions under Aruban law. This prohibition applies regardless of whether the activities are conducted in or outside of Aruba. The shares of an AEC cannot be held directly or indirectly by Aruban residents or by companies established in Aruba.

Checklist for AECs

- Formation of an AEC requires one founder only. The incorporation document does not have to be published in the *Official Gazette,* as is the case with NVs; there is also not any stamp duty on the incorporation document, as is required for NVs.
- Prior to formation, the corporate name must be checked in order to establish whether it is already in use. This check is carried out with the Justice Department.
- The required minimum authorized capital, which can be expressed in any currency, is Afl 10,000.
- The articles can provide for voting shares and for nonvoting shares. They can also provide for shares with limited voting rights. Shares can be issued either in registered form or to bearer. A share certificate can be issued. It is also possible to issue preferential and cumulative preferential shares.
- An AEC is managed by one or more managing directors, of whom at least one must be nominated at incorporation. Only individuals who are not resident in Aruba can act as directors.
- Each AEC must have at least one local legal representative. An AEC that does not comply with this regulation is not in good standing and can be dissolved by court decision upon application by the attorney general. Only Aruban corporations whose bylaws expressly authorize them to act as local

legal representatives of AECs and that are in possession of a business license may so act.

- An AEC does not have to file yearly financial reports with any official or government authority. There are also no audit requirements. The articles of association can even provide that the requirement to prepare financial reports be waived.
- The AEC is exempt from corporate tax. Shareholders are also exempt from personal income tax. There is no withholding tax on interest or on royalties, nor is there any withholding tax on dividends or other profit distributions paid to nonresident shareholders. Inheritance taxes are not levied on the death of nonresident shareholders of AECs.
- An AEC does not need a business license, a director's license, or a foreign exchange license to operate. There is thus no restriction as to an AEC's financial affairs, regardless of whether its transactions are carried out through an offshore bank in Aruba or a banking institution in any other part of the world.
- The commercial register is open to inspection by the public. It contains a copy of the articles of association of each AEC, the names of the managing directors, and the resident legal representative. Names and addresses of shareholders are not filed with any Aruban authority.

Fees and Costs

An AEC must pay an annual registration fee of US$285 to the government. It must also register at the commercial register. The registration fee is approximately US$40 annually, based on the minimum authorized capital.

Formation charges for an AEC are approximately US$1,000. This figure includes the notarial fees for incorporation, the first fixed registration fee due annually to the government, and the first registration fee at the commercial register. It does not include the registered agent or resident managing director fee, which is between US$250 and US$500 and is also payable annually.

Trusts

There are no trusts in Aruba.

Notes

1. See definitions under "Corporations."

CHAPTER EIGHTEEN

BAHAMAS

Background Information

Geographic and Demographic Data

Location	The Bahamas, an archipelago of some seven hundred islands, lies in the North Atlantic Ocean, southeast of Florida. It operates either on eastern standard time, which is five hours behind GMT, or, between the first Sunday in April and the last Sunday in October, on eastern daylight time, which is four hours behind GMT.
Capital	Nassau.
Area	5,359 square miles.
Population	275,941.
Languages	English is the national language. Creole is also spoken.
Access	The Bahamas is served by sophisticated modern airports, with daily direct flights to North American cities and good connections to other parts of the world.
Telecommunications	Excellent.

Government

The Commonwealth of the Bahamas is an independent state within the Commonwealth.

Political and Economic Stability

The Bahamas is politically stable. Its political system is based on the Westminster parliamentary system and the rule of law. The Queen of England is the head of state and is represented by a governor-general.

The Bahamas is an economically stable, developing nation with an economy heavily dependent on tourism and offshore banking. It is one of the largest offshore financial centers in the Caribbean and one of the largest Eurodollar centers in the world. The economy is closely linked to that of the United States. Tourism accounts for more than 50% of GDP and directly or indirectly employs 40% of the archipelago's labor force. The construction sector benefits from hotel rehabilitation and the government's ongoing housing development program. Unemployment currently runs at 15%.

Business Environment

Government attitude to offshore activities: The government is aware of the importance to the economy of the continued development of the country as a tax haven and as a base for foreign commercial and financial operations. It has introduced a national investment policy to encourage foreign investment, particularly in the areas of property development, information and business data processing services, ship registration, repair services, manufacturing, financial services, and offshore medical centers. The government is also committed to maintaining the Bahamas as an international financial center. Rules and regulations prevent the laundering of criminally derived assets and continue the enforcement of bank secrecy laws.

The Bahamas Investment Authority is a government agency that facilitates foreign and local investment. The authority provides guidance to the government in respect of investment policy, and it has the following duties:

(a) identifying financial services available within the Bahamas;
(b) promoting these services internationally;
(c) facilitating the smooth entry of respondents into the Bahamas business sector;
(d) encouraging growth of the financial services sector; and
(e) acting as a clearinghouse of interested respondents by conducting background checks on their financial soundness and business integrity.

Employment: It is government policy to advance Bahamians, and employers who wish to employ foreign staff must satisfy the government that there is no suitably qualified Bahamian for the position and that they have implemented a training program for Bahamians. A work permit is required for foreign workers. It is usually granted for a period of one year, but it can be extended to three years.

Local business requirements: A license is required to carry on any kind of business in the Bahamas, including practicing a profession.[1] It is also necessary to obtain a license to operate a hotel[2] or to carry on banking or trust business[3] within the Bahamas. In the Port Area of Freeport in Grand Bahama, a license must be obtained from the port authority to carry on any manufacturing, trading, financial, or professional activity.

Foreigners and Immigration

Persons who wish to reside in the Bahamas without working must apply for a residence permit from the Immigration Department. The government has enacted the International Persons Landholding Act 1993 to encourage investors to buy homes in the Bahamas. The act improves the approval and registration process in real estate transactions involving foreign persons or companies. Accelerated consideration of applications for annual or permanent residence is given to major international investors and approved owners of a residence valued at BAH 250,000 or more. Nonresidents who own homes in the Bahamas can apply to the director of immigration for an annual home owner resident card for BAH 500. Spouses and juveniles have entry on the same card.

Currency and Exchange Control

The Bahamian dollar (BAH) is fixed at US$1.00. Exchange control is administered by the Central Bank of the Bahamas, which also determines all questions of residency. The Bahamian currency is not freely convertible for residents of the Bahamas, but it is for nonresidents with approved investment status. International business companies have exchange control exemption for twenty years.

Disclosure of Information

Secrecy of information: Protection of confidentiality is the cornerstone on which the banking industry has been built. The duty is imposed on bankers, attorneys, auditors, and government officials. Disclosure is permissible with the client's consent and under compulsion of law. A code of conduct was created in 1985 by members of the Association of International Banks and Trust Companies (AIBT) to enhance the reputation of the Bahamas as a financial center, to prevent the use of banks and trust companies for criminal purposes, and to adhere to the principle of banking confidentiality. The code has, to a large extent, been replaced by the Money Laundering (Proceeds of Crime) Act 1995. The act has no bearing on tax or fiscal matters.

Disclosure in company formation and trust settlement: The beneficial owner of an offshore corporation need not be disclosed on formation of the corporation. Legislation governing the confidentiality of disclosure generally includes the International Business Companies Act, the Banks and Trust Companies Regulation Act, and the Statutory Duties of Confidentiality.

Corporate audits are not required, although a local registered agent is. Copies of the register of directors and officers, records, minutes, and an imprint of the common seal must be lodged with the agent. The agent will disclose beneficial ownership only pursuant to an order of the Supreme Court of the Bahamas. A trustee is not required to register the beneficiaries of a trust. Banks are required to maintain evidence of their customers' identities. This requirement also applies to limited partnerships and limited liability companies.

International cooperation measures: The Foreign Tribunals Evidence Act 1856, which extends to civil and criminal matters, has a procedure for cooperation with foreign states and investigators. Under this act, letters of request are taken out and an ex parte application is made to a judge or the registrar of the Supreme Court. An appeal against this procedure may be lodged with the court of appeal.

The mutual legal assistance treaties govern the exchange of information with the United States, Canada, and the United Kingdom. The Reciprocal Enforcement of Judgments Act 1924 governs the enforcement of judgments obtained in Commonwealth countries. The common law applies in respect of judgments obtained in other jurisdictions. The foreign judgment must be registered in the Supreme Court within twelve months of being awarded. It will then be enforced as though made by the Supreme Court. At common law, the judgment creditor must bring a new action on the foreign judgment. In both cases, the judgment cannot relate to revenue matters.

The Bahamas has not entered into any tax treaties. The mutual legal assistance treaties contain exchange of information agreements. All information, excluding tax matters, is covered under the agreements. Disclosure is limited to criminal matters, as tax evasion does not constitute a crime in the Bahamas. A request for assistance in an investigation into tax evasion would therefore be turned down by the authorities.

Legal System

General

Bahamian law is based on English common law, although there are numerous Bahamian statutes. The highest court is the court of appeal.

Legislation

The principal provisions affecting offshore operations and transactions are contained in the following:

- Banks Act Cap 285
- Companies Act Cap 279
- Exchange Control Regulations Act Cap 330
- External Insurance (Amendment) Act 1996
- Fiscal Measures (Miscellaneous Amendments) Act 1990
- Insurance Act 1969
- International Business Companies Act 1989
- Money Laundering (Proceeds of Crime) Act 1995
- Mutual Funds Act 1995

- Stamp Act Cap 334
- Trustee Act (1893) Cap 164
- Variation of Trusts Act Cap 166

Case Law

Important recent cases are

- *Private Trust Corporation v. Grupo Torras SA* (1997/1998) 1 OFLR 443 (Court of Appeal, Bahamas)
- *Grupo Torras v. Mees Pierson (Bahamas) Ltd.* (1998/1999) 2 OFLR 163 (Court of Appeal, Bahamas)

Treaties

Mutual legal assistance treaties have been signed with the United States, Canada, and the United Kingdom. There are no tax treaties.

Taxation

The Bahamas is known for its tax haven status. There are no corporate, personal income, capital gains, profit, sales, inheritance, or estate taxes. There are no withholding taxes on dividends, interest, or royalties or any payroll taxes. The following taxes are levied:

Customs Duties

Customs duties are the major source of government revenue and are levied under the Tariff Act 1975. Duty is charged on all imported goods, such as food items, 22.5%, and motor vehicles, 52.5%.

Stamp Duties

Stamp duties are levied under the Stamp Act Cap 334. Following an amendment, the rates now also apply to deeds of conveyance, assignment or transfer of realty, and shares. There is a limit on the duty levied on the issue of Eurocurrency bonds.

Real Estate Taxes

Real estate tax is levied annually. Land of any sort in the Family Islands and undeveloped land in New Providence is exempt from the tax. Commercial farming property is also exempt. Owner-occupied property is exempt from the tax in respect of the first BAH 100,000 of its value. The rates on owner-occupied property are as follows:

On the first BAH 100,000 of value	exempt
On value between BAH 100,001 and BAH 500,000	1%
On value over BAH 500,000	1.5%

The rates on undeveloped property owned by nonresidents are as follows:

On value less than BAH 3,000	BAH 30
On value between BAH 3,000 and BAH 100,000	1%
On value over BAH 100,000	1.5%

The rates on commercial property are as follows:

On value less than BAH 500,000	1%
On value more than BAH 500,000	2%

Casino Tax

License fees for gaming casinos are stipulated in the Lotteries and Gaming Act 1969. The Gaming Machines Act 1974 imposes a tax on gaming machines.

Insurance Tax

Registered insurers pay a tax of 1% on premiums collected in terms of the Insurance (Amendment) Act 1975. This tax applies only to domestic insurers authorized to do business in the Bahamas.

Hotel Tax

The Hotels Act 1970 imposes a hotel guest tax. The act also provides a scale of fees based on the number of bedrooms in the hotel.

Shipping Tax

All ships passing through Bahamian waters are subject to light dues under the Light Dues Act 1976.

Tax Treaties and Double Taxation

There are no tax treaties, and the Bahamas is not party to any double taxation agreement.

Other Treaties

Mutual legal assistance treaties have been signed with the United States, Canada, and the United Kingdom.

Incentives (Tax and Nontax)

Tax Incentives

Various concessions provide unique opportunities for manufacturers to establish profitable offshore plants in the Bahamas where they pay no taxes, operate under bond, and obtain duty-free entry for their goods to the leading industrial markets.

The Lomé Convention: This provides for trade cooperation, export earnings from commodities, and industrial, financial, and technical cooperation. The main benefit received by the Bahamas comes from trade cooperation, which provides that all manufactured and tropical agricultural products have free access to the European Union.

General system of preference (GSP): Semimanufacturing industry is encouraged under the GSP scheme, which is a vehicle for the expansion of the industrial and manufacturing sectors of developing (beneficiary) countries. It enables various beneficiary countries to augment their production with skills and material from other trading neighbors, so long as prescribed minimum values are added in the exporting country. Exports to developed (donor) countries or markets will qualify for duty-free or low duty treatment.

The USA Congress Trade Act 1974: This act provides duty concessions similar to those of the Lomé Convention with respect to free access to the U.S. markets for goods manufactured in designated countries, including the Bahamas. To qualify under this scheme, the exporting product must have a minimum of 35% Bahamian content of raw material and labor.

Organization of American States (OAS): The benefits to be derived from this association are in the areas of technical assistance in economic, social, and cultural development.

Caribbean Basin Initiative (CBI): The CBI is designed to promote growth in the Caribbean region by stimulating investment in nontraditional industries that produce goods for the U.S. market. Under the initiative, U.S. tariffs are removed on most products shipped from the Caribbean to the United States, which is the region's largest market. The Caribbean Basin Economic Recovery Expansion Act 1990 extends the original CBI legislation. The most important provision is the permanent extension of the duty-free treatment most goods produced in the region receive upon entry into the United States.

Cabican: Cabican is a Canadian program for trade investment and industrial cooperation for the Commonwealth Caribbean region. The main feature is the unilateral extension by Canada of the preferential duty-free access to the Canadian market for almost all imports from the Commonwealth Caribbean region.

Freeport

In 1955, the government entered into a ninety-nine-year agreement with the Grand Bahama Port Authority Limited, a private company, whereby the Port Authority was granted concessions with regard to the Port Area at Hawksbill Creek on Grand Bahama Island. The concession allows materials and supplies other than consumables to enter the Port Area free of customs duties and other taxes if imported by the Port Authority or a licensee. The agreement guaranteed the Port Authority against the imposition of real estate taxes, personal property taxes, rates, capital levies, and capital gains tax until 1990. Similar guarantees related to the earnings of the Port Authority and its licensees until 1990. There are further guarantees against the levying of excise taxes until 2054 upon or against goods other than consumables imported into the Port Area or manufactured within the Port Authority. Similar provisions apply with regard to export taxes.

Development Encouragement Incentives

Investment incentives, including exemption from customs duties on building materials, equipment, and raw materials; business licensing fees; and real estate taxes for a period of up to twenty years, are contained in the following statutes:

- Export Manufacturing Industries Encouragement Act
- Industries Encouragement Act
- Agricultural Manufacturers Act
- Tariff Act
- Free Trade Zone Act
- Hotels Encouragement Act
- Spirits and Beer Manufacturers Act

Corporations

(The domestic laws of the Bahamas refer to corporations as companies. This terminology is retained in this chapter.)

As the Bahamas is one of the newest Caribbean jurisdictions, it has benefited from the mistakes made by other jurisdictions and has implemented highly flexible legislation that allows operation of a company's affairs in the way most appropriate to the beneficial owner.

Types of Companies

Bahamian companies are incorporated under the Companies Act 1992. Such companies may carry on business with individuals resident in the Bahamas and may also carry on from within the Bahamas banking or trust business and insurance and reinsurance. With regard to the migration of companies, the registered office of a local company must be situated in the Bahamas, but its location may be changed from one part of the Bahamas to another.

International business companies (IBCs) are governed by the International Business Companies Act 1989. An IBC is a company that does not

(a) carry on business with persons resident in the Bahamas;
(b) own real estate in the Bahamas or lease property other than for use as an office;
(c) carry on banking, trust, insurance, or reinsurance business; or
(d) provide a registered office for companies.

Limited duration companies (LDCs) are similar to IBCs, but the company life is limited to a maximum of thirty years.

Checklist for IBCs

- Once incorporated, IBCs are very cost effective, and they are guaranteed tax exemption for twenty years. However, because of a lack of public registers, ownership is difficult to prove. IBCs are not recommended for high-profile trading operations.
- IBCs are governed by the International Business Companies Act 1989 and the common law.
- Certain words are prohibited from being used in the company name, for instance, Assurance, Bank, or Building Society. Names must end with an appropriate suffix such as Incorporated, Société Anonyme, or Limited.
- Incorporation takes one to two days. No minimum capital is required. There is no requirement regarding information being furnished to the authorities prior to incorporation or prior to tax status being granted.
- Shelf companies are available.
- Capital duty is payable on a sliding scale. From B$0 to B$5,000, duty is payable at B$100. From B$5,001 to B$50,000, duty is payable at B$300, and from B$50,001, it is payable at B$1,000.
- A minimum of one shareholder is required. Bearer shares and shares of no par value are allowed.
- A minimum of one director is required. Corporate directors are permitted, and there is no restriction on the residence of directors.
- A company secretary is not mandatory. A corporate secretary is permitted, and there is no restriction on the secretary's residence.
- An IBC must have a registered office and a registered agent.

- The memorandum and articles of association, the registered office, and the registered agent are on the public file. Copies of the register of members and register of directors must be kept at the registered office, with an impression of the company seal.
- The company must have a seal and registers of members and directors.
- There are no requirements regarding the keeping and filing of accounts. Annual returns are not required.
- There are no requirements regarding the holding of meetings.
- An annual fee of B$100 is payable to the government if the authorized capital does not exceed B$5,000.
- Exchange controls do not apply to IBCs. There are no double tax treaties.
- Migration of IBCs to and from the Bahamas is facilitated, also allowing for the immediate transfer in or out of assets.

Other Forms of Business Organization

Partnerships

Exempted limited partnerships (ELPs): The Exempted Limited Partnership Act 1994 allows a normal partnership to be structured in such a way that it provides more flexibility in transacting business. Like the IBC, the ELP is free to carry on lawful business anywhere in the world, except with the "public in the Bahamas." However, this does not specifically preclude doing business with IBCs or foreign companies registered in the Bahamas under the Companies Act 1992.

An ELP must have one or more persons as general partners, who assume responsibility for all debts and obligations of the partnership in the event the assets of the partnership are inadequate, and others who are limited partners, although a general partner may also have an interest as a limited partner. At least one general partner must be a resident of the Bahamas or be incorporated under the International Business Companies Act 1989 or the Companies Act 1992.

Every ELP must have a registered office in the Bahamas. All business of the partnership must be transacted by a general partner and not a limited partner, who may be held liable as a general partner if he so acts.

An ELP must be registered with the registrar of companies. Certain disclosures and undertakings must be made as to the nature of the business of the ELP and the names and addresses of all general partners.

An ELP is exempt for fifty years, from the issuance of the certificate of registration, from any business license fee, stamp duty, income tax, capital gains tax, or any other tax on income or distributions. It is also exempt from exchange control, except where a partner is a resident of the Bahamas for exchange control purposes. Partners, their executors, or administrators are also exempt from any estate, inheritance, succession, or gift tax on their interest in the partnership.

Foreign Companies

A foreign company is any incorporated or unincorporated body formed under the laws of a country outside the Bahamas. To be incorporated in the Bahamas, the foreign company must file a statement stating the following:

(a) the company name, the jurisdiction in which it was incorporated, and the date of its incorporation;

(b) the manner in which it was incorporated, the particulars of its corporate instruments, and the duration of the company;

(c) the extent to which the liability of the shareholders or members is limited;

(d) the business the company will carry on in the Bahamas and the date the company intends to commence its undertakings in the Bahamas;

(e) the authorized, subscribed, and paid-up or stated capital and the shares that the company is authorized to issue, and their nominal or par value, if any;

(f) the full addresses of the principal offices of the company in and outside the Bahamas; and

(g) the full names, addresses, and occupations of the directors.

Banks and Trust Corporations

Banks and trust companies are governed by the Banks and Trust Companies Act 1965 and by rules and regulations formulated by the Central Bank. To incorporate a bank or trust company in the Bahamas, application must be made in writing to the minister of finance. The application must contain the name of the bank or trust company; the address of the head or registered office or, if the head or registered office is outside the Bahamas, the address of the principal office in the Bahamas; the name of the officer who is to be the bank or trust company's authorized agent in the Bahamas; and the name of the officer who, in the absence or inability to act of the authorized agent, is to be the bank or trust company's authorized agent.

A bank or trust company may be issued the following licenses: dealer, agent, public licensee, resident, nonresident, restricted, nonactive, or nominee.

Insurance

An offshore insurance company is an insurance company incorporated in the Bahamas under the Companies Act 1992. Such a company is licensed under the Insurance Act 1969 or the External Insurance Act 1983, and it manages its business from the Bahamas but insures risks located outside the Bahamas.

To qualify for registration as an external insurer under the External Insurance Act, a company must show that the offshore or captive insurer will be accepting BAH 500,000 or more in insurance premiums from an affiliated company. All other applicants will be accommodated under the Insurance Act as nonresident insurers.

The provisions relating to offshore insurance companies under the Insurance Act and the External Insurance Act are as follows:

	Insurance Act	*External Insurance Act*
Minimum capital (general)	BAH 140,000	BAH 100,000
Net premium preferred (capital and surplus)	5:1 on net premium up to BAH 7 million	5:1 on net premium up to BAH 7 million
	10:1 on net premium in excess of BAH 7 million	10:1 on net premium in excess of BAH 7 million
Shareholders, directors, and officers	Names, addresses, and references	Names, addresses, and references
Local representation	Appoint principal representative	No specific reference
Lawyer	Not mandatory	Not mandatory
Accountant	Independent accountant	Independent and local
Actuary (life office)	Triennial valuation	No provision

Shipping

Offshore shipping companies are not subject to taxes. The Bahamian shipping register allows the nationals of any country to own and operate foreign-going Bahamian-registered ships without any residency requirements. There are also no restrictions on transferring ships to or from Bahamian registry. Ships over 150 gross tons are exempt from paying customs duties and stamp duty on the value of the ship.

Foreign-owned ships less than twelve years old at the time of registry may be registered in the Bahamas. Such vessels must be over 1,600 net registered tons and must be engaged in foreign trade.

Registration fees are payable as follows:

Ships under 5,000 net tons	BAH 1.20 per ton
Ships over 5,000 net tons	BAH 1.10 per ton
Ships up to 25,000 net tons	BAH 2,400 minimum fee
Ships over 25,000 net tons	BAH 27,500 maximum fee

The Bahamas has a flag of convenience register and does not impose minimum wage standards or nationality rules on its ships. However, in a commitment to the continued growth and reputable international profile of the rapidly growing ships register, the government has established the Bahamas Maritime Authority to promote, facilitate, and encourage the development of ship registration and maritime administration in the Bahamas and to regulate, control, and administer all matters related to merchant shipping provided for under the Merchant Shipping Act 1976 or any other related law.

Mutual Funds

The Mutual Funds Act 1995 introduces a reporting, disclosure, and monitoring requirement on all forms of mutual funds operating either in or from the Bahamas. "Mutual fund" refers to a company, trust, or partnership that issues equity interests, the purpose or effect of which is the investment of its funds with the aim of spreading investment risks and enabling investors in it to receive profits or gains. "Equity interest" refers to a share, trust, or partnership interest in a mutual fund that carries an entitlement to participate in the profits or gains of the fund and is redeemable or may be repurchased at the option of the investor.

A mutual fund must be licensed by either the Securities Board or a mutual fund administrator with an unrestricted license. The Securities Board is established under the Securities Board Act 1995. An application for a mutual fund license must be accompanied by

(a) the current "offering document";

(b) details necessary to satisfy the licensor that the applicant has a registered office in the Bahamas; and

(c) the application fee.

Before granting the license, the licensor must be satisfied by the applicant that each promoter is of sound reputation, that the administration of the fund will be undertaken by a person who has sufficient expertise to administer the fund and is of sound reputation, and that the business of the fund and any offer of equity interests in it will be carried out in the proper manner.

An "authorized mutual fund" is exempted from the approval process if it has a minimum equity interest purchase of BAH 50,000 or if its equity interests are listed on a recognized stock exchange. However, it must still file a current offering document with the Securities Board, register with the board, and pay the annual registration fee.

An "exempt mutual fund" is one in which the equity interests are held by not more than fifteen investors or which is licensed in a prescribed jurisdiction. Such a fund does not have to comply with the approval provisions.

Trusts

The law of trusts in the Bahamas is based on English common law, as amended by the Trustee Act 1893.

Stamp duties are payable on creation of and on transfer of assets to the trust. Bahamian trusts are not required to be registered. However, for the purposes of banking and exchange control, registration with the Bahamas Exchange Control authorities is required for designation and approval as a Bahamian nonresident trust.

The Trust (Choice of Governing Law) Act 1989 provides protection from forced inheritance claims against Bahamian trusts or settlers domiciled in civil law countries.

The Fraudulent Dispositions Act 1991 allows persons to create an asset protection trust while still preserving the ability of creditors to void a settlement where it is intended to defraud. The period of limitation for claiming against or attacking the trust is two years after the disposition of the assets. The burden of proof is on the claimant to show that the settlor knew of the specific claim and intended to commit a fraud.

The rule against perpetuities applies to Bahamian trusts. However, the rule against accumulations does not apply, provided the trust does not breach the rule against perpetuities.

At present, nonresidents and nonresident offshore trusts are not recognized in Bahamian law.

Notes

1. See the Shop Licenses Act Cap 341 (1987); the Liquor Licenses Act Cap 336 (1987); Cap 302 and 287 of 1987.
2. Hotels Act 1970: see Cap 262 (1987).
3. Banks and Trust Companies Regulation Act 1965.

CHAPTER NINETEEN

BARBADOS

Background Information

Geographic and Demographic Data

Location	Barbados is in the Eastern Caribbean, northeast of Venezuela. It is the easternmost island of the West Indies and is four hours behind GMT.
Capital	Bridgetown.
Area	166 square miles.
Population	258,756.
Language	English.
Access	There are daily nonstop flights to New York, Miami, Toronto, London, and Puerto Rico, and modern harbor and port facilities.
Telecommunications	Excellent.

Government

Barbados is an independent state. It is a member of the Commonwealth.

Political and Economic Stability

Barbados has a history of political and economic stability. It has a constitutional democracy based on the Westminster system. The Queen of England is the head of state and is represented by a governor-general. The economy was based historically on sugarcane cultivation but has diversified into manufacturing, tourism, and the offshore sector. The start of the Port Charles Marina project in Speightstown in 1996 has boosted the tourism industry. Unemployment currently runs at about 16%. The business and financial sectors are well established, with strong Canadian and British links.

Business Environment

Government attitude to offshore activities: The government actively promotes regional integration and direct foreign investment. It constantly reviews and improves offshore financial legislation. The Barbados Industrial Development Corporation provides information to and assists local and foreign investors.

Employment: Nonresidents must acquire work permits. Work permits are easily obtainable provided it can be shown that no suitably qualified Barbadian is available. Tax incentives are provided for nonresidents working in some of the offshore financial services sectors.

Local business requirements: Investors pay nominal license fees to the government to participate in the offshore financial services sector.

Foreigners and Immigration

Nonresidents may purchase real estate in Barbados provided it is purchased with foreign currency registered with the Central Bank. Foreign purchasers must pay a property transfer tax.

Currency and Exchange Control

The Barbadian currency is the Barbados dollar. The exchange rate is fixed against the U.S. dollar at US$1.00 to Bds$2.0113. In terms of the Exchange Control Act 1967, the Central Bank controls the flow of foreign exchange. As foreign investment is actively sought, the inflow of foreign exchange is encouraged and authorization easily obtained. Corporations operating in the offshore financial sector (international business companies, offshore banks, exempt insurance companies, and foreign sales corporations) are exempted from exchange control regulations in relation to their offshore activities. Exchange control permission is required for the following transactions:

(a) for a foreign investor to hold shares or debt in a corporation incorporated in Barbados;

(b) for a foreign individual or corporation to borrow funds in Barbados; and

(c) for the remitting of funds abroad. The repatriation of capital gains may be spread by the Exchange Control Authority over a period of time.

Nonresidents may hold foreign currency accounts in Barbados and external accounts. Residents and branches or subsidiaries of foreign corporations must have Central Bank authority to hold foreign currency accounts.

Disclosure of Information

Secrecy of information: There is no legislation specifically governing secrecy in Barbados. Civil and criminal remedies are available against those who breach confidentiality.

Banking secrecy: An offshore bank's customers' affairs are kept confidential in terms of the Offshore Banking Act 1985.

Disclosure in company formation and trust settlement: Barbadian law does not require the disclosure of the beneficial owner of an offshore corporation on its formation. However, an application for an international business license must give the names and addresses of the proposed shareholders. Such disclosure must be made to the Ministry of International Trade and Business. No other information about beneficial owners is required. The Offshore Banking Act 1985 and the International Trusts Act 1995 govern the confidentiality of disclosure generally.

Corporations must be audited, although, with regard to private corporations, an audit is only necessary if the gross annual revenue or assets exceed US$500,000. A local registered office is also required. Copies of the minute book, company seal, articles and bylaws, and registers of directors, shareholders, debentures, privilege, rights, and option holders must be lodged with the registered office.

Beneficial ownership may be disclosed under the Companies Act, which empowers the registrar to require any person to furnish information where there is satisfactory reason to inquire into beneficial ownership of a corporation.

Trustees do not have to register beneficiaries of trusts. International trusts are exempt from the requirement of registration under any law.[1] Banks opening a corporate account will require references from beneficial owners. Banks opening a trust account will not require references if the account is opened by a known trust corporation and does not refer to a specific trust. Societies with restricted liability have a confidentiality provision.

International cooperation measures: The Proceeds of Crime Act 1990 provides for cooperation with local investigators and allows the attorney general to make an order to assist foreign countries in an investigation. Such a procedure is also provided for in tax treaties. The cooperation procedure functions by means of monitoring orders, confiscation orders, and orders of disclosure from financial institutions and Inland Revenue authorities. Exchange of information is also provided for between the various tax treaty countries. There is no appeal procedure against such cooperation.

Foreign judgments are enforced under the Foreign and Commonwealth Judgments (Reciprocal Enforcement Act of Barbados Cap 201) 1922. In terms of this act, if the foreign country has agreed to enforce high court judgments obtained in Barbados against any of its nationals, then the governor-general of Barbados has the power to extend to foreign countries giving reciprocal treatment the enforcement of foreign judgments.

Barbados has entered into numerous tax treaties that contain exchange of information agreements. Such information necessary to carry out the agreements on double taxation and to enforce the domestic laws of the contracting states is covered in the agreements. Provisions for mutual legal assistance are contained in double taxation agreements.

The Proceeds of Crime Act 1990 covers money laundering as well as fiscal crime, to the extent that it allows the director of public prosecutions access to the records of Inland Revenue and of financial institutions. The Barbadian authorities are willing to cooperate with foreign investigations into tax evasion, and any such investigation would be treated favorably by the authorities.

Legal System

General

The legal system is based on English common law, although constitutional supremacy has replaced parliamentary supremacy.

Legislation

The principal provisions affecting offshore operations and transactions are contained in the following:

- Exempt Insurance Act 1983
- Foreign Sales Corporations Act 1984
- Income Tax (Amendment) Act 1996
- International Business Companies Act 1991
- International Trusts Act 1995
- Offshore Banking Act 1985
- Shipping (Incentives) Act 1982
- Societies with Restricted Liability Act 1995

Treaties

See "Tax Treaties and Double Taxation" and "Other Treaties."

Taxation (Direct and Indirect)

Income Tax

Individuals: Individuals resident and domiciled in Barbados are taxed on their worldwide income, regardless of whether the income is remitted to Barbados. Individuals resident but not domiciled in Barbados are taxed on all income derived from sources in Barbados, including income derived from employment and foreign unearned income remitted to Barbados. Nonresident individuals are taxed on income derived from sources in Barbados. Marginal tax rates range from 20% to

50% for income over Bds$55,000 per annum. The minimum personal allowance is Bds$15,000. Tax on salaries and wages is deducted on a "pay as you earn" basis.

Corporations: Resident corporations are taxed on all income, except income derived from a source in Barbados. Income is taxed at a flat rate of 35%. Nonresident corporations are taxed at a flat rate of 15% on dividends, interest, royalties, and management fees derived from a Barbados source.

Capital Gains Tax

There is no capital gains tax in Barbados.

Stamp Duties

Stamp duty of 1% is paid on certain documents, such as documents relating to the transfer of real estate and shares, and leases. An additional stamp duty is levied on bills of entry on imported goods. The levy is 10% on regional and 15% on nonregional goods.

Withholding Taxes

Tax is withheld on payments to nonresidents as follows:

Dividends	15%
Interest	15%
Personal services	15%
Rents	40%
Royalties	15%

The withholding rates on payments to residents of treaty countries are as follows:

Country	*Interest*	*Dividends*	*Royalties*
Canada	15%	15%	0%[2]
Finland	0% or 5%[3]	5% or 15%[4]	5% or 15%[5]
Norway	–	–	–
Switzerland	–	–	–
United Kingdom	15%	–	–[6]
United States	5%	5% or 15%[7]	5%

Estate, Inheritance, and Gift Taxes

There are no estate, inheritance, and gift taxes in Barbados.

Real Estate Taxes

A land tax is levied annually on landowners. The tax is based on the value of the land and improvements, and it is between 1% and 1.5%. If the owner is a foreigner, the rate is 3% for unimproved land and 2% for improved land.

Transfer Tax

The transfer of shares and freehold and certain leasehold property is subject to transfer tax. The rate is determined by the residence of the parties, and it is between 5% and 10%.

Sales Taxes and Value-Added Tax

A tax of 15% is levied on hotel income for rooms, food, and beverages, and for restaurant and certain club sales. An 8% tax is levied on car rentals and rental of nonbusiness premises.

VAT was introduced in 1997, at a standard rate of 15%.

Social Security Tax

Contribution to the national insurance scheme is compulsory. Employers pay 8.25% of wages and employees pay 9.75% of wages. Self-employed persons must contribute 13.25% to the scheme. Only monthly wages up to an amount of Bds$2,600 are subject to the tax.

Import Duties

Customs duty is payable on many imported goods. Rates are prescribed in the customs tariff.

Consumption Tax

Many imported and locally produced items are subject to consumption tax. The rate ranges from 6% to 30%.

Tax Incentives

See "Incentives (Tax and Nontax)."

Tax Treaties and Double Taxation

Barbados has entered into double taxation treaties with Canada, Finland, Norway, Sweden, Switzerland, the United Kingdom, and the United States. The treaties with Denmark, Norway, and Sweden have low withholding rates, tax sparing, and only limited potential for treaty shopping. The Canadian treaty provides for tax sparing. The double taxation treaty with the United States is a landmark treaty as it included an exchange of tax information agreement for the first time and was the first such treaty entered into by the U.S. government with a less developed country. Under the treaty, U.S. investors have the benefit of reduced withholding rates as well as exemption from accumulated earnings tax on profits earned in Barbados. The treaty is particularly attractive to U.S. manufacturers and persons investing in U.S. real estate.

In 1995, Barbados signed the Caribbean Common Market and Community (CARICOM) Double Taxation Treaty and the Reciprocal National Insurance Agreement. Barbados has also entered into mutual tax treaties with Caribbean countries such as Anguilla, Antigua, Belize, Dominica, Grenada, Guyana, Jamaica, Montserrat, St. Kitts and Nevis, St. Vincent, and Trinidad and Tobago.

Other Treaties

In 1994, Barbados concluded the Encouragement and Reciprocal Protection of Investments with Germany. Barbados concluded a bilateral investment treaty with the United Kingdom in 1995 and is negotiating similar treaties with the United States and France. A bilateral investment treaty with Italy has also recently come into force. In 1996, two Reciprocal Promotion and Protection of Investments Agreements came into force between Barbados and Canada, and Barbados and Cuba.

Incentives (Tax and Nontax)

The Fiscal Incentives Act 1974 grants an exemption from corporation tax and customs duty to new manufacturing operations for between six and ten years. Exemption from withholding taxes on dividends and carryforward of losses are also provided for. Other legislation provides for investment incentive allowances of up to 40% on new equipment, agricultural subsidies, and building allowances.

Regionally, CARICOM provides a duty-free market for goods produced within the region. The Caribbean Basin Initiative gives preferential access to the United States for products manufactured in Barbados, and the Generalized System of Preferences allows duty-free access to the United States in respect of certain goods. As far as Europe is concerned, the Lomé Convention grants privileged access rights to the European Union.

Two forms of training grants are available to manufacturers from the Barbados Investment and Development Corporation. These are training subsidies for new corporations and subsidies for upgrading skills.

Corporations

(The domestic laws of Barbados refer to *corporations* as *companies*. This terminology is retained in this chapter.)

The advantage of incorporating companies in Barbados is that Barbados is a stable, well-managed, democratic jurisdiction with an advanced legal system. Low tax rates apply, and there is a growing network of double taxation treaties. There are also few filing requirements.

Types of Companies

Companies are governed in Barbados by the Companies Act 1982. This act is based on the Canadian Business Corporation Act. There are various types of offshore companies. These include international business companies (IBCs), which are governed by the International Business Companies Act 1991, and foreign sales corporations (FSCs), which are governed by the Foreign Sales Corporations Act 1984.

To qualify as an IBC, a company must

(a) be incorporated in Barbados;

(b) if not so incorporated, then be managed and controlled in Barbados;

(c) have at least 90% of its shares owned by nonresidents; and

(d) not carry on business as an offshore bank, exempt insurance company, or a foreign sales corporation.

Barbados qualifies as a jurisdiction recognized by the United States for the incorporation and management of FSCs. To qualify as an FSC, a company must be incorporated under the Barbados Companies Act 1982 and satisfy the relevant U.S. regulations. FSCs may not do business with any of the CARICOM countries. FSCs are exempt from income tax, withholding tax, transfer tax, customs duty, and exchange controls. An FSC with an annual turnover below US$5 million pays an annual license fee of US$500. All other FSCs pay an annual license fee of US$1,000.

Regarding migration of companies, the corporate seat of a company incorporated in Barbados cannot be transferred to another jurisdiction. However, a foreign company can become a resident company by transferring its management and control to Barbados and by registering with the registrar of companies. Such a company can also transfer its residence from Barbados.

Checklist for IBCs

- The company name must end in *Incorporated*, *Corporation*, or *Limited*. Consent is required for the use of words such as *Bank* or *Insurance*. The registrar of companies often refuses to approve names with words such as *International* or *Global*.
- It takes two to three days to incorporate a company. Shelf companies are not available. The minimum capital requirement is US$1,000. Capital duty of US$390 is payable.
- Prior to granting of an IBC license, the details of shareholders must be submitted to the Ministry of Finance.
- At least one shareholder is necessary. Bearer sharers are not allowed, but shares of no par value are. It should be noted that Barbados law does not provide for shares of par value.
- At least one director is required. Corporate directors are allowed, and there is no restriction on directors' residence.
- A company secretary is mandatory. There is no restriction on the residence of the secretary.
- A registered office is required, although a registered agent is not. Statutory records and registers are lodged with the registered office.
- Audited accounts are required only when the total assets exceed US$500,000. They do not have to be filed. An annual return is not necessary.
- Directors are obliged to meet once a year, and shareholders are to meet within eighteen months of incorporation, and thereafter, within fifteen months of the previous meeting.
- An annual fee of US$100 is payable to the government.
- Exchange controls do not apply to IBCs.

Other Forms of Business Organization

Sole Proprietorships

Sole proprietorships are not regulated by statute in Barbados, but they are allowed and are governed by the common law. Registration is not necessary, but specialized tax returns must be filed.

Partnerships

The Partnership Act Cap 313 governs general partnerships in Barbados. Limited partnerships are governed by the Limited Partnership Act Cap 312. General partnerships may be created in writing or orally. The formation of limited partnerships is always in writing, and a maximum of twenty partners, one of whom must be a managing partner, is allowed. Limited partnerships must be registered for the partners to acquire limited liability. General partnerships need be registered only if they trade in a name other than the names of the partners. Management and capital requirements are determined by the partnership agreement. There are no accounting and auditing requirements for partnerships in Barbados, other than as determined in the partnership agreement. It is customary for at least one partner to be a resident of Barbados (usually an IBC). Barbados law is the proper law of all partnerships.

Offshore partnerships are not distinguished from onshore partnerships. Offshore status will be determined by residence and the source of the partnership's income. This will also determine whether there is any tax liability in Barbados.

Societies with Restricted Liability (SRLs)

The Societies with Restricted Liability Act 1995 governs SRLs. SRLs have a corporate life of fifty years. A registered office and agent are required in Barbados. The articles, bylaws, minutes, resolutions, registers, and accounting records must be kept at the registered office. An SRL with gross revenue and assets exceeding Bds$1 million is required to submit annual audited financial statements. SRLs are exempt from exchange controls and may migrate to and from Barbados. A guarantee of benefits may be obtained under the act for a period of up to thirty years. There are also exemptions on import duties on machinery and equipment used in Barbados by SRLs. SRLs are liable to annual tax, at a rate of 1.5% to 2.5% per US$5 million increment of profit, and at 1% over US$15 million.

Banks and Other Financial Institutions

Offshore Banks

Offshore banks are regulated by the Offshore Banking Act 1979. A license is required from the Minister of Finance. To qualify for the license, a company must

(a) be incorporated in Barbados or be a qualified foreign bank;

(b) maintain a minimum issued capital of up to Bds$1 million;

(c) pay an annual license fee of Bds$25,000; and

(d) maintain a reserve fund equal to issued capital and transfer at least 25% of profits to the reserve fund annually if the fund should fall below the level of issued capital.

Offshore banks are exempt from exchange control. Dividends and interest paid to nonresidents are exempt from withholding tax. Tax on the profits of offshore banks is payable at the following rates:

Up to Bds$10 million	1.5%
Between Bds$10 and $20 million	2%
Between Bds$20 and $30 million	1.5%
Over Bds$30 million	1%

Offshore Finance Companies

Offshore finance companies may qualify as investment IBCs. If they do, they are eligible for the same favorable rates of tax. Provided borrowed money is used to produce assessable income, there is no limit on the amount of interest that may be charged, whether or not it is paid at arm's length.

Insurance

Captive Insurance Companies

Captive insurance is governed by the Exempt Insurance Act and the Companies Act. There are approximately 327 captives established in Barbados. The total asset size of the captive sector is US$9.9297 billion. The total premium size is approximately US$1.9869 billion. The supervisor of insurance in the Ministry of Finance and Economic Affairs regulates the sector. An annual audit is required, as is a solvency certificate.

There are no regulatory concessions. Captives are exempt from tax.

The minimum capital requirements are as follows:

First year	US$125,000
NWP* US$125,000	Under US$750,000
NWP between US$750,000 and US$5 million	20% of premium
NWP over US$5 million	US$1 million + 10% of premiums over US$5 million

*Net written premium

Incorporation costs are US$390. An annual license fee of US$2,500 is payable. An additional legal fee of US$2,500 and an application fee of US$250 are also payable.

There are no special categories of captive. Provision is made for rent-a-captives but not for protected cell corporations.

Shipping

Ships Registry

In 1994, Barbados opened a new ships registry. The registry provides the provisional and statutory mortgage registration facilities that are in common usage in the Commonwealth. The ships registry program operates with the help of a London office, which is also the central registry office depository. Permanent vessel registration, mortgage registration, and mortgage cancellation can be effected through either the London or Bridgetown office.

The Shipping Act 1994 regulates the registration of ships under the Barbados flag and of foreign ships when they operate within Barbados's territorial waters. The Shipping (Oil Pollution) Act regulates the discharge of oil by any ships within Barbados's territorial waters and by Barbados-registered ships anywhere in the world. Barbados is also a party to twenty-two International Maritime Organization conventions relating to safety of life at sea and the protection of the marine environment.

Shipping Corporations

The Shipping Corporations Act 1996 regulates corporations that own and operate ships. Shipping corporations are accorded nonresidential status and are not liable to income tax. The provisions of the act overlap with the provisions of the Companies Act, but the Shipping Corporations Act provides a self-contained corporate structure for shipping corporations.

Licensing Corporations

Offshore licensing corporations are not specifically provided for in Barbados. Offshore licensing corporations that qualify as IBCs are taxed at a rate of 2.5%.

Trusts

The law of trusts in Barbados is based on the English common law. It is supplemented by the Trustees Act Cap 250 and the Offshore Banking Act 1985, in regard to offshore trusts. An offshore trust is defined as the acceptance in trust of

(a) amounts of money in foreign currencies or foreign securities or both;

(b) foreign personal or movable properties; or

(c) real or immovable property outside Barbados

from persons resident outside Barbados to be administered, managed, or invested or otherwise dealt with for the benefit of persons resident outside Barbados, and it includes any activities related, incidental, or ancillary thereto.[8]

A Barbados trust is one whose proper law is Barbados law. There are no registration requirements for trusts, although common trust funds must be registered. Confidentiality is therefore guaranteed. A common trust fund is defined as "a trust that operates by the process of pooling funds from a number of participants in the trust who share as beneficiaries under the trust in the income or other gains derived from the acquisition, holding, management or disposal of assets acquired for the trust."[9]

There are also no capital requirements.

Resident and nonresident individuals and corporations can act as trustees. In terms of the Offshore Banking Act, resident corporations acting as trustees of offshore trusts must hold a license to carry on offshore banking business in Barbados.

Trusts in Barbados can be either discretionary or fixed in relation to entitlement to trust assets and the vesting of the assets in particular beneficiaries. The beneficiaries of an offshore trust must be nonresidents.

Exchange control provisions apply to trusts. However, no direct taxes are levied against dividends, interests, or other returns from shares, securities, deposits, or other borrowings of a licensed trustee or any assets managed by a trustee, if the dividends, interests, or other returns are in respect of shares, securities, or deposits or other borrowings or assets beneficially owned by a nonresident.[10] Trusts may be migrated into and out of Barbados.

Checklist for Offshore Trusts

- There is no statutory schedule of standard trust powers.
- The maximum perpetuity period for noncharitable trusts is one hundred years.
- At least one resident trustee is required.
- Trusts need not be registered.
- Trust documents may be in any language, but an English translation is required.
- There is no stamp duty or registration fee.
- Barbados trust law has an English common law background.
- Appeal lies to the Privy Council.
- The Hague Convention has not been implemented.
- Specific provision is made for the exclusion of foreign inheritance laws.
- Specific provision is also made for the nonrecognition of foreign judgments.
- There is a specific "asset protection" provision protecting a disposition to a trust from challenge by creditors.
- Instant immunity is granted from creditors' claims.
- Provision is made for noncharitable purpose trusts.

Notes

1. International Trusts Act 1995, sec. 32.
2. A 10% withholding tax is levied on royalties on films and television shows.
3. The zero rate applies to interest to government agencies.
4. The 5% rate applies if the beneficial owner is a corporation owning 10% or more of the voting stock of the corporation paying the dividend.
5. The zero rate applies to copyright royalties.
6. A 15% withholding tax is levied on royalties on films and television shows.
7. The 5% rate applies if the beneficial owner is a corporation owning 10% or more of the voting stock of the corporation paying the dividend; the 15% rate applies to a U.S. regulated investment corporation; and a 15% rate applies to a U.S. real estate investment corporation where the beneficial owner is an individual holding less than a 10% interest, or else the rate applicable under domestic law applies.
8. Offshore Banking Act 1985, sec. 4(2).
9. Sec. 26(3).
10. Sec. 103(3).

CHAPTER TWENTY

BELIZE

Background Information

Geographic and Demographic Data

Location: Belize is in Central America, on the Caribbean coast, between Guatemala and Mexico. It is six hours behind GMT.

Capital: The new capital is Belmopan. Belize City, the hurricane-damaged former capital, remains the commercial center and is the country's major cargo port.

Area: 14,269 square miles

Population: 230,160.

Languages: English is the official language. Spanish, Mayan, and Garifuna are also spoken.

Access: The international airport outside Belize City has regular flights to North and Central American destinations. A new international airport is being built.

Telecommunications: Good.

Government

Belize has a parliamentary democracy. The constitution was adopted on September 21, 1981, when Belize gained independence from the United Kingdom. Queen Elizabeth II is the chief of state and is represented by a Governor General, who must be a Belizean. Belize is a member of the Commonwealth.

Political and Economic Stability

The small, essentially private enterprise economy is based primarily on agriculture, agro-based industry, and merchandising, with tourism and construction assuming greater importance. Sugar, the chief crop, accounts for more than one-third of exports, while the banana industry is the country's largest employer. The government's tough austerity program in 1997 resulted in an economic slowdown that is likely to continue. The trade deficit has been growing, mostly as a result of low export prices for sugar and bananas. The ruling in 1997 by the World Trade Organization against the European Union's banana import regime—which had granted Belize preferential treatment— is also hurting the prospects for growth and could contribute to an increase in unemployment, which already runs at a high of 13%.

Belize has enjoyed internal political stability since independence, but neighboring Guatemala continues to dispute its sovereignty.

Business Environment

Government attitude to offshore activities: The government encourages investment in agriculture, light manufacturing, and offshore assembly and offers tax concessions for battery assembly and for the production of plywood and veneers, matches, boats, beer, rum, and soft drinks. It is also encouraging the development of Belize as a tourist destination, to exploit the world's second largest barrier reef and Mayan ruins.

Employment: Belize suffers from a shortage of professional and technical workers. Where an employer can convince the government that there is a shortage of skilled workers in a particular area, the government will admit immigrant employees. Foreigners working for an Export Processing Zone business must obtain work permits from the Minister of Labor. Permits will be granted to applicants who serve the business in a senior management or technical capacity, while composing up to 20% of the corporation's employees. There are no fees regarding permits for zone personnel.

Foreigners and Immigration

Belize has an Economic Citizen Investment Program, in terms of which a qualified head of a household may obtain citizenship by investing Bz$50,000 in the Belize Economic Citizenship Investment Fund and paying a registration fee of Bz$50,000 into the Special Fund at the Central Bank. Spouses and children under 18 years old cost an additional Bz$10,000 each. Children over 18 cost an additional Bz$30,000 each. Dependent parents are entitled to citizenship in terms of the program on payment of an additional Bz$30,000. Single heads of households pay an investment fee of Bz$50,000 and a reduced registration fee of Bz$30,000, which covers dependents under 18.

Application for participation in the above program must be through a licensed immigrant consultant, who is entitled to charge up to 20% of the registration and investment fees. If the application is rejected, the government may retain a portion of the fee to cover its processing costs.

A person who acquires Belizean citizenship through the program is exempt from income tax and entitled to a Belizean passport.

Currency and Exchange Control

The currency is the Belizean dollar, which is linked to the U.S. dollar, both currencies circulating freely. Foreign exchange is freely transferable.

Disclosure of Information

Banking secrecy: Banking secrecy is tight in Belize. The Central Bank may seek information from a licensee but not from a customer unless there is a particularly large credit exposure.

International cooperation measures: The Belizean Central Bank is authorized under the Banks and Financial Institutions Act of 1995 to cooperate with foreign banking supervisory bodies with regard to drug trafficking and money laundering. This authority includes inspecting business records, entering premises, and providing information to law enforcement agencies. The Money Laundering Act of 1995 imposes heavy fines and/or imprisonment on persons found guilty of issuing false documents, failing to maintain records, and deriving proceeds from criminal activities. Belize has also signed an exchange of information agreement with the United States under the Caribbean Basin Initiative. The agreement provides for the exchange of information on tax matters relating to drug trafficking, money laundering, fraud, or other criminal activity.

Legal System

The legal system is based on the British system. The court system follows the British system closely, and the final court of appeal is the Privy Council in London.

Treaties

See "Tax Treaties and Double Taxation."

Taxation

Income Tax

Companies that are not subject to the IBC exemption pay corporate tax at a rate of 45%. Companies whose gross annual income is less than Bz$25,000 pay a reduced rate of 25%. Branches pay the same taxes as subsidiaries organized in Belize.

Individuals pay income tax on a sliding scale, commencing at 15% on up to Bz$12,000 and increasing to 45% on over Bz$60,000. Personal deductions are allowed to a maximum of Bz$1,200. Individuals whose total gross income is less than Bz$20,800 are exempt from income tax.

Withholding Tax

There is a 25% tax on mortgage and debenture interest, but the tax is reduced to 0% when paid to foreigners if it is paid on capital used in certain development projects. It is also reduced to 0% if the interest is subject to tax in the payee's country of residence. Royalties are taxed at normal rates and management fees are taxed if the management service is performed in Belize through a permanent establishment. A 5% withholding tax is levied on gross interest from time deposits.

Value-Added Tax

A value-added tax (VAT) was introduced in Belize in 1996 at a rate of 15%. Certain goods and services are exempt, such as staple foodstuffs, prescription medicine, exports, medical services, water and electricity provision, and residential rents.

Import Duties

Import duties range between 25% and 40% on the general list and 15% and 25% on preferential items.

Estate Duties

Estates are taxed on a sliding scale, beginning at 1% on estates up to Bz$500 and reaching a maximum of 25% on estates over Bz$50,000.

Other Taxes

Companies are not subject to capital gains tax, turnover tax, or headquarters tax.

Tax Incentives

See "Incentives."

Tax Treaties and Double Taxation

Initially Belize was party to double taxation treaties with the United States, Sweden, Norway, Denmark, and Switzerland as a result of the U.K. tax conventions with these countries. All of these treaties have been terminated and only the double taxation treaty with the United Kingdom remains in effect.

Incentives (Tax and Nontax)

Free Trade Zone

Legislation regarding duty-free Export Processing Zones was passed in 1990. The first such zone was established in the San Antonia area, a few miles south of the

Mexican border. An Export Processing Zone business may produce goods or services only for export or for sale to nonresidents, although a waiver may be obtained from the Minister of Trade and Commerce. All imports are exempt from customs duties, excise duties, trade turnover, foreign exchange, and tonnage taxes, excluding motor vehicles and fuel entering the zone, unless the vehicles are forklift or platform trucks. Exports are exempt from the same taxes, and export licenses are not required. The Export Processing Zone businesses are also exempt from income, withholding, and capital gains tax for at least the first 20 years of operation. This exemption may be extended. Dividends paid by zone businesses are exempt from tax in perpetuity.

Fiscal Incentives

The Fiscal Incentives Act of 1990 provides a 5-year tax holiday, renewable for a further 10 years. The holiday can be extended to a maximum of 25 years for a company involved in agriculture, agro-industry, marine culture, or manufacturing, if all output is exported or the business is labor intensive. The Act also provides for a waiver of import duties for up to 15 years, renewable for a further 10, on raw materials, capital equipment, and spare parts. The exemption can be extended to a maximum of 25 years for a company involved in agriculture, agro-industry, marine culture, or manufacturing, if all output is exported, or the business is labor intensive.

The income tax exemption period comes into operation when the approved enterprise begins production. This must be within 5 years of the enterprise being approved. Application fees for approval are as follows:

Investment of between Bz$250,000 and Bz$500,000	Bz$5,000
Investment of between Bz$500,000 and Bz$750,000	Bz$6,000
Over Bz$750,000	Bz$7,000

Approval takes up to two months, and thereafter there are further licensing and permit requirements. The period of the exemption will depend on the extent of local value added, the foreign exchange earnings, and the number of new jobs created. There are restrictions on the type of activities foreigners without permanent resident status may invest in.

Corporations

(The domestic laws of Belize refer to corporations as companies. This terminology is retained in this chapter.)

International Business Companies

Purposes: The International Business Companies Act of 1990 contains extremely liberal provisions as part of the government's policy to attract foreign investors and undercut competing Caribbean jurisdictions such as the Bahamas and the British Virgin Islands. An International Business Company (IBC) may be used for a number of purposes, including trusts, ship ownership and management, financial management, trading, offshore banking, and captive insurance. An IBC may not carry on business with Belizean residents or own real estate in Belize, although it may lease office premises. It may also not issue securities to a Belizean resident or domestic company or own shares in a domestic company.

Incorporation: An IBC is incorporated by submitting a Memorandum and Articles of Association to the Registrar of Companies. The Memorandum must contain the following Information:

1. The company name, which must end in "Limited," "Corporation," "Incorporated," "Societe Anonyme," "Sociedad Anonima," or their abbreviations;
2. The Belizean address of the company and its registered agent;
3. The company's objects or purposes;
4. The currencies in which its shares will be issued; and
5. Information regarding the shares.

Application can take as little as one hour.

There is no minimum capital requirement, but shares must be fully paid in. It takes only US$100 to register an IBC with up to US$50,000 authorized capital, where all shares have a par value. Registration costs US$1,000 if authorized capital is greater than US$50,000. Professional fees range between US$500 and US$1,000.

There are no requirements to hold annual general meetings, audit the IBC, or disclose its financial statements.

Redomiciliation: A company incorporated outside Belize may transfer its domicile to Belize. Likewise a company incorporated in Belize may migrate to another jurisdiction.

Taxation: IBCs, including trusts and public investment companies, are exempt from income and capital gains tax, and dividends, royalties, and interest paid to nonresidents are exempt from withholding tax. Stamp duty does not have to be paid on instruments relating in any way to an IBC's assets and activities, and there is no estate tax on an IBC's assets.

Public Licensed Investment Companies

Certified public licensed investment companies are entitled to a 30-year exemption from all taxes. Group benefits include the group's not being subject to exchange control regulations or dividend tax on intercompany dividends. Subsidiaries that are not exempt IBCs pay a reduced company tax of 15%. A Public

Licensed Investment Company (PIC) may own Belizean real estate.

In order to qualify as a PIC, a company must intend to be or be listed on an approved stock exchange, it must have conducted business in Belize, and it must employ a minimum of 50 Belizean workers. It may not have received fiscal or development incentives. There are also stringent financial requirements: the company must have a net tangible asset value of US$2.5 million, a gross tangible asset value of US$25 million, and an average net income of US$500,000 for the most recent financial year and US$375,000 for each of the two previous financial years.

Banks and Other Financial Institutions

The domestic banking industry is regulated by the Banks and Financial Institutions Act of 1995. The Offshore Banking Act of 1996 was introduced to attract foreign banks.

An unrestricted class A bank must have a minimum capital of US$500,000 if it is a local entity and US25 million if it is a foreign bank. A restricted class B bank must have a minimum capital of US$200,000 if it is a local entity and US$15 million if it is a foreign bank. A restricted bank is confined to offshore banking only and cannot receive deposits from the general public or take current account business.

Domestic banks must have a minimum paid-in capital of Bz$3 million. Other financial institutions must have a minimum paid-in capital of Bz$100,000. Subsidiaries of foreign banks are also subject to the minimum capitalization requirement of Bz$3 million, and their parent corporations must have paid-in and unencumbered capital of Bz$50 million. The equivalent capitalization for parents of other kinds of financial institutions is Bz$25 million, of which Bz$100,000 must be dedicated to the Belizean branch.

Shipping

The Registration of Merchant Ships Act of 1989 regulates shipping in Belize. Provisional registration costs US$500 per document. Application must be made to the International Marine Registry of Belize. Permanent registration is granted after one year, provided that the applicant has complied with the Act and paid the documentation fees. Registered vessels can obtain a second or dual registration for two years, for a documentation fee of US$500.

An owner of two or more vessels is eligible for a reduced registration rate of up to 75% of the registration fee and/or the first year's service tax.

Smaller vessels such as yachts and pleasure craft pay an initial registration fee of US$500 and US$1,000 annually. Commercial vessels under 500 gross tons pay a US$200 registration fee, with a maximum registration fee of US$3,000 for vessels over 3,000 tons. Commercial vessels pay an annual tax of US$0.10 per net ton.

Annual service taxes range from US$200 for vessels under 500 tons to US$3,000 for vessels over 10,000 tons. Inspection taxes range from US$500 for vessels under 1,500 gross tons to US$1,500 for vessels over 8,000 tons. Transfer of ownership costs US$1,000, deregistration US$750, and name reservation US$20 per month.

There are currently approximately 1,500 vessels registered in Belize, with a gross tonnage of over 1 million tons.

Trusts

The Trusts Act of 1992 permits the formation of offshore trusts in Belize that are exempt from income, estate, and gift taxes. The Act permits a life-spanned income accumulation of 120 years. Charitable trusts have an unlimited life-span.

The Act also permits the establishment of asset protection trusts. Belize law provides instant asset protection without the two-year or longer waiting period imposed by other jurisdictions. Trusts may be declared void by a court in Belize only if established by fraud or under duress, if they are immoral or contrary to public policy, or for vagueness.

A trust may be established orally or in writing. It can be private or registered with the Registrar of the Court. Registration requires a certified copy of the trust settlement, where applicable, in English, and costs Bz$200. The Act is particularly flexible regarding the choice of law governing the trust, which may even be changed during the life of the trust.

Noncharitable purpose trusts are permitted, provided certain conditions are met.

CHAPTER TWENTY-ONE

BERMUDA

Background Information

Geographic and Demographic Data

Location	Bermuda is a group of islands in the North Atlantic Ocean, east of North Carolina in the United States. It is four hours behind GMT.
Capital	Hamilton.
Area	20 square miles.
Population	62,569.
Languages	English is the official language, but Portuguese is also widely spoken.
Access	There are frequent flights to and from major cities in North America and the United Kingdom, and the islands are well serviced by international shipping lines.
Telecommunications	Excellent.

Government

Bermuda is a self-governing but dependent territory of the United Kingdom. It is a member of the Commonwealth.

Political and Economic Stability

Bermuda is a politically stable constitutional democracy, with a bicameral parliamentary system. The Queen of England is the head of state and is represented by a governor.

Bermuda enjoys one of the highest per capita incomes in the world, having successfully exploited its location by providing financial services for international firms and luxury tourist facilities for 200,000 visitors annually. The tourist industry attracts 91% of its business from North America. The industrial sector is small, and agriculture is severely limited by a lack of suitable land. About 80% of food needs are imported. International business contributes over 60% of Bermuda's economic output; a failed independence vote in late 1995 can be partially attributed to Bermudians' fear of scaring away foreign firms. Unemployment is negligible.

Business Environment

Government attitude to offshore activities: Government and the commercial sector have cooperated to develop an infrastructure and legislative framework that is highly attractive to foreign investors. Bermuda's reputation as an international offshore financial center is insured by its exclusion of foreign banks and by the strict supervision of the banking and corporate sectors by the Bermuda Monetary Authority, which screens all applications for incorporation of Bermuda corporations. Bermuda is also one of the largest insurance markets in the world. The Investment Business Act of 1998, which came into force on January 1, 1999, provides for investor protection. It contains a framework for regulating business investment carried on in and from Bermuda and was designed to meet international standards. The act depoliticizes licensing, establishes a supervisory body to regulate investment business, and provides criteria to ensure that investment advisors and intermediaries have the necessary experience and fitness. It also provides a mechanism for sharing information with local and international regulators.

Employment: Foreign employees require a work permit, for which a renewal fee is charged. An annual renewal is charged at Bd$440, and a five-year renewal is charged at Bd$2,200.

Currency and Exchange Control

The unit of currency is the Bermuda dollar. Parity is fixed with the U.S. dollar, and both currencies are accepted on the islands. Exchange controls apply only to the Bermuda dollar. They do not apply to international offshore operations. Exempt Bermuda corporations may open bank accounts anywhere in the world without any restrictions being imposed by Bermudian authorities.

Disclosure of Information

Secrecy of information: Employees of the Bermuda Monetary Authority and officials in the Ministry of Finance are sworn to secrecy in terms of the Official Secrets Act.

Disclosure in company formation and trust settlement: Beneficial ownership must be disclosed to the Bermuda Monetary Authority on incorporation, in the form of a personal declaration. The confidentiality of such disclosure is governed by the Monetary Authority Act 1969, section 31, and the Companies Act 1981, section 6(8).

Corporate audits are necessary, but the requirement may be waived on agreement by all members and directors. In terms of the Companies Act, a local registered office is required. Corporations falling under the Insurance Act 1978 must also appoint a principal representative. Minutes of directors' and members' meetings, financial statements, and auditors' reports must be lodged with the registered office. Beneficial ownership would be disclosed by the local office only under a properly constituted request by the authorities in terms of relevant legislation, such as the United States/Bermuda Tax Convention Act 1986.

Trustees do not have to register the beneficiaries of trusts. However, a trustee or corporation opening a bank account must disclose the beneficiaries or beneficial ownership. This requirement also applies to limited partnerships and corporations.

International cooperation measures: The United States/Bermuda Tax Convention Act and the Criminal Justice (International Cooperation) Act 1994 both provide procedures for cooperation with foreign states or investigators. Section 12 of the United States/Bermuda Tax Convention Act provides for judicial review by the Supreme Court of any act performed by the minister of finance or other person under the act.

Foreign judgments are enforced in terms of the Judgments (Reciprocal Enforcement) Act 1958. As a dependent territory of the United Kingdom, Bermuda is bound to abide by reciprocal provisions made by the legislature of any part of Her Majesty's dominions outside the United Kingdom for the enforcement within that part of the dominions of judgments obtained in the Supreme Court.

The United States/Bermuda Tax Convention Act 1986 represents a tax treaty entered into between Bermuda and the United States. The treaty contains an exchange of information agreement, in terms of which Bermuda is obliged to assist the United States in civil and criminal tax matters upon request from the U.S. government. Information provided is limited by solicitor-client privilege. Bermuda has not entered into any mutual legal assistance treaties.

Money laundering provisions were first contained in the Drug Trafficking Suppression Act of 1988, which allowed the authorities to confiscate property held by a person who had benefitted from drug trafficking. This was followed by the Criminal Justice (International Cooperation) (Bermuda) Act of 1994 and the Proceeds of Crime Act of 1997, whch was enacted to give effect to the United Kingdom's obligations under the Strasbourg Convention of 1990. The Proceeds of Crime Act of 1997 extends money laundering legislation beyond drug trafficking to cover offenses such as extortion, piracy, counterfeiting, forgery, and false accounting.

Banking secrecy: Banking secrecy is governed by the common law.

Legal System

General

The legal system in Bermuda is based on English common law. A constitution was adopted on June 8, 1968.

Case Law

Important recent cases include the following:

- *Berliner Bank v. Karageorgis & Silver Carriers* (1997/1998) 1 OFLR 145 (Supreme Court, Bermuda); and
- *Muhl v. Ardra Insurance Co. Ltd.* (1997/1998) 1 OFLR 198 (Supreme Court, Bermuda).
- *Thyssen-Bornemisza v. Thyssen Bornemisza* (1998/1999) 2 OFLR 98 (Supreme Court of Bermuda)

Treaties

See "Tax Treaties and Double Taxation."

Taxation (Direct and Indirect)

General

There is no income tax, corporation tax, capital gains tax, wealth tax, or inheritance tax on income, profits, dividends, or wealth in Bermuda.

Payroll Tax

A local employer must pay a payroll tax, which is levied at 12%, of which 4.5% can be recovered from the employee. Exempt corporation employers must pay 12% on a notional amount of Bd$66,000 per employee per annum, also of which 4.5% can be recovered from the employee. Their employees are also each liable for 4.5% of this amount.

Stamp Duties

Duty on a deceased estate in Bermuda is payable on Bermuda property at the following rates on application in Bermuda for probate, letters of administration, or resealing of a foreign grant:

Up to Bd$20,000	0%
Between Bd$20,000 and Bd$100,000	5%
Over Bd$100,000	10%

Shares in an exempt corporation are excluded from the deceased's estate for these purposes.

Real Estate Taxes

A land tax is imposed on all Bermudian property. The tax is on a sliding scale.

Import Duties

Duty is levied at varying rates on all imports to Bermuda.

Hotel Tax

Revenue from hotels and other forms of accommodation is taxed at 7.25%.

Departure Tax

A departure tax of US$20 is charged on all persons leaving Bermuda.

Betting Tax

A betting tax of 20% is levied in Bermuda.

Tax Incentives

See "Incentives."

Tax Treaties and Double Taxation

There are no double taxation treaties between Bermuda and other jurisdictions, as Bermuda does not impose direct taxation. A tax treaty between the United States and Bermuda exempts Bermudian insurance corporations from U.S. franchise taxes on premium remittances from the United States to Bermuda. It also grants U.S. tax deductions to U.S. corporations that hold conventions in Bermuda. An exchange of information provision is incorporated in the treaty.

Incentives

Few incentives apply in Bermuda. The notable exception is that import duties can be waived in full or in part on materials imported for construction or renovation of hotels.

Corporations

(The domestic laws of Bermuda refer to *corporations* as *companies*. This terminology is retained in this chapter.)

The advantages of incorporation in Bermuda are that it is a highly respected, politically stable jurisdiction, with modern business laws and excellent professional and judicial infrastructure. It also benefits from tax neutrality. Exchange controls do not apply to nonresident companies, and there is a stock exchange in Bermuda. It is conveniently situated for the North American and European markets and is well served by international air and shipping lines. It is also a well-known captive insurance jurisdiction. However, government fees are expensive, and incorporation can take up to five working days. The government is addressing these problems.

Types of Companies

Bermuda companies are either resident companies or offshore companies, which may be either exempt companies or foreign permit companies. Exempt companies are exempt from the restrictions on ordinary Bermuda companies relating to the portion of share capital that may be held by foreigners. Foreign permit companies are companies incorporated anywhere in the world that, on application, may be granted permits for places of business in Bermuda.

Checklist for Ordinary and Exempt Companies

- Bermuda ordinary and exempt companies are governed by the Companies Act 1981. Companies must include *Limited* or *Ltd.* in their names, and the use of words such as *Bank* is restricted.
- Incorporation can take up to five working days. Shelf companies are not available, although old companies may be. The identity of the beneficial owner must be disclosed to the authorities prior to incorporation.
- The minimum capital required is US$12,000, and capital duty of 0.25% is charged on the authorized capital. No duty is charged on exempt companies.
- A minimum of one shareholder is required. Bearer shares and shares of no par value are not permissible.
- A minimum of two directors is required. Corporate directors are not allowed, and Bermudian directors are no longer necessary. There are no restrictions on where meetings may be held.
- A local registered office is necessary, although a registered agent is only needed if resident directors are appointed. The share register, share certificate book, minutes of shareholders' and directors' meetings, and accounts must be kept at the registered office, although the accounts are not open to inspection.
- Corporate books and a seal are necessary, and they are usually kept at the registered office.

- A company secretary is mandatory. A corporate secretary is allowed, and there is no restriction on the secretary's residence.
- The share register, register of directors and officers, certificate of incorporation, and memorandum and articles of association are available on the public file.
- An annual return is not necessary for exempt companies.
- Provision is made for migration or redomiciliation.

Fees

A fee for either form of offshore company is paid annually. The fee is between US$1,680 and US$25,000. Resident companies are liable to an annual fee ranging between US$525 and US$15,000.

Other Forms of Business Organization

Partnerships

Bermudian law recognizes partnerships. Exempt partnerships are exempt from exchange control and local ownership requirements. They may be established by nonresidents and may operate from Bermuda. A fee of Bd$2,000 is payable annually to the government by exempt partnerships.

Foreign Companies

A permit is needed from the minister of finance before a foreign company can commence operations in Bermuda or open a branch in Bermuda. A fee of Bd$1,680 is payable annually to the government.

Banks and Trust Companies

Foreign banks are excluded from operating in Bermuda. There are three Bermudian banks, each with its own trust company. The banks operate a joint clearing system and are supervised by the Bermuda Monetary Authority, which issues and backs the Bermuda dollar.

Insurance

Captive Insurance Companies

Captives are permitted under the Insurance Act 1978, the Insurance Amendment Act 1996, and the Companies Act 1981. There are approximately one thousand captives established in Bermuda. The total asset size of the insurance sector is approximately US$95 billion. The total premium size of the insurance sector is approximately US$23.4 billion. The minister of finance and the registrar of companies regulate the sector. An annual audit is required, as is a solvency certificate. Auditors are required to comply with the relevant financial reporting legislation.

There are no regulatory concessions. Captives are taxed at a rate of 0%.

The minimum capital requirements are as follows:

General: single parent writing parent/affiliate risks	US$120,000
Multiowner or single parent writing connected income	US$250,000
Third party reinsurers	US$1 million
Long-term	US$250,000

Incorporation costs are approximately US$11,000. An annual license fee is payable and is between US$800 and US$2,500. There are no additional costs.

Provision is not made for special categories of captives. Rent-a-captives and protected cell companies are provided for.

Shipping and Aviation

Hamilton is a port of British registry. A Bermuda exempt company whose principal place of business is Bermuda or another of Her Majesty's dominions can register wholly owned vessels in Hamilton. Wholly owned aircraft may also be registered in Bermuda by exempt companies.

Licensing Companies

A Bermuda exempt company may be used to hold copyrights, patents, and trademarks. These can be registered in Bermuda and exploited worldwide.

Mutual Funds

Bermudian law allows the establishment of unit trusts and mutual funds. The over 350 collective investment schemes in Bermuda have assets worth approximately US$7 billion. Bermuda has been granted "designated territory status" under the Financial Services Act 1986 (United Kingdom). This means that mutual funds that are certified by Bermuda's minister of finance as U.K. class schemes can apply to the Securities and Investments Board in the United Kingdom to be classified as "recognized schemes." The implication of such classification is that the funds can be promoted to the public in the United Kingdom on a basis similar to U.K. authorized unit trusts.

Trusts

The law of trusts in Bermuda is based on the English common law and the doctrines of equity. The Trustee Act 1975, based on the English Trustee Act 1925, stipulates the powers and duties of trustees, although trustees' statutory investment powers are usually augmented in trust agreements.

The wide investment and administrative provisions of the Trusts (Special Provisions) Act 1989 can be incorporated by reference into trust agreements. The perpetuity period of trusts has been extended to one hundred years under the Perpetuities and Accumulations Act 1989. The perpetuity period does not apply to charitable trusts. Migration is provided for in that a trust governed by the law of Bermuda may change its governing law, provided that the new law recognizes the validity of the trust and the interests of the beneficiaries. Secrecy is insured as there is no register of trusts.

Checklist for Trusts

- There is a statutory schedule of standard trust powers for the Bermuda trust.
- The maximum perpetuity period for noncharitable trusts is one hundred years.
- At least one resident trustee is required.
- There is no requirement for the registration of trusts.
- Trust documents are normally in English.
- No stamp duty is charged.
- The law of trusts is based on English common law.
- Appeal lies to the Privy Council.
- The Hague Convention has been implemented in Bermuda.
- Specific provision is made for the exclusion of foreign inheritance laws.
- There is a specific provision dealing with the nonrecognition of foreign judgments.
- There is a specific "asset protection" provision (beyond that offered by general insolvency law) protecting a disposition to a trust from challenge by creditors.
- A special limitation period of six years is imposed on creditors' claims.
- Provision is made for (registrable) noncharitable trusts.

CHAPTER TWENTY-TWO

BRITISH VIRGIN ISLANDS

Background Information

Geographic and Demographic Data

Location	The British Virgin Islands (BVI) is situated in the northeastern Caribbean, approximately sixty miles east of Puerto Rico. The territory is five hours behind GMT.
Capital	Road Town.
Area	58 square miles.
Population	13,368.
Language	English.
Access	There are frequent flights from San Juan, Puerto Rico, with good connections.
Telecommunications	Excellent.

Government

The BVI is a British protected territory (Crown colony). The territory is self-governing and is a member of the Commonwealth.

Political and Economic Stability

The BVI is politically stable. Internal government is by locally elected representatives, and external affairs are the responsibility of the governor, who is appointed by the British government. The BVI is economically stable, with successful tourism and offshore financial services industries. The territory's main sources of revenue are fees from offshore companies, customs duties, and income tax.

Business Environment

Government attitude to offshore activities: The government has a long-standing policy of encouraging offshore financial activities. It also has an ongoing commitment to ensuring that regulatory structures are constantly being updated and modernized to keep pace with increasing competition between international offshore financial centers.

Employment: The Labor Code Ordinance 1975 regulates employment practices. A nonbelonger requires a work permit to work or be employed in the BVI. Such a permit will be granted only if the labor commissioner is satisfied that no British Virgin Islander is available to fill the position. Work permit fees are between US$100 and US$1,000, depending on the nature of the employment.

Local business requirements: A trade license is required by any person carrying on a business within the territory. However, a trade license is not required by an offshore corporation or other entity that does not have business operations in the territory. Corporations exempt from licensing requirements are those licensed under the Banks and Trust Companies Act 1990, the Company Management Act 1990, and the Insurance Act 1994.

Foreigners and Immigration

The government encourages persons with appropriate skills or persons bringing investment capital into the BVI that will create employment opportunities. Nonbelongers may purchase real estate personally or through a company, provided they hold a license. Licenses relating to vacant land are issued subject to a development commitment on the part of the purchaser.

Currency and Exchange Control

The currency in use in the territory is the U.S. dollar. There is no exchange control. Banks in the territory can offer accounts in all major currencies.

Disclosure of Information

Secrecy of information: There is no specific secrecy law. The inspector of banks and trust companies may seek information from licensees, but not information relating to clients of the licensees. Confidential information may be obtained only under a court order. Court orders may be obtained under the Drug Trafficking Offenses Act 1992 and the Criminal Justice (International Cooperation) Act 1993. Very little information is held on public record. Client confidentiality is also insured by the frequent use of nominees and the issue of bearer shares.

Disclosure in company formation and trust settlement: The disclosure to a public authority of the beneficial owner of an offshore corporation is not required. However, service providers in the private sector, as part of their due diligence procedures, would normally ascertain the beneficial ownership. The International Business Companies Ordinance Cap 291 and the Banks and Trust Companies Act 1990 govern the confidentiality of such disclosure. Corporations do not have to be audited, but a local registered agent and office are required. All particulars of the corporation, such as its name, share capital, and the persons requesting the formation of the corporation, must be lodged with the local registered agent. The local registered agent may be compelled to disclose beneficial ownership under an order of court or with the specific authorization of the client. A trustee is not required to register the beneficiaries of a trust. Although a bank may request a company or trustee opening a bank account to disclose the beneficial owners, this is not required by law.

International cooperation measures: The BVI has a procedure for cooperation with foreign states and investigators. This procedure functions through mutual legal assistance treaty arrangements. An appeal to the courts lies against the furnishing of information under such an arrangement. The Mutual Legal Assistance (US) Act 1990, the Criminal Justice (International Cooperation) Act 1993, and the gateway provisions in specific pieces of legislation such as the Insurance Act 1994 govern the exchange of information with foreign states.

The enforcement of foreign judgments is governed by the principles of law developed by the courts and by the Reciprocal Enforcement of Judgments Act Cap 65. A judgment can be registered and then enforced provided that (a) it is a final judgment; (b) it was given by a court of competent jurisdiction; and (c) the respondent had notice of the proceedings.

The Proceeds of Criminal Conduct Act 1997 (governing "all-crimes" money laundering) was passed on September 30, 1997, but is not yet in force. This act does not cover fiscal crime and tax evasion.

The BVI tax treaties contain an exchange of information provision. Tax matters are generally not included in the range of activities for which assistance is provided regarding foreign investigations into tax evasion. Requests for assistance in investigations into tax evasion are excluded from the ambit of the cooperation arrangements, although the authorities would probably facilitate access to such information as is available on the public record.

Legal System

General

The territory's legal system is based on English common law. Orders in council have extended the application of some English statutes to the BVI. The practice and procedure of the courts is based on English law.

Legislation

The principal provisions affecting offshore operations and transactions are contained in the following:

- Aliens Land Holding Regulations Act 1923
- Banks and Trust Companies Act 1990
- Companies Act 1885
- Encouragement of Industries Ordinance 1953
- Hotels Aid Ordinance 1953
- Income Tax Ordinance 1946
- Insurance Act 1994
- International Business Companies Ordinance 1984
- Limited Partnerships Act 1996
- Mutual Funds Act 1996
- Mutual Funds Amendment Act 1997
- Pioneer Services and Enterprises Ordinance 1966
- Proceeds of Criminal Conduct Act 1997
- Trustee (Amendment) Act 1993

Case Law

Important recent cases include the following:

- *Re TC Pagarani Deceased* (1997/1998) 1 OFLR 239 (High Court of Justice [Civil] BVI)
- *Moss & Pearce v. Integro Trust* (1997/1998) 1 OFLR 427 (High Court of Justice [Civil] BVI)
- *Floyd Koch v. Robert Chew* (1997/1998) 1 OFLR 537 (High Court of Justice [Civil] BVI)
- *Canada Trust v. Century Holdings* (1998/1999) 1 ITELR 56 (High Court of Justice [Civil Division])
- *Re TC Pagarini (deceased)* (1998/1999) 2 OFLR 1 (Court of Appeal, BVI)
- *Tel-Art Inc. v. Ming Kown Kooh* (1997/1998) 1 OFLR 870 (Court of Appeal, BVI)

Treaties

See "Tax Treaties and Double Taxation" and "Other Treaties."

Taxation (Direct and Indirect)

Income Tax

Under the Income Tax Ordinance 1946, persons, including companies resident and domiciled in the BVI, are liable to income tax on their worldwide income.

However, a company incorporated in the BVI but managed and controlled elsewhere is regarded as nonresident and taxed accordingly. A resident foreign company is not domiciled and is taxed only on income arising within or remitted to the BVI. An international business company (IBC) is totally exempt from income tax. Nonresidents are taxed only on income arising within the BVI.

Personal tax rates are as follows:

Income	*Percentage tax*
Up to US$2,500	3%
US$2,501 to US$7,500	6%
US$7,501 to US$15,000	10%
US$15,001 to US$25,000	15%
US$25,001 and above	20%

Withholding Taxes

Under the Income Tax Ordinance 1946, sec. 39, interest paid to nonresidents is not subject to income tax. See also "Tax Treaties and Double Taxation," below.

Employment Tax

Under the Employment Tax Ordinance 1968, an employer has to pay to government an employment tax.

Land Tax

Under the Land Tax Ordinance 1955, tax is payable by the owners of property in the BVI.

Stamp Duties

A schedule to the Stamp Duty Ordinance specifies instruments on which stamp duty is imposed.

Trade License Fees

License fees are payable under the Business, Professions, and Trade Licenses Act 1989.

Hotel Accommodation Tax

Under the Hotel Accommodation Taxation Ordinance 1969, a tax of 7% is levied on the accommodation proportion of hotel bills, which is charged to the guests.[1]

Other Taxes

There is no capital gains tax, net worth tax, gift tax, sales tax, turnover tax, or estate duty.

Tax Incentives

See *Incentives (Tax and Nontax).*

Insurance Companies

See "Taxation of Insurance Companies," under "Insurance."

Tax Treaties and Double Taxation

The treaties between the United Kingdom, Japan, and Switzerland have been extended to cover the BVI. At present there is no treaty with the United Kingdom. Credit is given for any foreign taxes suffered on income subject to income tax.[2]

Japan

With regard to dividends, withholding tax may not exceed 15% or 10% if the beneficial owner of the shares is a company that owns at least 25% of the voting power. With regard to interest, withholding tax may not exceed 10%. With regard to royalties other than mining and similar royalties, withholding tax may not exceed 10%.

Switzerland

Royalties other than mining and similar royalties are exempt from withholding tax.

Other Treaties

The BVI has entered into mutual legal assistance treaties. These contain exchange of information provisions in respect of criminal matters but not fiscal and taxation matters.

Incentives (Tax and Nontax)

Development encouragement incentives are provided under the following ordinances:

Encouragement of Industries Ordinance 1953

An industry that is not being conducted in the BVI on a commercial scale or at all and for which there are insufficient manufacturing facilities may be declared to be a pioneer industry by the governor. Customs duty relief may then be obtained for a period of five years on imported materials for the constructing and fitting of the pioneer factory. There is also a five-year exemption on income tax.

Hotels Aid Ordinance 1977

A license for relief from customs duty on building materials and equipment may be granted in respect of constructing and fitting out a hotel. Income of the licensee arising from the newly erected hotel is exempt from income tax for ten years. On transfer of ownership of such a hotel, the purchaser may apply for transfer of the license from the vendor.

Pioneer Services and Enterprises Ordinance 1966

Any business may be declared by the governor to be a pioneer service or enterprise if it is in the public interest to do so. Such a business will obtain relief from customs duty on materials and articles imported for constructing or equipping the pioneer works. There is also an exemption from income tax for ten years.

Corporations

(The domestic laws of the BVI refer to *corporations* as *companies*. This terminology is retained in this chapter.)

Types of Companies

Companies are incorporated under the International Business Companies Ordinance 1984 or the Companies Act 1885 (Cap 285 companies). They may be private or public, limited or unlimited, and with or without share capital. A private company is one that, by its articles of association,[3]

(a) restricts the right to transfer its shares;

(b) limits the number of its members, exclusive of employees, to fifty; and

(c) prohibits any invitation to the public to subscribe for any shares or debentures.

A public company must have at least five members; a private company, only two.

International Business Companies

Companies incorporated under the International Business Companies Ordinance 1984 are exempt from income tax. An IBC is defined as a company that does not

- carry on business with persons resident in the BVI;
- own an interest in real property situated in the BVI, other than a lease *(see list below);*
- carry on banking business unless it is licensed to do so under the Banking Act;
- carry on business as an insurance or reinsurance company; or
- carry on the business of riveting the registered office for companies.

IBCs are empowered to

- maintain a bank account;
- use the services of accountants and lawyers;
- maintain accounting records;
- hold meetings of shareholders and directors;
- hold a lease of property for use as an office; and
- hold shares and other securities.[4]

A resident of the BVI may hold shares in an IBC, whether as an individual or as a company.[5] An IBC can issue registered shares or bearer shares or both.[6] Shares may be issued with any kind of preferential or redemption rights.[7] The word *Limited, Corporation, Incorporated, Société Anonyme*, or *Sociedad Anonima* or abbreviations thereof must be part of the name.[8] The objects clause need only state that the company is to engage in an activity that is not illegal in the BVI.[9] The memorandum or articles may be amended by a resolution of members or, where permitted, by a resolution of directors.[10] An IBC may increase or reduce its share capital by resolution of the directors, subject to its memorandum or articles.[11] It is not necessary to file details of shareholders and directors with the registrar. A company incorporated under the Companies Act can transfer to the IBC register,[12] as can a company incorporated in a jurisdiction outside the BVI.[13] An IBC must have a registered agent in the territory who is licensed under the Banks and Trust Companies Act 1990 or the Company Management Act 1990. The International Business Companies (Amendment) Act 1990 provides for the optional filing with the registrar of companies or a register of mortgages and charges, and the register of directors or the share register.

Checklist for IBCs

- Prior approval of the name is required when registering a company. Some words are sensitive, e.g., *Royal* and *Imperial*. The name must end in *Limited, Corporation, Incorporated, Société Anonyme*, or *Sociedad Anonima*, or abbreviations thereof.
- It can take one day to incorporate a company. Shelf companies are available. The usual minimum capital required is US$50,000.

- The minimum number of shareholders required is one. Bearer shares or shares of no par value are possible.
- The minimum number of directors required is one. Corporate directors are allowed, and there is no restriction on the residence of directors.
- A company secretary is not mandatory. A corporate secretary is allowed, and there is no restriction on the place of residence of directors.
- There must be a registered office and a registered agent.
- No information is required by the authorities prior to incorporation or prior to tax status being granted. The memorandum and articles and the registered office and agent are available on the public file. Copies of the register of members and directors (if maintained) and an impression of the seal must be kept at the registered office. Both corporate books and a seal are required and may be kept anywhere.
- Accounts are not required and do not have to be filed anywhere. An annual return is not required.
- There are no restrictions on when meetings should be held.
- Migration and redomiciliation are not provided for.
- The annual license fee payable to the government is US$300 if the capital does not exceed US$50,000, and US$1,000 if it does. There is no filing fee.

Other Forms of Business Organization

Sole Proprietorships

There is no special legislation relating to sole proprietorships. If such a business is being carried on in the territory, a trade license may be required at the rates applicable to corporations.

Partnerships

Partnerships with corporate attributes: Partnerships do not have to be registered. All partners may be limited liability companies.

Partnerships without corporate attributes: Partnerships without corporate attributes are governed by the Partnership Act of 1996, which provides specifically for local and international limited partnerships. Limited partnerships must have a registered agent in the BVI and be registered with the Registrar of Limited Partnerships. There is a registration fee of US$500 and an annual license fee of US$500. Limited partnerships are prohibited from carrying on insurance, banking, or trust company business. An international limited partnership may not own real estate in the BVI or carry on business with persons in the BVI, although there are exceptions to this provision along the lines of those applying to IBCs.

Foreign Companies

A company that is incorporated in a country outside the BVI and has a place of business within the BVI must be registered with the registrar of companies as a foreign company. Companies so registered are liable for a license fee.[14] The fee is US$250 for nonresident companies, and US$25 or more for resident companies.

Banks and Trust Companies

In terms of the Banks and Trust Companies Act 1990, a license must be obtained before any person or trust company may conduct either banking or trust business in the BVI. This applies whether the business is to be carried on locally or outside the BVI.[15]

Banking licenses are classified as follows:

(a) a general banking license, allowing full banking activities both onshore and offshore—US$10,000 per annum;

(b) a restricted Class I banking license, which allows full offshore banking activities but does not allow the licensee to take deposits from persons resident in the BVI other than another licensee or an IBC, and it does not allow investment in any asset that represents a claim on any person in the BVI other than another licensee or government body—US$8,000 per annum; and

(c) a restricted Class II banking license, which allows offshore banking activities only with persons or entities nominated in the license application—US$6,000.

The minimum paid-up capital for a bank with a general license is US$2 million and for a bank with a restricted license of either Class I or II is US$1 million.

Trust licenses are divided into a general trust license that allows the carrying on of trust business without any restriction and a restricted trust license that allows the carrying on of trust business only with the persons or entities nominated in the license application. The minimum paid-up capital for a trust company with a general trust license is US$250,000.

Insurance

General

In terms of the Insurance Act 1994, application must be made for a license to carry on any form of insurance business in or from the BVI. The minimum paid-up share capital requirements for insurers range from US$100,000 to US$300,000. The annual fees are US$2,000 for insurers and US$500 for insurance brokers, agents, or managers. Minimum margins of solvency for insurers range from a flat US$250,000 to 10% or 20% of net retained annual premium, depending on the type of business insured and the amount of net retained annual premium income.

Licensed insurers must have an insurance manager, duly licensed and registered in the BVI. They are also required to submit annual audited financial statements to the commissioner of insurance.

Captive Insurance Companies

Captive insurance is governed by the Insurance Act 1994. There are approximately 125 captives established in the BVI. The total asset size of the captive sector is approximately US$400 million. The total premium size is approximately US$233 million. The Financial Services Department (Insurance Division) regulates the sector. An annual audit is required, as is a compliance (solvency) certificate.

Regulatory concessions are made under sec. 74(3) of the act. Captives are exempt from tax.

The minimum capital requirements are as follows:

General	US$100,000
Long-term	US$200,000
General and long-term	US$300,000

Incorporation costs are between US$500 and US$1,500. An annual license fee of US$2,000 is payable. There are no additional costs.

Provision is not made for special categories of captives.

Taxation of Insurance Companies

Life insurance: A life insurance company is taxable on its investment income less the management expenses, and when premiums are received from outside the BVI, the taxable income is the same proportion of the total investment income as the premiums received in the BVI bear to the total premiums received.

Other insurance: Where other insurance companies have profits arising in part outside the BVI, tax is payable on the gross premiums and other income receivable in the BVI and deducting attributable expenses, and also a reserve for unexpired risks at the percentage adopted by the company as a whole.

Shipping

Ships may be registered in the BVI, but they must be owned by a person or company resident in the territory or any other British territory. Road Town is a port of British registry.

Mutual Funds

Mutual funds domiciled or carrying on business in the BVI are regulated by the Mutual Funds Act of 1996 and the Mutual Funds (Amendment) Act of 1997, which came into force on January 1, 1998. The latter act distinguishes among private, professional, and public funds. A private fund has a maximum of 50 private investors; a professional fund offers its shares only to professional investors whose net worth is greater than US$1 million; and a public fund is neither of the above and offers its shares to the public.

Private and professional funds must apply for recognition, and funds that are not domiciled in the BVI must pay an application fee of US$350. All private and professional funds must pay an annual fee of US$350.

A public fund must apply for registration, a more complex procedure than the recognition procedure, and pay an application fee of US$500. Public funds must also submit audited annual accounts and are required to pay an annual fee of US$500.

The Mutual Funds (Amendment) Act of 1997 also regulates managers and administrators of funds domiciled or carrying on business in the BVI. Managers and administrators must be licensed under the Act. The application fee for a license is US$250, and the annual fee thereafter is US$500.

Trusts

The basic principles of English trust law apply in the BVI, subject to the Trustee Ordinance 1961 and the Trustee (Amendment) Act 1993. Registration is not required but can be effected without undue delay.

A trust may be established by instrument in writing, either by an instrument of settlement, in which the person establishing the trust transfers assets to the trustee to be held on the terms of the instrument, or by a declaration of trust, in which there is no settlor and the trustee simply executes a declaration creating trusts of specified property.

A fee of US$50 is payable to the government on setting up a trust, and professional fees of about US$500 will be levied. There are no annual fees payable to the government, but professional fees of about US$500 are leviable annually. The same applies to termination costs.

Foreign trusts may be registered if the deed or instrument creating the trust is suitably executed and there are no special requirements.

The Trustee (Amendment) Act 1993 provides for fixed term perpetuity not exceeding one hundred years. It also provides for the establishment of purpose trusts, the disposition of personal property, and the avoidance of forced heirship. It introduces the notion of "wait and see" and provides statutory exemption from all taxes.

Checklist for Offshore Trusts

- The maximum perpetuity period for noncharitable trusts is one hundred years.
- A resident trustee is not required.
- There is no requirement for the registration of trusts.
- Trust documents are normally in English.
- Stamp duty of US$50 is charged.
- The law of trusts is based on English common law.
- The Hague Convention has been implemented in the BVI.
- Specific provision is made for the exclusion of foreign inheritance laws.
- There is no specific provision dealing with the nonrecognition of foreign judgments.
- There is no specific "asset protection" provision (beyond that offered by general insolvency law) protecting a disposition to a trust from challenge by creditors.
- There is no special statute of limitations period for creditors' claims.
- Provision is made for noncharitable purpose trusts.

Notes

1. Hotel Accommodation Taxation (Amendment) Ordinance 1977, sec. 2.
2. Income Tax Ordinance 1946, sec. 54.
3. Companies Act 1885, sec. 2.
4. Sec. 5.
5. Sec. 5(g).
6. Sec. 9(1).
7. Sec. 9.
8. Sec. 11(1).
9. Sec. 12(2).
10. Sec. 16(1).
11. Sec. 24(1).
12. Sec. 84(1).
13. Secs. 84(2), 85.
14. Companies Act (Amendment) (No. 2) Ordinance 1977, sec. 14.
15. Banks and Trust Companies Act 1990, sec. 3.

CHAPTER TWENTY-THREE

CAYMAN ISLANDS

Background Information

Geographic and Demographic Data

Location	The Cayman Islands is a group of three islands in the western Caribbean, south of Miami. The islands are five hours behind GMT.
Capital	George Town.
Area	100 square miles.
Population	36,153.
Language	English.
Access	The islands are served by six major airlines, with daily flights to Miami and weekly flights to major North American and European cities.
Telecommunications	Excellent.

Government

The Cayman Islands is a self-governing but dependent territory of the United Kingdom. It is a member of the Commonwealth.

Political and Economic Stability

The Cayman Islands is politically stable, and there is no desire for independence from Britain. It has a unicameral legislature and is subject to a constitution. The Queen of England is the head of state and is represented on the islands by a governor.

With no direct taxation, the Cayman Islands is a thriving offshore financial center: Twenty-eight thousand foreign companies do business with the six hundred registered banks and trust companies, and banking assets exceed US$500 billion. Tourism is also a mainstay, accounting for about 70% of the GDP and 75% of foreign currency earnings. The tourist industry is aimed at the luxury market and caters mainly to visitors from North America. Total tourist arrivals exceed 1 million visitors annually. About 90% of the islands' food and consumer goods must be imported. The Caymanians enjoy one of the highest outputs per capita and one of the highest standards of living in the world. Unemployment is about 7%.

Business Environment

Government attitude to offshore activities: The government actively encourages offshore activities and is constantly revising corporate, trust, banking, insurance, partnership, and mutual fund legislation. A Monetary Authority was established in 1997 under the Monetary Authority Law 1996. It is a separate legal entity, wholly owned by the government, and its functions are to deal with the local currency, maintain monetary stability, advise the government on banking and monetary issues, and regulate the financial sector. A stock exchange was also established in 1996.

Employment: A work permit is required for persons without "Caymanian status" wishing to work in the Cayman Islands. Caymanian status is granted on a quota basis to British citizens, British dependent territory citizens, and citizens from countries such as Australia, the Bahamas, Barbados, Belize, Canada, Jamaica, New Zealand, the Republic of Ireland, Trinidad and Tobago, and the United States. Work permits and related matters are regulated under the Immigration Law 1992.

Local business requirements: In terms of the Trade and Business Licensing Law (1995 Revision), any individual or corporation engaged locally in business must hold a license. To hold such a license, an individual must have Caymanian status or hold a work permit; a corporation must be beneficially owned and controlled by persons having Caymanian status, or it must hold a license under the Local Companies (Control) Law (1995 Revision). Licenses under the Trade and Business Licensing Law range from CI$50 to CI$10,000 annually, and CI$50,000 for bulk storers of petroleum. Licenses under the Local Companies (Control) Law cost CI$200 annually. Licenses are also required under other legislation and are charged on issue and annually as follows:

Banks and Trust Companies Law (1995 Revision)

Class A license	CI$42,000
Class B or trust license:	
Unrestricted	CI$12,600
Restricted	CI$6,000
Restricted (trust license)	CI$1,640

Insurance Law (1995 Revision)	
Class A license	CI$5,000
Class B license	CI$4,500
Mutual Fund Law (1996 Revision)	
Unrestricted	CI$5,000
Restricted	CI$2,000 plus CI$500 for each fund under administration
Single fund exemption	CI$200
Companies Management Law (1996 Revision)	
On issue	CI$500
Annually	CI$300 plus CI$10 for each company managed
Immigration Law 1992	CI$100 to CI$6,000 annually

Currency and Exchange Control

The local currency is the Caymanian dollar. It is tied to the U.S. dollar at CI$1.00 to US$1.20. There is no exchange control.

Disclosure of Information

Secrecy of information: Confidentiality is protected in the Cayman Islands under, among others, the Monetary Authority Law 1996, section 42; the Banks and Trust Companies Law (1995 Revision), section 13; and the Confidential Relationships (Preservation) Law (1995 Revision), section 5. These laws impose penalties on professional persons and government officials who disclose information without authorization. Banker-client confidentiality is also protected at common law.

Disclosure in company formation and trust settlement: Disclosure of the beneficial owner of a corporation is not required on incorporation in the Cayman Islands, unless a licensed bank, trust corporation, insurance corporation, insurance manager or broker, mutual funds administrator, or corporate manager is involved. No other information about the beneficial owner is required, although the local registered office will have its own due diligence requirements with regard to the identity of the beneficial owner, in order to comply with money laundering legislation. The Confidential Relationships (Preservation) Law (1995 Revision) governs the confidentiality of disclosure generally.

Corporations do not have to be audited, but a local registered office is required. The registered office will hold the registers of shareholders, directors, and officers, and mortgages and charges. It will disclose information under a court order made in terms of the Confidential Relationships (Preservation) Law (1995 Revision), the Mutual Legal Assistance (USA) Law 1986, the Proceeds of Criminal Conduct Law 1996, the Misuse of Drugs Law (1995 Revision), or the Misuse of Drugs (International Cooperation) Law 1997.

A trustee does not have to register the beneficiaries of a trust. However, a corporation or trust opening a bank account will have to disclose the beneficial owners or beneficiaries in order for the bank to meet the due diligence standards of the Proceeds of Criminal Conduct Law 1996. A bank may waive this requirement in certain circumstances, depending on the source and the standing of the business. This requirement also applies to limited partnerships and corporations.

International cooperation measures: Procedures for cooperation with foreign states and investigators are provided for in the Evidence (Proceedings in Other Jurisdictions) Act 1975, the Confidential Relationships (Preservation) Law (1995 Revision), the Mutual Legal Assistance (USA) Law 1986, the Proceeds of Criminal Conduct Law 1996, and the Misuse of Drugs (International Cooperation) Law 1997. The procedures are enforced by means of letters of request between courts, pursuant to a court order or governor's order, or with the approval of the relevant authority. An appeal against the procedure lies in certain circumstances. Exchange of information with foreign states is also dealt with in the Banks and Trust Companies Law (1995 Revision), the Insurance Law (1995 Revision), the Mutual Fund Law (1996 Revision), and the Monetary Authority Law 1996.

Foreign judgments are enforced under the following:

(a) the Foreign Judgments Reciprocal Enforcement Law (1996 Revision);
(b) the Foreign Arbitral Awards Enforcement Law (1996 Revision);
(c) the Misuse of Drugs Law (1995 Revision);
(d) the Proceeds of Criminal Conduct Law 1996; and
(e) the common law.

In terms of (a) above, the jurisdiction must be designated by the governor. In terms of (b) above, only arbitration awards in a jurisdiction party to the New York Convention of 1958 may be enforced; in terms of (c) and (d) above, foreign restraint orders of the United States and the United Kingdom can be enforced; and in terms of (e) above, a foreign civil judgment for a liquidated sum can usually be enforced.

The Cayman Islands has not entered into any tax treaties. It has entered into a mutual legal assistance treaty with the United States, which contains an exchange of information agreement. All crimes except those relating to taxes are covered in this agreement.

Banking secrecy: Banking secrecy in relation to offshore banking is covered by the Banks and Trust Companies Law (1995 Revision), the Confidential Relationships (Preservation) Law (1995 Revision), and the Monetary Authority Law 1996. The Proceeds of Criminal Conduct Law 1996 is an "all-crimes" money laundering statute. It was amended in 1998, the amendment coming into effect early in 1999, to remove the clause in the original law providing for a specific exemption for fiscal offenses among the serious crimes under which the legal authorities would assist in the enforcement of foreign "freezing" and confiscation orders at the request of designated countries, currently the United States and the United Kingdom. Alleged offenses must still meet a dual criminality test and be indictable under Cayman law.

The local authorities will not cooperate with foreign investigations into tax evasion and will not consider requests for assistance in this regard.

Legal System

General

The legal system in the Cayman Islands is based on English common law, with the addition of a local constitution and local statutes. The practice and procedure in the courts is based on English law.

Legislation

The principal provisions affecting offshore operations and transactions are contained in the following:

- Banks and Trust Companies Law (1995 Revision)
- Cayman Islands Stock Exchange Law 1996
- Companies Law (1995 Revision)
- Companies Management Law (1996 Revision)
- Exempted Limited Partnership Law 1991
- Immigration Law 1992
- Insurance Law (1995 Revision)
- Land Holding Companies Share Transfer Tax Law (1996 Revision)
- Local Companies (Control) Law (1995 Revision)
- Misuse of Drugs (International Cooperation) Law 1997
- Misuse of Drugs Law (1995 Revision)
- Monetary Authority Law 1996
- Mutual Fund Law 1993 (1996 Revision)
- Mutual Legal Assistance (USA) Law 1986
- Partnership Law (1995 Revision)

- Perpetuities Amendment Law 1997
- Perpetuities Law 1995
- Proceeds of Criminal Conduct Law 1996
- Registration of Merchant Ships Law 1991
- Special Trust (Alternative Regime) Law 1997
- Stamp Duty Law (1995 Revision)
- Stock Exchange Company Law 1996
- Tax Concessions Law (1995 Revision)
- Trade and Business Licensing Law (1995 Revision)
- Trusts Law (1996 Revision)

Case Law

Important recent cases are

- *Deloitte & Touche v. Johnson & Dinan* (1997/1998) 1 OFLR 285 (Court of Appeal, Cayman Islands).
- *AG Cayman Islands v. McCorkle* (1998/1999) 1 ITELR 3 (Court of Appeal, Cayman Islands)
- *DI Brian Gibbs & Others v. John Mitchell Rea* (1997/1998) 1 OFLR 719 (Privy Council)
- *Evan Wahr-Hansen v. Bridge Trust Co. Ltd.* (1997/1998) 1 OFLR 787 (Court of Appeal, Cayman Islands)
- *Re Ansbacher (Cayman) Ltd.* (1998/1999) 2 OFLR 123 (Grand Court of the Cayman Islands)
- *Re Dunnes Payments Enquiry* (1998/1999) 2 OFLR 202 (Grand Court of the Cayman Islands)
- *William J. McCorkle et al. v. Attorney General* (1997/1998) 1 OFLR 753 (Grand Court of the Cayman Islands)

Treaties

The Cayman Islands has not entered into any tax treaties with other jurisdictions.

In 1984, the United Kingdom, acting on behalf of the Cayman Islands, entered into the Narcotics Agreement with the United States. The Narcotic Drugs (Evidence) (USA) Law 1984 was subsequently enacted in the Cayman Islands to enforce the agreement by providing a mechanism for evidence to be obtained for U.S. federal and grand jury investigations and federal court proceedings relating to activities falling within the Single Convention on Narcotic Drugs 1961.

In 1986, the Cayman Islands entered into a mutual legal assistance treaty with the United States, the terms of which are set out in the Schedule to the Mutual

Legal Assistance (USA) Law 1986. The Cayman Mutual Legal Assistance Authority (i.e., the chief justice or a judge designated by him) was set up in terms of the act. The treaty specifically excludes matters relating to tax evasion.

Taxation (Direct and Indirect)

The following taxes do not apply in the Cayman Islands:

Business tax
Capital gains tax
Capital or wealth tax
Corporation tax
Gift tax
Income tax
Inheritance tax or estate duty
Payroll tax
Real estate tax
Sales tax
Transfer tax (except where the transfer is chargeable to stamp duty)
Turnover tax
Withholding tax

Stamp Duties

Stamp duty is charged at a rate of 7.5% on the value of the consideration on a conveyance or transfer on the sale of real estate within the islands. If the land is owned by a corporation or other body corporate, the stamp duty is payable if shares are transferred for value. No other land taxes are charged.

Mortgages, promissory notes, and other legal documents require payment of stamp duty at rates up to 1% ad valorem. The maximum stamp duty on a mortgage of movable property in the Cayman Islands is CI$500 if the mortgage is granted by an exempt corporation, an ordinary nonresident company, or a company incorporated outside the Cayman Islands.

Certain instruments or notes and any secured or unsecured global instruments, and assignments or transfers of such instruments, are exempt from stamp duty, provided

(a) the instruments or notes are issued as part of a series of instruments of equal rank;

(b) the issuer is an exempt company, an ordinary nonresident company, or a company incorporated outside the Cayman Islands;

(c) the issuer paid a duty of CI$500 in respect of the issue; and

(d) the issue is not secured by real estate in the Cayman Islands.

Import Duties

Varying rates of duties are levied on all imports into the islands.

Tax Incentives

See "Incentives."

Incentives

Few incentives apply in the Cayman Islands. The notable exception is that import duties may be waived on materials imported for the construction of new hotels or industrial premises for businesses that employ Caymanians.

Corporations

(The domestic laws of the Cayman Islands refer to *corporations* as *companies*. This terminology is retained in this chapter.)

Although an expensive Caribbean jurisdiction, the Cayman Islands is a well-established offshore center, with sophisticated banking and legal infrastructure and a flexible approach to legislative alterations.

Types of Companies

In terms of the Companies Law (1995 Revision) and the Local Companies (Control) Law (1995 Revision), there are three basic types of companies capable of registration: the ordinary company, the ordinary nonresident company, and the exempt company. For an ordinary company to be designated nonresident in terms of the Local Companies (Control) Law, it must not carry on business within the islands. Such designation is granted by certificate issued by the financial secretary. In terms of the Companies Law, exempt companies may not carry on business within the islands except in furtherance of their business abroad. Ordinary nonresident companies may convert to exempt companies. Exempt companies have a maximum life of thirty years.

Ordinary nonresident and exempt companies are not subject to the licensing requirements of the Local Companies (Control) Law and so are the vehicles most commonly used for offshore operations.

There is no special provision for migration or redomiciliation of companies.

Fees and Costs

Ordinary companies with no registered capital or capital not exceeding CI$42,000 pay an incorporation fee of CI$150 and an annual fee of CI$150. Ordinary companies with a registered capital over CI$42,000 pay an incorporation fee of CI$250 and a further CI$250 annually.

Nonresident companies with no registered capital or capital not exceeding CI$42,000 pay an incorporation fee of CI$350 and an annual fee of CI$350. Nonresident companies with a registered capital over CI$42,000 pay an incorporation fee of CI$492 and a further CI$492 annually.

Exempt companies with no registered capital or capital not exceeding CI$42,000 pay an incorporation fee of CI$410 and an annual fee of CI$410. Exempt companies with a registered capital over CI$42,000 but below CI$1.7 million pay an incorporation fee of CI$574 and a further CI$574 annually. Exempt companies with a registered capital exceeding CI$1.7 million pay an incorporation fee of CI$1,435 and a further CI$1,435 annually.

Checklist for Nonresident and Exempt Companies

- A nonresident company's name must end with *Limited* or *Ltd*. There is no restriction on the ending of exempt companies' names. The use of words such as *Bank* and *Insurance* is restricted.
- It takes three to five days to incorporate a company. Shelf companies, although unusual, are available. Prior to incorporation, an undertaking must be made not to engage in local business.
- The usual minimum capital required for exempt companies and for nonresident companies is US$50,000. Capital duty on incorporation of an exempt company is a minimum of US$500, and for a nonresident company, a minimum of US$427.
- At least one shareholder is required. With regard to exempt companies, bearer shares and shares of no par value are allowed, but no such shares are possible for nonresident companies.
- There must be at least one director. Corporate directors are allowed, and there is no restriction on the place of residence of the directors.
- A company secretary is not necessary. Corporate secretaries are permissible, and there is no restriction on the secretary's residence.
- There must be a registered local office, but there is no requirement for a registered agent.
- No documents are required to be kept at the registered office in respect of exempt companies, but the registers of members, directors, mortgages, and charges must be kept in respect of nonresident companies.
- The address of the registered office and a copy of the memorandum and articles of association are available on the public file.
- Corporate books and a seal are required in both cases.
- An audit is not necessary, but books reflecting the true financial state of the company must be kept, although there are no filing requirements.

- A limited form of annual return is required for exempt companies, and a full form is required for nonresident companies.
- There are no restrictions on the meetings of nonresident companies. With regard to exempt companies, one directors' meeting per year must be held in the islands, but there is no restriction on annual general meetings.

Other Forms of Business Organization

Sole Proprietorships

The Cayman Islands recognizes sole proprietorships but does not have any specific legislation governing them. Aspects of sole proprietorship are regulated under the common law, and the sole proprietor's liability is unlimited.

Limited Partnerships

Limited partnerships may be registered under the Partnership Law (1995 Revision) or the Exempted Limited Partnership Law 1991. A limited partnership is the combination of one or more partners whose liability for the obligations of the firm is unlimited (the general partners) together with one or more partners whose liability is limited in amount (the limited partners). The right to take part in the management of the affairs of the firm is strictly confined to the general partners. The limited partners have no control over the assets or affairs of the partnership.

To establish a limited partnership under the Partnership Law, all of the general partners must make a sworn declaration containing the following:

(a) the name of the firm;

(b) the general nature of its business;

(c) the principal place of its business;

(d) the full name of each of the partners and their respective places of business;

(e) the term, if any, for which the partnership is entered into and the date of its commencement;

(f) a statement that the partnership is limited and the description of every limited partner as such;

(g) the amount of capital contributed by each limited partner; and

(h) a statement that the sum referred to in (g) above as having been contributed by each of the limited partners has actually and in good faith been paid in cash.

This declaration must be filed with the registrar of limited partnerships, and the information contained in it must also be published in the *Cayman Gazette*.

An existing limited partnership may reregister as an exempted limited partnership.

To establish an exempted limited partnership, a general partner must file a signed statement with the registrar of limited partnerships containing the following:

(a) the name of the exempted limited partnership, which must contain the words *Limited Partnership* or *LP;*

(b) the general nature of the business;

(c) the address of the registered office in the Cayman Islands;

(d) the term, if any, of the partnership;

(e) the names and addresses of the general partners; and

(f) a declaration that the partnership will not do business with the public in the Cayman Islands except in furtherance of its business outside the Cayman Islands.

The above information is open to public inspection. The general partner must maintain at the registered office a register of limited partnership interests and a register of mortgages of such interests, both of which are public documents.

An exempted limited partnership may obtain a fifty-year undertaking against the future imposition of taxation.

Foreign Companies

Under the Companies Law (1995 Revision), foreign companies are companies incorporated outside the Cayman Islands that establish a place of business or carry on business in the Cayman Islands. "Carrying on business" includes the sale by or on behalf of the foreign company of its shares or debentures or the establishment of a share transfer or registration office.

All foreign companies must be registered in the Cayman Islands. This is done by filing the following with the registrar of companies:

(a) a certified copy of the memorandum and articles of association;

(b) a list of the directors; and

(c) the name and address of one, or more than one, person resident in the Cayman Islands authorized to accept service of process or notices on behalf of the company.

A registration fee of CI$850 is also payable. A foreign company must also pay an annual fee of CI$500.

Banks and Trust Companies

Banks and trust companies must be licensed under the Banks and Trust Companies Law (1995 Revision). Without a license, no company may carry on any banking or trust business or use words in its name such as *Bank, Trust* or *Savings and Loan.*

There are two types of bank license. An "A" license permits unrestricted domestic and offshore business; a "B" license permits only offshore business. The holder of a B license may have an office in the Cayman Islands and conduct business with other licensees and offshore companies but may generally not do business with residents of the islands. A B bank and a trust licensee may be restricted or unrestricted. An unrestricted B bank or trust licensee needs a minimum paid-up capital of US$500,000, and there is no restriction on the number of customers. A restricted B bank or trust licensee requires a minimum paid-up capital of US$25,000 or its equivalent, but a list must be given of those persons or companies from whom it will solicit or receive funds by way of trade or business (in the case of a bank) or for whom it will undertake trust business (in the case of a trust company). This list forms part of the license and any alteration requires approval of the Monetary Authority.

A licensee need not be a Cayman Islands company, and a foreign bank or trust company may be licensed and registered under the Companies Law as a foreign company. In such cases, an appropriate guarantee of the branch's obligations will be required to be given by its head office.

Insurance

General

The Insurance Law (1995 Revision) requires all persons carrying on insurance (including reinsurance) business in or from within the Cayman Islands to be licensed. Licenses are granted by the governor-in-council. Applications are scrutinized by the Monetary Authority.

There is a distinction between a Class A insurer's license and a Class B insurer's license (which may be restricted or unrestricted). The Class A license permits the holder to carry on insurance business generally and to underwrite Cayman Islands domestic business. Persons intending to engage in insurance business from within the Cayman Islands but not to engage in domestic business may obtain a Class B license. All forms of reinsurance business are specifically excluded from the definition of domestic business.

A restricted Class B insurer's license is designed for the insurer formed essentially as a single parent "captive" or as a "mutual" by a common interest group to write insurance, other than domestic insurance, only for its parent or members or such other persons as may be approved by the Cayman Islands authorities.

No insurer's license other than a restricted Class B license will be granted unless the insurer demonstrates a minimum net worth of CI$100,000 in the case of an insurer effecting general business but not long-term business; CI$200,000 in the case of an insurer effecting long-term business (for instance, life policies, annuity contracts, or personal injury policies in excess of five years) but not general business; and CI$300,000 in the case of an insurer effecting general business and long-term business.

A licensed insurance manager must maintain full and proper records of the business of the insurer at its office in the Cayman Islands.

Auditors must be appointed and the financial statements of the insurer audited annually. Annual accounts need not be filed with the Cayman Islands authorities, although this is normal practice.

Captive Insurance Companies

Captive insurance is regulated by the Insurance Law (1995 Revision). There are approximately 424 captives established in the Cayman Islands. The total asset size of the captive sector is approximately US$7.231 billion. The total premium size is approximately US$1.885 billion. The Monetary Authority regulates the sector. An annual audit is required, as is a compliance certificate.

There are no regulatory concessions. Captives are taxed at a zero tax rate.

The minimum capital requirements are as follows:

General	US$120,000
Long-term	US$240,000
General and long-term	US$360,000

Incorporation costs are US$2,000. An annual license fee of US$6,097.56 is payable, as is an annual return fee of US$701.20.

Legislation is pending with regard to rent-a-captives and protected cell corporations.

Shipping and Aviation

Shipping

George Town is a port of British registry. The Merchant Shipping Act 1894 (United Kingdom) as amended by the Merchant Shipping Act 1988 (Cayman Islands) Order 1988 provides for the registration of ships and mortgages. The Admiralty provisions of the Administration of Justice Act 1956 (United Kingdom) have also been extended to the Grand Court of the Cayman Islands, which is a colonial court of Admiralty within the meaning of the Colonial Courts of Admiralty Act 1890 (United Kingdom).

A Cayman Islands company may be a qualified person under the terms of the Merchant Shipping Act 1894, even though the owners of the company are not qualified persons. To be a qualified person, the company must have its principal place of business in the Cayman Islands, the United Kingdom, the Isle of Man, the Channel Islands, or any other British colony.

A ship may be registered in the Cayman Islands if a majority interest in the ship is owned by one or more qualified persons. Qualified persons include British citizens, nationals of a member state of the European Union, and bodies corporate incorporated in a member state of the European Union having their principal place of business in any part of the European Union.

The Registration of Merchant Ships Law 1991 provides for the registration of vessels over 1,600 gross tons that are chartered by demise for a period of at least three years to a person qualified to own a British ship. This law also provides for a vessel over 1,600 gross tons registered in the Cayman Islands to be granted dispensation from the Cayman Islands merchant shipping laws and regulations where the vessel is chartered by demise and is to be registered at the same time under the flag of another country. The Registration of Merchant Ships Law also facilitates the registration of vessels by allowing the bill of sale and carving and marking note to be produced to the registrar of shipping within twenty-one days of registration rather than prior to registration.

Government registration fees and tonnage taxes are minimal. The maximum fee payable upon first registration of a vessel is now CI$500. Thereafter, tonnage taxes are payable annually according to the gross registered tonnage of the vessel. For vessels not exceeding 200 gross tons, CI$60 is payable each year. For vessels exceeding 200 and not exceeding 1,000 gross tons, the annual tonnage tax is assessed at CI$0.30 per ton; for vessels exceeding 1,000 gross tons, the annual tonnage tax is CI$300 plus CI$0.10 per ton in excess of 1,000 tons.

The Merchant Shipping Law of 1997 was expected to come into force in September 1998. The law, based on the U.K. Merchant Shipping Act of 1995, updates and streamlines the existing legislation and reflects all applicable maritime conventions, except the conventions on marine pollution, which will be dealt with in a separate piece of legislation. The law provides for the registration of ships, including a bareboat charter registration regime. The qualifications for owning a Cayman Island ship have been expanded to enable persons (natural and corporate) from a wider global range to have access to the registry. It also provides statutory protection for first mortgages, where the mortgage contract contains a negative covenant prohibiting the creation of subsequent mortgages or the transfer of ownership or registration.

Aviation

The Aircraft Navigation (Overseas Territories) Order 1989 sets out the requirements in respect of the registration of aircraft on the Cayman Islands' Register of

Civil Aircraft. The Civil Aviation Authority of the Cayman Islands is responsible for the maintenance of the register and all matters such as licensing, certification, and regulation of aircraft and aircrews. The Civil Aviation Authority maintains an aircraft mortgage register.

A Cayman Islands company may be a "qualified person" under the Aircraft Navigation (Overseas Territories) Order 1989 even though the owners of the company are not qualified persons. To be a "qualified person," the company must have its principal place of business within the Commonwealth. Registration is discretionary, and the Civil Aviation Authority must be satisfied as to the proposed ownership structure and operation of the aircraft, together with full information regarding pilots and maintenance personnel.

The policy of the Civil Aviation Authority is not to encourage the registration of civil aircraft operating passenger services. Most aircraft registered in the Cayman Islands' Register of Aircraft are private jet aircraft.

Registration fees are between CI$150 and CI$300, based on the weight of the aircraft. The fee for the issue of a certificate of airworthiness is CI$200 plus a charge of CI$150 in respect of each 500 kg., or part thereof, of the aircraft, or a charge of CI$150 plus an amount equal to the cost of making the investigation by the Civil Aviation Authority.

Mutual Funds

The Mutual Fund Law (1996 Revision) requires those persons engaged in mutual fund administration to be licensed. Licenses are granted by the governor-in-council, and applications are scrutinized in detail by the Monetary Authority. Restricted licenses are available to those administering a small number of regulated mutual funds. The initial and annual license fee for a mutual fund administrator is CI$5,000; for a restricted mutual fund administrator, it is CI$2,000. Each must also pay an additional initial and annual fee of CI$500 per regulated mutual fund under administration. Those administrating only one regulated mutual fund may be exempted from licensing and pay an initial and annual exemption fee of CI$200.

Open-ended companies, trusts, or partnerships established in the Cayman Islands to operate as investment or mutual funds with more than fifteen investors are now regulated. All must prepare and file an offering document and register with the Monetary Authority, as well as file annual audited accounts. In addition, they must either be specifically licensed as mutual funds or appoint licensed mutual fund administrators to provide a principal office, unless there is a minimum investment per investor of CI$40,000 or its equity interests are quoted on a recognized stock exchange or market. To be specifically licensed, a mutual fund must demonstrate that its promoters and managers are of sound repute, that its managers have the necessary experience, and that its business will be properly run.

Regulated mutual funds must pay an initial and annual fee of CI$500.

Trusts

The Trusts Law (1996 Revision) Part V provides for the registration of exempted trusts. All the trust documents must be delivered to the registrar of trusts together with a fee of CI$400.[1] The registrar retains the originals and issues a certificate of registration. An annual fee of CI$100 is payable to the registrar.[2]

The main advantage conferred on an exempted trust is a fifty-year undertaking from the governor to the trustees that no law subsequently enacted "imposing any tax or duty to be levied on income or on capital assets gains or appreciation or any tax in the nature of estate duty or inheritance tax shall apply to any property comprised in or any income arising under such exempted trust or to the trustees or the beneficiaries thereof in respect of any such property or income."[3]

Exempt or ordinary nonresident Cayman Islands companies may qualify as beneficiaries of exempted trusts.

The Special Trust (Alternative Regime) Law, 1997 (Law 18 of 1997) introduced a special trust law to permit the "creation of non-charitable purpose trusts" that cover "incidental and connected purposes." Special trusts may therefore be created for any objects as long as they are "lawful and not contrary to public policy."

In 1998 the Trusts (Amendment) (Immediate Effect and Reserve Powers) Law was passed to regulate the position with regard to "sham trusts." The act identifies the powers that can be reserved by the settlor of a trust without risking that the arrangement is deemed an agency rather than a trust.

Checklist for Trusts

- There is no statutory schedule of standard trust powers for trusts or exempted trusts.
- The maximum perpetuity period for noncharitable trusts is 150 years.
- A resident trustee is not required.
- Exempted trusts have to be registered.
- Trust documents are usually in English.
- A registration fee of US$48 is charged.
- The law of trusts is based on English common law.
- Appeal lies to the Privy Council.
- The Hague Convention has been implemented in the Cayman Islands.
- Specific provision is made for the exclusion of foreign inheritance laws.
- Specific provisions deal with the nonrecognition of foreign judgments.
- There is a specific "asset protection" provision (beyond that offered by general insolvency law) protecting a disposition to a trust from challenge by creditors.

- There is a special limitation period of six years for creditors' claims.
- Provision is made for noncharitable purpose trusts.

Notes

1. Secs. 70 and 71.
2. Sec. 74.
3. Sec. 77.

CHAPTER TWENTY-FOUR

COOK ISLANDS

Background Information

Geographic and Demographic Data

Location	The Cook Islands is situated in the South Pacific Ocean, approximately halfway between Hawaii and New Zealand. It is ten hours behind GMT.
Capital	Avarua.
Area	93 square miles.
Population	19,776.
Languages	English is the official language. Maori is also spoken.
Access	Direct flights are available to and from Auckland, Fiji, Tahiti, and Honolulu.
Telecommunications	Excellent.

Government

The Cook Islands is a self-governing parliamentary democracy, in free association with New Zealand. It has the right at any time to declare unilateral independence.

Political and Economic Stability

The Cook Islands is a politically stable constitutional democracy, based on the Westminster model. The Queen of England is the head of state and is represented by the queen's representative.

Like other South Pacific island nations, the Cook Islands' economic development is hindered by the isolation of the country from foreign markets, its lack of natural resources, periodic devastation from natural disasters, and inadequate infrastructure. Agriculture provides the economic base with major exports made up of copra and citrus fruit. Manufacturing activities are limited to fruit-processing plants and several clothing factories. Trade deficits are made up for by remittances from emigrants and by foreign aid, largely from New Zealand. In 1996, the government declared bankruptcy, citing a US$120 million public debt.

Efforts to exploit tourism potential and to expand the mining and fishing industries have not been enough to deal adequately with the financial crisis. In an effort to stem further erosion of the tenuous economic situation, the government slashed public service salaries by 50%, condensed the number of government ministries from fifty-two to twenty-two, reduced the number of civil servants by more than half, began selling government assets, and closed all overseas diplomatic posts except for the one in New Zealand.

Business Environment

Government attitude to offshore activities: The government actively encourages foreign investment in the Cook Islands and grants incentives and concessions, including reductions in tax, to foreign investors. Business licenses are required, and the amount payable to the government varies according to the type of business. The licensing requirement does not apply to international and foreign companies.

Currency and Exchange Control

The New Zealand dollar and the local Cook Islands currency are legal tender in the Cook Islands. There is no exchange control.

Disclosure of Information

Secrecy of information: Strong confidentiality provisions apply to the offshore sector. Government officials and trust company and bank employees are compelled to observe secrecy, and failure to do so leads to penal sanctions. The offshore registries are not open to general public search; they may be searched only by persons showing to the registrar good and cogent reason for doing so. Fraud constitutes one such reason.

The Trustee Companies (Due Diligence) Regulations 1996 require a trust company to be satisfied that assets are not derived from activities such as drug trafficking prior to registering an international trust. In terms of the Offshore Industry (Criminal Provisions) Act 1995–1996, trust companies are required to report suspicion or knowledge of drug trafficking and other criminal activities to the Monetary Board. A trust company failing to comply with this provision could lose its license, and an offshore corporation that the Monetary Board reasonably believes to be involved in serious criminal activity will be deregistered.

Disclosure in company formation and trust settlement: The disclosure of the beneficial owner of an offshore corporation or trust is not required on its formation in the Cook Islands. No other information is required about the beneficial owner. The International Companies Act 1981–1982 and the Trusts Act 1984 govern the confidentiality of such disclosure. Audits are not required, unless the corporation involved also holds an offshore banking license or an offshore insurance license.

International corporations must have a resident corporate secretary. International trusts must have, as one of their trustees, a licensed Cook Islands trust corporation or a Cook Islands international corporation. The statutory registers and similar documents must be lodged with the local agent. Details of international trusts cannot be disclosed under any circumstances. Beneficial ownership of a corporation may be disclosed by the local agent with the consent of all the directors. A trustee does not have to register the beneficiaries or settlor of a trust.

The law does not require a corporation or trust opening a bank account to disclose beneficial ownership or the beneficiaries; however, banks may require disclosure to satisfy their own due diligence requirements. The same applies to limited partnerships.

International cooperation measures: The Cook Islands does not have a procedure for cooperation with foreign investigators, unless the case involves drug trafficking or money laundering. The procedure involves making an application to the high court for a direction to an officer of the corporation under investigation. A decision of the high court is subject to an appeal to the court of appeal and ultimately to the Privy Council in the United Kingdom. The International Companies Act 1981–1982, section 227(4)(c), governs the exchange of information with foreign states with regard to drug trafficking. No similar legislation exists with regard to international trusts.

An enforcement mechanism only exists in the Cook Islands in relation to judgments of the courts of New Zealand. The procedure involves a registration process. The Cook Islands is not party to any exchange of information agreements or to any tax treaties. The islands' confidentiality provisions do not permit the disclosure of information relating to taxation matters, and the authorities would therefore not consider a request for assistance in an investigation into tax evasion favorably unless the evasion was also related to activities such as drug trafficking or fraud.

The legislation does not cover fiscal crime, unless it is related to proven criminal activity.

Legal System

General

The legal system in the Cook Islands is based on English common law. Certain New Zealand statutes were once part of the law of the Cook Islands, but since independence in 1965, the Cook Islands parliament is sovereign.

Legislation

The principal provisions affecting offshore operations and transactions are contained in the following:

- International Companies Act 1981–1982, with regulations passed in 1997
- International Partnership Act 1984
- International Trusts Act 1984
- International Trusts Act Amendments 1995
- Offshore Banking Act 1981
- Offshore Industry (Criminal Provisions) Act 1995
- Offshore Insurance Act
- Trustee Companies Amendment Act 1995–1996
- Trustee Companies (Due Diligence) Regulations 1996

Case Law

An important recent case is *South Orange Grove* (No. 2) (1997/1998) 1 OFLR 3 (Court of Appeal [Civil Division], CI).

Treaties

The Cook Islands is not party to any treaty arrangements, tax or otherwise, with other countries.

Taxation (Direct and Indirect)

Corporation Tax

Cook Islands companies are subject to tax at a rate of 20% on their worldwide income. Nonresident companies registered under the Domestic Companies Act 1971–1972 are not subject to tax, except regarding income and profit sourced in the Cook Islands. International companies and foreign companies registered under the International Companies Act 1981–1982 are exempt from all taxes in the Cook Islands.

Turnover Tax

All businesses in the Cook Islands, except for international and foreign companies, pay a turnover tax of 10%. The tax is levied on gross turnover and is payable on a monthly basis.

Bonus Issue Tax

There is no capital gains tax in the Cook Islands. However, there is a bonus issue tax that applies to domestic companies when making a bonus issue to shareholders. The tax does not apply to international and foreign companies.

Stamp Duties

Some documents executed in the Cook Islands are subject to stamp duty.

Withholding Taxes

International and foreign companies are not subject to withholding taxes, although these taxes do apply to dividends, interest, and royalties paid by Cook Islands companies to nonresidents.

Import Duties

Most goods imported to the Cook Islands are subject to import duties.

Tax Incentives

See "Incentives (Tax and Nontax)."

Incentives (Tax and Nontax)

As the Cook Islands is a dependent economy, the government offers incentives to encourage business activities that will reduce its dependence on foreign aid. In particular, it encourages the manufacturing and offshore financial sectors. Incentives that are available include tax incentives, such as reduced import duty and income tax concessions in cases in which the minister of finance believes that the business venture will contribute significantly to the development of the Cook Islands. Applications for tax concessions are made to the Monetary Board and the cabinet.

Corporations

(The domestic laws of the Cook Islands refer to *corporations* as *companies*. This terminology is retained in this chapter.)

The advantages of incorporation in the Cook Islands are that no taxes of any kind are payable for international and foreign companies and there is a high degree of confidentiality. Flexible shareholding and debt structuring methods are also available. However, the Cook Islands is in an inconvenient time zone, particularly for European clients, and is at present suffering the negative aftereffects of defaulting on loans from Nauru and the rescheduling of loans from other banks.

Types of Companies

Domestic companies are governed by the Companies Act 1971–1972. They are required to register with the registrar of companies their name, memorandum and articles of association, notice of registered office, notice of particulars of directors and the secretary, and a certificate of due compliance with the statutory provisions. An incorporation fee is payable based on the authorized capital, and a business license fee is payable annually.

International companies are the most commonly used offshore entities. They are governed by the International Companies Act 1981–1982. A great deal of flexibility is permitted to these companies, and the memorandum of association empowers them to carry on any business other than a business prohibited by the act. Prohibited businesses are those relating to banking, insurance, and trust companies, unless the international company has a license from the Monetary Board to carry on such a business. Typically, incorporation costs will be in the range of US$500, with additional professional fees of between US$500 and US$1,000. Annual fees include statutory fees of US$500 and administration fees of approximately US$1,000.

Registered listed companies are international companies that are listed on approved stock exchanges[1] and are registered under the International Companies Act 1981–1982 Part VIA. Such companies may be subject to scrutiny by inspectors with wide powers of examination, within or outside the Cook Islands. Registration excludes listed companies from certain statutory restrictions, such as the restrictions against search and the provisions altering the traditional rules of capital maintenance and permitting indirect returns of capital. Particular rules apply to the buyback of shares and the distribution of share premiums.

Checklist for International Companies

- The registrar's approval of the company name is required, and words such as *Bank, Trust,* and *Insurance* are restricted to use by special license holders.
- It takes one day to incorporate an international company. A limited number of shelf companies are available. No information is required by the authorities prior to incorporation.
- The usual minimum capital required is US$1 million. Fees charged are not based on the company's capital.
- No capital duty is charged.
- A minimum of one shareholder is required. Bearer shares and shares of no par value are possible.
- A minimum of one director is required. Corporate directors are allowed, and there is no restriction on the directors' residence.
- A company secretary is mandatory. Corporate secretaries are allowed, and at least one joint secretary must be a Cook Islands resident.
- A registered office is required, but a registered agent is not. The registered office must keep registers of directors, members, secretary, and charges, as well as the company books and seal.

- The company name and registered office are available on the public file.
- Accounts must be maintained, but they need not be filed. An audit is not required. An annual return is required.
- There is no restriction on the holding of meetings.
- Provision is made for the migration and redomiciliation of companies.

Foreign Companies

Foreign companies are companies that are incorporated outside the Cook Islands and are registered as foreign companies under the International Companies Act 1981–1982. A company is not required to register as a foreign company if it is conducting an offshore transaction on a one-off basis and the transaction is completed within thirty-one days. Registration enables a foreign company to have a physical place of business in the Cook Islands. On registration, the registrar issues the company with a certificate that is renewable annually on payment of a prescribed fee.

Foreign companies, whether or not they have registered under the act, are exempt from tax.

Typically, incorporation costs will be in the range of US$500, with additional professional fees of between US$500 and US$1,000. Annual fees include statutory fees of US$500 and administration fees of approximately US$1,000.

Offshore Finance Companies

An international company may be formed to operate as an offshore finance company. Such a company will not be liable to tax on its profits or income and will not have to pay withholding taxes, stamp duty, issues taxes, imposts, or levies of any kind. An offshore finance company is also not subject to debt/equity requirements or to thin capitalization rules. Depending on the activities engaged in by the company, it may be subject to the licensing requirements under the Offshore Banking Act 1981.

Insurance

Captive Insurance Companies

Captive insurance is governed by the Offshore Insurance Act. The number of captives established in the jurisdiction and the total asset and premium size of the sector have not been disclosed. The Monetary Board regulates the sector. An annual audit is required, but a compliance certificate is not.

There are no regulatory concessions. Captives are exempt from tax.

The minimum capital requirement is US$2 million, and incorporation costs are between US$1,500 and US$2,000. The license fee is US$2,000 in the first year and US$500 annually thereafter. A reregistration fee of between US$1,500 and US$2,000 is also payable annually.

Provision is not made for special categories of captives. Legislation is pending with regard to protected cell companies.

Licensing Companies

International companies may be formed to operate as offshore licensing companies. Intellectual property rights are recognized and can be registered in the Cook Islands, which is a signatory to most of the international protocols and agreements relating to copyrights, patents, trademarks, and other intellectual property. Royalties are not taxed in the Cook Islands, and there are no rules relating to arm's length transactions or valuations with regard to the transfer of intellectual property rights to or from a company in the Cook Islands.

There are no taxes on the holding or acquisition of intellectual property rights, copyrights, patents, and trademarks by an international company. Income accumulated in the Cook Islands from royalties, licensing agreements, and franchising arrangements is also not subject to tax.

Trusts

International trusts are governed by the International Trusts Act 1984. This act governs the registration of trust deeds and provides that registration must be renewed annually upon payment of a fee, and can be for a period of up to five years. A registered international trust has no tax liability in the Cook Islands and is not subject to any filing requirements with regard to returns, reports, and records. The act also alters the common law with regard to the following:

(a) the rule against accumulations;
(b) the rule against perpetuities;
(c) the rule against double possibilities;
(d) the rules limiting the extent of charitable purposes; and
(e) the rules against purpose trusts.

Checklist for International Trusts

- There is no statutory schedule of standard trust powers.
- The maximum perpetuity period for noncharitable trusts is over one hundred years.

- A resident trustee is usually required.
- Registration is required in that a certificate must be filed with the registrar of international trusts.
- Trust documents are in English.
- A registration fee of US$200 is charged.
- The law of trusts is based on English common law.
- Special leave is required to appeal to the Privy Council.
- The Hague Convention has not been implemented in the Cook Islands.
- Specific provision is made for the exclusion of foreign inheritance laws.
- Specific provisions deal with the nonrecognition of foreign judgments.
- There is a specific "asset protection" provision (beyond that offered by general insolvency law) protecting a disposition to a trust from challenge by creditors.
- There is a statutory limitation period of two years for creditors' claims.
- Provision is made for noncharitable trusts.

Notes

1. That is, Australia, Canada, France, Hong Kong, Indonesia, Japan, Luxembourg, Malaysia, the Netherlands, New Zealand, Singapore, South Africa, Taiwan, Thailand, the United Kingdom, and the United States.

CHAPTER TWENTY-FIVE

COSTA RICA

Background Information

Geographic and Demographic Data

Location	Costa Rica is situated in Central America, between Nicaragua and Panama. It is bordered by the Pacific Ocean and the Caribbean Sea, and it is six hours behind GMT.
Capital	San José.
Area	19,730 square miles.
Population	3,534,174.
Languages	Spanish is the official language. English is widely spoken in the commercial sector.
Access	There are regular flights.
Telecommunications	Excellent.

Government

Costa Rica is a democratic republic.

Political and Economic Stability

Costa Rica is the most politically stable country in Latin America, and it abolished its army in 1948. Its basically stable and progressive economy depends especially on tourism and the export of bananas, coffee, and other agricultural products. Poverty has been substantially reduced over the past fifteen years, and a strong social safety net has been put in place. Unemployment appears moderate, at little more than 5%, but substantial underemployment continues. Furthermore, large government deficits have undermined efforts to maintain the quality of social services.

Business Environment

Government attitude to offshore activities: The government has recently begun to encourage international operations in Costa Rica. Previously, there were no limitations on activities in which foreigners could invest, and Costa Rican legislation tended toward tax haven status, but the government is now actively encouraging investment in certain areas.

Employment: The sophisticated Labor Code and social security system result in a stable, well-regulated workforce, with little influence from trade unions.

Local business requirements: A license is required from the local municipality for certain commercial activities, such as running stores and restaurants.

Foreigners and Immigration

Foreigners may acquire residence under either the Retirement Law 1971 or the Residence Law 1950. Under the former, applicants are classified as pensioner residents or annuitant or investor residents, depending on whether their foreign income is derived from retirement income or permanent investments, whether local or foreign. A foreigner who has either type of foreign source income may obtain residence in Costa Rica and may invest in local business activities and serve on corporate boards, but a foreigner may not take employment that would displace local workers.

Residence under the Residence Law is granted without employment limitations, but it is only granted on a selective basis to professionals and businesspeople.

Currency and Exchange Control

The Costa Rican col6n (¢) is the local currency. There is no exchange control.

Disclosure of Information

Secrecy of information: Professional privilege insures the secrecy of information given to local attorneys. Violation of secrecy provisions leads to civil and criminal sanction.

Banking secrecy: The law requires banks to maintain absolute secrecy with regard to their clients, although normal banking operations are reported to the Central Bank. The Central Bank does not pass such information on to the Tax Department.

Legal System

General

The Costa Rican legal system is based on the Spanish civil law system. The 1948 constitution is the supreme law. The Commercial Code 1964 governs corporate law, trust law, loans, and securities. The Civil Code governs all other matters.

Legislation

The principal provisions affecting offshore operations and transactions are contained in the following:

- Civil Code
- Commercial Code 1964
- Free Export Zone Law
- Retirement Law 1971
- Tax Adjustment Law 1995
- Tax Justice Law 1996

Treaties

Costa Rica is not party to any double taxation agreements or any other treaty arrangements with any other country.

Taxation (Direct and Indirect)

Income Tax

All resident persons and businesses in Costa Rica are liable to income tax on income earned in Costa Rica. Nonresident persons and businesses must pay income tax on property or business income earned in Costa Rica. Income earned from a foreign source is tax-exempt. The annual personal income tax rates are as follows:

From 0 to ¢679,000	exempt
Between ¢679,001 and ¢1,016,000	10%
Between ¢1,016,001 and ¢1,694,000	15%
Between ¢1,694,001 and ¢3,395,000	20%
Above ¢3,395,000	25%

Capital Gains Tax

There is no capital gains tax in Costa Rica.

Conveyance Tax

A conveyance tax is imposed on the higher of the values of property as recorded at the Tax Administration or by the parties. The tax is at a flat rate of 3.01%.

Stamp Duties and Annual Fees

The Stamp Duty for Education and Culture Law 1976 imposes a duty on all domestic corporations or branches of foreign corporations registered in the public registry (mercantile section). Each entry in the registry by such a corporation is subject to a stamp duty of ¢750.

Corporations also pay an annual fee based on their net capital. The fee is calculated as follows:

Capital	*Fee*
Below ¢1,000,000	¢3,000
Between ¢1,000,001 and ¢2,000,000	¢6,000
Above ¢2,000,000	¢9,000

Withholding Taxes

A withholding tax of 15% is imposed on all dividends or corporate participations to shareholders. However, if the shares are registered on the stock exchange, the tax rate is 5%. A withholding tax of 15% is also imposed on interest on deposits, loans, commissions, and other financial expenses. However, a business based in Costa Rica that pays interest and other financial expenses to a foreign bank recognized by the Central Bank as a bank that finances international operations is exempt from the tax. The exemption also applies to the leasing of capital goods and the payment of interest on loans in relation to industrial or agricultural activities in Costa Rica.

A withholding tax of 15% is imposed on interest paid on any kind of securities by a public or private enterprise. However, if the securities are listed on a recognized stock exchange or are issued by certain registered financial institutions, the tax is reduced to 8%. Income derived from bills of exchange, promissory notes, and mortgage bonds is exempt from this tax.

Foreigners providing any form of service in Costa Rica are subject to a withholding tax of 15% of their gross income, before deductions. Foreigners who provide such services in a relationship of dependency pay a reduced tax of 10%. Foreigners who provide technical, financial, or administrative services are subject to a withholding tax of 25%.

Payments for the use of patents, formulas, trademarks, franchises, privileges, and royalties are subject to a 25% withholding tax over the amount remitted.

Real Estate Taxes

An annual tax is levied on real estate under the Land Territorial Tax Law 1939. The tax ranges from 0.3% to 1% and is assessed by and paid to the local municipality.

Sales Taxes and Consumer Taxes

Sales tax of 15% is levied on the sale of products or articles and services rendered in restaurants, bars, hotels, motels, auto repair shops, photo development shops, and dry cleaning services, and on telephone, cables, telex, and imported goods.

A consumer tax is also imposed under the same law,[1] and it applies to goods as stated in lists approved by the executive.

Vehicles Tax

A tax based on the weight and fair market value of a vehicle is levied on all owners of vehicles registered in the public registry of vehicles. The tax is payable annually.

Tax Incentives

See "Incentives."

Incentives

The Incentives to Tourist Development Law 1985 granted a tax holiday to enterprises engaged in hotel services, air transportation, water transportation, or car rental. These enterprises are also exempt from import duty. Any person purchasing stock in one of these corporations may deduct from their income tax an amount of up to 50% of the value of the share, in a proportion of up to 25% of their annual tax payment.

Corporations

Types of Corporations

Costa Rican law recognizes three types of corporations: the collective corporation (*sociedad en nombre colectivo*), the limited liability corporation (*sociedad de resonsabilidad limitada*), and the stock corporation or chartered corporation (*sociedad anonima*).

The collective corporation does not limit the owners' liability and has thus become a redundant corporate form in Costa Rica.

The limited liability corporation limits the investors' liability to the extent of their capital investment. In terms of the Commercial Code, article 104(a), at least two persons are required to form a limited liability corporation, but one person may thereafter become sole owner of the corporation's shares. Shares must be registered and can only be assigned by one person to another. The corporation requires only a manager with broad powers of attorney to administer it and is therefore similar to partnerships and close corporations in common law countries.

The stock corporation is the most common form of business organization in Costa Rica and is used most frequently in offshore activities.

Checklist for Stock Corporations or Chartered Corporations

- Formation requires at least two incorporators, who may be natural or legal persons, but thereafter a single person may become sole owner of all the shares.
- A stock corporation can do business in any part of the world and can also be organized as a banking corporation. A stock corporation requires special authorization from the Central Bank to operate as a bank in Costa Rica. However, if it is going to operate as a bank in other countries, it does not require such authorization. Finance or credit corporations that take funds from the public require a minimum capital of ¢300,000,000.
- The directors' and stockholders' meetings may be held anywhere in the world, provided that the cities where such meetings may be held are indicated in the incorporation charter.
- The time necessary for incorporation is approximately four weeks.
- The Commercial Code does not establish a minimum authorized capital, but it does provide that at least 25% of the capital must be paid up on incorporation.
- The capital is represented by registered shares, but these shares are transferable in "blank," which virtually makes them bearer. No par value shares are not permissible.
- At least three directors are necessary. They may be nonresident foreigners and need not be shareholders. At least one director must have managing power and is called the president. The president is assisted by the treasurer and the secretary. The meetings of the board of directors may be held anywhere in the world.
- The Commercial Code provides that a statutory comptroller ("fiscal") and a resident agent have to be appointed. The resident agent must be a lawyer.
- At least one annual general stockholders' meeting must be held. As with the board of directors, as long as the charter provides for meetings in other cities of the world and states the names of those cities, the stockholders' meetings may be held outside of Costa Rica.
- A stock corporation must keep three sets of minute books and three sets of accountancy books. The minute books are required for the board of directors' meetings, the stockholders' meetings, and the stockholders' registry book.
- Except for the filing of an income tax return once a year, there are no reporting requirements in Costa Rica. If the corporation has had only

foreign source income, it will not be taxed on such income, but the return still has to be filed.

- The corporation is required to maintain a registered office in Costa Rica.
- The costs of a corporation in Costa Rica vary depending on the amount of the incorporation capital. Unless a corporation is created for a specific purpose that requires a high capital, it is normal for a corporation to be formed with a low capital in order to keep the costs low.

Stock Corporation of Open Capital

Stock corporations of open capital were introduced in 1990 for trading on the stock exchange. Their shares can be negotiated freely on the stock exchange. Stock corporations of open capital must have a minimum social capital of ¢50 million and at least ten shareholders, and they are under the permanent supervision of the National Securities Council, which is controlled by the Central Bank.

Migration and Redomiciliation

Provision is made under the Commercial Code, article 227, for the migration of corporations to Costa Rica and for redomiciliation, the latter effected by presentation of a stockholders' resolution to the mercantile registry. Migration does not require the dissolution of the corporation in its country of origin or the incorporation of a new corporation in Costa Rica.

Other Forms of Business Organization

Sole Proprietorships

The sole proprietorship, or individual enterprise with limited liability (*empresa individual de responsabilidad limitada*), is recognized in Costa Rica under the Commercial Code. Liability is limited to the amount of capital assigned to the business, and the owner is thus relieved from any other liability. However, if bankruptcy is declared fraudulently, the civil judge is empowered to decree attachment of all the owner's assets.

A sole proprietorship requires only a manager with broad powers of attorney. The manager may be the owner or another person. Profits may only be distributed to the owner in the form of a dividend when the yearly statement shows a profit.

Limited Partnerships

Costa Rican law recognizes a limited partnership (*sociedad en commandita*), but it has become an unusual form of business entity. One financial associate (*commanditaire,* or limited partner) and one working associate (general partner) are required to form a limited partnership. The limited partner's liability is limited to the extent of his capital investment, and the general partners are jointly and severally liable for the partnership's debts. However, if the limited partner participates actively in the administration of the partnership, his liability will be equal to that of the general partner.

Foreign Corporations

Foreign corporations may operate in Costa Rica through either a branch or a subsidiary. A branch must be registered in Costa Rica in terms of the Commercial Code, article 226. For registration, a general stockholders' resolution is required and should be authenticated by the Costa Rican consul in the country of residency. Subsidiaries may be formed through local stock corporations without any such restrictions.

Branches are subject to a 15% withholding tax on all remittances to the head office, which is payable monthly, whereas subsidiaries are eligible for the more favorable tax treatment granted to Costa Rican corporations. A subsidiary is entitled to retain its gains as reserves, and tax is only assessed on payment on dividends.

Trusts

The Commercial Code, articles 633 to 662, deals with the establishment of trusts in Costa Rica and contain flexible provisions, particularly concerning the proper law of the trust, the jurisdiction, and situs of its administration.

Notes

1. Law 6828 of November 10, 1982.

CHAPTER TWENTY-SIX

CYPRUS

Background Information

Geographic and Demographic Data

Location	Cyprus is an island in the Eastern Mediterranean Sea, south of Turkey. It is two hours ahead of GMT.
Capital	Nicosia.
Area	3,570 square miles.
Population	752,808.
Languages	Greek is the official language. English is also widely spoken.
Access	Access to Cyprus by sea and air is excellent.
Telecommunications	Excellent.

Government

Cyprus is a democratic republic. It is a member of the Commonwealth.

Political and Economic Stability

In 1974, hostilities between Greece and Turkey divided the island into two de facto autonomous areas: a Greek area controlled by the Cypriot government (59% of the island's land area) and a Turkish-Cypriot area (37% of the island), which are separated by a United Nations buffer zone (4% of the island). There are two U.K. sovereign base areas within the Greek Cypriot portion of the island, which is now considered to be politically stable.

The Greek Cypriot economy is small and prosperous. Industry contributes 23% to GDP and employs 25% of the labor force, while the service sector contributes 72% to GDP and employs 62% of the labor force. Erratic growth rates in the 1990s reflect the economy's vulnerability to swings in tourist arrivals, caused by fluctua-

---

This chapter does not relate to the northern part of Cyprus, which has been under Turkish occupation since 1974.

tions in political and economic conditions in Western Europe and the Middle East, and the need for structural changes in the economy. In 1996, Cyprus fully satisfied all the Maastricht convergence criteria. Unemployment runs at 2.3%.

Business Environment

Government attitude to offshore activities: The government has a policy of actively encouraging shipping and offshore activities and offers numerous tax incentives to local industries and tourist operations.

Employment: Foreigners require a permit from the Immigration Department to work in Cyprus. Foreign employees are allowed if they are necessary for a business (i.e., executive or technical staff) or if they have skills that are not available locally.

Local business requirements: Foreign investors may invest in many sectors in Cyprus. Foreign participation of up to 49% is allowed in agriculture, forestry, fishing, hunting, mining, and quarrying, but the total investment must be over C£100,000. Foreign participation of up to 100% is allowed in the construction and manufacturing sectors. In other sectors, foreign participation between 49% and 100% is allowed, with investment minimums being required between C£50,000 and C£750,000.

In the banking sector, a license is required from the Central Bank to establish an offshore bank. The license costs US$15,000 annually.

Foreigners may also invest in companies listed on the stock exchange, provided that the foreign holding is not more than 49% of the issued capital and that individual shareholdings by nonresidents do not exceed 5%. Foreign investment in local banks is limited to a total holding of 15% and individual holdings of 0.5%.

Following an amendment to the Income Tax Law in 1998, offshore companies, partnerships, and branches may now acquire shares of Cyprus companies listed on the Cyprus Stock Exchange. Dividends and gains are fully tax exempt.

Foreigners and Immigration

Immigration to Cyprus is not encouraged, except in the case of foreign employees and retired persons. Both categories require a permit from the Immigration Department. Foreigners who retire in Cyprus are eligible for significant tax benefits.

A foreigner, whether resident or nonresident, requires a permit from the Council of Ministers to purchase real estate in Cyprus. A limit of 2,600 square meters (or 4,000 square meters in rare cases) is usually imposed on the size of the property, and it should be intended for temporary or permanent residence. It should be noted that new regulations governing the issue and renewal of temporary residence and employment (TRE) permits have been introduced, and the relevant authority should be consulted in this regard.

Currency and Exchange Control

The currency is the Cyprus pound; the Turkish lira is used in the area under Turkish occupation. Cyprus is not in the sterling area.

Exchange control is governed by the Exchange Control Law Cap 199 and is administered by the Central Bank. Permission is required from the Central Bank for residents to transact with nonresidents. A resident is defined as a person whose normal residence has been in Cyprus for the previous four years. All foreign incorporated corporations are nonresident. Corporations incorporated in Cyprus by foreigners are also nonresident. They may open bank accounts abroad and do not require Central Bank permission to transact outside Cyprus or with nonresidents. Where there is foreign participation in a local corporation that is intended for local operations, exchange control permission is required.

Disclosure of Information

Disclosure in company formation and trust settlement: The beneficial owner of an offshore corporation must be disclosed to the Central Bank of Cyprus on incorporation. Bank or other references may also be required with regard to the beneficial owner. The Central Bank Law 1993 governs the confidentiality of such disclosure.

Corporate audits are required, as are local registered offices and agents. The identity of the beneficial owner, memorandum and articles of association, the identity of nominees, and the director and secretary must be lodged with the local agent. The agent may be compelled to disclose beneficial ownership only under a court order.

A trustee is not required to register the beneficiaries of a trust, but a corporation or trustee opening a bank account must disclose beneficial ownership or the beneficiaries. This applies to limited partnerships and corporations as well.

International cooperation measures: Income tax laws, double taxation agreements, and mutual legal assistance treaties govern the exchange of information with foreign states and contain exchange of information agreements. The twenty-seven double taxation agreements are based on the OECD Model Convention. The mutual legal assistance treaties contain provisions with regard to the service of documents, the admission of evidence, the recognition of judgments, and the general exchange of information. Normal court procedures apply in respect of appeal against such cooperation procedures.

Foreign judgments are enforced under the Foreign Judgments (Reciprocal Enforcement) Law Cap 10. In terms of this law, foreign judgments may be registered and enforced by virtue of reciprocity.

Requests for information by treaty partners accompanied by explanations of the request are met with the taking of reasonable steps toward securing the information. Requests for assistance in investigations into tax evasion are considered within the remit of the relevant tax treaty agreement and with reference to domestic law.

The Confiscation of Proceeds of Trafficking of Narcotic Drugs and Psychotropic Substances Law of 1992 criminalizes money laundering and provides for the confiscation of proceeds from drug trafficking. Suspicions of money laundering must be reported to the police, and this will not be treated as a breach of banking confidentiality. Banks may also be compelled by court order to disclose information relevant to investigations into drug money laundering. This legislation does not cover fiscal crime.

Legal System

General

The legal system in Cyprus is based on English common law, with some civil law input with regard to administrative matters. U.S. constitutional law has considerable influence.

Legislation

Recent provisions affecting offshore operations and transactions are contained in the following:

- Banking Law 1997
- Liberalisation of Investment Laws 1997
- Prevention and Suppression of Money Laundering Law 1996

Treaties

See "Tax Treaties and Double Taxation" and "Other Treaties."

Taxation (Direct and Indirect)

Income Tax

Individuals: Personal income over C£5,000 per annum is taxed in Cyprus. The minimum tax rate is 20% on income over C£5,000 and below C£8,000. The maximum tax rate is 40% on income over C£11,000.

Corporations: Corporations and other bodies corporate are taxed at 20% of annual profits up to C£40,000, and 25% for annual profits exceeding C£40,000.

Capital Gains Tax

Capital gains tax applies to gains from real estate, which includes shares in a corporation owning real estate. The tax is at 20%. For individuals, the first C£10,000 profit is exempt from the tax. For farmers, the exemption increases to C£15,000, and for residential property that has been used by the owner as his residence for the past five years, the exemption increases to C£50,000.

Capital gains tax does not apply to profits from the sale of real estate abroad by nonresidents, by residents who were not resident when they purchased the property, or by offshore corporations or branches.

Stamp Duties

Stamp duty is payable at varying rates on documents executed in Cyprus and on documents executed outside of Cyprus that relate to matters or property within Cyprus.

Business License Tax

Municipal councils and village improvement boards impose professional taxes at varying rates.

Withholding Taxes

Dividends paid to shareholders are subject to a 20% withholding tax, although such tax may be set off against income tax. See also "Tax Treaties and Double Taxation," below.

Estate Duties

Estate duty applies as follows:

(a) If a person was domiciled in Cyprus at the time of his death, the tax is imposed on all property, no matter where it is situated, except property acquired in Cyprus after January 1, 1976, from funds emanating from abroad, if the deceased was previously not a permanent resident of Cyprus; and

(b) if a person was not domiciled in Cyprus at the time of his death, the tax is imposed on all property in Cyprus.

Gifts made within three years before death are subject to estate duty, but discretionary trusts may be used to avoid the tax. The tax is not applied to residential property up to C£150,000 in value, although any amount above C£150,000 is subject to the tax.

Estate duty is levied on the following scale:

Up to C£20,000	nil
C£20,001 to C£25,000	20%
C£25,001 to C£35,000	13%
C£35,001 to C£55,000	15%
C£55,001 to C£80,000	17%
C£80,001 to C£105,000	20%
C£105,000 to C£150,000	23%
Over C£150,000	30%

Gift Tax

There is no gift tax in Cyprus. However, where real estate is transferred as a gift, the usual transfer fees apply. If the property is a gift transfer to children, the fee is 4%, and if it is from spouse to spouse or relative to relative, the fee is 8% on the value appearing on the title deeds, which is usually far less than the market value.

Real Estate Taxes

Rates imposed by municipal councils and village improvement boards vary between 0.1% and 0.5% of assessed value. There is also an annual real estate tax based on the market value of the property. The tax is imposed on the following scale:

Up to C£100,000	nil
C£100,001 to C£250,000	0.2%
C£250,001 to C£500,000	0.3%
Over C£500,000	0.35%

Transfer fees range from 5% on sums up to C£10,000 to 8% on sums over C£75,000. A fee of 1% is charged for the registration of a mortgage, based on the amount secured by the mortgage.

Value-Added Tax

VAT in Cyprus currently runs at 8%. In line with the European Union VAT directive, the tax is not imposed on basic goods.

Offshore entities do not have to register for VAT or charge or collect VAT. They and their foreign employees are exempt from paying VAT on the purchase of certain goods, such as cars, office equipment, and household equipment. Telecommunication services are also exempt from VAT when given to offshore entities.

Import Duties

The Customs and Excise Duties Law 34 of 1975 imposes import duties on items following the Brussels Tariff Nomenclature. Import duty has been abolished on most European Union goods by virtue of the customs union agreement with the European Union.

Items imported for offshore entities and their foreign staff are exempt from import duty. Such items include cars and office and household equipment but do not include furniture. Cars imported by persons retiring to Cyprus are also exempt from the tax.

The manufacture of cigarettes, matches, and alcohol are subject to excise duties.

Tax Incentives

See "Tax Incentives" under "Incentives (Tax and Nontax)."

Tax Treaties and Double Taxation

Cyprus has entered into a significant number of double taxation agreements with other countries, namely, Austria, Belgium, Bulgaria, Canada, China, the Czech Republic, Denmark, Egypt, France, Germany, Greece, Hungary, India, Ireland, Italy, Kuwait, Malta, Norway, Poland, Romania, Slovakia, South Africa, Sweden, Syria, the United Kingdom, the United States, and Yugoslavia. Treaties with Thailand and Singapore are being negotiated, and a treaty with Belgium is awaiting signature and ratification. Most of the treaties are based on the OECD Model, although the treaty with the United States is based on the most recent model of United States Agreements.

The effect of these treaties is that, in many cases, Cyprus-registered offshore and shipping companies that already have partial or full tax exemption in Cyprus will also have partial or full tax exemption in a treaty country in respect of income derived in the treaty country.

Other Treaties

Cyprus is party to mutual legal assistance treaties, which contain provisions with regard to the service of documents, the admission of evidence, the recognition of judgments, and the general exchange of information. It has a customs union agreement with the European Union.

Incentives (Tax and Nontax)

Tax Incentives

Offshore entities: Cyprus-registered offshore companies that are fully owned by foreigners pay tax at a reduced rate of 4.25% on profit. Dividends are paid after tax and are not subject to any additional taxes. Cyprus-registered shipping companies, regardless of ownership, are fully tax-exempt. In addition, estate duty is not charged upon the inheritance of shares in offshore and shipping companies, and the sale or transfer of assets of such companies is immune from capital gains and other taxes, except for real estate in Cyprus.

The partners that are in partnerships with only foreign partners and that are engaged only in offshore activities are fully exempt from tax.

Branches of foreign corporations registered in Cyprus and engaged only in offshore activities are fully tax-exempt. If the company registering the branch is deemed to be managed and controlled from Cyprus, then it is taxed at 4.25% on worldwide profits.

The above provisions apply to offshore banks and offshore branches of foreign banks and to captive insurance companies that have a minimum paid capital of C£10,000.

The application of article 28A of the Income Tax Law has recently been extended to continue the current tax rate for offshore companies until 2007.

Certain VAT exemptions apply. (See "Value-Added Tax" under "Taxation [Direct and Indirect]" above.)

Foreign employees: A foreign employee of an offshore or shipping company, offshore partnership, or offshore branch of a foreign company or company established within Larnaca, the free industrial zone, is eligible for a 50% reduction in tax on his salary. Where the employee renders services outside Cyprus, the employee is subject to tax at 10% of local rates. In addition, certain VAT and import duty exemptions apply to foreign employees in relation to cars and household and office equipment (but not furniture), provided their salaries are over a fixed amount, which is currently under revision by the authorities.

Retired persons: Foreign investment income that is remitted to Cyprus is tax-exempt on the first C£2,000 and is thereafter taxed at a flat rate of 5%. Income in the form of royalties is included in this provision. Pensions received in Cyprus in respect of services rendered outside Cyprus are tax-exempt on the first C£2,000 and thereafter are taxed at the rate of 5 cents for every pound. Foreigners retiring in Cyprus are also allowed to import cars duty-free, if the car is for personal use.

Free Trade Zones

Free zones are established in Cyprus under the Free Zones Law 69 of 1975. There are free trade zones at Limassol Port and at Larnaca. Goods may be transshipped, manufactured, processed, or warehoused in these zones duty-free, provided a permit has been granted.

"Bonded" factories are also allowed to encourage export industries where raw materials are subject to import duty. Such factories may store raw materials in bonded stores exempt from import duty, provided they are used in the manufacture of goods intended for export.

Development Encouragement Incentives

An investment allowance of 40% is given in the first year of use on robots, computers, and operating software. Investment allowances also apply at varying rates to other assets. Annual wear and tear allowances are also granted in relation to assets and are calculated on the "straight line" basis. Plant, machinery, and raw materials not locally available may be imported duty-free. Protective tariffs and drawbacks of import duty also encourage local industry.

Corporations

(The domestic laws of Cyprus refer to *corporations* as *companies*. This terminology is retained in this chapter.)

The advantage of incorporation in Cyprus is that the network of twenty-seven double taxation treaties can be used by nonresident companies. Company law is based on the English common law, and there is a good professional infrastructure. However, documentation must be presented to the companies registry in Greek, and Cyprus is a relatively expensive jurisdiction.

Types of Companies

The various types of companies are regulated by the Companies Law Cap 113, which is based on the English Companies Act 1948. The first type of company is the public company limited by shares, which may be listed on the Cyprus Stock Exchange. The second type, which is commonly used for offshore activities and shipping companies, is the private company limited by shares, which, when fully owned by foreigners, is referred to as an "offshore company." There are also two types of companies limited by guarantee: the company limited by guarantee not having a share capital and the company limited by guarantee having a share capital. They are also regulated by the Companies Law Cap 113.

Checklist for Offshore Companies

- Prior reservation of the company name is required, and many words are considered sensitive. The name must end with *Limited.* Prior to offshore status being granted, bank references and copies of passports must be given to the Cyprus Central Bank.
- It takes two to three days to incorporate an offshore company. Shelf companies are available. The usual minimum capital is C£1,000, and in the case of offshore companies, this must be issued.

- The minimum number of shareholders is two. Bearer shares and shares of no par value are not allowed.
- A minimum of one director is required. Corporate directors are not allowed, and there is no restriction on the directors' residence.
- A company secretary is mandatory. A corporate secretary is allowed, and there is no restriction on the secretary's residence.
- Offshore companies need a local registered office, but there is no need for a registered agent. The registered office must keep the company register.
- The memorandum and articles of association, directors, secretary, shareholders, share capital, registered office, mortgages and charges, and sometimes accounts are available on the public file.
- Corporate books and a seal are necessary and are kept at the registered office.
- Accounts are required and must be filed, but they are not available to the public. An annual return is also required.
- There is no restriction on the holding of meetings.
- There is no provision for migration or redomiciliation.

Other Forms of Business Organization

Partnerships

General partnerships: General partnerships offer tax planning advantages for offshore activities. They are governed by the Partnerships and Business Names Law Cap 116, which is based on the equivalent English legislation. A general partnership may have between two and twenty partners, all of whom have unlimited liability.

A general partnership must be registered and must submit a return to the registrar of partnerships indicating its name, its objects, its partners, which of the partners may bind the partnership by their signatures, and the partnership's duration.

Foreigners may become partners in a Cyprus partnership fully or partially owned by foreigners but only after an exchange control permit is obtained.

The registration fee is C£30. The legal fees for registration range from C£300 upward.

Limited partnerships: Limited partnerships are also governed by the Partnerships and Business Names Law Cap 116. They must have at least one general partner who has unlimited liability and one or more limited partners whose liability is limited to the amount declared in the return filed with the registrar of partnerships.

Limited partnerships may be used in conjunction with offshore companies to obtain almost total tax exemption for the limited partner, instead of the 4.25% tax chargeable on offshore companies. An individual limited partner with an offshore company as an unlimited partner (with a very limited participation in the profits) may obtain fully tax-free profits for himself.

Foreign Companies

Foreign companies may be registered in Cyprus under the Companies Law Cap 113. Foreign insurance and banking companies usually register under these provisions.

Within one month after a foreign company establishes (with exchange control approval) a place of business in Cyprus, it must register, but registration as a foreign company does not carry with it a right to operate locally owing to exchange control restrictions.

Under the Income Tax (Amendment) Law 15 of 1977, branches of foreign companies may be used for offshore activities, including regional offices and offshore banking units, free from any tax incidence. However, if the foreign company is deemed to be managed and controlled from Cyprus, a 4.25% tax is imposed on its profits. Branches may be used for those wishing to take advantage of Cyprus's network of double taxation agreements, as such foreign companies are considered resident in Cyprus for the purposes of these agreements.

One of the disadvantages of incorporation in Cyprus is that annual accounts translated into Greek must be submitted by foreign companies.

The official registration fee for branches is C£100, and it costs C£20 to file annual accounts. Registration fees charged by lawyers are about C£500, and annual representation fees are the same as in the case of companies.

Insurance

Captive Insurance Companies

Captive insurance is governed by the Insurance Companies Laws 1984 to 1990 and the Insurance Regulation of 1995. There are approximately twenty captives established in Cyprus. The total asset size and premium size of the captive sector are not known. The superintendent of insurance, under the Ministry of Finance, regulates the sector. An annual audit and an annual license renewal are required, as is confirmation of the directors and principal officers and bank references for the beneficial owners.

There are regulatory concessions in the form of reduced share capital costs, and there is no requirement for the maintenance of deposits in Cyprus. A captive that is an offshore company is taxed at a rate of 4.25%. A captive that is an offshore branch managed from abroad or an offshore partnership is tax-exempt.

Incorporation costs are C£10,000. An annual license fee of about C£3,600 is payable. An additional registration fee of C£300 is also payable.

There are no special categories of captives. No provision is made for rent-a-captives and protected cell corporations.

Shipping

Registration of ships under the Cyprus flag is in terms of the Merchant Shipping (Registration of Ships, Sales, and Mortgages) Law 45 of 1963. The Merchant Shipping (Fees and Taxing Provisions) Law 38(I) of 1992 grants full tax exemption on profits derived by owners or bareboat charterers of Cyprus ships and on dividends distributed to shareholders. As a result, at the end of 1997, more than 2,500 ships were registered under the Cyprus flag, with a gross tonnage of over 25.5 million, ranking Cyprus fifth in the world in terms of ship registration.

Registration fees for cargo vessels are calculated as follows:

For each ton gross up to 5,000	C£0.10
For each ton gross between 5,001 and 10,000	C£0.08
For each ton gross over 10,000	C£0.04
Minimum fee	C£125
Maximum fee	C£3,000

For passenger ships, the fee is C£0.15 per gross ton, with a minimum fee of C£250.

All annual fees payable to the Cyprus shipping authorities have been consolidated into one annual fee known as annual tonnage tax. The annual tonnage tax is calculated as follows:

Basic tax	C£100
plus	
For each ton gross up to 1,600	C£0.26
For each ton gross between 1,601 and 10,000	C£0.16
For each ton gross between 10,001 and 50,000	C£0.06
For each ton gross in excess of 50,000	C£0.04

The result is then increased or decreased by multiplying it by the relevant factor depending on the age of the ship, as follows:

Age of Ship	*Factor*
Up to 10 years	0.75
Between 11 and 20 years	1.00
Over 20 years	1.30

The tax is reduced by 30% if the ship is technically managed and crewed by a Cyprus-based ship management company, by 2.5% per month for each Cypriot employed as an officer or cadet officer, and by 1.5% per month for each Cypriot employed as a rating on board a ship.

For a ship to qualify as a Cyprus ship, it must belong to a Cypriot or a company incorporated in Cyprus must own more than half of the shares in the ship. All non-Cypriot owners who wish to register their ships under the Cyprus flag must form a Cyprus company to acquire the title in the ship. A special type of Cyprus shipping company has evolved, namely, a company limited by shares that has a nominal share capital of C£1,000, divided into 1,000 shares of C£1 each. These companies, as with other Cyprus companies, must have at least two shareholders, one director, and one secretary. Approximately 11,400 shipping companies have been registered thus far.

The directors and secretary may be of any nationality. There are also no restrictions as to the nationality of the shareholders who usually hold, directly or indirectly, shares in the company pro rata to the shares they own in the ship. Exchange control regulations require that the shares in a Cyprus shipping company must be owned directly or indirectly by nonresidents. Where this is the case, the company is considered for exchange control purposes as nonresident and can enter freely into any transactions with other nonresidents of Cyprus, without exchange control permission.

Mutual Funds

In September 1998 a bill on mutual funds was introduced for consideration by the legislature.

Trusts

Trustees are regulated by the Cyprus Trustee Law Cap 193, which is based on the English Trustee Act 1925. Since 1992, international trusts may be created under the International Trusts Law 69(I) of 1992. There are therefore three types of trusts in Cyprus:

The "local trust": The International Trusts Law does not apply to the "local trust," which is governed by the English common law and the Trustee Law. The local trust and the property settled in the trust are subject to exchange controls. Unless special permission is given by the Central Bank of Cyprus, the settlor as well as the beneficiaries must be residents of Cyprus.

The "offshore trust": Offshore trusts are subject to exchange controls and must be established with the approval of the Central Bank of Cyprus. They are, in effect, the same as local trusts but have as beneficiaries only nonresidents, and all their activities must be outside Cyprus.

The "international trust": To qualify as an international trust, a trust must comply with the following requirements:

(a) The settlor may not be a resident of Cyprus for exchange control purposes;
(b) the beneficiaries, with the exception of any charity in Cyprus, must be nonresidents;
(c) at least one of the trustees must be a resident of Cyprus, whether the trustee is a legal or a natural person; and
(d) the assets of the trust may not include any immovable property situated in Cyprus.

Checklist for International Trusts

- There is no statutory schedule of standard trust powers.
- The maximum perpetuity period for noncharitable trusts is one hundred years.
- At least one resident trustee is required.
- Trusts need not be registered.
- Trust documents are in English.
- A stamp duty of US$550 is payable.
- Cyprus trust law has a mixed common and civil law background.
- There is no right of appeal to the Privy Council.
- The Hague Convention has not been implemented.
- Specific provision is made for the exclusion of foreign inheritance laws.
- Specific provision is also made for the nonrecognition of foreign judgments.
- There is a specific "asset protection" provision protecting a disposition to a trust from challenge by creditors.
- A limitation period of two years is imposed on creditors' claims.
- Provision is made for noncharitable purpose trusts.

CHAPTER TWENTY-SEVEN

GIBRALTAR

Background Information

Geographic and Demographic Data

Location	Gibraltar is a peninsula on the southern coast of Spain. It borders the Strait of Gibraltar, which links the Mediterranean Sea and the North Atlantic Ocean. In winter, it is one hour ahead of GMT; in summer, it is two hours ahead.
Capital	Gibraltar.
Area	2.75 square miles.
Population	28,913.
Languages	English is the official language, but Spanish is widely spoken.
Access	There are several flights daily between London and Gibraltar. Connections to other international destinations may be made in Spain. Gibraltar also has good harbor and port facilities.
Telecommunications	Excellent.

Government

Gibraltar is a self-governing but dependent territory of the United Kingdom. It is a member of the European Union and the Commonwealth.

Political and Economic Stability

Gibraltar is politically stable, although relations with Spain historically have been tense. It is a constitutional democracy with a unicameral House of Assembly.

Gibraltar is economically stable and benefits from an extensive shipping trade, offshore banking, and its position as an international conference center. The British military presence has been sharply reduced and now contributes about 11% to the local economy. The financial sector accounts for 15% of GDP;

tourism, shipping services fees, and duties on consumer goods also generate revenue. Because more than 70% of the economy is in the public sector, changes in government spending have a major impact on the level of employment.

Business Environment

Government attitude to offshore activities: The government actively promotes foreign investment in the territory in order to generate employment opportunities. It offers tax concessions to light manufacturers who wish to export from Gibraltar.

Local business requirements: Some businesses require licenses to operate in Gibraltar, and local advice should be sought in this regard.

Foreigners and Immigration

Nonresidents require a permit to work in Gibraltar, but a work permit cannot be denied to a national of a European Union country. Such nationals may enter Gibraltar for a period of six months in order to find employment and thereafter are entitled to residential permits for five or ten years. They may also acquire real estate in Gibraltar. Other nationals may be granted residential permits renewable on a monthly, quarterly, or annual basis and may be refused permission to purchase real estate in Gibraltar.

Currency and Exchange Control

The Gibraltarian currency is the Gibraltar pound, which is on a par with the British pound. There is no exchange control.

Disclosure of Information

Banking secrecy: The Banking Ordinance 1992 protects banking secrecy and confidentiality, although the Drug Trafficking Ordinance 1989 contains certain exceptions to banking secrecy. Applications for banking licenses are confidential, but customer confidentiality depends on the bank's normal due diligence procedures.

Disclosure in company formation and trust settlement: Corporations applying for exempt or qualifying status must disclose the beneficial owner to the financial and development secretary. No other corporation is required to do so on formation. A reference for the beneficial owner is also required, normally from a professional body. The Companies (Taxation and Concession) Ordinance, section 14, and the Income Tax (Qualifying Companies) Rules, rule 8, govern the confidentiality of such disclosure in relation to exempt and qualifying companies, respectively.

A corporate audit is required, but private companies do not have to file accounts to Company's House.

A company incorporated in Gibraltar must have at least a registered office in Gibraltar. The minute book, register, and seal of the company must be kept at the registered office. The local office would disclose the beneficial ownership of the company where the company sought exempt or qualifying status or on the direction of the Supreme Court.

A trustee is not required to register the beneficiaries of a trust. A trust or company opening a bank account is required, in the case of the trust, to disclose the settlor's identity and, in the case of the company, to disclose the beneficial owner's identity. This requirement also applies to limited partnerships and companies.

International cooperation measures: The Mutual Assistance Directive on the Exchange of Tax Information with Member States of the European Union of October 1, 1997, applies in Gibraltar and provides for cooperation with foreign states and investigators. Since the directive is recent, no arrangements for procedures under the directive have yet been made, but in Gibraltar the nature of the information that will be made available will be limited by the ambit of the information powers of the commissioner of income tax. Judicial review of the actions of officials involved may be possible, but there is no appeal procedure. The authorities will respond to requests for assistance in investigations into tax evasion by foreign authorities under the Mutual Assistance Directive, where mutual arrangements have been made. However, compliance with the directive has not yet been put to the test in Gibraltar.

There is no legislation in Gibraltar governing the exchange of information with foreign states or governing the enforcement of foreign judgments. Reciprocity of judgment arrangements exists with a few jurisdictions, such as the United Kingdom and Australia. In terms of these arrangements, the foreign judgment is entered into court without relitigation.

Gibraltar has not entered into any tax treaties with other countries. It has also not entered into any mutual legal assistance treaties.

Legislation relating to money laundering is contained in the Criminal Justice Ordinance 1995, which incorporates E.C. Directive 91/308 into Gibraltarian law, and provides for the confiscation of the proceeds of drug trafficking offenses and other criminal conduct. It does not cover tax evasion.

Legal System

General

The Gibraltarian legal system is based on English common law. There are four courts: the Court of First Instance, the Magistrates Court, the Supreme Court, and the Court of Appeal.

Legislation

The principal provisions affecting offshore operations and transactions are contained in the following:

- Banking (Amendment) Ordinance
- Banking (Auditors and Information) Ordinance
- Banking (Extension to Building Societies) Ordinance
- Banking Ordinance
- Companies Ordinance
- Companies (Taxation and Concessions) Ordinance
- Control of Employment Ordinance
- Deposit Guarantee Scheme Ordinance
- Development Aid Ordinance
- Estate Duties Ordinance
- Financial Institutions (Prudential Supervision) Ordinance
- Financial Services Ordinance
- Income Tax Ordinance
- Insurance Companies Ordinance
- Trustees (and Corporations) Ordinance

Treaties

Gibraltar has not entered into tax treaty arrangements or mutual legal assistance treaties with any other countries. It is a member of the European Union but by agreement (the Parent Subsidiary Directive 90/435) is excluded from the common customs union, the requirement to levy VAT, and the Common Agricultural Policy.

Taxation (Direct and Indirect)

Income Tax

Individuals: Individuals pay income tax at the following rates:

Up to G£1,500	at 20%
The next G£5,500	at 30%
The next G£5,500	at 35%
The next G£3,500	at 40%
The next G£3,500	at 45%
Thereafter	at 50%

Corporations: Any corporation resident in Gibraltar (i.e., managed and controlled in Gibraltar) is liable for tax on its worldwide profits at a rate of 35%. Nonresident companies are liable for tax on all Gibraltar source income, except for interest from banks and building societies. Exempt companies are not subject to local taxes and duties, including estate duties on their shares. Qualifying companies pay tax at between 2% and 3%, at the taxpayer's option.

Stamp Duties

Certain documents that are executed in Gibraltar are subject to stamp duties at varying rates.

Withholding Taxes

Interest paid by a resident corporation to resident or nonresident individuals is subject to a 30% withholding tax. Interest paid by a resident corporation to resident or nonresident corporations is subject to a 35% withholding tax. Dividends paid to residents or nonresidents by a resident corporation are subject to a 35% withholding tax. Dividends paid to a qualifying shareholder in another state in the European Union are tax-exempt, following the Parent/Subsidiary Directive. Dividends paid by a 1992 company to a non–European Union shareholder are subject to a withholding tax of 1%.

Management or consulting fees and royalties that are paid to nonresident individuals are subject to a withholding tax of 30%. Management or consulting fees and royalties that are paid to nonresident corporations are subject to a withholding tax of 35%.

Exempt companies are free of all withholding taxes.

Payments from qualifying companies to nonresidents are subject to withholding tax as follows:

(a) Interest is subject to a withholding tax at the same rate at which the company is taxed;

(b) dividends are subject to a withholding tax at the same rate at which the company is taxed; and

(c) management or consulting fees and royalties are subject to a withholding tax determined in consultation with the commissioner of income tax. This amount may not be less than 2%.

Estate Duties

Gibraltarians are liable to estate duty of between 5% and 25%. Nonresidents' estates are liable to estate duty on real and personal property in Gibraltar only. Such property excludes bank and building society deposits but includes gifts made within three years prior to death.

Real Estate Taxes

Anyone occupying property in Gibraltar must pay rates. The amount is calculated on the value of the property or the rental paid.

Import Duties

Most goods imported to Gibraltar are subject to a 12% import duty.

Other Taxes

There is no capital gains tax, sales tax, or VAT in Gibraltar. There are also no gift or wealth taxes.

Tax Incentives

See Incentives.

Incentives

The Development Aid Ordinance governs tax incentives. A corporation that is granted a development aid license by the governor for a development project that will benefit Gibraltar economically is exempt from paying income tax on profit resulting from the development until such time as the total gains from the development exceed the percentage of approved capital expenditure. To qualify for a license, the project must be one that will

(a) create a tangible and immovable asset in Gibraltar;
(b) provide two or more housing units in Gibraltar;
(c) contribute materially to the development of Gibraltar's tourism industry;
(d) provide new industry in Gibraltar;
(e) afford new employment opportunities or career prospects in Gibraltar; or
(f) materially improve the economic or financial infrastructure of Gibraltar.

Corporations

(The domestic laws of Gibraltar refer to *corporations* as *companies*. This terminology is retained in this chapter.)

Gibraltar is probably the most cost-effective European jurisdiction for the incorporation of companies. It was the first European jurisdiction to offer the exempt company, which allows a company to be managed and controlled from Gibraltar and still enjoy preferential tax status there. The exempt certificate gives the company a twenty-five-year guarantee of exemption from Gibraltarian taxes.

The disadvantages of incorporation in Gibraltar are that it is not as well established as its European competitors as an offshore center and, as a full member of the European Union, pressure may be brought to bear in the future to force Gibraltar to harmonize its taxes with other member states.

Types of Companies

Under the Companies Ordinance, four types of companies are recognized:

(a) the company limited by shares;
(b) the company limited by guarantee having a share capital;
(c) the company limited by guarantee not having a share capital; and
(d) the unlimited company, which may or may not have share capital.

Companies may also be either private or public. Private companies limit the number of members to fifty, restrict the free transfer of shares, and restrict the right of the public to subscribe for shares. Public companies are companies that are not private companies.

Gibraltar 1992 companies: Gibraltar 1992 companies were introduced as a result of E.C. Parent Subsidiary Directive 90/435. The 1992 company is an ordinary resident company that may take advantage of the directive, in terms of which,

(a) dividends between companies of two member states are exempt from withholding taxes; and
(b) a participation exemption is granted where dividends are received from a subsidiary in another member state.

In addition, the 1992 company must only pay a withholding tax of 1% on dividends paid to residents of non–European Union countries. To qualify as a 1992 company, a company must meet the following requirements:

(a) be incorporated or registered under the Companies Ordinance after January 1, 1992;
(b) be ordinarily resident in Gibraltar;
(c) have a real physical presence in Gibraltar (i.e., at least 400 square feet of office premises and two employees);
(d) maintain a reasonable debt/equity ratio;
(e) have as its principal object to hold participations in other companies (at least 5% is required by the directive); and
(f) be beneficially owned by nonresidents of Gibraltar.

There are three types of offshore companies in Gibraltar: nonresident companies, exempt companies, and qualifying companies. Only companies with a share capital may apply for a tax-exempt or qualifying certificate.

Nonresident companies: Nonresident companies are companies that are incorporated in Gibraltar but are managed and controlled outside of Gibraltar by nonresidents of Gibraltar and beneficially owned by nonresidents of Gibraltar. They may not carry on business in Gibraltar and are not subject to the provisions of the Income Tax Ordinance or the Companies (Taxation and Concession) Ordinance.

Exempt companies: Exempt companies are the entity most commonly used for offshore operations in Gibraltar. These may be managed and controlled in Gibraltar, but may not be beneficially owned by a resident of Gibraltar or do business with a resident of Gibraltar. Exemption certificates are granted by the Financial and Development Secretary, and they last for twenty-five years. Applications must be accompanied by a bank or professional person's reference concerning the beneficial owner and the activity the company wishes to engage in. Such information is treated with the strictest confidentiality. Exemption certificates entitle companies to exemption from local taxes and duties, including estate duty on their shares, and freedom from withholding taxes. Exempt companies are taxed at a flat rate of G£200 or G£225 annually, depending on whether they are nonresident or resident, respectively.

Qualifying companies: Qualifying companies may also not be beneficially owned by residents of Gibraltar. These companies are subject to the ordinary income tax rates in respect of Gibraltar resident business (35%) but to concessionary rates of between 2% and 3% in respect of nonresident business. Payments by qualifying companies to nonresidents are subject to withholding tax, usually at the same rate as the company is taxed.

Migration of Companies

In terms of the Companies (Redomiciliation) Regulations of 1996, a company domiciled in the following states may establish its domicile in Gibraltar, provided the law of its jurisdiction of incorporation allows it to do so:

1. European Economic Area states
2. British Commonwealth member states
3. Liberia, Panama, and Switzerland
4. Anguilla, Bermuda, the British Antarctic Territory, the British Indian Ocean Territory, the British Islands, the Cayman Islands, the Falkland Islands, South Georgia and the South Sandwich Islands, Hong Kong, Montserrat, Pitcairn, St. Helena, the Turks and Caicos Islands, and the British Virgin Islands.

Similarly, a company incorporated or domiciled in Gibraltar may establish domicile outside Gibraltar but is limited to territories in the European Economic Area.

Checklist for Companies

- Prior approval of the company name is not required, but it must end with *Limited*. Many words are sensitive, such as *Royal, Holdings, Group, Gibraltar, International, Bank,* and *Insurance*.
- It takes five to seven days to incorporate a company, although same-day incorporation can be obtained for an additional fee of G£30. Shelf companies are available, but application for exemption may only be made after acquisition of the company.
- Exempt companies must have at least G£100 of paid-up share capital or its currency equivalent. Capital duty of 0.5% is payable.
- At least one shareholder is required, but it is more usual to have two shareholders. Bearer shares are possible but impractical, and shares of no par value are not allowed.
- A minimum of one director is required. Corporate directors are allowed, and directors may be residents of Gibraltar.
- A secretary is mandatory only for exempt companies. Corporate secretaries are allowed, and they must be residents of Gibraltar.
- A registered office in Gibraltar is required, but a registered agent is not. References with regard to the beneficial owner must be supplied to the agents and may be required by the authorities before exemption is granted. The registers of members, directors, mortgages, and charges must be kept at the registered office.
- The directors, shareholders, registered office, memorandum and articles of association, annual return, mortgages, and charges are available on the public file.
- Corporate books and a seal are required and are usually retained at the registered office.
- Accounts are required but need not be filed. An annual return is required.
- There is no restriction on the holding of meetings.
- Tax of G£225 (or G£200 for a nonresident exempt company) is payable annually. A filing fee of G£26 is also charged for the annual returns.

Other Forms of Business Organization

Sole Proprietorships

Sole proprietorships are recognized in Gibraltarian law, and anyone may start a business, subject to immigration control and the Trade Licensing Ordinance. A sole trader must submit an annual return to the commissioner of income tax.

Partnerships

Gibraltar recognizes both general and limited partnerships. General partnerships are regulated by the Partnership Ordinance, which is based on the English Partnership Act 1890. Limited partnerships are regulated by the Limited Partnership Ordinance, which is based on the English Limited Partnership Act 1907. A limited partnership is defined in the Ordinance as "a partnership consisting of one or more general partners, liable for all debts and obligations of the firm, and one or more limited partners who contribute a sum as capital, or contribute property valued at a stated amount at the time of entering the partnership, and who are not liable for the debts or obligations of the firm beyond the amount so contributed."

General partnerships need not be in writing, but it is usual for the partners to execute a partnership agreement. Limited partnerships must comprise a statement, signed by all partners, that includes details of the firm's name, nature and place of business, the names of each partner, whether he is a general or a limited partner, the amount of his contribution to partnership capital, and the term of the partnership.

If either a general or limited partnership trades in a name other than that of the actual partners themselves, the name of the partnership must be registered under the Business Names Registration Ordinance. Limited partnerships must file a statement with the registrar of companies. Until such statement is filed and the partnership is registered, the limited partners do not have the protection of limited liability.

There are no capital requirements for general partnerships. For limited partnerships, capital may be in cash or in kind, the amount and nature being determined by the partnership agreement. Limited partners must actually transfer the capital on formation (or on the introduction of a new limited partner).

For a general partnership, the minimum number of partners is two. For a limited partnership, the minimum is also two (at least one general and one limited partner). As a general rule, the maximum number of partners is twenty, although this restriction does not apply to professional firms of lawyers, doctors, and accountants. Corporate partners are permitted.

A general partnership is managed by each of the general partners, unless stated otherwise in a partnership agreement. Only the general partners may manage the affairs of a limited partnership. If a limited partner purports to manage the partnership, he runs the risk of losing the protection of limited liability.

There are no specific rules as to residency of partners. A limited partnership must have its principal place of business in Gibraltar.

There is no requirement for the preparation or audit of partnership accounts, other than as determined by the partnership agreement, but if the partnership is resident in Gibraltar, then proper accounts must be submitted to the commissioner of income tax.

Insurance

General

Insurance companies are regulated by the Insurance Companies Ordinance of 1987. The regulatory authority is the Commissioner of Insurance, who is a member of the Financial Services Commission.

Gibraltar has modeled its insurance legislation on the United Kingdom provisions. In 1997 the government of the United Kingdom recognized the Gibraltar Commissioner of Insurance as a competent authority for the supervision of insurance companies, enabling Gibraltar insurance companies to write cross-border business within the EU member states without further authorization being necessary. Gibraltar has also adopted all the EU Insurance Directives.

Captive Insurance Companies

Captive insurance is governed in Gibraltar by the Insurance Companies Ordinance 1987. There are six captives established thus far in Gibraltar. The total asset and premium sizes of the captive sector are not available. The commissioner of insurance regulates the sector. An annual audit is required, as are annual supervisory returns and a statement of shareholder controllers.

Section 113 of the ordinance provides regulatory concessions. Captives that are exempt companies pay G£225 tax per year; captives that are qualifying companies pay a negotiated rate of between 0% and 35%.

There are no statutory capital requirements. Solvency margins and minimum guarantee fund requirements must be met.

Incorporation costs vary. The annual license fee is G£2,000. In addition, an application fee of G£500 is payable, as is stamp duty of 0.5% on the authorized capital, and an annual filing fee.

There are no special categories of captive. Provision is made for rent-a-captives and protected cell companies.

Shipping

The Gibraltar ship register is part of the British Register, and any ship registered in Gibraltar is considered to be a British ship and may fly the Red Ensign. A vessel may be registered in Gibraltar if the owner is a British subject or a corporation incorporated in any British territory that has its principal place of business in that territory.

Mutual Funds and Collective Investment Schemes

Collective investment schemes are regulated by the Financial Services (Collective Investment Schemes) Regulations 1991. The regulations were introduced to implement the E.C. Directive on Undertakings for Collective Investments in Transferable Securities (UCITS). Application to have Gibraltar collective investment schemes accepted as UCITS is pending. Collective investment schemes can be set up as either unit trusts and common or mutual funds, or public investment companies.

Unit Trusts and Common or Mutual Funds

If a scheme is created under Part II of the Financial Services (Collective Investment Schemes) Regulations as a unit trust, it must be established by a trust deed between the manager and the trustee. If the scheme is created as a common or mutual fund, it must be established either by a trust deed, in the same manner as a unit trust, or by way of fund rules, which must be set out in the formation documents of the company. If a company is to act as a common or mutual fund, it must be incorporated under the Gibraltar Companies Ordinance.

Public Investment Companies

A public investment company (PIC) must be incorporated under the Companies Ordinance, and its head office must be in Gibraltar. The company must have a paid-up capital of not less than G£50,000. The property of a PIC must be held by a custodian pursuant to an agreement among the custodian, the PIC, and the manager. The PIC may be exempted from this requirement if it is publicly listed on an authorized exchange and meets auditing and certain other requirements regarding the calculation and publication of its net asset value. The regulations also provide for open-ended investment companies.

UCITS

Part V of the regulations relates to schemes for undertakings for collective investments in transferable securities (UCITS). A UCITS scheme must be an open-ended scheme, with investments limited to transferable securities, which are

(a) listed on a stock exchange in the European Union;
(b) traded on another regulated market in the European Union;
(c) listed on an approved stock exchange or traded on an approved regulated market outside the European Union;
(d) recently issued securities; and
(e) approved publicly traded debt instruments.

Trusts

Gibraltar trust law is based on the English common law. The following legislation also applies:

- Perpetuities and Accumulations Ordinance
- Trustee Investments Ordinance
- Trustee Ordinance
- Trusts (Recognition) Ordinance
- Variation of Trusts Act 1958 (UK)

Only charitable trusts have to be registered in Gibraltar. All other trusts are private and therefore completely confidential. Asset protection trusts have been recognized since 1990, in terms of amendments to the Bankruptcy Ordinance. The transfer of assets to an asset protection trust must be registered with the Financial Services Commission to qualify for the statutory protection now granted. The Financial Services Commission licenses firms especially to act as trustees of asset protection trusts, and the requirements relating to such trustees are generally higher than those relating to regular trustees.

Offshore or nonresident trusts and resident trusts are governed by the same rules, and the only difference is in the incidence of tax. In terms of the Income Tax (Amendment) Ordinance 1983, income received by a trust or a beneficiary of a trust is exempt from income tax if

(a) the trust is created by or on behalf of a nonresident person;

(b) the income accrues or is derived from outside of Gibraltar, or, where it is received directly by the beneficiary, it is exempt from tax under the ordinance; and

(c) the terms of the trust expressly exclude residents of Gibraltar as persons who are or may be beneficiaries.

Offshore trusts are commonly used in Gibraltar for estate planning, asset protection, asset accumulation, and unit trusts.

Checklist for Trusts

- There is no statutory schedule of standard trust powers.
- The maximum perpetuity period for noncharitable trusts is one hundred years.
- At least one resident trustee is required.
- Trusts need not be registered.
- Trust documents are in English.
- There is no stamp duty or registration fee.
- Gibraltarian trust law has an English common law background.
- Appeal lies to the Privy Council.
- The Hague Convention has been implemented.

- No specific provision is made for the exclusion of foreign inheritance laws.
- No specific provision is made for the nonrecognition of foreign judgments.
- There is a specific "asset protection" provision protecting a disposition to a trust from challenge by creditors.
- There is no limitation period on creditors' claims.
- No provision is made for noncharitable purpose trusts.

CHAPTER TWENTY-EIGHT

GUERNSEY

Background Information

Geographic and Demographic Data

Location	The Guernsey bailiwick includes the Channel Islands of Guernsey, Alderney, Herm, and Sark, which are situated in the English Channel, northwest of Cherbourg in France. The islands are on GMT; in the summer, they are one hour ahead.
Capital	Saint Peter Port.
Area	75 square miles.
Population	63,731.
Languages	English is the main language in Guernsey, although French is also widely spoken.
Access	There are frequent flights between Guernsey, Paris, and London. The flights take approximately one hour.
Telecommunications	Excellent.

Government

The Guernsey bailiwick is a British Crown dependency, although in practice it is self-governing, particularly regarding fiscal policies. Britain is responsible for external affairs, including negotiating Guernsey's unique position with the European Union, in particular its exclusion from the policy of harmonizing taxation within member states.

Political and Economic Stability

Guernsey is politically stable, with a democratically elected, unicameral legislature. The Queen of England is the head of state and is represented by a lieutenant governor.

The economy is stable, with an expanding financial services sector that now accounts for over 50% of Guernsey's income. Tourism is also an important source of revenue, as is the receipt of investment income from abroad by wealthy immigrants. Unemployment is low (between 3% and 4%), and the government pursues a prudent economic policy that maximizes scarce resources and maintains a low tax regime.

Business Environment

The political and economic stability in Guernsey, its consistently low tax status, the control exercised by the government over the financial services sector to combat fraud and other criminal activities, and the excellent professional services available have made it an attractive option to foreign investors and workers. As a result, the government has had to restrict the number of businesses and individuals wishing to migrate to the islands. A further result is that the government does not consider it necessary to offer exemptions, grants, or incentives to attract further investment.

Guernsey has "designated territory" status under the United Kingdom Financial Services Act of 1986, which means that investor protection in Guernsey is at least as good as that available in the United Kingdom.

Currency and Exchange Control

The currency is the Guernsey pound, which is on a par with the British pound. There is no exchange control.

Disclosure of Information

Secrecy of information: Professional privilege also exists between professional advisors, including advocates, and their clients. This privilege may be breached only where the law compels disclosure.

Banking secrecy: The identity of the holder of a bank account can be concealed under certain circumstances. Banking is governed by the Banking Supervision Law 1994, but there is no specific banking secrecy legislation.

Disclosure in company formation and trust settlement: Disclosure of the beneficial owner of an offshore company must be made on formation of the company to the Financial Services Commission. Other information that is required includes the owner's address, date of birth, nationality, permanent residence, country of domicile, and occupation. Such disclosure is made in terms of the Financial Services Commission Law 1987.

All companies except dormant and asset holding companies must be audited. A local registered office is required, and the names and addresses of the directors and the memorandum and articles of association must be lodged at the office. Beneficial ownership will be disclosed by the local office under an order of court.

A trustee does not have to register the beneficiaries of a trust. A company or trustee opening a bank account is required in terms of the Guidance Notes on the Prevention of Money Laundering to disclose beneficial ownership or the beneficiaries. This provision also applies to limited partnerships.

International cooperation measures: Procedures exist for cooperation with foreign states and investigators, in terms of which information can be disclosed to the courts or authorities of other jurisdictions by means of commissions rogatoire and court orders under the Banking Supervision Law 1994, the Company Securities (Insider Dealing) Law 1996, the Drug Trafficking Offences Law 1988, the Criminal Justice (Fraud Investigation) Law 1991, the Money Laundering (Disclosure of Information) Law 1995, and the Prevention of Terrorism Law 1990. Professional privilege may be a ground for nondisclosure in these cases. The Financial Services Commission Law 1987 also governs the exchange of information with foreign states.

Under the Judgment (Reciprocal Enforcement) Law 1957, judgments of reciprocating foreign states may be registered. Application for registration must be made to the Commission or the Law Offices, HM procureur, or HM comptroller.

Guernsey has entered into double taxation treaties with Jersey and the United Kingdom. These treaties contain exchange of information agreements, which cover such information as is available under the respective taxation laws. Guernsey has not entered into mutual legal assistance treaties, although Guernsey courts may make orders to assist U.K. courts in insolvency matters. There is money laundering legislation in the pipeline.

Guernsey authorities will only cooperate with treaty partners' investigations into tax evasion, provided that the evasion also comprises a criminal offense.

Legal System

General

The islands of Guernsey, Alderney, and Sark each have their own legal systems, which differ from English law and the law of the other Channel Islands. They also have their own courts. The Guernsey legal system is based on the customary law of Normandy, particularly regarding real estate and inheritance. However, legislation is now often based on English principles. Precedent is drawn from both Normandy and England.

Legislation

Recent provisions affecting offshore operations and transactions are contained in the following:

- Amalgamation of Companies Ordinance 1997

- Collective Investment Schemes (Qualifying Professionals Investor Funds) (Class Q) Rules 1998
- Companies (Enabling Provisions) Law 1996
- Companies Law 1994
- Company Security (Insider Dealing) Law 1996
- Guarantee Companies Ordinance 1997
- Limited Partnerships Law 1995
- Migration of Companies Ordinance 1997
- Protected Cell Companies Ordinance 1997
- Protection of Investors Law 1987

Case Law

Important recent cases are

- *Century Holdings v. HM Procureur* (1997/1998) 1 OFLR 220 (Royal Court of Guernsey)
- *Cross v. Benitrust International* (1998/1999) 2 OFLR 32 (Royal Court of Guernsey [Ordinary Division])

Treaties

See "Tax Treaties and Double Taxation."

Taxation (Direct and Indirect)

Income Tax

Individuals: Guernsey residents pay income tax at a rate of 20%. Overseas employees who do not perform any of their duties on Guernsey are not subject to income tax.

Corporations: Guernsey companies are liable to income tax at 20% on their worldwide income. Exempt Guernsey companies pay a flat rate of G£600 per annum. International companies pay 30%, or a lower rate negotiated with the Income Tax Authority, on their total income if they are Guernsey bodies or on the total of Guernsey sourced income if they are any other bodies.

Capital Gains Tax

A Guernsey nonexempt company is not taxed on its capital gains if they were incidental as opposed to fundamental to a transaction. Where capital gains are taxed, they are taxed at a rate of 20%.

Dwellings Profit Tax

The profits of a sale of a dwelling in Guernsey or Alderney may be taxed at 100%, unless the property has been occupied by the owner continuously for twelve months or owned for more than five years. Provision is made, when deducting the tax, for inflation, improvements, and the costs of the sale.

Stamp Duties

The transfer of shares, securities, checks, and other legal documents is not subject to stamp duty. The initial authorized share capital of a company is subject to a 0.5% stamp duty, and conveyances of real estate are subject to stamp duty of 2.5%.

Withholding Taxes

Withholding tax is not imposed on dividends, but they are subject to income tax at 20%. Where payment of interest is made to a nonresident by a Guernsey nonexempt company, income tax is deducted at 20%. However, interest on deposits paid by Guernsey banks to nonresidents is exempt from income tax, including where it is payable to exempt-status companies. Royalties are taxed on the same basis as payments of interest.

Import Duties

Comparatively low import duties are levied on goods imported into Guernsey.

Other Taxes

There are no taxes on capital or wealth or on estate duty in Guernsey. There is also no sales tax or VAT.

Tax Treaties and Double Taxation

Guernsey has entered into double taxation treaties with Jersey and the United Kingdom. The agreement with the United Kingdom does not provide for a reduction in withholding taxes.

Corporations

(The domestic laws of Guernsey refer to *corporations* as *companies*. This terminology is retained in this chapter.)

It should be noted that the islands of Guernsey and Alderney have different company laws and that Sark has no company law at all. Incorporation in Guernsey is advantageous in that it is a highly respected jurisdiction in international financial circles, and many of the world's most respected institutions, particularly in the banking and trust sectors, are based in Guernsey. Another advantage is that new legislation allows exempt companies to be managed and controlled in Guernsey. However, the well-regulated nature of the jurisdiction means that it is also expensive.

Types of Companies

Company law in Guernsey is governed by the Companies Law 1994–1996, and in Alderney, it is governed by the Companies Law 1994. In Guernsey, all companies are limited liability companies, and there is no distinction between private and public companies. In Alderney, a distinction is made between public and private companies. Furthermore, companies limited by guarantee and hybrid companies are also recognized. Alderney has also reduced the minimum number of members to one and simplified the incorporation procedure, as well as introduced a standard set of articles of association.

Companies in Guernsey may either be resident or income tax companies, exempt companies, or international companies (ICs). Resident companies are those controlled in the bailiwick or maintaining a place of business there (excluding Sark) and conducting a substantial part of their activities there. They are taxed at 20% of their worldwide profits.

Exemption must be applied for annually. Exempt companies are those that

1. have not changed beneficial ownership since last notified to the Financial Services Commission or, where changes have been made, have notified the commission of the changes;
2. do not have shares beneficially owned by a resident of the bailiwick other than as a shareholder or debenture holder in a company quoted on a stock exchange that has a beneficial interest in the company seeking exemption;
3. have notified the administrator of income tax of Guernsey sourced income in the previous year; and
4. have fully paid all income tax relating to previous years.

Exempt companies pay a tax of G£500 annually. They usually do not trade in the bailiwick.

International companies are those that, whether incorporated in Guernsey or not, are wholly beneficially owned outside of Guernsey. ICs may carry on business in Guernsey but must trade exclusively with nonresidents or other ICs, and they must be able to show to the administrator of income tax that their activities warrant registering as an IC. ICs are taxed at 30% or lower, and the rate is subject to review every five years. ICs are typically used for group financing operations, captive insurance companies, industrial and commercial activities, and overseas investment companies. Exempt companies, banks, and some insurers do not qualify for IC status.

Migration of Companies

The Migration of Companies Ordinance 1997 enables Guernsey or foreign coporations to be incorporated under the laws of another jurisdiction.

Checklist for Companies

- Prior approval is required for a company name. Words such as *Insurance* and *Assurance* require additional approval. The company name must end with *Limited.*
- Incorporation takes seven to thirteen days. Shelf companies are not available. Beneficial ownership, as well as the intended trading activities of the company, must be disclosed to the authorities prior to incorporation or exempt status being granted.
- The usual minimum capital is G£10,000. A capital duty of 0.5% is payable, with a minimum of G£50.
- The minimum number of shareholders is two. Bearer shares and shares of no par value are not allowed.
- A minimum of one director is required. Corporate directors are allowed, and there is no restriction on the directors' residence.
- A company secretary is mandatory. Corporate secretaries are allowed, and there is no restriction on the secretary's residence.
- A registered office is required, but a registered agent is not. The registers of directors and members, the secretary's details, and the minute books must be kept at the registered office.
- The share capital, registered office, shareholders, and directors are available on the public file.
- Corporate books and a seal are required and are usually kept at the registered office.
- Active resident companies must keep accounts and file them with the revenue authority. Exempt companies must also keep accounts but do not need to file them. Annual returns are required.
- There is no restriction on the holding of meetings.
- Exempt companies pay G£500 annually. A filing fee of G£100 is payable by those companies required to file accounts.

Other Forms of Business Organization

Sole Proprietorships

Local residents are entitled to carry on business as sole traders, but sole proprietorships have no implications for offshore operations.

Partnerships and Joint Ventures

The Partnership Law 1995 governs general partnerships in Guernsey. In such partnerships, the partners have joint and several liability for partnership debts, and there are no statutory auditing or accounting requirements. Annual accounts should be submitted to the Income Tax Authority, but the partners are taxed individually.

The Limited Partnerships Law 1995 governs limited partnerships. Limited partnerships must be registered with the Greffier and the name must include *Limited Partnership* or *LP*. On registration, the Greffier issues a certificate of registration. Limited partnerships must have a registered office in Guernsey.

A limited partnership has both general and limited partners. The liability of the general partners is unlimited and is both joint and several. Limited partners are not liable beyond the amount contributed to the capital of the partnership.

There are certain audit requirements in relation to limited partnerships. The general partners must appoint an auditor who must be an English, Scottish, or Irish chartered accountant, a certified or public accountant, or a person authorized by the Advisory and Finance Committee to audit partnership accounts. Limited partnerships must also keep minutes of partners' meetings.

Joint ventures are not treated as separate entities in Guernsey. They are treated instead as the conduit through which the participators in the joint venture receive their share of income.

Foreign Companies

A foreign company that is managed and controlled outside of Guernsey and does not trade within the island does not have to register or file an annual return in Guernsey. However, it will be liable for income tax on profits earned in Guernsey by one of its branches. Companies incorporated in other jurisdictions are often administered from Guernsey, taking advantage of the stability and excellent infrastructure of the Channel Islands and the flexibility of other tax regimes.

Insurance

General

The insurance industry is regulated by the Insurance Business Law 1986. A company may not carry on insurance business in or from within Guernsey unless it is registered. Registration must relate to the category of insurance business undertaken, namely, domestic, long-term, or general.

A registered insurer must have a minimum share capital of G£100,000 and must appoint a general representative to act on the insurer's behalf. Such person must be either an executive director of the insurer ordinarily resident in Guernsey or an employee ordinarily resident in Guernsey.

Captive Insurance Companies

Captive insurance is also regulated by the Insurance Business Law 1986. There are approximately 339 captives established in Guernsey. The total asset size of the captive sector is approximately G£6.80 billion. The total premium size of the captive sector is approximately G£1.834 billion. The Financial Services Commission regulates the sector. An annual audit is required, as is a solvency calculation, a certificate of accordance with application, an up-to-date business plan, claims schedules, bank and investment schedules, and actuarial certificates (for life insurance companies).

There is a flexible approach to registration. Captives are taxed at the following rates, depending on the nature of the insurance company:

International company	negotiated rate between 0% and 30%
Exempt company	0% with an annual fee of G£500
Sliding scale basis	tax charges on income investment derived from shareholders' equity and other non-insurance-related income
Other	20%

The minimum capital requirement is G£100,000 or its currency equivalent. Incorporation costs about G£1,000, and an annual license fee of G£1,650 is payable. A fee of G£1,650 is payable to register an offshore insurance company.

There is financial guarantee insurance legislation in place, and provision is made for rent-a-captives and protected cell companies.

Mutual Funds and Collective Investment Schemes

The regulation of collective investment schemes is by the Financial Services Commission, which has published a series of rules in this regard, namely, the Collective Investment Scheme Rules 1988 (known as the "Class A Rules"), the Collective Investment Schemes (Designated Persons) Rules 1988, the Collective Investment Schemes (Compensation of Investors) Rules 1988, the Licensees (Notification) Rules 1989, the Collective Investment Schemes (Class B) Rules 1990, and the Licenses (Conduct of Business and Notification) (Non-Guernsey Schemes) Rules 1994.

A collective investment scheme may take the form of either a corporate vehicle (i.e., an open-ended investment company or a unit trust) or a limited partnership.

There are three classes of authorization in Guernsey:

(i) Class A1 authorization, which implies full compliance with the Class A Rules and qualifies a fund for eligibility as a "recognized scheme" under section 87 of the Financial Services Act 1986 (United Kingdom), as well as gives protection under the compensation scheme established by the Financial Services Commission;

(ii) Class A2, which implies compliance, except for some exceptions to the Class A Rules, and also qualifies a fund under section 87 of the Financial Services Act and gives it protection under the compensation scheme; and

(iii) Class B, which implies limited compliance with the rules, offering greater flexibility without qualifying the fund under the Financial Services Act.

No person may carry on any activity in connection with a collective investment scheme except under a license. A person licensed to conduct such activities may engage in such activities only in connection with a collective investment scheme that is authorized as above. An annual license fee is payable in this regard.

Trusts

The Trusts Law 1989 codifies the common law in Guernsey in relation to trusts, which was largely based on the English common law; resolves many uncertainties; and increases the protection afforded to beneficiaries. The Trusts Law does not apply in Alderney and Sark, but it may have persuasive influence in judicial proceedings.

There is no government duty payable upon creation of a trust. There are also no registration requirements.

A Guernsey trust is one whose proper law is the law of Guernsey. If the beneficiaries of a Guernsey trust are nonresident, income arising from sources outside Guernsey is not liable to income tax in Guernsey, and neither are distributions to the beneficiaries. Interest on bank deposits made by the trustees of a nonresident trust is also not taxed. This is because of a government concession. Trust assets are immune from capital gains tax, estate or probate duty, and gift tax. The trustees of a nonresident trust are not required to make returns or provide accounts of the trust to the administrator of income tax. Trust accounts must be kept but do not have to be audited.

Migration of trusts is possible. A Guernsey trust may be "exported" by replacing Guernsey trustees with nonresident trustees and changing the proper law of the trust; a trust established in another jurisdiction may migrate to Guernsey by appointing Guernsey resident trustees.

Checklist for Trusts

- There is no statutory schedule of standard trust powers in Guernsey.
- The maximum perpetuity period for noncharitable trusts is one hundred years.
- A resident trustee is not required.
- Registration of a trust is not necessary.

- Trust documents are in English.
- There is no stamp duty or registration fee.
- The law of trusts in Guernsey has a mixed common law and civil law background.
- Appeal lies to the Privy Council.
- The Hague Convention has been implemented.
- Specific provision is made for the exclusion of foreign inheritance laws.
- Specific provisions deal with the nonrecognition of foreign judgments.
- There is no specific "asset protection" provision (beyond that offered by general insolvency laws) protecting a disposition to a trust from challenge by creditors.
- There is no special limitation period for creditors' claims.
- No provision is made for noncharitable purpose trusts.

CHAPTER TWENTY-NINE

HONG KONG

Background Information

Geographic and Demographic Data

Location	Hong Kong is on the southeast coast of China, bordered by the South China Sea. It is eight hours ahead of GMT.
Capital	Victoria.
Area	420 square miles.
Population	6,547,189.
Languages	Cantonese Chinese and English are the official languages of Hong Kong.
Access	Hong Kong is a popular stopover for international flights and is well served by numerous international airlines.
Telecommunications	Excellent.

Government

Hong Kong was a British dependent territory until June 30, 1997, when it reverted to Chinese sovereignty. It is now a special administrative region (SAR) of the People's Republic of China.

Political and Economic Stability

In accordance with the provisions of the agreement negotiated by Britain and the People's Republic of China in 1984, the social, legal, and economic systems in place in Hong Kong at the time of handover in 1997 are to remain in place for fifty years. This should insure political and economic stability for the foreseeable future. Hong Kong has retained its status as a free port and a separate customs territory and continues to operate as one of the largest financial centers in the world, ranking alongside New York and London in terms of infrastructure. Hong Kong has a thriving economy and low unemployment, in the region of 3%.

Business Environment

Government attitude to offshore activities: The government does not consider Hong Kong to be a tax haven but rather an area with a low tax regime. The low taxes make it an attractive base for international operations, and it is also a gateway to other markets in Asia and the Pacific Rim. The economy is very open, and there are no restrictions on foreign investment or the transfer of income and capital in foreign currencies. Although the government actively encourages foreign investment, it does not offer any special incentives or grants, considering the low tax liability, which is based on source and not residence, and the SAR's position as a leading financial center to be adequate incentives.

Employment: The Employment Ordinance governs conditions of employment in Hong Kong. There is no comprehensive social security scheme, although legislation establishing a mandatory provident fund has been approved but not yet implemented. Foreigners wishing to be employed in Hong Kong must apply for a work permit, which can take up to three months to be issued. Executives entering Hong Kong for relatively short periods will obtain work permits with comparative ease.

Local business requirements: Every company incorporated or registered in Hong Kong under the Companies Ordinance must also register under the Business Registration Ordinance, even though the company may not trade in Hong Kong. The certificate is renewable annually at a cost of HK$2,250.

Foreigners and Immigration

Foreigners wishing to enter Hong Kong for purposes of residence or employment must be in possession of a visa. British citizens may stay in Hong Kong as visitors without visas for up to six months. Those who wish to take up employment, study, or settle in Hong Kong must now apply for the appropriate visa prior to arrival in Hong Kong.

There are no residence or nationality restrictions on the ownership of Hong Kong real estate. There is no freehold land, and land is leased from the SAR government. Leases may extend beyond the fifty-year agreed period ending in 2047, as the majority are for seventy-five years, with a right of renewal for a further seventy-five years.

Currency and Exchange Control

The local currency is the Hong Kong dollar, which is tied to the U.S. dollar at about HK$7.80 to US$1.00. There are no exchange controls.

Disclosure of Information

As Hong Kong has not entered into any tax treaties and has a sophisticated banking system, a considerable degree of confidentiality is maintained.

Legal System

General

The Hong Kong legal system is based on the English common law, supplemented by legislation passed by the Legislative Council.

Case Law

Important recent cases include the following:

- *Commissioner of Inland Revenue v. Magna Industrial Company* (1997/1998) 1 OFLR 33 (Court of Appeal, Hong Kong)
- *Commissioner of Inland Revenue v. Orion Caribbean* (1997/1998) 1 OFLR 457 (Privy Council)
- *Harvest Sheen Ltd. & Another v. CSR* (1997/1998) 1 OFLR 669 (High Court, Hong Kong)
- *Re Pong Ten Un (deceased)* (1998/1999) 1 ITELR 79 (High Court of the SAR)

Treaties

Hong Kong has not entered into any tax treaties, and double taxation treaties entered into by the People's Republic of China do not apply in the Hong Kong SAR. On April 1, 1998, the Hong Kong government implemented the Memorandum of Understanding with China based on the OECD tax treaty model. The memorandum, which was implemented on July 1, 1998, clarifies many areas of double taxation by providing for a tax credit system and emphasizing the "one country, two systems" principle enshrined in the Joint Declaration and set out in the Basic Law. The main omissions from the memorandum concern withholding taxes on dividends, interest and royalties, and capital gains. These are not taxed in Hong Kong but are treated as gains on revenue in China.

Taxation (Direct and Indirect)

Profits Tax

Individuals, corporations, trustees, and partnerships are liable to tax on profits arising in or derived from Hong Kong. The tax is imposed equally on residents and nonresidents, and resident and nonresident corporations, although some exceptions to the source rule apply to shipping and air transport corporations. Income that arises outside of Hong Kong is exempt from the tax, even though it may also be exempt at source. Where business is transacted in Hong Kong, any profits arising from the transaction are deemed to arise in Hong Kong. The rate of profits tax on corporations is 16%. The rate for individuals is 15%.

With regard to shipping, as of April 1, 1992, most income derived from the international operation of ships is exempt from Hong Kong profits tax. The Double Taxation Relief (Income from Shipping Operations) (USA) Order 1989 provides for the exemption from tax by one territory of income from the international operation of ships accruing to a resident of the other territory.

With regard to aircraft, as of May 17, 1996, resident aircraft owners will be taxed on income earned in territories with which Hong Kong has a double taxation agreement and when the income is not taxed in the other territory. Treaties have thus far been entered into with Canada, Germany, the Netherlands, New Zealand, the United Kingdom, and South Korea, and fourteen other treaties are in the pipeline.

Stamp Duties

Stamp duty is levied on the transfer of shares and securities at a rate of 0.25%. The sale of real estate is also subject to stamp duty at the following rates:

Up to HK$1 million	HK$100
From HK$1 million to HK$2 million	0.75%
From HK$2 million to HK$3 million	1.5%
From HK$3 million to HK$4 million	2%
Above HK$4 million	2.75%

The transfer of real estate and shares between associated companies with a prescribed level of common ownership is exempt from stamp duty.

Estate and Inheritance Taxes

Estate duty is levied on the principal value of property situated in Hong Kong, which passes on a person's death. The duty is levied at the following rates:

Up to HK$7.5 million	nil
From HK$7.5 million to HK$9 million	5%
From HK$9 million to HK$10.5 million	10%
Above HK$10.5 million	15%

Gifts made within three years prior to the death are included in the value of the estate for the purposes of the tax. This includes property, where full consideration in value was not transferred on transfer of the property.

Real Estate Taxes

A property tax is levied on the owner of land and buildings situated in Hong Kong, excluding certain properties in the new territories. The tax is levied on the net assessable value of the property (i.e., rental income less rates, less an allowance of 20%). The tax rate is 15%. Property owned by a corporation carrying on business in Hong Kong and occupied by that business for the purposes of trade is exempt from the tax. In addition, individuals, partnerships, and joint ventures, as well as corporations that have not claimed exemption, may set off the property tax against profits tax, and any excess of property tax over profits tax will be refunded.

In terms of the Rating Ordinance, rates are levied at 4.5% of the annual value of the premises. They are payable by the occupant of the premises.

Salaries Tax

Under the Inland Revenue Ordinance, any income earned in Hong Kong, including from pensions, is subject to salaries tax. However, an individual with Hong Kong sourced employment is not subject to the tax if he performs all of his duties outside of Hong Kong. Taxable income includes wages, salary, leave pay, fees, commissions, bonuses, gratuities, perquisites, and allowances. Certain pensions are exempt from the charge. The standard tax rate is 15%.

Other Taxes

There are no withholding taxes or capital taxes, although a capital fee of 0.25% is levied on the authorized share capital of a registered company. There is also no capital gains tax in Hong Kong.

The Hotel Accommodation Ordinance imposes a hotel accommodation tax of 3% on accommodation charges paid by guests.

Certain goods such as vehicles, tobacco, and liquor are subject to customs and excise duties. There is also a betting tax.

Corporations

(The domestic laws of Hong Kong refer to *corporations* as *companies*. This terminology is retained in this chapter.)

A company that is incorporated in Hong Kong will not automatically be seen as a "tax haven" company because of Hong Kong's trading tradition. Also, such a company will benefit from Hong Kong's strong professional infrastructure, and if it does not earn income within Hong Kong, it can avoid all taxation. However, an annual audit is required, and the difference in time between Europe and Hong Kong can cause problems.

Types of Companies

There are no special categories of companies in Hong Kong. Corporate structure is regulated by the Companies Ordinance, and a company may be either private or public. There are no particular provisions recognizing offshore companies, except that Hong Kong companies may be owned by nonresidents and trade in jurisdictions other than Hong Kong, to benefit from the fact that Hong Kong does not tax foreign sourced income.

A private company is one that restricts the right to transfer its shares, limits the number of members to fifty, and prohibits any invitation to the public to subscribe for its shares. A public company must support any invitation to the public to subscribe for its shares by a prospectus, or a statement in lieu of a prospectus, which must be given to the registrar of companies.

Checklist for Companies

- All company names must end with the word *Limited.* Words such as *Royal* and *Imperial* are not permitted.
- It takes two to three weeks to incorporate a company, and shelf companies are available. No information is required by the authorities prior to incorporation.
- The usual minimum authorized share capital is HK$10,000. Capital duty of 0.6% is payable.
- At least two shareholders are required. Bearer shares and shares of no par value are not permitted.
- At least two directors are necessary. Corporate directors are allowed, and there is no restriction on their residence.
- A company secretary is mandatory. Corporate secretaries are allowed, and the secretary must be in Hong Kong.
- A company must have a registered office in Hong Kong, but there is no need for a registered agent. The registered office must keep the registers of members, secretaries, directors, mortgages, and charges and the minute book.
- The memorandum and articles of association and information as to directors, the secretary, shareholders, the registered office, annual returns, and mortgages and charges are available on the public file.
- An annual return is required.
- There is no restriction on the holding of meetings.
- Companies that do not earn income in Hong Kong are exempt from tax. An annual return filing fee of HK$75 is payable, as is a business registration fee.
- No provision is made for the migration or redomiciliation of companies.

Other Forms of Business Organization

Sole Proprietorships

A sole proprietorship may be established in Hong Kong but is subject to the Business Registration Ordinance and must obtain a registration certificate within one month of starting business in Hong Kong. There are no residence or nationality requirements in respect of sole proprietorships.

Partnerships

Partnership law in Hong Kong is contained in the Limited Partnerships Ordinance and the Partnership Ordinance.

In terms of the Limited Partnerships Ordinance, a limited partnership may not consist of more than twenty persons, one or more of whom must be a general partner, whose liability for the debts of the firm is unlimited. A limited partner's liability for the debts of the firm is limited to the amount contributed by him at the inception of the partnership.[1] No withdrawal of the whole or any part of the initial amount contributed by a limited partner is permitted during the existence of the partnership.[2] Limited partners are not permitted to take any part in the management of the firm, nor can they bind the firm in any way.[3]

Limited partnerships must be registered with the registrar of companies under the provisions of the Limited Partnerships Ordinance. Failure to register results in the partnership being deemed a general partnership with unlimited liability on each partner.[4]

Partnerships may be set up for a certain or an indefinite period, or they will dissolve upon the completion of a specific venture if the partnership was initially conceived for that venture.[5] All partnerships must be registered under the Business Registration Ordinance. However, a formal partnership agreement is not required.

Foreign Companies

Companies that are incorporated outside of Hong Kong and establish a place of business within Hong Kong must register with the registrar of companies within one month of establishing the place of business in Hong Kong. The application for registration must be accompanied by the following:

1. a copy of the memorandum and articles of association, with a translation if the originals are not in English;
2. particulars regarding the directors and secretary of the company;
3. the name and address of the company's agent in Hong Kong, and the address of the company in its principal place of business and in Hong Kong;

4. a power of attorney or other document authorizing the agent to accept service of process and any notices required to be served on the company in Hong Kong;
5. a copy of the certificate of incorporation of the company, with a translation if the certificate is not in English; and
6. where the company is a public company, a copy of the latest accounts, with a translation if the accounts are not in English.

Where the company is required to publish its accounts in its place of incorporation, copies of the annual financial statements and annual return must also be filed with the registrar of companies in Hong Kong. The company will also be liable for the annual return filing fee of HK$140.

Insurance

Captive Insurance Companies

Captive insurance is governed by the Insurance Companies Ordinance 1997. Thus far, no captives have been established. The sector will be regulated by the Hong Kong Insurance Authority. An annual audit will be required, but there are no other reporting requirements.

Captive insurance companies will be eligible for lower minimum capital requirements and solvency margins. They will also be exempt from the requirement of holding assets in Hong Kong and from the Valuation Regulation. Captives will be taxed at the corporate rate of 16.5%. Offshore income will be exempt from tax, and there is no VAT or capital gains tax applicable.

The minimum capital requirement is HK$2 million, and all captives will be restricted to nonstatutory general business.

Incorporation costs are HK$1,580 with an additional HK$3 per HK$1,000 of capital. An annual license fee is under consideration. There are no additional costs.

Provision is not made for special categories of captives. There is no provision for rent-a-captives and protected cell companies.

Shipping and Aviation

There are no special rules regarding offshore shipping and air transport corporations, except that the worldwide profits of nonresident shipping and aircraft companies are taxable in Hong Kong. The Inland Revenue Ordinance apportions the Hong Kong sourced income against the worldwide income, and assessable profits are the proportion that Hong Kong profit bears to worldwide income. If such apportionment is too complex, 10% of income will be taxed in Hong Kong, as that is deemed to be a fair allocation of Hong Kong sourced income.

Trusts

The Hong Kong law of trusts is based on English law. Ordinances regulating the administration of trusts are the Trustee Ordinance, which is modeled on the English Trustee Act 1925, and the Trustee (Amendment) Ordinance.

The accumulation period is restricted, as in England, but this can be overcome by providing in the trust deed for the incorporation of companies that do not distribute their profits to the trustees until such time as the trustees consider it desirable. Provisions are often made in settlement trust deeds for the transfer of the forum of administration to another area, which is usually a tax haven.

As there is a free exchange market, trustees may invest in any currency and in any market in the world.

As far as taxes are concerned, estate duty is payable only on such trust assets as are in Hong Kong in the event that an estate duty liability arises. If trust assets are invested abroad, no estate duty is payable in Hong Kong. In addition, no tax is charged in Hong Kong on capital or dividends.

Checklist for Trusts

- There is no statutory schedule of standard trust powers.
- The maximum perpetuity period of noncharitable trusts is eighty years.
- A resident trustee is not required.
- There is no requirement for the registration of trusts.
- Trust documents are in English and Chinese.
- There is no registration fee or stamp duty.
- The law of trusts is based on English common law.
- Appeal does not lie to the Privy Council.
- The Hague Convention has been implemented.
- No specific provision is made for the exclusion of foreign inheritance laws.
- There is no specific provision dealing with the nonrecognition of foreign judgments.
- There is no specific "asset protection" provision (beyond that offered by general insolvency law) protecting a disposition to a trust from challenge by creditors.
- There is no special statute of limitations period for creditors' claims.
- No provision is made for noncharitable purpose trusts.

Notes

1. Limited Partnerships Ordinance, sec. 3(2).
2. Sec. 3(3).

3. Sec. 5(1).
4. Sec. 4.
5. Partnership Ordinance, sec. 34.

CHAPTER THIRTY

IRELAND

Background Information

Geographic and Demographic Data

Location	Ireland occupies five-sixths of the island of Ireland in the North Atlantic Ocean, west of Great Britain. It is in the GMT zone.
Capital	Dublin.
Area	27,450 square miles
Population	3,619,480.
Languages	English is the language of general usage, although Irish is also an official language.
Access	There are daily direct flights to the United Kingdom, Europe, and North America, and the harbor and port facilities are excellent.
Telecommunications	Excellent.

Government

Ireland is an independent republic. Its form of government is a parliamentary democracy based on free elections. It joined the European Union in 1973.

Political and Economic Stability

Ireland is politically stable compared with its neighbor, Northern Ireland.

Its economy has benefited from entering the European Union. Agriculture, once the most important sector, is now dwarfed by industry, which accounts for 38% of GDP, about 80% of exports, and employs 27% of the labor force. Although exports remain the primary engine for Ireland's robust growth, the economy is also benefiting from a rise in consumer spending and recovery in both construction and business investment. Since the 1980s, inflation has fallen sharply and chronic trade deficits have been transformed into annual surpluses. Unemployment remains a serious problem, however, and job creation is the main focus of government policy. To ease unemployment, Dublin aggressively courts foreign investors and recently created a new Industrial Development Agency to aid small indigenous firms. Unemployment currently runs at about 11.8%.

Business Environment

Government attitude to offshore activities: Government agencies actively seek foreign investment and offer sophisticated grant aid systems for capital investment and employment creation. Considerable tax and investment incentives are offered to foreign investors.

Employment: Work permits are not required for workers from other European Union countries but must be obtained to employ personnel from non-EU members. The permits are for one-year periods and may be extended thereafter. They are easily obtained for managerial personnel.

Local business requirements: No licenses are required for businesses to commence trading in Ireland, with the exception of banks and insurance companies.

Currency and Exchange Control

The currency is the Irish pound. There are no exchange control regulations in Ireland.

Disclosure of Information

Banking secrecy: There is no specific legislation governing banking secrecy. Numbered bank accounts are not available.

International cooperation measures: There are exchange of information provisions in double taxation treaties between Ireland and numerous other countries. Measures were introduced in 1994 to counter money laundering. Financial institutions must report any knowledge or suspicion of money laundering to the Money Laundering Investigations Unit of the Garda.

Legal System

General

The legal system is derived from and based on the British system. It is a mix of common and statute law.

Legislation

The principal provisions affecting offshore operations and transactions are contained in the following:

- Capital Acquisitions Tax Act 1976
- Capital Gains Tax Acts 1975 to 1978
- Central Bank Act 1971
- Companies Acts 1963 to 1990
- Corporation Tax Act 1976
- Income Tax Act 1967
- Insurance Act 1936
- Partnership Act 1890
- Trustee (Authorized Investments) Act 1980
- Trustee Act 1893

Treaties

See “Tax Treaties and Double Taxation.”

Taxation

Income Tax

The current rate of tax on the income of corporations is 32%. A lower rate of 25% applies to the first IR£50,000 of taxable profit.

A special 10% rate of corporate tax is applicable to corporate income from manufacturing activities, some export-oriented service activities, and international financial services provided within specified zones. This rate is available to December 31, 2010 for manufacturing companies and to December 31, 2005 in the case of certain Shannon Airport Zone activities and operations licensed to operate in the International Financial Services Center.

Subsidiaries of foreign corporations operating in the International Financial Services Center can apply to be taxed at a higher rate if their parent is resident in a jurisdiction that penalizes subsidiaries taxed at low rates.

As of January 1, 2003 a new tax rate of 12.5% will be available for all corporations on their trading income. This rate will also apply to existing 10% corporations when the 10% tax regime ends. Corporations that did not qualify for the 10% rate as of July 22, 1998 but qualify thereafter will benefit from the 10% regime only until January 1, 2003, after which the 12.5% rate will apply.

Individual income is taxed on a sliding scale to a maximum rate of 48%. All persons resident in Ireland are subject to the tax. Income derived in Ireland by nonresidents is also subject to the tax, although double taxation treaties may mitigate the situation. An individual is regarded as being resident for income tax purposes if he or she spends more than 183 days of the tax year in Ireland, or more than 280 days in Ireland in the tax year and the preceding tax year.

Capital Gains Tax

Corporate capital gains are taxed at a rate of 20%. Capital gains tax on development land is 40%, unless planning permission has been obtained for residential development, in which case the rate is 20%.

Migrating corporations are subject to capital gains tax on their assets unless the parent is resident in Ireland or in a treaty country.

Withholding Tax

Withholding taxes are imposed on interest, annual payments, rent paid to nonresidents, some construction payments, and fees paid to certain professionals. The rate is generally 24%, although construction payments to subcontractors are taxed at 35%.

Value-Added Tax

VAT is imposed at rates of between 0% and 21% on goods and services. Banking and insurance companies are exempt from VAT and may therefore not reclaim VAT charged to them. Irish incorporated nonresident companies cannot register for VAT in Ireland unless taxable supplies for VAT purposes are made in Ireland. A company engaged in cross-border trading must register for EU VAT in order to receive goods from its suppliers free of VAT. A trader may register for VAT in any EU country in which supplies are made.

Inheritance and Gift Taxes

Capital acquisitions tax is levied on recipients of certain dispositions, at a maximum rate of 40%.

Customs and Excise Duties

Customs duties are imposed on certain goods imported into Ireland from outside the European Union. Excise duties are imposed on alcohol, tobacco, and mineral oils.

Tax Incentives

See "Incentives (Tax and Nontax)."

Tax Treaties and Double Taxation

Ireland has entered into double taxation treaties with a number of countries as shown in Table 30-1.

Table 30-1. Limits on Rates of Withholding

Country	*Interest*	*Royalties*
Australia	10%	10%
Austria	0%	0%
Belgium	15%	0%
Canada	24%	24%
Cyprus	0%	0%
Czech Republic	0%	10%
Denmark	0%	0%
Finland	0%	0%
France	0%	0%
Germany	0%	0%
Hungary	0%	0%
Israel	10%	10%
Italy	10%	0%
Japan	10%	10%
Korea	0%	0%
Luxembourg	0%	0%
The Netherlands	0%	0%
New Zealand	10%	10%
Norway	0%	0%
Pakistan	0%	0%
Poland	10%	10%
Portugal	15%	0%
Russia	0%	0%
Spain	0%	10%
Sweden	0%	0%
Switzerland	0%	0%
United Kingdom	0%	0%
United States	0%	0%
Zambia	0%	0%

Incentives (Tax and Nontax)

Grants and Free Zones

In order to attract foreign investment, the Industrial Development Authority gives cash grants to manufacturing companies, export-oriented service companies, and international financial services companies. The grants are nonrefundable and generally take the form of a percentage contribution to the cost of new fixed assets.

The Shannon Free Airport Development Company also offers similar incentives to companies operating in the Shannon zone, which is a customs free zone. Companies located in the Shannon zone are subject to tax at a reduced rate of 10%.

Exemptions and Relief

There are reductions on municipal rates available for up to ten years to persons resident in certain parts of Ireland, including some areas of Dublin.

Tax exemption is available for entities involved in the collective investment in transferable securities of capital raised from the public. Such entities are those that are managed by a company licensed to operate in the Shannon zone or the Financial Services Center in the Custom House Docks Area of Dublin and are confined to nonresident investors.

A scheme of tax incentives for investment in property in certain urban renewal areas was introduced on August 1, 1998. The qualifying period runs to December 31, 1999 for industrial and commercial premises, and July 31, 2000 for residential premises. The scheme entails an allowance of 25% on the building cost of new industrial buildings in the first year and an annual allowance of 4% thereafter, until 100% of the cost is written off. The initial allowance for owner/occupiers is raised to 50%.

Capital Allowances for Hotels

There is a capital allowance for hotels in the form of a seven year straight line write-down. The allowance for each of the first six years is 15%, and for the seventh year 10%.

Corporations

(The domestic laws of Ireland refer to corporations as companies. This terminology is retained in this chapter.)

Types of Companies

Republic of Ireland companies: Companies are generally regulated by the Companies Act of 1963. Republic of Ireland companies may be either limited or unlimited. In the case of a limited company the shareholders' liability for company debts is limited to the amount of capital contributed.

Companies that are incorporated in Ireland must register with the Companies Office. Registration is only possible once the company name has been approved by the Registrar of Companies. Incorporation usually takes 10–15 working days. Shelf companies can be purchased. Incorporation will cost between IR£300 and IR£1,200. There is also a capital duty of 1% on the paid-up share capital of limited companies. There are no capital requirements.

It is possible to incorporate a single member private limited company with only one shareholder, but such company must have two directors. Public limited companies must have at least seven shareholders with a minimum share capital of IR£30,000. It is usual for shares to be registered. Bearer shares are allowed but are unusual in Ireland.

The company register contains details of company directors and registered shareholders. There is no requirement that any of the directors must be Irish nor that at least one director must be resident in Ireland.

Accounts must be audited. Limited companies must file audited accounts with the Registrar for public inspection. Unlimited companies must also make disclosure in certain circumstances.

Investment companies with variable capital: The Companies Act of 1990 makes provision for foreign investment companies engaged in the advertising and marketing of shares in Ireland. These investment companies with variable capital must have Central Bank approval. They are not subject to certain disclosure requirements.

Migration and Redomiciliation

It is possible to transfer the corporate seat into and out of Ireland, but there is capital gains tax on the assets of companies migrating from Ireland in certain circumstances.

Other Forms of Business Organization

Partnerships

The Partnership Act of 1890 governs partnerships. Limited partnerships are rare in Ireland. General partnerships may have no more than 20 members, although firms of accountants and solicitors are exempt from this provision. The partnership name must be registered under the Registration of Business Names Act unless it comprises the surnames or corporate names of all partners.

The Investment Limited Partnership Act of 1994 allowed for the introduction of investment limited partnerships, which are collective investment undertakings designed to attract nonresident investors.

Joint Ventures

The Industrial Development Authority actively encourages Irish companies to seek overseas joint venture partners and technology transfer agreements. Ireland passed legislation in 1898 concerning European Economic Interest Groupings, which are enterprises of two or more EU member states. These enterprises act as vehicles enabling international cooperation between businesses across borders within the European Union. The enterprises must be registered in a member state and operate with unlimited liability to provide common, nonprofit-making support to their members, whether they be individuals, firms, or companies.

Insurance

Captive insurance companies are encouraged to set up in Ireland because of the low income tax rate of 10% and the fact that Irish captives are allowed to write coverage directly for sister companies in the European Union. Ireland is the only country in the EU in which it is possible to write policies across European borders.

The Irish Development Agency reviews applications and forwards them to the Certification Advisory Committee for approval. Approval generally takes four to six weeks. A 1% stamp duty on the company's share capital is due upon acceptance, and a fee of IR£30,000 is payable to the captive's manager for guiding the application through the various official channels.

Captives owned by industrial companies are allowed to build up reserves quickly to cover potential disasters by not paying income tax on underwriting profits for five years.

Trusts

Trusts in Ireland are still based on the English Trustee Act of 1893. Foreign settlers' trusts for nonresident beneficiaries are exempt from taxation if they are established under Ireland's Financial Services Center. Distributions to beneficiaries are taxed at 27%, or 48% if the trust is located in Ireland and the income is Irish sourced, even though the trust may be managed abroad.

There is no fee to establish a trust in Ireland, and there are no capital requirements. A noncharitable trust is not required to be registered. There are no auditing requirements, but where an Irish resident trust is concerned, an annual return of income and accounts must be filed.

The common law of perpetuities is followed, so that a trust is voided if powers transferred to it or conferred by it continue for more than 21 years after the end of a life in being at the time the trust was created.

In terms of the Finance Act of 1993, foreign trusts will be exempt from income and capital gains taxes when the requisite legislation is approved by the Central Bank.

No tax charges arise on the migration of a trust.

CHAPTER THIRTY-ONE

ISLE OF MAN

Background Information

Geographic and Demographic Data

Location	The Isle of Man is an island in the Irish Sea, between Great Britain and Ireland. It is on GMT; in summer, it is one hour ahead.
Capital	Douglas.
Area	227 square miles.
Population	74,504.
Languages	English is the official language. A Manx dialect is also spoken.
Access	There are regular flights between cities in the United Kingdom and Ireland and the Isle of Man. It is also accessible by ferry.
Telecommunications	Excellent.

Government

The Isle of Man is a self-governing British Crown dependency. It has a special relationship with the European Union, although it is not a member of the European Union. It enjoys free trade as far as agricultural and industrial products are concerned, but it is out of the union in regard to its fiscal policies.

Political and Economic Stability

The Isle of Man is politically stable. The Queen of England is the head of state and is represented by a lieutenant governor. The island's bicameral legislature, Tynwald, passes its own legislation, although U.K. legislation is sometimes applied by agreement between the governments of the United Kingdom and the Isle of Man.

The Manx economy is stable. Offshore banking, manufacturing, and tourism are key sectors of the economy. The government's policy of offering incentives to high-technology companies and financial institutions to locate on the island has paid off in expanding employment opportunities in high-income industries. As a result, agriculture and fishing, once the mainstays of the economy, have declined in their shares of GDP. Banking now contributes about 45% to GDP. Trade is mostly with the United Kingdom. Unemployment currently runs at about 1%.

Business Environment

Government attitude to offshore activities: As the Manx economy depends heavily on the offshore financial sector, the government actively protects the sector through legislative innovations aimed at regulating the sector and eliminating the use of the island for money laundering. To counter the island's dependency on the financial sector, the government actively encourages the manufacturing industry by providing a range of incentives and grants. Since the 1970s, the government has also encouraged shipping by introducing legislation concerning the establishment of ship management companies and by developing the register of ships.

Employment: The Control of Employment Acts regulate the employment of British and European Union nationals on the Isle of Man. Such persons must apply for a control of employment work permit, although doctors, dentists, police, and ministers of religion are exempt from this requirement. Nationals of other countries must apply for a work permit under the Immigration Rules.

Local business requirements: Most businesses do not require licenses to commence trading, although banks and insurance and investment companies do. Business names must be registered.

Foreigners and Immigration

The Manx government actively encourages immigration and allows nonresidents to purchase and own real estate on the island.

Currency and Exchange Control

The local currency is the Manx pound, which is at a par with the British pound. There is no exchange control.

Disclosure of Information

Secrecy of information: The Criminal Justice (Money Laundering Offenses) Act of 1998 was brought into force on July 1, 1998. Based on the UK Criminal Justice Act of 1993, it extends existing laws against laundering the proceeds of drug trafficking and terrorism to cover the proceeds of all crimes. This includes fiscal offenses such as tax evasion. An Anti-Money Laundering Code has since been brought in under the Criminal Justice (Money Laundering Offenses) Act of 1998. The Code came into operation on December 1, 1998, and provides for identification procedures, record keeping, reporting, and education and training. It applies to all individuals engaged in banking and insurance, and extends to bookmakers, casinos, estate agents, and the post office. The Code also applies to such professionals as accountants and advocates, business promoters, company secretaries, and registered agents. Any suspicion of money laundering must be reported to the police, and anyone found guilty of money laundering is liable to a maximum fine of £5,000 or imprisonment for a maximum of six months.

Banking secrecy: There are no banking secrecy or confidentiality laws on the Isle of Man. Local banks have resisted pressure to disclose account details to the United Kingdom Inland Revenue Service. Numbered accounts are not available on the island.

Disclosure in company formation and trust settlement: The Isle of Man does not require disclosure of beneficial ownership on formation of an offshore company. No other information about the beneficial owner is therefore required.

Companies must be audited, unless they are tax-exempt companies, nonresident companies, family investment companies, or companies with an annual turnover of £45,000 or less.

A local registered office is required. The statutory records and company registers must be kept at the local office. Disclosure of beneficial ownership would be made by the local office under a court order.

A trustee is not required to register the beneficiaries of a trust. A company or trustee opening a bank account is not required by law to disclose beneficial ownership or the trustees, although most banks have their own internal procedures for identifying clients. The same applies to limited partnerships, although in this case the register of members is a matter of public record.

International coopertion measures: The island does not have a statutory procedure for cooperation with foreign investigators, although a full cooperation policy is in operation. The nature of the procedure will vary depending on the circumstances of the case. There is also no specific appeal procedure against cooperation.

The double taxation treaty with the United Kingdom is the only treaty governing the exchange of information with foreign states. The treaty concerns information relating to the prevention of fraud and tax avoidance. The Isle of Man has not entered into mutual legal assistance treaties. However, local authorities will cooperate as fully as possible with foreign investigators where specifically requested to in cases of tax evasion.

Foreign judgments are enforced by registration in the local court.

Legal System

General

The Isle of Man has its own courts and legal system and passes its own laws. The legal system has been influenced very much by English law, so the ancient customary law that derived from Scandinavian law has almost disappeared. English common law and equity is applied by the Manx courts when Manx customary law or case law is silent.

Legislation

Recent provisions affecting offshore operations and transactions are contained in the following:

- Drug Trafficking Act 1996
- Financial Supervision (Professional Investor Fund) (Exemption) Order 1995
- Insurance Act Amendment 1996
- Insurance Intermediaries (General Business) Act 1995
- Limited Liability Company Act 1996
- Purpose Trust Act 1996
- Trust Act 1995
- Value Added Tax (Financial Services) (Amendment) Order 1996

Case Law

Important recent cases include the following:

- *Aall Trust v. McCormick* (1998/1999) 2 OFLR (High Court of Justice [Common Law Division])
- *Barlow Clowes v. Eurotrust* (1998/1999) 2 OFLR 42 (High Court of Justice [Staff of Government Division])
- *Molyneux-Webb v. Price Waterhouse* (1997/1998) 1 OFLR 810 (High Court of Justice [Staff of Government Divison])
- *Re the Petition of John William McClean* (1997/1998) 1 OFLR 818 (High Court of Justice [Common Law Division])
- *Cusack & Cotter v. Pannell Kerr Forster & Crowe* (1997/1998) 1 OFLR 409 (Staff of Government Divisions, Isle of Man)
- *Cusack & Cotter v. Scroop Ltd.* (1997/1998) 1 OFLR 68 (Common Law Division, Isle of Man)
- *Re The Attorney General of the Isle of Man* (1997/1998) 1 OFLR 49 (Chancery Law Division, Isle of Man)
- *Re The Attorney General of the Isle of Man* (1997/1998) 1 OFLR 419 (Staff of Government Divisions, Isle of Man)
- *SIB v. Braff—Note of Oral Judgment* (1997/1998) 1 OFLR 553 (Chancery Law Division, Isle of Man)
- *William Katz v. George Moore* (1997/1998) 1 OFLR 500 (Staff of Government Division, Isle of Man)

Treaties

The only treaty in force is a double taxation treaty with the United Kingdom.

Taxation (Direct and Indirect)

Income Tax

Income tax is levied under the Income Tax Act 1970. Resident individuals and corporations are liable for income tax on their worldwide income. Resident corporations are those controlled and managed in the Isle of Man. Nonresidents are liable for income tax on income derived from the Isle of Man. The tax rates are the same for residents and nonresidents. The rates are as follows:

- A *standard rate* of 15% is charged on the taxable income of individuals up to £9,500 for single persons and £19,000 for married persons.
- A *higher rate* of 20% is charged on the taxable income of individuals exceeding the standard rate thresholds.
- The taxable income of trusts and resident nonexempt companies and branches is subject to tax at the higher rate of 20%.
- The taxable income of nonresident companies is subject to tax at the higher rate of 20%.

Interest from banks and building societies and dividends paid by listed companies are exempt from income tax. The profits of new companies may be exempted from income tax for a period of up to five years by resolution of the Treasury.[1] Certain industrial undertakings carried on on the island are also exempt from income tax for up to five years.[2] First year allowances of 100% are available for industrial building machinery, agricultural land, and scientific research. Tourist premises are eligible for an additional incentive allowance to the first year allowance mentioned in respect of industrial buildings. The 100% first year allowance does not apply to motor cars, although these qualify for a writing down allowance subject to a maximum amount.

Other classes of Manx corporations are taxed as follows:

- Nonresident controlled companies are liable to a duty of £750, payable to the registrar of companies. They are exempt from income tax.[3]
- Companies that are exempt from income tax[4] are liable to an annual fee of £400.
- International companies not receiving income from the Isle of Man are liable to a minimum tax charge of £400.

Withholding Taxes

Companies have to deduct withholding tax from payments made to nonresidents in respect of dividends, interest, profit shares, and directors' remuneration. However, payments made by exempt insurance companies, exempt companies, and exempt banks are excluded from liability to withholding tax. The government also offers concessions in regard to interest paid to nonresidents by banks, dividends paid to nonresidents by listed investment companies, and interest paid to nonresidents on shares, deposits, and loans from building societies.

Real Estate Taxes

Rates are levied on property according to the nature and location of the property. Each property is accorded a gross annual value, based on the national annual rent that could be charged for the property. The amount is then reduced by a fifth to arrive at the net annual value, on which the rates are charged.

Value-Added Tax and Customs and Excise Duties

For the purposes of VAT and trade in the European Union, the Isle of Man and the United Kingdom form a single area. As a result, there are no customs barriers between the United Kingdom and the Isle of Man. In terms of a customs and excise agreement between the two governments, the Isle of Man has undertaken to keep its VAT and customs and excise duties provisions in line with those of the United Kingdom. VAT is currently levied at a rate of 17.5%. A lower rate of 8% applies to domestic fuel. There is also a special concession relating to holiday accommodation, excluding time-share. The reduced rate is 5%.

The Isle of Man's VAT and customs and excise duties are collected and put into a "common purse" with those of the United Kingdom. The proceeds are then shared between the two countries according to an agreed formula, based on their respective populations.

The special relationship the Isle of Man has with the European Union also falls under this heading. In terms of Protocol 3 of the United Kingdom Act of Accession to the Treaty of Rome, the Isle of Man enjoys free trade with member states of the European Union but makes no payments to the union and receives no grants from it.

National Insurance Contributions

Employers, employees, self-employed persons, and nonemployed persons contribute to the national insurance fund on the same basis as contributions are required to be made in the United Kingdom. Social security benefits and state pensions paid by the Isle of Man's government are generally in line with benefits paid by the government of the United Kingdom.

Other Taxes

The Isle of Man does not impose capital or wealth tax, capital gains tax, inheritance tax or death or estate duty, stamp duty, gift tax, corporation tax other than a standard rate income tax, or payroll tax.

Tax Incentives

See "Tax Incentives" under "Incentives (Tax and Nontax)."

Tax Treaties and Double Taxation

In 1955, the Isle of Man entered into a double taxation treaty with the United Kingdom. This is the only taxation treaty in force. The treaty deals with the granting of double taxation relief in respect of income passing between the two countries, although it excludes dividends and debenture interest. It also contains a provision concerning the exchange of information between the authorities in each country to counter fraud and tax avoidance. In 1991, the treaty was amended to include references to the continental shelf in the definition of *United Kingdom*. The amendments also established new arrangements in respect of income derived from services provided in connection with offshore installations.

Incentives (Tax and Nontax)

Tax Incentives

Temporary exemption for certain industrial undertakings: The Isle of Man Treasury may, after consultation with the Department of Industry, exempt for a period of up to five years the whole or part of the profits or income of any industrial undertakings from liability to income tax. The Treasury may only exercise this power if it is satisfied that

(a) it is in the interests of the economy of the island;

(b) it is necessary for the purposes of establishing or developing any industrial undertaking in the Isle of Man; and

(c) it will enable the undertaking to provide additional productive employment in the island.

Allowable payments made by individuals: Payments made by individuals to approved pension schemes or personal pension arrangements are allowed as deductions from the relevant earnings. In addition, payments made by individuals in respect of

(a) interest;

(b) maintenance paid by one party to a marriage to or for the benefit and maintenance of the other party or a child of the family under a court order or a written agreement;

(c) covenanted payments to charities; and

(d) educational covenanted payments for children and grandchildren up to a maximum of £4,500 each year for each donee,

which conform with the criteria laid down in the Income Tax (Deductions) (Prescribed Cases) Order 1989, are allowed as deductions from the total income of an individual residing in the Isle of Man in the computation of taxable income.

Personal allowance: A resident individual may claim certain personal allowances. The total amount of personal allowance is deducted from total income in the computation of taxable income. Personal allowances include the following:

(a) a single person's allowance;

(b) married couples' allowances;

(c) a single parent's allowance; and

(d) a blind person's allowance.

In addition, life assurance relief calculated at 50% of allowable premiums is deducted from the total amount of the taxable income before income tax is calculated at the applicable rate.

The film industry: The government actively supports developing a film industry and has established the Isle of Man Film Commission to this end. Attractive tax incentives are available for both companies and individuals wishing to use the island as a location and production base and for companies acting as managers or coordinating producers of off-island productions.

Free Trade Zones and Free Ports

The Isle of Man Freeport, which is Europe's first and only free port, is adjacent to the airport. It is an enclosed area that is treated by the customs authorities as being outside the home territory. Goods may be manufactured, processed, and stored in the free port area. Goods imported into the free port area may remain indefinitely without incurring import duty, VAT, or other levies. No quota restrictions apply while the goods remain within the free port area. The free port has been successful since its development was passed to a private company in 1986. It is currently occupied by ten approved traders, but there is capacity for further development. Accommodation and support services are of a high standard, and as a free port in an offshore jurisdiction, it is unique.

Development Encouragement Incentives

The government encourages the creation of new businesses and industries in the Isle of Man. Substantial assistance is available to both existing and new businesses if the following criteria are met:

(a) the development does not adversely affect the existing amenities of the Isle of Man or its environment;

(b) the goods produced will have a high added value; and

(c) there will be a good level of profitability and high return on capital investment.

If all conditions are satisfied, the following incentives are available:

Investment grants	40% of the cost of new building and plant and machinery
First year grants	40% of nonrecurring commissioning and running-in expenditure, including business plan preparation costs and personnel transfer costs
Training costs	50% of approved training costs
Loans	50% of working capital requirements
Rent reduction	a rental grant is available where premises are rented, rather than purchased or built, to reflect the capital grant forgone

Corporations

(The domestic laws of the Isle of Man refer to *corporations* as *companies*. This terminology is retained in this chapter.)

The advantage of incorporation in the Isle of Man is that the different tax statuses available allow businesspeople to obtain the correct corporate structure depending on their needs. In addition, the Isle of Man provides a sophisticated infrastructure and a high degree of respectability. No stamp duty, estate duty, or capital gains tax is payable. However, the Isle of Man can be expensive for nontrading operations.

Types of Companies

Companies are governed by the Companies Acts 1931 to 1993, in particular, the Companies Consolidation Act 1931. The types of companies that are available are resident or nonresident, exempt, or international companies. Companies may either be public, in which case at least two members are required, or private, in which case one member is required and the public may not be invited to subscribe for shares. It must also be stated in the memorandum of association that the company is a private company. In addition, companies may be limited by shares, in which case the liability of members is limited to the amount that is unpaid on shares held by them; limited by guarantee, with or without share capital, in which case the liability of members is limited to the amount they undertake to contribute in the event of being wound up; or unlimited, in which case the liability of members is unlimited.

In addition, since 1996, limited liability companies may be established in terms of the Limited Liability Company Act 1996. A limited liability company must have at least two members, whose liability is limited to the extent of the capital they contribute to the company. Profits are divided among the members and are taxed in their hands, as for a partnership. The company has a limited duration of thirty years. Limited companies are governed by articles of organization, as opposed to a memorandum and articles of association. There are no directors or secretary, but the company must have a registered local office and agent in the Isle of Man. The profits of members of an international limited liability company are exempt from income tax in the Isle of Man.

The limited liability company (LLC) (officially called an International LLC) is exempt from payment of Isle of Man income tax by the company and its partners, provided that it is composed of nonresident members and does not do business in the Isle of Man. The LLC is fiscally transparent in the United States, which means that each member can be taxed on his or her income but the company is not taxed on its income. All members are able to participate in the management of an LLC. An LLC may undertake any lawful activity, trade, or business, except for banking, insurance, and investment.

A resident company is taxed at the rate of 20% of profits. A nonresident company is one that is controlled and managed from somewhere other than the Isle of Man. It is taxed at a flat rate of £750 per annum. An exempt company is one that, under the Income Tax (Exempt Companies) Act 1984, is exempted from income tax on payment of an annual fee of £400. An exempt company must have at least one director resident in the Isle of Man, and the secretary must be professionally qualified. The resident director must certify annually to the assessor of income tax that no resident is beneficially interested in the shares of the company and that the income of the company arises outside the Isle of Man. An international company is one that is not incorporated in the Isle of Man. It must pay an annual fee of £400 and may be subject to an income tax rate if so elected. The applicable rate is negotiable.

Migration of Companies

The Companies (Transfer of Domicile) Act of 1998 provides for the migration of certain qualifying companies between the Isle of Man and other jurisdictions without the need for dissolution and winding up. The legislation facilitates the ease of migration and reduces the costs of moving domicile where this is commercially desirable.

Checklist for Companies

- Company law is based on English common law, as codified in the Companies Acts 1931 to 1993.
- Prior approval of the company name is necessary, and many words are sensitive, for instance, *International, Bank, Royal, Trust, Holdings,* and *Group*. The name must end with *Limited* or *Public Limited Company*.
- It takes two to four days to incorporate a company in the Isle of Man. Shelf companies are available, but application for nonresident or exempt or international status must be made after acquisition. No information is required by the authorities prior to incorporation or prior to tax status being granted, except with regard to banking, insurance, and some other finance-related operations.
- It is customary to have at least two shareholders. Bearer shares are possible, but shares of no par value are not.
- All companies, whether resident, nonresident, international, or exempt, must have at least two directors. Corporate directors are not allowed. With resident companies, the directors are normally resident. With nonresident companies, the directors must be nonresident. With international and exempt companies, at least one director must be resident.
- All companies, whether resident, nonresident, international, or exempt, must have a secretary. With resident and nonresident companies, corporate secretaries are allowed, and there is no restriction on the secretary's residence. With international and exempt companies, corporate secretaries are not allowed, and the secretary must be resident and professionally qualified.
- Registered offices are required in all cases, but registered agents are not. The registers of directors, secretaries, members, mortgages, and charges must be kept at the registered office.
- The registered office, directors, shareholders, secretary, memorandum and articles of association, annual return, mortgages, and charges are available on the public file.
- A corporate seal is not necessary. The corporate books and seal are usually kept at the registered office.
- International and resident companies must file accounts with the revenue authority, but these are not on public record. Nonresident and exempt companies must also maintain accounts, but they do not need to have them audited or file them with the revenue authority.

- An annual return is required in all cases. The annual return filing fee is £42.
- Nonresident companies may not hold meetings on the Isle of Man. There is no restriction on the location of meetings for all other companies.

Other Forms of Business Organization

Sole Proprietorships

In terms of the Registration of Business Names Acts 1918 and 1954, a sole trader who carries on business in the Isle of Man under a name that is not his surname must register at the general registry. Profits derived from a sole trader's trade or profession are subject to Manx income tax and therefore must be included in the annual return submitted to the assessor of income tax.

Partnerships

General: Partnerships are governed by the Partnership Act 1909, which is based on the Partnership Act 1890 (United Kingdom) and the Limited Partnership Act 1907 (United Kingdom). There is no limit to a partner's personal liability for the liabilities of a general partnership, unless the liability is limited in accordance with the terms of the Partnership Act 1909.

In terms of the Registration of Business Names Acts 1918 and 1954, partnership names must be registered at the general registry if they differ from the surnames of the partners. Partnership agreements and financial accounts do not have to be filed at the general registry. An annual return must be submitted to the assessor of income tax. The assessor usually requires returns to be accompanied by copies of the relevant annual accounts and details of the manner in which profits or losses are shared.

The amount of the trading profits or losses is divided among the partners according to their profit-sharing arrangements for the accounting year and assessed on the respective partners for the year of assessment of which the partnership's accounting year forms the basis of assessment for each individual partner.

Limited partnerships: In banking, limited partnerships may consist of not more than ten partners. In all other cases, limited partnerships may consist of not more than twenty partners. A limited partnership must consist of one or more general partners, who are liable for all the firm's debts and obligations, and one or more limited partners, who are liable only for debts and obligations equal to the amount contributed. A limited partner has no part in the management of the partnership and is not entitled to dissolve the partnership by notice. A body corporate may be a limited partner. A limited partnership must be registered as such, failing which it will be deemed to be a general partnership. A statement should be sent to the registrar, signed by all the partners, stating the name, nature, and place of business; the name of each partner; and the terms and sums contributed. Notice of change should be registered within seven days and published in two Isle of Man newspapers.

The International Limited Partnership has the status of a nonresident partnership for tax purposes.

Foreign Companies

In terms of the Companies Act 1931, an overseas company is a company incorporated in a jurisdiction other than the Isle of Man that establishes a place of business within the Isle of Man. Such a company must furnish the registrar with a copy of the charter, memorandum and articles of association, and names of directors and the Manx resident representing the company within one month of establishing a place of business on the island. Overseas companies may hold land in the Isle of Man, and where they do not establish a place of business, land held will be deemed to be such a place of business.

Banks and Financial Services

Banking is regulated by the Banking Act 1975, which governs the licensing of banks, the inspection of their records, and the control of advertising and other activities. All banks and deposit takers must be licensed and must furnish the Financial Supervision Commission with the necessary information. However, such information is subject to secrecy provisions.

The Financial Supervision Act 1988 governs financial services generally and establishes the regulatory body—the Financial Supervision Commission. The Isle of Man is a designated territory for insurance business and authorized collective investment schemes in terms of the Financial Services Act 1986 (United Kingdom).

Insurance

General

The insurance business is regulated by the Insurance Act 1986. The act also provides for the licensing of insurance companies. Application is made to the Insurance Authority, which must be satisfied as to the company's financial standing. The application costs £1,000, and a further £500 is payable annually for renewal of the authorization. A fee of £2,000 is payable annually by companies applying for exemption from Manx income tax.

Captive Insurance Companies

Captive insurance is regulated by the Insurance Act 1986, as amended by the Insurance (Amendment) Act 1995 (Redomiciliation of Captives). There are approximately 160 captives established in the Isle of Man. The total asset size of the captive sector is approximately £4.23 billion. The total premium size is approximately £9.56 million. The Government Insurance and Pensions Authority regulates the sector. An annual audit is required, as is an analysis of the business written, the claims run off, the net retention, the reinsurance arrangements, letters of credit, and the calculation of solvency margin.

There are no regulatory concessions. Captives can apply to be totally or partially exempt from tax on profits under the Income Tax (Exempt Insurance Companies) Act 1981.

The minimum capital requirements are as follows:

General: captive	£50,000
General: reinsurer	£100,000
Long-term	£500,000

Incorporation costs are £150 plus £14 per £1,000 share capital in excess of £2,000. An annual license fee of £2,500 is payable or, where the company is not exempt, £500. A registration fee of £1,000 is also payable.

There is no provision for special categories of captives. Provision has been made for rent-a-captives but not for protected cell companies.

Shipping

Shipping was perceived in the 1970s as one of the areas of new business that could be developed on the island. The Merchant Shipping (Registration) Act 1984 was passed in consultation with the government of the United Kingdom to encourage the registration of ships in the Isle of Man. The Isle of Man is a flag of convenience registry, and the United Kingdom owns eleven ships, Switzerland owns two, and South Africa, Denmark, and the Netherlands each own one.

Trusts

The law of trusts is based on the English law and is governed by the following acts:

- Purpose Trusts Act 1996
- Trustee Act 1961
- Trusts Act 1995
- Variation of Trusts Act 1961

There are no formal requirements for the formation of a trust, and trusts do not need to be registered, unless they involve Manx real estate, in which case settlements *inter vivos* must be registered in the deeds registry. There are no capital requirements in respect of a trust, unless it is to be a unit trust authorized as a collective investment scheme under the Financial Supervision Act 1988. The Trusts Act 1995 provides for the forced heirship provisions of civil law jurisdictions to be overridden and the Isle of Man law to be the governing law of the trust. Provision also exists for changing the governing law. The Purpose Trusts Act 1996 allows a trust to be established as a valid purpose trust not exceeding eighty years' duration, provided the purposes of the trust are lawful, certain, reasonable, and possible.

Charitable trusts are governed by the Public Charities Act 1922, the Charities Act 1962, and the Charities Act 1986.

A trust is regarded as resident in the Isle of Man for the purposes of income tax if the management and control is in the island. A resident trust must make annual returns of income to the assessor of income tax. Trust income that arises outside the Isle of Man to the benefit of a beneficiary who does not reside in the Isle of Man is generally exempt from assessment.

Checklist for Trusts

- There is no statutory schedule of standard trust powers.
- The maximum perpetuity period for noncharitable trusts is eighty years.
- A resident trustee is not required.
- Trusts do not have to be registered.
- Trust documents are in English.
- No registration fee or stamp duty is payable.
- The law of trusts is based on English common law.
- Appeal lies to the Privy Council.
- The Hague Convention has been implemented.
- No specific provision is made for the exclusion of foreign inheritance laws.
- No specific provisions deal with the nonrecognition of foreign judgments.
- There is no specific "asset protection" provision (beyond that offered by general insolvency law) protecting a disposition to a trust from challenge by creditors.
- There is no special limitation period for creditors' claims.
- No provision is made for noncharitable purpose trusts.

Notes

1. Income Tax Act 1970, sec. 2A.
2. General Development Act 1964.
3. See the Nonresident Company Duty Act 1986.
4. In terms of the Income Tax (Exempt Companies) Act 1984.

CHAPTER THIRTY-TWO

JAMAICA

Background Information

Geographic and Demographic Data

Location	Jamaica is an island in the Caribbean Sea, south of Cuba. It is five hours behind GMT.
Capital	Kingston.
Area	4,243 square miles.
Population	2,615,582.
Languages	English is the official language. A local Creole dialect (Patois) is also spoken.
Access	Jamaica has two international airports that are served by major international airlines. It also has excellent port facilities.
Telecommunications	Good.

Government

Jamaica is an independent parliamentary democracy. It is a member of the Commonwealth.

Political and Economic Stability

Jamaica is politically stable. It has a bicameral parliament based on the Westminster model. The Queen of England is the head of state and is represented by a governor-general.

Key sectors in the economy are bauxite (alumina and bauxite account for more than half of exports) and tourism. Since assuming office in 1992, Prime Minister Percival J. Patterson has consolidated the market-oriented reforms initiated by his predecessor to make Jamaica a regional leader in economic reform. Most price controls have been eliminated, tax schedules streamlined, and government enterprises privatized. Tight monetary and fiscal policies under an International Monetary Fund program have helped slow inflation and stabilize the exchange rate, but, as a result, economic growth has slowed down and unemployment remains high.

Business Environment

Government attitude to offshore activities: The government encourages free enterprise and has passed legislation[1] in this respect. Ventures with foreign investors are encouraged.

Employment: Foreign nationals, including Commonwealth citizens, may not work in Jamaica unless they hold a valid work permit. Work permits are granted for a period of five years, but they may be extended. The Foreign Nationals and Commonwealth Citizens (Employment) Act provides certain exceptions to the above rule.

Local business requirements: The Financial Institutions Act 1992 contains stringent provisions requiring all companies that accept deposits to be licensed. Failure to comply with the act leads to legal penalties. The Bank of Jamaica and the Ministry of Finance are involved in the issuing of licenses. A deposit-taking institution requires a minimum subscribed capital of J$25 million to qualify for a license, and it may not commence trading until such sum has been paid in cash.

Currency and Exchange Control

The local currency is the Jamaican dollar. Since 1991, the government has implemented an aggressive open market policy, which includes liberalizing exchange control. In terms of this policy, exporters and other foreign exchange earners may hold their earnings in foreign exchange accounts anywhere in the world, including Jamaica, and pay for raw materials purchased abroad from these accounts. In addition, foreign investors are assured repatriation of the following:

(a) equity capital;

(b) dividends on equity capital;

(c) loans from foreign sources; and

(d) capital equipment brought in as part of equity or debt.

However, authorized dealers in foreign exchange will continue to implement due procedures to prevent money laundering and other criminal activities. In addition, regulations require the reporting of the import of currency notes exceeding US$10,000 and the export of currency notes exceeding J$150,000.

Disclosure of Information

Secrecy of information: In terms of the Official Secrets Act, it is an offense for government officials to disclose information obtained in their official capacity without authorization.

Banking secrecy: The Banking Act contains secrecy provisions. In addition, professional codes of confidentiality pertain in banking and in other spheres.

Legal System

General

The legal system is based on English common law. A constitution is also in place.

Treaties

See "Tax Treaties and Double Taxation."

Taxation (Direct and Indirect)

Income Tax

Resident companies, that is, companies incorporated and managed and controlled in Jamaica, are liable to income tax on their worldwide income. Overseas companies are liable only on their Jamaican sourced income. All individuals and bodies corporate, excluding building societies and life assurance companies, pay income tax at a flat rate of 33.33%. Building societies pay tax at a rate of 30%. Life assurance companies are subject to special, more favorable provisions in the Income Tax Act.

Resident individuals are allowed a tax-free deduction of J$14,352 before income tax is applied.

Withholding Taxes

In general, dividends; payments to shareholders, holders of securities, and principal members; and repatriation of company profit to nonresidents are subject to withholding tax. Individuals pay tax at the rate of 25%, and companies at 33.33%. Royalties, annuities, rent, professional consulting fees, and managerial fees paid to nonresidents are also subject to the tax.

Distributions made by nonresident companies out of foreign income to nonresident shareholders are exempt from withholding tax. Such distributions to resident shareholders form part of the shareholders' income for the purposes of Jamaican income tax.

Interest paid to a nonresident from

(a) investments or deposits in a building society;

(b) investments in a scheme under the Housing Act; or

(c) investments in an approved public utility, an approved hotel development or extension under the Hotels (Incentives) Act, or a recognized resort cottage development or extension under the Resort Cottages (Incentives) Act is exempt from Jamaican tax in terms of the Income Tax Act. The act also exempts interest paid to an "approved overseas organization" by a local bank or company licensed under the Protection of Depositors Act and approved by the minister of finance on sums made available by the overseas organization to the local bank or company.

Real Estate Taxes

A transfer tax of 7.5% is payable by the transferor on any consideration or land disposed of. There is also a property tax on the unimproved value of land.

Other Taxes

There is no capital gains tax in Jamaica. Excise duties are imposed on goods manufactured locally, and a customs duty is imposed on goods that are imported. There is also a general consumption tax of 12.5% on goods and services. Certain documents are subject to stamp duty. Payroll taxes to be paid by employers are governed by the National Insurance Act, the National Housing Trust Act, the Education Tax Act, and the Human Employment and Resource Training Act. Employees pay taxes under all but the Human Employment and Resource Training Act.

Tax Incentives

See "Incentives."

Tax Treaties and Double Taxation

Jamaica has entered into double taxation treaties with Canada, Denmark, the Federal Republic of Germany, Israel, Norway, Sweden, the United Kingdom, and the United States. In addition, the Income Tax Act provides for some relief in respect of Commonwealth income tax. The treaties also provide for the exchange of information between the contracting parties necessary for implementing the treaties, and for preventing fraud or tax evasion.

Canada

The Double Taxation Relief (Taxes on Income) (Canada) Order 1978 covers Canadian and Jamaican income tax and transfer tax and any identical or substantially similar tax imposed after the signing of the treaty. Withholding tax rates are as follows:

Interest	15% or 33.33%
Dividends	15% or 22.5%

Royalties	10% or 33.33%
Management fees and rental payments	12.5%

Business profits are taxable in one state only, unless the business is carried on through a permanent establishment in the other state.

Denmark

The Double Taxation Relief (Taxes on Income) (Denmark) Order 1950 was made between the governments of the United Kingdom and Denmark, with application to Jamaica. The taxes covered are Danish and Jamaican income tax and other taxes of a substantially similar character imposed after the signing of the treaty. Withholding tax rates are as follows:

Interest	33.33%
Dividends	33.33%
Royalties	nil or 33.33%
Management fees	15%

Business profits are taxable in one state only, unless the business is carried on through a permanent establishment in the other state.

Germany

The Double Taxation Relief (Taxes on Income) (Federal Republic of Germany) Order 1974 covers German income tax, corporation tax, capital tax, and trade tax, and Jamaican income tax and transfer tax. The treaty also covers any identical or substantially similar taxes subsequently imposed. It does not apply to companies entitled to special tax benefits under the Jamaican International Finance Companies (Income Tax Relief) Act 1971. Withholding tax rates are as follows:

Interest	12.5% or 10% (in the case of a bank)
Dividends	10% and 15%
Royalties	10%
Management fees	10%

Business profits are taxable in one state only, unless the business is carried on through a permanent establishment in the other state.

Israel

The Double Taxation Relief (Taxes on Income) (State of Israel) Order 1984 covers Israeli income tax (including capital gains tax and company tax), tax on gains from the sale of real estate and under the Land Appreciation Tax Law, and Jamaican income tax and transfer tax. It also applies to any identical or substantially similar taxes subsequently imposed. Withholding tax rates are as follows:

Interest	15%
Dividend	15% or 22.5%
Royalties	10%
Management fees	33.33%

Business profits are taxable in one state only, unless the business is carried on through a permanent establishment in the other state.

Norway

The Double Taxation Relief (Taxes on Income) (Norway) Order 1951 was made between the governments of the United Kingdom and Norway, with application to Jamaica. The Norwegian taxes covered are national income tax, national defense tax on income, communal income tax, old-age pension tax, war pension tax, seamen's tax, and national property tax. The Jamaican tax covered is income tax. Withholding tax rates are as follows:

Interest	33.33%
Dividends	33.33%
Royalties	nil or 33.33%
Management fees	15%

Business profits are taxable in one state only, unless the business is carried on through a permanent establishment in the other state.

Sweden

The Double Taxation Relief (Taxes on Income) (Kingdom of Sweden) Order 1985 covers Swedish state income tax (including sailors tax and coupon tax), communal income tax, tax on public entertainers, tax on the undistributed profits of companies, and tax on distribution in connection with reduction of share capital or in winding up of a company, and Jamaican income tax and transfer tax. It applies to any identical or substantially similar taxes subsequently imposed. Withholding tax rates are as follows:

Interest	12.5%
Dividends	10% or 22.5%
Royalties	10%
Management fees	10%

Business profits are taxable in one state only, unless the business is carried on through a permanent establishment in the other state.

United Kingdom

The United Kingdom Double Taxation Relief (Taxes on Income) (United Kingdom) Order 1973 covers U.K. income tax, capital gains tax, and corporation tax, and Jamaican income tax and transfer tax. Withholding tax rates are as follows:

Interest	12.5%
Dividends	15% and 22.5%
Royalties	10%
Management fees	12.5%

Business profits are taxable in one state only, unless the business is carried on through a permanent establishment in the other state.

United States

The Double Taxation Relief (Taxes on Income) (United States) Order 1980 covers U.S. federal income taxes imposed by the Internal Revenue Code, excluding accumulated earnings tax and personal holding company tax, and Jamaican income tax and profits tax. Withholding tax rates are as follows:

Interest	12.5%
Dividends	10% or 15%
Royalties	10%
Management fees	15%

Business profits are taxable in one state only, unless the business is carried on through a permanent establishment in the other state.

Incentives

The Jamaican government has provided tax incentives that are available to approved enterprises engaged in specific activities. Activities included are agriculture, bauxite mining, export, factory construction, film production, hotels, international finance, manufacturing, petroleum refining, resort cottages, and shipping. Most incentives are only available to companies, and they provide for the following:

(a) exemption from income tax for set periods;
(b) exemption from customs duties on imports of equipment and materials during the concession period;
(c) exemption from tax on dividends received by residents and nonresidents; and
(d) carryforward of losses incurred during the concession period.

The statutory concession periods are as follows:

Export Industry Encouragement Act	5 to 10 years
Hotels (Incentives) Act	10 to 15 years
Industrial Incentives Act	5 to 10 years
Industrial Incentive (Factory Construction) Act	15 years
International Finance Companies (Income Tax Relief) Act	while the company remains an approved company
Jamaica Free Zone Act	while the company remains an approved enterprise
Motion Picture Industry Encouragement Act	variable
Petroleum Refining Industry (Encouragement) Act	7 years
Resort Cottages (Incentives) Act	7 years
Shipping (Incentives) Act	10 years

A company that is incorporated in Jamaica, is resident in Jamaica, and engaged or proposing to engage in venture capital transactions in Jamaica may be granted approved venture capital status by the minister of finance, in which case it will be entitled to special income tax treatment. Venture capital transactions are such investment activities (including loan financing) that would, in the minister's opinion, by their influence on new or developing enterprises, be beneficial to the economic development of Jamaica. The special tax treatment may include the following:

(a) deduction of any distribution made by the company in arriving at its chargeable income;

(b) relief from income tax for any year of assessment in which it made distributions of at least 90% of its chargeable income before deduction of the distributions; and

(c) relief or partial relief from income tax in respect of dividends received by a nonresident shareholder who resides in a country with which Jamaica has a double taxation treaty.

An investment allowance may be obtained in respect of capital expenditure on building and structures and plant and machinery by businesses engaged in specified industries. Where the allowance is granted, the business will receive total allowances of 120% or 140% of the cost of the asset.

Corporations

(The domestic laws of Jamaica refer to *corporations* as *companies*. This terminology is retained in this chapter.)

Types of Companies

The Companies Act governs companies in Jamaica. The most common form of company is the company having a share capital and conferring limited liability on its shareholders. This may be either private, in which case it may have from two to twenty members, or public, in which case it must have a minimum of seven members and an unlimited maximum.

Migration of Companies

In terms of the Income Tax Act, a resident company (i.e., a company whose central control and management are in Jamaica) may not cease to be resident in Jamaica or transfer part of its business to a nonresident individual without the written consent of the minister of finance.

Checklist for Companies

- On incorporation, a list of directors must be filed with the registrar of companies. Overseas companies must also file the name of an agent who will accept service of process and notices on behalf of the company.
- No minimum share capital is prescribed.
- A private company must have at least two shareholders, and a public company must have at least seven.
- There is no local presence requirement for either local or overseas company directors.
- All companies must keep accounts and returns. Where records are kept overseas, they must be sent to Jamaica every six months. Annual returns must be filed with the registrar of companies. In addition, certain statutory registers and minute books must be kept.
- Company financial statements must be audited by registered public accountants.

Foreign Companies

Offshore companies are not defined in Jamaican law. Companies are therefore local or overseas companies. Overseas companies are companies that are incorporated overseas and whose management and control is overseas. Within a month of such a company establishing a place of business in Jamaica, it must file the following with the registrar of companies:

(a) a copy in English of its charter, statutes or memorandum and articles of association, or a certified translation;
(b) a list of directors, giving their full names, addresses, nationalities, and occupations; and
(c) the name and address of at least one person resident in Jamaica who will accept service and notices on behalf of the company.

All income of an overseas company arising in Jamaica is liable to income tax, unless it is exempt under a double taxation treaty or a statutory incentive scheme.

Offshore Finance Companies

In terms of the International Finance Companies (Income Tax Relief) Act 1971, the minister of finance may grant a certificate to an international finance company designating it an "approved company" in relation to the financial operations described in the certificate. For the purposes of this act, an international finance company means a body corporate, no matter where it is incorporated, that is engaged primarily in financial transactions. The following conditions must also be met:

(a) Not less than 95% of the issued share capital and voting power must be held by persons not resident in Jamaica;
(b) in the event of a liquidation, Jamaican residents would not be entitled to receive more than 5% of sums receivable for share or loan capital or of assets available for distribution after payment of credits; and
(c) Jamaican residents would not receive more than 5% of the interest payable on its loans and loan capital, the dividends payable on its preference share capital, or the dividends payable on its share capital.

The definition of financial transactions includes the following activities:

(a) buying, selling, holding, or managing securities;
(b) accepting deposits, borrowing, or lending money;
(c) placing deposits;
(d) issuing guarantees, letters of credit, and acceptances;
(e) underwriting, collecting, and transmitting funds;
(f) discounting;
(g) foreign exchange dealings;
(h) buying receivables;
(i) leasing of property;
(j) conducting trust business; and
(k) providing management consultant services.

An approved company is liable to pay income tax at the rate of 2.5% on the portion of its chargeable income that relates to its prescribed financial operations. An approved company that is resident in Jamaica is entitled to deduct tax at 2.5% from dividends paid to a nonresident of Jamaica and to retain the tax deducted. Where an approved company makes a payment to a nonresident in respect of interest, royalty, annuity, or other annual payment; rent accruing from property in Jamaica; or the provision of industrial or commercial information or advice, it is not obliged to deduct tax.

Shipping and Aviation

The Income Tax Act contains special income tax provisions for shipping and air transport. If the principal place of business of an owner or charterer of a vessel or aircraft is not Jamaica, sums arising in Jamaica in respect of fares, freight, or mail shipped in Jamaica will be taxed in the proportion that such sums bear to total profits worldwide. This provision applies subject to a certificate being produced from the taxing authority of the principal place of business.

Profits arising from shipping or air transport carried on by a nonresident will be exempt from income tax if the minister of finance is satisfied that a similar exemption is granted by that person's country of residence to persons in Jamaica or the United Kingdom (where that country is not the United Kingdom). A company is deemed to be resident for this purpose in the country in which the central control and management of its business is situated.

Licensing Companies

Licensing companies are not defined for the purposes of the Income Tax Act. Licensing fees from trademarks, patents, secret processes, royalties, rentals, industrial and commercial information, and advice are liable to income tax in Jamaica where such payments arise in Jamaica. Payments of such fees to nonresidents are subject to withholding tax at the higher rate of 33.3%, although in some cases the provisions may be varied by double taxation agreements.

Notes

1. That is, the Fair Competition Act 1993.

CHAPTER THIRTY-THREE

JERSEY

Background Information

Geographic and Demographic Data

Location	The Jersey bailiwick is an island in the English Channel, northwest of France. It is the southernmost of the Channel Islands. It is on GMT; in summer, it is one hour ahead.
Capital	Saint Helier.
Area	45 square miles.
Population	88,510.
Languages	English and French are both official languages, and both are widely used. A Norman-French dialect is spoken in country areas.
Access	Jersey is within one hour's flying time of London and Paris.
Telecommunications	Excellent.

Government

The Jersey bailiwick is a British Crown dependency, although in practice it is self-governing, particularly regarding fiscal policies. Britain is responsible for external affairs, including negotiating Jersey's unique position with the European Union, in particular, its exclusion from the policy of harmonizing taxation within member states.

Political and Economic Stability

Jersey is politically stable, with a democratically elected, unicameral legislature. The Queen of England is the head of state and is represented by a lieutenant governor.

The economy is stable and is based largely on financial services, agriculture, and tourism. Potatoes, cauliflower, tomatoes, and flowers are important export crops, shipped mostly to the United Kingdom. The Jersey breed of dairy cattle is known worldwide and represents an important export earner. Milk products go to the United Kingdom and other European Union countries. In 1986, the finance sector overtook tourism as the main contributor to GDP, accounting for 40% of the island's output. In recent years, the government has encouraged light industry to locate in Jersey, with the result that an electronics industry has developed alongside the traditional manufacturing of knitwear. All raw material and energy requirements are imported, as is a large share of Jersey's food needs.

Business Environment

Government attitude to offshore activities: Jersey's political and economic stability, its consistently low tax status, and its international reputation make it an attractive prospect to foreign investors and workers. The government actively promotes Jersey as an international financial center rather than as a tax haven. The growth of reputable business in the offshore financial sector is encouraged, and business of insufficient quality is discouraged. However, to protect its limited resources, the authorities discriminate between direct foreign investment of an "active" nature (including new businesses and permanent immigration) and of a "passive" nature (including purchasing real estate for investment rather than for personal residential purposes, or purchasing an existing business). It exercises control over the former by licensing the establishment of new businesses, controlling the number of staff employed in existing businesses, and regulating the occupation of residential accommodation. The general policy is to discourage new business that is controlled by nonresidents. As a result, the government does not consider it necessary to offer exemptions, grants, or incentives to attract further investment.

The economy of the United Kingdom benefits from Jersey's status as an international financial center. The United Kingdom negotiated special arrangements to preserve Jersey's fiscal autonomy with regard to the then European Economic Community. However, in 1998, the European Commission proposed measures aimed at reducing "harmful tax competition" from Jersey. These measures propose to impose on the U.K. government an obligation to ensure that its offshore dependent territories and Crown Peculiarities such as Jersey do not offer preferential tax regimes. Jersey has responded to these proposals by declaring that neither the United Kingdom nor the European Union is empowered to force Jersey to amend its tax regime.

Employment: Employment contracts are regulated by the Terms of Employment Regulations 1992. A social security scheme provides sickness, pension, and other benefits. There is no unemployment benefit.

Local business requirements: As a result of the government's policy of protecting Jersey's limited resources, foreign applicants are seldom granted licenses to commence business. Banks and insurance companies require special consent to commence activities in Jersey, and licenses will only be granted to individuals and organizations providing financial services if it can be shown that the services will extend the range of services offered on the island, including geographical areas covered by banking institutions, and not simply duplicate services that are already on offer. Licenses of new undertakings are granted under the Regulation of Undertakings and Development Laws 1973 and 1975. In deciding whether to grant a license, the benefits that will flow to the Jersey community will be assessed against the cost that the development will impose on the community. Application is free and is made to the Chief Advisor's Department of the Finance and Economics Committee.

In terms of the Registration of Business Names Law 1956, every individual, partnership, or body corporate carrying on business in Jersey under a name that is not a true surname and having a place of business on the island must register with the registry of business names. It costs J£20 to register the name and J£10 to alter the particulars thereafter.

Foreigners and Immigration

In regard to nationals of European Union member states, a right of free movement for the purposes of work and establishment pertains. Non–European Union members may establish themselves or work in Jersey only on the granting of permission from the States Defense Committee of the Aliens Office. A work permit will be granted only if no suitably qualified local exists or for seasonal work. In regard to applications for permanent residence in which the applicant does not seek employment and meets certain financial requirements, preference is given to U.K. and other European Union nationals.

Housing controls are exercised by the Housing Committee under the Housing Law 1949. Transactions involving Jersey real estate are subject to consent, although some exceptions apply to established residents. Consent is usually granted in respect of commercial property, but there are limited categories of persons to whom consent will be granted in respect of residential property. Consent must be justifiable on grounds of benefit to the island, particularly regarding revenue from tax receipts. Applicants must show that they will incur substantial liability to Jersey tax if consent is given. The number of consents granted per year is restricted, recently to eight applicants, and applicants must purchase a luxury dwelling.

Currency and Exchange Control

The local currency is the Jersey pound, which is at a par with the British pound. There is no exchange control.

Disclosure of Information

Banking secrecy: No legislation governs bank secrecy, but it is possible to have a numbered bank account in Jersey. Professional privilege pertains between professional advisors and their clients. Such confidentiality is limited by the fact that disclosure may be compelled by court order, where there is a duty to the public to disclose suspicious transactions, or where the customer has consented. Bankers and other professional advisors offer full nominee services.

Disclosure in company formation and trust settlement: The beneficial owner of an offshore company must be disclosed to the Financial Services Department on formation. The owner's address must also be furnished. There is no legislation governing the confidentiality of such disclosure, but a duty of confidentiality exists.

Public companies are required to be audited. Companies must have a Jersey-registered office. The registers of members, directors, and secretaries as well as the minute books must be kept there. A local agent would disclose beneficial ownership only under a court order.

A trustee does not have to register the beneficiaries of a trust. A company or trustee opening a bank account does not have to disclose the beneficial owners or beneficiaries. Limited partnerships also do not have to make such disclosure.

International cooperation measures: Jersey has procedures in place for cooperation with foreign investigators. How the procedure functions depends on the nature of the investigation. For example, in matters concerning a fraud, the attorney general will be approached; for insider dealing, contact will be made between regulators. Regarding appeal against these procedures, the normal court procedures apply. There is no mechanism for the enforcement of foreign judgments.

Legislation exists in Jersey concerning the exchange of information with foreign states in respect of drug trafficking, terrorism, fraud, insider dealing, banking, insurance, collective investment schemes, and companies. Jersey has also entered into tax treaties with the United Kingdom and Guernsey. These treaties do not contain exchange of information agreements. There are no mutual legal assistance treaties between Jersey and other countries.

The Drug Trafficking Offenses Law of 1988 will be extended to cover the laundering of proceeds from all criminal conduct. To this end the Proceeds of Crime Law of 1998 was introduced for debate in the second half of 1998. The law will criminalize any arrangement that is intended to deal in and disguise the origin of the proceeds of any serious criminal activity.

Legal System

General

Jersey has its own legal system, which is different from that of the other Channel Islands and the United Kingdom. Customary law derives mostly from the customary law of Normandy, particularly as regards real estate, hypothecation, and inheritance. However, English legislation has been assimilated into Jersey law and has persuasive influence where there is no Jersey precedent.

Legislation

The principal provisions affecting offshore operations and transactions are contained in the following:

- Banking Business Law 1991
- Collective Investment Funds Law 1988
- Companies Law 1991
- Income Tax Law 1961
- Insurance Business Law 1996
- Limited Partnerships Law 1994
- Registration of Business Names Law 1956
- Regulation of Undertakings and Development Laws 1973 and 1975
- Trusts Law 1984

Case Law

Important recent cases include the following:

- *Re The Den Haag Trust; Bhader v. Barclays Private Bank & Trust* (1997/1998) 1 OFLR 495, 497 (Royal Court of Jersey, Samedi Division)
- *Krohn v. Varna Shipyards* (*Nos. 1 & 2*) (1997/1998) 1 OFLR 471 (Royal Court of Jersey, Samedi Division)
- *Lloyds Bank v. Cala Cristal SA* (1997/1998) 1 OFLR 91 (Royal Court of Jersey, Samedi Division)
- *Solvalub Ltd. v. Match Investments Ltd.* (1997/1998) 1 OFLR 152 (Court of Appeal, Jersey)
- *Barclays v. Bhander* (1998/1999) 1 ITELR 46 (Royal Court of Jersey [Samedi Division])
- *Floor Khan v. Leisure Enterprises Ltd.* (1997/1998) 1 OFLR 771 (Royal Court of Jersey [Samedi Division])
- *Re Morgan & Chase Corp. (A Liberian Co.)* (1998/1999) 2 OFLR 111 (Royal Court of Jersey [Samedi Division])
- *Yachi v. Levi* (1998/1999) 2 OFLR 88 (Royal Court of Jersey [Samedi Division])

Treaties

See "Tax Treaties" and "Double Taxation."

Taxation (Direct and Indirect)

Income Tax

Individuals who are Jersey residents are liable to income tax in respect of income arising worldwide. The rate is 20%. Nonresidents are liable to Jersey income tax for all income from real estate, trade, profession, or employment arising in Jersey, including pension.

Jersey resident companies are liable to income tax at 20% on their worldwide income. A company is resident for these purposes if it is registered in Jersey and beneficially owned by Jersey residents, or if its central management and control are exercised in Jersey and exempt status has not been granted to the company for the year of assessment. This provision includes companies incorporated elsewhere that are managed and controlled in Jersey and have not applied for exempt status. A Jersey branch of a foreign corporation is liable to the standard rate income tax on profits arising in Jersey, provided the overall management and control of the company are outside Jersey. A branch may apply to be taxed as an international business company (IBC).

A foreign corporation that has applied for international business company status is liable for income tax at a rate of only 2% or less on profits arising outside of Jersey. IBCs are subject to a minimum annual tax liability of J£1,200. The diminishing sliding scale applicable to IBCs is as follows:

Up to J£3 million profit	2%
Following J£1.5 million	1.5%
Following J£5.5 million	1.0%
Thereafter	0.5%

Profits arising to IBCs within Jersey are subject to income tax at the standard rate of 20%.

Exempt companies pay tax at a flat rate of J£500 per annum.

Capital gains that are incidental to a transaction are not taxed. If the comptroller of income tax considers that the gain was fundamental to the transaction, the profit will be taxed as trading or dealing income, at the standard rate of 20% or the lower rate applicable to IBCs.

Withholding Taxes

Withholding tax is not imposed on dividends, but they are deemed to have borne income at 20% for a resident company, or at the lower rate payable by an international business company. Income tax is deducted at the standard rate of 20% from any payment of interest by a Jersey income tax paying company, irrespective of whether the payment is made to a resident or a nonresident. An IBC is not obliged to deduct tax when paying interest. Interest payments are deductible as trading or management expenses when calculating the profits chargeable to income tax for an IBC. A concession applies to deposit interest from Jersey banks payable to nonresidents. This is exempt from Jersey income tax. Royalties are treated for the purposes of tax in the same manner as interest.

Other Taxes

There are no taxes upon capital, capital gains, inheritances, gifts, sales or turnover, or deceased estates. Excise duties on spirits, wines, beer, tobacco, and petrol and import duties on foreign products are at comparatively low levels. There is no stamp duty payable on the transfer of shares and securities, checks, or other legal documents. Legal conveyances of real estate and mortgages registered against any real property bear court stamps levied at 0.5%.

Tax Treaties and Double Taxation

Jersey has a policy of not entering into tax treaties. However, it has double taxation agreements with the United Kingdom and France and a limited agreement with France relating to the exemption of profits from ships and aircraft. In terms of the double taxation agreements, industrial or commercial profits of a business in one country will not be taxed in the other country, unless the business also engages in commercial activity in the other country through a permanent establishment. If it does, it will be taxed by that country on as much of the profit as is attributable to the permanent establishment. A permanent establishment will include a branch but not an agency. The agreement with the United Kingdom specifically excludes dividends and debenture interest from its provisions.

Corporations

(The domestic laws of Jersey refer to *corporations* as *companies*. This terminology is retained in this chapter.)

Jersey offers a sophisticated infrastructure of trust companies, banking services, lawyers, accountants, and other professionals. It has also recently introduced legislation that allows for control and management of exempt companies from Jersey. However, it is an expensive jurisdiction, and disclosure of beneficial ownership must be made to the authorities, but not to the public.

Types of Companies

Companies incorporated in Jersey are governed by the Companies Law 1991, which is based largely on the Companies Act 1985 (United Kingdom). Companies in Jersey may only be limited liability companies; they may not be companies that are unlimited or limited by guarantee. Limited liability companies may be either public or private. A public company is one that has more than thirty members or that states in its memorandum that it is a public company. A private company is any company that is not a public company.

Public companies are required to file audited accounts with the registrar of companies, whereas private companies are not. Only a public company may issue a prospectus and offer its shares for subscription to the public.

Limited liability companies may be broken down into further categories on the basis of how they are treated for tax purposes. They may be resident, in which case they pay 20% income tax on annual worldwide profits; exempt, in which case they pay a flat rate annual tax of J£500; or international business companies, in which case they pay tax on a diminishing sliding scale of 2% or less on profits arising from international activities, subject to a minimum of J£1,200.

To be granted status as an exempt company, the following conditions must be met:

(a) Application must be lodged with the comptroller of income tax, together with J£500;

(b) no Jersey resident may have an interest in the company's share capital, unless it is a collective investment fund;[1]

(c) disclosure of beneficial ownership must be made to the Financial Services Department;

(d) the company must have paid its previous years' taxes in full; and

(e) the company must not have been an exempt company in a previous year of assessment.

On being granted exempt status, the company is treated as if it were nonresident, and it does not pay tax on income arising outside Jersey or on interest arising from bank and building society deposits in Jersey. An exempt company also does not have to deduct income tax from dividends or interest paid by it or file an annual income tax return.

To be granted international business company status, the following conditions must be met:

(a) Application must be lodged with the comptroller of income tax, together with J£1,200;

(b) no Jersey resident may have an interest in the company concerned;

(c) disclosure of beneficial ownership must be made to the Financial Services Department; and

(d) the company may not have had any tax status in Jersey in any previous year other than as an IBC.

Migration and Redomiciliation

An exempt company automatically becomes an income tax paying company if it fails to apply annually for exempt status. The same applies to IBCs. Once IBC status is lost, it cannot be regained. Income tax companies can acquire exempt status, but exempt or income tax paying companies cannot ordinarily become IBCs.

Redomiciliation legislation is in the pipeline.

Checklist for Companies

- Resident companies are taxed at a rate of 20% of profits. Exempt companies pay a flat rate of J£500 per annum.
- The Companies Law 1991 governs companies in Jersey.
- Company names must be approved in advance. Certain words are considered sensitive, such as *Royal* and *International.* All names must finish with the word *Limited* or its abbreviated form.
- It takes about three days to incorporate a company, although same-day service is available at an additional cost of J£40. Shelf companies are not available. Beneficial ownership must be disclosed to the authorities prior to incorporation or to tax status being granted, and references may also be required.
- The usual minimum capital is J£2. A capital duty of 0.5% is charged, with a minimum of J£50.
- At least two shareholders are required. Bearer shares and shares of no par value are not possible.
- A minimum of one director is required. Corporate directors are not allowed, and there is no restriction on the directors' residence.
- A company secretary is mandatory. A corporate secretary is allowed, and there is no restriction on the secretary's residence.
- A registered office is required in Jersey, but a registered agent is not.
- The registered office, shareholders, annual return, and memorandum and articles of association are available on the public file.
- Corporate books and a seal are required and are usually kept at the registered office.
- Resident companies must keep accounts that must be filed with the revenue authorities. Exempt companies also have to keep accounts, but they do not have to be filed.
- An annual return is required. The annual return filing fee is J£120.
- There is no restriction on the holding of meetings.

Other Forms of Business Organization

Sole Proprietorships

A Jersey resident may carry on business as a sole trader.

Partnerships and Joint Ventures

General partnerships: In the absence of legislation in Jersey governing ordinary partnerships, the law is similar to English common law as codified in the Partnership Act 1890. A general partnership is one that arises from the association of two or more persons (which may include companies) with a view to carrying on business for profit. The liability of each partner is unlimited.

One or more partners must be Jersey residents, or the partnership must carry on business in Jersey. It is possible to register a partnership without a Jersey partner under the Registration of Business Names Law 1956. As long as the management and control of the partnership is exercised outside Jersey, the partnership will not be resident for Jersey income tax purposes and will not be liable to income tax in respect of profits arising outside of Jersey. There is no restriction on the nationality of the partners. Partnership agreements do not have to be registered and therefore remain strictly confidential. Nonresident partners are not liable to Jersey income tax on profits arising outside of Jersey. Resident partners are liable to income tax on profits arising worldwide.

Limited partnerships: Limited partnerships are governed by the Limited Partnerships Law 1994. Limited partnerships allow institutional investors to become partners in the ownership of less conventional assets, including venture capital and development funds, management buyouts, and real property.

A limited partnership is not formed until a declaration has been filed with the registrar of limited partnerships and the registrar has issued a certificate that he has received the declaration. The declaration must give the partnership's name (which must end with the words *Limited Partnership* or its abbreviation, *LP*), its registered office, the name and address of each general partner (in the case of a general partner that is a company, its place of incorporation and registered or principal office), and the duration for which the partnership is established. It is not necessary to file a copy of the partnership agreement or the names of the limited partners. The partnership agreement is not available for inspection by anyone other than the partners. A registration fee of J£500 is payable to the registrar, and there is no annual registration fee.

Limited liability partnerships: The controversial Limited Liability Partnerships Law of 1997 came into force on September 9, 1998. The act is based on legislation in the State of Delaware (USA) and was specifically developed to permit large U.K. partnerships to register in Jersey with limited liability status. The partnership remains totally liable for its debts, and all partnership assets are available to creditors, but the assets of individual partners who have not been negligent are protected from debts arising from negligence. Each partnership must provide J£5 million for judgments that may be made against the partnership.

Joint ventures: Joint ventures are not treated as separate ventures in Jersey but as the conduit through which the participators in the venture receive their share of the joint income.

Foreign Companies

A foreign company does not have to register its corporate details or file an annual return in Jersey. However, if it intends to trade within Jersey in its own name or to establish a branch or a permanent place of business in Jersey, it is subject to the same consents and license requirements that apply to resident companies.

A company incorporated outside Jersey will be liable only to Jersey income tax on the profits earned from trading activities within the island by its branch or local establishment. Foreign corporations that are managed and controlled outside of Jersey and do not trade in Jersey are not liable to income tax or the flat rate annual tax on profits.

A nonresident private investment company may be managed and controlled by resident directors and hold its board meetings in the island but be exempt from Jersey income tax, including the flat rate annual fee, by government concession. The company must make written application to the comptroller of income tax confirming that the beneficial owners are nonresidents, that the company is not carrying on trade, and that the company is not in receipt of Jersey source income, other than bank interest.

A nonresident trading corporation wishing to be managed and controlled from Jersey must elect for either exempt tax status (that is, the paying of an annual flat rate tax of £500) or international business company status (that is, the paying of income tax on its profits at the rate of 2% or less). In return, the foreign corporation may appoint Jersey directors and hold its board meetings on the island without becoming liable to the full income tax rate of 20%.

A Jersey branch of a nonresident company can apply to be taxed as an international business company.

Banks and Trust Companies

Banking and other categories of deposit-taking business are governed by the Banking Business Law 1991. Banks and other licensed deposit takers must register with the Financial Services Department. A registration fee of J£7,500 is payable. Audited accounts and other information must be filed with the Financial Services Department, and an annual fee of J£7,500 is payable.

Trust companies do not require specific authorization to carry on business in Jersey, although it may be desirable to be registered as a trust corporation under the provisions of article 12 of the Probate Law 1949 for the purposes of taking out Jersey probates and letters of administration.

Insurance

General

Insurance business is regulated by the Insurance Business Law 1996. This law prohibits the carrying on of insurance business in or from within Jersey except by persons or companies that are registered to carry on insurance business or particular classes of insurance business in the United Kingdom or another member state of the European Union, unless that person or company has a permit under the law to carry on that business in Jersey. Permits extend only to restricted insurance business, namely, captive insurance and reinsurance. They remain in force until canceled. The restrictions mean that direct or nonadmitted insurance, other than pure captive business, is not permitted.

On July 17, 1998, the U.K. government granted Jersey "designated territory" status for long-term insurance business under Section 130(3) of the U.K. Financial Services Act of 1986. Designation enables insurance companies registered in Jersey to promote or advertise their products in the United Kingdom.

Captive Insurance Companies

Captive insurance is regulated by the Insurance Business Law 1996, the Insurance Business (General Provisions) (Jersey) Order 1996, and the Insurance Business (Solvency Margin) Order 1996. There are eight captives established in Jersey. The total asset and premium size of the sector is not available. The director of insurance in the Financial Services Department regulates the sector. An annual audit is required, as are semiannual unaudited accounts and confirmation that permit conditions are being complied with.

As far as regulatory concessions are concerned, all permits are subject to conditions that may be varied. A captive that is an international company is taxed at a negotiated rate, between 0% and 30%. A captive that is an exempt company is tax-exempt but must pay an annual fee of J£500.

The minimum capital requirement is J£100,000 or its currency equivalent. Incorporation costs J£120 plus a stamp duty on authorized capital at a rate of 0.5%, to a maximum of J£2,500. The annual license fee is J£5,000 for long-term business and J£2,500 for any other class. Professional fees and application fees are also payable, the latter on the same basis as the annual fees.

No provision is made for special categories of captives. There is no provision concerning rent-a-captives and protected cell companies.

Shipping and Aviation

A register of British ships is kept at Saint Helier. Ships of up to 150 tons may be registered in Jersey. U.K. legislation pertaining to merchant shipping, such as the Merchant Shipping Acts 1894 to 1958 and the Carriage of Goods by Sea Act 1924, apply in Jersey, as do requirements of the U.K. Department of Trade and Industry. Jersey-registered ships fly under the British flag. Registration costs approximately J£280. No annual fees are payable.

Aircraft may not be registered in Jersey.

Mutual Funds and Collective Investment Schemes

The Collective Investment Funds Law 1988 regulates mutual funds. The act is intended to protect investors in mutual funds by licensing and regulating all functionaries of every Jersey-based fund, as well as any Jersey functionary of funds established elsewhere. The level of protection afforded by the act has allowed the government of the United Kingdom to grant Jersey "designated territory" status under the Financial Services Act 1986 (United Kingdom). As a result, Jersey-based "recognized funds" can be marketed freely in the United Kingdom. Jersey-based fund management groups are aiming to obtain similar freedom to market funds in other jurisdictions.

The two most commonly used legal structures for establishing open-ended collective schemes are

(i) investment companies with redeemable share capital; and

(ii) unit trusts, whose units may be issued and redeemed.

Open-Ended Investment Companies

Most mutual funds established in Jersey for retail clients are open-ended investment companies with redeemable share capital. In terms of the Companies Law 1991, the redeemable share capital need not be preference shares. The shares can be issued and redeemed at a price relative to the underlying net asset value. Investment companies enter into management agreements with Jersey management companies whereby the latter act as investment advisors and sales agents and undertake the general administration of the companies' business.

Corporate mutual funds are liable to a registration fee and stamp duty calculated by reference to the authorized capital. Most mutual funds established through an open-ended investment company claim exemption from Jersey income tax, even if there are resident shareholders. However, Jersey income tax is deducted from dividends paid to residents, and the tax is accounted for to the comptroller of income tax.

Unit Trusts

A unit trust is established by a written trust instrument that is entered into between a Jersey trustee and a Jersey management company. The trustee acts as the custodian trustee and holds the proceeds of the sale of units and the investments purchased with such proceeds. The trustee has a duty to insure that the management company carries out its obligations to unit holders under the terms of the trust instrument. The management company attends to the general administration of the mutual fund and may also act as investment advisor or sales agent.

The trustee is usually a subsidiary of one of the English clearing banks. The day-to-day administration of the fund may be delegated by the management company, but the administration must be carried out in Jersey by a company with a proven record of unit trust administration.

There are no government fees, taxes, or duties payable in respect of this type of mutual fund, either upon establishment or annually. The Collective Investment Funds Law requires all persons and companies that are involved in the promotion, management, and administration and in the safekeeping of assets of a mutual fund that is established in or managed from Jersey to be registered as a functionary under the law. An annual fee of J£1,080 is payable by each functionary.

Trusts

The Trusts Law 1984 codified the English-based common law, resolving many uncertainties and increasing the protection afforded to beneficiaries.

There is no government duty payable upon creation of a trust. There are also no registration requirements.

A Jersey trust is one whose proper law is the law of Jersey. If the beneficiaries of a Jersey trust are nonresident, income arising from sources outside Jersey is not liable to income tax in Jersey, nor are distributions to the beneficiaries. Interest on bank deposits made by the trustees of a nonresident trust is also not taxed. This is because of a government concession. Trust assets are immune from capital gains tax, estate or probate duty, and gift tax. The trustees of a nonresident trust are not required to make returns or provide accounts of the trust to the comptroller of income tax. Trust accounts must be kept but do not have to be audited.

Migration of trusts is possible. A Jersey trust may be "exported' by replacing Jersey trustees with nonresident trustees and changing the proper law of the trust; a trust established in another jurisdiction may migrate to Jersey by appointing Jersey resident trustees.

Since 1995 noncharitable purpose trusts may be created in Jersey. A purpose trust is one that has a specific purpose stated in the trust deed for which there are no ascertainable beneficiaries.

Checklist for Trusts

- There is a statutory schedule of standard trust powers.
- The maximum perpetuity period for noncharitable trusts is one hundred years.

- A resident trustee is not required.
- Registration of a trust is not necessary.
- Trust documents are normally in English.
- There is no stamp duty or registration fee.
- The law of trusts in Jersey has a common law background.
- Appeal lies to the Privy Council.
- The Hague Convention has been implemented.
- Specific provision is made for the exclusion of foreign inheritance laws.
- Specific provisions deal with the nonrecognition of foreign judgments.
- There is no specific "asset protection" provision (beyond that offered by general insolvency laws) protecting a disposition to a trust from challenge by creditors.
- There is no special limitation period for creditors' claims.
- Provision is made for noncharitable trusts.

Notes

1. As to which, see the Collective Investment Funds Law 1988.

CHAPTER THIRTY-FOUR

LABUAN

Background Information

Geographic and Demographic Data

Location	Labuan is an island off the coast of the Malaysian state of Sabah, northwest of Borneo. It is seven hours ahead of GMT.
Capital	Labuan.
Area	37 square miles.
Population	57,000.
Languages	Bahasa Malaysia is the official language, but English is widely spoken in the commercial sector.
Access	There are daily flights from Kuala Lumpur to Labuan, and efforts are being made to improve its accessibility from Hong Kong, Singapore, and Tokyo.
Telecommunications	Excellent.

Government

Labuan is a federal territory directly under the control of the Malaysian government. Malaysia itself is a constitutional monarchy with a democratically elected bicameral parliament. It is a member of the Commonwealth.

Political and Economic Stability

Despite the recent economic crisis in Southeast Asia, Malaysia remains politically stable. The Labuan economy is based on offshore oil and gas operations, shipbuilding, manufacturing, and import and export activities.

Business Environment

Government attitude to offshore activities: Since 1990, the Malaysian government has actively developed Labuan as an international offshore financial center. The government is committed to upgrading the infrastructure, including transport and telecommunications, to facilitate this development. In particular, offshore banking, trust and fund management, offshore insurance, and offshore investment holding companies are encouraged. There are no incentives relating to industrial or manufacturing activities.

Local business requirements: Offshore companies may not purchase real estate in Malaysia except for use as business premises or as accommodation for employees.

Foreigners and Immigration

Foreign nationals require work permits to work in Malaysia. A liberal immigration policy has been adopted in Labuan with regard to expatriates, who will be issued with multiple-entry visas where they have work permits with offshore companies in Labuan. They are also subject to liberal exchange control policies.

Currency and Exchange Control

The local currency is the Malaysian ringgit. Malaysian exchange controls do not apply to licensed offshore banks, insurance companies, and other offshore companies operating in Labuan. Nonresident individuals are also exempt from all exchange controls.

Under the Foreign Exchange of Malaysia (ECM) Notice No. 15 issued by the Bank Negara Malaysia (Central Bank), offshore companies, foreign offshore companies, and licensed offshore banks and offshore insurance entities may open external accounts in Malaysia solely for the purpose of defraying their administrative and statutory expenses, including the granting of loans to staff pursuant to the terms and conditions of service. As a result of speculative trading in the ringgit, as of September 1, 1998, licensed offshore banks are no longer entitled to trade in instruments denominated in ringgit, and the exchange rate has been pegged to the U.S. dollar at RM3.80. Licensed offshore insurance entities may also open external accounts for the purpose of reinsurance of domestic insurance business, provided the external account is funded from the sale of foreign currencies or the proceeds of approved credit facilities in ringgit. Offshore banks may also receive fees and commission in ringgit on transactions denominated in ringgit as a way of reducing the cost of business.

In terms of the same notice, offshore entities may open foreign currency accounts in or outside Malaysia and buy, borrow, sell, or lend foreign currency with an authorized dealer, a licensed offshore bank, or any nonresident.

The notice also permits licensed offshore banks to buy, borrow, sell, or lend foreign currency and to do any act connected with buying, borrowing, selling, or lending any foreign currency, provided that they

(a) open only foreign currency accounts, including current accounts but excluding checking accounts, for any nonresident and resident;

(b) extend only foreign currency credit facilities to nonresidents and residents;

(c) undertake foreign exchange transactions, including forward and spot purchases and sales, with nonresidents and authorized dealers only;

(d) make payments on behalf of nonresidents;

(e) make payments to nonresidents on behalf of residents, provided that the funds for the payment are proceeds of approved foreign currency facilities obtained by residents from licensed offshore banks or funds in permitted foreign currency accounts and that the payments to Malaysia are only for credit into the resident's own foreign currency accounts with authorized dealers or payment to authorized dealers or licensed merchant banks in relation to foreign currency credit facilities obtained from the latter institutions, unless permitted otherwise by the comptroller of foreign exchange; and

(f) are permitted to use the ringgit in their external accounts, to be placed in interest-bearing external accounts.

The prior permission of Bank Negara Malaysia is required for

(a) offshore entities to fund their external accounts in ringgit, otherwise than as permitted above;

(b) licensed offshore banks to undertake any foreign exchange transaction, including remittances (other than as permitted above), forward and spot purchases, and sales with or on behalf of residents other than an authorized dealer; and

(c) all transactions of offshore entities with Israel, Serbia, or Montenegro, or in the currencies of Israel, Serbia, or Montenegro.

Disclosure of Information

Secrecy of information: The Secrecy Act prohibits the release of information relating to offshore companies to the public. The Labuan authorities endeavor to provide foreign investors with maximum confidentiality, while preventing the island from being used for money laundering or other criminal activities. Disclosure of shareholdings or beneficial ownership is prohibited, and public inspection of company records is limited. Court proceedings involving offshore companies are held in camera, and disclosure of company records can be compelled by court order only.

Banking secrecy: Banking secrecy and confidentiality are governed by the Offshore Banking Act of 1990, the Offshore Companies Act of 1990, and the Offshore Insurance Act of 1990. Total banking secrecy is not provided, but legitimate customers are assured of confidentiality. Trust companies must ascertain beneficial ownership but may not disclose such information except in criminal proceedings.

Disclosure in company formation and trust settlement: The disclosure of beneficial ownership of an offshore company must be made to the trust company on formation. No other information is required regarding beneficial ownership. The confidentiality of such disclosure is governed by the Offshore Companies Act 1990, the Offshore Banking Act 1990, the Offshore Insurance Act 1990, the Labuan Offshore Trust Act 1996, the Labuan Limited Partnership Act 1997, and the Labuan Trust Companies Act 1990.

Companies may choose whether or not to be audited. An offshore company must have a Labuan trust company as its agent. The registered address of the offshore company must be the address of the Labuan trust company. All company secretarial and accounting records must be lodged with the agent. The agent may disclose beneficial ownership only under an order of the high court.

A trustee may choose whether or not to register the beneficiaries of a trust. A company or trustee opening a bank account must disclose beneficial ownership or the identity of the beneficiaries to the bank. This does not apply to limited partnerships.

International cooperation measures: Labuan does not have a procedure for cooperation with foreign investigators. There is no legislation governing the exchange of information with other states. Foreign judgments are enforced in terms of the Reciprocal Enforcement of Foreign Judgments Act 1958. A foreign judgment must be registered in a Malaysian court and will be enforced by that court.

Labuan is subject to the tax treaties entered into between Malaysia and other countries. These treaties contain exchange of information agreements, which vary depending on the agreement. Malaysia has not entered into any mutual legal assistance treaties.

"All-crimes" money laundering legislation is under consideration. The response of the authorities to a request for assistance from foreign investigations into tax evasion would depend upon government policy.

Legal System

General

The Malaysian legal system is based on English common law, although local custom is increasingly being incorporated.

Legislation

The principal provisions affecting offshore operations and transactions are contained in the following:

- Labuan Limited Partnership Act 1997

- Labuan Offshore Business Activity Tax Act 1990
- Labuan Offshore Financial Services Authority Act 1995
- Labuan Offshore Limited Partnership Act 1997
- Labuan Offshore Securities Industry Act 1998
- Labuan Offshore Trust Act 1996
- Labuan Trust Companies Act 1990
- Offshore Banking Act 1990
- Offshore Companies Act 1990
- Offshore Insurance Act 1990
- Offshore Insurance (Amendment) Act 1997
- Offshore Limited Partnership Act 1997
- Offshore Trusts Act 1996

Treaties

See "Tax Treaties and Double Taxation."

Taxation (Direct and Indirect)

Income Tax

Labuan resident companies incorporated under legislation such as the Companies Act 1965 are not recognized as offshore companies for income tax purposes, and they pay Malaysian corporate tax, which is at a rate of 28%. Branches of Malaysian banks and insurance companies that are licensed to carry on offshore business also pay Malaysian corporate tax at 28%.

In terms of the Offshore Business Activity Tax Act 1990, an offshore company may pay either RM 20,000 or 3% of audited net profit on income from offshore trading activities. These include banking, insurance, trading, management, and other activities that are not nontrading activities, but not activities relating to shipping and petroleum. Nontrading activities are those that relate to the holding of investments in securities, stocks, shares, loans, deposits, and immovable properties by an offshore company on its own behalf. Offshore nontrading activities do not incur liability to tax unless they are carried on along with offshore trading activities, in which case the company will be deemed to be carrying on offshore trading activities.

If an offshore company elects to pay the RM 20,000 rather than the 3%, it will not have to submit an annual return.

Resident individuals pay income tax on a sliding scale of 2% to 30%. Nonresidents are taxed at a flat rate of 30%.

Capital and Capital Gains Taxes

There are no corporate capital taxes. There is a capital gains tax on transactions involving real estate situated in Malaysia.

Stamp Duties

Offshore companies are exempt from stamp duty on all instruments that are made in connection with an offshore business activity.

Withholding Taxes

The following payments are exempt from withholding tax:

(a) interest paid by a Malaysian resident to an offshore company carrying on offshore banking business in Labuan;
(b) royalties paid by an offshore company to another offshore company or nonresident individual; and
(c) interest paid by an offshore company to another offshore company or nonresident individual.

Furthermore, where income received from a Labuan offshore company is tax-exempt, withholding provisions do not apply.

Other Taxes

As Labuan is a free port, there is no customs duty. This provision does not apply to petroleum products. There is also no service tax.

Tax Incentives

See "Tax Incentives" under "Tax Incentives (Tax and Nontax)."

Tax Treaties and Double Taxation

Labuan itself has not entered into any tax treaties with other countries. However, Malaysia has entered into approximately forty-four double taxation treaty agreements (some of these are not yet in force). Malaysia's treaty partners may be reluctant to recognize Labuan offshore legislation as Malaysian tax covered under the double taxation agreements. Sweden has already implemented legislation that treats Swedish companies that operate in Labuan as not being domiciled in Malaysia at all for treaty purposes.

Tax Incentives (Tax and Nontax)

Tax Incentives

Distributions made by an offshore trust are not subject to income tax in the hands of the beneficiary.

Income derived by a person or his employee or a company from qualifying professional services rendered to an offshore company in Labuan is exempt from tax up to an amount equivalent to 50% of the adjusted income from that source. "Qualifying professional services" are legal, accounting, financial, or secretarial services and include the services provided by a Labuan trust company.

Interest received from an offshore company by a resident person (other than interest received by licensed banks and insurance companies) is exempt from tax.

From the year of assessment 1991, amounts received from an offshore company by a nonresident person or another offshore company in consideration of services, advice, or assistance specified in paragraphs (i) and (ii) of section 4A of the Malaysian Income Tax Act 1967 are exempt from tax. Specifically, these sections apply to amounts paid in consideration of

(a) services rendered by persons or their employees in connection with the use of property or rights belonging to, or the installation or operation of, any plant, machinery, or other apparatus purchased from such persons; and

(b) technical advice, assistance, or services rendered in connection with technical management or administration of any scientific, industrial, or commercial undertaking, venture, project, or scheme.

Free Port

Labuan enjoys free port status, with the exception of petroleum products.

Corporations

(The domestic laws of Malaysia refer to *corporations* as *companies*. This terminology is retained in this chapter.)

Offshore companies that are incorporated in Labuan benefit from preferential tax treatment, namely, 3% of net audited profits or RM 20,000 per annum, and from the fact that there is no stamp duty. To benefit from these tax incentives, the company must be beneficially owned by a nonresident, must carry on financial and investment business only, and may not invest in the Malaysian market. Offshore companies may not trade with Malaysians and must deal only in foreign currency, except for statutory fees and administrative costs.

Types of Companies

Offshore companies are incorporated under the Offshore Companies Act 1990. They are regulated by the Labuan Financial Services Authority, which was established under the Labuan Offshore Financial Services Authority Act 1995. The authority is also responsible for licensing of offshore businesses.

Offshore companies are limited by share capital and may only be incorporated by nonresidents.

Migration and Redomiciliation

Offshore companies may migrate to other jurisdictions with the approval of the registrar of companies, the new jurisdiction, and the directors, shareholders, and debenture holders. Similarly, foreign companies may migrate to Labuan.

Checklist for Companies

- Company names must be reserved to check for availability. Some words are sensitive and require the minister of finance's approval, for example, *Finance*, *Bank, Trust, Royal, Insurance*, and *Security*.
- Incorporation takes three to five days. Shelf companies are not available. Offshore companies in general need not furnish the authorities with information as to beneficial ownership prior to incorporation, although banks and insurance companies must.
- The usual minimum capital is between US$18,000 and US$20,000. There is no capital duty.
- At least one shareholder is required. Bearer shares and shares of no par value are not allowed.
- At least one director is required. Corporate directors are allowed, and there is no restriction on the directors' residence.
- A secretary is mandatory. Corporate secretaries are allowed, and offshore companies must have a resident secretary.
- Offshore companies must have a registered office but need not have a registered agent. The registers of directors, secretaries, members, transfers, mortgages, debentures, debenture holders, and interest holders must be kept at the registered office. Corporate books and a seal are also usually kept at the registered office.
- No information is available on the public file.
- Trading companies must keep accounts. These do not have to be filed if the company elects to pay RM 20,000 tax per annum.
- An annual return is required. An annual return filing fee of RM 100 is payable.

- There are no restrictions on the holding of meetings, unless proof of residency is required, in which case meetings must be held in Labuan.
- Trading companies must pay either 3% of net audited profits or RM 20,000 per annum in tax.

Other Forms of Business Organization

Partnerships

The Labuan Offshore Limited Partnerships Act of 1997 regulates offshore limited partnerships. An offshore limited partnership must consist of not less than two partners and not more than twenty partners, at least one of whom must be a general partner and one a limited partner.

Offshore limited partnerships must be registered with the Labuan Offshore Financial Services Authority and must have a registered office in Labuan, which must also be the registered office of a trust company. Documents required to be filed, lodged, or registered with the Labuan Offshore Financial Services Authority must be filed, lodged, or registered through a trust company to ensure their validity.

Partnership accounts do not have to be audited but must be submitted annually to the Inland Revenue Board, together with the income tax return form.

Foreign Companies

Foreign companies must register under the Offshore Companies Act 1990. They may have names in a foreign language, provided they use roman characters, and must use the services of a trust company to fulfill their statutory obligations.

Banks and Trust Companies

Offshore banks are incorporated in terms of the Offshore Companies Act 1990 and are licensed in terms of the Offshore Banking Act 1990. They must have a minimum paid-up capital and reserves of RM 10 million or its currency equivalent. They are liable to an annual license fee of RM 60,000. Licenses are issued by Bank Negara Malaysia (Central Bank). Offshore banks may accept deposits and grant loans in foreign currency to both residents and nonresidents, but where loans of over RM 1 million are granted to residents, the approval of the Central Bank is required.

Trust companies are incorporated in terms of the Companies Act 1965 and are licensed in terms of the Labuan Trust Companies Act 1990. They must have a minimum authorized capital of RM 500,000, with RM 150,000 paid up. A security deposit of RM 100,000 must also be lodged. Trust companies may carry on business as trustee, agent, or administrator. Activities include share registration;

transfer office operation; the provision of management and accounting services, directors, and secretarial services; and providing registered offices for offshore and foreign companies, as well as for branches of foreign companies.

Insurance

Offshore insurance companies are incorporated in terms of the Offshore Companies Act 1990 and licensed in terms of the Offshore Insurance Act 1990. Applications for licenses must be made to the minister of finance through the Bank Negara Malaysia. Annual license fees are as follows:

Life and general insurance	RM 60,000
Life insurance	RM 30,000
General insurance	RM 30,000
Captive insurance	RM 10,000
Offshore insurance management	RM 5,000
Offshore insurance underwriting management	RM 5,000
Offshore insurance brokerage	RM 5,000

The following activities are permitted:

(a) captive insurance;
(b) direct insurance of foreign risks;
(c) reinsurance, including of Malaysian risks;
(d) insurance management;
(e) underwriting management; and
(f) insurance brokering.

The following minimum working funds are prescribed for offshore insurers:

Life and general business	RM 7.5 million
Reinsurance business	RM 10 million
Captive insurance	RM 1 million

Mutual Funds

The Labuan Offshore Securities Industry Act of 1998 defines a "mutual fund" as an offshore company, company incorporated under the laws of a recognized jurisdiction, partnership, or unit trust that:

(a) collects and pools funds for the purpose of collective investment with the aim of spreading investment risk; and
(b) issues shares that entitle the holder to receive on demand an amount computed by reference to the value of a proportionate interest in the whole or part of the net assets of the company, partnership, or unit trust.

The trustee of a public fund must be a trust company formed under the Labuan Trust Companies Act of 1990. The custodian of a mutual fund must be a trust company or offshore bank licensed under the Offshore Companies Act of 1990.

There are separate registers for pirvate funds, public funds, managers, and administrators. The manager of a public fund must be an offshore company that has been granted a license to act as manager. The administrator of a public fund must be a company or trust company registered as an administrator. An offshore bank, trust company, or management company licensed under the Offshore Companies Act of 1990, section 130C, is exempt from these requirements.

A registered fund must keep accounting records and financial statements at its place of business in Labuan. The statements must be audited annually.

Trusts

The law of trusts in Labuan was based on English common law but has since been codified in the Labuan Offshore Trust Act 1996. Offshore trusts (i.e., trusts created in Labuan in which the settlor and beneficiaries are nonresidents) are eligible for the preferential tax treatment granted to offshore companies. Offshore trusts that elect to pay tax at the rate of 3% of net audited profits must submit audited accounts to the tax authorities.

Trusts that are not offshore trusts are taxed at domestic income tax rates, namely, 30%. A trust is regarded as being resident in Malaysia if any of the trustees are resident in Malaysia. However, if the trust was created outside of Malaysia, the income is wholly derived from outside Malaysia, the trust is administered entirely outside Malaysia, and at least half of the trustees are nonresident, it will not be regarded as resident for tax purposes. Resident and nonresident trusts are taxed at the same rate (30%). However, nonresident trusts are taxed only on income arising in Malaysia, whereas resident trusts are taxed on income arising in Malaysia and income received in Malaysia but arising outside Malaysia.

Offshore trusts do not have to be registered, although they may be registered with the Labuan Financial Services Authority. Where a nonresident trustee opens a bank account with an offshore bank, there are no exchange controls. Where a Labuan trust company is the trustee, exchange control approval is required from the Bank Negara Malaysia.

At least one trustee must be a trust company registered under the Labuan Trust Companies Act 1990.

Checklist for Offshore Trusts

- There is a statutory schedule of standard trust powers.
- The maximum perpetuity period for noncharitable trusts is life plus twenty-one years.
- A resident trustee is not required.
- Trusts do not have to be registered.
- Labuan trust documents may be in any language.
- There is no stamp duty or registration fee.
- The law of trusts is based on English common law.
- There is no right of appeal to the Privy Council.
- The Hague Convention has not been implemented.
- Specific provision has not been made for the exclusion of foreign inheritance laws.
- No specific provision deals with the nonrecognition of foreign judgments.
- There is no specific "asset protection" provision (beyond that offered by general insolvency law) protecting a disposition to a trust from challenge by creditors.
- There is no special limitation period for creditors' claims.
- Provision is not made for noncharitable purpose trusts.

CHAPTER THIRTY-FIVE

LIBERIA

Background Information

Geographic and Demographic Data

Location	Liberia is on the west coast of Africa, between the Ivory Coast and Sierra Leone. It is on GMT.
Capital	Monrovia.
Area	37,741 square miles.
Population	2,602,068.
Language	English.
Access	Monrovia is a free port that is one of the most modern ports on the west coast of Africa. There was easy access by air to major international commercial centers, but this has been affected by continued civil unrest.
Telecommunications	Poor.

Government

Liberia is an independent republic that has historically had, and continues to have, a long and beneficial association with the United States.

Political and Economic Stability

Civil order ended in 1990 with civil war. The Abuja II peace accord was signed in August 1996, and national elections were scheduled for May 30, 1997, but long-term prospects for political stability remain poor.

The civil war has destroyed much of Liberia's economy, especially the infrastructure in and around Monrovia. Businessmen have fled the country, taking capital and expertise with them. Many will not return. Richly endowed with water, mineral resources, forests, and a climate favorable to agriculture, Liberia had been a producer and exporter of basic products, while local manufacturing, mainly foreign owned, had been small in scope. Political and economic instability—

including the stripping of resources by local warlords—threatens prospects for reconstruction as well as for the repatriation of an estimated 750,000 Liberian refugees who have fled to neighboring countries. The continued political turmoil has prevented restoration of normal economic life, including the reestablishment of a strong central government with effective economic development programs.

Business Environment

The government began its maritime and corporate programs in 1948 and has actively pursued them ever since. It also established the International Trust Company of Liberia, which acts as the maritime administrator and provides corporate formation and registered agency services for nonresident corporations. Political unrest in Liberia has not affected the operation of the corporate and maritime programs or the operation of the International Trust Company of Liberia.

Currency and Exchange Control

The local currency is the Liberian dollar, although the U.S. dollar is also legal tender. There are no exchange controls pertaining to business corporations.

Legal System

General

The Liberian legal system is a dual system of statutory law based on Anglo-American common law for the modern sector and customary law based on unwritten tribal practices for the indigenous sector.

Legislation

The principal provisions affecting offshore operations and transactions are contained in the following legislation, which is published by authority granted to the International Trust Company of Liberia by the Liberian government:

(a) the Liberian Code of Laws Revised 1978, which contains Title 5 (associations law), dealing with business corporations (Part I), not-for-profit corporations (Part II), and partnerships (Part III), and Title 37 (revenue and finance law), dealing with the Internal Revenue Code (Part II);

(b) the Liberian Corporation Law 1948, dealing with corporations formed before 1977; and

(c) the Liberian Code of Laws 1956, which contains Title 22 (maritime law).

Treaties

See "Tax Treaties and Double Taxation."

Taxation (Direct and Indirect)

Income Tax

In terms of the Internal Revenue Code—Income Tax, Liberian corporations are exempt from income tax provided that

(a) no more than 25% of the total combined voting power and no more than 25% of the total value of the outstanding equity stock is owned, directly or indirectly, by Liberian residents; and

(b) the company does not carry on operations in Liberia.

A corporation that qualifies for exemption from income tax does not have to file an annual return.

Stamp Duties and Annual Fees

On incorporation, a nonresident domestic corporation is liable for stamp duty of US$43.50 and capital duty of at least US$100. Additional capitalization tax is payable when stock with par value over US$50,000 is issued or when over five hundred shares of stock with no par value are issued. A fee of US$550 is also payable to the International Trust Company of Liberia. This includes a fee of US$200 for the company's first year of services as statutory registered agent. Furthermore, US$20 must be paid to the government for telecommunications services.

Thereafter, annual fees of US$150 are payable to the government, and annual fees of US$300 are payable to the International Trust Company of Liberia.

Withholding Taxes

Dividend remittances are not taxed in Liberia. However, a withholding tax may be levied on dividends, interest, and managerial fees where the income arises within Liberia. Dividends paid by a nonresident Liberian corporation to another nonresident Liberian corporation are exempt from tax if the income arises from sources that are generally exempt from Liberian tax.

Tax Incentives

See "Incentives."

Tax Treaties and Double Taxation

Liberia has entered into double taxation treaty agreements with Germany and Sweden.

Incentives

Tax incentives include that Monrovia is a free port. In addition, nonresident domestic corporations are exempt from Liberian income tax.

Corporations

Liberia is a well-established jurisdiction for the incorporation of companies, and, as it is run predominantly from outside the country, investors avoid the communications problems that would otherwise occur. It is widely used for shipping purposes. However, because of the lack of a public register, Liberian corporations are not recommended for high-profile trading activities. Furthermore, recent civil strife has led to a decline in popularity of the jurisdiction.

Types of Corporations

Nonresident domestic corporations are governed by the Business Corporations Act 1976. A nonresident domestic corporation is a corporation for profit that does not trade in Liberia and of which 75% of the total combined voting power and total value of outstanding equity stock is owned, directly or indirectly, by nonresident persons. In addition, the corporate income must be derived from sources outside of Liberia. A nonresident domestic corporation is exempt from Liberian income tax.

Checklist for Corporations

- Any name that is not in use may be used. The name must end with a word such as *Limited* or *Incorporated*. The name may be in any language.
- Same-day incorporation is possible through the International Trust Company of Liberia. Documents are available within two to three days. Shelf companies are available. The authorities do not require any information prior to incorporation.
- There is no usual minimum capital. No capital duty is payable.
- At least one shareholder is required. Bearer shares and shares of no par value are possible.
- If the number of shareholders is less than three, there may be the same number of directors. If the number of shareholders is three or more, there must be at least three directors. Corporate directors are allowed, and there is no restriction on the directors' residence.
- A secretary is mandatory. Corporate secretaries are not allowed, and there is no restriction on the residence of the secretary.
- Corporations do not need a registered office in Liberia, but they must have a registered agent (the International Trust Company of Liberia).

- The registered agent's address and articles of association are available on the public file.
- Accounts do not have to be kept or filed. An annual return is also not required.
- Corporate books and a seal are necessary but may be kept anywhere.
- There is no restriction on the holding of meetings.
- An annual fee of US$150 is payable to the government.

Other Forms of Business Organization

In terms of the Associations Law, provision is made for not-for-profit corporations (Part II) and general and limited partnerships (Part II). Not-for-profit corporations may be nonresident domestic corporations and so qualify for exemption from income tax. Partnerships may also register for exempt status.

Shipping

In 1948, Liberia enacted the Maritime Law, encouraging the registration of ships under the Liberian flag. The Liberian Maritime Administrator is responsible for the recording of mortgages and registration of ships and operates through its correspondent offices in London; New York; Reston, Virginia; Hong Kong; Tokyo; Zurich; Piraeus; and Rotterdam.

Intended Registry

Prospective owners of a vessel that is being built may obtain a certificate of intended registry for use during the period of construction or until the delivery date. This document is often valuable to lenders, builders, and owners. To obtain a certificate of intended registry of newbuilding during construction at a builder's yard, the prospective owner must submit an application form, the appropriate fees, and a letter from the shipbuilder confirming that a contract has been signed between the proposed owner and the yard, along with the date of such contract, the vessel's hull number, the expected date of delivery, and the estimated gross tonnage. The certificate is valid for the period of construction or until the expected date of delivery, whichever is later.

Registration Procedure

In general, for a vessel to be registered, it must be owned by a Liberian citizen or national, which includes a juristic person. However, registration by a non-Liberian entity may be allowed provided the owner registers in Liberia as a foreign maritime entity. Liberian corporations are convenient and efficient vehicles for the ownership of vessels as they are easily and quickly created and are inexpensively maintained.

Vessels should not be over twenty years old at the time of registration. However, older vessels may be registered if the application by the owner is accompanied by an advice from the vessel's classification society confirming that the vessel is in class and that the society will be willing to issue all statutory certificates to the vessel. All vessels must be classed by a classification society that is a full member of the International Association of Classification Societies.

Vessels are usually only eligible for registration in Liberia providing they are over 1,600 gross tons.

Provisional registry: The provisional certificate of registry is the temporary document issued by Liberia to a vessel that is either under construction or is being transferred from another registry. An unexpired provisional certificate of registry has the same validity as a permanent certificate of registry.

The application for registration must be submitted with the following proof of ownership:

(a) with respect to an existing vessel, the bill of sale that transfers title;

(b) with respect to a newbuilding, the builder's certificate or master carpenter's certificate; or

(c) where the owner owns the vessel under a foreign flag and is transferring it to the Liberian flag without change of ownership, the proof of ownership.

Registration fees and tonnage tax are payable when the vessel to be registered is a newbuilding or an existing ship transferred from a foreign registry.

A provisional certificate of registry and a temporary radio authority are issued upon acceptance of the completed application, appropriate documents, and fees. The certificate of registry is valid for a period of twelve months. The temporary radio authority is valid for ninety days.

Bareboat charter registration: A vessel registered in another jurisdiction can be bareboat registered in Liberia, giving it the right to fly the Liberian flag. During this period, Liberian law will apply to all aspects of the vessel's operation, navigation, and management. However, the law of the foreign state will apply to the vessel's mortgage. During the period of bareboat charter registration under the Liberian flag, the vessel may not fly any other flag nor show any home port other than Monrovia, Liberia. Registration is in the name of the bareboat charterer.

Permanent Registration

A permanent certificate of registry is the navigational document issued by Liberia to an owner with a provisional certificate of registry who has all of the following additional documents:

(a) certified copies of certificates of classification;

(b) a Liberian certificate of tonnage measurement, either national or 1969 convention;

(c) a Liberian certificate issued under the provisions of the International Convention on Load Lines 1966;

(d) Liberian certificates issued under the International Convention for the Prevention of Pollution from Ships (MARPOL 73/78), Annex I and II;

(e) Liberian certificates issued under the International Convention for the Safety of Life at Sea (SOLAS) 1974;

(f) Liberian National or International Maritime Organization Code or resolution certificates;

(g) a report of satisfactory completion of the Liberian safety inspection;

(h) a Liberian ship radio station license;

(i) a certificate of cancellation of the vessel's former registry, which is necessary for vessels transferring to Liberia from another country of registry; and

(j) a civil liability certificate for oil pollution damage (1969), which is only required for vessels carrying 2,000 tons or more of oil in bulk as cargo.

The permanent certificate of registry is valid for an indefinite period.

Foreign Maritime Entities

If a vessel is not owned by a Liberian citizen or national, registration can be through a foreign maritime entity. A foreign maritime entity is a non-Liberian entity that is registered in Liberia for the purpose of owning and operating a vessel under the Liberian flag. The foreign entity need only be recognized by the foreign state to have the power to own or operate vessels. A completed application must be submitted with the registration fee of US$1,525. Annual fees are US$500.

Fees

The following fees are required at registration:

Registration fee	US$2,500
Annual tonnage tax, per net ton	US$0.40
Annual fee: marine investigations, nautical training, and international participation	US$1,000
plus US$0.07 per net ton	
Marine inspection (each)	US$1,200

Provisional certificate of registry	US$200
Permanent certificate of registry	US$200
Temporary radio authority	US$100
Combined publications folder (CPF)	US$50
Oil record book (nontankers)	US$5
Oil record book (tankers), two each at US$5	US$10
Articles of agreement (one only)	US$2

Where an application is made for permission for foreign bareboat charter registration, the following fees are due:

Certificate of permission for foreign bareboat charter registration	US$225
Restricted certificate of registry	US$200

CHAPTER THIRTY-SIX

LIECHTENSTEIN

Background Information

Geographic and Demographic Data

Location	The Principality of Liechtenstein is in Central Europe, situated between Switzerland and Austria. In winter, it is one hour ahead of GMT; in summer, it is two hours ahead.
Capital	Vaduz.
Area	62 square miles.
Population	31,389.
Languages	German is the official language. An Alemannic dialect is also spoken.
Access	By virtue of its location in Central Europe, Liechtenstein is easily accessible from all major commercial and financial centers.
Telecommunications	Excellent.

Government

The Principality of Liechtenstein has a hereditary constitutional monarchy and a democratically elected parliament.

Political and Economic Stability

Liechtenstein maintains a neutral status and is politically stable. Despite its small size and limited natural resources, Liechtenstein has developed into a prosperous, highly industrialized, free-enterprise economy with a vital financial service sector and living standards on a par with the urban areas of its large European neighbors. Low business taxes and easy incorporation rules have induced about 25,000 holding or so-called letter box companies to establish nominal offices in Liechtenstein, providing 30% of state revenues. The country participates in a customs union with Switzerland and depends on Switzerland for its national defense. It imports more than 90% of its energy requirements. Liechtenstein has been a member of the European Economic Area (an organization serving as a bridge between the European Free Trade Association and the European Union) since May 1995. The government is working to harmonize its economic policies with those of an integrated Europe.

Foreigners and Immigration

Foreign investments are welcome in Liechtenstein, although there are restrictions imposed on the purchase of real estate and the ownership of banks by foreigners.

Currency and Exchange Control

The Swiss franc is the official currency of Liechtenstein. There is no exchange control.

Disclosure of Information

Secrecy of information: Liechtenstein provides a high degree of confidentiality regarding both banking and tax matters. Absolute tax secrecy exists in terms of the Act relating to Local and National Taxation 1961 concerning taxes payable by holding companies, pensioners, and domiciliary enterprises. The principality has not entered into any exchange of information treaties with other countries.

Banking secrecy: Banking secrecy falls under the Act concerning Banks and Savings Funds 1960. The act provides heavy penalties for breaches of professional secrecy.

Disclosure in company formation and trust settlement: There is no requirement for disclosure of beneficial ownership to any authority prior to incorporation. Companies must be audited, and a local registered agent or office is required. The articles of incorporation must be lodged with the registrar of companies. The local agent may be compelled to disclose beneficial ownership in a Penal Code matter where legal assistance is sought between courts.

A trustee has to register the beneficiaries of a trust. Companies or trustees opening bank accounts do not have to disclose beneficial ownership or the identity of the beneficiaries.

International cooperation measures: Procedures for cooperation with foreign investigators are contained in the Cooperation in Criminal Matters (Penal Code). In terms of the code, foreign investigators may request in court that certain investigations be performed by the Liechtenstein authorities. Provision is made for an appeal against this procedure. The exchange of information with foreign states is contained in the European Convention on Cooperation in Criminal Matters and the Law on International Cooperation in Criminal Matters. Foreign judgments are also enforced in terms of this legislation.

A comprehensive double taxation agreement exists between Austria and Liechtenstein. This contains a limited exchange of information agreement in that only information concerning the wages of commuters working in Liechtenstein and living in Austria is covered. Liechtenstein has not entered into any mutual legal assistance treaties.

The Law on Banks makes it a criminal offense to disclose confidential information obtained in a position as an employee, auditor, director, manager, or agent of a bank. The Penal Code and the Law on Due Diligence contain provisions regarding money laundering. These provisions do not cover tax evasion. There is no agreement regarding cooperation with foreign investigators on tax evasion, and the authorities will reject requests for cooperation in these matters.

Legal System

General

Liechtenstein has a liberal and modern legal system, particularly in regard to the codification of individual and corporate law. It adopted most of its laws from Austria and Switzerland. Its criminal law and criminal and civil procedure derive from Austrian law and its civil law is a mix of Austrian and Swiss law. Some of its commercial law is based on the law of Germany, but there are certain commercial concepts that are unique to Liechtenstein, such as its law of associations and the company without juridical personality.

Legislation

The principal provisions affecting offshore operations and transactions are contained in the following:

- Act concerning Banks and Savings Funds 1960
- Act relating to Local and National Taxation 1961
- Due Diligence Act 1996, made effective by the Due Diligence Ordinance 1997
- Insurance Supervision Act 1995
- Investment Companies Act 1996
- Law concerning the Trust Enterprise 1928
- Law on Persons and Companies (PGR[1] Code) 1926
- Penal Code

Treaties

See "Tax Treaties and Double Taxation."

Taxation (Direct and Indirect)

Profits and Capital Tax

Corporations and other corporate bodies are resident in Liechtenstein for tax purposes, regardless of where their effective management and control are, if they are registered or incorporated in Liechtenstein. Liechtenstein resident corporations are taxed as follows:

(a) Corporations carrying on business operations in Liechtenstein pay a capital tax of 0.2%. Income tax on profits is charged at a rate of half of the percentage of the net earnings as these are a percentage of the taxable paid capital. The minimum is 7.5% of net revenue and the maximum is 15%. In regard to domestic and foreign corporations whose business extends abroad, capital and profits tax are levied proportionately to the extent that the business in Liechtenstein relates to the whole.

(b) Domiciliary and holding companies pay a reduced capital tax of 0.1%, subject to a minimum levy of CHF 1,000. They do not pay income tax on profits. *Anstalten* having similar activities are eligible for similarly beneficial tax treatment.

(c) A *Stiftung* is taxed on a similar basis to domiciliary and holding companies, except that the net worth tax of 0.1% is reduced to 0.075% where the capital is between 2 and 10 million Swiss francs, and further reduced to 0.05% where capital is over 10 million Swiss francs. A *Stiftung* is also subject to the minimum levy of CHF 1,000.

Capital Gains Tax

The capital gains of corporations are taxed on the same basis as ordinary income is taxed.

Turnover Tax

A securities turnover tax at rates of between 0.15% and 0.30% is levied on domestic securities dealers.

Stamp Duties

As of 1998, the stamp duty on the issue of capital of a corporation, registered trust, or establishment (*Anstalt*) is reduced to 1%, subject to an allowance of CHF 250,000, which is exempt from liability to tax. With regard to an *Anstalt* or registered trust, the rate is reduced to 0.5% for capital exceeding CHF 5 million and to 0.3% for capital over CHF 10 million. Noncommercial (family) foundations pay stamp duty of 0.2% on formation, subject to a minimum of CHF 200.

The issue of bonds is also liable to stamp duty. The rate is 0.12% annually for long-term bonds and 0.06% for medium- and short-term bonds.

Coupon (Withholding) Tax

Coupon tax is levied at a rate of 4% on certain securities, bonds, unit bonds, and other financial instruments. If the capital of Liechtenstein public and private companies is distributed in share form, the tax is also levied on the coupons of shares.

If one of the parties to a loan agreement is entered in the public register or carries on commercial activities and the loan is granted for more than two years and the loan balance is over CHF 50,000, the interest is subject to the coupon tax.

The coupon tax also applies to domiciliary and holding companies whose capital is divided into shares.

Estate Tax

The Liechtenstein estate tax is a combination of estate duty and inheritance tax. It is levied at the following rates:

First CHF 200,000	1%
Next CHF 400,000	2%
Next CHF 600,000	3%
Next CHF 800,000	4%
Any amount in excess of CHF 2 million	5%

In some cases, namely, where the estate is transferred to the spouse, children, or parents of the deceased, the duty is levied at half of the above rates.

Inheritance and Gift Taxes

Liechtenstein residents are liable to inheritance and gift taxes at between 0.5% and 18%, depending on the relation to the donor. The scale is as follows:

Recipient	*Rate*
Children, grandchildren, parents, spouses	0.5%
Grandparents, brothers, and sisters	2%
Children of in-laws, stepchildren, nephews, and nieces	5%
Uncles and aunts	9%
Other blood relatives and relatives by marriage to the second degree	12%
Other persons	18%

Real Estate Gains Tax

Any natural or juristic person who makes a profit from the sale of real estate in Liechtenstein is liable to a tax on the profit. The profit is the amount by which the proceeds of the sale exceed the invested cost. The rate is that fixed by parliament each year for income tax.

Value-Added Tax

As of January 1, 1995, and in terms of the Law on Value Added Tax, VAT replaced turnover tax. The tax is levied at a rate of 6.5% on domestic and foreign goods and services. Liability to VAT is imposed on private individuals, corporations, and other entities and their branches resident or domiciled in Liechtenstein or Switzerland. Goods such as food, medicine, and newspapers are subject to VAT at a reduced rate of 2%. Activities that are exempt from VAT include the export of certain goods and services, medical services, educational services, and change of ownership in buildings and real estate.

Customs Duties

Customs duty is the same as that applying in Switzerland.

Unearned Income Tax

Persons resident or domiciled in Liechtenstein who live off the proceeds of investment or other unearned income from abroad are subject to tax, currently at a rate of 15%.

Tax Treaties and Double Taxation

Liechtenstein entered into a comprehensive double taxation treaty with Austria in 1970. In 1995, it entered into limited double taxation agreements with Switzerland, which cover items such as employment income, interest on mortgages, and pensions. The agreements are between Liechtenstein and the cantons St. Gallen and Graubünden, and Liechtenstein and the cantons Freiburg and Schaffhausen.

Other Treaties

Liechtenstein and Switzerland entered into a Customs Treaty in 1923 according to which the principality joined the Swiss customs area and adopted the Swiss franc as its official currency. A monetary agreement entered into between the two countries in 1980 now supplements the Customs Treaty.

Corporations

(The domestic laws of Liechtenstein refer to *corporations* as *companies*. This terminology is retained in this chapter.)

Liechtenstein's company law is flexible and liberal and contains few mandatory provisions. The principality provides a high degree of political stability as well as banking secrecy, as beneficial ownership need not be disclosed to banks. In addition, the monetary customs union with Switzerland provides a high degree of economic stability. However, offshore companies cannot benefit from double taxation agreements and the jurisdiction can be expensive for nontrading operations or companies with small assets.

Types of Corporations

Liechtenstein corporate law is contained in the Law on Persons and Companies (PGR Code) 1926 and the Law concerning the Trust Enterprise 1928. These laws provide for the following associations of persons:

- the company limited by shares,
- the private limited company,
- the establishment (*Anstalt*),
- the foundation (*Stiftung*), and
- the trust enterprise.

The above entities may also be either holding companies or domiciliary enterprises. The distinction is made for Liechtenstein tax purposes. Holding companies are defined by the Tax Act as "juridical persons entered in the public register and nonregistered foundations whose objects are exclusively or predominantly the management of assets, participation in other enterprises, or the permanent management of holdings in other enterprises." Domiciliary enterprises are defined in the same act as "juridical persons entered in the public register which have only their domicile in Liechtenstein whether an office is kept or not and carrying on no commercial or trading activities in the country." Domiciliary and holding companies qualify for exempt tax status regarding all taxes except capital tax, which is levied at a beneficial rate.[2]

The company limited by shares: In terms of the PGR Code, a company limited by shares is an association with its own trade name whose predetermined capital is divided into shares and whose liability is borne by its assets only. A limited company is a separate legal person and may carry on any lawful commercial or noncommercial activity.

The private limited company: The private limited company may be formed by two or more members whose individual liability is limited to a specified amount.

The establishment (*Anstalt*): An establishment is an autonomous fund with its own independent legal and corporate personality. It may own its own property and assets. An establishment has no members, shareholders, or other participants and therefore its capital is not divided into shares. Establishments have beneficiaries who gain economic benefit from them.

The foundation (*Stiftung*): The PGR Code defines a foundation as being "set up by individuals or by associations of persons or by firms by the endowment of assets (the foundation property) for a specifically prescribed purpose." The assets thus endowed become an autonomous juridical entity devoted to a specific purpose. If the founder is resident abroad, the transfer of the assets to the foundation does not incur liability for Liechtenstein death duty or gifts tax. A foundation exists solely to realize the wishes of the founder as prescribed in the foundation deed and the statutes. In particular, family foundations, mixed family foundations, and ecclesiastical foundations cannot be formed to pursue commercial activities.

The trust enterprise: The trust enterprise is comparable to the business (Massachusetts) trust. It is a legally independent undertaking conducting commercial or other activities under a trade name and endowed with funds in favor of its beneficiaries. The trust enterprise may be organized with or without a separate legal personality. Trust enterprises without personality are "active trusts" and trusts with personality are "nonactive trusts." Only the trust enterprise with its own juridical personality is of significance, particularly as a vehicle for pursuing economic objectives. Trust enterprises are usually formed for the investment of assets, the distribution of income from property, and the merger of enterprises, although they can be formed for family, charitable, and other personal objects.

Migration

A limited company may be transferred out of or into Liechtenstein with the prior approval of the government, in the former case, and the court, in the latter case. An *Anstalt*, as a form of entity specific to Liechtenstein, is unlikely to be capable of migration unless it converts to another form of entity. The same applies to the *Stiftung*.

Checklist for Corporations

- The corporate name may contain any words and be in any language, but the name of the corporate body (such as *Akteingesellschaft, Limited,* or *Anstalt*) must be registered in full.
- Incorporation takes five to ten days. Shelf companies are available.
- The establishment, foundation, and trust enterprise must have a minimum capital of CHF 30,000. The limited company must have a minimum capital of CHF 50,000.

- A capital duty of 3% is payable, although there are some exceptions for foundations and trust enterprises.
- A minimum of one member or founder is required. Bearer shares and shares of no par value are allowed, although it is more usual to have bearer shares.
- A holding or domiciliary company must have one resident director who is professionally qualified. The same applies to a trust enterprise. There are no residency requirements for members of a foundation council or the founder of an establishment. Corporate directors are allowed.
- There are no legislative provisions regarding secretaries.
- Companies with exempt status must have a local trustee or lawyer, who will charge a representation fee. Registered and nonexempt companies do not have to have local agents.
- No information is required by the authorities prior to exempt status being granted. For resident and nonexempt companies, a business license may be required where the company is engaged in banking, insurance, or other commercial activities.
- The corporate name, domicile, type, date of registration, board members, signatory rights of board members, purpose, representation, and share capital are available on the public file.
- Resident and nonexempt companies must keep certification at their registered offices that all prerequisites concerning nationality and professional qualifications have been met. In general, the memorandum and articles of association, registration correspondence, and confirmation that the minimum formation capital has been deposited with a bank must also be kept.
- Corporate books and a seal are not required.
- All companies that are engaged in commercial activity, whether within or outside Liechtenstein, must maintain and file accounts. Exempt companies that are not engaged in commercial activity (for instance, foundations, trust settlements, holding companies, and companies engaged in personal asset management) do not have to file accounts.
- Resident companies must file an annual return. Exempt companies do not have to comply with this provision.
- There is no restriction on the holding of meetings.
- Resident and nonexempt companies pay tax of between 7.5% and 20% on profits and 0.2% tax on capital, including reserves. Exempt companies pay a flat rate of 1% on their capital and surplus, with a minimum of CHF 1,000 per annum.

Trusts

Liechtenstein is the only country on the Continent to have codified the law of trusts in the PGR Code. Contrary to its English counterpart, the Liechtenstein trust is not prohibited from accumulating income and there are no rules against perpetuity.

If a trust is created to last for longer than twelve months, it must be registered in the public trust register or deposited with the court. On registration, the trust name, date of creation, duration, and trustee details must be furnished. Deposited documents are not open to public inspection.

At least one trustee must be resident in the principality. The resident trustee may also be a juristic person.

Liechtenstein trusts may migrate without prior authorization. No tax is charged on departure, and once the registration or deposit of the trust is canceled, no future annual tax liability is incurred.

Checklist for Trusts

- There is no statutory schedule of standard trust powers.
- The perpetuity period of noncharitable trusts is unlimited.
- At least one resident trustee is required.
- It is compulsory to register trusts.
- Trust documents may be in German or any other language.
- A registration fee of US$200 is payable.
- The law of trusts has a civil law background.
- The Hague Convention has not been implemented.
- No specific provision is made for the exclusion of foreign inheritance laws.
- There is no specific provision dealing with the nonrecognition of foreign judgments.
- There is no specific "asset protection" provision (beyond that offered by general insolvency law) protecting a disposition to a trust from challenge by creditors. However, a Liechtenstein *Stiftung* generally provides excellent asset protection.
- A special statute of limitations period of one year exists for creditors' claims.
- Provision is made for noncharitable purpose trusts.

Notes

1. *Personen-und Gesellschaftsrecht.*
2. See" Taxation (Direct and Indirect)."

CHAPTER THIRTY-SEVEN

LUXEMBOURG

Background Information

Geographic and Demographic Data

Location	The Grand Duchy of Luxembourg is situated in Western Europe, between France and Germany. In winter, it is one hour ahead of GMT; in summer, it is two hours ahead.
Capital	Luxembourg.
Area	1,000 square miles.
Population	420,416.
Languages	French and German are the official languages. The national language is Luxembourgish. English is also widely spoken.
Access	There are excellent air, rail, and road links to Luxembourg.
Telecommunications	Excellent.

Government

Luxembourg is a constitutional monarchy. It is a member of the European Union.

Political and Economic Stability

Luxembourg is politically and economically stable. The prosperous economy features moderate growth, low inflation, and low unemployment, currently at a rate of 3%. Agriculture is based on small family-owned farms. The industrial sector, until recently dominated by steel, has become increasingly more diversified. Growth in the financial sector has more than compensated for the decline in steel. Services, especially banking, account for a growing proportion of the economy. Luxembourg has participated since 1948 in an economic union with Belgium on trade and most financial matters, is closely connected economically to the Netherlands, and, as a member of the European Union, enjoys the advantages of the open European market.

Business Environment

Government attitude to offshore activities: Luxembourg is not a tax haven as such, as it has high personal and corporate tax rates. Exceptions are the Luxembourg holding company, created in terms of legislation passed in 1929, and the investment fund, both of which are exempt from income tax, wealth tax, and withholding taxes. However, the government has seen the need to encourage foreign investment and has developed less onerous and more flexible tax and legal systems for reinsurance, shipping, and group finance companies, among others. It also strives to maintain a high professional standing and financial backing among banks, insurance companies, and other financial institutions.

Employment: Work permits are not required for persons from European Union countries.

Local business requirements: Any person or company wishing to commence business that is not a reserved activity in Luxembourg must apply for permission to the *Ministre des Classes Moyennes* (Ministry of Middle Classes). Reserved activities are activities such as state matters (e.g., defense) and matters governed by professional bodies (e.g., the medical and legal professions). It takes between two and four months for a permit to be granted. Application must be made by the individual trader or the company's managing director or manager, as the permit is personal to the grantee. Permits are granted for an indefinite period but lapse if they are not used within two years of issue. Trading without a permit constitutes an offense, and the permit number must be displayed on all company correspondence. Foreign companies setting up a branch in Luxembourg are subject to similar permit requirements.

Currency and Exchange Control

The local currency is the Luxembourg franc, which is at a par with the Belgian franc, which circulates freely in Luxembourg. There is no exchange control.

Disclosure of Information

Banking secrecy: Banking secrecy is very strict in Luxembourg and is governed by the Banking Secrecy Law 1993. Breach of the statutory duty is a criminal offense under the *Code Penal*. A Grand-Ducal Regulation of 1989 prohibits bank, investment fund, or holding company staff from disclosing information regarding a taxpayer to the tax authorities. The tax authorities are also prevented from using such information. However, disclosure can be compelled in the event of the death of a Luxembourg resident and where a banker is a witness in criminal proceedings.

Disclosure in company formation and trust settlement: Disclosure and publication of company founders are required upon formation. Where shares are issued in bearer form, a subsequent sale need not be disclosed. Disclosure must be made to the registry office of the companies registry. No further details about the beneficial owner are required. No legislation governs the confidentiality of such disclosure.

An audit is required if the net asset value is greater than LUF 77 million, the sales volume is greater than LUF 160 million, or the corporation has more than fifty employees. A registered office is also required. Luxembourg law does not recognize the registered agent. All legal and accounting documents relating to the activities of the company must be lodged at the registered office.

A trustee is not required to register the beneficiaries of a trust. However, a company or trustee opening a bank account is required to disclose the beneficial owner or the beneficiaries. These provisions also apply to limited partnerships and are governed by European Directive June 1991, in terms of which clients must be identified with an approval document.

International cooperation measures: Luxembourg has a procedure for cooperation with foreign investigations into money laundering. The procedure is in terms of the Basle Convention, the European Directive, and the Strasbourg Convention 1978. All double taxation agreements also contain an exchange of information agreement, and the additional protocol of the Strasbourg Convention has further exchange of information measures. No specific appeal procedure is contained in the above conventions and directive.

Foreign judgments are enforced in terms of the *exequatur* procedure whereby they are recognized by the Luxembourg court. The foreign judgment must be presented to the local judge before it can be applied in Luxembourg.

The double taxation agreements to which Luxembourg is party contain exchange of information agreements in relation to money laundering and tax fraud. Luxembourg is also party to mutual legal assistance treaties, namely, the European Directive and the additional protocol to the Strasbourg Convention 1997. Disclosure may be permitted in terms of these provisions where the alleged crime falls within Luxembourg anti–tax fraud law.

Money laundering provisions do not cover fiscal crime and tax evasion. When the local authorities are requested to cooperate with foreign investigations into tax evasion, they will require clear evidence of tax fraud as defined under Luxembourg law. Unless the tax evasion is linked to money laundering activities, the authorities will be unlikely to violate banking secrecy.

Legal System

General

The legal system is based on the Napoleonic code, although the fiscal system is based entirely on German law. Company law is similar to the law of Belgium.

Treaties

See "Tax Treaties and Double Taxation."

Taxation (Direct and Indirect)

Income Tax

Resident individuals are taxed on their worldwide income on a sliding scale, with a maximum rate of 47.15% on income over LUF 2.64 million for a single person and LUF 5.28 million for a married couple. There is a capital gains allowance of LUF 2 million for a single person and LUF 4 million for a married couple every ten years. Nonresidents are taxed only on income arising in Luxembourg. The minimum tax rate on nonbusiness income is 15%.

Luxembourg resident companies (i.e., companies incorporated or registered in Luxembourg) are liable to profits tax on their worldwide income. They escape double taxation as a result of numerous double taxation treaties. A nonresident or foreign company is taxed only on income arising in Luxembourg. Holding companies have tax-free status.

The tax rate is on a sliding scale, with a maximum rate of 30% on income and gains over LUF 600,000. As a result of a 4% surcharge applied in favor of an unemployment fund, the effective maximum rate is 31.2%. There is also a municipal tax on profits over LUF 700,000, at a rate of approximately 10%. As a result, the combined maximum rate is 37.45%. The municipal tax does not apply to holding companies, investment funds, or shipping companies.

Capital and Capital Gains Taxes

Luxembourg resident companies pay an annual net worth tax of 0.5% on their worldwide assets less liabilities. Foreign assets may be exempted by treaty. Holding companies do not pay capital tax. Foreign companies are taxed only on assets in Luxembourg. A minimum of LUF 2,500 applies to a *société anonyme*, and a minimum of LUF 1,000 applies to a *société à responsabilité limiteé.*

Capital gains are taxed as normal income. See, however, "Participation Exemptions."

Stamp Duties

A stamp tax is payable on documents having a probatory force.

Withholding Taxes

Withholding tax of 25% is imposed on dividends and other profit distributions from Luxembourg companies. If the dividend is paid to a European Union parent company, it is exempt from withholding tax. A tax of 10% to 12% is levied on royalties, and there is no withholding tax on interest. Management fees are subject to a withholding tax of 28.2% and auditors' fees to a withholding tax of 39.7%. (See also "Tax Treaties and Double Taxation.")

Value-Added Tax

Any business with an annual turnover of over LUF 400,000 must register for VAT. VAT is charged at 15%, 12%, 6%, and 3%. Companies with a turnover between LUF 4.5 million and LUF 25 million must submit quarterly returns, but companies with a turnover of less than LUF 4.5 million need only submit annual returns.

Participation Exemptions

As a result of the Tax Reform Law of December 6, 1990, there are two related regimes conferring tax benefits on parent-subsidiary relationships. One relates to dividends while the other relates to capital gains.

Participation exemption on dividends: This beneficial regime applies where a Luxembourg company, an indigenous permanent establishment of a company listed in EU Directive 90/435/CEE, or an indigenous permanent establishment of a company with which Luxembourg has a double tax treaty (a "Luxco") owns a qualifying participation in a subsidiary (a "Subco") and receives dividends from it. The portion of Luxco's income that has been taxed in Subco is excluded from Luxco's taxable income under this regime.

For a participation in Subco to be a qualifying participation, it must cost more than LUF 50 million, or represent 10% of the share capital in a Subco that is either a fully taxable resident company, or a nonresident company that is fully taxable under a foreign regime similar to Luxembourg's, or a company listed in EU Directive 90/435/CEE.

If these exemptions are to apply, the investment must have been held for at least twelve consecutive months preceding the end of the company's accounting period.

Capital gains exemption: The capital gains regime is new. Luxembourg does not have separate capital gains tax provisions and treats gains as income. As a result of the reform, where a Luxembourg company has an investment in a subsidiary of 25%, or that costs more than LUF 250 million,

(a) realized gains on the sale of the subsidiary are excluded;
(b) unrealized losses on the subsidiary investment are allowable against income; but
(c) on the eventual sale of the subsidiary, realized losses will be disallowed if previously allowed while unrealized. This is a kind of claw-back.

If this exemption is to apply, the investment must have been held for at least twelve months prior to the beginning of the accounting period when the disposal occurred.

Tax Incentives

See "Tax Incentives" under "Incentives (Tax and Nontax)."

Tax Treaties and Double Taxation

Luxembourg has entered into over thirty double taxation agreements, based on the OECD Model. The treaties do not apply to Luxembourg holding companies.

In general, income from real estate is taxed in the country in which it is situated. Profits accruing to a resident of one country from commercial or business activities in another country are taxed in the other country only to the extent to which they can be attributed to the permanent establishment of the enterprise there. Dividends received are taxed in the country in which the recipient is resident. The country in which the dividends are paid may levy withholding tax, but at lower rates. Similar provisions apply to interest payments.

Table 37.1 shows withholding tax rates that apply in general, although specific conditions pertain to each country and the relevant treaty should be consulted in each case.

Treaties are also being negotiated with Argentina, Iceland, Mongolia, Uzbekistan, Portugal, South Africa, Tunisia, Turkey, and the Ukraine.

Other Treaties

An extradition treaty between Luxembourg and the United States was ratified in September 1996.

Incentives (Tax and Nontax)

Tax Incentives

The Laws of July 28, 1923, and July 27, 1972, and the Tax Reform Law of December 6, 1990, grant partial exemption from corporate taxation to companies

Table 37.1 Withholding Tax Rates

	Share ownership more than 25%		
	Dividends	*Interest*	*Royalties*
Austria	0/5%	15%	0/10%
Belgium	0/10%	15%	0%
Brazil	15%	25%	25/15%
Bulgaria	5%	15%	5%
Canada	5%	15%	10/0%
China	5%	15%	10/6%
Czech Republic	5%	15%	10/0%
Denmark	0/5%	15%	0%
Finland	0/5%	15%	5/0%
France	0/5%	15%	0%
Germany	0/10%	15%	5%
Greece	0/7.5%	7.5%	5/7%
Hungary	5%	15%	0%
Indonesia	10%	15%	0%
Ireland	0/5%	15%	10/12%
Italy	0/15%	15%	10%
Japan	5%	15%	10%
Korea	10%	15%	10/12%
Malta	5%	15%	10%
Mauritius	5%	10%	0%
Morocco	10%	15%	10%
Netherlands	0/2.5%	15%	0%
Norway	5%	15%	0%
Poland	5%	15%	10%
Romania	5%	15%	10%
Russia	10%	0%	0%
Singapore	0/5%	15%	10%
Slovak Republic	5%	15%	10/0%
Spain	0/5%	15%	10%
Sweden	0/5%	15%	0%
Switzerland	0/5%	15%	0%
Thailand	5%	10%	15%
United Kingdom	0/5%	15%	5%
United States	5/5%	15%	0%
Vietnam	5/10%	7%	10%

that are developing Luxembourg economically by creating, extending, nationalizing, or reorienting industrial and service companies. No distinction is made between foreign or domestic investors in the granting of the following tax incentives:

(a) An investment tax credit of up to 14% is allowed in respect of additional investments in depreciable fixed assets other than land and buildings.

(b) There are tax holidays, tax reductions, or special concessions determined on a discretionary basis for a determined period.

(c) Foreign investors receive assistance from the various government departments, and there are no restrictions on foreign ownership. The government has also set up a development program supported by a number of incentives offered to investors, provided their projects contribute to the development and extension of the Luxembourg economy and create new employment.

Development Encouragement Incentives

The government actively encourages foreign investment and offers a range of investment incentives. Nontax investment incentives are granted to industrial entities and some economically important service companies. Incentives include interest rate rebates on loans from subsidized credit institutions for the acquisition of tangible or intangible assets, investments for the protection of the environment, or the cost of training staff. Government guarantees, cash grants, intervention in the acquisition of equipment, industrial rights, and buildings are also available.

Corporations

Types of Companies

Luxembourg law recognizes two types of companies: the limited liability company in the form of a *société anonyme* (SA) and the limited liability company in the form of a *société à responsabilité limiteé* (SARL).

An SA limits the shareholders' liability to the amount of their subscribed capital. The minimum capital requirement is LUF 1.25 million, and registered and bearer shares are permitted. An SA must have at least three directors and two shareholders, who may be resident or nonresident persons or juridical entities. A general meeting must be held annually, and where the company exceeds the small company limits, a qualified Luxembourg auditor must be appointed.

A SARL limits the shareholders' liability to the extent of their paid-up capital. The minimum paid-up capital requirement is LUF 500,000, and only registered shares are permitted. A SARL may have between one and forty shareholders, who may be resident or nonresident persons or juridical entities. If there are fewer than twenty-five members, an annual general meeting is not required. A qualified auditor is only necessary where the small company limits are exceeded.

A small company is one that has not exceeded two of the following three requirements: a balance sheet total of LUF 93 million, a turnover of LUF 186 million, or fifty employees.

Registration and Migration

A company must have a registered office in Luxembourg, which may be changed temporarily in times of war, civil unrest, or due to an act of God. If the address of the registered office is changed, notification of the change must be published in the *Gazette*.

Checklist for Companies

- Name clearance can be obtained by phone.
- Incorporation takes two days.
- The statutes must be published in French or German.
- Different classes of shares are permitted.
- Directors must supply their full names, addresses, and occupations.
- A registered office in Luxembourg is required. Only the share register must be kept at the registered office.
- Accounts must be kept, but whether an audit is required is determined by the size of the company. Accounts must be filed with the registrar of companies and are open to public inspection.

Other Forms of Business Organization

Sole Proprietorships

Luxembourg law recognizes the sole proprietor.

Partnerships

Luxembourg law recognizes the following partnerships: the general partnership, which may be a *société civile* (e.g., a firm of attorneys) or a *société en nom collectif* (e.g., a family business), and the limited partnership, which may be a *société en commandite simple* or a *société en commandite par actions*. In a general partnership, the partners are jointly and severally liable for partnership obligations; in a limited partnership, the general or managing partner has unlimited liability, while the limited partner is only liable up to the amount contributed. In a *société en commandite par actions*, the sleeping partner is issued with shares.

All partnerships must be registered with the Greffe du Tribunal de Commerce. Partnerships limited by shares require a minimum capital of LUF 1.25 million and are subject to the same accounting rules and regulations that apply to limited liability companies (SAs).

Foreign Companies

A foreign company is liable to Luxembourg tax when it has a permanent establishment in Luxembourg through which it does business. A permanent establishment would be a branch office, manufacturing facility, or business project lasting longer than six months. Tax liability is limited to the profits arising from the Luxembourg unit. If there is a double taxation agreement between the foreign company's headquarter country and Luxembourg, it will ordinarily specify that the foreign company will only be liable to Luxembourg tax if it is a branch, a permanent establishment, or a permanent representative. The company will be taxed on either the Luxembourg sourced profit as a separate unit or on a share of the worldwide profit adjusted for the Luxembourg unit. The same rates apply as for Luxembourg companies, and capital gains are taxed at the normal tax rates.

Holding Companies

Luxembourg domestic company law does not recognize the concept of an offshore company. However, the Holding Company Law of July 31, 1929, granted a favorable fiscal status to companies established as holding companies. A Luxembourg holding company is a company domiciled in Luxembourg but restricted to certain activities, namely, the following:

(a) acquiring, holding, and disposing of shares and bonds of Luxembourg or foreign companies;

(b) holding cash and foreign currencies, gold, and negotiable securities, and placing funds on deposit with financial institutions;

(c) acting as a financier to subsidiaries or companies in which the holding company has a direct shareholding;

(d) holding and licensing patents and receiving income from granting licenses abroad;

(e) issuing bonds by public or private subscription of up to ten times the amount of its paid-up capital and, in addition, borrowing up to three times its issued capital; and

(f) buying back up to 10% of its own shares where permitted by its statutes and agreed by a general meeting of shareholders.

A Luxembourg holding company is prevented from engaging in the following activities:

(a) being an active member of a general partnership or partnership limited by shares;

(b) carrying on any industrial or commercial activity;

(c) carrying on brokerage or banking activities;

(d) granting loans to a company that is not a direct subsidiary (unless it is a financial holding company); or

(e) owning real estate, except the premises used for its own offices (though it may hold shares in real estate companies).

Holding companies are exempt from income tax or tax on capital gains. They are also exempt from stamp duties. There are no withholding taxes on dividends or bond interest paid to nonresidents. Holding companies are liable to capital registration duty on incorporation and subsequent increases of capital, and an annual capital tax. Capital registration duty is levied at a rate of 1% of the value of the subscribed capital. Annual capital tax is levied at a rate of 0.2% per annum and is payable in quarterly installments. Different rates apply to "Milliard" holding companies, namely, those with a share capital of LUF 1,000 million or over.

Luxembourg holding companies may not benefit under double taxation treaties.

Financial Holding Company

A financial holding company is formed by a group of companies with similar financial or industrial interests to float an international bond issue, the proceeds of which will be invested within the group. "Group" refers to either all fellow subsidiaries having one common parent or companies with substantial (25%) mutual shareholdings that do not have a common parent but that maintain close financial and business contacts.

Bonds issued by a financial holding company in Luxembourg are attractive to foreign investors, as interest payments are exempt from withholding taxes.

A financial holding company must

(a) be incorporated as a *société anonyme* and the parent or members of the group must appear as the founders in its articles of association;

(b) have shares in registered form that cannot be freely transferred to third parties until loans have been fully repaid;

(c) have a minimum issued capital of LUF 50 million;

(d) have a minimum of 10% of share capital invested in shares issued by companies within the group within three months from the date of formation; and

(e) use funds raised only for the benefit of the group.

It may also carry out ordinary holding company activities apart from its main object. It can issue bonds up to a maximum of ten times its paid-in capital and borrow up to three times its issued capital. It may also act as a factor to its subsidiaries at market or lower rates.

"Milliard" Holding Companies

Special provisions were introduced in 1977 for the calculation of the annual tax payable by holding companies with a share capital of LUF 1,000 million or over. The tax is calculated on interest paid to bondholders, dividends distributed to shareholders, and fees paid to directors and *commissaires* not fully resident in Luxembourg.

If the total bond interest paid exceeds LUF 100 million, the rates are as follows:

- 3% on interest
- 1.8% on dividends and directors' and auditors' fees of up to LUF 50 million
- 0.1% on the excess over LUF 50 million of dividends and directors' and *commissaires'* fees

If the total bond interest paid is less than LUF 100 million, the rates are as follows:

- 3% on interest
- 3% on dividends and directors' and *commissaires'* fees of up to the amount equal to the difference between LUF 100 million and the total interest payment
- 1.8% on excess of dividends and fees over LUF 100 million up to LUF 150 million
- 0.1% on the excess of dividends and fees

The minimum tax payable is LUF 2 million per annum. Application is made to the Finance Ministry, which will only grant this tax status for a full accounting year. The Finance Ministry may grant the tax status retroactively in some cases.

Licensing Companies

Licensing companies are subject to the same rules that apply to financial holding companies. Luxembourg holding companies are entitled to hold and license patents and receive income from the granting of licenses to subsidiaries, but they cannot acquire and hold licenses, except when these are needed for granting licenses to subsidiaries. Buying and selling licenses and patents to third companies is prohibited unless a reinvestment of the price is made in the year; otherwise, it will be considered a commercial activity, which is not permitted under holding company rules.

Insurance

Captive Insurance Companies

Captive insurance is governed by the Insurance Supervisory Law 1991. There are approximately 243 captives established in Luxembourg. The total asset size of the captive sector is approximately LUF 213.06 million. The total premium size is approximately LUF 78.89 million. The *Commissariat aux Assurances* regulates the sector. An annual audit is required, as is general information on the insurer and a special report to the *Commissariat aux Assurances*.

There are no regulatory concessions, and captives are taxed at the corporate rate of 30%.

The minimum capital requirement is LUF 50 million. Incorporation costs LUF 50,000 plus a 1% tax on capital. An annual license fee of LUF 100,000 is payable. There are no additional costs.

Provision is made for a compulsory catastrophe reserve. Rent-a-captives and protected cell companies are not provided for.

Shipping

Although Luxembourg is a landlocked country, it has a maritime shipping register, complementing its register of inland vessels. The register was introduced in 1990. The governing authority is the *Commissariat aux Affaires Maritimes*. All registered vessels must fly the Luxembourg flag and carry the name "Luxembourg" on their hull. Ship management, including the payment of crew, must be undertaken in Luxembourg by an approved ship management company, although subcontractors and agents outside Luxembourg may also be used.

Luxembourg offers specific benefits to shipowners, including the following:

(a) fiscal advantages;

(b) flexible labor laws;

(c) favorable social security rules;

(d) respectability as a financial center;

(e) minimal bureaucracy; and

(f) possible evolution into a European Union flag.

Wages of crew who are nonresidents are subject to income tax at a flat rate of 10%. Luxembourg shipping companies are exempt from municipal business tax. They are also eligible for investment tax credits of up to 14% of the amount invested in movable tangible property, including ships, carried forward for a maximum period of ten years. Accelerated depreciation of between 24% and 30% is also available. Capital gains realized on the eventual sale of a vessel are tax-free, provided they are used within two years to purchase a new vessel. Tax losses can be carried forward indefinitely, unless the company changes its activity.

Mutual Funds and Collective Investment Schemes

Luxembourg's 1988 law relating to undertakings for collective investments in transferable securities (UCITS) was designed to develop Luxembourg's position as a fund center and to implement the European Union UCITS directive. It also introduced the concept of multiple compartment umbrella funds, thus giving the legal certainty that was previously lacking.

UCITS are exempt from all Luxembourg taxes other than a one-off capital duty of LUF 50,000 and an annual subscription at a rate of 0.06% of net assets.

There are approximately 3,900 authorized undertakings for collective investments. The majority take the corporate form, while the remainder are established under contract and are similar to unit trusts. There are two different legal forms available for a fund in Luxembourg:

(i) the *fond commun de placement*, which resembles a unit trust; and

(ii) the *société d'investissement*, which is a corporate entity and can be either a *société d'investissement à capital variable*, which is an open-ended vehicle with a variable share capital that is always equal to the net asset value, or a *société d'investissement à capital fixte*, which is a closed-ended vehicle, usually for private placements.

Trusts

As Luxembourg is a civil law country, it does not have legislation pertaining to trusts. However, it recognizes foreign trusts and may implement the Hague Convention, which it has signed but not ratified. A specific law of July 19, 1983, enables financial institutions to hold assets in a fiduciary capacity.

CHAPTER THIRTY-EIGHT

MADEIRA

Background Information

Geographic and Demographic Data

Location	Madeira is part of an archipelago in the Atlantic Ocean, northwest of Africa. It is on GMT; in the summer, it is one hour ahead.
Capital	Funchal.
Area	314 square miles.
Population	300,000.
Languages	Portuguese is the official language. English is also widely spoken.
Access	There are direct daily flights to most major European cities.
Telecommunications	Excellent.

Government

Madeira is an autonomous region within Portugal. It has its own legislature and government that are subject to the authority of the central Portuguese government. Portugal is a member of the European Union.

Political and Economic Stability

Madeira is politically stable. The economy has traditionally relied heavily on tourism, the wine industry, and agricultural products. It is also benefiting from the development of Madeira as an offshore financial center. Since the adoption of free trade zone legislation, many Portuguese banks and some international banks have been granted offshore banking licenses to operate in Madeira.

Foreigners and Immigration

The government actively encourages foreign investment. Foreigners may own land in Madeira without any restrictions and may also own shares in local companies.

Currency and Exchange Control

The local currency is the Portuguese escudo. There are minimal exchange control provisions that are regulated by the Portuguese Central Bank. Residents making outward investments in foreign currencies are required to report these transactions to the Monetary Authority for statistical purposes only. In terms of its free trade zone status, Madeira enables banks with offshore banking licenses to open accounts for nonresident individuals and companies incorporated under the free trade zone legislation in any currency. Licensed banks may also deal freely in foreign currencies.

Disclosure of Information

Banking secrecy: Bank secrecy is governed by the Banking Secrecy Law, and penalties are imposed both at civil and criminal law for anyone breaching the confidentiality provisions. However, bank officials can be compelled in criminal proceedings to disclose information relating to clients in connection with drug trafficking or money laundering.

Disclosure in company formation and trust settlement: Beneficial ownership does not have to be disclosed to any authorities on formation of an offshore company. Confidentiality in this regard is governed by Decree Law 298/92. Companies are required to be audited, and they must maintain a local registered office. A copy of the memorandum and articles of association must be lodged with the local office or agent. Disclosure of beneficial ownership will be made by a local agent under a court order only where there is clear evidence of drug or weapons trafficking.

A trustee is not required to register the beneficiaries of a trust. A company or trustee opening a bank account does not have to disclose beneficial ownership or the beneficiaries to the bank.

International cooperation measures: Portugal has a range of double taxation agreements with other countries, which provide procedures for cooperation with foreign investigators. In addition, all relevant European Union directives apply. The way the procedure functions depends on the treaty involved. Appeals may be lodged with the local court of appeal. Some of the tax treaties contain exchange of information agreements. Information covered is limited to information relating to drug and weapons trafficking. Portugal has not entered into any mutual legal assistance treaties.

Foreign judgments relating to drug or weapons trafficking may be enforced by a local court order. The foreign judgment is registered in the Portuguese court and is then enforced by a local court order.

The local authorities will not cooperate with foreign investigations into tax evasion.

Legal System

General

Madeira is a civil law jurisdiction. Private law in particular derives from the Napoleonic code.

Legislation

Recent provisions affecting offshore operations and transactions are contained in the following:

- Banking Secrecy Law
- Decree Law 31/97
- EU Regulation 122/96
- EU Regulation 1482/97

Treaties

See "Tax Treaties and Double Taxation."

Taxation (Direct and Indirect)

General

A company that is incorporated under Madeira's free trade zone legislation is exempt from capital gains tax, corporate tax, import duties, inheritance tax, investment income tax, property transfer tax, stamp duty, and withholding tax on dividends or interest. However, it must submit a VAT return.

Income Tax

Madeira resident companies are taxed under the Corporate Tax Code but are fully exempt from tax until 2011. Portuguese companies pay corporate tax at 36%.

Capital Gains Tax

Madeira companies are fully exempt from capital gains tax. Portuguese companies are taxed on capital gains at a rate of 36%.

Stamp Duties

There is no stamp tax levied on documents and transactions of Madeira companies unless entities resident in mainland Portugal act as intermediaries or recipients.

Withholding Taxes

The following withholding tax rates apply:

	Residents	*Nonresidents*
Dividends	15%	25%
Royalties	15%	15%
Interest	20%	20%

Madeira company shareholders are not subject to the above withholding taxes. However, income arising in mainland Portugal is subject to the rates applicable to nonresidents with regard to normal Portuguese companies.

It should be noted that the above rates may be lower where the dividends, royalties, or interest is received by a person resident in a country that is party to a double taxation agreement with Portugal.

Real Estate Taxes

An annual tax is levied on the net worth value of real estate. The tax ranges from 0.7% to 1.3%.

Transfer tax is payable on the acquisition value of real estate. For urban property, the rate is 8%, and for rural property, the rate is 10%. If the property is to be used as the head office of a Madeira company, the company is exempt from paying transfer tax.

Value-Added Tax

VAT in mainland Portugal is charged at a rate of 17%. VAT in Madeira is charged at a lower rate of 12%.

Tax Incentives

See "Incentives."

Tax Treaties and Double Taxation

Portugal has an extensive network of double taxation agreements with other countries. In terms of these treaties, residents of the treaty countries are subject to withholding tax at the rates shown in Table 38.1.

Table 38.1 Tax Rates for Treaty Country Residents

	Interest	*Dividends*	*Royalties*
Austria	10%	15%	5/10%
Belgium	15%	15%	5%
Brazil	15%	15%	10/15%
Bulgaria	10%	10/15%	10%
Czech Republic	10%	10/15%	10%
Finland	15%	10/15%	10%
France	10/12%	15%	5%
Germany	10/15%	15%	10%
Hungary	10%	10/15%	10%
Ireland	15%	15%	10%
Italy	15%	15%	12%
Korea	15%	10/15%	10%
Mozambique	10%	15%	10%
Norway	15%	10/15%	10%
Spain	15%	10/15%	5%
Switzerland	10%	10/15%	5%
United Kingdom	10%	10/15%	5%
United States	10%	15%	10%

Madeira companies are subject to withholding tax in the treaty countries at the rates shown in Table 38.2.

However, where the income accrues from activities carried on in the free trade zone or abroad, interest, dividends, and royalties paid by Madeira companies to nonresidents are not subject to withholding tax.

Portugal also entered into a double taxation agreement with Poland that came into force in 1998.

Table 38.2 Tax Rates for Madeira Companies in Treaty Countries

	Interest	*Dividends*	*Royalties*
Austria	10%	15%	5/10%
Belgium	15%	15%	5%
Brazil	15%	15%	10/15%
Bulgaria	10%	10/15%	10%
Czech Republic	10%	10/15%	10%
Finland	15%	10/15%	10%
France	12%	15%	5%
Germany	15%	15%	10%
Ireland	15%	15%	10%
Italy	12.5/15%	15%	12%
Mozambique	10%	15%	10%
Norway	0%	10/15%	0%
South Korea	15%	10/15%	10%
Spain	15%	10%	5%
Switzerland	10%	10/15%	0%
United Kingdom	10%	0%	5%
United States	10%	15%	10%

Incentives

Free Trade Zone

Madeira has adopted free trade zone legislation that has been approved by the European Union. In terms of the legislation, exemptions are guaranteed until 2011. These exemptions relate to the production and movement of goods undertaken in the designated area of Madeira and are as follows:

(a) Materials and goods imported into the free trade zone are exempt from customs duty; and

(b) goods produced in the free trade zone and exported to European Union member states are exempt from customs duty, provided the components from which they were made came from the European Union. If some of the raw materials came from outside the European Union, customs duty is payable on a proportionate basis.

International service activities, namely, trading, holding company activities, investment, and management consulting, can be undertaken anywhere in Madeira and still benefit from the free trade zone exemptions.

The free trade zone legislation also covers offshore banking. Branches of Portuguese and foreign banks may operate anywhere in Madeira or abroad without exchange controls and provide banking and other services for companies operating within the free trade zone legislation.

The free trade zone provisions in Madeira are available to Portuguese residents.

Corporations

The advantage of incorporation in Madeira is that it is a new offshore center with European Union status offering full tax exemption until 2011. A VAT number is provided with the incorporation of any company, and Madeira companies are not subject to exchange controls. They also benefit from a network of double taxation agreements between Portugal and other countries. However, the jurisdiction is relatively expensive and activities undertaken in Portugal are subject to tax.

Types of Companies

Under Portuguese company law, the following types of entities are possible in Madeira:

(a) the private limited liability company (*sociedade por quotas*), and

(b) the stock corporation (*sociedade anonima*).

Madeira companies are thus companies that are incorporated and governed by the same principles as Portuguese companies, but they may apply to operate under the free trade zone legislation. A Madeira company that is licensed to operate in the free trade zone has full exemption from tax liability until 2011 on activities carried out abroad or with other companies licensed to operate in the free trade zone.

Migration and Redomiciliation

Portuguese law allows a company to transfer its seat to another jurisdiction, provided the other jurisdiction has suitable legislation and a resolution has been passed to this end by at least 75% of the shareholders. Companies may redomicile in Portugal if similar conditions are met and provided the country of origin accepts the redomiciliation.

Checklist for Companies

- Prior approval of the company name is required. Foreign names are permitted, but the name must include the main activity of the company.
- Incorporation takes four to six weeks. Shelf companies are available. No information is required by the authorities prior to incorporation.
- The minimum capital required for stock corporations is Esc 5 million, and for limited liability companies, Esc 400,000. There is no capital duty.
- Limited liability companies must have at least one shareholder, and stock corporations must have five or more. Stock corporations may issue bearer shares after the initial share capital is paid up in full, but shares with no par value are not permitted.
- At least one director is required for either form of company, and there is no restriction as to the directors' place of residence. Stock corporations may have corporate directors, but limited liability companies may not. Madeira companies do not have secretaries.
- A registered office is necessary. All legal documents, minute books, and official accounting books and records must be kept at the registered office.
- The registered office, directors, shareholders, mortgages, object clause, share capital, and form of binding are available on the public file.
- Annual accounts and a tax return must be filed with the tax authorities. These are not a matter of public record for limited liability companies, but they are for stock corporations.
- Meetings must be held at the registered office.
- An annual filing fee of US$1,000 is payable to the government.

Other Forms of Business Organization

Portuguese law also recognizes general partnerships (*sociedades em nome colectivo*), limited partnerships (*sociedade em comandita*), and sole traders.

Holding Companies

Holding companies (*sociedades gestoras de participações sociais*) are governed by Decree Law 495/88 of Portugal. They are entitled to a 95% deduction of taxable income derived from dividends received to reduce double taxation of such income and are effectively taxed at a rate of 36% of 5%, which is 1.8%. Capital gains are taxed at the standard rate of 36%, although there are exceptions where the gains are reinvested in the acquisition of other shareholdings. In terms of an amended tax regime applicable to holding companies incorporated in Madeira and operating in the free trade zone, such companies are liable to corporate tax on profits from shareholdings located in Portugal and other European Union member states, but dividends from shareholdings in companies in non–European Union states qualify for full tax exemption. However, nonresident shareholders of such companies are entitled to full exemption from withholding taxes on dividends distributed to them by Madeira holding companies, including profits related to all European Union shareholdings except Portuguese shareholdings.

A Madeira holding company is allowed to engage in holding activities only. A holding activity is defined as a shareholding that endures for at least one year and reaches at least 10% of the voting capital of the participated company. A holding company may not

(a) purchase its own quotas or shares;

(b) purchase bonds issued by companies in which it does not participate, although there are limited exceptions to this rule;

(c) sell or create a lien over its own bonds that have not been subscribed;

(d) grant loans, except to companies in whose capital it subscribes; or

(e) sell or create liens over shareholdings of more than 10% of the voting capital of the participated company that have been purchased less than one year before their disposition, although there are also limited exceptions to this rule.

Madeira holding companies may be either stock corporations or private limited liability companies, and the name must contain the abbreviation *SGPS*. An official auditor must be appointed. Shareholders in a holding company may be of any nationality, and in general there is no restriction on the place of the investments.

Finance Companies

Decree Law 10/94 authorizes the incorporation of international and Portuguese banks in Madeira as well as the establishment of branches. Offshore banks and financial branches are exempt from withholding tax and stamp duty and have a 0% corporation tax rate until 2011. In terms of Decree Law 10/94, offshore banks or financial branches may undertake banking activity, financing, insurance, and fund management.

The minimum share capital required for a bank is Esc 3 billion. Formal authorization for incorporation is required from the Ministry of Finance and the Bank of Portugal. Branches of financial institutions operating in other European Union member states are subject to less stringent authorization requirements than non–European Union financial institutions. It takes between five and seven months for the license application to be processed, and the application must be conducted by a Portuguese representative.

Shipping

In terms of the free trade zone legislation, Madeira has opened an international ships registry. Under these provisions, vessels and yachts may be registered under the Portuguese flag provided they are not intended for transportation between Portuguese ports, although they may travel between one Portuguese port and a foreign port. Shipping companies are eligible for the following incentives:

(a) They do not pay corporation tax on profits made from ships flying the Portuguese flag that operate in international waters or ships registered elsewhere;

(b) there is no inheritance tax on their shares;

(c) there is no capital gains tax on the sale or transfer of their shares or the sale or transfer of a ship;

(d) officers and crew of ships operating in international waters do not pay income tax on their salaries and wages; and

(e) they are eligible for benefits under the network of Portuguese tax treaties.

Licensing Companies

A Madeira licensing company may hold patents and trademarks and may make use of the network of double taxation treaties between Portugal and other countries by licensing the patents and trademarks they hold to countries where withholding tax on royalties applies.

Trusts

As Madeira is an autonomous region operating under Portuguese law, and as Portugal is a civil law jurisdiction, the trust is unknown. However, free trade zone legislation has been enacted to cover offshore trusts, namely, trusts whose property is located and income derived from outside Portugal. An offshore trust is not liable to tax on its trading or investment income. Trust income that accrues in Portugal is taxable in the hands of the trustees. Trusts and trust companies are not subject to exchange control.

An offshore trust whose duration is more than one year must register in the private registry of the Madeira free trade zone. However, the beneficiary's name need not be registered. The settlor and beneficiary may not be residents of Portugal.

There are no capital requirements, but only corporate bodies may act as trustees and must be either companies incorporated in Madeira under the free trade zone legislation or branches of offshore trust corporations. The latter must be stock corporations. Trust corporations must have a minimum share capital of Esc 20 million, and at least 51% of the share capital must be represented by nominative shares.

Trusts are subject to an annual license fee of US$250, which must be guaranteed by the trustee. Offshore trust companies and branches pay an application fee of US$750 and an annual license fee of US$2,000.

Trusts that are created in or transferred to Madeira may emigrate without prior authorization by substituting the law governing the trust with the law of another jurisdiction.

CHAPTER THIRTY-NINE

MALTA

Background Information

Geographic and Demographic Data

Location	Malta is a group of islands in the Mediterranean Sea, south of Sicily. In winter, it is one hour ahead of GMT; in summer, it is two hours ahead.
Capital	Valletta.
Area	124 square miles.
Population	377,177.
Languages	Maltese and English are both official languages. Italian is also widely spoken.
Access	Malta has a modern airport that is served by several international airlines. Direct flights are available to major European cities, as well as to cities in the Middle East and North America. It also has excellent harbor and port facilities.
Telecommunications	Excellent.

Government

The republic of Malta is a parliamentary democracy. It is a member of the Commonwealth and has applied for full membership in the European Union.

Political and Economic Stability

Malta is politically stable and is a declared neutral territory. However, it is divided politically over the question of joining the European Union.

As far as the economy is concerned, Malta is in the range of the less affluent European Union countries. Significant resources are limestone, a favorable geographic location, and a productive labor force. Malta produces only about 20% of its food needs. It has limited freshwater supplies and has no domestic energy sources. The economy is dependent on foreign trade, industry (especially electronics and textiles), and tourism. The state-owned Malta dry docks employ about

3,800 people. In 1995, over 1.1 million tourists visited the island. Unemployment runs between 3% and 4%.

Business Environment

Government attitude to offshore activities: The Maltese government actively encourages foreign investment and offers various incentives to foreign entrepreneurs. Industrial enterprises may be wholly owned by foreigners and need only acquire exchange control permission under the Exchange Control Act.

In 1988, the government set up an "international business center" to attract both trading and nontrading companies. It also passed the International Business Activities Act, setting up the Malta International Business Authority, an autonomous regulatory body. The authority's function is to develop and regulate offshore banking, insurance, and trading companies.

Currency and Exchange Control

The local currency is the Maltese lira. Exchange control is regulated by the Central Bank of Malta. The relevant legislation is the Exchange Control Act. Exchange control provisions do not apply to international trading companies, international holding companies, collective investment schemes (including unit trusts), mutual funds, and investment companies. Exchange control permission is required, but is readily granted, for the repatriation of earnings and capital from Malta and for the investment of foreign capital in Maltese industry.

Disclosure of Information

Secrecy of information: Offshore banking secrecy and confidentiality are governed by the Banking Act of 1994, the Financial Institutions Act of 1994, the Professional Secrecy Act of 1994, the Prevention of Money Laundering Act of 1994, the regulations under that act, and the Malta Financial Services Center Act of 1994.

The Professional Secrecy Act of 1994 governs the right to privacy in Malta and was enacted to complement the existing provisions of the Criminal Code. The duty of professional secrecy extends to government officials and their employees and agents. Disclosure may be made only when it is absolutely necessary for the functioning of the fiscal system or when it is authorized. Unlawful disclosure leads to penal sanctions. In terms of the Prevention of Money Laundering Act of 1994, which follows European Union precedents, money laundering is an offense. Conviction under the act may lead to a fine of up to Lm 1 million and/or imprisonment of up to fourteen years. In addition, all property of the convicted person may be confiscated, since it is presumed to have been obtained illegally.

Disclosure in company formation and trust settlement: Disclosure of beneficial ownership on formation of a company is not an absolute requirement, as licensed nominees may be used. Where nominees are used, disclosure need only be made to them. Disclosure is generally made to the Central Bank of Malta for exchange control purposes. Where disclosure is required, this will include personal details and bank references. The Professional Secrecy Act 1994 and the Malta Financial Services Center Act 1994 govern the confidentiality of such disclosure.

Companies must be audited. A local registered office is required for companies incorporated and registered under the Companies Act 1995, while a local representative is required for overseas companies establishing a place of business in Malta. In the case of overseas companies, the memorandum and articles of association, directors and company secretary, local representatives, and accounts must be lodged with the registrar of companies. Disclosure may only be compelled under the Prevention of Money Laundering Act 1994.

A trustee does not have to register the beneficiaries of a trust. A company or trustee opening a bank account is not required to disclose beneficial ownership or the beneficiaries.

International cooperation measures: Malta has procedures for cooperation with foreign investigators, but they are subject to domestic legislation. The procedures are to be found in the Banking Act 1994, the Financial Institutions Act 1994, and the Investment Services Act 1994, as well as the various double taxation treaties. An appeal may be lodged against such cooperation in the courts. The above acts also contain exchange of information provisions.

Foreign judgments are enforced according to the provisions of the Code of Organization and Civil Procedure. In terms of these provisions, a request for enforcement must be made to the Maltese court.

Malta has entered into numerous double taxation agreements that contain exchange of information provisions. All information necessary for the carrying out of the provisions of the treaties is covered in the agreements. Malta has not entered into any mutual legal assistance treaties.

Requests for assistance by foreign investigators into tax evasion will be dealt with by the Maltese authorities according to the relevant double taxation treaty provisions.

Legal System

General

The legal system is based on Roman civil law and the Napoleonic code, although it has been strongly influenced by English common law, particularly regarding public and commercial law.

Legislation

The principal provisions affecting offshore operations and transactions are contained in the following:

- Banking Act 1994
- Companies Act 1995
- Financial Institutions Act 1994
- Freeport Act 1989
- Industrial Development Act 1988
- Investment Services Act
- Malta Financial Services Center Act 1994
- Prevention of Money Laundering Act 1994
- Professional Secrecy Act 1994

Treaties

See "Tax Treaties and Double Taxation."

Taxation (Direct and Indirect)

Income Tax

Maltese resident companies are subject to tax on their worldwide income. The tax is at a flat rate of 35%. Foreign companies are subject to Maltese income tax on income arising in Malta, in respect of both one-off transactions and agency or branch profits.

Capital Gains Tax

A Maltese resident company is liable to capital gains tax at a flat rate of 35% on gains arising worldwide, subject to tax treaty provisions. Nonresidents do not pay capital gains tax on gains arising outside Malta.

Withholding Taxes

There is no withholding tax on dividends, interest, or royalties payable to nonresidents. Dividends payable by a Maltese company to residents are subject to tax at a rate of 35% if paid out of taxed profits or 15% if paid out of untaxed profits. The tax at source is credited to the shareholder. (See also "Tax Treaties and Double Taxation.")

Value-Added Tax

VAT is levied at a rate of 15% in Malta.

Other Taxes

Other taxes levied in Malta include customs and excise duties, stamp duty on certain documents, and social security contributions.

Nonresident individuals are exempt from tax on interest and royalty payments received by them, unless from a trade that is permanently established in Malta, and on profits and capital gains received in respect of the disposal of shares in a Maltese company.

Tax Incentives

See "Tax Incentives" under "Incentives (Tax and Nontax)."

Tax Treaties and Double Taxation

Malta has entered into double taxation agreements with Australia, Austria, Belgium, Bulgaria, Canada, China, Cyprus, the Czech Republic, Finland, France, Germany, Hungary, India, Italy, Korea, Libya, Luxembourg, Malaysia, the Netherlands, Norway, Pakistan, Poland, Romania, South Africa, Sweden, and the United Kingdom. All but the agreement with Switzerland are OECD based. Dividend, interest, and royalty payments from Malta to nonresidents are not subject to withholding taxes. Withholding tax rates on payments from treaty countries to Maltese residents are shown in Table 39.1.

Incentives (Tax and Nontax)

Tax Incentives

A Maltese-registered company whose objects are limited to trading activities of an international nature may be classified as an international trading company. Special provisions in the Income Tax Act apply to international trading companies, the most important being that such a company may request Inland Revenue to confirm its status by means of an advance revenue ruling. In addition, the international trading company is a tax-efficient vehicle for nonresident shareholders since the net tax payable in Malta is 4.17%.

In terms of the Income Tax Act, special provisions also apply to participating holdings held by a Maltese company in an overseas company. Income received by a Maltese company from its participating holdings is allocated to a foreign income account and is taxed in the normal way. This includes the ability to claim double taxation relief or the flat rate foreign tax credit. However, when profits derived by a Maltese company from its participating holdings are subsequently distributed to a nonresident shareholder (or to a Maltese company that is 100% owned by nonresidents), there will be a full repayment of the Malta tax suffered on the income or gain.

There is also a package of fiscal incentives that is designed to attract to Malta the management and administrative support required for Maltese funds. Maltese investment service companies that are licensed under the Investment Services Act

Table 39.1
Withholding tax Rates on Payments from Treaty Countries to Maltese Residents

	Dividends (minor share-holding)	*Dividends (major share-holding)*	*Dividends (percentage to qualify for major share-holding)*	*Interest*	*Royalties*
Australia	15%	15%	N/A	15%	10%
Austria	15%	15%	N/A	5%	10%
Belgium	15%	15%	N/A	10%	10%
Bulgaria	0%	0%	N/A	—	10%
Canada	15%	15%	N/A	15%	10%
China	10%	10%	N/A	10%	10%
Cyprus	15%	15%	N/A	10%	10%
Czech Republic	5%	5%	N/A	0%	5%
Finland	15%	5%	25%	10%	10%
France	15%	5%	10%	10%	10%
Germany	15%	5%	25%	10%	10%
Hungary	15%	5%	25%	10%	10%
India	15%	10%	25%	10%	15%
Italy	15%	15%	N/A	10%	10%
Korea	15%	5%	25%	10%	0%
Libya	15%	15%	N/A	15%	15%
Luxembourg	15%	5%	25%	0%	10%
Malaysia	—	—	N/A	15%	15%
The Netherlands	15%	5%	25%	10%	10%
Norway	15%	15%	N/A	10%	10%
Pakistan	—	15%	20%	10%	10%
Poland	15%	5%	20%	10%	10%
Romania	5%	5%	N/A	5%	5%
South Africa	15%	5%	N/A	10%	10%
Sweden	15%	0%	10%	0%	0%
United Kingdom	—	—	N/A	10%	10%

are eligible for generous additional deductions for tax purposes, including double deduction on building occupancy costs (e.g., rent and heating) and on salaries paid to Maltese staff for the first ten years, as well as tax relief on excess funds invested in their own schemes.

Under the Malta Financial Services Center Act 1994, only licensed nominee companies may serve as nominees for subscribers to the memorandum of companies or as "agents" for nonresidents in relation to companies and trusts.

Nominee companies must be managed by professional persons of integrity and competence, such as accountants and advocates. Licensed nominee companies must be granted a warrant by the Malta Financial Services Center.

Free Trade Zones and Free Ports

The Malta Freeport Act 1989 introduced a free port that is a customs-free zone to take advantage of Malta's position on the major sea routes between the Atlantic, the Black Sea, and the Suez Canal. The zone is known as Marsaxlokk Bay. The free port provides various storage facilities, including container and break-bulk terminals and a mineral oil terminal. It also offers labeling, packing, repacking, assembly, and processing facilities, as well as ship servicing facilities.

A Freeport Authority has been created to administer the free port and to process license applications from companies wishing to operate in the free port zone. The license application costs Lm 1,000, and a further Lm 1,000 is payable annually. Companies that are licensed to operate in the free port zone are exempt from customs and excise duties, income tax, stamp duties, exchange control, and death and donation duties. The exemption is guaranteed between the company and the authority for a period of fifteen years. Expatriate employees also qualify for tax benefits in that income tax will be charged at a maximum of 30 cents per Maltese lira and personal belongings that are brought into Malta within six months of the employee's taking up residence in Malta are exempt from customs duty.

The free port exemptions do not apply to licensed companies in which Maltese citizens or companies are entitled to over 40% of the normal value of issued share capital.

Development Encouragement Incentives

Development incentives are contained in the Industrial Development Act 1988 and include the following:

(a) a ten-year tax holiday to industrial enterprises that export at least 95% of their products;

(b) tax exemption on an increase of profits from export sales over sales in a previous year;

(c) financing at low interest rates;
(d) factory premises at relatively low rentals;
(e) grants for training and management services; and
(f) investment allowances and accelerated rates of depreciation.

Corporations

(The domestic laws of Malta refer to *corporations* as *companies*. This terminology is retained in this chapter.)

The advantages of incorporation in Malta are that the English language is used and Malta has a European culture and falls within the European time zone. It also has excellent telecommunications. Disclosure is required with the regulator but not with the public.

As of the end of 1996, offshore companies may no longer be registered in Malta. However, previously registered companies may continue to benefit from regulatory concessions until March 31, 2004.

In terms of the new Companies Act, which came into effect in 1997, various types of commercial entities may be formed, namely, a partnership *en nom collectif*, a partnership *en commandite,* and a partnership *anonyme*, or limited liability company. The latter is the most commonly used form of business enterprise.

Fees

The following registration and annual fees are payable by the existing types of offshore companies:

	Registration fee	*Annual fee*
Offshore bank	Lm 25,000	Lm 25,000
Offshore insurance company	Lm 5,000	Lm 5,000
Offshore trading company for collective investments	Lm 5,000	Lm 5,000
Offshore captive insurance company	Lm 1,000	Lm 1,000
Offshore general trading company	Lm 1,000	Lm 1,000
Offshore nontrading company	Lm 500	Lm 500
Shipping company	Lm 100	Lm 100

The following fees pertain to new companies registered under the new Companies Act and to existing companies registered under the old Commercial Partnerships Ordinance. They do not apply to existing offshore companies.

Registration of Company

Share capital	*Fee*
Up to Lm 2,000	Lm 100
Lm 5,000 and over	Lm 100 + Lm 6 per every additional Lm 1,000
Lm 100,000	Lm 116 + Lm 1 per every additional Lm 1,000
Over Lm 100,000	Lm 213 + Lm 0.40 per every additional Lm 1,000 to a maximum of Lm 573

Registration of Annual Return

Share capital	*Fee*
Lm 5,000	Lm 50
Lm 50,000	Lm 100
Lm 100,000	Lm 150
Lm 500,000	Lm 200
Over Lm 500,000	Lm 250

Checklist for Companies

- The company name must end with *Limited* or *Ltd.*
- Incorporation takes seven to ten days. Shelf companies are not available.
- The minimum capital required is Lm 500 or its foreign currency equivalent. No capital duty is payable.
- At least two shareholders are necessary. Bearer shares and shares of no par value are not allowed.
- A minimum of one director is required. Corporate directors are permitted, and there is no restriction on the directors' residence.
- A company secretary is mandatory. Use must be made of a Maltese nominee company.
- A registered office is necessary, as is a registered agent that must be a Maltese nominee company. The share register must be kept at the registered office.
- The memorandum and articles of association are available on the public file, but beneficial ownership is not disclosed.
- A corporate seal is not necessary.
- Corporate accounts must be kept but need not be filed.

- An annual return must be made with a declaration that the company still satisfies the relevant regulations.
- There is no restriction on the holding of meetings.
- Trading companies pay an annual fee of Lm 1,000 and are taxed at a rate of 5%. Nontrading companies pay an annual fee of Lm 500 and are exempt from tax. Shipping companies pay an annual fee of Lm 100 and are also exempt from tax.

Banks

Banks are regulated by the Banking Act 1994, which was enacted in line with European Union banking directives. The responsibility for banking services has been passed to the Malta Financial Services Center, which has the following functions:

(a) to promote Malta as an international financial center;
(b) to assist those establishing financial services activities in Malta;
(c) to coordinate the financial services sector;
(d) to advise the Maltese government on financial services matters; and
(e) to supervise offshore activity in Malta.

In terms of the act, applicants for a banking license, whether local or foreign banks, must have a minimum capital of 5 million ECU. Foreign banks may establish branches in Malta provided that the Malta Financial Services Center is satisfied that the parent company is supervising the branch adequately and supplying it with sufficient capital.

The Central Bank of Malta controls interest rates.

Insurance

In 1998 the following changes occured in the insurance industry. The Insurance Business Act of 1998 and the Insurance Brokers and Other Intermediaries Act of 1998 replaced the Insurance Business Act of 1981. The acts raised Maltese regulatory standards to the international level and incorporate a number of EU directives. The Investment Services Act (Amendment) Regulations of 1998 now permits persons licensed under the Investment Services Act of 1994 to offer linked, long-term contracts of insurance.

In addition, the Income Tax Act has been amended to remove the distinction between offshore and onshore insurance activities. For long-term business, life insurance companies will be taxed on the profits attributable to shareholders plus the surplus in the life funds after deducting all mathematical and participation reserves. Policyholders' funds may accumulate tax free, but a 15% tax will be levied on the insurance company on profits made by the insured in the event of a maturity or surrender of a long-term contract. For general business, the items of income and deductions in arriving at chargeable income will include all technical provisions and equalization reserves. For linked long-term insurance products, the tax treatment will be similar to that for collective investment schemes:

(a) capital gains on maturity or surrender will be chargeable at a rate of 15% withheld at source;

(b) where benefits are determinded wholly by reference to securities listed on the Malta Stock Exchange, the relative transfer, including maturity or surrender, will be tax exempt; and

(c) no tax will be chargeable on receipt of a lump sum on death.

Shipping

A company that is registered under the Maltese Companies Act and owns and operates an exempted ship (i.e., a ship that is registered in Malta under the Merchant Shipping Act) is exempt from tax on the profits derived from the ownership or operation of the ship, as well as inheritance tax, stamp duty, and withholding taxes. A company that is registered but not resident in Malta and owns and operates a ship registered outside Malta is not subject to income tax on its foreign source income other than that remitted to Malta. A ship-owning company is also totally exempt from exchange control restrictions in respect of its dealings with nonresidents, provided Maltese residents do not hold more than 20% of its share capital.

Ships are registered in Malta under the Merchant Shipping Act, which is based on the English equivalent. A ship will be eligible for registration in Malta if it is wholly owned by citizens of Malta or a body corporate registered in Malta.

A company that owns a Maltese ship must have its principal place of business in Malta or have a place of business or registered office in Malta. Such a company must also satisfy the authorities that it will ensure due observance of Malta's merchant shipping laws.

There are no statutory restrictions on the nationality of the master, officers, and crew engaged on Maltese ships. There are also no restrictions on the sale and mortgaging of ships, minimal restrictions on the sale or transfer of shares in ship-owning companies, and no age limit for the registration of ships.

The registration procedure comprises two phases: provisional registration and permanent registration. Provisional registration is valid for six months, although it may be extended. Application for provisional registration must include the ship's name, present flag, and tonnage, as well as a declaration of ownership and proof of seaworthiness. It is usually sufficient to show that the ship possesses valid Safety of Life at Sea (SOLAS) and load-line certificates or that it is classed with an approved classification society.[1] Once a provisional certificate of registration has been issued, the vessel may fly the Maltese flag.

Within *one* month of provisional registration, the registrar of shipping must be presented with the following:

(a) a builder's certificate or bill of sale;
(b) proof that the foreign registry has been closed;
(c) proof of marking in terms of law; and
(d) proof of the state of registered encumbrances on the ship.

Within *six* months of provisional registration, the registrar of shipping must be presented with the following:

(a) a list of crew signed by the master and endorsed by the port authorities of any port of call;
(b) a copy of the certificate of competency in respect of every officer of the ship;
(c) copies of the SOLAS and load-line certificates;
(d) a tonnage measurement certificate and a certificate of survey issued by a surveyor of ships; and
(e) a carving and marking note.

Mutual Funds and Collective Investment Schemes

Collective investment schemes are licensed in terms of the Investment Services Act. They are exempt from all liability to tax. A fund may elect to waive the exemption and be taxed on its income at a rate of 25%. Where the right to waiver is used, the fund can benefit from Malta's double taxation agreements.

The following deductions apply to investment services companies:

(a) 200% on rent, lighting, building maintenance, and insurance for the first ten years;
(b) 100% on wear and tear of plant, machinery, and business premises for the first five years;
(c) any amount invested by a fund management company in one of its own schemes during the first five years that is not sold for at least two years;
(d) 200% deduction on resident employees' salaries; and
(e) other expenses incurred for the purposes of trade.

Trusts

Although Malta is a civil law jurisdiction, the Offshore Trusts Act 1988 recognizes and regulates offshore trusts. An offshore trust is defined as one in which the settlor and beneficiaries are nonresidents and the trust property does not include real estate situated in Malta. Offshore trusts must be registered with the Malta International Business Authority. Registration costs Lm 200. There are no annual fees, but tax at a flat rate of Lm 200 is levied annually on trust income. At least one of the trustees must be a Maltese nominee company.

The Recognition of Trusts Act 1994 was passed in order for Malta to become party to the Hague Convention. The Offshore Trusts Act 1988 was amended as a result to provide for the recognition of foreign trusts governed by foreign law. Offshore trusts that are governed by foreign law and are already registered in Malta have been given a fixed period in which to register as foreign trusts under the new regime.

Notes

1. That is, the American Bureau of Shipping, the Bureau Veritas, Det Norske Veritas, Germanischer Lloyd, the Hellenic Register of Shipping, Lloyd's Register of Shipping, Nippon Kaiji Kyokai, and Registro Italiano Navale.

CHAPTER FORTY

MARSHALL ISLANDS

Background Information

Geographic and Demographic Data

Location	The Marshall Islands are located in Oceania. They are a group of atolls and reefs in the North Pacific Ocean, about halfway between Hawaii and Papua New Guinea. The islands are 12 hours ahead of GMT.
Capital	Majuro.
Area	70.8 square miles.
Population	63,031.
Languages	English is universally spoken and is the official language. Two major Marshallese dialects from the Malayo-Polynesian family, and Japanese, are also in use.
Access	The republic has its own air carrier, Air Marshall, which flies between Majuro and Honolulu. There are also flights to Hawaii, Micronesia, the west coast of the United States, Australia, and New Zealand.
Telecommunications	Excellent.

Government

Originally a United Nations Trust Territory under the jurisdiction of the United States, the Marshall Islands were granted independence in 1986 under the Compact of Free Association with the United States. The Marshall Islands belatedly joined the United Nations in 1991, after the then Soviet Union dropped its objections. A parliamentary system of government with a constitution blends the U.S. and British models of government.

Political and Economic Stability

U.S. government assistance is the mainstay of the economy, constituting an important supplement to GDP. Agricultural production is concentrated on small farms, and the most important commercial crops are coconuts, tomatoes, melons, and breadfruit. Small-scale industry is limited to handicrafts, fish processing, and copra. The tourist industry, now a small source of foreign exchange employing less than 10% of the labor force, remains the best hope for future added income. The islands have few natural resources, and imports far exceed exports. The government is drafting economic reforms designed to increase revenue and compensate for reductions in U.S. government grants—in 1995/1996, the U.S. government provided grants of US$68 million, equal to roughly 70% of the country's GDP. More than 25% of the government's budget for the same period was devoted to debt repayment. In 1996, efforts to stabilize the economy included a 27% reduction in the government's work force and a 10% cut in the budget. High unemployment, which exceeds 20%, is a serious problem.

The government is reasonably stable. The United States continues to maintain a military base on Kwajalein Island.

Business Environment

In 1990 laws were introduced to promote the Marshall Islands as a flag of convenience nation and offshore business center. The Marshall Islands legislature passed legislation granting freedom from income, asset, withholding, and stamp taxes to foreign maritime entities, as well as nonresident corporations, partnerships, trusts, and associations.

After an offshore banking scandal, offshore banks had their licenses revoked. There is no banking, insurance, or free trade zone legislation in place, and captive insurance companies are unlikely to transfer to the Marshall Islands yet.

Currency and Exchange Control

The Marshallese currency is the U.S. dollar. There are no exchange controls.

Disclosure of Information

Disclosure in company formation and trust settlement: Disclosure requirements for corporations are minimal. Annual reports need not be filed, and the names of shareholders, directors, and officers do not have to be disclosed. Confidentiality provisions with regard to trusts is excellent. Disclosure of information is forbidden except under court order. Any violation of these provisions is a criminal offense.

International cooperation measures: The Marshall Islands has an exchange of information agreement with the United States that calls for mutual assistance in tax matters.

Legal System

The legal system is administered by independent courts whose judges are appointed by the cabinet. The court system consists of local courts of first instance, a Traditional Rights Court with jurisdiction over real property matters, and a High Court with maritime jurisdiction. Appeal lies to the Supreme Court in all cases.

Taxation

The waiver on profits, income, withholding, asset, and stamp taxes applies only to nonresident entities that cannot do business in the Marshall Islands.

Income tax

Nonresident individuals are subject to income tax at a rate of 10%. U.S. citizens who are employees of the U.S. military are subject to 5% tax. Resident companies are subject to corporate tax at a rate of 12%. The tax on income of unincorporated businesses is 8% on the first US$6,000 and 12% thereafter.

Land Tax

There is a tax on immovable property at a rate of 10%.

Customs and Import Duties

Ad valorem taxes are imposed on food, building materials, earth-moving equipment, heavy machinery, vehicles, household appliances, textiles, clothing, furniture, and rubber and plastic goods. The taxes range from 5% to 10% on these items. Considerably higher duties are imposed on television sets (20%), jewelry (30%), perfume and cosmetics (40%), video games (50%), and tobacco products (75%).

Import duties are levied on gasoline (25% per gallon), jet fuel (15% per gallon), and wine (US$10 per gallon).

Tax Incentives

See "Incentives (Tax and Nontax)."

Incentives (Tax and Nontax)

Under the Associations Law of 1990, nonresident corporations, partnerships, trusts, and associations are exempt from corporate tax, profits tax, income tax, withholding tax, asset tax, stamp duty, and reporting requirements. Interest, dividends, royalties, rents, payments, and compensation paid by a nonresident corporation to another nonresident corporation, other entity, or individual are exempt from all taxes, including withholding tax in the Marshall Islands.

Incorporated and unincorporated entities that carry on business in the Marshall Islands are entitled to a 5-year tax holiday on income earned in the Marshall Islands, provided they pay a minimum of US$150,000 in wages to Marshallese citizens or invest a minimum of US$1 million.

Exemption from import duties is granted on machinery, equipment, furniture, and fixtures imported for the construction of factories, hotels, and resorts. Raw materials used in manufacturing are also exempt.

Corporations

Incorporation

The Associations Law of 1990 governs resident and nonresident business entities. Part I of the law comprises The Business Corporations Act, which applies to domestic and foreign corporations, banks and insurance companies, and foreign maritime entities. The legislation is based to some extent on Delaware and New York State legislation and provides that a corporation may be formed by one or more incorporators, who may be individuals, partners, associations, or corporations of any nationality or domicile. The corporate name must include "corporation," "incorporated," "company," "limited," or their abbreviations.

The articles of incorporation must be in English and must include the duration of the corporation (if its life span is not perpetual), the purpose of the corporation, the name and address of the registered agent (which is always the Trust Company of the Marshall Islands, Inc. for nonresident corporations), and information regarding authorized capital and share classes.

The Trust Company acts as Registrar for nonresident corporations. There is another Registrar for resident and authorized foreign corporations. Incorporation can be completed in one day.

There is no minimum capital requirement. Shares may be issued with or without par value but may not be issued at discount. Only nonresident corporations can issue bearer shares.

A corporation must have at least one director. There are no nationality or residence requirements for directors. Meetings can be held anywhere in the world. A shareholders' meeting should be held annually, but failure to do so does not affect otherwise valid corporate acts.

Annual reports are not required, and the names of the shareholders, directors, and officers need not be disclosed.

The initial registration fee is US$650, with an annual fee thereafter of US$450. The initial fee includes the cost of the Trust Company's first year as registered agent. There are no other fees.

Migration and Redomiciliation

Redomiciliation provisions in the Business Corporations Act allow foreign corporations to transfer their domicile to the Marshall Islands by filing Articles of

Domestication and the original articles of incorporation, translated into English where necessary. Domestic corporations may migrate from the Marshall Islands provided they have met their domestic financial obligations. When a domestic corporation migrates from the Marshall Islands it must appoint a registered agent to serve the Marshall Islands corporation for at least three years.

Other Forms of Business Organization

Partnerships

The Associations Law of 1990, Part II, governs partnerships, including joint ventures, and unincorporated associations. General partnerships and limited partnerships are formed by execution of a written agreement to carry on a business for profit. The agreement must be filed with the Registrar of Corporations. In a general partnership, each partner is jointly and severally liable for the partnership's debts. In a limited partnership, there is at least one general partner who has unlimited liability, and one or more limited partners whose liability is limited to the amount of their capital contributions and who may be excluded from management of the firm.

Associations

An unincorporated association must also execute a certificate, which is filed with the Registrar of Corporations. The association may hold property and sue and be sued. Its members will be personally liable for its debts if it engages in business for profit.

Foreign Corporations

The Limited Liabilities Companies Law of 1996 allows company members to be governed by an agreement similar to a partnership agreement, while benefiting from the limited liability accorded to a corporation's shareholders.

In order for a foreign limited liability company to conduct business in the Marshall Islands it must register with the Registrar of Corporations. The following information must be supplied:

- The name of the company and the name it proposes to use in the Marshall Islands
- Its place of formation, date of formation, and proof of corporate existence from a person authorized in that jurisdiction to furnish such information
- The nature of the business it wishes to conduct in the Marshall Islands
- The name and address of a registered agent
- The date on which it intends to commence business in the Marshall Islands

The company name must include "Limited Liability Company" or its abbreviation. The filing fees are the same as those for corporations governed by the Business Corporation Act.

Shipping

In 1990 the Marshall Islands legislature passed legislation to turn the country into a flag of convenience nation, with Majuro as the home port. Seagoing vessels registered in the Marshall Islands that are engaged in foreign trade and owned by a foreign entity are exempt from all income, profit, withholding, stamp, and wealth taxes.

In order for a vessel to be eligible for registration it must weigh more than 500 tons and be less than 20 years old. The fees are as follows:

Initial registration fee	US$2,500
Annual fee thereafter	US$1,000
Annual tonnage tax per gross registered ton	US$0.25 (minimum of US$1,000)
Marine inspection fee	US$725
Provisional certificate of registry	US$200
Permanent certificate of registry	US$200
Foreign bareboat registration	US$225

The Marshall Islands ship registry program has aroused considerable interest, particularly in Japan. Currently there are more than 150 ships registered.

Trusts

The Marshall Islands passed the Trust Act of 1994, changing from a common law system to one of the most modern trust law systems in the world, containing asset protection provisions in the statute. Two regulatory statutes were also passed, namely the Trustee Licensing Act of 1994 and the Trust Companies Act of 1994.

A Marshall Islands trust may be created by conduct, the oral grant of authority to a trustee, or an instrument in writing. Two trustees are required, one of whom must be a licensed trust company, a Marshall Islands company, or a foreign company registered in the Marshall Islands.

The trust must be registered with the Registrar of Trusts within 30 days of establishment, either by filing a trustee's certificate or by filing a copy of the trust instrument. When registration is complete a Registrar's certificate is issued. This certificate is valid for one year but will be renewed annually. There are no government fees for registration and renewal.

A nonresident trust is usually free from taxes but will pay a 12% tax on any real estate it owns in the Marshall Islands or if it engages in business.

The beneficiaries of a Marshall Islands trust must be nonresidents. The perpetuity and accumulation period is a maximum of 100 years, although charitable trusts have indefinite existence.

There are no financial disclosure provisions in the Trust Act of 1994, but at common law the trustees must provide accounts to the beneficiaries.

The asset protection provisions state that a creditor bringing suit to recover property from a Marshall Islands trust on the grounds of alleged fraud must do so within two years from the time the transfer occurred or the trust was settled.

Forced heirship provisions of another jurisdiction are nullified because transfers to a Marshall Islands trust are valid even if contrary to inheritance or succession laws in the settler's jurisdiction of domicile.

CHAPTER FORTY-ONE

MAURITIUS

Background Information

Geographic and Demographic Data

Location	Mauritius is an island in the southern Indian Ocean, east of Madagascar. It is four hours ahead of GMT.
Capital	Port Louis.
Area	710 square miles.
Population	1,154,272.
Languages	English is the official language, although French, Creole, and several Indian and Chinese languages are also spoken.
Access	Mauritius is served by ten international airlines, and Port Louis Harbor is served by twenty-five international shipping lines.
Telecommunications	Good.

Government

Mauritius has a parliamentary democracy. It is a member of the Commonwealth and the Association of Francophone Countries.

Political and Economic Stability

Mauritius is politically stable, with a system of government based on the Westminster model. Since independence in 1968, Mauritius has developed from a low-income, agriculturally based economy to a middle-income, diversified economy with growing industrial, financial services, and tourist sectors. For most of the period, annual growth has been about 5% to 6%. This remarkable achievement has been reflected in increased life expectancy, lowered infant mortality rates, and a much-improved infrastructure. Sugarcane is grown on about 90% of the cultivated land area and accounts for 25% of export earnings. The government's development strategy centers on industrialization (with a view to modernization and to exports), agricultural diversification, and tourism. Economic performance in the 1990s has continued strong with solid growth and low unemployment.

Currency and Exchange Control

The local currency is the Mauritian rupee. There is no exchange control.

Disclosure of Information

Banking secrecy: Confidentiality provisions relating to offshore banks are contained in the Banking Act 1988.

Disclosure in company formation and trust settlement: Disclosure of beneficial ownership is required on formation of an offshore company, but not on formation of an international company. Disclosure must be made to the Mauritius Offshore Business Activities Authority. In addition, sources of income and bank references must also be made available. In terms of the Mauritius Offshore Business Activities Authority Act, offshore entities, their beneficial owners, and shareholders are considered to be protected persons, and no information will be divulged in this regard except by order of the director of public prosecutions on proof that the information relates to drug or weapons trafficking.

Offshore companies must file annual audited accounts. Branches must file annual audited accounts for the past three years when applying for registration in Mauritius.

Offshore companies must have a registered office in Mauritius. International companies and branches of foreign companies must have a registered agent in Mauritius. Accounts, minute books, and the register of shareholders must be lodged with the registered office or agent. The local registered agent is bound by law not to disclose any information unless under a court order or where instructed to do so by the beneficial owner.

A trustee does not have to register the beneficiaries of a trust. A company or trustee opening a bank account must disclose the beneficial owners or beneficiaries. Similar requirements apply to limited partnerships.

International cooperation measures: Mauritius does not have a specific procedure for cooperation with foreign investigators, but well-established networks exist between the different regulatory bodies for the purposes of such investigations. Inquiries between authorities are treated on a case-by-case basis in strict confidence. No appeal procedures apply, and there is no legislation governing the exchange of information with foreign states.

The Reciprocal Enforcement of Judgment Act 1923 applies in respect of U.K. and other British colony judgments. For other countries, the common law rule of *exequatur* will apply. For non-Commonwealth countries, a judgment must be obtained from a Mauritian court establishing the validity of the foreign judgment before it can be applied in Mauritius.

Mauritius has entered into numerous tax treaties, and many more await ratification. All of the treaties that have been ratified and signed are OECD Model–based treaties and contain a provision on exchange of information. The exchange of information provision is restricted to the interaction of the tax authorities of the respective treaty countries on the working and implementation of the treaty itself. Mauritius has not entered into any mutual legal assistance treaties.

Wherever a double tax avoidance or other convention exists with another country, the authorities will cooperate fully in relation to the exchange of such information as is necessary for the purposes of giving effect to the convention or for the prevention of evasion of taxes that are subject to the convention.

Legal System

General

The Mauritian legal system is a hybrid of English common law and French civil law. Company law is based on English law, as is procedural law. Substantive law is based mostly on the Napoleonic code.

Legislation

The principal provisions affecting offshore operations and transactions are contained in the following:

- Banking Act 1988
- Finance Act 1996
- Income Tax Act 1995
- International Companies Act 1994
- Offshore Business Activities Act 1992
- Offshore Trust Act 1992
- Trust Companies Act 1989

Case Law

An important recent case is *State Bank International v. Pershing* (1997/1998) 1 OFLR 170 (Supreme Court, Mauritius).

Treaties

See "Tax Treaties and Double Taxation."

Tax Treaties and Double Taxation

Mauritius has an extensive network of at least twelve double taxation agreements, including treaties with the Republic of China, Italy, Pakistan, Madagascar, Botswana, Singapore, Luxembourg, Sri Lanka, and South Africa. The treaty with India is particularly important as it provides for substantial short-term capital gains tax reduction from 30% to 0% when leaving India, making Mauritius a particularly tax-efficient route for nonresident Indians to invest in their own country. The maximum withholding tax rates imposed by treaty partners are shown in Table 41.1.

Incentives (Tax and Nontax)

Tax Incentives

The following tax incentives are available to offshore entities in Mauritius:

(a) There is zero income tax on net profits arising from offshore operations, although an entity may choose to pay tax at rates between 0% and 35%;

(b) expatriate staff are taxed at half the normal personal income tax rates (the current maximum rate is 15%);

Table 41.1 Maximum Withholding Tax Rates Imposed by Treaty Partners

Country	*Dividends*	*Interest*	*Royalties*
China	15%	0%	10%
France	15%	0%	15%
Germany	15%	0%	15%
India	15%	0%	15%
Malaysia	15%	0%	15%
Pakistan	10%	0%	12.5%
South Africa	15%	0%	15%
Swaziland	15%	0%	7.5%
Sweden	15%	0%	15%
United Kingdom	15%	0%	15%
Zimbabwe	20%	0%	15%

(c) documents relating to offshore operations are exempt from stamp duty;

(d) cars and household equipment for two expatriate employees per offshore company are exempt from customs duty, and the exemption may also apply to imported office equipment;

(e) interest on deposits raised from nonresidents by offshore banks is not subject to withholding tax;

(f) dividends and benefits payable by offshore entities are not subject to withholding tax;

(g) there is no inheritance tax or estate duty levied on the inheritance of shares in an offshore entity;

(h) there is no capital gains tax; and

(i) double taxation treaties exist with at least twelve countries.

Free Trade Zones and Free Ports

The free port was established under the Freeport Act 1992. Free port licensed operatives are eligible for the following incentives:

(a) exemption from corporate tax;

(b) preferential rates for warehousing and storage;

(c) reduced port charges for goods destined for reexport;

(d) exemption from customs duty, import duty, and sales tax on all finished goods, machinery, equipment, and materials imported into the free port zone;

(e) access to offshore banking facilities, including the holding of foreign currency accounts;

(f) the sale of a percentage of turnover of the local market;

(g) offshore entity advantages where the company is engaged exclusively in reexport business; and

(h) the possibility of 100% foreign ownership.

The Mauritius Freeport Authority has so far issued 250 licenses, but as a result of warehousing shortages, only 50 are operational.

Mauritius also has an export processing zone, which is the largest employer of labor in the country. The objective is to encourage export-oriented industries and international trade. Manufacturers in the zone are eligible for African Preferential Trade Area (the African equivalent of the European Union) tariff privileges and have access to an enormous regional market of developing countries.

Goods manufactured in the export processing zone have quota-free access to the European Union market, since Mauritius is a signatory to the Rome Convention. In addition, they enter the European Union duty-free. Under the general system of preferences, eligible products may be exported to the United States duty-free or with reduced tariffs.

Numerous local tax and other incentives apply to manufacturers in the export processing zone, including the availability of residence and work permits for expatriate workers, income tax exemption for the first ten years, a nominal 15% corporate tax for the life of the company, and free repatriation of capital, profits, and dividends.

Development Encouragement Incentives

New investment is encouraged by a 50% depreciation allowance on plant and machinery costs.

Corporations

(The domestic laws of Mauritius refer to *corporations* as *companies*. This terminology is retained in this chapter.)

Mauritius offers offshore companies the following advantages:

(a) a zero tax rate on net profits arising from offshore business operations;
(b) no withholding tax on dividends and benefits payable by offshore entities;
(c) no estate duty or inheritance tax on the inheritance of shares in an offshore entity; and
(d) no capital gains tax.

Types of Companies

Mauritius provides two types of offshore companies: the offshore company (previously the offshore status company) and the international company.

International companies are governed by the International Companies Act 1994, which provides for a hybrid type of company that is a corporate body but has the limited liability characteristics of a partnership. International companies are prohibited from engaging in the following activities:

(a) raising capital by public subscription;
(b) banking, insurance, or reinsurance business;
(c) owning real property in Mauritius;
(d) holding or managing a collective investment fund as a professional functionary;
(e) operating in the free port zone or benefiting from double taxation agreements; or
(f) providing registered office or nominee services.

International companies may transfer their assets to trusts and may act as trustees to no more than three trusts.

Offshore companies are governed by the Offshore Business Activities Act 1992 and are engaged in activities such as banking, insurance, funds management, and raising capital from the public. Offshore companies are prohibited from engaging in the following activities:

(a) transacting business with Mauritian residents;
(b) holding real property in Mauritius or shares, debentures, or any interest in a locally incorporated company;
(c) holding accounts in a domestic bank and dealing in Mauritian rupees, unless under a day-to-day transaction in Mauritius; and
(d) issuing bearer shares.

Taxation of Companies

As of July 1, 1998, the new tax regime applicable to offshore companies came into force. An offshore company operative before that date could annually elect its immediate income tax rate between 0% and 35% on submission of its tax return. Typically, an offshore company opted to be taxed at a nomimal rate of 0.1%. In practice this dispensation will continue to apply to an offshore company registered before July 1, 1998, even if no transactions took place before the cut-off date. An offshore company registered after July 1 will be known as an incentive company and will be liable to tax in Mauritius at a rate of 15%. Mauritius will grant the incentive company a deemed foreign tax credit equal to 90% of taxable income, resulting in an effective annual tax rate of 0.15%.

Redomiciliation of Companies

A foreign company (i.e., a company incorporated in another jurisdiction) may be redomiciled in Mauritius on application to the registrar of companies accompanied by the resolution authorizing the continuation of the company in Mauritius and a certificate of incorporation.

Checklist for International Companies

- International companies are not resident for tax purposes.
- Prior approval of the company name is required, and words such as *Assurance, Chartered*, and *Bank* are sensitive.
- Incorporation takes two days, and shelf companies are available. No information is required by the authorities prior to incorporation.
- There is no usual minimum capital and no capital duty.
- At least one shareholder is required. Bearer shares and shares of no par value are allowed.

- At least one director is required. Corporate directors are allowed, and there is no restriction on the directors' place of residence.
- A company secretary is not mandatory. Corporate secretaries are allowed, and there is no restriction on the secretary's residence.
- A registered office and agent are necessary. All documents must be kept at the registered office.
- No information is available on the public file.
- Corporate books and a seal may be kept at the registered office.
- Accounts are not necessary and do not have to be filed.
- An annual return is not required.
- There is no restriction on the holding of meetings.
- An annual fee of US$100 is payable to the government.
- An international company does not have access to double taxation treaties.

Checklist for Offshore Companies

- Offshore companies are resident for tax purposes.
- Prior approval of the company name is required, and words such as *National, Chartered*, and *Government* are sensitive.
- Incorporation takes approximately two weeks, and shelf companies are not available. Disclosure of beneficial ownership is required by the authorities prior to incorporation.
- There is no usual minimum capital and no capital duty.
- At least two shareholders are required, although one corporate shareholder is permitted after incorporation. Bearer shares and shares of no par value are not allowed.
- At least two directors are required. Corporate directors are not allowed, and at least two directors must be resident to benefit from double taxation agreements.
- A company secretary is mandatory. Corporate secretaries are allowed, and the secretary must be resident in Mauritius.
- A registered office and agent are necessary. The registers of shares, directors, secretary, and members must be kept at the registered office.
- No information is available on the public file.
- Corporate books and a seal may be kept at the registered office, although the official seal may be dispensed with.
- Accounts are necessary and must be filed with the Mauritius Offshore Business Activities Authority, although they are not on public record.
- An annual return is not required.

- Directors' meetings must be in Mauritius if the company is to be tax resident there. There is no restriction on the holding of shareholders' meetings.
- An annual fee of US$1,500 is payable to the government.
- An offshore company has access to numerous double taxation treaties.

Banks

Offshore banking is regulated by the Banking Act 1988. Licenses are granted by the Central Bank and entitle offshore banks to conduct banking business with nonresidents in currencies other than the Mauritian rupee. They must maintain capital or paid-up capital of US$1.4 million after the deduction of accumulated losses and may be established as a branch, subsidiary, or joint venture with a local bank.

Offshore banks are entitled to the same tax incentives as other offshore companies. Interest paid on deposits to nonresidents is exempt from withholding tax, and documents are exempt from stamp duty. Offshore banks are also free from exchange control.

An application fee of US$3,000 is payable for the offshore banking license, and thereafter a fee of US$20,000 is payable annually.

Insurance

Offshore insurance is regulated by the Offshore Insurance Regulations of 1992. Offshore insurance is insurance business concerning risks outside Mauritius that is conducted with nonresidents in foreign currencies. Offshore insurance companies may be foreign insurance companies, their subsidiaries, locally incorporated offshore companies, or captive insurance companies.

On March 19, 1998, Mauritius introduced new guidelines for the regulation and supervision of captive insurance under the Offshore Insurance Regulations of 1992. It is also drafting new protected cell companies legislation, based on the Guernsey model, to enhance flexibility for captives. There is no restriction on the forms of captive permissible in Mauritius or the lines of business that a captive inurance company can write. Insurers must maintain a margin of solvency whereby the value of the captive's admitted assets must exceed the amount of its admitted liabilities by not less than US$100,000 or 15% of net premium. Minimum statutory capital must be fully paid up.

The registration process involves incorporation of an offshore company and application for an offshore license. Offshore companies established under the protected cell company legislation are also allowed, but each cell must have a solvency margin of 15% and maintain a capital requirement of US$100,000. The application fee for formation of a captive insurance company is US$1,500. Two captives have been registered since the start of 1998.

Shipping and Aviation

Shipping

Recent amendments to the Merchant Shipping Act 1986 enable shipping companies to benefit from the incentives offered to offshore entities. The amendments include the introduction of an open registry, parallel registration of ships, bareboat chartering, and regulation of ship mortgaging.

Ships registered in Mauritius are exempt from tax on freight earnings. Their stores, consumables, spare parts, and bunkers are exempt from customs and excise duties. In addition, seamen working on ships flying the Mauritian flag are not liable to income tax. Foreign seamen are exempt from work permit requirements.

Ships under parallel registration pay the following annual fees:

Up to 10,000 gross tons	US$0.30 per ton
From 10,001 to 50,000 gross tons	US$0.20 per ton
Above 50,000 gross tons	US$0.10 per ton

Aviation

New legislation for the registration and financing of foreign aviation equipment was announced in the 1998/1999 budget speech. The objective of the legislation is to develop Mauritius as a reputable aircraft registry and finance center. The legislation covers the organization of aircraft mortgages and leases in Mauritius, the maintenance and administration of aircraft registers, the maintenance of a register of charges created on foreign aviation equipment, and the establishment of a register of aviation equipment leases.

Mutual Funds and Collective Investment Schemes

Mauritius does not have legislation specifically dealing with collective investment schemes as yet, although it is in the pipeline. However, the establishment and operation of such funds in Mauritius is regulated by the Mauritius Offshore Business Activities Authority. The regulations concern due diligence requirements regarding disclosure, conducting back office operations in Mauritius, and quarterly reporting. Offshore funds may be listed on the Mauritius Stock Exchange.

An offshore company, branch of a foreign company, or subsidiary of a fund established in a foreign jurisdiction must apply to the Mauritius Offshore Business Activities Authority, which is responsible for granting offshore certificates to offshore funds. Investment funds and collective investment schemes must lodge a prospectus including the following details:

(a) the basis of the net asset value calculation;

(b) its borrowing policy;
(c) the type and status of the fund;
(d) its investment policy;
(e) the remuneration of investment advisors, directors, managers, custodians, and administrators;
(f) the conditions relating to shares; and
(g) the name and details of the custodian bank, auditor, investment manager, advisor, directors, and administrators.

A fund whose effective management and control is in Mauritius will qualify for a tax resident certificate from the commissioner of income tax and may then benefit under the double taxation agreements.

Trusts

The law of trusts in Mauritius is regulated by statute but is similar to that of English common law jurisdictions. Offshore trusts are governed by the Offshore Trust Act 1992 and are defined as trusts in which

(a) the settlor is not at any time a resident of Mauritius, although offshore companies incorporated in Mauritius may be settlors of offshore trusts;
(b) at least one trustee is resident in Mauritius or is an offshore company authorized by the Mauritius Offshore Business Activities Authority to act as a trustee; and
(c) the trust property does not include property situated in Mauritius.

Trusts may be registered by registering a declaration of trust with the Mauritius Offshore Business Activities Authority and paying a fee of US$250.

Checklist for Offshore Trusts

- There is a statutory schedule of standard trust powers.
- The maximum perpetuity period for noncharitable trusts is fifty years.
- One resident trustee is required.
- Minimal registration provisions pertain.
- Trust documents may be in any language.
- Mauritian trust law has a civil law background.
- No registration fee or stamp duty is payable.
- Appeal lies to the Privy Council.
- The Hague Convention has not been implemented.

- Specific provision is made for the exclusion of foreign inheritance laws.
- Specific provisions deal with the nonrecognition of foreign judgments.
- There is a specific "asset protection" provision (beyond that offered by general insolvency law) protecting a disposition to a trust from challenge by creditors.
- A special statute of limitations period of two years exists for creditors' claims.
- Provision is made for noncharitable purpose trusts.

CHAPTER FORTY-TWO

MONACO

Background Information

Geographic and Demographic Data

Location	The principality of Monaco is situated on the south coast of France, near the Italian border. In winter, it is one hour ahead of GMT; in summer, it is two hours ahead.
Capital	Monaco-Ville.
Area	0.73 square miles.
Population	31,892.
Languages	French is the official language. English and Italian are also widely spoken.
Access	Monaco has a regular helicopter link with the French city of Nice, which has regular direct flights to major European, North American, and Asian cities. There are also good rail and road connections.
Telecommunications	Excellent.

Government

The principality of Monaco has a constitutional monarchy.

Political and Economic Stability

Although independent, the principality has a close relationship with France. The relationship is formalized in several treaties, and Monaco has a full customs and monetary union with France.

Monaco, surrounded as it is by the French Riviera, is a popular resort, attracting tourists to its casino and pleasant climate. The principality has successfully sought to diversify from casino operations into services and small, high value-added, nonpolluting industries. Monaco has no income tax and low business taxes and thrives as a base for both individuals who have established residence and foreign companies that have set up businesses and offices. About 55% of Monaco's annual revenue comes from value-added tax on hotels, banks, and the industrial sector; about 25% of revenue comes from tourism. Living standards are high, and unemployment is low.

Business Environment

Government attitude to offshore activities: The government actively discourages the perception that Monaco is a tax haven. Instead, it has limited international offshore center characteristics. In addition, foreign investment in light, nonpolluting manufacturing and service industries is encouraged.

Employment: A foreigner seeking to work in Monaco must submit a contract of employment with the application for a visa. The application normally takes three months. Once the applicant has a fixed address in Monaco, further application may be made for a residence permit. There are no quotas for the hiring of foreign nationals, but priority is given to Monegasque nationals, their spouses, residents of Monaco, and residents of areas surrounding Monaco.

Local business requirements: The consent of the government is required for foreigners wishing to undertake commercial, industrial, or professional activity in Monaco, including through a branch of a foreign company. Authorization can take several months. Many sectors have special provisions governing the grant of consent, and approval is usually granted only to companies showing at least three years of successful operations. Monaco holding companies are not permitted.

Foreigners and Immigration

Visitors to Monaco are subject to the same rules that apply to foreigners traveling in France. A French visa must be acquired before a foreigner can take up residence in Monaco. A bank certificate stating that the applicant has sufficient funds may also be required.

At least ten years' residence is usually required before Monegasque nationality will be granted.

Foreign nationals may freely purchase real estate in Monaco. Property owned by a French resident is subject, in the event of his death, to estate duties in Monaco rather than France.

Currency and Exchange Control

The local currency is the French franc. Monaco is part of the French Franc Zone and is subject to French exchange controls. The controls do not apply to most offshore financial center transactions, but there are reporting requirements and controls regarding large cash transactions and inward investment. The French

Franc Zone includes France, Monaco, French overseas departments and territories, and numerous African countries.

A company's residence for exchange control purposes is determined by its head office and place of business activity, as opposed to the residence of the shareholders and directors. An individual's residence for exchange control purposes terminates as soon as the individual becomes resident outside the French Franc Zone. Two years' residence is required in the French Franc Zone before an individual is deemed to be resident for exchange control purposes.

The movement of funds, shares, or valuables by residents and nonresidents is not subject to exchange control restrictions. Direct investments by residents of over 20% of capital in foreign companies or foreign-controlled companies are also not restricted. Investors and companies controlled by individuals resident in the European Union may acquire shares in French or Monaco companies without authorization, although a declaration of European Union status must be made to the relevant French minister. Other direct investments of over 20% of capital require prior authorization.

Disclosure of Information

International cooperation measures: Monaco has no double taxation treaties or mutual legal assistance treaties, except for with France. The police have wide search and seizure powers.

Banking secrecy: As Monaco is within the French Franc Zone, the Bank of France has significant control over its banking system. As a result, there is less banking confidentiality in Monaco than in many other offshore financial centers. Bank records are open to inspection by local customs officials, and there is no provision for numbered accounts.

Legal System

General

Monaco is a civil law jurisdiction, with a system based largely on the French system. Many French laws apply automatically in Monaco, especially in the sphere of commercial law. This is particularly so concerning French monetary, exchange control, and banking regulations, and French customs regulations.

Treaties

Monaco has no double taxation agreements, although its treaty with France, signed in 1963, contains provisions regarding a local profit tax. It also has no mutual legal assistance treaties. Monaco has a full customs and monetary union with France and therefore is indirectly subject to several European Union directives, although it is not a member of the union.

Taxation (Direct and Indirect)

Income Tax

Individuals of all nationalities resident in Monaco are immune from income tax. However, French nationals resident in Monaco are deemed to be domiciled in France for income tax purposes, unless they fall into one of the categories below:

(a) persons habitually resident in Monaco on October 13, 1962;
(b) persons holding dual nationality;
(c) persons attached to the prince's household; or
(d) French spouses married to foreigners before January 1, 1986.

Profit Tax

For the purposes of the profit tax, no distinction is made between sole practitioners and business entities. The tax is imposed on residents and nonresidents and applies to the following:

(a) entities engaged in industrial or commercial activities in Monaco whose turnover is derived either directly or indirectly by at least 25% from sources outside Monaco; and
(b) entities receiving royalties or other intellectual property income in Monaco (e.g., the proceeds from licensing or selling copyrights, patents, and trademarks).

Thus, entities whose total income arises in Monaco are not subject to the tax. In addition, foreign companies that are administered in Monaco but do not engage in industrial or commercial activities in Monaco are free of the tax. The test for whether an entity is engaged in industrial or commercial activity in Monaco is whether its effective place of management is in Monaco. The following factors are to be considered:

(a) the residence of the directors and officers of the entity;
(b) the residence of the main shareholders of the entity; and
(c) the location of board meetings.

Industrial and commercial activities are contrasted with those that entail the carrying on of a civil activity, such as the practicing of a civil profession, passive investment, or purchase and sale of real estate. Such activities are not subject to the profit tax.

As there is no income tax in Monaco, it is common practice to pay out most of the profits of a business entity as salaries or management fees.

Profit tax is levied at a rate of 35% of net worldwide profits, although profits from certain operations undertaken outside Monaco are excluded.

Capital Gains Tax

There is no capital gains tax in Monaco. However, capital gains and losses are included in net profit and may be subject to tax at 35%, depending on whether the entity is liable to profit tax.

Registration Tax and Stamp Duties

Documents that are executed and registered for the creation, transfer, or disposal of title to property are subject to registration tax as follows:

Disposal of a business	7.5%
Disposal of real estate	6.5% plus 1%
Ordinary leases	1%
Long-term leases	6.5%
Incorporation of company	1% of share capital
Issue of shares	0.5%

Withholding Taxes

There are no withholding taxes in Monaco.

Value-Added Tax

VAT is applied in Monaco as it is in France and is a major source of revenue for Monaco. Goods that are exported are not subject to VAT unless they are delivered to an entity in the European Union and are not registered for VAT in their country of origin. Services rendered to an entity that is established out of Monaco and the European Union are also not subject to VAT. Services that are rendered to an entity established in the European Union and that are liable to VAT in the entity's country of establishment are not subject to VAT. In addition, lower rates apply to goods such as newspapers and medicine.

Customs and Excise Duties

All French laws relating to customs and excise apply in Monaco. French officials operate the customs service in Monaco, and the French Treasury collects customs duties and other taxes, which are then rebated to Monaco according to a special formula.

Inheritance and Gift Taxes

Assets situated in Monaco at the time of a person's death or at the time a gift is made are subject to inheritance or gift tax. The rates are based on the relationship of the beneficiary to the deceased or the donor and are as follows:

Direct line and spouses	0%
Brothers and sisters	8%
Uncles, aunts, nieces, and nephews	10%
Other relations	13%
Unrelated persons	16%

The taxes do not apply to assets that are left to charitable organizations or the commune of Monaco.

Social Security

Social security contributions are particularly high in Monaco, with the employer's contribution being over 40% of the gross salary. Thus, although there is no individual income tax, the cost of employing staff is relatively high. Employees contribute up to 10% of the gross salary.

Tax Incentives

Monaco offers the following tax incentives:

(a) freedom from individual taxation;

(b) a low tax headquarters base from which international operations may be conducted;

(c) a low tax industrial site for the manufacturing of electronics, cosmetics, and pharmaceutical products; and

(d) no stamp duties and withholding taxes in order to encourage offshore banking.

Corporations

Monaco corporations are not of particular relevance to offshore operations because of the high profit tax, numerous administrative controls, and time taken for incorporation. Company law is based on the law of France, and, as with all civil law jurisdictions, the objects specified in the statutes must be limited. Prior authorization of the government is required for incorporation unless the company is being established by Monegasque citizens. Authorization can take up to twelve months. Shelf companies are not available.

Types of Companies

The company limited by shares (*société anonyme monégasque* [SAM]) is the usual form of company.

Checklist for SAMs

- On incorporation, a SAM must publish its authorization and statutes in the Official Journal and register with the government.
- If the SAM does not commence trading within two years of government authorization, the authorization will be revoked.
- There is no minimum share capital, but in practice authorizations will not be granted to SAMs with less than FF 1 million.
- At least two shareholders are required. Registered shares and bearer shares are permitted.
- At least two directors are required, one of whom must be a resident of Monaco.
- A company secretary is not necessary.
- A local office is required prior to authorization being granted.
- Accounts must be kept and must be audited.
- Migration and redomiciliation are possible.

Other Forms of Business Organization

Sole Proprietorships

Sole proprietors are recognized in Monaco. They require a license to trade.

Partnerships

Monaco law recognizes the partnership limited by shares (*société en commandite par actions*), the limited partnership (*société en commandite simple*), and the civil partnership (*société civile*). The latter is often formed for real estate activities or to hold passive investments.

Foreign Corporations

The local manager, who must be resident in Monaco, must request an authorization to open a branch of a foreign corporation. The corporate documents, audited financial statements for the past three years, a report describing the proposed activities of the branch, and proof of premises in Monaco must be filed with the request. There is no minimum share capital requirement, but the branch must have sufficient funds allocated to it. A branch is usually granted a two- or three-year license, which is not necessarily renewed.

It is also possible for foreign corporations to be administered or managed by a Monaco management company instead of establishing a Monaco branch. Profit tax at 35% will generally apply to a branch but not to a foreign company that is merely administered from Monaco.

Insurance

Prior authorization is required from the government for companies wishing to conduct insurance or reinsurance business in Monaco. French rules govern the insurance industry, but the reinsurance industry is not regulated. No specific provisions pertain to offshore insurance companies, but the high costs, profit tax, strict authorization requirements, and regulatory provisions prevent Monaco from being used as an offshore insurance center.

Licensing Companies

Companies that receive intellectual property income, whether they are Monaco companies, branches of foreign companies, or offshore licensing companies, are liable to profit tax at a rate of 35%. An offshore licensing company cannot benefit from the treaties governing the recognition of intellectual property rights to which Monaco is party, and Monaco is therefore not an ideal location for licensing companies.

Mutual Funds and Collective Investment Schemes

The *fond commun de placement* may be created in Monaco. Because of the strict reporting requirements, administrative costs are generally high. In addition, there are severe limits imposed on the investment of funds and the *fond commun de placement* therefore has little relevance to international offshore financial center activities.

Trusts

As a civil law jurisdiction, Monaco does not have its own law of trusts. However, it does in limited circumstances recognize two forms of trusts: foreign trusts registered but not formed under the laws of Monaco (Law 214 trusts) and foreign trusts administered from but not registered in Monaco (offshore trusts). Law 214 trusts may not be registered in Monaco unless the settlor is resident in Monaco, and they therefore have little application to international offshore financial center planning. In addition, Law 214 trusts may incur considerable tax liability in Monaco.

A Law 214 trust must be registered. Its validity in terms of the law of the country of creation must be certified by an approved lawyer, and it must have an approved corporate trustee. Registration tax is payable on the value of settled property, at rates of 1.3%, 1.5%, or 1.7%, depending on whether there are one, two, or three or more beneficiaries. The rate is reduced to 0.25% or 0.45% if the property comprises Monaco real estate. However, the trust can instead make provision for an annual tax of 0.2% on the value of the trust fund. There are no capital requirements for either type of trust.

Checklist for Trusts

- There is no statutory schedule of standard trust powers.
- The perpetuity period of a noncharitable trust is unlimited.
- All trustees must be approved by the government.
- Registration of the trust is compulsory.
- Law 214 trust documents must be in French. Other trust documents may be in any language.
- No registration fee or stamp duty is payable.
- There is no appeal to the Privy Council.
- The Hague Convention has not been implemented.
- No specific provision has been made for the exclusion of foreign inheritance laws.
- There is no specific provision dealing with the nonrecognition of foreign judgments.
- There is no specific "asset protection" provision (beyond that offered by general insolvency law) protecting a disposition to a trust from challenge by creditors.
- No provision is made for noncharitable purpose trusts.

CHAPTER FORTY-THREE

NAURU

Background Information

Geographic and Demographic Data

Location	The Nauru Republic is an island in the South Pacific Ocean, south of the Marshall Islands. It is eleven hours ahead of GMT.
Capital	There is no official capital.
Area	8 square miles.
Population	10,390.
Languages	Nauruan is the official language. English is widely used for government and commercial purposes.
Access	Regular flights connect Nauru with Australia, Fiji, Hong Kong, Honolulu, and Manila.
Telecommunications	Adequate.

Government

Nauru has a parliamentary democracy. It is a member of the Commonwealth.

Political and Economic Stability

The Nauru republic is the smallest country in the world and is politically stable. Its economy depends on the export of phosphates, the reserves of which are expected to be exhausted by the year 2000. Phosphates have given Nauruans one of the highest per capita incomes in the Third World, but incomes will probably drop sharply in the future. Few other resources exist, so most necessities must be imported, including freshwater from Australia. The rehabilitation of mined land and the replacement of income from phosphates are serious long-term problems. Substantial amounts of phosphate income are invested in trust funds to help cushion the transition. However, dividends from the trusts have declined sharply since 1990 and the government has been borrowing heavily from the trusts to finance fiscal deficits. In an effort to stem further escalation of fiscal problems, the 1996/1997 budget called for a freeze on government wages for two years, a reduction of overstaffed public service departments, drastic cutbacks in hiring new government staff, privatization of numerous government agencies, and closure of some overseas consulates.

Business Environment

The government actively encourages Nauru's status as a tax haven. Activities such as investment and trust management, manufacturing, trading, banking, and insurance are encouraged through no tax structure and no exchange control. Nauru legislation differs from that governing other tax havens and is designed to assist entrepreneurs in expanding and maximizing profits. However, the government is also concerned with preventing corporations from conducting criminal activities from or within Nauru.

The Nauru Agency Corporation arranges incorporation of trading and holding corporations. It is also responsible for the issuing of licenses for the establishment of trusts, banks, and insurance companies under the Nauru Corporation Act 1972, the Banking Act 1975, and the Insurance Act 1974. In addition, the Nauru Agency Corporation and other corporations such as the Nauru Trustee Corporation, which was established under the Nauru Trustee Corporation Act 1972, provide corporate services for business entities incorporated in Nauru. These services include the provision of directors, initial subscribers, resident secretaries, and trustees.

Currency and Exchange Control

The local currency is the Australian dollar. There is no exchange control.

Disclosure of Information

Holding corporations are insured confidentiality in that records maintained by the Nauru Agency Corporation are not available for inspection by the public. Confidentiality in this regard is provided for by statute. Trading corporation documents filed with the registrar of corporations are open to public inspection, but documents filed with the Nauru Agency Corporation are not open to inspection by a third party except with the consent of the promoters or sponsors of the corporation.

Legal System

General

The Nauruan legal system is based on English common law.

Legislation

The principal provisions affecting offshore operations and transactions are contained in the following:

- Bank of Nauru Act 1975
- Banking Act 1975
- Insurance Act 1974
- Nauru Corporation Act 1972
- Nauru Insurance Corporation Act 1974
- Nauru Trustee Corporation Act 1972
- Republic of Nauru Finance Corporation Act 1972

Treaties

Nauru is not party to any treaty arrangements with other countries.

Taxation (Direct and Indirect)

The Nauru republic does not have an individual or corporate tax structure.

Corporations

The Corporation Act 1972 governs the incorporation of companies in Nauru.

A holding corporation may undertake any lawful activity except trading, commercial activities, or business as a broker, manufacturer, or dealer of goods. It may not have more than twenty members and may convert itself into a trading corporation. It may issue shares of any class and may deal in its own shares.

A trading corporation may undertake any lawful trading, manufacturing, or other activity. It may not convert to a holding corporation, and there is no restriction on the number of shareholders. It may issue shares of any class but may not deal in its own shares. A trading corporation may issue debentures to the public.

Fees

The following fees are payable to the registrar of corporations by holding and trading corporations on incorporation in Nauru:

Incorporation fee	A$250
Filing fee	A$45
Special article filing fee	A$15
Copy of documents (one set)	A$22.50

Thereafter, an annual renewal fee of A$250 and an annual return filing fee of A$30 are payable to the registrar of corporations.

The following fees are payable to the Nauru Agency Corporation by holding and trading corporations on incorporation in Nauru:

Initial fee	A$250
Registered office fee	A$300
Registered secretary fee	A$300
Registered director fee	A$100
Resident director fee	A$100
Initial subscriber fee	A$50

Thereafter, the following fees are payable to the Nauru Agency Corporation annually:

Registered office fee	A$300
Registered secretary fee	A$300
Registered director fee	A$100
Resident director fee	A$100
One subscriber/shareholder's fee	A$50

Migration and Redomiciliation

The Corporation Act 1972 permits foreign corporations to transfer domicile to Nauru and permits Nauru corporations to migrate to other jurisdictions.

Checklist for Trading and Holding Corporations

- Nauru law recognizes trading and holding corporations with limited liability.
- The name must end with *Corporation, Corp., Incorporated*, or *Inc.*
- Incorporation takes twenty-four hours.
- A holding corporation requires at least one shareholder and one director. A trading corporation must have at least two shareholders and two directors. A registered director is required on adoption of standard articles of association.
- A holding corporation may adopt standard articles of association as provided in Table B of the Corporation Act 1972, Schedule 2. A trading corporation may adopt standard articles of association as provided in Table A of the Corporation Act 1972, Schedule 2.
- A resident secretary is a statutory requirement.

- A corporate seal is required and is usually kept at the registered office in Nauru.
- There is no minimum capital requirement, although the Nauru Agency Corporation expects a holding corporation to have at least A$100 and a trading corporation to have at least A$1,000.
- Bearer shares may be issued by a holding corporation but not by a trading corporation.
- The accounts of a holding corporation need not be audited by a registered corporation auditor. There are statutory provisions relating to the audit of trading corporations' accounts, but these have not yet come into force.
- Annual returns must be filed for license renewal purposes.
- The central management and control of either corporation may be anywhere in the world.
- There is no restriction on the holding of meetings for either corporation.

Foreign Corporations

Foreign corporations may be registered in Nauru on lodging the documents prescribed by the Corporations Act 1972, section 225.

Banks and Other Financial Institutions

The Bank of Nauru Act 1975 established the Bank of Nauru, which conducts all Nauru's national banking operations as well as being an international bank. The Republic of Nauru Finance Corporation Act 1972 established the Republic of Nauru Finance Corporation, which carries on the business of finance and investment in Nauru.

In terms of the Banking Act 1975, a trading corporation that is incorporated in Nauru may operate as a commercial and trading bank, a savings bank, or a financial institution, provided it has obtained a license to do so. A license will be granted only to persons with sufficient expertise, financial standing, and reputation. Application must be made in the prescribed form, accompanied by the following documents:

(a) a summary of the applicant's professional qualifications and banking experience;

(b) reports on creditworthiness from two international banks;

(c) the most recent audited financial statements;

(d) a government certificate showing the lack of a criminal record; and

(e) a testimonial from a reputable firm of solicitors certifying the antecedents and business activities of the prospective licensee.

License applications are usually processed within the month. A license costs A$1,000, which is payable to the registrar of banks. An additional A$1,000 is payable annually. A special fee of A$200 is payable to the Nauru Agency Corporation regarding the license application, and the same amount is due annually to the Nauru Agency Corporation.

Licenses are usually granted subject to the following conditions:

(a) A minimum paid-up capital of US$100,000 must be raised within two years from the date of issue of the license;

(b) audited balance sheets and profit and loss accounts must be furnished annually to the registrar of banks; and

(c) bank operations must be in-house, that is, the bank should not raise deposits from the public, either in Nauru or elsewhere.

Insurance

The Nauru Insurance Corporation Act 1974 established the Nauru Insurance Corporation, which carries on insurance and reinsurance business in Nauru and elsewhere.

An insurance corporation that is incorporated in Nauru is subject to the same conditions that apply to banks. (See *Banks and Other Financial Institutions.*) Insurance licenses are governed by the Insurance Act 1974 and are granted subject to certain conditions, including that audited balance sheets and profit and loss accounts be submitted annually to the registrar of insurances. An insurance license costs A$1,000, which is payable to the registrar of insurances. An additional A$1,000 is payable annually. A special fee of A$200 is payable to the Nauru Agency Corporation regarding the license application, and the same amount is due annually to the Nauru Agency Corporation.

Corporations in possession of an insurance license are required to be audited annually.

Trusts

The law of trusts in Nauru is based on English common law, as modified by the Nauru Foreign Trusts, Estates, and Wills Act 1972. The Nauru Trustee Corporation was established under the Nauru Trustee Corporation Act 1972 and may act as trustee for all types of trusts, including purposes trusts under the Foreign Trusts, Estates, and Wills Act 1972. It may also hold property of statutory purpose trusts.

A Nauru Trustee Corporation that is established under the Corporation Act 1972 to manage trusts must obtain a trustee license, which is valid for five years. The license costs A$1,000. The trustee corporation is also liable to an annual government fee of A$1,000.

Checklist for Trusts

- The rule against perpetuities does not apply.
- Trusts may be created with perpetual duration.
- Noncharitable purpose trusts are permitted.
- There is no registration requirement.
- There are no nationality or residence requirements for settlors, beneficiaries, or trustees.

CHAPTER FORTY-FOUR

NETHERLANDS

Background Information

Geographic and Demographic Data

Location	The Netherlands is on the west coast of Europe, bordering the North Sea, between Belgium and Germany. It is one hour ahead of GMT.
Capital	Amsterdam.
Area	16,221 square miles.
Population	15,731,112.
Language	Dutch.
Access	The Netherlands is traditionally considered the gateway to Europe, as two of Europe's principal rivers and waterways, the Rhine and the Meuse, flow into the North Sea at the Dutch coast. Rotterdam has long been the world's busiest port, and the Netherlands has excellent road, rail, and air communications systems.
Telecommunications	Excellent.

Government

The Kingdom of the Netherlands is a constitutional monarchy, with its seat of government at The Hague. Queen Beatrix is the hereditary, constitutional monarch.

Political and Economic Stability

This highly developed and affluent economy is based on private enterprise. The government makes its presence felt, however, through many regulations, permit requirements, and welfare programs affecting most aspects of economic activity. Industrial activity features food processing, oil refining, metalworking, agro-industries, engineering products, electrical machinery and equipment, chemicals, petroleum, fishing, construction, and microelectronics. The highly mechanized agricultural sector employs only 2% of the labor force but provides large surpluses for export and the domestic food-processing industry. The Netherlands ranks third worldwide in value of agricultural exports, behind the United States and France. Sharp cuts in subsidy and social security spending have been accompanied by sustained growth in output and employment. Unemployment now runs at 6.9%.

Political stability has been a hallmark of the Netherlands government since the end of World War II, which has enabled the Dutch economy to achieve sustained growth.

Business Environment

The Netherlands is one of the few industrial nations to be labeled a tax haven, with an open-door policy to foreign investors. Dutch authorities welcome foreign enterprises as part of the policy of stimulating industrial expansion and offer incentives to foreign base subsidiaries and direct manufacturing operations. The Industrial Projects Division is the body that provides foreign investors with information and assistance.

Foreigners and Immigration

Foreign nationals who wish to remain in the Netherlands for more than 3 months must apply for permission to do so. This does not apply to citizens of the United States or members of the European Union. Foreign nationals who wish to work in the Netherlands must obtain a work permit, which is usually valid for one year but can be extended. Permits are generally granted without delay.

Currency and Exchange Control

The currency is the Netherlands guilder. The Netherlands Central Bank administers exchange control regulations.

Disclosure of Information

The Netherlands is party to a mutual assistance agreement with the United States, which provides for cooperation between the two countries regarding supervision, implementation, and compliance of customs with regard to exchange of information.

Legal System

General

The Netherlands has a civil law system incorporating French penal theory.

Treaties

See "Tax Treaties and Double Taxation," below.

Taxation

Income Tax

Corporate income tax for resident companies, branches, and open funds for joint accounts other than the exempt substantial holding companies and investment organizations is at a rate of 35% on net profit from worldwide income and 37% on the first 100,000 Dutch guilders. The rate also applies to partnerships and sole proprietorships.

Foreign branches remitting profits to a Netherlands parent company do not pay company tax.

Individuals are taxed on their worldwide income on a sliding scale ranging from 6.35% to 60%.

Capital Tax

There is a capital tax of 0.7% on all capital owned by individuals, although a system of tax allowances is in place. Corporations pay a 1% initial tax on paid-up nominal capital and 0.25% on unpaid subscribed capital.

Capital Gains Tax

The normal tax rate applies to capital gains. Individual capital gains arising from a merger are taxed at between 25% and 50%.

Withholding Tax

A 25% withholding tax is imposed on dividends from corporations resident in the Netherlands, unless the continuous and substantial interest of 5% exemption applies. (See, however, "Tax Treaties and Double Taxation," below.)

Value-Added Tax

VAT is charged at a rate of 17.5%. A reduced rate of 6% is levied on food, gas, water, coal, oil, some medicines, books, newspapers, artworks, advertising, and some legal and transport services. The rate on farm goods is 10.8%. Exempt services include medical, dental, educational, insurance, broadcasting, telecommunications, postal, credit, collection, and monetary services. Exports are not subject to VAT. Insurance premiums are taxed at 7%.

Land Tax

There is a 0.8% tax on real estate. There is also a rental tax of between 4.5% and 4.7% and a 1.5% levy on the value of furniture. A federal real estate tax is levied on landowners amounting to 4.86% of the sales value of improved property and

6% on unimproved property. A 5% transfer duty is payable on purchase of immovable property.

Tax Incentives

See "Incentives," below.

Tax Treaties and Double Taxation

The Netherlands ranks in the top three nations in the world with regard to the number of double taxation treaties signed. It has treaties in force with Argentina, Aruba, Australia, Austria, Belgium, Brazil, Bulgaria, Canada, China, Croatia, the Czech Republic, Denmark, Finland, France, Germany, Greece, Hungary, India, Indonesia, Ireland, Israel, Italy, Japan, Korea (South), Luxembourg, Macedonia, Malaysia, Malta, Mexico, Morocco, the Netherlands Antilles, New Zealand, Nigeria, Norway, Pakistan, the Philippines, Poland, Romania, Singapore, the Slovak Republic, Slovenia, South Africa, Spain, Sri Lanka, Surinam, Sweden, Switzerland, Thailand, Turkey, the United Kingdom, the United States, Venezuela, Yugoslavia (suspended), Zambia, and Zimbabwe.

Incentives (Tax and Nontax)

Participation Exemption

A foreign base company organized in the Netherlands is not taxed on profits on income received from a foreign branch or subsidiary 5% or more owned by the Dutch corporation. The exemption applies only if the nonresident corporation in which the resident corporation holds a "continuous and substantial interest" is subject to similar tax levied outside the Netherlands. "Continuous and substantial interest" means interest in the principal of at least 5%. As a result of this provision the Netherlands is a recognized center for the incorporation of holding companies, because incorporators can avoid or minimize the tax on dividend income or capital gains by virtue of the extensive double taxation treaty network the Netherlands is party to, which does not distinguish between holding and other types of companies. Group financing deductions are available in connection with the participation exemption scheme.

Investment Organizations

A resident "investment organization" may qualify for complete tax exemption by reducing its tax rate to 0% if its activities and objects consist of investment funds to the extent of 90% of all investments in securities, real estate, and secured loans. The investment organization will also be exempt from withholding tax received from Netherlands corporations. In order to qualify for the exemption, all of the organization's profits must be distributed to shareholders within an 8-month period from the fiscal year end and the organization may not invest as much as 25% in a nonresident company, fund, or joint account or individual through direct participation or in the total of all the organization's participations of resident entities and individuals through foreign companies or funds for joint account. Foreign investment funds or trusts do not qualify for this tax exemption.

Free Port

The Netherlands has no free trade zones but Rotterdam is a *de facto* "free port," although there is no legislation regulating it. It has an extensive network of customs bonded warehouses in which goods can remain without immediate payment of duties. The warehouses are divided into the following classification: public bonded warehouses, private bonded warehouses, merchant controlled bonded warehouses, and factory bonded warehouses.

Investment Incentives

New manufacturing establishments may obtain a cash grant of 25% from the government of the value of all fixed assets, including the site, buildings, and machinery, up to 4 million Dutch guilders for each new project in Groningen, Friesland, and Drenthe, part of Overijssel, Tilburg, and South Limburg, in addition to the usual 50% reduction on the cost of the site. The investment should be at least 200,000 Dutch guilders and 35% must be financed from own resources. The government will grant subsidies of 15% of the amount invested in fixed assets in North Holland, provided the new investment is 500,000 Dutch guilders or more. The maximum grant is 5 million Dutch guilders, and 35% must be financed from abroad.

There are also export incentive schemes whereby the government will provide up to 20% of export promotion expenses. Tax reductions are also available on export income channeled through a foreign base company.

Accelerated depreciation is available and there are tax incentives for certain skilled foreign employees, as well as for individuals and corporations engaged in sea transportation.

Corporations

Types of Corporation

The two most important forms of corporation in the Netherlands are the *Naamloze Vennootschap* (NV), which is the equivalent of the limited liability company in the United States, and the *Besloten Vennootschap met beperkte aansprakeliykheid* (BV), the private company.

Incorporation

Requirements for an NV: Two or more individuals or corporations may form an NV by executing a deed of incorporation before a notary. The articles of association must be in Dutch and must be filed with the Commercial Trade Register for public inspection. The following information must be contained in the deed of association (which contains the articles of association):

(a) the corporate name, which must end with "Naamloze Vennootschap" or the abbreviation "NV";

(b) the Netherlands address of the registered office;

(c) the objects of the company;

(d) the share capital; and

(e) the directors' names.

The minimum authorized capital and minimum paid-up capital must each be 100,000 Dutch guilders. Shares must have a par value, usually a minimum of 10 Dutch guilders, and may be registered or bearer.

The shareholders' meeting must be held in the Netherlands. NV's must have their accounts audited and must file them for public inspection with the Commercial Trade Register. If the company's stock is traded on the stock exchange, the annual report must be in Dutch unless otherwise agreed at an annual meeting.

A Dutch resident company must submit the books of its nonresident parent company and its nonresident subsidiaries to the Dutch tax authority.

Requirements for a BV: The BV is distinguished from the NV in that its shares can only be registered ones and it does not have to file annual accounts unless its total assets exceed 3 million Dutch guilders or more than 50 employees or net reserves of more than 6 million Dutch guilders. There are some exceptions to the reporting requirements where the BV is a bank or insurance company and is a subsidiary.

The transfer of shares in a BV is also strictly regulated. Minimum authorized capital and minimum paid-up capital must each be 40,000 Dutch guilders.

The BV must also file particulars concerning share capital, its registered office, and officers' powers with the Commercial Trade Register.

General requirements: There are no nationality requirements for officers of either form of company. The notarial registration fee is based on the authorized capital. The minimum charge is 2,000 Dutch guilders.

up to 100,000 guilders	2,000 guilders
between 100,000 and 200,000 guilders	2,000 guilders + 0.3% of capital over 100,000 guilders

between 200,000 guilders and 1 million guilders	2,300 guilders + 0.1% of capital over 200,000 guilders
between 1 million guilders and 10 million guilders	2,300 guilders + 0.01% of capital over 1 million guilders
over 10 million guilders	9,000 guilders + 0.01% of capital over 10 million guilders

There are also fees of 150 guilders for filing documents with the Ministry of Justice, and 200 guilders for trademark name investigation by the Chamber of Commerce. A newly incorporated company must register in the Register of Trade Names, which is kept by the Chamber of Commerce. An annual fee is charged for this, which varies depending on the long-term capital of the enterprise or its annual turnover.

Foreign Corporations

Companies organized under the laws of another jurisdiction may carry on business in the Netherlands through either form of Netherlands company, or through a branch. Foreign corporations that wish to establish a subsidiary in the Netherlands or to cooperate with a Dutch corporation must acquire an exchange license issued by the Netherlands Bank. The license entitles the holder to all benefits regarding the transfer of profits and retransfer of capital under the legal regulations administered by the Netherlands Bank. It should always be borne in mind that foreign branches of Netherlands companies have considerable advantages over subsidiary operations, as branch earnings remitted to Dutch parent companies are exempt from Netherlands taxation provided the profits have been taxed, however minimally, overseas.

CHAPTER FORTY-FIVE

NETHERLANDS ANTILLES

Background Information

Geographic and Demographic Data

Location	The Netherlands Antilles consists of two island groups in the Caribbean Sea. One includes Curaçao and Bonaire, north of Venezuela; the other includes St. Martin, St. Eustatius, and Saba, east of the Virgin Islands. The Netherlands Antilles is four hours behind GMT.
Capital	Willemstad.
Area	370 square miles.
Population	211,093.
Languages	Dutch is the official language, but the Papiamento dialect is commonly used. English and Spanish are also widely spoken.
Access	There are daily flights to major cities in Europe, North and South America, and the Caribbean. The Netherlands Antilles also has international port and harbor facilities.
Telecommunications	Excellent.

Government

The Netherlands Antilles is a parliamentary democracy. It has full autonomy over its internal affairs but forms part of the kingdom of the Netherlands, which controls its defense and foreign relations. It has been an associate member of the European Union as an overseas country and territory since 1964.

Political and Economic Stability

The Netherlands Antilles is politically stable. The Queen of the Netherlands is the head of state and is represented by a governor-general.

Tourism, petroleum transshipment, and offshore finance are the mainstays of the small economy. The islands enjoy a high per capita income and a well-developed infrastructure as compared with other countries in the region. Almost all consumer and capital goods are imported, with Venezuela and the United States being the major suppliers. Poor soils and inadequate water supplies hamper the development of agriculture. Unemployment runs at about 13%.

Business Environment

The government actively encourages foreign investment and does not impose restrictions on foreign ownership of business enterprises. The business climate is internationally oriented, with strong links to the Netherlands and the United States. The Netherlands Antilles has a highly sophisticated financial structure, based on the Netherlands model, as well as a well-established network of professional advisors.

Currency and Exchange Control

The local currency is the Netherlands Antilles guilder, which is fixed to the dollar at US$1.00 to NAf 1.79. (Note: the terms *guilder* and *florin* are used interchangeably.)

Exchange control is regulated by the Central Bank of the Netherlands Antilles. Offshore companies (that is, companies owned by nonresidents that do not carry on business in the Netherlands Antilles) may acquire a license on incorporation exempting them from all exchange control requirements.

Imports and exports may be undertaken in any convertible currency other than Netherlands Antilles guilders. Foreign exchange transactions must be reported for statistical purposes only.

The investment of foreign capital into the Netherlands Antilles may only be undertaken by a license holder, but a license will be granted if the investment is in the economic and social interests of the Netherlands Antilles. A license is also required for the repatriation of capital and earnings from the Netherlands Antilles. These licenses are usually granted as of right, as there are no laws prohibiting or limiting such repatriation.

Disclosure of Information

Banking secrecy: Banking secrecy is not guarded by any particular legislation, but penal sanctions are imposed under the Criminal Code for breaches of confidentiality.

Disclosure in company formation: Disclosure of beneficial ownership is not required on formation of an offshore company. However, professional service providers are required to "know their customers" and keep certain documents such as passports on file. Some form of identification and a letter of introduction issued by a reputable bank are needed when opening a bank account.

Offshore companies in general are not required to be audited, unless they are offshore banks or offshore insurance companies. A local registered office is required. The local office or agent would disclose beneficial ownership in the case of a criminal or fiscal investigation covered by treaty.

International cooperation measures: The Netherlands Antilles has procedures for cooperation with foreign states, including with Aruba for the collection of taxes, tax assessments, and other penalties and with its kingdom partners. With regard to the collection of taxes, a formal request must be made to the Ministry of Finance. An appeal procedure is provided.

Exchange of information provisions are contained in the intrakingdom tax treaty between Aruba, the Netherlands, and the Netherlands Antilles, and a double taxation treaty between Norway and the Netherlands Antilles. The tax treaty is along the lines of the OECD Model. Information covered includes the collection of taxes and the establishment of tax assessments or connected penalties. Foreign judgments are enforced in terms of the Hague Treaty on Enforcement of Foreign Judgments and a treaty with the United Kingdom. Mutual legal assistance treaties have been entered into only with regard to criminal investigations.

Money laundering is dealt with in three ordinances: the National Ordinance on Penalization of Money Laundering 1993, the National Ordinance for the Reporting of Unusual Transactions 1996, and the National Ordinance for Identification When Rendering Financial Services 1997. These provisions do not cover tax evasion. The National Ordinance on Penalization of Money Laundering provides for penalties of up to sixteen years' imprisonment and a fine of up to NAf 1.25 million for international money laundering, and up to four years' imprisonment and a fine of up to NAf 250,000 for negligently being in possession of money derived from criminal acts. The National Ordinance for the Reporting of Unusual Transactions sets up reporting mechanisms for financial service providers. Failure to report an unusual transaction can lead to up to four years' imprisonment and a fine of up to NAf 500,000. The National Ordinance for Identification When Rendering Financial Services extends identification requirements applicable to banks to all financial service providers. Passports must be provided as a means of identification, and the ordinance stipulates client information that must be kept on file. Failure to comply with these provisions can lead to up to four years' imprisonment and a fine of up to NAf 500,000.

Requests for assistance by foreign investigators into tax evasion would only be considered by the authorities if they came from treaty partners, namely, the Netherlands, Aruba, and Norway.

Legal System

General

The Netherlands Antilles is a civil law jurisdiction. The legal system is based on the Netherlands system.

Treaties

See "Tax Treaties and Double Taxation."

Taxation (Direct and Indirect)

Profit Tax

Companies that are resident in the Netherlands Antilles are subject to profit tax on their worldwide income. A Netherlands Antilles company is resident if it is incorporated in the Netherlands Antilles, regardless of the location of its effective management and control. A foreign corporation is resident if its effective management and control are in the Netherlands Antilles. Nonresident companies are liable to tax only on profits arising in the Netherlands Antilles. Tax on onshore companies is levied at the following marginal rates:

NAf 0–NAf 40,000	32%
NAf 40,001–NAf 50,000	35%
NAf 50,001–NAf 60,000	38%
NAf 60,001–NAf 70,000	41%
NAf 70,001–NAf 80,000	44%
NAf 80,001–NAf 90,000	46%
NAf 90,001–NAf 100,000	48%
NAf 100,001–NAf 1 million	38%
Over NAf 1 million	39%

A 15% municipal surcharge is added to the profit tax calculation.

Offshore companies (i.e., companies incorporated in the Netherlands Antilles but owned by nonresidents and whose income arises outside the Netherlands Antilles) are entitled to tax concessions guaranteed to 1999, depending on the nature of their activities.[1] Nonresident shareholders are fully tax-exempt regarding payments from offshore companies.

Capital Gains Tax

Netherlands Antilles companies are not taxed on their capital or capital gains.

Stamp Duties

Certain documents executed in the Netherlands Antilles are subject to stamp duty.

Withholding Taxes

There are no withholding taxes in the Netherlands Antilles.

Inheritance and Gift Taxes

Netherlands Antilles residents are liable to inheritance and gift taxes to a maximum rate of 24%.

Real Estate Taxes

An annual real estate tax is levied in Curaçao and Bonaire on the value of improved real property. The rate is 0.6%. Unimproved property is taxed at a rate of 0.05%. In addition, Curaçao imposes a surcharge of 15% on the amount of real estate tax. There is also an annual occupancy tax levied on houses and buildings at a rate of 5% of rental value.

Import Duties

Certain goods imported into Curaçao and Bonaire are subject to import duty, ranging from 4.5% to 14%.

Tax Incentives

See "Incentives (Tax and Nontax)."

Tax Treaties and Double Taxation

The Netherlands Antilles is currently party to tax treaties with the Netherlands and Norway. The treaties with the United States, the United Kingdom, and Denmark have all been terminated. There is also the *Belastingregeling voor het Koninkrijk* (BRK), which is an agreement governing the tax regulations of the Netherlands, the Netherlands Antilles, and Aruba with treatylike arrangements.

Norway

The tax treaty between the Netherlands Antilles and Norway came into force in 1990. The terms of the treaty reduce the withholding tax on dividends from a Norwegian company from 25% to 15% if paid to a resident of the Netherlands Antilles. There is no withholding tax in Norway, nor in the Netherlands Antilles, on interest or dividends. The treaty does not apply to the following:

(a) Netherlands Antilles companies that do not have a "genuine business purpose" in the Netherlands Antilles;

(b) Netherlands Antilles companies in which less than 50% of the beneficial ownership is held by individuals resident in one of the contracting states (this does not apply if the company has a genuine business purpose in the Netherlands Antilles, if its shares are regularly traded on a recognized stock exchange, or if it is a direct or indirect subsidiary of a company whose shares are so traded); and

(c) Netherlands Antilles companies that claim the benefits of the reduced tax rates under articles 14 and 14A of the National Ordinance on Profit Tax 1940.

The Netherlands

The BRK was amended in 1997 as follows:

(a) The normal rate of Netherlands withholding tax on dividends is 25%. This rate is reduced under the BRK, and a distinction is made between the payment of a portfolio dividend and a dividend from a participation.
(b) A portfolio holding exists when a Netherlands Antilles company holds less than 25% of the paid-up capital of a Netherlands company. Under the BRK, withholding tax on dividends paid by the Netherlands company is reduced to 15% of the amount of dividends paid.
(c) A participation holding exists when a Netherlands Antilles company holds 25% or more of the paid-up capital of a Netherlands company. In this situation, withholding tax on dividends paid by the Netherlands company to its Netherlands Antilles shareholder is reduced to either 7.5% or 5%.
(d) There are no withholding taxes on interest and royalty payments by Netherlands companies.

Incentives (Tax and Nontax)

Free zone companies are exempt from import duties and pay a reduced profit tax of 2%. Tax holidays are granted for up to a period of eleven years on new industries and hotel duties. The holiday will apply to import duties, profit tax, real estate tax, and occupancy tax.

As an associate member of the European Union as an overseas territory, the Netherlands Antilles has the following benefits:

(a) free access into the European Union for products imported into the Netherlands Antilles from non–European Union states and then reexported without added working or procession, provided similar tariffs apply to the goods in the Netherlands Antilles as apply in the European Union; and
(b) free access into the European Union for all products that originate in the Netherlands Antilles. Products imported from non–European Union states into the Netherlands Antilles are deemed to have originated in the Netherlands Antilles if they have been sufficiently worked or processed there or meet the criterion of "substantial economic transformation."

Corporations

The advantage of incorporation in the Netherlands Antilles is that it is a low tax jurisdiction forming part of the kingdom of the Netherlands. There are no withholding taxes, and advance tax rulings are possible. It has a strong professional infrastructure, but there is no provision for tax-exempt companies, except with regard to real estate income.

Types of Companies

The Commercial Code provides for standard limited liability companies (NVs) with offshore status. Netherlands Antilles companies must be registered with the commercial register of the Chamber of Commerce. Articles of incorporation must be in Dutch, but it is customary to attach an English or other translation. Companies must obtain business licenses, managing directors' licenses, and foreign exchange exemption licenses. These licenses are issued routinely after incorporation.

Migration and Redomiciliation

It has always been possible to transfer the seat of a Netherlands Antilles company to the Netherlands in the event of an emergency, but as of December 1986, it has been possible for a corporation to freely transfer its corporate seat into and out of the Netherlands Antilles, on the condition that the other jurisdiction involved has suitable legislation.

Checklist for Companies

- The corporate name must be cleared with the Ministry of Justice. Words such as *Royal* and *Bank* are prohibited. The name must end with *NV*.
- Incorporation takes five to ten days. Shelf companies are available. No information is required by the authorities prior to incorporation.
- The usual minimum capital is US$30,000, which must be issued and paid up to US$6,000. There is no capital duty.
- At least one shareholder is required. Bearer shares are possible, but shares of no par value are not.
- At least one director is necessary. Corporate directors are allowed, and there is no restriction on the directors' location, but a local representative is required.
- The concept of the company secretary is not known to Netherlands Antilles law.
- Companies must have a registered office in the Netherlands Antilles but need not have a registered agent. The registered office must keep the share

register, minutes and resolutions, share transfer documents, and administrative and bookkeeping records.

- The articles of association, address, capital, purpose clause, and personal details of the supervisory directors, managing directors, and attorneys are available on the public file.
- The concept of the corporate seal is not known under Netherlands Antilles law.
- Accounts must be kept but need not be filed.
- An annual return must be filed.
- There are no restrictions on the holding of board meetings, but shareholders' meetings must be held within the Netherlands Antilles.
- An annual contribution is payable to the Chamber of Commerce.

Other Forms of Business Organization

Foundation *(Stichting)*

Unlike the common law trust, the foundation (*stichting*) is a legal entity in its own right. Foundations were originally set up for private and state nonprofit or welfare purposes. They may act as trustees of assets transferred to them for investment or management purposes to the benefit of third parties, and they have developed into vehicles that are commonly used to control shares in companies. Shares in a company are transferred to the foundation, which issues the former shareholders with certificates of participation entitling them to the benefits from the shares. These certificates are in either nominative or bearer form and are freely transferable.

Foundations must be registered with the commercial register of the Chamber of Commerce. There is no minimum capital requirement, although in practice the minimum is US$100. Foundations may not have members or shareholders and are managed by directors who cannot share in the profits or assets. At least one director must be resident in the Netherlands Antilles. Corporations may function as directors.

Accounts must be kept and filed but need not be audited. The identity of beneficiaries or holders of certificates of participation need not be disclosed.

As of December 1986, a foundation may freely transfer its seat into and out of the Netherlands Antilles, on condition that the other jurisdiction involved has suitable legislation.

In terms of the National Ordinance on Profit Tax 1940, unless a foundation is created for charitable purposes, its profits will be taxed in all regards as a corporation is taxed. An offshore foundation that is created for noncharitable purposes will be taxed in all regards as an offshore corporation is taxed.

Private Foundation

The foundation has been used in the Netherlands Antilles as a vehicle for non-profit-making purposes. As a result, the concept of a private foundation has been introduced, to use the foundation vehicle for private purposes. The private foundation may have any legal purpose, excluding the running of a business or enterprise. However, in terms of its Articles, it may manage funds, hold shares in a corporation that does run a business, and make distributions under its purpose clause.

Private foundations must be registered with the Chamber of Commerce in Curacao. The register is open for public inspection. There are no minimum capital requirements, and no residency rules applicable to foundations.

In terms of the Ordinance on the Transfer of a Seat, a foreign entity may transfer its seat to the Netherlands Antilles, and a foundation existing under the laws of the Netherlands Antilles may transfer its seat to another country.

The private foundation is exempt from all profits tax in the Netherlands Antilles, provided it does not carry on a commercial business or enterprise. There is no capital tax payable on establishment of a private foundation, and distributions to nonresident beneficiaries are exempt from withholding taxes.

Partnerships

There are no capital requirements or residency rules for Netherlands Antilles partnerships, although it is usual for one of the partners to be resident in the Netherlands Antilles, for tax purposes. There are also no accounting or auditing requirements. Partnerships are regarded as see-through entities for tax purposes. The following types of partnerships are recognized in the Commercial Code:

The general partnership: The general partnership (*vennootschap onder firma*) is one in which all partners are jointly and severally liable for the obligations of the partnership. A general partnership must be registered with the commercial register of the Chamber of Commerce and the identity of all members must be disclosed.

The limited partnership: The limited partnership (*commanditaire vennootschap*) is one in which there are managing (general) and limited partners. The general partners manage the partnership and are severally liable for its debts. The limited partners' liability is limited to the extent of the capital contributed. They are not entitled to participate in the management of the partnership. Limited partnerships can issue shares to the partners. They must also be registered with the commercial register of the Chamber of Commerce, but the identity of the limited partners need not be disclosed.

Insurance

Offshore insurance is supervised by the Central Bank of the Netherlands Antilles, following the implementation in 1992 of the Insurance Supervision National

Ordinance 1990. Offshore captive insurance companies and reinsurance companies (i.e., companies that insure risks outside the Netherlands Antilles) must obtain a license from the Central Bank. Only companies incorporated in the Netherlands Antilles as limited liability companies with registered shares or as mutual assurance companies will qualify for licenses.

The minimum authorized capital required is NAf 200,000. Day-to-day management must be conducted in the Netherlands Antilles by at least one natural person approved by the Central Bank as having sufficient experience and expertise. All books and records must be maintained in the Netherlands Antilles.

Foreign companies may carry on insurance business in the Netherlands Antilles, provided that the business is done through an establishment in the Netherlands Antilles that meets the same requirements and is subject to the same supervision as a Netherlands Antilles insurance company.

By special concession, the profits of all qualifying offshore captive insurance companies and reinsurance companies that do not receive any treaty-related income will be deemed to be NAf 100,000 taxable at the rate of 2.4%. This limits the tax payable by such offshore captive insurance or reinsurance companies to NAf 2,400.

Shipping and Aviation

Companies that have as their purpose shipping or aviation business, including the letting or chartering of oceangoing vessels or aircraft, may qualify for concessional tax treatment, provided that they are incorporated and conduct their daily management in the Netherlands Antilles. In addition, the vessels or aircraft must be registered in the kingdom of the Netherlands (although chartered vessels may qualify in certain circumstances).

The following tax provisions apply to profits derived outside the Netherlands Antilles:

(a) 80% of profits are taxed at 2.76% to 3.45%;
(b) the balance is taxed at 27.6% to 34.5%;
(c) capital gains are taxable and capital losses deductible;
(d) an investment allowance of 8% is provided for the first two years after the investment is made (provided the investment is held for ten years);
(e) accelerated depreciation of one-third of the purchase price of the vessel or aircraft is allowed;
(f) losses can be carried forward for six years (losses incurred in the first six years can be carried forward an unlimited number of years), and there is no carryback of losses;
(g) a company can create a reserve for replacement or reparation in the event of expropriation, loss, or damage; and
(h) bareboat charter income is only subject to tax at the rate of 2.4% to 3%.

The National Ordinance on Ship Registration Tax 1987 provides that a Netherlands Antilles shipping company may choose alternative tax treatment on the basis of the gross tonnage of each ship registered, at the rate of NAf 0.40 per gross registered ton, with a minimum tonnage tax of NAf 1,000 per annum.

Holding Companies

The National Ordinance on Profit Tax 1940 defines an offshore holding company or an offshore investment company as one that has the "exclusive or almost exclusive purpose of investing its assets in securities, including shares and other certificates of participation and bonds, as well as other claims for interest bearing debts however nominated and in whatever form." Such offshore companies are taxed at a rate of 2.4% on the first NAf 100,000 of income and at a rate of 3% on the remainder, unless a double taxation agreement applies.

Licensing Companies

The National Ordinance on Profit Tax 1940, article 14A, defines an offshore licensing company as a corporation that exclusively or almost exclusively acquires

(a) revenues derived from the alienation or leasing of the right to use copyrights, patents, designs, secret processes or formulas, trademarks, and other analogous properties;
(b) royalties, including rentals, in respect of motion picture films or for the use of industrial, commercial, or scientific equipment as well as for the operation of a mine or a quarry, or of any other extraction of natural resources and other immovable properties; or
(c) considerations paid for technical assistance received from outside the Netherlands Antilles.

Offshore licensing companies are subject to profit tax at 2.4% to 3% unless otherwise provided by treaty.

Mutual Funds and Collective Investment Schemes

A mutual fund or other collective investment vehicle established in the Netherlands Antilles is exempted from all profit tax on non-treaty-related income if it meets the following criteria: The mutual fund should have either minimum net assets of US$50 million, a participation of at least fifty shareholders, and four local employees, or minimum net assets of US$300 million and two local employees.

If a mutual fund does not meet these requirements, it will be taxed on non-treaty-related income based on its average net assets in each financial year, as follows:

Up to US$25 million	1%
Between US$25 million and US$40 million	0.5%
US$40 million and above	0.25%

The result will be taxed at the rates of 2.4% to 3% (2.4% on the first NAf 100,000 of taxable income and 3% on the balance) with a minimum charge to tax in any financial year of US$1,000 and a maximum of US$10,000.

Income received by a Netherlands Antilles mutual fund from treaty-related sources or from the Netherlands will be taxed at the applicable treaty rates or pursuant to the provisions of the BRK, as the case may be.

Trusts

As the Netherlands Antilles is a civil law jurisdiction, the common law concept of the trust is not recognized. However, the Netherlands Antilles legal system provides for entities that may fulfill a similar function, namely, the *stichting* and the limited and general partnerships. (See "Other Forms of Business Organization" above.)

Notes

1. See "Insurance," "Shipping and Aviation," "Holding Companies," "Licensing Companies," and "Mutual Funds and Collective Investment Schemes."

CHAPTER FORTY-SIX

NEVIS

Background Information

Geographic and Demographic Data

Location	Nevis is an island in the Caribbean Sea, approximately 250 miles southeast of Puerto Rico. It is four hours behind GMT.
Capital	Charlestown.
Area	36 square miles.
Population	9,000.
Language	English is the official language.
Access	Nevis is linked by air to nearby islands with major international airports, such as St. Kitts, St. Martin, and Antigua.
Telecommunications	Excellent. Nevis is linked to the U.S. telephone system and has a U.S. dialing code.

Government

Nevis is an independent parliamentary democracy. It is part of the federation of St. Kitts and Nevis, although it may elect to leave the federation by a two-thirds majority in a public referendum. Recently a referendum on secession was defeated.

Political and Economic Stability

Nevis is politically stable and has been declared by the Freedom Foundation in the United States to be one of the ten most free nations in the world.

The Nevis economy traditionally depended on the growing and processing of sugarcane; decreasing world prices have hurt the industry in recent years. Tourism and export-oriented manufacturing have assumed larger roles. Most food is imported. The newly elected government has undertaken a program designed to revitalize the faltering sugar sector. It is also working to improve revenue collection to better fund social programs.

Business Environment

Government attitude to offshore activities: Since 1984, the government has actively developed Nevis as an offshore financial center. It encourages foreign investment in production facilities in Nevis. Tax incentives, including an exemption from customs duty for businesses beneficial to the island, are considered on an individual basis. A tax holiday may be granted for up to ten years.

Employment: Minimum wages are set for certain categories of workers, but they are relatively low. There is a social security system. Employers contribute 6% of annual wages and employees contribute 5% plus a 2% levy.

Local business requirements: Every business enterprise must have a business license. A license costs EC$200 per annum.

Currency and Exchange Control

The local currency is the Eastern Caribbean dollar, which is fixed against the U.S. dollar at US$1.00 to EC$2.70. The federation is one of eight Caribbean islands using the currency, which is extremely stable. There is no exchange control.

Disclosure of Information

Secrecy of information: Secrecy of information is governed by the Confidential Relationship Act 1985. The act provides prison sentences for violation of secrecy provisions and insures complete confidentiality where foreign authorities seek private banking and financial records. Nevis has not entered into any exchange of information agreements.

Banking secrecy: Banking secrecy is governed by the Nevis Offshore Banking Ordinance 1996.

Disclosure in company formation and trust settlement: Disclosure of beneficial ownership is not required on incorporation of a company. Confidentiality is governed by the Confidential Relationship Act 1985.

Companies are not required to be audited, but they must have a local registered office. The name and address of the person or entity forming the company must be kept at the local office.

A trustee is not required to register the beneficiaries of a trust. Moreover, a company or trustee wishing to open a bank account need not disclose the beneficial owner or beneficiaries. This provision applies to limited partnerships as well.

The federal government and parliament, resident in St. Kitts, have authority over foreign affairs and therefore over procedures for cooperation with foreign investigators. The Mutual Assistance in Criminal Matters Act 1993 governs the exchange of information with foreign states. Foreign judgments are enforced in terms of the Foreign Judgments (Reciprocal Enforcement) Act 1969. The act extends the final judgment of a superior court of a foreign country, provided there is satisfactory evidence of sufficient reciprocity relating to enforcement of local judgments in that foreign jurisdiction.

There are no mutual legal assistance treaties in force between the federation and other countries. The federation does have a double taxation treaty with the United Kingdom, which contains an exchange of information agreement. The treaty is based on the OECD Model.

Anti–money laundering provisions are contained in the Proceeds of Crime Act 1993. The act does not cover fiscal crime.

Requests for assistance in an investigation into tax evasion will be dealt with by the Offshore Finance Authority in terms of the Confidential Relationship Preservation (International Finance) Act 1996. Any assistance given will be in terms of the provisions of the act.

Legal System

General

The legal system is based on English common law. Nevis is part of the West Indies court system, and the Privy Council is the final court of appeal.

Legislation

The principal provisions affecting offshore operations and transactions are contained in the following:

- Banking Act
- Confidential Relationship Act 1985
- Income Tax Act
- Nevis Business Corporation Ordinance 1984
- Nevis International Exempt Trust Ordinance 1994
- Nevis Limited Liability Company Ordinance 1995
- Nevis Offshore Banking Ordinance 1996

Treaties

The federation of St. Kitts and Nevis has entered into a double taxation treaty with the United Kingdom, based on the OECD Model.

Taxation (Direct and Indirect)

Nevis taxes income on a source basis. Income earned outside Nevis is not taxed in Nevis.

There is no Nevis income tax for individuals.

Corporations incorporated under the Nevis Business Corporation Ordinance 1984 do not have to submit annual returns and are exempt from Nevis tax. Corporations incorporated under the Companies Act 1885 are subject to a profit tax levied at a rate of 50%. Such companies may qualify for a tax holiday of up to fifteen years for an approved project, as well as for exemptions on customs duty on imported goods. Limited liability companies incorporated under the Nevis Limited Liability Company Ordinance 1995 are fully exempt from corporate tax, income tax, withholding tax, stamp duty, asset tax, or other taxes on income originating outside Nevis.

There is no capital gains tax or withholding tax in Nevis. Nevis nationals pay a social services levy of 2% and a social security tax of 5%. There are import duties on certain goods, and there is a land tax that is based on the rental value of buildings and land.

Corporations

(The domestic laws of Nevis refer to *corporations* as *companies*. This terminolgy is retained in this chapter.)

Nevis law recognizes the following types of corporations:

(a) companies incorporated under the Companies Act 1885;
(b) companies incorporated under the Nevis Business Corporation Ordinance 1984; and
(c) companies incorporated under the Nevis Limited Liability Company Ordinance 1995.

Companies incorporated under the Companies Act 1885 are businesses operating locally, such as hotels, real estate owning companies, and commercial enterprises. The act is based on its English equivalent. Such companies are taxed at a rate of 50%, unless they have been granted a tax holiday.

International business companies (IBCs) are incorporated under the Nevis Business Corporation Ordinance 1984. The ordinance is based largely on the company law of the state of Delaware in the United States, but provision is also made for English common law conventions. IBCs are entitled to total tax exemption as their profits are not generated in Nevis, provided they conduct limited activities that are not considered to be "doing business" in Nevis. These activities are as follows:

(a) maintaining bank accounts;
(b) holding meetings of directors or shareholders;
(c) maintaining corporate or financial records;
(d) maintaining an administrative or managerial office;
(e) maintaining a registered agent; or
(f) investing in stocks of Nevis corporations, being a partner in a Nevis partnership, or being a beneficiary of a Nevis trust or estate.

Migration and redomiciliation of an IBC out of and into Nevis are quick, easy, and inexpensive. A unique feature of the Nevis Business Corporation Ordinance is the emergency provision whereby a foreign corporation can apply for emergency transfer of domicile to Nevis on filing of the necessary supporting documents.

Checklist for IBCs

- The company name cannot be in conflict with a preexisting company. The words *Bank* and *Insurance* and their derivatives are prohibited. The name must end with *Limited, Inc., Corporation*, or *SA*.
- Incorporation takes a few hours. Documents are returned within five to seven days. Fax copies of documents are available immediately. Shelf companies are available. No information is required by the authorities prior to incorporation.
- There is no minimum capital requirement. Capital duty of at least US$200 is payable, based on an authorized share capital of 1,000 shares at no par value or US$100,000 of par value shares.
- At least one shareholder is required. Bearer shares and shares of no par value are possible.
- If the number of shareholders is less than three, the number of directors may equal the number of shareholders. Corporate directors are permitted, and there is no restriction on the directors' residence.
- A company secretary is mandatory. Corporate secretaries are permitted, and there is no restriction on the secretary's residence.
- An IBC does not need a registered office in Nevis, but it must have a registered agent.
- The address of the registered agent and the articles of incorporation are available on the public file.
- No documents are required to be kept at a local office. There is no need for corporate books and a seal to be kept in Nevis.

- Accounts are not required, nor is an annual return.
- There is no restriction on the holding of meetings.
- An annual fee of US$200 is payable to the government.

The Nevis limited liability company, incorporated under the Nevis Limited Liability Company Ordinance 1995, is a unique company form providing limited liability without shareholders' restriction. Such companies are analogous to limited liability companies in the United States. They may be used for any business venture or professional practice and are fully exempt from tax on all assets or income originating outside of Nevis. Limited liability companies' management vests in the members. A sole member limited liability company is permitted under the ordinance.

Foreign limited liability companies may transfer domicile to Nevis. Limited liability companies have a limited life.

Checklist for Limited Liability Companies

- The company name must include *LLC* or *LC*.
- Same-day incorporation is provided for. Shelf companies are not available. No information is required by the authorities prior to incorporation.
- There is no minimum capital requirement and no capital duty.
- At least one member is required.
- There are no shares in the company.
- Management is by members, who may be located anywhere in the world.
- There is no company secretary.
- There is no need for a registered office in Nevis, but a registered agent is required.
- The articles of organization and the registered agent are available on the public file.
- No documents are required to be kept in Nevis. The corporate books and seal may be maintained anywhere in the world.
- Accounts need not be maintained or filed. An annual return is also not required.
- There is no restriction on the holding of meetings.
- A fee of US$200 is payable to the government on registration and annually thereafter.

Banks and Trust Companies

The Nevis Offshore Banking Ordinance 1996 was passed to facilitate the providing of financial services in Nevis, rather than to establish Nevis as an offshore banking center. It allows onshore banks to establish offshore banking units in Nevis. To qualify for an offshore banking license, a bank must be registered under the Banking Act, and must be regulated by the Eastern Caribbean Central Bank or must hold a license in its jurisdiction of incorporation to accept deposits from members of the public.

An offshore bank is required to file quarterly financial statements and an annual audited statement and must have a resident director in Nevis. Profits are taxed at the following rates:

Up to EC$10 million	2.5%
Above EC$10 million to EC$20 million	2%
Over EC$20 million	1.5%

Under the Nevis Business Corporation Ordinance 1984, an international business company using the words *Trust Company* in its name may be incorporated without disclosing beneficial ownership or obtaining government permission. Trust companies may administer trust assets or undertake related activities in Nevis but may not conduct public business or operate locally in Nevis. The management of offshore trust assets may be done in Nevis or elsewhere without incurring tax liability in Nevis.

Insurance

In terms of the Nevis Business Corporation Ordinance 1984, Nevis international business companies may engage in reinsurance business and use the word *Reinsurance* in their names. There is no licensing requirement for reinsurance companies in Nevis, but a standard disclaimer clause must be included in the articles of association forbidding the company from conducting insurance underwriting or public business.

Mutual Funds

Mutual funds are established under the Business Corporation Ordinance of 1984. However, there are as yet no laws governing the administration of funds in Nevis, and the funds that are currently registered in Nevis are therefore administered from other offshore jurisdictions. This absence of security laws and regulations is one of the advantages of using Nevis companies as mutual fund entities. Other advantages are:

(a) the absence of restrictions on using such words as "mutual fund," "unit fund," or "securities" in company names;

(b) the fact that the Business Corporation Ordinance allows companies to buy their own shares or redeem shares out of surplus;

(c) the fact that the Business Corporation Ordinance allows for flexible share structures; and

(d) low incorporation and annual renewal fees, regardless of the authorized or issued share capital.

Trusts

Up until 1994, trusts in Nevis were governed by the Trustee Ordinance 1961, which did not provide for trusts with international assets. The Nevis International Exempt Trust Ordinance 1994 was enacted to provide for and regulate trusts whose assets are located worldwide.

The registrar of trusts maintains a register of international trusts. To register a trust, the following must be submitted:

(a) the registration fee of US$200;

(b) the name and registered office of the trust; and

(c) a certificate from a trustee company, barrister, or solicitor certifying that the trust will be an international trust.

A trust renewal fee of US$200 is payable annually.

The Statute of Elizabeth does not apply to trusts created under the Nevis International Exempt Trust Ordinance 1994. Forced inheritance rights also do not apply. Legal action by a creditor against trust property in a Nevis court is subject to a bond of EC$25,000 for costs. There is a statute of limitations period of one year for creditors' claims.

The property of trusts registered in terms of the Nevis International Exempt Trust Ordinance 1994 is exempt from income tax, inheritance tax, and stamp duty.

An international trust is a registered trust of which at least one trustee is a corporation incorporated under the Nevis Business Corporation Ordinance 1984 or a trust company doing business in Nevis. In addition, the settlor and beneficiaries must at all times be nonresident, and the trust property may not include land situated in Nevis.

There are no specific accounting or auditing provisions and no capital requirements on creation of a trust.

CHAPTER FORTY-SEVEN

NIUE

Background Information

Geographic and Demographic Data

Location	Niue is an island in the South Pacific Ocean, east of Tonga. It is eleven hours behind GMT.
Capital	Alofi.
Area	100 square miles.
Population	1,700.
Languages	English is the official language, although most islanders also speak Niuean, a Polynesian dialect.
Telecommunications	Excellent.

Government

Niue is a self-governing parliamentary democracy, based on the Westminster system, in free association with New Zealand, which is responsible for its defense and foreign affairs. Niue is a member of the Commonwealth.

Political and Economic Stability

Niue is politically stable. The Queen of England is the head of state and is represented by the New Zealand high commissioner.

The economy is heavily dependent on aid from New Zealand as Niue has no indigenous export product. Government expenditure regularly exceeds revenues, with the shortfall made up by grants from New Zealand. The grants are used to pay wages to public employees. However, Niue has recently cut government expenditure by reducing the public service sector by almost half. The agricultural sector consists mainly of subsistence gardening, although some cash crops are grown for export. Industry consists primarily of small factories to process passion fruit, lime oil, honey, and coconut cream. The sale of postage stamps to foreign collectors is an important source of revenue. The island in recent years has suffered a serious loss of population because of migration of Niueans to New Zealand.

Business Environment

The government actively encourages foreign investment into Niue, and it may provide incentives and concessions in particular cases. However, given the island's limited resources, it is not intended to create a large industrial sector in Niue, and concessions will be restricted to activities such as tourism, fishing, and agriculture.

Currency and Exchange Control

The local currency is the New Zealand dollar. There is no exchange control.

Disclosure of Information

Secrecy of information: Companies incorporated under the International Business Companies Act 1994 are granted total secrecy in terms of the Offshore Center (Miscellaneous Provisions) Act 1994. It is an offense under this act to breach confidentiality. However, the court may order disclosure if it is satisfied that the information is required for investigation or prosecution of offenses such as drug trafficking and money laundering. Confidentiality provisions relating to trusts are contained in the Trustee Companies Act 1994 and the Trusts Act 1994.

Banking secrecy: Confidentiality and secrecy provisions relating to banks are contained in the Niue Bank Act 1994 and the Offshore Banking Act 1994.

Disclosure in company formation and trust settlement: Disclosure of beneficial ownership is not required on incorporation of an exempt company. No other information is required by the authorities. The Offshore Center (Miscellaneous Provisions) Act 1994 governs confidentiality relating to companies. Companies are not required to be audited. A local registered office and agent are required. In practice, the agent often provides the local office. There is no requirement for information to be lodged with the local agent. The local agent would be compelled to disclose beneficial ownership only if relating to a conviction for an offense committed in any jurisdiction for which the offender has been sentenced to a term of imprisonment of three years or more, providing such an offense would carry a similar penalty if committed in Niue.

Trustees must register the beneficiaries of a trust. Registration is completely confidential and is carried out by the registrar of the Niue high court. Companies or trustees opening a bank account must disclose beneficial ownership or the beneficiaries, but the information is recorded under terms of absolute secrecy. The same applies to limited partnerships.

International cooperation measures: Niue has no procedures for cooperation with foreign investigators and would not cooperate with a request for assistance concerning a foreign investigation into tax evasion. It also has no legislation concerning the enforcement of foreign judgments. It has not entered into any double taxation treaties or mutual legal assistance treaties. There is no specific anti–money laundering legislation in force.

Legal System

General

The Niue legal system is based on English common law.

Legislation

The principal provisions affecting offshore operations and transactions are contained in the following:

- International Business Companies Act 1994
- Niue Bank Act 1994
- Offshore Banking Act 1994
- Offshore Center (Miscellaneous Provisions) Act 1994
- Trustee Companies Act 1994
- Trusts Act 1994

Treaties

Niue has not entered into any double taxation treaty arrangements, although the taxation authority is empowered to do so.

Taxation (Direct and Indirect)

Income Tax

Income tax is levied under the Income Tax Ordinance 1961. International business companies (IBCs) are wholly exempt from tax in Niue. All other Niue resident companies (i.e., companies whose effective management and control are in Niue) are expected to file annual returns and are taxed on their worldwide income at the rate of 30%. Individuals are taxed on their worldwide income at the following rates:

Up to NZ$5,000	10%
NZ$5,001 to NZ$15,000	30%
NZ$15,001 to NZ$35,000	40%
Over NZ$35,000	50%

Where foreign source income has been subject to foreign taxes, some form of unilateral relief may be granted, although Niue is not party to any double taxation agreements.

Withholding Taxes

Payments made from Niue are exempt from withholding tax. Dividends received by a Niue resident company are subject to withholding tax, unless the company is an international business company. Relief is available for foreign taxes already paid in respect of the dividend income. Dividends paid by a Niue resident company to a resident individual are subject to tax.

Other Taxes

There are no capital gains taxes in Niue and no other forms of tax.

Corporations

(The domestic laws of Niue refer to *corporations* as *companies*. This terminology is retained in this chapter.)

The advantage of incorporation in Niue is that it is a new jurisdiction that has benefited from the experience of other international offshore financial centers. It provides total secrecy and anonymity to beneficial owners, and incorporation documents may be drafted in English or any other language, with an English translation. However, Niue is not a well-known jurisdiction and does not have the reputation and standing of some other international offshore financial centers.

Types of Companies

Niue domestic companies are governed by the Companies Act 1955 (New Zealand). Such companies are liable to the reporting and filing requirements applicable in New Zealand and to taxes and duties imposed in Niue. They are not typically used as offshore vehicles.

The International Business Companies Act 1994 provides for the incorporation of international business companies, which are exempt offshore companies. Such companies may not

(a) carry on business with Niue residents;

(b) own an interest in real estate in Niue, except hold a lease for office purposes;

(c) carry on banking or trust business without a license;

(d) carry on insurance or reinsurance business without a license; or

(e) provide registered offices and agents to companies incorporated in Niue, unless registered to do so.

IBCs are required to pay an annual license fee of US$150.

Migration and Redomiciliation

The International Business Companies Amendment Act of 1998 was enacted to waive the fees payable for companies redomiciling in Niue. Formerly a fee of US$500 was payable to the Registrar for companies with standard authorized capital of less than US$50,000 and US$1,000 for companies with standard authorized capital of more than US$50,000.

Checklist for IBCs

- Company names may be in Chinese characters or Cyrillic script, provided an English translation is given. A name can be reserved without payment for seven days and for up to sixty days on payment of US$25. The name must end with an abbreviation signifying limited liability, such as *Ltd., Corp., Inc., SA, A/S, AG, NV, BV, GmbH,* or *Akteingesellschaft.*
- Incorporation takes one day. Shelf companies are available. No information is required by the authorities prior to exempt status being granted.
- There is no minimum capital requirement. The usual authorized capital is US$50,000 divided into 50,000 shares with a par value of US$1.
- A registration fee of US$150 is payable on capital of up to US$50,000 par value shares, and US$1,000 is payable on capital over US$50,000. A fee of US$200 is payable on capital with no par value shares up to US$50,000.
- At least one shareholder is required. Bearer shares and shares of no par value are permitted.
- At least one director is required. Corporate directors are allowed, and there is no restriction on the directors' location.
- A company secretary is not mandatory. Corporate secretaries are allowed, and there is no restriction on the secretary's location.
- An IBC must have a registered office and a registered agent. There is no requirement regarding the keeping of documents at the registered office.
- The memorandum and articles of association, registered office, and registered agent are available on the public file.
- The company's books may be kept anywhere in the world. A corporate seal is optional.

- Accounts do not have to be kept or filed.
- An annual return is also not required.
- There is no restriction on the holding of meetings.

Other Forms of Business Organization

Partnerships

The Niue legal system recognizes three forms of partnerships: the general partnership, the special partnership, and the limited liability partnership. The Partnership Amendment Act 1994 governs general and special partnerships, supplemented by the provisions of the Partnership Act 1908 that are not in conflict with the 1994 act. Part III of the Partnership Amendment Act 1994 governs limited liability partnerships.

The various types of partnerships may be distinguished according to the partners' liability. In the general partnership, all partners are jointly and severally liable for the partnership's obligations. In the special partnership, the general partner is liable for all obligations and the limited partner is liable only to the extent of his contribution. In a limited partnership, the partners each guarantee an amount of US$250, and their liability is limited to that amount.

The limited liability partnership is the only type of partnership of relevance to offshore operations. Such partnerships are required to be registered with the registrar of the high court. A registration fee of US$250 is payable, and an annual renewal fee of US$100 is payable thereafter. The application for registration must contain several guarantees from the partners to a minimum of US$250 each. There are no minimum capital requirements and no statutory accounting or auditing requirements. There are also no residency requirements.

Nonresident or offshore partners are not subject to tax in Niue, and distribution by the partnership will not be subject to Niue withholding tax or exchange controls.

Banks and Trust Companies

Banks

The Niue Bank was established as the central bank in terms of the Niue Bank Act 1994. The bank supervises the offshore financial sector and determines Niue's monetary policy. In addition, companies carrying on domestic banking activities must be registered by the Niue Bank under the Niue Bank Act 1994, and companies wishing to carry on offshore banking activities are required to obtain a license under the Offshore Banking Act 1994. The latter type of license may be granted only to international business companies or foreign incorporated companies.

In deciding whether to register a bank, the Niue Bank must consider the expertise of the applicant and, in the case of a company registered outside Niue, the extent of the regulatory requirements relating to the bank in its home jurisdiction.

An offshore bank must apply for an "A," "B," or "C" license under the Offshore Banking Act 1994. These licenses only entitle the holder to carry on offshore banking business. An A class license entitles the holder to carry on offshore banking business while maintaining a permanent establishment in Niue. A B class license entitles the holder to carry on offshore banking business provided that such business may be transacted only in specified currencies. In addition, the holder may transact business only through a Niue trustee company. A C class license entitles the holder to carry on offshore banking business with the restriction that he may not issue checks or drafts. All business of the licensee must be done with the knowledge of a director resident in Niue.

Licenses granted under the Offshore Banking Act 1994 must be renewed each year.

There are no capitalization requirements for a registered bank. However, when considering an application for registration, the Niue Bank must consider the size of the applicant's business, the applicant's ability to carry on its business in a prudent manner, and the standing of the applicant in the financial market. Specific capitalization requirements exist in respect of offshore license holders:

(a) A class A license holder that is not an IBC must have a surplus of tangible assets of not less than US$2.5 million. A class A license holder that is an IBC must have a paid-up capital of not less than US$2.5 million or a bank guarantee of not less than US$2.5 million.

(b) A class B license holder that is not an IBC must have a surplus of tangible assets of not less than US$500,000. A class B license holder that is an IBC must have a paid-up capital of not less than US$500,000 or a bank guarantee of not less than US$500,000.

(c) A class C license holder must be an IBC. It must have a paid-up capital of US$50,000 and must pay a deposit of US$5,000 to the government.

A registered bank must maintain fully audited financial statements. The information is open to public inspection. The holders of offshore banking licenses must file annual audited accounts with the Niue Bank.

A registered bank is liable to taxation in Niue. The holders of offshore banking licenses are expressly exempt from Niue taxes.

Trustee Companies

Companies carrying on trust business in Niue are governed by the Trustee Companies Act 1994. In addition, the Niue Bank is empowered to supervise their activities in terms of the Niue Bank Act 1994. Such companies must be registered under the Trustee Companies Act 1994. Only companies incorporated under the

Companies Act 1955 (New Zealand) or the International Business Companies Act 1994 may apply to be registered under the act.

Provisional registration is granted for two years, after which application to be registered permanently can be made. Registration is granted for one year and must be renewed annually. Every company making an application to be registered as a trustee company must have a minimum share capital of US$250,000. Once registered, a trustee company must be resident in Niue.

Accounts must be audited and must be submitted annually to the registrar of trustee companies. All registered trust companies are subject to taxation in Niue.

Insurance

Insurance activities in Niue are regulated by the Offshore Insurance Act 1994. In addition, the Niue Bank is empowered in terms of the Niue Bank Act 1994 to supervise the insurance sector.

A company wishing to carry on insurance or reinsurance business in Niue must apply to the Niue Bank for a license under the Offshore Insurance Act 1994. A license is not required in the following cases:

(a) if the business is between international business companies;

(b) if the companies are controlled by the same person; or

(c) if the companies have a relationship of parent and subsidiary.

Only an international business company or a foreign corporation may apply for a license. Licenses are renewable annually. To qualify for a license, an applicant must have a surplus of tangible assets over liabilities in excess of US$500,000.

The holder of an offshore insurance license must file audited accounts annually to the Niue Bank but is expressly exempt from taxation in Niue.

Trusts

Trusts are governed by the Trustee Act 1956 (New Zealand) and the Trusts Act 1994. Trusts established prior to the enactment of the Trusts Act 1994 continue to be governed by the Trustee Act 1956 (New Zealand) and have little relevance to offshore operations.

The Trusts Act 1994 codifies the English common law on trusts as well as incorporating various modern concepts. Trusts are required to be registered with the registrar of the high court. A registration fee of NZ$300 is payable. Entries in the register are confidential, unless the court orders disclosure where it is satisfied that the information is necessary for an investigation or prosecution of an offense such as drug trafficking or money laundering. There are no statutory capital requirements or accounting and auditing requirements.

A trust may be migrated out of Niue by appointing a trustee resident in another jurisdiction and changing the proper law of the trust. Similar procedures apply to trusts migrating to Niue. The Trusts Act 1994 contains specific entry and exit provisions in this regard.

Offshore trusts are governed by the Trusts Act 1994. They must be registered and are required to pay a registration fee of US$300.

Trustees of trusts established under the Trusts Act 1994 are not liable to tax. However, trust income of resident trusts established under the Trustee Act 1956 (New Zealand) is liable to tax.

Checklist for Trusts

- The maximum perpetuity period for noncharitable trusts is 120 years.
- A resident trustee is not required but in practice is usually appointed.
- Trusts must be registered.
- A registration fee of NZ$300 is charged.
- The law of trusts is based on English common law.
- The Hague Convention has been implemented.
- There is a specific "asset protection" provision (beyond that offered by general insolvency law) protecting a disposition to a trust from challenge by creditors.
- Provision is made for noncharitable purpose trusts.

CHAPTER FORTY-EIGHT

PANAMA

Background Information

Geographic and Demographic Data

Location	Panama is in Central America, between Costa Rica and Colombia. It is bordered by the Caribbean Sea and the North Pacific Ocean, and it is five hours behind GMT.
Capital	Panama City.
Area	30,193 square miles.
Population	2,693,417.
Languages	Spanish is the official language, but English is also widely spoken.
Access	Panama's international airport is served by many international carriers, with daily flights to most major centers in the world. The ports of Balboa and Cristobal are served by the major international shipping lines.
Telecommunications	Excellent.

Government

Panama is a constitutional democracy.

Political and Economic Stability

Because of its key geographic location, Panama's economy is service based, heavily weighted toward banking, commerce, and tourism. Panama's former protectionist policies have taken their toll, and the economy has been sluggish the past few years. Although the government has advanced an economic reform program designed to liberalize the trade regime, attract foreign investment, privatize state-owned enterprises, institute fiscal reform, and encourage job creation through Labor Code reform, the positive effects of this program have not yet been felt at the macroeconomic level. In 1996, the government concluded a Brady-type plan to restructure the country's commercial debt—one of the highest in the world in per capita terms—allowing it to reenter international financial markets. Panama also completed all requirements to join the World Trade Organization and is awaiting legislative ratification to become a full member. Unemployment runs at 14%.

Business Environment

Government attitude to offshore activities: The Panamanian government actively encourages foreign investment and free enterprise.

Local business requirements: There are no joint venture requirements for foreigners. The only restriction on foreign business activities is that only Panamanians may carry out retail business.

Currency and Exchange Control

The local currency is the balboa, but it is not available in denominations over US$1.00. As a result of a bilateral agreement with the United States, the dollar is the legal tender in Panama and circulates freely. The balboa is at par with the U.S. dollar. There is no central bank and no exchange control.

Disclosure of Information

Banking secrecy: Banking secrecy is insured under the Banking Law, which penalizes government officials who disclose information without authorization. There is a code of confidentiality regarding the secrecy of clients' affairs, and numbered accounts are possible. However, where criminal investigations are being undertaken in Panama, confidentiality may be pierced. The new Banking Law of 1998 provides that banks must disclose the identity of clients and the nature of their transactions to the Superintendence of Banks where their assets are under investigation by the Superintendence.

Disclosure in company formation and trust settlement: Disclosure of beneficial ownership need not be made on formation of a Panamanian corporation. No other information is required by the authorities. The Commercial Code, articles 88 and 89, and the Penal Code, article 170, govern confidentiality. Companies are also not required to be audited.

A local registered agent is required but a local registered office is not. No information need be lodged with the agent. The agent would only disclose beneficial ownership if required by a prosecutor investigating a criminal act perpetrated in Panama relating to drug trafficking or money laundering.

A trustee is not required to register the beneficiaries of a trust. In addition, a company or trustee opening a bank account does not have to disclose beneficial ownership or the beneficiaries. However, limited partnerships and limited liability companies do have to disclose the names of their members.

International cooperation measures: Panama has entered into several mutual legal assistance agreements. The procedures for cooperation with foreign states in terms of these treaties preclude the need for letters rogatory to be sent to the Supreme Court and provide for a Central Authority to facilitate the submission of evidence. Provision is made for appeal against the cooperation procedure. Treaties have been entered into with the United States, Costa Rica, El Salvador, Guatemala, Honduras, Nicaragua, and Colombia.

Foreign judgments are enforced by the *exequatur* mechanism, contained in article 1409 of the Judicial Code. In terms of this procedure, the sentence issued by a foreign court is sent to the Panamanian Supreme Court through diplomatic channels. The court then accepts or rejects the sentence.

Panama has not entered into any double taxation treaties. The mutual legal assistance treaties listed above contain limited exchange of information provisions. Information exchange is restricted to information extracted from the carrying out of prosecution procedures, not including tax matters.

Anti–money laundering provisions are contained in Law 23 of December 30, 1986. The law does not cover fiscal crime.

The local authorities would not grant a request for assistance in an investigation into tax evasion. A request for cooperation would have to be made by petition.

Legal System

General

Panama is a civil law jurisdiction. The basic statutes are the Civil Code and the Commercial Code.

Treaties

Panama has not entered into any double taxation treaties with other countries. It has signed an investment treaty with China, in terms of which the Panamanian government protects the investments of Chinese citizens in Panama. Panama has also entered into mutual legal assistance treaties with the United States, Costa Rica, El Salvador, Guatemala, Honduras, Nicaragua, and Colombia.

Taxation (Direct and Indirect)

Income Tax

As Panama has adopted the territorial principle of taxation, income tax is levied only on income derived from operations within Panama. In terms of the Fiscal Code, article 694, the following income is expressly excluded:

(a) invoicing from an office in Panama the sale of merchandise for a sum greater than that for which it was invoiced against such office, provided the merchandise only moves outside of Panama;
(b) directing operations outside of Panama from an office in Panama; and
(c) distribution of dividends derived from income not arising in Panama, including income from the activities listed in (a) and (b) above.

Thus, a Panama corporation that has an office in Panama, employees in Panama, and a license to do business in Panama will not pay tax in Panama if the office merely directs purchases and sales that are completed abroad. A corporation that engages in business both within and outside of Panama will be taxed only on the portion of income arising in Panama.

Income tax is charged at a flat rate of 30% for all corporations. Individuals are charged on a sliding scale.

Business Tax

An annual business tax is levied at a flat rate of 1% of the net worth of the business, up to a maximum of US$20,000. The tax does not apply to Colon Free Zone companies or to offshore companies. There is also a municipal tax levied on businesses, which varies according to the nature of the business and the municipality concerned.

Capital Gains Tax

Capital gains from the sale of real estate in Panama are subject to tax, based on the amount left after the purchase price and cost of improvements have been deducted from the sale price. There is also an allowance of 10% of the basic cost per annum. The gain is divided by the number of years of ownership. The resulting amount is then added to the seller's taxable income to determine the rate at which the gains will be taxed.

Stamp Duties

Contracts that are executed and performed in Panama and checks and bills of exchange are subject to stamp duties that may be fixed or ad valorem, depending on the type of document. Stamp duty is not levied on contracts that are to be performed elsewhere.

Withholding Taxes

Dividends are taxed at a flat rate of 10% where they are paid to holders of nominative shares and a flat rate of 20% where they are paid to holders of bearer shares. The income from which the distribution is made must have arisen in Panama. Dividends that are so taxed are not included in the stockholders' taxable income.

Inheritance and Gift Taxes

There are no inheritance taxes in Panama.

Gifts of property situated in Panama that are made *inter vivos* are subject to tax at varying rates, depending on the degree of kinship between the donor and the donee. The rates are between 4% on US$4,000 of value if the gift is made to a next of kin and 33.75% on over US$400,000 of value if the gift is made to an individual removed by more than four degrees of consanguinity.

Real Estate Taxes

An annual property tax is levied on real estate situated in Panama. The tax is based on official valuations and ranges from 1.4% on the first US$10,000 of value to 2.1% on value over US$75,000.

A flat rate transfer tax of 2% is levied on the transfer of realty. This amount is credited to the capital gains tax discussed above.

Sales Taxes

The transfer of personalty, whether by way of sale, rental, or gift, is subject to sales tax. The rate is 5%. Certain goods are excepted, such as foodstuffs, medicines, and imports into the Colon Free Zone.

Import Duties

Import duties are imposed at varying rates on certain goods imported into Panama. The rates are published by the Council of Ministers.

Social Security Tax

Employees make a social security contribution of 7.25% of their salaries, and employers contribute 10.75%. There is also a 2% education tax levied on salaries, of which the employer contributes 0.25% and the employee the remainder.

Tax Incentives

See "Tax Incentives" under "Incentives (Tax and Nontax)."

Incentives (Tax and Nontax)

Tax Incentives

In terms of Law 3 of 1986, Panama offers the following incentives to investment in industrial activities:

(a) full exemption from import duties and sales tax on machinery and equipment used in the manufacturing process;

(b) full exemption from income tax, except regarding activities that exploit natural resources;
(c) full exemption from export tax;
(d) full exemption from sales tax;
(e) full exemption from capital duty, except regarding license fees and real estate taxes; and
(f) partial exemption from restrictions in the Labor Code.

A company that is registered with the official registry for national industry will normally qualify automatically for the above incentives.

The above incentives have been granted continued validity in terms of Law 28 of 1995, which offers the following further incentives:

(a) full exemption from income taxes till December 31, 2002, with regard to export activities;
(b) a uniform fixed import rate on materials and assets required for manufacturing; and
(c) tax credits till December 31, 2002, to companies involved in the development of technological infrastructure.

The Colon Free Zone

The Colon Free Zone is in a specially designated area in the city of Colon on the Atlantic entrance to the Panama Canal. The zone was created by Law 18 of June 17, 1948, and there are over 1,000 companies established there, handling more than US$9 billion of shipments annually.

The law defines the permissible activities in the Colon Free Zone as follows:

> To bring in, store, display, unpack, manufacture, put in containers, mount, assemble, refine, purify, blend, alter, and, in general, carry out operations with and handle all kinds of merchandise, products, raw materials, containers, and other articles of commerce, with the sole exception of articles the importation of which is prohibited by the laws of Panama.

Companies in the Colon Free Zone may sell wholesale to foreign countries (external operations) or to Panamanian businesses (internal operations). However, as the principal purpose of the Colon Free Zone was to establish a base for companies to engage in external operations, most operations now carried out are external, principally, the reexport of merchandise.

As of January 1, 1997, companies established in the Colon Free Zone are exempted from all taxes, including income tax. Income resulting from internal operations is taxed at the normal rates. Withholding tax on dividends is generally not applicable to Colon Free Zone companies on the distribution of profits derived from external operations. However, distribution of dividends from profits derived from internal operations will be subject to dividends tax. Employees in the Colon Free Zone are subject to income tax and social security contributions at current rates on their salaries.

Colon Free Zone companies carrying out both internal and external operations must maintain separate accounting for both kinds of operations.

Export Processing Zones

Since 1992, regulations have created special tax, licensing, and labor incentives for the operation of export processing zones. Concessions may be obtained for businesses wishing to establish and operate special export processing zones in any part of Panama. The intention is to attract export-oriented businesses that will take advantage of the extensive real estate facilities being turned over to Panama with the implementation of the 1977 Panama Canal Treaties.

All activities and transactions, including the transfer of movables or immovables, the importation of equipment or raw materials, as well as all services required for the operation of the zones, are exempt from tax. The transfer of assets between companies located in the special processing zones is also deemed to be an export operation and is exempted from taxation. In addition, interests and dividends paid by shares, bonds, and other securities issued by companies established in the special processing zones, as well as gains realized on their sale or disposition, are also exempted from taxation.

Corporations

Panama is a well-established jurisdiction for offshore corporations that has acquired a high reputation over the years. The legal and professional infrastructure is excellent, and the professionals within Panama have marketed the jurisdiction actively and aggressively over an extended period. It is also a well-known flag of convenience for shipping purposes. However, Panama is one of the few non–English language international offshore financial centers.

Types of Corporations

The Commercial Code and the Corporation Law 1927 provide for joint stock partnerships, which are limited partnerships where the partners' capital is represented by shares; limited liability companies, where the members' liability is limited to their share of the capital; and Panamanian corporations (*sociedades anónimas*), which are the most common vehicles for offshore operations.

Migration and Redomiciliation

A foreign corporation may be continued in Panama as a Panama corporation, and it may change its corporate seat to Panama if the law of its country of origin permits it to do so.

Checklist for Corporations

- The corporation's name may be in any language but must end with a word or abbreviation such as *Corporation* or *SA*.
- Incorporation takes three days. Shelf companies are available. No information is required prior to incorporation.
- There is no required minimum capital, but the usual authorized capital is US$10,000.
- A registration fee of US$60.20 is payable on a capital of US$10,000. A sliding scale operates for amounts above this.
- At least two subscribers are required, but after incorporation only one ongoing shareholder is necessary. Bearer shares and shares of no par value are permitted.
- At least three directors are necessary. Corporate directors are not allowed, and there is no restriction on the directors' location.
- A company secretary is mandatory. Corporate secretaries are not allowed, and there is no restriction on the secretary's location.
- A corporation must have a registered agent but need not have a registered office in Panama. No documents are required to be kept by the agent.
- The deed of incorporation, names and addresses of the directors, and the registered agent are available on the public file.
- A minute book and stock register must be kept at any location in the world. There is no need for a corporate seal.
- Accounts do not have to be maintained or filed.
- An annual return is also not required.
- There is no restriction on the holding of meetings.
- An annual franchise duty of US$150 is payable.

Other Forms of Business Organization

Partnerships and Joint Ventures

The Commercial Code recognizes general partnerships. General partnerships are those in which the liability of the partners is unlimited. The Limited Liability Partnership Law 1966 provides for limited partnerships, those in which the general or managing partners are jointly and severally liable for the partnership's debts and the limited partners are liable only to the extent of their capital contributions. Participatory accounts or joint ventures are also possible, in terms of which two or more individuals or companies form a joint venture by private agreement. The business is conducted by one member on behalf of himself and the other members, and the profits and liabilities are distributed as per the agreement. Liability to third parties is unlimited.

Private Foundations

Unlike the common law trust, a private foundation created under the Private Foundation Law 1995 is an autonomous legal entity, without members or shareholders. A private foundation may not have a profit motive or conduct business activities. Private foundations are generally used as asset protection vehicles.

The foundation charter must be registered at the public registry. There is a minimum capital requirement of US$10,000. The founder must appoint at least three members of the Foundation Council, who will administer the property of the foundation on behalf of the beneficiaries. Accounts do not have to be maintained or filed, and an audit is not required. Only income generated within Panama is subject to income tax in Panama.

There are no forced heirship laws in Panama and no estate duties. Therefore, to the extent that Panamanian law is applicable to the foundation, the foundation, founder, and beneficiaries will not be subject to testamentary limitations or taxes in Panama.

Private foundations may be transferred to other jurisdictions, if this is provided for in their foundation charter. Foundations created under the laws of another jurisdiction may likewise migrate to Panama.

Foundations are subject to the annual franchise duty of US$150. In addition, the resident agent will charge an annual fee of between US$150 and US$250. Costs relating to the registration of the foundation charter are as follows:

Stamp duty	US$75
Notarial fees	US$70
Translation costs, if the charter is in a language other than Spanish	US$50

Capital duty on the first US$10,000 is US$60. Thereafter, it is charged on a sliding scale.

Foreign Corporations

A foreign corporation may establish a branch or agency in Panama and engage in business in Panama provided it registers the following documents at the public registry:

(a) articles of incorporation;

(b) a resolution authorizing its registration in Panama;

(c) copies of the most recent financial statements;

(d) a certificate of validity in its country of origin, authenticated by the Panamanian Consul; and
(e) the portion of capital assigned to the branch or agency.

Registration duty is payable on the portion of capital assigned to the Panama operation. Foreign corporations are also subject to the annual franchise duty of US$150.

Banks

Panama has traditionally been regarded as an international banking center. Its development as such has been encouraged by the absence of exchange controls, the absence of a central bank, the free circulation of the U.S. dollar, and the territorial principle of taxation. The banking regime was changed by the introduction of Decree Law 9 of February 1998, which implements the principles of the Basle Accord. The new law allows banks to establish their own interest rates without limitation or restriction on loans or deposits. It also replaces the National Banking Commission with the Superintendence of Banks. The Superintendence is not a central bank but is the agency responsible for controlling Panama's banking system. The Superintendence is also responsible for granting banking licenses. There are three types of banking licenses:

(i) the general license, for banks that are authorized to engage in banking business both in Panama and elsewhere;
(ii) the international license, for offshore business only; and
(iii) the representation license, for banks organized under foreign law that maintain representation offices in Panama.

To apply for the appropriate license, the following documents and information must be filed with the Superintendence:

(a) the articles of incorporation;
(b) the resolution of the board of directors stating the amount of capital set aside for the operation in Panama;
(c) a copy of the last balance sheet certified by a public accountant;
(d) certification from the appropriate authorities at the place of incorporation (in the case of foreign banks) to the effect that it has been validly constituted in accordance with the laws of that place;
(e) a business plan and feasibility study;
(f) certification from the banking authority of the jurisdiction where the head office is incorporated as to its good standing and license to carry on banking activities;

(g) a power of attorney in favor of two individuals enabling them severally to represent the bank, one of whom must be a Panama national and both of whom must be residents of Panama; and

(h) a certified check in favor of the National Banking Commission in the amount of US$1,000 in the case of a general license and in the amount of US$500 in the case of an international license or representation license.

An international license allows a bank to conduct offshore banking business from an office in Panama. The bank must maintain a sum of not less than US$500,000 at all times in Panama.

A bank's tax liability will depend on the nature of the business. As Panamanian income tax is territorially based, only banks operating under a general license are liable to tax, and then only as to profits arising within Panama. Loans made from Panama to be used outside of Panama are not considered local operations. As a result, the interest earned on them is not subject to tax. Interest paid on deposits made with any bank in Panama is specifically exempted from income tax to further attract deposits to Panama.

Banks operating under a general license must maintain separate accounting records for their local and offshore operations since they are subject to tax only on their local operations.

Insurance

Captive Insurance Companies

Captive insurance companies are companies that are authorized by the superintendent of insurance and reinsurance of the Ministry of Commerce and Industry of Panama to insure or reinsure foreign risks from an office in Panama. A captive insurance company must obtain a license from the superintendent of insurance and reinsurance. The following documents must be submitted with the application:

(a) articles of incorporation, a good-standing certificate, a resolution of the board of directors authorizing the opening of an office in Panama, appointing a resident manager or "attorney-in-fact," and authorizing the amount of capital to be used to carry out business in Panama;

(b) banking and personal letters of reference for all shareholders and directors of the company;

(c) the company's official address and the name of the resident manager or attorney-in-fact;

(d) a technical report, which must state the types of risks to be insured or reinsured and the insurance or reinsurance activities to be undertaken; and

(e) a certified check for US$1,000 to cover administrative and due diligence expenses of the superintendent.

A registration fee of US$1,000 is payable, and thereafter a license fee of US$2,000 is payable annually to the superintendent.

A company that intends to carry out the insurance of general risks must have a paid-up capital of US$150,000. A company that intends to carry out the insurance of long-term risks must have a paid-up capital of US$250,000.

As a captive insurance company can only insure or reinsure foreign risks, the premiums received by the company in Panama are not subject to income tax and the income earned by the company for offshore insurance and reinsurance activities is tax-exempt. Similarly, dividends paid by captive insurance companies to their shareholders are not subject to income or dividends withholding tax because those dividends are earned from offshore activities. Captives must, however, pay an annual general corporate tax of US$150.

Shipping

Panama is one of the most prominent vessel registries. Any natural or legal person may register a vessel in Panama, regardless of his nationality or domicile. There are also no restrictions as to age, type, or size of the vessel. In addition, the definition of *vessel* is wide enough to include a variety of floating structures, including platforms and drilling rigs that are not considered to be vessels by other jurisdictions.

Vessels are taxed on their net and gross registered tonnage rather than on an earned income basis. Further, as income tax is territorially based, income derived by Panama-registered vessels from international trade is not subject to income tax.

Registration

Once a vessel is provisionally registered or flagged in Panama, a provisional patent, valid for six months, and a radio permit, valid for three months, will be issued. Both documents are renewable. The patent costs US$500 and is renewable at US$50 per month. The radio permit costs US$150 quarterly. Thereafter, the ship is permanently documented and issued with a regulation patent of navigation, which is valid for a renewable four-year period, except in the case of pleasure yachts, in which case the registration is granted for renewable two-year periods.

Provisional registration is effected through lawyers in Panama. The following information is required:

(a) the ship's name;

(b) the owner's name and address outside Panama;

(c) the previous nationality of the ship;

(d) the place and date of construction;

(e) the builder's name;

(f) the number of decks, masts, and chimneys;

(g) the type of vessel;
(h) the hull material;
(i) the service;
(j) the length, width, and height;
(k) the gross and net tonnages;
(l) the type of engine, number, and name of manufacturer;
(m) the number of cylinders;
(n) the horsepower;
(o) the speed;
(p) unless the vessel is not an oceangoing vessel, the name and complete address of the company responsible for the radio charges, to be chosen from the list of qualified radio accounting agencies, such as ITT MacKay, Debeg GmbH, Radio Holland BV, Kyoritsu Radio Service Co. Limited, etc.;
(q) the name of the classification society, such as Lloyd's Register of Shipping, the American Bureau of Shipping, Bureau Veritas, Det Norske Veritas, Nippon Kaiji Kyokai, etc.; and
(r) the International Maritime Organization (IMO) number for the vessel.

A registration fee based on gross registered tons (GRT) is payable upon provisional registration as follows:

Up to 2,000 GRT	US$500
From 2,001 GRT to 5,000 GRT	US$2,000
From 5,001 GRT to 15,000 GRT	US$3,000
Over 15,000 GRT	US$3,000 plus US$0.10 per GRT or fraction thereof up to a maximum of US$6,500

The following duties are payable annually:

(a) Consular Tasa

For vessels engaged in maritime commerce, the duties are as follows:

Up to 1,000 GRT	US$1,200
From 1,001 GRT to 3,000 GRT	US$1,800
From 3,001 GRT to 5,000 GRT	US$2,000
From 5,001 GRT to 15,000 GRT	US$2,700
Over 15,000 GRT	US$3,000

For barges, pontoons, and vessels dedicated to scientific research or other nonprofit, noncommercial activity, the duties are as follows:

Up to 500 GRT	US$850
From 501 GRT to 1,000 GRT	US$1,400
Over 1,000 GRT	US$1,800

(b) Annual Inspection Tasa, which ranges between US$500 and US$1,800 depending on the type of vessel and gross registered tonnage

(c) Tasa for Accident Investigation and Government Participation in International Treaties and Conferences

For tankers, drilling rigs, passenger ships, gas carriers, and chemical transports, the duty is US$850 plus US$0.03 per net registered ton.

For other vessels, the duties are as follows:

Up to 500 GRT	US$300 plus $0.03 per net ton
From 501 GRT to 10,000 GRT	US$400 plus $0.03 per net ton
Over 10,000 GRT	US$500 plus $0.03 per net ton

Pleasure vessels, non-self-propelled vessels, and other vessels used for nonprofit activities are exempted.

For permanent registration to be granted, the following documents must be submitted to the Panama Bureau general of consular affairs and shipping at the time of the provisional registration or within thirty days thereafter:

(a) a power of attorney in favor of lawyers in Panama to act as the legal representatives of the vessel;

(b) a bill of sale, or builder's certificate in the case of a new construction, and acceptance of title;

(c) the deletion certificate of the vessel from the previous registry, where applicable;

(d) the admeasurement or international tonnage certificate and a class certificate issued by an authorized classification or surveyor agency; and

(e) a special inspection if the vessel is twenty years old or more.

Registration of Ships under Charter

Charterers of vessels registered elsewhere may register them in Panama for renewable two-year periods, provided that the country where the vessel is registered grants its consent. No bills of sale or other evidence of title or liens may be registered in Panama in respect of such vessels. Registration costs US$150 plus US$0.20 per GRT or fraction thereof.

Pleasure Vessels

Registration of pleasure boats costs US$1,500. This fee will be reduced to US$1,000 if the shipowner is a Panama national. The registration fee is payable on provisional registration and every two years thereafter on renewal of the patent of navigation. No other fees are charged with respect to pleasure vessels.

Trusts

The Trust Law 1984 was passed to update Panama's law of trusts and incorporate modern concepts. There are no registration requirements and no capital requirements. A trust will be exempt from Panamanian tax provided it involves

(a) real property located abroad;

(b) money deposited by persons, whether natural or juridical, whose income is not derived from Panamanian sources or taxed in Panama; or

(c) stock issued by corporations whose income does not arise in Panama, although the stock may be deposited in Panama.

A Panamanian trust may migrate to another jurisdiction if this is provided for in the trust deed. Foreign trusts may be governed by Panamanian law if this is provided for in the trust deed and Panamanian formalities are complied with.

Any breach of confidentiality with regard to a trust-related transaction may be penalized with up to six months' imprisonment and a fine of up to US$50,000.

Checklist for Trusts

- There is no statutory schedule of standard trust powers.
- There is an unlimited perpetuity period for noncharitable trusts.
- A resident trustee is not required.
- The trust must be registered only if land is held.
- Trust documents may be in English or Spanish.
- There is no registration fee or stamp duty payable.
- The law of trusts has a civil law background.
- The Hague Convention has not been implemented.
- Specific provision has not been made for the exclusion of foreign inheritance laws.
- There is no specific provision dealing with the nonrecognition of foreign judgments.
- There is no specific "asset protection" provision (beyond that offered by general insolvency law) protecting a disposition to a trust from challenge by creditors.

- There is no special statute of limitations period for creditors' claims.
- Provision is made for noncharitable purpose trusts.

CHAPTER FORTY-NINE

SAMOA

Background Information

Geographic and Demographic Data

Location	Samoa is a group of islands in the South Pacific Ocean, halfway between Hawaii and New Zealand. It is eleven hours behind GMT.
Capital	Apia.
Area	1,100 square miles.
Population	219,509.
Languages	The official language is Samoan, although English is widely used in the commercial sector.
Access	Direct flights are available to destinations in New Zealand, Australia, Hawaii, Fiji, and Tonga, with ongoing connections to other international centers.
Telecommunications	Excellent.

Government

Samoa is a constitutional monarchy. It is a member of the Commonwealth.

Political and Economic Stability

Samoa is a stable democracy with a written constitution and a parliamentary system based on the Westminster model. One of the four paramount chiefs is head of state.

The economy of Samoa has traditionally been dependent on development aid, private family remittances from overseas, and agricultural exports. However, tourism is becoming a significant source of revenue. While registering an overall economic improvement, the country continues to struggle with the results of a series of natural disasters in the early 1990s that wiped out the nation's infrastructure as well as its then major export crop, taro root. Agriculture continues to be a key source of wealth for Apia, employing more than one-half of the labor force and furnishing 90% of exports. The bulk of these export earnings comes from the sale of coconut cream, coconut oil, and copra. Family remittances also play a key role in economic viability for the island nation—in 1995, remittances totaled $34.9 million, four times export earnings.

Business Environment

The government of Samoa actively encourages foreign investment and grants concessions and incentives to enterprises that will enhance economic development. Samoa also has strong links with the major Pacific Rim centers.

A business license is required to carry on business in Samoa. The fee depends on the nature of the business conducted.

Currency and Exchange Control

The local currency is the tala. Exchange control is regulated by the Central Bank. The bank's approval must be obtained for direct investment into Samoa and for overseas borrowing by a resident of Samoa. The remittance of dividends, profits, interest, royalties, and other payments out of the country is not restricted, although Central Bank approval is required. Approval will generally be granted unless the foreign currency is not available.

Disclosure of Information

Banking secrecy: Banking secrecy and confidentiality are governed by the Financial Institutions Act of 1996 and the Offshore Banking Act of 1987.

Secrecy of information: The offshore sector has strong confidentiality provisions, and penal sanctions apply to government officials and professionals who breach client confidentiality. Offshore registries are not open to the public, although the registrar will allow searches of international companies' memorandums and articles of association on request and provided that confidentiality is insured.

Disclosure in company formation and trust settlement: Disclosure of beneficial ownership is not required on formation of an international company, but companies applying for an offshore banking or insurance license must disclose beneficial ownership to the registrar as part of the application process. No other information is required. Confidentiality provisions relating to offshore operations are contained in the International Companies Act 1987, the Offshore Banking Act 1987, the International Trusts Act 1987, the Trustee Companies Act 1987, and the International Insurance Act 1988.

In general, international companies are not required to be audited, although licensed offshore banks, international insurance companies, and trustee companies must submit annual audited accounts to the government regulator. International companies must have a registered office in Samoa at which the register of directors and secretaries and the register of debentures must be lodged. Information will be disclosed in this regard only under an order of the Supreme Court of Samoa. Information can also be disclosed by the registered agent to the minister of finance if it is in the best interests of Samoa to uphold the integrity of the jurisdiction as an international offshore financial center.

A trustee is not required to register the beneficiaries of a trust. In addition, a company or trustee opening a bank account does not have to disclose beneficial ownership or the beneficiaries. The same provisions apply to limited partnerships in terms of the draft International Partnership and Limited Partnership Bill.

International cooperation measures: Samoa does not have any formal procedure for cooperation with foreign investigators, but there is a high level of contact within the financial community, regulator to regulator. The regulator is subject to stringent confidentiality provisions. There is also no legislation governing the exchange of information between states, although draft amendments to the Offshore Banking Act 1987 and the International Insurance Act 1988 include gateway provisions for disclosure between regulators for the purposes of the regulators only.

Foreign judgments are enforced under the Reciprocal Enforcement of Judgments Act 1970, in terms of which the foreign judgment can be registered in Samoa and enforced as a judgment of the Supreme Court of Samoa. The act does not apply to judgments obtained in respect of taxes or related charges and at present applies only to judgments granted in the superior courts of New Zealand and Western Australia.

Samoa has not entered into any double taxation agreements or mutual legal assistance treaties.

The Samoan authorities would not cooperate or assist in the investigation of tax-related matters in other jurisdictions.

Legal System

General

The legal system is based on English common law and local custom, with some input from New Zealand statutes.

Legislation

The principal provisions affecting offshore operations and transactions are contained in the following:

- Financial Institutions Act 1996
- International Companies Act 1987

- International Insurance Act 1988
- International Trusts Act 1987
- Offshore Banking Act 1987
- Trustee Companies Act 1987

Case Law

An important recent case is *Commercial Bank Platina v. Mytischinki Bank* (1997/1998) 1 OFLR 697 (Supreme Court, Samoa).

Treaties

Samoa has not entered into any double taxation agreements with other countries.

Taxation (Direct and Indirect)

International companies and foreign companies registered under the International Companies Act 1987 are exempt from all taxes in Samoa.

Income Tax

Under the Income Tax Act 1974, Samoan domestic companies are liable to tax on their worldwide income. Nonresident companies incorporated under the Domestic Companies Order 1935 are taxed on their income arising in Samoa only. A corporation is resident in Samoa for tax purposes if it is incorporated in Samoa or has its head office in Samoa. The corporate tax rate for resident companies operating in the domestic jurisdiction is 39%; for nonresident companies operating in the domestic jurisdiction, it is 48%.

Capital Gains Tax

There is no capital gains tax in Samoa.

Stamp Duties

Legal documents executed in Samoa are subject to stamp duty at varying rates.

Withholding Taxes

International and foreign companies are exempt from withholding taxes. Withholding taxes are imposed on dividends, interest, or royalties paid to nonresidents by domestic corporations at the rate of 15%, and in some cases, payments to residents also attract withholding taxes at the rate of 10%. Intercompany dividend payments attract withholding tax of 10%.

Goods and Services Tax

Accommodation, entertainment, food, and liquor are subject to a goods and services tax levied at the rate of 10%.

Import Duties

Most goods that are imported into Samoa are subject to customs duty at varying rates.

Tax Incentives

See "Incentives (Tax and Nontax)."

Incentives (Tax and Nontax)

Incentives are granted under the Enterprises Incentives Act 1965 and the Industrial Free Zone Act. They are granted to both local and foreign investors in the form of tax holidays, tax concessions, exemptions from import duty, concessions on building equipment and raw materials, and relief from withholding taxes.

Corporations

(The domestic laws of Samoa refer to *corporations* as *companies*. This terminology is retained in this chapter.)

Samoa offers international companies incorporated in the jurisdiction the option of paying government fees five, ten, or twenty years in advance. No additional fees are imposed on companies with large authorized share capital, and the certificate of incorporation may be written in Chinese characters if desired. However, Samoa is far ahead of the European time zone and its infrastructure is fairly basic.

Types of Companies

Companies may be either incorporated or registered under the Domestic Companies Order 1935 or the International Companies Act 1987. A company incorporated under the Domestic Companies Order 1935 must file its memorandum and articles of association with the registrar of companies and pay an incorporation fee based on its authorized capital. It must also apply for a business license and renew the license annually. Domestic companies are subject to all taxes in Samoa, and nonresident companies registered under the order are subject to Samoan taxes on all Samoan sourced income.

The International Companies Act 1987 provides for the incorporation of international companies and the registration of foreign companies. Limited life international companies are also possible under the act. International companies may carry on any lawful business activity, except that companies carrying on banking, insurance, or trustee company business must be duly licensed to do so.

The International Companies Amendment Act of 1998, which came into force on July 17, 1998, provides for companies limited by guarantee, and hybrid companies limited by shares and guarantee. The act also provides for the redomiciliation of companies into Samoa without the need for the consent of the home jurisdiction.

Migration and Redomiciliation

Companies that are incorporated outside Samoa may transfer their domicile to Samoa, and companies incorporated under the International Companies Act 1987 may transfer domicile to any jurisdiction that permits redomiciliation.

Checklist for International Companies

- Prior approval of the company name is required. Names can be in any language.
- Incorporation takes one day. Shelf companies are available. Banks, trust companies, and insurance companies are required to furnish information to the authorities prior to incorporation.
- There is no minimum capital requirement and no capital duty.
- At least one shareholder is required. Bearer shares are permitted, but shares of no par value are not.
- At least one director is required. Corporate directors are allowed, and there is no restriction on the directors' place of residence.
- A company secretary is mandatory. Corporate secretaries are allowed, and there is no restriction on the secretary's location.
- International companies must have a local registered office and agent in Samoa. Copies of the registers must be kept at the local office.
- The memorandum and articles of association and registered office and agent are available on the public file.
- Corporate books and a seal are required but may be kept anywhere.
- Accounts need not be kept or filed.
- Annual returns are also not required.
- There is no restriction on the holding of meetings.
- An annual fee of US$300 is payable to the government.

Other Forms of Business Organization

Partnerships

The International Partnership Act of 1998 and Limited Partnership Act of 1998 provide for the creation of new tax-exempt statutory investment vehicles. Both must have all nonresident partners and must not carry on business or engage in trade in Samoa and must have at least one general partner that is an international, foreign, or trustee company registered in Samoa. English common law continues to apply to international partnerships except where there are inconsistencies with the new Act. Registration and annual fees are US$150 per annum.

Foreign Companies

Foreign companies may be registered under the International Companies Act 1987 instead of as overseas companies under the Domestic Companies Order 1935. Registration is necessary if the company has a permanent establishment or is carrying on business in Samoa. The following documents must be lodged with the registrar of companies:

(a) a copy of the certificate of incorporation;

(b) copies of the memorandum and articles of association;

(c) a list of directors;

(d) a memorandum of appointment of power of attorney to a trustee company;

(e) the address of the registered office; and

(f) a declaration of the authorized capital.

Registration entitles the foreign company to full tax exemption.

Licensing Companies

As Samoa is an English common law jurisdiction, it recognizes and provides for intellectual property rights. International companies incorporated under the International Companies Act 1987 may hold intellectual property rights, copyrights, patents, and trademarks, and the income from these rights may be accumulated free of tax. Royalties are not taxed, and there are no capital gains taxes and no requirements as to arm's length transactions or valuations in respect of the transfer of intellectual property rights to or from the international company.

Trusts

The International Trusts Act 1987 governs international trusts, which are required to be registered in terms of the act. International trusts have no tax liability in

Samoa, and there is no requirement regarding the filing of records, returns, or reports. On the contrary, resident trusts need not be registered, but the trustees must pay tax on the trust's worldwide income. There are no formal accounting or auditing requirements for trusts in Samoa.

Registration of an international trust is effected by the trustee company making application to the registrar of international trusts and certifying that there is a trust deed in existence whose registration will bring the trust within the ambit of the International Trusts Act. Registration must be renewed annually upon payment of a fee. The registry is not open to inspection by the public.

The International Trusts Act alters the common law in regard to the rules restricting the extent of charitable purposes and the rules against purpose trusts.

Migration of a trust may be effected by altering the residence of the trustee. Trustee companies must be registered under the Trustee Companies Act 1987.

Checklist for International Trusts

- There is no statutory schedule of standard trust powers.
- The maximum perpetuity period is life plus twenty-one years.
- At least one resident trustee is required.
- Registration of the trust is compulsory.
- Trust documents are normally in English.
- A registration fee of US$150 is charged.
- The law of trusts is based on English common law.
- The Hague Convention has not been implemented in Samoa.
- Specific provision has not been made for the exclusion of foreign inheritance laws.
- There is no specific provision dealing with the nonrecognition of foreign judgments.
- There is specific "asset protection" provision (beyond that offered by general insolvency law) protecting a disposition to a trust from challenge by creditors.
- There is no special statute of limitations period for creditors' claims.
- Provision is made for noncharitable purpose trusts.

CHAPTER FIFTY

SWITZERLAND

Background Information

Geographic and Demographic Data

Location	Switzerland is situated in central Europe, east of France and north of Italy. It is one hour ahead of GMT.
Capital	Bern.
Area	16,516 square miles.
Population	7,260,357.
Languages	Switzerland is a multilingual country, with German, French, Italian, and Romansch being spoken. English is also widely used.
Access	Switzerland has excellent railway and freeway systems, and the airports at Zurich, Geneva, and Basle provide daily flights to European and other international destinations. Inland water traffic handles about 40% of Swiss foreign trade, with daily shipments reaching Belgium, Holland, Germany, and France via a system of lakes, rivers, and canals.
Telecommunications	Excellent.

Government

Switzerland is a federal republic divided into 26 cantons. Since 1815 it has pursued a policy of armed neutrality, linked with a readiness to collaborate with all nations, although it is not a member of the United Nations or the European Union.

Political and Economic Stability

Switzerland is a fundamentally prosperous and stable modern economy, oriented toward foreign trade. Its per capita GDP is about 10% above that of the other major West European economies, although it has recently experienced some difficulties.

Its leading sectors include financial services, biotechnology, pharmaceuticals, watch-making, and special-purpose machines. The unemployment rate is 5%.

Switzerland has been Europe's most stable economy for fifty years and has enjoyed a century and a half of political peace, both on the domestic and international fronts.

Business Environment

Government attitude to offshore activities: Flowing from its policy of neutrality, Switzerland is traditionally hospitable to foreign investment.

Employment: The scarcity of workers in Switzerland is a major constraint on the expansion of domestic production and contributes to the inflationary problem currently being experienced. The acute labor shortage is exacerbated by the difficulty foreign workers experience in obtaining work permits. When it is impossible to obtain Swiss work permits, some executives resort to living in France near the Swiss border and obtaining frontier work permits enabling them to commute to work in Geneva.

Foreigners and Immigration

The acquisition of Swiss nationality by foreigners is a complex procedure, requiring residency of at least 12 years. There are simplified naturalization procedures in special cases. A foreigner must have authorization before taking up residency in Switzerland. Resident foreigners may now freely acquire their homes, but nonresident foreigners require permission to do so. There are no longer restrictions on the acquisition of commercial property for business purposes.

Currency and Exchange Control

The currency is the Swiss franc. There are no exchange controls.

Disclosure of Information

Banking secrecy: Switzerland is renowned for its banking secrecy, which is protected not only by criminal law but also by administrative law. Banking secrecy cannot be lifted by tax authorities if it is a matter of tax assessment or tax evasion.

Secrecy of information: Switzerland introduced new money laundering legislation on April 1, 1998, in the form of the Combat of Money Laundering in the Financial Sector Act 1998, increasing and refining due diligence measures in order to ensure the lawful origin of funds received. The law applies not only to banks but to all "financial intermediaries," namely fund managers, insurance companies, brokers, and asset managers, and imposes a duty on them to report any knowledge or suspicion that clients' assets are derived from criminal activities.

International cooperation measures: Switzerland has a mutual legal assistance treaty with the United States, which covers tax cases only when major organized crime figures are involved.

Legal System

Switzerland has a civil law system, with some customary law influences.

Treaties

See "Tax Treaties and Double Taxation," below.

Taxation

Because of Switzerland's federal structure, taxes are levied simultaneously at three levels, namely the federal level, cantonal level, and communal (municipal) level. Considerable differences exist in tax rates at the cantonal and communal levels, although efforts are being made at tax harmonization, which should be in place by the end of the year 2000.

The federal level has the exclusive right to levy customs duty, VAT, taxes on liquor and tobacco, withholding tax, and stamp duties. The right to levy income tax on individuals and corporations is held by all three levels. The cantons and communes levy a wealth tax, among others.

Income Tax

Individuals resident in Switzerland are taxed on their worldwide income, excluding income from enterprises, permanent establishments, and real estate situated abroad. The federal tax rate is between 0% and 11.5%. The cantonal and communal rates are approximately double.

Similarly, Swiss resident companies are liable to corporation tax on all sources of income, wherever arising, unless specifically exempted, such as income from enterprises, permanent establishments, and real estate situated abroad. A company is resident in Switzerland if it is incorporated in Switzerland or managed in Switzerland. Federal tax is levied at a flat rate of 8.5% on taxable income. The effective rate is 7.8% because the tax is tax-deductible. Associations and foundations are taxed at a rate of 4.25% at the federal level. Cantonal and municipal taxes vary between 17% and 32%.

Capital Tax

The federal government does not impose a tax on capital, but the cantons levy capital taxes ranging between 1% and 3%.

Withholding Tax

Federal withholding tax is levied at the following rates: 35% on investment income and lottery gains, 15% on pension fund benefits, and 8% on other insurance benefits. Nonresidents may obtain partial or full refund of the Swiss withholding tax only on the basis of double taxation treaties.

Value-Added Tax

Federal VAT was introduced in Switzerland in 1995. The standard rate for 1999 is 7.5%, although such goods as food, medicine, books, and newspapers are taxed at a rate of 2.3%. Accommodation is taxed at 3.5%. There are two exempt categories: where the input tax is not recoverable, and where the exemption is with credit of the input tax. VAT registration is compulsory on a minimum turnover of SF75,000 consisting of transactions in Switzerland.

Land Tax

The cantons impose tax on property located within their areas.

Inheritance and Gift Taxes

Most cantons levy inheritance and gift taxes. They are not levied at the federal level. The rates are progressive and depend on the value of the estate and the relationship between the deceased and the heir.

Stamp Duties

A federal stamp tax is levied on the issue of shares, bonds, and financial paper by Swiss companies, the transfer of ownership of securities, and the payment of certain insurance premiums.

Other Taxes

Compensation paid to executives is subject to federal direct tax and cantonal taxes at source for foreigners and employees who are resident abroad. The rate may be between 20% and 25%. Payments that are considered as hidden profit distribution are subject to the 35% withholding tax. These would include excessive salary payments and excessive interest on loans.

Tax Incentives

See "Incentives," below.

Table 50-1. Tax Treaty Arrangements in Switzerland

Country	*Dividends*	*Interest*	*Royalties*
Argentina	10%/15%	0%	0%
Australia	15%	10%	0%
Austria	5%	5%	0%
Belgium	10%/15%	10%	0%
Bulgaria	5%/15%	10%	0%
Canada	5%/15%	15%	0%
China	10%	10%	0%
Czech Republic	5%/15%	0%	0%
Denmark	0%	0%	0%
Ecuador	15%	10%	0%
Egypt	5%/15%	0%/15%	0%
Finland	5%/10%	0%	0%
France	5%/15%	10%	0%
Germany	5%/15%	0%	0%
Greece	5%/15%	10%	0%
Hungary	10%	10%	0%
Iceland	5%/15%	0%	0%
India	15%	10%/15%	0%
Indonesia	10%/15%	10%	0%
Ireland	0%/15%	0%	0%
Italy	15%	12.5%	0%
Ivory Coast	15%	15%	0%
Jamaica	5%/10%	10%	0%
Japan	10%/15%	10%	0%
Korea (South)	10%/15%	10%	0%
Luxembourg	0%/5%/15%	10%	0%
Malaysia	5%/15%	10%	0%
Mexico	5%/15%	10%/15%	0%
Morocco	7%/15%	10%	0%
The Netherlands	0%/15%	5%	0%
New Zealand	15%	10%	0%
Norway	5%/10%/15%	0%	0%
Pakistan	15%/35%	15%/35%	0%
Poland	5%/15%	10%	0%
Portugal	10%/15%	10%	0%

Romania	10%	10%	0%
Russia	5%/15%	10%	0%
Singapore	10%/15%	10%	0%
Slovak Republic	5%/15%	10%	0%
Slovenia	5%/15%	5%	0%
South Africa	7.5%	10%/35%	0%
Spain	10%/15%	10%	0%
Sri Lanka	10%/15%	5%/10%	0%
Sweden	0%/15%	5%	0%
Thailand	10%/15%	10%/15%	0%
Trinidad and Tobago	10%/20%	10%	0%
Tunisia	10%	10%	0%
United Kingdom	5%/15%	0%	0%
United States	5%/15%	0%	0%
Venezuela	0%/10%	5%	0%
Vietnam	7%/10%/15%	10%	0%

Tax Treaties and Double Taxation

The tax treaty arrangements apply in Switzerland are shown in Table 50-1.

Incentives (Tax and Nontax)

Free Trade Zones

Switzerland has more free ports or free zones than most countries in the world. It has 19 free zones: 4 at Basle, 3 at Geneva, 2 each at Zurich and St Margarethen and 1 each at Aarau, Bern, Chiasso, Lausanne, St Gallen, Brig, Buchs, and Cadenazzo. Goods may be warehoused in the free zones for an unlimited period without being subject to Swiss customs duties. The airports of Geneva and Zurich house free port areas.

Participation Exemptions

At the federal level a reduction of profit tax is possible by reference to the ratio between the net earnings generated by qualifying participations and total net profit. Participations of at least 20% in the share capital of another company or with the market value of more than SF2 million are qualifying participations. Earnings generated from participations include ordinary dividend distributions as well as constructive dividend distributions, liquidation proceeds, and bonus shares.

Capital gains on participations of at least 20% held for at least one year are also taken into account as privileged holding income.

Grants and Incentives

Some rural cantons grant a tax holiday of up to 10 years to newly incorporated companies that provide employment and industrial development for the canton. The tax holiday does not affect the company's federal tax liability. It may be a total or partial exemption from cantonal tax. There are no other special incentives in the form of accelerated depreciation, investment allowances, or grants.

Corporations

Types of Corporations

The limited liability company (*Gesellschaft mit beschränker Haftung* (GmbH)) is an association of two or more corporations or persons under a corporate name. The association has a fixed capital, the quota, which must be at least SF20,000 but no more than SF2 million. The limited liability company is not used for offshore financial activities as it does not offer any specific advantages.

The corporation (*Aktiengesellschaft* or *société anonyme* (AG or SA)) is the more common corporate form and is used for holding and investment companies. It corresponds to the American joint stock company. A business license is not required, unless the corporation engages in banking or insurance business. At least three founders are required to form a corporation. They meet before a notary to adopt the statutes and appoint the necessary bodies. Registration usually follows within two days, at which time the corporation comes into being.

The minimum share capital for a corporation is SF100,000, and the shareholders' liability is limited to their subscription for share capital. The corporation can issue ordinary and preference shares, which may be to bearer and/or registered. The minimum nominal par value per share is SF10, and the shares may be issued at a premium. There are no residence or nationality requirements regarding shareholders, but a corporation must have a registered address in Switzerland.

The majority of directors of a corporation must be Swiss nationals and be domiciled in Switzerland. Only shareholders may be elected to the board. Where there is only one director, that director must be a Swiss national resident in Switzerland. Members must hold a meeting once a year.

Swiss law does not require corporate seals. Annual audited financial statements are required, and at least one auditor must have a domicile, registered office, or a registered branch office in Switzerland.

Migration and Redomiciliation

The migration of corporations is not penalized financially under federal or cantonal law. The Swiss Federal Council will grant a corporation, having its domicile abroad, permission to transfer it to Switzerland without liquidation, provided the corporation has legal personality according to the laws of its former jurisdiction of domicile, the last approved balance shows that the capital stock is fully covered by assets, and the transfer of the domicile has been validly resolved in accordance with its bylaws. If such special permission is refused, the foreign corporation must be liquidated and reincorporated.

Other Forms of Business Organization

Sole Proprietorships

A sole owner carrying out business must be entered in the commercial register. A capital structure is not required and liability is unlimited.

Partnerships

General partnership: The *Kollecktivgesellschaft* (KOLG) is a partnership corresponding roughly to the American partnership. A minimum of two partners is required, and the partnership contract is filed with the commercial register.

Limited partnership: The *Kommanditgesellschaft* (KG) corresponds roughly to the American limited partnership. At least one partner must be fully liable for the firm's debts, the others being liable only to the extent of their contributions.

Limited partnership corporation: The *Kommanditaktiengesellschaft* (Komm AG) is a hybrid of the corporation and the limited partnership.

Ordinary partnership: The *einfache Gesellschaft* (eG) is a loose, unregistered association, which need not be formed with a view to making a profit or carrying on business.

Foreign Corporations

A foreign company may carry on business in Switzerland through a Swiss branch. The Swiss branch must be entered in the Register of Commerce and its representation must be in the hands of an authorized person resident in Switzerland.

Trusts

Switzerland being a civil law jurisdiction, the concept of the trust is unknown. However, a foreign trust will be recognized by Swiss courts if it has been properly established under the laws of a foreign jurisdiction, and particularly if the settlor has a connection with that foreign jurisdiction. It is therefore possible for a Swiss company to be a trustee of a settlement properly created under the laws of another jurisdiction. Trust assets may be held in and controlled from Switzerland.

The foundation (*Stiftung*) is the Swiss legal concept bearing the closest resemblance to the common law trust. Once funds are transferred to a foundation, they cannot revert to the donor and must be used for the foundation's purposes. Foundations are either charitable or are used as vehicles for pension and provident schemes. Family foundations are not allowed by Swiss law.

CHAPTER FIFTY-ONE

TURKS & CAICOS ISLANDS

Background Information

Geographic and Demographic Data

Location	The Turks & Caicos Islands consists of two island groups in the Caribbean Sea, southeast of the Bahamas. The islands are five hours behind GMT.
Capital	Cockburn Town.
Area	166 square miles.
Population	14,631.
Language	English is the official language.
Access	There are three international airports, with Miami being the main gateway to the islands. Charter flights from New York and Canada serve the Club Med and other hotels on Providenciales. The national airline provides regular flights to other Caribbean destinations.
Telecommunications	Excellent.

Government

The Turks & Caicos Islands is a self-governing dependent territory of the United Kingdom.

Political and Economic Stability

The Turks & Caicos Islands is politically stable. The Queen of England is the head of state and is represented by a governor.

The stable Turks & Caicos economy is based on tourism, fishing, and offshore financial services. Most food for domestic consumption is imported, although there is some subsistence farming, mainly of corn, cassava, citrus, and beans. The

United States is the leading source of tourists, accounting for more than 70% of arrivals. Major sources of government revenue include fees from offshore financial activities and customs receipts, as the islands rely on imports for nearly all consumption and capital goods. Unemployment runs at approximately 12%.

Business Environment

Government attitude to offshore activities: The decision to develop the Turks & Caicos Islands as an international offshore financial center was made by the British government following a report in 1970. Development in this direction has therefore been steady and well regulated. The local government continues to actively encourage the Turks & Caicos Islands' status as an international offshore financial center. Responsibility for administering the center now lies with the Offshore Finance Center Unit, which processes license applications and supervises banks, insurance companies, and trust companies. The Offshore Finance Center Unit is also responsible for promoting the Turks & Caicos Islands as an offshore center. Incentives are offered for developments that are deemed to be beneficial to the islands. It is usually a requirement that belongers are trained or participate in the new enterprise. The government also actively promotes the islands as a tourist destination.

Employment: The immigration authorities welcome qualified persons wishing to establish business enterprises or undertake employment in the islands, and it is relatively easy to obtain a work permit. However, a list of reserved activities has been published to ensure the hiring of belongers. Work permits are granted for up to three years and cost up to US$2,000 annually.

Local business requirements: In terms of the Business Licensing Ordinance 1983, anyone wishing to engage in a business or profession in the islands must obtain a business license.

Foreigners and Immigration

As a result of the Aliens Property Ordinance 1953, there is no restriction on the ownership of land by foreigners. Residence permits are readily granted to foreigners wishing to buy or build homes in the islands.

Currency and Exchange Control

The local currency is the U.S. dollar. There is no exchange control.

Disclosure of Information

Banking secrecy: Banking confidentiality and secrecy are governed by the Confidential Relationships Ordinance 1979, which provides penalties of up to US$10,000 and three years' imprisonment for professionals, including government officials, who make unauthorized disclosure of confidential information.

Secrecy of information: A professional company that makes unauthorized disclosure may be fined US$50,000. The Companies Ordinance 1981, sections 199 to 204, contains confidentiality provisions in relation to exempted companies. The common law privilege of confidentiality also imposes civil liability on breaches of professional privilege.

Disclosure in company formation and trust settlement: Disclosure of beneficial ownership is not required on formation of an exempt company. No other information is required by the authorities. The Confidential Relationships Ordinance 1979 governs the confidentiality of this information.

Turks & Caicos Islands companies do not have to be audited. They must have a local registered agent, who has a duty of due diligence with regard to knowing client details. The agent may be compelled to disclose beneficial ownership under a court order.

A trustee does not have to register the beneficiaries of a trust. Companies or trustees opening bank accounts are required to make disclosure of beneficial ownership or the beneficiaries to the bank. This provision also applies to limited partnerships.

International cooperation measures: The islands have a procedure for cooperation with foreign states, contained in the mutual legal assistance treaty between the United Kingdom and the United States. The treaty does not extend to fiscal crime. The islands have not entered into any double taxation agreements and will not cooperate with requests by foreign investigators for assistance in investigations into tax evasion.

Anti–money laundering provisions are contained in the Proceeds of Crime Bill, which is due to come into force in 1998.

Legal System

General

The legal system is based on English common law, although there is also a written constitution in place.

Legislation

The principal provisions affecting offshore operations and transactions are contained in the following:

- Banking Ordinance 1979
- Companies Ordinance 1981

- Confidential Relationships Ordinance 1979
- Insurance Ordinance 1989
- International Financial Institution (Exemption) Ordinance 1979
- Limited Partnerships Ordinance 1992
- Trustees (Licensing) Ordinance 1992
- Trusts Ordinance 1990

Treaties

The islands are not party to any double taxation treaties. However, as a British dependent territory, the Turks & Caicos Islands is party to the mutual legal assistance treaty between the United Kingdom and the United States. The agreement does not extend to assistance regarding tax offenses.

Taxation (Direct and Indirect)

The Turks & Caicos Islands does not levy the following taxes:

capital gains tax
capital or wealth tax
corporation tax
gift tax
income tax
inheritance tax or estate duty
payroll tax
real estate tax
sales tax
social security tax
transfer duty
turnover tax
undistributed profits tax
withholding tax

Taxes that are levied are probate fees of 2% of the value of the deceased estate, to a maximum of US$550; stamp duty on certain documents and transactions; import duties on goods imported into the islands, unless pursuant to a development order; hotel tax at 8%; departure tax of US$15 per person; and a business license fee of up to US$4,000 for professionals.

The Companies Ordinance 1981, section 197, provides exempt companies with an automatic twenty-year guarantee from the government against possible future taxes. Development projects may be granted a tax holiday of up to thirty-five years.

Tax Incentives

See "Incentives (Tax and Nontax)."

Incentives (Tax and Nontax)

In terms of the Encouragement of Development Ordinance 1972, approved development projects are granted relief from import duties and possible future direct taxes for a period of ten years. The period may be extended to a total of thirty-five years.

The development of hotels and tourist amenities is encouraged on government land, which may be acquired under favorable long-term concessionary leases or conditional purchase leases. The provisions do not apply to private residences.

The government established the Turks & Caicos Islands Investment Agency in 1994 as a "one-stop shop" for investors. The agency will assess the feasibility of projects and convey this to the government, and negotiate the awarding of incentives to approved projects, which are contained in development orders. The Civil Service Consultative Group has also been set up to provide developers with a direct line of communication with government officials.

Proposals are dealt with on a case-by-case basis, and the developer must have visited the islands before consideration will be given to any proposal.

Corporations

(The domestic laws of the Turks & Caicos Islands refer to *corporations* as *companies*. This terminology is retained in this chapter.)

The Turks & Caicos Islands is a forerunner of the British Virgin Islands and the Bahamas as far as incorporation of international business companies (IBCs) is concerned. The islands' legislation is extremely flexible, and a twenty-year government guarantee can be obtained with regard to exemption from future taxes and increases in existing taxes. Incorporation procedures are also very quick. However, the jurisdiction has not been promoted as successfully as some of the other Caribbean jurisdictions and does not have as high a profile as some of its neighbors.

Types of Companies

Companies in the Turks & Caicos Islands are governed by the Companies Ordinance 1981 and by English common law. There are five types of companies: the ordinary (nonexempted) company, the exempted (international business) company, the limited life company, the foreign company, and the incorporated nonprofit organization.

No distinction is made between private and public companies. All five types of companies may be companies limited by shares, companies limited by guarantee, or unlimited companies. Companies limited by shares are the most common.

Ordinary companies: Ordinary companies are used for local business and investment activity and for holding land in the islands. Details of the company's capital, shareholders, and officers are a matter of public record, and an annual return disclosing details of the share capital must be filed with the companies registry. Ordinary companies are not subject to direct taxes, but they must pay stamp duty, customs duty, and licensing fees. The government guarantee against the imposition of taxes is not available to ordinary companies.

Exempted companies (IBCs): To be registered as an international business company, a company must carry on its business mainly outside the Turks & Caicos Islands. An ordinary company can become an exempted company and vice versa. Exempt companies offer flexibility and anonymity, as well as a twenty-year guarantee against tax.

Limited life company: A limited life company is the equivalent of the U.S. limited liability company, which is recognized as a partnership by the Internal Revenue Service for income tax purposes. It thus has the tax benefits of a partnership as well as the advantages of corporate identity. A limited life company must be formed by at least two subscribers for a life of not more than 50 years, although the life may be extended to 150 years. An additional incorporation fee of US$100 is payable on top of the incorporation fee payable by an exempt company.

Incorporated associations: Non-profit-making organizations such as clubs and professional bodies may be registered under the Companies Ordinance 1981. They are exempt from filing requirements and do not use the word *Limited* in their name.

Migration and Redomiciliation

The Companies Ordinance 1981, section 205, provides a simple procedure in terms of which a foreign company may transfer its domicile to the Turks & Caicos Islands. Similarly, a company incorporated in the islands may migrate to another jurisdiction. It is also possible to obtain a standby permit authorizing a company to move its domicile to the islands within three years of the permit's issue, which is useful for companies incorporated in unstable jurisdictions. A foreign company may register as an exempted company provided that it has the consent of its shareholders and creditors and that the company law of its country of origin does not expressly prohibit migration. The company must file a copy of its certificate of incorporation with the registrar of companies in Grand Turk and pay the necessary incorporation fee (US$150). There is no fee for outward redomiciliation.

Checklist for IBCs

- Prior approval of the company name is required. The name may be in any language and need not end with *Limited.*
- Incorporation takes one to two days. Shelf companies are available. No information is required prior to exempt status being granted.
- There is no minimum capital requirement and no capital duty.
- At least one shareholder is required. Bearer shares and shares of no par value are permitted.
- At least one director is required. Corporate directors are allowed, and there is no restriction on the directors' location.
- A company secretary is mandatory. Corporate secretaries are allowed, and there is no restriction on the secretary's location.
- IBCs must have a local registered office but do not need a registered agent. No documents are required to be kept at the registered office.
- The articles of incorporation and registered office are available on the public file.
- An IBC should have a seal but need not maintain company records.
- Accounts do not have to be kept or filed.
- An annual declaration that the company continues to comply with the Companies Ordinance 1981 is required.
- There are no restrictions on the holding of meetings.
- IBCs pay an annual fee of US$300.

Other Forms of Business Organization

Sole Proprietorships

Sole proprietorships are recognized in the Turks & Caicos Islands but are not the subject of separate legislation. They are subject to the common law of contract and agency, and the liability of the sole proprietor is unlimited.

Partnerships

General partnerships are governed by English common law. Since 1992, the Limited Partnerships Ordinance 1992 has provided for the registration of limited partnerships. Limited partnerships must have at least one general and one or more limited partners, with a maximum of one hundred partners. The general, or managing, partner is liable for all partnership debts, while the limited partners are only liable to the extent of the amount of capital contributed to the partnership. At least one general partner must be resident or incorporated in the Turks & Caicos

Islands. Limited partnerships must have the words *Limited Partnership* or abbreviation *LP* in their names and must have registered offices in the islands.

Registration of a limited partnership is effected by filing with the registrar of companies a statement containing the following information:

(a) the name of the firm;

(b) the general nature of its business;

(c) the address of its registered office;

(d) the duration of the partnership; and

(e) the full name and address of each partner.

A registration fee of US$500 is payable.

An exempt limited partnership, which is a partnership that carries on its business outside the islands, may acquire a fifty-year government guarantee against taxation. It also does not have to file the partners' details with the registrar of companies, although these must be kept at the registered office.

Foreign Companies

The Companies Ordinance 1981 recognizes foreign companies. A company incorporated in a foreign jurisdiction that wishes to carry on business or hold land in the Turks & Caicos Islands must register as a foreign company with the registrar of companies within a month of undertaking such activity in the islands. Documentation to be filed includes the following:

(a) a copy of the charter, statute, or memorandum and articles of association;

(b) directors' names and personal details; and

(c) the name of a person resident in the islands who will accept service of process on behalf of the foreign company.

Registration costs US$250, and an annual fee of US$250 is payable thereafter.

Banks and Trust Companies

Banks

Banking in the Turks & Caicos Islands is regulated by the Banking Ordinance 1979, which provides that no company may use the word *Bank* or *Savings and Loan* in its name or undertake banking business without a license.

A license may be either an overseas banking license or a national banking license. The national banking license entitles the licensee to carry on banking business within the Turks & Caicos Islands with islanders and other residents. The overseas banking license permits banking business from within the islands, but the license holder may not accept deposits from, or lend to, a resident of the islands. A combined license is also possible.

An application for a national banking license may be made only in respect of branches or subsidiaries of established banks that are subject to effective consolidated supervision by their home supervisory authority, except where the bank is predominantly locally owned and doing business primarily within the Turks & Caicos Islands. An application for an overseas banking license may be made from

(a) banks that, although not subsidiaries, are closely associated with an overseas bank and that, by agreement, will be included within the consolidated supervision of the overseas bank's home authority; and
(b) subsidiaries of major corporations whose bank is to undertake and manage in-house financial and banking activity.

The national banking license fee is US$15,000. The overseas banking license fee is US$10,000. The combined license fee is US$20,000.

Annual license fees are as follows:

National banking license	US$10,000
Overseas banking license	US$7,500
Combined banking license	US$17,000

A national banking license holder must file monthly and quarterly statements. An overseas banking license holder is required to file less detailed returns on a quarterly basis. All banks must also submit annual audited accounts.

Trust Companies

The Trustees (Licensing) Ordinance and Regulations 1992 provide for the licensing and regulation of trust companies and professional trustees. Two types of licenses are available: restricted trustee licenses that permit the trustee to act as a professional trustee only in respect of a named trust or trusts and unrestricted trustee licenses that are issued with no restrictions. The application fee for an unrestricted license is US$500, and for a restricted license it is US$200. The annual fees are US$3,000 and US$750, respectively.

Insurance

General

The Insurance Ordinance 1989 and the Insurance Regulations 1990 regulate insurance business in the Turks & Caicos Islands. No person or company may use the word *Insurance, Reinsurance, Indemnity, Guarantee, Underwriting, Surety*, or

Casualty in its name or transact any insurance business or brokering without possessing a license.

There are different categories of licenses for insurers, brokers, managers, principal representatives, agents, and subagents. License applicants must supply references and evidence of character and relevant experience for owners, directors, and management. Application fees cost between US$300 for an agent's license and US$500 for an insurer's license. Annual fees are as follows:

Domestic insurers	US$2,500
Captive insurers	US$2,000
Credit life reinsurers	nil
Other insurers	US$500
Brokers	US$1,000
Managers	US$3,500
Principal representatives	US$1,000
Agents	US$100
Subagents	US$50

Capital requirements for insurers vary, but companies engaged in reinsurance, life, or general (domestic or international) business should have a minimum paid-up capital of US$100,000. Insurers must submit annual audited profit and loss statements and balance sheets, as well as specified reports.

Captive Insurance Companies

Captive insurance is governed by the Insurance Ordinance 1989 and the Insurance Regulations 1990. Approximately sixty captives have been established in the Turks & Caicos Islands. The Financial Services Commission (Insurance Division) regulates the sector. An annual audit is required, as are solvency statements and confirmed conformity to an approved business plan. Notification must be made of changes to the business plan.

Insurers formed under section 7(11) of the ordinance (i.e., for reinsurance of risks covered by an acceptable named insurer) may be subject to fewer reporting requirements. Captives are exempt from tax.

The minimum capital requirements are US$100,000 for general insurance and US$180,000 for long-term insurance.

A registry fee of US$100 and an insurance application fee of US$500 are payable. There is also an annual license fee of US$2,000. There are no additional costs.

Provision is not made for special categories of captives.

Shipping

The Turks & Caicos Islands is a British port of registry. Ships of up to 150 gross tons can be registered on payment of a flat fee of US$250 each. Only British-owned ships may be registered. British ownership includes ownership by companies incorporated in the United Kingdom, Turks & Caicos Islands, or any other dependent territory. The crew may be of any nationality.

Mutual Funds and Collective Investment Schemes

The Companies Ordinance 1981 governs mutual funds and open-ended investment companies. Unit trusts are subject to the general laws of equity and trusts, including the Trusts Ordinance 1990. An ordinance regulating mutual funds is in the pipeline.

Trusts

The Turks & Caicos law of trusts is contained in the Trusts Ordinance 1990, supplemented by English common law. The Trusts Ordinance has been approved for the purposes of the Hague Convention.

Trusts do not have to be registered, and there are no minimum capital requirements. There are also no residency requirements. Trustees must keep accurate accounts and records, but the accounts do not have to be audited. No tax is payable in the Turks & Caicos Islands on either trust or beneficiary income, and the trust funds may be moved freely into and out of the islands.

With regard to asset protection, the ordinance provides that a creditor may not set aside a settlement made by a settlor who is an individual, unless the creditor can prove that at the time the settlement was made, the settlor was insolvent. A statute of limitations period of six years applies to such claims. The application of foreign laws is expressly excluded, and the rule against perpetuities is abolished.

A Turks & Caicos Islands trust may be changed to a foreign trust and vice versa, provided that the terms of the trust provide for the law to be changed and that the change does not invalidate any terms of the trust. The change must also be consistent with the wishes of the settlor.

CHAPTER FIFTY-TWO

VANUATU

Background Information

Geographic and Demographic Data

Location	Vanuatu is a group of islands in the South Pacific Ocean, about three-quarters of the way from Hawaii to Australia. It is eleven hours ahead of GMT.
Capital	Port-Vila.
Area	5,700 square miles.
Population	181,358.
Languages	English and French are the official languages. Bislama, a sophisticated form of pidgin English, is also spoken.
Access	Flights are available to major Pacific Rim destinations such as Auckland, Brisbane, Fiji, Melbourne, Nouméa, and Papua New Guinea, from which connections are available to other international destinations.
Telecommunications	Excellent.

Government

Vanuatu is a parliamentary democracy based on the Westminster system.

Political and Economic Stability

Vanuatu has recently had periods of political instability, although a reform program has been implemented to encourage long-term stability and economic growth.

The economy is based primarily on subsistence or small-scale agriculture, which provides a living for 65% of the population. Fishing and tourism are the other mainstays of the economy. Mineral deposits are negligible, and the country has no known petroleum deposits. A small light industry sector caters to the local market. Tax revenues come mainly from import duties. Economic development is hindered by dependence on relatively few commodity exports, vulnerability to natural disasters, and long distances from main markets and between constituent islands. The activities of the international financial center also make a significant contribution to the economy.

Business Environment

Government attitude to offshore activities: The government actively encourages growth in the agricultural, tourism, and finance sectors and welcomes foreign investment in these areas. The Financial Services Commission was established in terms of the Financial Services Commission Act to supervise the financial services sector and to administer the related legislation. In August 1998 the Foreign Investment Act came into effect. A Foreign Investment Board was established by the act to facilitate and promote foreign investment in Vanuatu. The procedure under the act is that once an investor is issued an Approval Certificate, other approvals relating to residence and work permits and business licenses are usually issued automatically.

Employment: Employment is governed by the Employment Act and the Labor (Work Permits) Act. Foreigners will be granted a work permit provided there is no suitably qualified Ni-Vanuatu applicant available. There is a minimum wage of VT 16,000 and contributions to a superannuation fund are deducted from all salaries.

Local business requirements: In terms of the Business Names Act 1990, all business names, except those reflecting the names of the principals in the business, must be registered with the Financial Services Commission. Registration costs VT 5,000 annually. In addition, any business activity in Vanuatu must be licensed in terms of the Business Licenses Act. The fee depends on the type of business being conducted. An exception is made for international business companies. Additional licensing requirements are imposed on banks, insurance companies, and trust companies, whether they are fully licensed or exempt.

Foreigners and Immigration

Applications for citizenship may be made only after ten years of residence. Residency permits are granted concurrently with work permits and cost VT 20,000. Residency permits are also granted to investors, the length of the permit being proportionate to the amount of the investment, under the rules of the Vanuatu Immigration Service. Residency permits are also granted to retired persons with a net worth equivalent to VT 12 million.

Investors in property do not have to be resident in Vanuatu. However, only leasehold title is available, for a maximum of seventy-five years, with an option to renew. A land lease charge is payable annually. The charge is relatively low but is subject to review every five years.

Currency and Exchange Control

The local currency is the vatu. It floats against a secret basket of currencies, with the dollar as the major component. There is no exchange control on foreign currency accounts, although there are some restrictions on the conversion of the vatu to foreign currency.

Disclosure of Information

Secrecy of information: The Official Secrets Act governs secrecy generally. The act requires all government employees to sign a declaration prohibiting the release of classified information to unauthorized persons. In terms of the International Companies Act, it is a criminal offense to disclose information regarding an international company to any person. There are similar secrecy provisions in the Companies Act and the Trust Companies Act. However, disclosure may be compelled by court order. Court proceedings relating to international or exempt companies are heard in camera.

Banking secrecy: Banking secrecy and confidentiality are provided for in the Banking Act, the Companies Act, and the Offshore Banking Act, which is in the pipeline. Anti–money laundering provisions are contained in the Serious Offences (Confiscation of Proceeds) Act. In certain circumstances, fiscal crime may be covered by the provisions of this act, but it is unlikely that tax evasion would be covered.

Disclosure in company formation and trust settlement: Disclosure of beneficial ownership is not required on formation of an international or exempt company, and no other information is required by the authorities. Companies are also not required to be audited. They must have a local registered office in Vanuatu. The company's constitution and registers of members and debentures must be held at the local office. The local agent will disclose beneficial ownership only with the consent of the beneficial owner or under an order of court.

Trustees do not have to register the beneficiaries of trusts. A trustee opening a bank account also is not required to disclose the beneficiaries to the bank. However, a company opening a bank account must disclose beneficial ownership. This provision also applies to limited partnerships.

International cooperation measures: A procedure for cooperation with foreign investigators is contained in the Mutual Assistance in Criminal Matters Act. The foreign investigator must make application for assistance to the attorney general. In some circumstances, a person from whom evidence is taken pursuant to a request from a Commonwealth country may lawfully refuse to answer questions by application to the Supreme Court.

There is no mechanism for the enforcement of foreign judgments in Vanuatu. Vanuatu has also not entered into any double taxation agreements.

The Vanuatu authorities would not assist in an investigation into tax evasion as there are no tax laws in Vanuatu, and hence tax evasion is not an offense.

Legal System

General

The legal system in Vanuatu is based on English common law, with some influence from the French civil system. Vanuatu also has a written constitution.

Legislation

The principal provisions affecting offshore operations and transactions are contained in the following:

- Banking Act Cap 63
- Business Names Act 1990
- Companies Act Cap 191
- Financial Services Act 1993
- Insurance Act Cap 82
- International Companies Act 1992
- Maritime Act Cap 131
- Prevention of Fraud (Investments) Act Cap 70
- Stamp Duties Act Cap 68
- Trust Companies Act Cap 69

Treaties

Vanuatu has not entered into any double taxation agreements with other countries.

Taxation (Direct and Indirect)

Vanuatu does not levy direct taxes. There is therefore no income tax, corporation tax, capital gains tax, wealth tax, inheritance tax, or estate duty. There are also no withholding taxes.

Residency Permit Fees

Residency permit fees are charged at the following rates based on the term of the permit:

1 year	VT 20,000
3 years	VT 90,000
5 years	VT 130,000
10 years	VT 230,000
15 years	VT 330,000

Stamp Duties

Stamp duty is charged on the transfer of land leases at a rate of 5%. Land leases are registered, and there is an additional Land Records Office fee of 2%. Stamp duty is charged at varying rates on legal documents such as mortgages, powers of attorney, and promissory notes. The maximum rate is 1%. Share transfers are subject to stamp duty at US$6 for every US$1,000.

Business License Tax

Business licenses cost between VT 20,000 and VT 100,000. Depending on the type of business, there is an additional fee of up to 4% of turnover.

Business Name Registration Fee

Businesses that are required to register under the Business Names Act pay an annual registration fee of VT 5,000.

Tourist Tax

Revenue from bars, hotels, and other accommodations is subject to a 10% tourist tax. A 15% turnover tax is charged on rental accommodation. There is also a departure tax of VT 2,500.

Import and Export Duties

Many goods imported into Vanuatu are subject to import duty at a rate equal to a percentage of the CIF value. The amount varies depending on the nature of the goods.

Many goods exported from Vanuatu are subject to export duty at a rate of 5% of the FOB value of the goods.

Value-Added Tax

Value-added tax is levied at a rate of 12%.

Tax Incentives

See "Incentives (Tax and Nontax)."

Incentives (Tax and Nontax)

Development incentives are offered by the government of Vanuatu in the form of exemptions from import and export duties. Developments are considered on a case-by-case basis and will only be considered where they can be shown to benefit Vanuatu economically. Relief from customs duty is granted under the Import Duties Act to goods imported for manufacturing or processing purposes. Relief from export duty is granted under the Export Duties Act.

Duty-free trade of goods between certain Pacific Island countries is possible in terms of the 1996 Melanesian Spearhead Agreement between Papua New Guinea, Fiji, the Solomon Islands, and Vanuatu.

Corporations

(The domestic laws of Vanuatu refer to *corporations* as *companies*. This terminology is retained in this chapter.)

Vanuatu provides companies with modern, flexible legislation. The jurisdiction is in a good time zone for the Far East and provides suitable distancing from Europe where this is required. All companies are tax-exempt: There is no income tax, corporate tax, estate duty, or capital gains tax. International companies may obtain a twenty-year guarantee against taxation.

Types of Companies

All companies except international companies are governed by the Companies Act. These companies may be limited by shares, by guarantee, or be unlimited, and they may be public or private. A private company may only have a maximum of fifty shareholders and may not invite the public to subscribe for shares. In addition, these companies may be local companies or exempt. Local companies are used for operations in Vanuatu and are incorporated and registered in a manner similar to U.K. companies. Exempted companies were used for offshore operations prior to the enactment of the International Companies Act. They are seldom used nowadays, and most exempted companies have converted to international companies. Exempted companies may not conduct business in Vanuatu, offer shares to the public in Vanuatu, or own an interest in nonexempt companies operating in Vanuatu. Exempted companies are subject to less stringent reporting requirements than local companies, but those holding banking, insurance, or trust company licenses must file annual audited accounts. Exempted companies must hold annual general meetings and at least one directors' meeting in Vanuatu.

Of more importance to international offshore operations is the international company, which is governed by the International Companies Act 1992. International companies do not have authorized capital and may be limited by shares, guarantee, or both. They have constitutions rather than memorandums and articles of association, and incorporators rather than subscribers. A registration fee of US$150 is payable. Thereafter, an annual fee of US$300 is due.

Companies that offer their shares to the public; hold banking, trust, or insurance licenses; or operate within Vanuatu may not be registered as international companies and must register instead under the Companies Act.

All companies are tax-exempt in Vanuatu. However, international companies have the advantages of being exempt from stamp duty, taxes, and exchange control for a period of twenty years and of having minimal reporting requirements and low fees.

Migration and Redomiciliation

International companies may migrate into and out of Vanuatu provided the other jurisdiction does not expressly prohibit this. Exempted and local companies may also migrate and redomicile freely.

Checklist for International Companies

- The company name may be in any language or script, with any common ending. There is rapid feedback as to availability.
- Incorporation takes one day. A one-hour special service is available at an extra cost of US$100. Shelf companies are available. No information is required prior to incorporation.
- There is no authorized minimum capital, although US$100 is standard. There is also no capital duty. Capital can be in any currency.
- At least one shareholder is required. Bearer shares and shares of no par value are possible.
- At least one director is required. Corporate directors are allowed, and there is no restriction on the directors' place of residence.
- There is no requirement for a company secretary. Corporate secretaries are allowed, and there is no restriction on the secretary's location.
- Companies must have a registered office and a registered agent. Documents do not have to be kept at the registered office.
- The constitution, registered office, and registered agent are available on the public file.
- A company seal is optional.
- Accounts do not have to be kept or filed.
- An annual return is also not required.
- There is no restriction on the holding of meetings.
- An annual fee of US$300 is payable.

Other Forms of Business Organization

Sole Proprietorships

Vanuatu does not have separate legislative provisions for sole traders. In terms of the Business Names Act, sole traders must register their business name, and in terms of the Business Licenses Act, they must apply for a business license.

Partnerships

The Partnerships Act regulates partnerships in Vanuatu. All partnerships must have a business license in terms of the Business Licenses Act, and the name must be registered in terms of the Business Names Act.

General partnerships: General partners are jointly and severally liable for the partnership's obligations. General partnerships do not have to be registered with the Financial Services Commission or pay annual fees.

Limited partnerships: A limited partnership must have at least one general partner and one limited partner. It may not have more than twenty members in total. The general partners are jointly and severally liable for the partnership's obligations, whereas limited partners are liable to the extent of their capital contribution. Limited partnerships must be registered with the Financial Services Commission and pay VT 100,000 annually.

Foreign Companies

The Companies Act provides for foreign companies, which are called overseas companies. Overseas companies are tax-exempt.

Banks, Trust Companies, and Other Financial Institutions

Banks and Other Financial Institutions

Banking is regulated by the Banking Act, which differentiates between banks carrying on business within Vanuatu ("local banks") and those carrying on business outside Vanuatu ("exempted banks"). Exempted banks may not do business within Vanuatu unless with other exempted companies or in furtherance of the business carried on outside Vanuatu. Most international banking and finance groups choose to use Vanuatu exempted companies, in terms of which the licensees are exempt from any reserve and equity ratio requirements and from the need to submit detailed statistical returns.

Two types of licenses are available:

(i) "financial institution" licenses, which cover any company whose business includes accepting deposits (withdrawn or repaid on demand, after a fixed period or after notice) and the employment of those deposits by lending or any other means; and

(ii) "banking" licenses, which give the licensee the rights of a financial institution as well as the power to accept deposits withdrawable by check.

The choice of a banking license as opposed to a financial institution license confers the right to use the word *Bank* in the company name. The granting of either license to an exempted company does not prevent the company from carrying on other business permitted by its memorandum of association. Thus, an exempted bank or financial institution may also be an investment, holding, or trading company.

A company that is promoted by a recognized international bank or financial institution would more easily satisfy the minister of finance as to capital and management requirements in deciding whether to grant a license. Conversely, where the proposed company is to be owned by individuals or groups of individuals (or by them, through private companies or nominees), the following criteria would apply to activities of an "in-house" nature:

(a) a minimum paid-up capital of US$150,000;

(b) evidence of suitable experience for day-to-day management;

(c) involvement in the bank's operations by local professionals;

(d) bank and personal references as to the good character and bona fides of the ultimate beneficial owners of the company;

(e) evidence that the beneficial owners are people of substance;

(f) a written statement confirming the "in-house" nature of the company and detailing its intended activities;

(g) the approval of the banking authority in the jurisdiction where the bank will be based;

(h) copies of passports and police clearances for all managers and beneficial owners;

(i) a business plan; and

(j) prior approval of the minister before any change in the beneficial ownership of the bank takes place.

If the proposed company's activities are such that it may wish to solicit funds from the general public, then the above criteria will be more strictly applied together with more stringent requirements where deemed necessary.

Trust Companies

The Trust Companies Act regulates Vanuatu trust companies. Any company that acts as a trustee, executor, or administrator from within Vanuatu must be licensed under the act. To obtain a license, a trust company must have the following:

(a) a minimum paid-up capital of VT 12.5 million if its head office is in Vanuatu, or VT 50 million if elsewhere;

(b) a head office or "principal office" in Vanuatu; and

(c) at least two resident officers, one of whom must be the authorized agent of the company and the other an alternate.

Trust companies are liable to a government registration fee of VT 30,000 (for authorized capital of up to VT 35 million) on incorporation and annually thereafter as well as a license fee of VT 200,000 on incorporation and annually thereafter.

Insurance

Captive Insurance Companies

Captive insurance is governed by the Insurance Act. There are approximately twenty-five captives established in Vanuatu. The Financial Services Commission regulates the sector. An annual audit is required.

There are no regulatory concessions since captive insurance companies are tax-exempt. The minimum capital requirements are determined on a case-by-case base, as are the reporting requirements.

Incorporation costs approximately US$3,000. The annual license fee costs US$2,000. There are no additional costs.

Provision is not made for special categories of captives.

Shipping

Vanuatu established a flag of convenience shipping registry in 1981. The registry is administered by Vanuatu Maritime Services Limited, which has its headquarters in Port-Vila, although the actual work of maintaining the registry is carried on in New York.

Shipping companies are exempt from stamp duties on shipping documentation. They also do not have to submit audited financial statements. In addition, the finance minister may reduce or waive fees in special circumstances.

The requirements for registration of ships under the Vanuatu flag are as follows (although in some cases, the conditions may be waived):

(a) The ship must be owned by a citizen of Vanuatu or a Vanuatu corporation;
(b) the vessel must be in a safe and seaworthy condition;
(c) if the vessel is under 500 net tons, it will pay fees based on 500 net tons;
(d) ships of over twenty years of age may not be registered; and
(e) documents must be submitted in duplicate.

Licensing Companies

Offshore licensing companies are not covered by specific legislation in Vanuatu. They are exempt from all taxes. The Registration of United Kingdom Trade Marks Act Cap 81 provides for a system extending to Vanuatu the effect of rights under U.K. patents and trademarks. Extensions are recorded in a register in Vanuatu and remain valid for as long as the rights in the United Kingdom remain in force. Registration costs US$15. No provision is made for the registration of copyright in Vanuatu.

Trusts

The law of trusts in Vanuatu is based on English common law, as supplemented by the Perpetuities and Accumulations Regulation 1974 and the Succession Probate and Administration Regulation 1972. The following U.K. legislation applies in Vanuatu: the Settled Land Act 1925, the Law of Property Act 1925, the Trustee Act 1925, and the Variation of Trusts Act 1958.

Trusts do not have to be registered. All trusts are subject to a stamp duty at the rate of $0.50 for every US$100. Trusts that are registered are subject to a stamp duty of VT 7,500. There are no minimum capital requirements.

The initial trustee is usually a trust company incorporated in Vanuatu. However, there are no residency rules. The trustee must keep proper books of account, but there are no audit requirements.

Trustees may migrate to any other jurisdiction.

Checklist for Trusts

- There is no statutory schedule of standard trust powers in Vanuatu.
- The maximum perpetuity period for a noncharitable trust is eighty years.
- A resident trustee is not required.
- There is no requirement for the registration of trusts.
- Trust documents may be in French or English.
- Stamp duty of US$130 is charged.
- The law of trusts is based on English common law.
- The Hague Convention has not been implemented.
- Specific provision has not been made for the exclusion of foreign inheritance laws.
- There is no specific provision dealing with the nonrecognition of foreign judgments.
- There is no specific "asset protection" provision (beyond that offered by general insolvency law) protecting a disposition to a trust from challenge by creditors.
- There is no special statute of limitations period for creditors' claims.
- No provision is made for noncharitable purpose trusts.

APPENDIXES

EXAMPLES OF OFFSHORE DISCRETIONARY TRUST DEEDS AND LETTERS OF WISHES

1. Introductory Note

The trust is a master product of Anglo-Saxon legal genius—so much so that today there is an estimated US$2 trillion in offshore trusts. This amounts to approximately one-quarter of all the money in the world.

The trust deed and, where applicable, the letter of wishes or letter of intent should be drafted every bit as carefully as a last will and testament (mostly referred to simply as a "will") and should cover all of the matters that would normally be incorporated in a will.

A discretionary trust gives the trustees very considerable powers to deal with the interests of the beneficiaries in an arbitrary manner. For this reason, a discretionary trust is usually accompanied by a letter of wishes giving guidance to the trustees with regard to the manner in which they should exercise their discretion. The letter of wishes is not, strictly speaking, binding in law and can be changed at any moment by the settlor or other person expressing wishes to the trustees.

Normally, a letter of wishes would not be given to the trustees unless the trust were a discretionary trust.

2. Example of a Letter of Wishes/Letter of Intent (A)

To: The Trustees

Dear Sirs:

I thought it might help you in the exercise of your discretion under the above-named Settlement to know how I would have acted had I been the Trustee of this Settlement.

This letter is not in any way to detract from your discretion or to have any legal effect, but only to give some guidance in the exercise of your powers and to enable you to know how I would have administered or distributed the assets, had I been in the position to do so.

During the lifetime of XXX, it is my wish that you should apply the income and capital of the Trust Fund in the manner directed by XXX, who may write to you at subsequent times requesting that you give your consideration to making distributions of either income or capital.

After the death of XXX, I should like the capital of the Trust Fund to be distributed as follows:

> The capital of the Trust Fund should be divided into equal portions and distributed to each of the persons named as Beneficiaries in Schedule I of the Trust Deed ("the Beneficiaries").
>
> If any of the Beneficiaries should predecease XXX, that Beneficiary's share should be distributed to that Beneficiary's children in equal shares, or, if such Beneficiary should die without leaving children, then to the other Beneficiaries in equal shares per stirpes.
>
> Please note that the term "child" includes an adopted child.

Yours truly

[normally signed by the Settlor or the principal Beneficiary or a nominee of the Settlor or principal Beneficiary]

3. Letter of Wishes/Letter of Intent "B"

To: The Trustees

You are the present trustees of the above named Instrument of Trust created by me, which sets out the Trusts upon which the Trustees thereof are to hold certain assets received by them.

I appreciate that my wishes are in no way binding upon you or in any way enforceable. However, I hope that my views will assist you in deciding how to exercise the various powers and discretions conferred upon you.

During my lifetime, I would like you to deal with the income and capital of the settlement in accordance with such wishes as I shall express to you from time to time. In addition, I would like you to consider implementing any proposals which my personal tax advisor may suggest in connection with this settlement.

Upon my death, I would like you to use your discretionary powers to pay to my current wife, any interim payments of capital, and/or income, as the trustees think fit.

This Letter of Wishes can be changed by me during my lifetime and replaced by a new Letter of Wishes.

Yours truly

[normally signed by the Settlor or the principal Beneficiary or a nominee of the Settlor or principal Beneficiary]

4. Example of a Discretionary Trust Deed

This settlement is made the _____ day of __________, 2000

BETWEEN: The Settlor:

The Original Trustee:

WHEREAS: The Settlor has paid the sum of US$____ to the Original Trustee to be held upon the trusts declared by this Deed.

NOW THIS DEED WITNESSES AS FOLLOWS:

(1) In this Deed the following expressions shall have the following meanings:

  (a) "The Trustees" means the Original Trustee or the other Trustee or Trustees for the time being hereof.

  (b) "The Beneficiaries" means the persons named as such in the First Schedule hereto or from time to time comprised in the class or classes of persons specified in the First Schedule hereto.

  (c) "The Trust Fund" means the said sum paid to the Original Trustee all property at any time added thereto by way of further settlement accumulation of income capital accretion or otherwise and all property from time to time representing the premises respectively.

  (d) "The Perpetuity Date" means the day on which the period of 80 years from the date hereof shall expire.

(2) The Trustee shall hold the Trust Fund upon the trusts and with and subject to the powers and provisions hereinafter contained.

(3) Until the Perpetuity Date the Trustees shall have the following powers exercisable from time to time:

  (a) power to appoint by deed or deeds revocable or irrevocable that the whole or any part or parts of the Trust Fund and the income thereof shall thenceforth be held upon such trusts for the benefit of such one or more of the Beneficiaries at such ages or times and in such shares as the Trustees shall think fit;

  (b) power to pay transfer or apply the whole or any part or parts of the capital of the Trust Fund to or for the benefit in any manner of such one or more of the Beneficiaries for the time being in existence as the Trustees shall think fit;

  (c) power by deed or deeds to extinguish (or restrict the future exercise of) either or both of the foregoing powers or any other power or powers conferred on the Trustees by this Deed.

(4) Subject to any and every exercise of the powers contained in clause 3 hereof the Trustees until the Perpetuity Date:

(a) may pay or apply the whole or such part or parts of the income of the Trust Fund as the Trustees shall from time to time think fit to or for the benefit of all or such one or more of the Beneficiaries for the time being in existence in such proportions or manner as the Trustees shall from time to time think fit, and

(b) shall deal with the income of the Trust Fund (or so much thereof as shall not be paid or applied as aforesaid) by accumulating the same as an accretion to the capital of the Trust Fund.

(5) Subject as aforesaid the Trustees shall from and after the Perpetuity Date hold the capital and income of the Trust Fund upon trust for such of the Beneficiaries as shall be in existence and ascertained on the Perpetuity Date and if more than one in equal shares per capita.

(6) If on the Perpetuity Date property remains in the Trust Fund but no Beneficiary appointed pursuant to the First Schedule is in existence the Trustee shall distribute the Trust Fund to the Organizations named in the Third Schedule.

(7) The powers and provisions set out in the First Second and Third Schedules hereto shall be construed and have effect as if contained in this Deed.

IN WITNESS WHEREOF this Deed has been executed the day and year first before written.

SCHEDULE I

NAMES AND/OR CLASSES OF BENEFICIARIES

____

____

____

SCHEDULE II

(1) The Trustees shall have (in addition to all other powers vested in them by this Deed or by law) all the powers of investment management sale exchange partition mortgage leasing insurance protection improvement equipment dealing and disposition of an absolute beneficial owner of the Trust Fund and in particular (but without prejudice to the generality of

the foregoing powers) the Trustees shall have over and in respect of the Trust Fund and every part thereof the following powers:

(a) To retain any property forming part of the Trust Fund in the actual state or condition in which the same is received by the Trustees for so long as the Trustees shall think proper;

(b) To invest trust moneys in the acquisition by purchase or otherwise or upon the security of such property or upon such personal credit (with or without security) as the Trustee shall think fit to the intent that the Trustee shall have the same full and unrestricted power of investing and varying investments in all respects as a beneficial owner and so that:

   (i) the expression "property" in this paragraph shall mean property of whatever nature and wherever situated and (without prejudice to the generality of the foregoing definition) shall include all or any one or more (and any share or interest in any one or more) of the following, namely: stocks funds shares securities commodities land chattels assurance policies annuities goodwill reversions and rights of every description;

   (ii) the acquisition with trust moneys of property with a view to its enjoyment in kind by any person or persons for the time being entitled (or capable by the exercise of any power or discretion of becoming entitled) to the income of such moneys shall for the purposes of this Deed be deemed to be an authorized investment of such moneys;

   (iii) the acquisition with trust moneys of property not producing an income property involving liability or property of a wasting character shall for the purposes of this Deed be deemed to be an authorized investment of such moneys;

   (iv) the improvement repair insurance (in any value) decoration or restoration with trust moneys of property subject to the trusts of this Deed shall for the purposes thereof be deemed to be an authorized investment of such moneys.

(c) To pay out of the income or capital of the Trust Fund all the costs of and incidental to the preparation execution and stamping of this Deed.

(d) To employ and pay any agents advisors managers servants workpeople and employees whatsoever.

(e) To incorporate any company or companies in any place in the world at the expense of the Trust Fund with limited or unlimited liability for any purpose including that of acquiring the whole or any part of the Trust Fund and so that the consideration on the sale of the Trust

Fund or any part thereof to any company incorporated pursuant to this paragraph may consist wholly or partly of shares debentures stock or other securities of the company and may be allotted to or otherwise vested in the Trustees and shall be capital moneys in the Trustees' hands.

(f) To borrow money on the security of the Trust Fund at any time and from time to time and to pay or apply the money so raised in any manner in which money forming part of the capital of the Trust Fund may be paid or applied.

(g) To hold the whole or any part of the Trust Fund in the name or names of any nominee of the Trustees.

(h) To invest any part of the Trust Fund in the securities of any company without being obliged in any way to attend to or interfere with the management of such company or its affairs or to secure representation on its board of directors.

(i) To allot appropriate partition or apportion any property whatever which (or the future proceeds of sale of which) are for the time being subject to the trusts hereof in or towards satisfaction of any share or interest in the Trust Fund or the income thereof in such manner as the Trustee shall (without the necessity of obtaining any consent) consider just according to the respective rights of the persons interested.

(j) To be employed and remunerated as a director or other officer or employee or as an agent or advisor of any company or other corporation or undertaking or firm whatsoever at any time or in any way connected with the Trust Fund or dealing with or acquiring any property to the Trustees and to retain as his absolute property (and without being liable to account therefor) any remuneration fees or profits received by him in any such capacity notwithstanding that his situation or office as such director officer employee agent or advisor may have been obtained or may be held or retained in right or by means of his position as one of the Trustees or any shares stock property rights or powers belonging to or connected with the Trust Fund.

(2) The Trustees may exercise any power of appointment conferred on them by this Deed by appointing that the whole or any part of the Trust Fund shall thenceforth be held upon the trusts and with and subject to the powers and provisions of any other trust not infringing the rule against perpetuities applicable to this trust and approved by the Trustees and for the benefit of all or any one or more exclusively of the others or other of the Beneficiaries and upon any such appointment being made the Trustees may transfer to the Trustees for the time being of the said other trust the property comprised in the said appointment and thereupon the trusts

herein declared concerning such property shall cease and determine and the said property shall for all purposes be subject to the trusts powers and provisions contained in the said other trust and be subject to and governed by the proper law of the said other trust whether such proper law shall be the proper law of this trust or not.

(3) The Trustees shall have power by deed to retire as Trustees and to appoint a new Trustee or new Trustees as Trustees hereof and to declare that the trusts hereof shall be read and take effect according to the law of the country of the residence or incorporation of such new Trustee or Trustees and upon such appointment being made the Trustees shall immediately stand possessed of the Trust Fund upon trust for the new Trustee or Trustees and shall transfer the same to the new Trustee or Trustees as soon as possible so that the Trust Fund shall continue to be held upon the trusts hereof but subject to and governed by the law of the country of residence or incorporation of such new Trustee or Trustees and thereafter the rights of all persons and the construction and effect of each and every provision hereof shall be subject to the exclusive jurisdiction of and construed only according to the law of the said country which shall become the forum for the administration of this trust.

(4) The Trustees shall keep accurate accounts of the trusteeship and may have them audited annually at the expense of the Trust Fund or the income thereof as the Trustees shall determine by a firm of accountants selected by the Trustees.

(5) (a) Any Trustee being a corporation shall be entitled to charge and to be paid out of the Trust Fund and the income thereof remuneration in accordance with its scale of fees from time to time in force and may without accounting for any resultant profit act as banker and perform any service on behalf of the trust estate and on the same terms as would be made with a customer.

(b) Any Trustee being a lawyer chartered accountant or other person engaged in any profession or business shall be entitled to charge and be paid all usual professional and other charges for business transacted time spent and acts done by him or any partner of his in connection with the trusts hereof including acts which a Trustee not being in any profession or business could have done personally.

(6) The Trustees shall not be required to give bond or security for the due and faithful administration of the Trust Fund or for the discharge of the trusts hereby created.

(7) Every discretion or power hereby or by law conferred on the Trustees shall be an absolute and uncontrolled discretion or power and no Trustee shall be liable for any loss or damage arising by reason of the Trustee exercising or failing to exercise or concurring or failing to concur in any exercise of any such discretion or power.

(8) No Trustee hereof shall be liable for any loss or damage which may happen to the Trust Fund or any part thereof or the income thereof at any time or from any cause whatsoever unless such loss or damage shall be caused by his own actual fraud.

(9) Any Trustee hereof who is a corporation may exercise or concur in exercising any discretion or power hereby or by law conferred on the Trustees by a resolution of such corporation or its board of directors or governing body or may delegate the right and power to exercise or concur in exercising any such discretion or power to any one or more of its directors officers or employees.

(10) Subject to paragraph 3 hereof and to any deed made thereunder this Deed shall be construed and take effect in accordance with the laws of [state the country] which shall be the forum for the administration thereof.

SCHEDULE III

NAMES AND/OR CLASSES OF BENEFICIARIES IF NONE OF THE SCHEDULE I BENEFICIARIES SHOULD BE IN EXISTENCE AT THE PERPETUITY DATE

____

____

____

SETTLOR:

SIGNED, SEALED, and DELIVERED

by the said ______________________________________

in the presence of:

____

Witness

____

Witness

TRUSTEE:

SIGNED, SEALED, and DELIVERED

by the said ______________________________________

in the presence of:

____

Witness

____

Witness

5. Commentary

(1) The language of all trust deeds tends to be archaic. Commas and the like are usually omitted in order to prevent dishonest persons from tampering with the original meaning by the introduction of internal punctuation.

(2) All of the essential elements for the validity of the trust and the trust deed are present in the above example. An additional element could be a protector who would normally have the right to replace the trustees and/or change the location of the trust.

(3) The main body of the trust deed is supplemented by:

- Schedule I listing the names and/or classes of beneficiaries.
- Schedule II setting out the powers and limitations of the trustees and the general provisions relating to the administration of the trust.
- Schedule III containing a fallback list of names and/or classes of beneficiaries if none of the Schedule I beneficiaries should be in existence at the perpetuity date.

(4) Clause 3 of Schedule III is a so-called Cuba Clause, i.e., a clause that makes possible the instant relocation of the trust to a new jurisdiction by the simple stratagem of the appointment of new trustees in a different jurisdiction.

(5) The trust is a "discretionary trust." Since the trustees will frequently find it increasingly difficult (and cumbersome) to be called upon to exercise many of their discretionary powers, it is a fairly frequent occurrence for the settlor or the principal beneficiary or a nominee to send a letter of wishes or letter of intent to the trustee.

(6) This letter of wishes is not binding and can be disregarded by the trustee.

(7) Since the trustee does usually follow the recommendations contained in the letter of wishes, the revenue may sometimes treat these recommendations as if they formed part of the trust deed.

6. Example of Deed Amending a Settlement / Declaration of Trust

THIS DEED is made the _____ day of __________, 2000

BY [ ] of [ ] (the "Trustee")

SUPPLEMENTAL TO:

(i) a [settlement/declaration of trust] dated [ ] [ ] 19 [ ] and made [between] [and/by] the Trustee and known as "The [ ] Trust" wherein trusts were declared concerning certain property therein described (the "Settlement"); and

(ii) [insert details of supplemental deeds]

WHEREAS:

A. The Trustee is the present trustee of the Settlement.

B. By clause [ ] of the Settlement the Trustee has power [by instrument in writing to make any alterations or additions to the provisions of the Settlement (whether of a beneficial or administrative nature) which is considers in its absolute discretion to be for the benefit of any one or more of the Beneficiaries].

C. The Trustee is desirous of exercising the power set out above in such manner as herein appears.

D. Where the context admits words and phrases used herein shall bear the same meaning herein as in the Settlement.

NOW THIS DEED WITNESSETH that in exercise of the power conferred upon [it/him] by clause [ ] of the Settlement the Trustee HEREBY [REVOCABLY] DECLARES that the Settlement shall be henceforth read and construed as if the provision specified in the Schedule hereto were expressly incorporated in the Settlement.

IN WITNESS WHEREOF this deed has been executed by the Trustee the day and year first above written.

THE SCHEDULE

[e.g. Before sub-clause ... there shall be inserted the following additional sub-clause: " _____________"]

THE COMMON SEAL of ________ was hereunto affixed in the presence of:

________________________ ________________________

Authorized signatory Authorized signatory

OR

SIGNED by the said [ ] in the presence of:

Witness' signature: ____________________

Witness' name: _______________________

Witness' address ______________________

____

Witness' occupation: ____________________

7. Example of Deed of Retirement of Trustee and Appointment of New Trustee by Trustee

THIS DEED OF RETIREMENT AND APPOINTMENT is made the _____ day of __________, 2000

BETWEEN

[ ] of [ ] (the "Retiring Trustee");

AND

[ ] of [ ] (the "New Trustee")

SUPPLEMENTAL TO:

(i) A [settlement/declaration of trust] dated [ ] and made [by/between [ ] and [ ] and known as ("The Trust") wherein trusts were declared concerning certain property therein described (the "Settlement"); and(insert details of supplemental deeds)

WHEREAS:

A. The Retiring Trustee is the present trustee of the Settlement.

B. By clause [ ] of the Settlement the Retiring Trustee has the power of appointing new trustees of the Settlement in the place of any trustee giving [not less than thirty days] notice of a desire to resign and be discharged from the trusts thereof.

C. The Retiring Trustee wishes to resign from the trusts of the Settlement and is desirous of appointing the New Trustee to be trustee in [his/its] place.

D. It is intended that the assets subject to the trust of the settlement (the "Trust Fund") shall forthwith be transferred into the name of the New Trustee in consideration for the covenants and indemnities set out below.

E. Where the context admits words and expressions used herein shall bear the same meaning herein as in the Settlement.

NOW THIS DEED WITNESSES as follows:

1. In exercise of the power conferred upon (him/it) by clause [ ] of and the[ ] Schedule to the Settlement and of every other power enabling it to do so the Retiring Trustee hereby appoints the New Trustee to be trustee of the Settlement and the New Trustee hereby accept such appointment.
2. The Retiring Trustee hereby resigns and is discharged from the trusts of the Settlement.
3. The parties hereby declare that the property comprised in the Trust Fund shall upon execution hereof vest in the New Trustee and the New Trustee hereby covenants and undertakes to execute all documents and take such other action as is necessary for the vesting of the Trust Fund in the New Trustee.
4. The New Trustee in [his/its] capacity as trustee of the Settlement hereby covenants and undertakes [for himself and his heirs assigns personal representatives and estate] [for itself its successors and assigns] to indemnify keep indemnified and hold harmless the Retiring Trustee [his heirs, assigns, personal representatives and estate] [its successors and assigns and its officers and employees and their respective heirs, assigns, personal representatives and estates] to the extent of the Trust Fund under [his/its] control from time to time against all actions, claims, costs, demand, loss or damage of any kind whatsoever and wheresoever arising directly or indirectly out of or in connection with the Settlement the Trust Fund or this deed whether the same shall be enforceable in law or not and in particular (but without prejudice to the generality of the foregoing) all taxes, duties and fiscal impositions (including all interest, costs, charges and expenses or other sums incurred in connection therewith) by the revenue authorities of any government in any part of the world EXCEPTING ONLY such actions, claims, cost, demands, loss or damage arising from any fraud, willful misconduct or [gross] negligence on the part of the Retiring Trustee.
5. The New Trustee hereby covenants further with the Retiring Trustee that:-
   (i) in the event of the New Trustee ceasing to be trustee of the Settlement then the New Trustee will cause [his/its] successor as trustee of the Settlement to enter into a covenant and indemnity with the Retiring Trustee covering the same matters as are covered by this

deed. In the event that the New Trustee fails to obtain the covenant and indemnity referred to in this sub-clause 5(i) then the limitation of liability contained in clause 4 hereof shall not apply and the New Trustee shall be deemed to have entered into the covenants and indemnities contained herein in a personal capacity as well as in [his/its] capacity as a trustee; and

(ii) if after the date hereof any person or persons (including a body corporate) becomes absolutely entitled to the Trust Fund or any part thereof (whether by way of a distribution or otherwise but not in the case of a distribution of trust income only) the New Trustee will not part with the Trust Fund or such part thereof except upon terms that such person or persons as aforesaid shall indemnify and keep indemnified the Retiring Trustee in respect of the same matters as are covered by this deed and shall give such security for the said indemnity as the Retiring Trustee shall reasonably require and such indemnity as the Retiring Trustee shall reasonably require and such indemnity in the case of a person or persons becoming absolutely entitled to part only of the Trust Fund to be in respect only of such actions, proceedings claims, demand, costs and expenses as aforesaid as shall relate to that part of the Trust Fund to which such person or persons becomes absolutely entitled. In the event that the New Trustee fails to obtain the covenant and indemnity referred to in this sub-clause 5 (ii) then the limitation of liability contained in clause 4 hereof shall not apply and the New Trustee shall be deemed to have entered into the covenants and indemnities contained herein in a personal capacity as well as in [his/its] capacity as a trustee.

6. This deed of retirement and appointment shall be governed by and construed in accordance with the laws of the Island of jersey and the parties hereto irrevocably submit to the non-exclusive jurisdiction of the courts of the said Island.

IN WITNESS whereof these present have been executed by the parties hereto the day and year first above written.

THE COMMON SEAL of [ ] was hereunto affixed in the presence of:

____________________ ____________________

Authorized signatory Authorized signatory

OR

SIGNED by the said [ ]in the presence of:

Witness' signature: ____________________

Witness' name: ______________________

Witness' address ______________________

____

Witness' occupation: ______________________

8. Example of Definitions of "Charitable Purpose" and "Excluded Persons"

"Charitable Purpose" means any purpose which is recognized as exclusively charitable under the laws of .... and (if different) the Proper Law of this Settlement;

"Excluded Persons" means:

1. all and any persons and classes of persons specified in the ..... Schedule hereto; and
2. such other persons and classes of persons as are added to the class of Excluded Persons in exercise of the powers conferred upon the Trustees under this Settlement;

"the Protector" means the protector appointed in accordance with the provisions hereof;

9. Example of Clause Relating to Proper Law

This Settlement is established under the laws of .... and subject to any change in the Proper Law of this Settlement duly made according to the powers and provisions hereinafter declared the Proper Law of this Settlement shall be the law of the .... and the courts of the said .... shall be the forum for the administration hereof.

10. Example of Clause Relating to Payments to Those Under Incapacity and to Charities

(a) Where the Trustees are authorized or required to pay or apply any income or capital of the Trust Fund to or for the benefit of any person who is a minor the Trustees shall have power in their absolute discretion either to pay the same to him as his absolute property notwithstanding that he is a minor and the receipt of any such minor Beneficiary shall be a good discharge to the Trustees therefore or to pay the same to any parent or lawful guardian of such minor or to apply the same in such manner as may be directed in writing by such parent or guardian and the receipt of such parent or guardian in either case shall be a sufficient discharge to the Trustees for any income or capital so paid or applied.

(b) Where the Trustees are authorized or required to pay or apply any income or capital of the Trust Fund to or for the benefit of any Beneficiary who is incapable by reason of mental disorder or otherwise the Trustees shall have power to pay the same to any curator guardian or other legal representative in any jurisdiction or to apply the same in such manner as may be directed in writing and authorized by such curator guardian or other legal representative and the receipt of such person in all cases shall be a sufficient discharge to the Trustees for any capital or income so paid or applied.

(c) Where the Trustees are authorized or required to pay or apply any income of the Trust Fund to or for the benefit of any charity the Trustees shall have power to accept the receipt of any person purporting to be the treasurer or other proper officer or one of the trustees or a sole trustee for the time being of any such charity and so that any such receipt shall be an effectual discharge to the Trustees for any sum of income or capital paid or applied to or for the benefit of such charity hereunder.

11. Example of Clause Relating to Power of Exclusion

(a) The Trustees may by deed made at any time during the Trust Period declare that any person or member of a class named or specified (whether or not ascertained) in such declaration who is would or might but for this clause be or become a Beneficiary:-

(i) shall be wholly or partially excluded from future benefit hereunder; or

(ii) shall cease to be a Beneficiary; or

(iii) shall be an Excluded Person

and any such declaration may be irrevocable or revocable during the Trust Period and shall have effect from the date specified in the said declaration provided that this power shall not be capable of being exercised so as to derogate from any interest to which any Beneficiary has previously become indefeasibly entitled whether in possession or in reversion or otherwise.

(b) Any person of full age to whom or for whose benefit any capital or income of the Trust Fund is or may become liable whether directly or indirectly to be appointed transferred or applied in any manner whatsoever by or in consequence of an exercise of any trust power or discretion vested in the Trustees or in any other person may by declaration in writing during the Trust Period either:

(i) irrevocably disclaim his whole interest; or

(ii) irrevocably or revocably disclaim part of his interest (but revocable during the Trust Period only); or

(iii) declare that he shall either permanently or for such period as therein stated cease to be a Beneficiary; or

(iv) declare that he shall either permanently or for such period as therein stated be an Excluded Person

and so that any such declaration shall apply whether or not the Beneficiary has received some benefit from his interest.

12. Example of Clause Relating to Power of Addition

(a) The Trustees shall have power at any time during the Trust Period to add as a Beneficiary such person or class of persons (not being an Excluded Person) as the Trustees shall in their absolute discretion determine.

(b) Any such addition shall be made by deed signed by the Trustees and:-

(i) name or describe the person or class of persons to be thereby added as a Beneficiary; and

(ii) specify the date (not being earlier than the date of the deed but during the Trust Period) from which such person or class of persons shall be so added.

13. Example of Clause Relating to Power to Change Proper Law

The Trustees may at any time during the Trust Period by deed declare that the Proper Law of this Settlement shall from the date of such deed or from such date as is specified therein or upon the occurrence of such circumstances as are specified therein be the law of some other jurisdiction and that the forum for the administration thereof shall thenceforth be the courts of that jurisdiction but subject to the power conferred by this clause and until any further declaration be made hereunder PROVIDED ALWAYS that so often as any such declaration as aforesaid shall be made the Trustees shall be at liberty to make such consequential alterations or additions in or to the trusts powers and provisions of the Settlement as the Trustees may consider necessary or desirable to ensure that the trusts powers and provisions of this Settlement shall (mutatis mutandis) be as valid and effective as they are under the Proper Law of this Settlement.

14. Example of Clause Relating to Power of Appointment of New or Additional Trustees

(a) If any Trustee whether original additional or substituted shall die or being a company shall be dissolved or shall give notice of desire to withdraw and be discharged from the trusts hereof under the provisions of sub-clause (b) of this clause or shall refuse or become unfit to act then the persons specified in the ..... Schedule hereto in order of priority may by deed appoint one or more other persons wheresoever resident but subject to any exclusions or provisions specified in the ..... Schedule to be a Trustee hereof in place of the trustee so deceased dissolved desiring to withdraw and be discharged refusing or becoming unfit to act.

(b) If any Trustee hereof shall at any time desire to withdraw and be discharged from the trusts hereof he may (subject to any exclusions or provisions specified in the ..... Schedule) so do by notice in writing executed by himself given to his co-trustees (if any) or failing which to the person having for the time being power to appoint new or additional Trustees hereof and:-

 (i) upon the expiration of any period specified therein; or subject thereto

 (ii) upon the delivery of such notice the Trustee so doing shall cease to be a Trustee hereof to all intents and purposes except as to acts and deeds necessary for the proper vesting of the Trust Fund in the continuing or new Trustee or otherwise as the case may require.

(c) The person for the time being having the power to appoint new Trustees hereof shall (subject always to any exclusions and provisions specified in the ..... Schedule have power to appoint one or more other persons wheresoever resident or situate to be additional Trustees hereof.

(d) Acts and deeds done or executed for the proper vesting of the Trust Fund in new additional or continuing Trustees shall be done or executed by the continuing or retiring Trustee at the expense of the income or capital of the Trust Fund.

(e) There shall be no obligation to have more than one Trustee of this Settlement.

15. Example of Clause Relating to Power to Remove Trustees

(a) The persons specified in the ..... Schedule hereto in order of priority may at any time by notice in writing given to the Trustees remove one or more of such Trustees (the "relevant trustee") with effect from the date specified in such notice not being earlier than 30 days from the date on which such notice is provided to the relevant trustee whereupon the relevant trustee shall execute such documents and do such things as may be necessary to give proper effect to such removal.

(b) The power to remove Trustees shall not be exercised so as to reduce the number of Trustees of this Settlement beneath the minimum number permitted under the Proper Law provided always that should the person specified in the ..... Schedule hereto as having power for the time being to remove Trustees (for the purposes of this sub-clause only hereinafter referred to as the "Appointor") desire to remove the Trustees in such a manner as would result in such a reduction the Appointor shall have power to appoint an additional Trustee of this Settlement provided always that the Appointor shall then exercise the power to remove the Trustees so desired to be removed.

(c) Acts and deeds done or executed by the relevant trustee for the proper vesting of the Trust Fund in the continuing or new Trustee or Trustees or otherwise as the case may require shall be done or executed by the relevant trustee at the expense of the income or capital of the Trust Fund.

16. Example of Clause Relating to the Protector

(a) The first Protector shall be the person or persons named in the ..... Schedule hereto who shall signify his or their willingness to act in such capacity by declaration in writing to the Trustees.

(b) A new Protector shall be appointed whenever the Protector for the time being (being an individual) dies or wishes to be discharged from the position of Protector or (being a company) is put into liquidation (whether voluntary or compulsory) or is declared en désastre or otherwise ceases to exist or passes a resolution to the effect that it desires to be discharged from the position of Protector.

(c) Such new Protector shall be appointed by declaration in writing or by will or codicil signed by the person making such appointment and the same shall be effective at the time or upon the occurrence of the events mentioned in the declaration or (in the event that no such time or event is mentioned) when the declaration or certified copy thereof effecting the same is received by the Trustees who shall cause a memorandum of such appointment to be endorsed on this Settlement.

(d) Power to appoint a new Protector shall be vested in such persons as are specified in the ..... Schedule hereto in the order of priority and in the manner and subject to such conditions (if any) therein specified.

(e) If at any time there is for a period of six months no Protector the Trustees shall from the expiration of that period and unless and until a Protector is appointed under sub-clause (d) of this clause have power themselves to appoint a person other than one of the Trustees to be the Protector and any appointment duly made by them under this power shall have effect in all respects as if it had been duly made under sub-clause (d) of this clause.

17. Example of Clause Relating to Powers of Protector

(a) Notwithstanding anything herein contained and in particular anything conferring an absolute or uncontrolled discretion on the Trustees hereof all and every power and discretion vested in the Trustees by such provisions of this Settlement as are specified in the ..... Schedule hereto shall only be exercisable by them with the prior or simultaneous written consent of the Protector PROVIDED THAT if the Trustees shall not have received a written consent or refusal of the Protector within thirty days of the Trustees requesting such consent in writing to the last known address of the Protector the Protector shall be deemed to have consented thereto for the purposes of this clause.

(b) Any written consent of the Protector required under the terms of this Settlement may be given either specifically in relation to any particular matter or by general written consent referring to one or more matters or to circumstances generally and such general consent may be given either permanently or for such period or periods as shall be specified in the consent.

18. Example of Clause Relating to Release or Abeyance of the Protector's Powers

(a) The Protector may from time to time by written notice to the Trustees (a memorandum of which shall be endorsed on or permanently attached to this Settlement) declare (either generally or in relation to any particular act or acts and either permanently or for such period as shall be specified in the notice) that any act or acts herein declared to require the consent of the Protector shall not require such consent and the said notice shall be effective according to its terms.

(b) If and whenever and so long as there is no Protector capable of acting a memorandum to that effect shall be endorsed on or permanently attached to this Settlement and all the provisions of this Settlement (other than the provisions relating to the appointment of a new Protector and this present clause) shall be read and have effect as though references to the Protector or the consent of the Protector were omitted.

19. Example of Schedule for Appointment of New or Additional Trustees

[The following persons in the following order of priority shall have the power to appoint new or additional Trustees:

1.
2.
3. The Trustees or the personal representative or liquidator of the last remaining Trustee.]

20. Example of Schedule for Removal of Trustees

[The following persons in the following order of priority shall have the power to remove Trustees:

1.
2.
3.]

21. Example of Schedule for Consent of Protector

The following powers shall not be exercised by the Trustees without the prior or simultaneous written consent of the Protector:

[LIST THESE AND REFER TO CLAUSES ________]

THE COMMON SEAL of [   ] was hereunto affixed in the presence of

________________________ ________________________

Authorized signatory Authorized signatory

OR

SIGNED by the said [   ]in the presence of:

Witness' signature: ______________________

Witness' name: ________________________

Witness' address _______________________

____

Witness' occupation: ___________________

APPENDIX II

HAGUE CONVENTION ON THE LAW APPLICABLE TO TRUSTS AND ON THEIR RECOGNITION

Chapter I—Scope

Article 1

This Convention specifies the law applicable to trusts and governs their recognition.

Article 2

For the purposes of this Convention, the term "trust" refers to the legal relationship created—inter vivos or on death—by a person, the settlor, when assets have been placed under the control of a trustee for the benefit of a beneficiary or for a specified purpose.

A trust has the following characteristics—

(a) the assets constitute a separate fund and are not a part of the trustee's own estate;

(b) title to the trust assets stands in the name of the trustee or in the name of another person on behalf of the trustee;

(c) the trustee has the power and the duty, in respect of which he is accountable, to manage, employ or dispose of the assets in accordance with the terms of the trust and the special duties imposed upon him by law.

The reservation by the settlor of certain rights and powers, and the fact that the trustee may himself have rights as a beneficiary are not necessarily inconsistent with the existence of a trust.

Article 3

The Convention applies only to trusts created voluntarily and evidenced in writing.

Article 4

The Convention does not apply to preliminary issues relating to the validity of wills or of other acts by virtue of which assets are transferred to the trustee.

Article 5

The Convention does not apply to the extent that the law specified by Chapter II does not provide for trusts or the category of trusts involved.

Chapter II—Applicable Law

Article 6

A trust shall be governed by the law chosen by the settlor. The choice must be express or be implied in the terms of the instrument creating or the writing evidencing the trust, interpreted, if necessary, in the light of the circumstances of the case.

Where the law chosen under the previous paragraph does not provide for trusts or the category of trust involved, the choice shall not be effective and the law specified in Article 7 shall apply.

Article 7

Where no applicable law has been chosen, a trust shall be governed by the law with which it is most closely connected.

In ascertaining the law with which a trust is most closely connected reference shall be made in particular to—

(a) the place of administration of the trust designated by the settlor;

(b) the situs of the assets of the trust;

(c) the place of residence or business of the trustee;

(d) the objects of the trust and the places where they are to be fulfilled.

Article 8

The law specified by Article 6 or 7 shall govern the validity of the trust, its construction, its effects and the administration of the trust.

In particular that law shall govern—

(a) the appointment, resignation and removal of trustees, the capacity to act as a trustee, and the devolution of the office of trustee;

(b) the rights and duties of trustees among themselves;

(c) the right of trustees to delegate in whole or in part the discharge of their duties or the exercise of their powers;

(d) the power of trustees to administer or to dispose of trust assets, to create security interests in the trust assets, or to acquire new assets;

(e) the powers of investment of trustees;

(f) restrictions upon the duration of the trust, and upon the power to accumulate the income of the trust;

(g) the relationship between the trustees and the beneficiaries including the personal liability of the trustees to the beneficiaries;

(h) the variation or termination of the trust;

(i) the distribution of the trust assets;

(j) the duty of trustees to account for their administration.

Article 9

In applying this Chapter a severable aspect of the trust, particularly matters of administration, may be governed by a different law.

Article 10

The law applicable to the validity of the trust shall determine whether that law or the law governing a severable aspect of the trust may be replaced by another law.

Chapter III—Recognition

Article 11

A trust created in accordance with the law specified by the preceding Chapter shall be recognised as a trust.

Such recognition shall imply as a minimum that the trust property constitutes a separate fund, that the trustee may sue and be sued in his capacity as trustee, and that he may appear or act in this capacity before a notary or any person acting in an official capacity.

In so far as the law applicable to the trust requires or provides, such recognition shall imply in particular—

(a) that personal creditors of the trustee shall have no recourse against the trust assets;

(b) that the trust assets shall not form part of the trustee's estate upon his insolvency or bankruptcy;

(c) that the trust assets shall not form part of the matrimonial property of the trustee or his spouse nor part of the trustee's estate upon his death;

(d) that the trust assets may be recovered when the trustee, in breach of trust, has mingled trust assets with his own property or has alienated trust assets. However, the rights and obligations of any third party holder of the assets shall remain subject to the law determined by the choice of law rules of the forum.

Article 12

Where the trustee desires to register assets, movable or immovable, or documents of title to them, he shall be entitled, in so far as this is not prohibited by or inconsistent with the law of the State where registration is sought, to do so in his capacity as trustee or in such other way that the existence of the trust is disclosed.

…

Article 14

The Convention shall not prevent the application rules of law more favourable to the recognition of trusts.

Chapter IV—General Clauses

Article 15

The Convention does not prevent the application of provisions of the law designated by the conflicts rules of the forum, in so far as those provisions cannot be derogated from by voluntary act, relating in particular to the following matters—

(a) the protection of minors and incapable parties;
(b) the personal and proprietary effects of marriage;
(c) succession rights, testate and intestate, especially the indefeasible shares of spouses and relatives;
(d) the transfer of title to property and security interests in property;
(e) the protection of creditors in matters of insolvency;
(f) the protection, in other respects, of third parties acting in good faith.

If recognition of a trust is prevented by application of the preceding paragraph, the court shall try to give effect to the objects of the trust by other means.

Article 16

The Convention does not prevent the application of those provisions of the law of the forum which must be applied even to international situations, irrespective of rules of conflict of laws.

Article 17

In the Convention the word "law" means the rules of law in force in a State other than its rules of conflict of laws.

Article 18

The provisions of the Convention may be disregarded when their application would be manifestly incompatible with public policy.

...

Article 22

The Convention applies to trusts regardless of the date on which they were created.

APPENDIX III

STATUTE OF ELIZABETH

TEXT OF THE STATUTE OF ELIZABETH 1571 (13 ELIZ., C.5) (WITH MODERN SPELLING)

An Act against fraudulent deeds, alienations, etc.

For the avoiding and abolishing of feigned, convinous and fraudulent feoffments, gifts, grants, alienations, conveyances, bonds, suits, judgments and executions, as well as lands and tenements, as of goods and chattels, more commonly used and practised in these days than hath been seen or heard of heretofore: (2) which feoffments, gifts, grants, alienations, conveyances, bonds, suits, judgments and executions, have been and are devised and contrived of malice, fraud, covin, collusion or guile, to the end, purpose and intent, to delay, hinder, or defraud creditors and others of their just and lawful actions, suits, debts, accounts, damages, penalties, forfeitures, heriots, mortuaries and reliefs, not only to thc lct or hindrance of the due course and execution of law and justice, but also to the overthrow of all true and plain dealing, bargaining, and chevisance between man and man, without the which no commonwealth or civil society can be maintained or continued:

1. Be it therefore declared, ordained and enacted, by this Present Parliament, That all and every feoffment, gift, grant, alienation, bargain and conveyance of lands, tenements, hereditaments, goods and chattels, or of any of them, or of any lease, rent, common or other profit or charge out of the same lands, tenements, hereditaments, goods and chattels, or any of them, by writing or otherwise, (2) and all and every bond, suit, judgment and execution, at any time had or made sithence the beginning of the Queen's majesty's reign that now is, or at any time hereafter to be had or made, (3) to or for any intent or purpose before declared and expressed, shall be from henceforth deemed and taken (only as against that person or persons, his or their heirs, successors, executors, administrators and assigns, and every of them, whose actions, suits, debts, accounts, damages, penalties, forfeitures, heriots, mortuaries and reliefs, by such guileful, covinous or fraudulent devies and practices, as is aforesaid, are, shall or might be in any wise disturbed, hindered, delayed or defrauded) to be clearly and utterly void, frustrate, and of none effect; any pretence, colour, feigned considerations, expressing of use, or any other matter or thing to the contrary notwithstanding.

2. And be it further enacted by the authority aforesaid, That all and every the parties to such feigned, covinous or fraudulent feoffment, gift, grant, alienation, bargain, conveyance, bonds, suits, judgments, executions and other things before expressed, and being privy and knowing of the same, or any of them; (2) which at any time after the tenth day of June next coming shall wittingly and willingly put in use, avow, maintain, justify or defend the same, or any of them, as true, simple, and done, had or made bona fide and upon good consideration; (3) or shall alien or assign any the lands, tenements, goods, leases or other things beforementioned, to him or them conveyed as is aforesaid, or any part thereof; (4) shall incur the penalty and forfeiture of one year's value of the said lands, tenements, and hereditaments, leases, rents, commons or other profits, of or out of the same; (5) and the whole value of the said goods and chattels; (6) and also so much money as are or shall be contained in any such covinous and feigned bond; (7) the one moiety whereof to be to the Queen's majesty, her heirs and successors, and other moiety to the party or parties grieved by such feigned and fraudulent feoffment, gift, grant, alienation, bargain, conveyance, bonds, suits, judgments, executions, leases, rents, commons, profits, charges and other things aforesaid, to be recovered in any of the Queen's courts of record by action of debt, bill, plaint or information, wherein no essoin, protection or wager of law shall be admitted for the defendant or defendants; (8) and also being thereof lawfully convicted, shall suffer imprisonment for one half year without bail or mainprise.

3. Provided always, and be it further enacted by the authority aforesaid, That whereas sundry common recoveries of lands, tenements and hereditaments have therefore been had, and hereafter may be had against tenant in tail, or other tenant of the freehold, the reversion or remainder, or the right of reversion or remainder, then being in any other person or persons; (2) that every such common recover heretofore had, and hereafter to be had, of any lands, tenements or hereditaments shall as touching such person and persons which then had any remainder or reversion, or right of remainder or reversion, and against the heirs of every of them, stand, remain and be of such like force and effect, and of none other, as the same should have been if this act had never had not made.

4. Provided always, and be it further enacted by the authority aforesaid. That this act, or any thing therein contained, shall not extend to make void any estate or conveyance, by reason whereof any person or persons shall use any voucher in any writ of Formedon, now depending or hereafter to be depending, but that all and every such vouchers in any writ of Formedon shall stand and be in like force and effect, as if this Act had never been had not made, any thing before in this act contained to the contrary notwithstanding.

5. Provided also, and be it enacted by the authority aforesaid, That this act, or any thing therein contained, shall not extend to any estate or interest in land, tenements, hereditaments, leases, rents, commons, profits, goods or chattels, had, made, conveyed or assured, or hereafter to be had, made, conveyed or assured, which estate or interest is or shall be upon good consideration and bona fide lawfully conveyed or assured, to any person or persons, or bodies politic or corporate, not having at the time of such conveyance or assurance to them made, any manner of notice or knowledge of such covin, fraud or collusion as is aforesaid; any thing before mentioned to the contrary hereof notwithstanding.

6. This act to endure unto the end of the first session of the next Parliament.

APPENDIX IV

EXCHANGE OF INFORMATION UNDER ARTICLE 26 OF THE OECD MODEL CONVENTION

Article 26 of the OECD Model Convention

" Exchange of information

1. The competent authorities of the Contracting States shall exchange such information as is necessary for carrying out the provisions of this Convention or of the domestic laws of the Contracting States concerning taxes covered by the Convention insofar as the taxation thereunder is not contrary to the Convention. The exchange of information is not restricted by Article 1. Any information received by a Contracting State shall be treated as secret in the same manner as information obtained under the domestic laws of that State and shall be disclosed only to persons or authorities (including courts and administrative bodies) involved in the assessment or collection of, the enforcement or prosecution in respect of, or the determination of appeals in relation to, the taxes covered by the Convention. Such persons or authorities shall use the information only for such purposes. They may disclose the information in public court proceedings or in judicial decisions.
2. In no case shall the provisions of paragraph 1 be construed so as to impose on a Contracting State the obligation:
   (a) to carry out administrative measures at variance with the laws and administrative practice of that or of the other Contracting State;

   (b) to supply information which is not obtainable under the laws or in the normal course of the administration of that or of the other Contracting State;

   (c) to supply information which would disclose any trade, business, industrial, commercial or professional secret or trade process, or information, the disclosure of which would be contrary to public policy (ordre public)."

OECD Commentary on Model Article 26

1-4 (Preliminary remarks : not reproduced)

Commentary on paragraph 1

5. The main rule concerning the exchange of information is contained in the first sentence of the paragraph. The competent authorities of the Contracting States shall exchange such information as is necessary to secure the correct application of the provisions of the Convention or of the domestic laws of the Contracting States concerning taxes covered by the Convention even if, in the latter case, a particular Article of the Convention need not be applied. In order to keep the exchange of information within the framework of the Convention, a limitation to the exchange of information is set so that information should be given only insofar as the national tax in question is covered by the Convention and the taxation under the domestic taxation laws concerned is not contrary to the Convention. An illustration may be cited in this connection: a request for the imposition of a sales tax need not be complied with by the requested State as it is not covered by the Convention.

6. The following examples may clarify the principle dealt with in para 5 above. In all such cases information can be exchanged under para 1.

7. Application of the Convention.

(a) When applying Art 12, State A where the beneficiary is resident asks State B where the payer is resident, for information concerning the amount of royalty transmitted.

(b) Conversely, in order to grant the exemption provided for in Art 12, State B asks State A whether the recipient of the amounts paid is in fact a resident of the last-mentioned State and the beneficial owner of the royalties.

(c) Similarly, information may be needed with a view to the proper allocation of taxable profits between associated companies in different States or the adjustment of the profits shown in the accounts of a permanent establishment in one State and in the accounts of the head office in the other State.

8. Implementation of the domestic laws.

(a) A company in State A supplies goods to an independent company in State B. State A wishes to know from State B what price the company in State B paid for the goods with a view to a correct application of the provisions of its domestic laws.

(b) A company in State A sells goods through a company in State C (possibly a low-tax country) to a company in State B. The companies may or may not be associated. There is no convention between State A and State C, nor between State B and State C. Under the convention between A and B, State A, with a view to ensuring the correct application of the provisions of its domestic laws to the profits made by the company situated in its territory, asks State B what price the company in State B paid for the goods.

(c) State A, for the purpose of taxing a company situated in its territory, asks State B, under the convention between A and B, for information about the prices charged by a company in State B, or a group of companies in State B with which the company in State A has no business contacts in order to enable it to check the prices charged by the company in State A by direct comparison (eg prices charged by a company or a group of companies in a dominant position). It should be borne in mind that the exchange of information in this case might be a difficult and delicate matter owing in particular to the provisions of para 2(c) relating to business and other secrets.

9. The rule laid down in para 1 allows information to be exchanged in three different ways—

(a) on request, with a special case in mind, it being understood that the regular sources of information available under the internal taxation procedure should be relied upon in the first place before request for information is made to the other State;

(b) automatically, for example when information about one or various categories of income having their source in one Contracting State and received in the other Contracting State is transmitted systematically to the other State;

(c) spontaneously, for example in the case of a State having acquired, through certain investigations, information which it supposes to be of interest to the other State.

10. The manner in which the exchange of information agreed to in the Convention will finally be effected can be decided upon by the competent authorities of the Contracting States.

11. Reciprocal assistance between tax administrations is feasible only if each administration is assured that the other administration will treat with proper confidence the information which it will receive in the course of their co-operation. At the same time maintenance of such secrecy in the receiving Contracting State is a matter of domestic laws. It is therefore provided in para 1 that information communicated under the provisions of the Convention shall be treated as secret in the receiving State in the same manner as information obtained under the domestic laws of that State. Sanctions for the violation of such secrecy in that State will be governed by the administrative and penal laws of that State.

12. The information obtained may be disclosed only to persons and authorities involved in the assessment or collection of, the enforcement or prosecution in respect of, or the determination of appeals in relation to, the taxes covered by the Convention. This means that the information may also be communicated to the taxpayer, his proxy or to the witnesses. The information received by a Contracting State may be used by such persons or authorities only for the purposes mentioned in para 1. If the information appears to be of value to the receiving State for other purposes than those referred to, that State may not use the information for such other purposes but it must resort to means specially designed for those purposes (e.g., in case of a nonfiscal crime, to a treaty concerning judicial assistance).

13. As stated above, the information obtained can be communicated to the persons and authorities mentioned but it does not follow from this that it can be disclosed by them in court sessions held in public or in decisions which reveal the name of the taxpayer. The last sentence of the paragraph, however, opens up this possibility. Once information is used in public court proceedings or in court decisions and thus rendered public, it is clear that from that moment such information can be quoted from the court files or decisions for other purposes even as possible evidence. But this does not mean that the persons and authorities mentioned in para 1 are allowed to provide on request additional information received. If either or both of the Contracting States object to the information being made public by courts in this way, or, once the information has been made public in this way, to the information being used for other purposes, because this is not the normal procedure under their domestic laws, they should state this expressly in their convention.

Commentary on paragraph 2

14. This paragraph contains certain limitations to the main rule in favor of the requested State. In the first place, the paragraph contains the clarification that a Contracting State is not bound to go beyond its own internal laws and administrative practice in putting information at the disposal of the other Contracting State. However, types of administrative measures authorized for the purpose of the requested State's tax must be utilized, even though invoked solely to provide information to the other Contracting State. Likewise, internal provisions concerning tax secrecy should not be interpreted as constituting an obstacle to the exchange of information under the present Article. As mentioned above, the authorities of the requesting State are obliged to observe secrecy with regard to information received under this Article.

15. Furthermore, the requested State does not need to go so far as to carry out administrative measures that are not permitted under the laws or practice of the requesting State or to supply items of information that are not obtainable under the laws or in the normal course of administration of the requesting State. It follows that a Contracting State cannot take advantage of the information system of the other Contracting State if it is wider than its own system.

16. Information is deemed to be obtainable in the normal course of administration if it is in the possession of the tax authorities or can be obtained by them in the normal procedure of tax determination, which may include special investigations or special examination of the business accounts kept by the taxpayer or other persons, provided that the tax authorities would make similar investigations or examination for their own purposes. This means that the requested State has to collect the information the other State needs in the same way as if its own taxation was involved, under the proviso mentioned in para 15 above.

17. The requested State is at liberty to refuse to give information in the cases referred to in the paragraphs above. However if it does give the requested information, it remains within the framework of the agreement on the exchange of information which is laid down in the Convention; consequently it cannot be objected that this State has failed to observe the obligation to secrecy.

APPENDIX V

OECD REPORT ON HARMFUL TAX COMPETITION—AN EMERGING GLOBAL ISSUE

Recommendations concerning domestic legislation and practices

1. ***Recommendation concerning Controlled Foreign Corporations (CFC) or equivalent rules: that countries that do not have such rules consider adopting them and that countries that have such rules ensure that they apply in a fashion consistent with the desirability of curbing harmful tax practices.***

Under Controlled Foreign Corporations (CFC) rules, certain income of a CFC is attributed to and taxed currently in the hands of its resident shareholders. Because CFC rules are intended to eliminate the benefits of the deferral of domestic tax on some or all of the foreign source income of a CFC in most countries that have already implemented CFC rules, the rules primarily serve the function to counter tax avoidance by discouraging the legal migration of certain types of income, e.g., base company and passive income to non-resident companies. Many of them extend the rules to foreign trusts that are used for the same purpose.

CFC rules have been developed for a variety of purposes in the light of the overall international tax policies of member countries. In some cases, the policy focus is on tax avoidance transactions and in others represents a broader limitation on the deferral of tax on income realized through foreign subsidiaries. Such rules are an effective tool to deal with harmful tax practices. However, their effectiveness is reduced by the fact that they are not applied by all countries and even in those countries that do apply them, they do not cover all situations of harmful tax practices. While the Recommendation only applies in the context of curbing harmful tax practices, CFC rules may also apply in situations which do not involve harmful tax practices as defined in this Report. It is recognized that countries retain their right to use such rules in such situations.

A 1996 OECD Report on Controlled Foreign Company Legislation showed that 14 OECD Member countries had CFC legislation.[1] Although there is considerable

---

1. Controlled Foreign Company Legislation, Studies in Foreign Source Income (OECD 1996). Korea and Mexico adopted CFC legislation in 1997.

variation in the technical details of this legislation, the objectives set for these regimes are remarkably similar in almost all countries and the structural features are quite similar in many countries.

The Recommendation is twofold. First, countries that do not have CFC rules are asked to consider adopting CFC rules or equivalent rules as one measure to counter harmful tax competition. Whether a country feels the need for such rules will depend in part upon its evaluation of the effectiveness of its existing measures. Second, countries are asked to consider applying their CFC or equivalent rules in appropriate cases to income and entities covered by tax practices considered, on the basis of the factors developed ... to constitute harmful tax competition. While the specificities of domestic tax systems do not allow for the harmonization of CFC rules or for the development of model CFC provision, greater co-ordination in targeting such domestic rules will be a useful improvement. Accordingly, Member countries are urged, with the continued co-ordination by the OECD, to try for congruence of results of their respective CFC or equivalent legislation in a manner consistent with the objectives of this Report. Further work may enable the Committee to elaborate on some minimum standards for the design of such regimes in terms of their effectiveness in counteracting harmful tax practices. Moreover, it would also be useful to examine more closely the interrelationship between CFC, Foreign Investment Fund and Foreign Trust legislation in order to improve their overall effectiveness in combating harmful tax practices. However, this should not delay action on the part of countries which do not now have CFC or equivalent rules.

2. ***Recommendation concerning foreign investment fund or equivalent rules: that countries that do not have such rules consider adopting them and that countries that have such rules consider applying them to income and entities covered by practices considered to constitute harmful tax competition.***

In general, CFC rules that subject the CFC's income to current tax apply only to foreign corporations controlled by resident shareholders that own a significant interest in a CFC (for example, 10 per cent or greater). Thus, residents may defer domestic tax by acquiring shares in foreign mutual funds. If such funds are widely owned, they will not be controlled by a small group of resident shareholders; nor will any one resident shareholder own a significant interest in the fund. Thus, owners of foreign mutual funds will not be subject to the anti-abuse protections afforded by resident countries' CFC rules. To counter this situation, several countries have adopted foreign investment fund (FIF) or equivalent rules to deal with this situation although they are not yet widespread in Member countries. In some countries, the underlying policy of the FIF rules is to supplement the CFC rules. In other countries, the policy of FIF rules is much broader; they are intended to eliminate the benefit of deferral for virtually all passive investments in foreign entities.

FIF rules constitute an effective tool against regimes that offer favorable tax treatment in order to attract foreign passive investment from resident individual, rather than corporate, shareholders. As such they should be encouraged as a way to address one form of harmful tax competition.

The Recommendation mirrors that related to CFC or equivalent rules. First, countries that do not have FIF or equivalent rules are asked to consider adopting such rules. Second, countries are asked to consider applying such rules in appropriate cases to income and entities covered by tax practices considered, under the criteria developed ... to constitute harmful tax competition.

3. Recommendation concerning restrictions on participation exemption and other systems of exempting foreign income in the context of harmful tax competition: that countries that apply the exemption method to eliminate double taxation of foreign source income consider adopting rules that would ensure that foreign income that has benefited from tax practices deemed as constituting harmful tax competition do not qualify for the application of the exemption method.

Most, if not all, exemption countries have certain limitations applicable to their exemption system. These measures include, for example, restricting the exemption to active business income and taxing passive income regardless of its source.

On the basis of restrictions that already exist in the legislation of Member countries, possible "minimum" restrictions could be designed on the basis of:

— the countries from which the foreign income originates: for example, it could be decided that income originating from a country that is included in a list of tax havens or from listed harmful preferential tax regimes should not be granted exemption;

— the type of income: foreign income that clearly could be attributed to practices constituting harmful preferential tax regimes would not be entitled to exemption;

— the effective rate of tax to which the income has been subjected: restrictions based on a minimum rate of foreign tax effectively paid are often found in participation exemption systems. They should, however, be linked to the other aspects of harmful preferential tax regimes ...

4. Recommendation concerning foreign information reporting rules: that countries that do not have rules concerning reporting of international transactions and foreign operations of resident taxpayers consider adopting such rules and that countries exchange information obtained under these rules.

This Recommendation aims at introducing measures that will assist countries in obtaining information about the foreign activities of their residents which may be relevant to counteracting harmful tax practices (e.g., transactions with related foreign payers, the ownership of foreign property such as financial accounts of any kind, transfers to and distributions from certain foreign entities, etc.). Tax authorities require information in order to be able to administer the income tax system properly. Obtaining information concerning taxpayers' foreign activities is especially difficult because such information is often located outside a country's jurisdiction and is often held by a separate legal entity. As a result, some countries have enacted special information reporting requirements with respect to international transactions and foreign operations of resident taxpayers.

The Recommendation is to the effect that countries that do not have such rules consider introducing them with respect to harmful tax practices and that the information obtained under these rules be shared with any other countries for which it is relevant through exchanges of information on the basis of the provisions of Article 26 of the OECD Model Tax Convention, due account being taken of administrative and compliance costs and the need to respect confidentiality.

5. ***Recommendation concerning rulings: that countries, where administrative decisions concerning the particular position of a taxpayer may be obtained in advance of planned transactions, make public the conditions for granting, denying or revoking such decisions.***

The absence of details concerning certain administrative practices through which taxpayers' positions are determined, in particular on issues such as the arm's length value of certain services or the allocation of profits or losses between associated enterprises or between head offices and their permanent establishments, contributes to making a tax system non-transparent. This results in distortions in relation to States which, under their legal system, are required to apply their tax regimes in the same way vis-à-vis all taxpayers.

The ignorance of the existence of a regime for obtaining administrative decisions on specific planned transactions, or of the conditions for granting or denying such decisions, may result in unequal treatment of taxpayers since the lack of public information on this regime may put taxpayers in different positions when determining their tax situation. Greater transparency concerning the conditions for eligibility to a particular regime will therefore favor a greater equality of treatment of taxpayers in a similar position.

The publication, in a way that protects taxpayer confidentiality, of the substantive and procedural conditions for granting or denying individual tax rulings, ensures a greater transparency of countries' tax policies concerning certain activities that may easily be re-located, and is essential to the application of measures to prevent harmful tax competition from being developed individually or collectively by countries. Without it, measures which are now "transparent" may well be transformed into non-transparent regimes.

6. ***Recommendation concerning transfer pricing rules: that countries follow the principles set out in the OECD's 1995 Guidelines on Transfer Pricing and thereby refrain from applying or not applying their transfer pricing rules in a way that would constitute harmful tax competition.***

A country may decide to deviate from the arm's length principle as set out in the OECD 1995 Guidelines as a means of making that country a tax-favored intermediary. Such action can constitute harmful tax competition. This Recommendation is directed at eliminating such behavior and encourages all countries to follow consistently the principles set out in the 1995 Guidelines both for resident and non-resident taxpayers. it applies in particular to regimes under which the specific position of a taxpayer is determined by administrative decision. These considerations will be taken into account by the Committee in the process of monitoring the implementation of the 1995 Guidelines.

7. ***Recommendation concerning access to banking information for tax purposes: in the context of counteracting harmful tax competition, countries should review their laws, regulations and practices which govern access to banking information with a view to removing impediments to the access to such information by tax authorities.***

Whilst recognizing the confidential nature of the relationship between a bank and its clients, countries agree that, in the context of harmful tax competition, provisions which unduly restrict access by tax authorities to banking information required for the assessment of taxes are a serious impediment to the fair and effective implementation of tax rules and may distort the allocation of financial flows between countries by providing an unfair competitive advantage to those financial centers which operate such provisions (see, however, paragraph 12 for a discussion of how withholding taxes interact with exchange of information). The new Forum will be used to review progress made in the removal of provisions that impede access to banking information in the context of counteracting harmful tax practices. The Committee will complete ... a survey of provisions governing access to banking information by tax authorities in force in Member countries and has begun preparing a broad set of proposals on how to improve the access of tax authorities to banking information.

Recommendations concerning tax treaties

This section sets out a series of Recommendations by which countries can use their tax treaties to counter harmful tax practices. Recommendations, 8, 9, 10 and 11 are closely interrelated and are aimed at ensuring that tax treaties are not used to facilitate harmful tax practices.

8. ***Recommendation concerning greater and more efficient use of exchanges of information: that countries should undertake programs to intensify exchange of relevant information concerning transactions in tax havens and preferential tax regimes constituting harmful tax competition.***

Information on foreign transactions and taxpayers is essential for certain domestic counteracting measures to work properly, but is notoriously difficult to obtain with respect to tax havens and certain harmful preferential tax regimes.

The Recommendation aims at improving the situation by ensuring that information obtained by a country is shared with any other country that may be concerned. This can be done through making greater use of the exchange of information provided for in tax treaties, as well as through the Multilateral Convention for Mutual Assistance in Tax Matters recently developed by the OECD and the Council of Europe which is now signed and ratified by Belgium (signed but not ratified), Denmark, Finland, Iceland, the Netherlands, Norway, Poland, Sweden and the United States.

Countries should also make available to other countries information on preferential tax regimes defined by way of administrative decisions for which their taxpayers are eligible. Such information should indicate the particular measure from which the taxpayer benefited as well as the regime under which the measure was granted.

As a first step to facilitate exchanges of information, the Committee has decided to amend Article 26 of the Model Tax Convention so as to extend its scope to taxes not otherwise covered by the Convention.

9. ***Recommendation concerning the entitlement to treaty benefits: that countries consider including in their tax conventions provisions aimed at restricting the entitlement to treaty benefits for entities and income covered by measures constituting harmful tax practices and consider how the existing provisions of their tax conventions can be applied for the same purpose; that the Model Tax Convention be modified to include such provisions or clarifications as are needed in that respect.***

Countries that have introduced regimes constituting harmful tax competition often view the development of their network of tax conventions as an asset that facilitates and encourages the use of these regimes by residents of third countries. A wide treaty network may therefore have the unintended consequence of opening up the benefits of harmful preferential tax regimes offered by treaty partners.

Various approaches have been used by countries to reduce that risk. In some cases, countries have been able to determine that the place of effective management of a subsidiary lies in the State of the parent company so as to make it a resident of that country either for domestic law or treaty purposes. In other cases, it has been possible to argue, on the basis of the facts and circumstances of the cases, that a subsidiary was managed by the parent company in such a way that the subsidiary had a permanent establishment in the country of residence of the parent company so as to be able to attribute profits of the subsidiary to that latter country. Another example involves denying companies with no real economic function treaty benefits because these companies are not considered as beneficial owner of certain income formally attributed to them. The Committee intends to continue to examine these and other approaches to the application of the existing provisions of the Model Tax Convention, with a view to recommending appropriate clarification to the Model Tax Convention.

There are, however, a number of additional provisions, such as limitation of benefits rules, which have been included in some tax treaties to specifically restrict access to their benefits. The Committee has also been reviewing these provisions with a view to propose changes to the Model Tax Convention aimed at denying the tax treaty benefits to entities and income covered by practices constituting harmful tax competition. The Committee intends to continue its work in this area with a view to modify the Model Tax Convention or the Commentary so as to include such provisions that countries will be able to incorporate in their tax treaties.

10. ***Recommendation concerning the clarification of the status of domestic anti-abuse rules and doctrines in tax treaties: that the Commentary on the Model Tax Convention be clarified to remove any uncertainty or ambiguity regarding the compatibility of domestic anti-abuse measures with the Model Tax Convention.***

The domestic tax laws of member countries include various anti-abuse rules and doctrines which are used to counteract harmful tax practices. CFC rules, for example, may be used to deny the benefits of deferral or exemption with respect to income accruing in a subsidiary located in a country that has introduced such practices and sham, alter ego or business purpose doctrines may be used to disregard the existence of any entity set up in such a country merely to act as a conduit.

Tax treaties generally include no general and few specific anti-avoidance rules. The issue sometimes arises as to whether domestic anti-abuse rules and judicial doctrines are compatible with tax treaties. For instance, where a transaction is ignored or re-characterized under domestic anti-avoidance rules or doctrines, the issue is whether such re-characterization can be applied for purposes of the provisions of a tax treaty without resulting in a treaty override.

In various reports, the conclusions of which have been incorporated in different parts of the Commentary on the Model Tax Convention, the Committee has discussed the interaction of domestic anti-avoidance rules (e.g. thin capitalization,

CFC rules, general anti-abuse rules) with tax treaties and has generally concluded that these were compatible with tax treaties. These conclusions, however, are sometimes unclear or expressed in mitigated terms. For example, while paragraphs 22 and 23 of the Commentary on Article 1 indicate that a majority of countries considers that CFC rules do not violate tax treaties and paragraph 37 of the Commentary on Article 10 (Dividends) indicates that CFC rules are not contrary to paragraph 5 of Article 10, the issue of whether such rules are compatible with Article 7 (Business Profits) is not discussed.

The Model Tax Convention does not deal with certain domestic anti-abuse provisions and it could be appropriate to provide that tax treaties should generally accommodate the application of such rules. This is an area that has been identified for further study.[2]

The Recommendation is to the effect that the Commentary to the Model tax Convention be clarified to remove any uncertainty or ambiguity regarding the compatibility of domestic anti-abuse measures with the Model Tax Convention. This Recommendation will help ensure that domestic anti-abuse and judicial doctrines are compatible with tax treaties.

11. ***Recommendation concerning a list of specific exclusion provisions found in treaties: that the Committee prepare and maintain a list of provisions used by countries to exclude from the benefits of tax conventions certain specific entities or types of income and that the list be used by Member countries as a reference point when negotiating tax conventions and as a basis for discussions in the Forum.***

Various treaties include provisions denying specified entities or types of income the benefits of tax treaties. As these specific exclusion provisions vary considerably and different treaties treat similar entities or types of income differently, they show different ways to approach the same problems.

The Recommendation aims at ensuring greater co-ordination in the use of these provisions by having the Committee prepare and maintain a list of the exclusion provisions found in tax treaties concluded by Member countries. Member countries can then use the list as a reference point when negotiating tax conventions and, where appropriate, for purposes of obtaining agreement from a treaty partner to add similar provisions in an existing convention, such agreement to amend the treaty along the lines of what has been agreed with other treaty partners being presented as preferable to the termination of a treaty that facilitates harmful tax competition.

---

2. See Chapter 14, section 5, "Topics for Further Examination and Report by the Forum on Harmful Tax Practices"

A preliminary version of the list has already been prepared by the Committee. This list will be finalized ... and periodically updated.

12. ***Recommendation concerning tax treaties with tax havens: that countries consider terminating their tax conventions with tax havens and consider not entering into tax treaties with such countries in the future.***

Some countries have terminated their treaties with certain tax havens. Most countries recognize that termination of a treaty may raise significant political and diplomatic difficulties both for the countries concerned and possibly for other countries as well. It may also raise broader economic considerations. Experience has shown that it is usually very difficult to take such action alone, despite the fact that most tax treaties explicitly provide for the possibility of termination. While termination of a treaty is a matter to be decided by each party to that treaty, the possibility that many countries could adopt the same position vis-à-vis treaties entered into by a tax haven would increase the credibility of such action.

The Recommendation is to the effect that countries consider terminating their treaties with tax havens and not entering into treaties with these countries. The criteria for identifying tax havens which are developed ... and the list of such jurisdictions would provide a consistent basis for countries to assist them in making that decision. The Forum referred to in Recommendation 15 will also be useful in providing a mechanism through which countries can exchange views in that rcspcct.

In considering whether they should terminate, or not enter into, a tax treaty with a tax haven, countries should take account of all relevant factors, including the effect of their decision on exchange of information. If the exchange of information provision of a tax treaty with a tax haven can be used effectively to obtain information, if no other mechanisms (such as an agreement limited to the exchange of information) can be used to obtain that information and if the treaty includes safeguards to prevent it from being used to the detriment of other countries, the benefits of the treaty in relation to the exchange of information may offset the disadvantages of that treaty for countries as a whole.

The Recommendation implicitly requests countries to ensure that the territorial scope of their tax conventions does not extend to dependencies that constitute tax havens, whether these dependencies are their own or those of the countries with which they negotiate tax conventions.

13. ***Recommendation concerning co-ordinated enforcement regimes (joint audits; co-ordinated training programmes, etc.): that countries consider undertaking co-ordinated enforcement programs (such as simultaneous examinations, specific exchange of information projects or joint training activities) in relation to income or taxpayers benefiting from practices constituting harmful tax competition.***

Since the late 1970s, a number of countries have developed simultaneous or joint audit programs under which the tax authorities of both countries audit the tax returns of affiliated corporations for the same taxation year. This form of co-operation should be intensified since such audit programmes can help achieve the objectives of this Report.

Other types of co-operation between tax authorities are also likely to be effective in improving international tax compliance. For example, the international features of a country's tax system are among its most technical and complex aspects. It is often difficult for tax departments to ensure that their international audit staff have the proper training to deal with the issues adequately. Joint training activities on topics such as audit strategies, transfer pricing, treaty issues, sophisticated transactions, the design and implementation of CFC and FIF rules, etc. could improve compliance by disseminating successful audit practices and by promoting closer contacts between tax inspectors dealing with international transactions. These could take place under the auspices of the Committee and its subsidiary bodies.

The Recommendation is aimed at further developing collaboration in that respect. The efforts that will be taken under this Recommendation will typically result in countries combining their information and audit powers in order to better apply domestic tax rules vis-à-vis income from, or entities of, other countries from which such information cannot be obtained. Simultaneous examinations based upon the 1992 OECD Model Agreement should be encouraged.

14. ***Recommendation concerning assistance in recovery of tax claims: that countries be encouraged to review the current rules applying to the enforcement of tax claims of other countries and that the Committee pursue its work in this area with a view to drafting provisions that could be included in tax conventions for that purpose.***

Harmful tax competition which leads to tax evasion by taxpayers of other countries may be encouraged if one country will not enforce the tax claims of another country. This position is based on concerns about the extra-territorial enforcement of tax claims, the lack of reciprocity, and procedural fairness. Also, the counteracting measures of some countries may be prevented from applying where a taxpayer has moved assets from one jurisdiction to another for tax evasion purposes.

In an era of globalization and increased mobility for taxpayers, traditional attitudes towards assistance in the collection of taxes may need to change. The purpose of the Recommendation is to encourage countries to review the current rules in this area with a view to encouraging the enforcement of tax claims of other countries. The committee intents to speed up its work in this area.

Recommendations to intensify international co-operation in response to harmful tax competition

Although one country's actions can be influential in curbing harmful tax practices, it is difficult for the actions of any single country to eliminate harmful tax practices. In fact, for many reasons, individual countries may not have a strong incentive to take action against harmful tax practices since, by so doing, they can worsen their position relative to where they would have been if they had not acted at all. For example, as a result of some of the defensive measures an individual country takes to counteract harmful tax practices, the targeted activity may simply move to another location that is not taking measures to combat such practices. Thus, individual actions do not completely solve the problem; they may merely displace it. For this reason, a multilateral approach is required and the OECD is the most appropriate forum to undertake this task.

The present Report provides a useful starting point for improving international co-operation to counter harmful tax competition. The effectiveness of many of the Recommendations concerning domestic legislation and tax treaties described in sections II and III will depend to a large extent on whether the measures concerned can be taken in a co-ordinated fashion. As explained in the introduction to this Chapter, a co-ordinated response to the problem of harmful tax competition will greatly reinforce the effectiveness of unilateral measures. Such a response will involve a number of elements, the most important of which are:

— The adoption of a set of Guidelines (reproduced in Box) intended to ensure that member countries refrain from adopting preferential tax regimes constituting harmful tax competition and gradually eliminate those harmful preferential tax regimes that currently exist;

— The creation of a subsidiary body of the Committee, the Forum on Harmful Tax Practices, to allow, among other things, for an on-going discussion of experiences with the problems posed by tax havens and harmful preferential tax regimes and of the effectiveness of measures taken in response to such practices. The Forum will monitor the implementation of the Recommendations set out in the earlier sections of this Chapter and the accompanying Guidelines as well as;

— The preparation of a list of jurisdictions constituting tax havens; and

— The development and active promotion of principles of Good Tax Administration relevant to counteracting harmful tax practices.

15. ***Recommendation for Guidelines and a Forum on Harmful Tax Practices: that the Member countries endorse the Guidelines on harmful preferential tax regimes set out in the following Box and establish a Forum to implement the Guidelines and other Recommendations in this Report.***

The OECD has successfully developed guidelines in a number of areas including taxation. This Recommendation builds upon this successful experience. The Guidelines in Box set out a general framework within which member countries can implement a common approach to restraining harmful tax competition using the analysis set out in this Report. The Guidelines are non-binding and will form the basis for the review procedures outlined below and will evolve as the Committee gains experience in their application.

The Guidelines will in themselves provide the principles which would guide action in this area, with the other Recommendations in this Report translating these principles into concrete practices. The review procedures outlined below are seen as an essential feature of implementing the Guidelines.

At the same time as the Guidelines are endorsed, a Forum will be created under the auspices of the Committee to undertake an on-going evaluation of existing and proposed regimes in member and non-member countries, to analyze the effectiveness of counteracting measures, including non-tax measures, and to propose ways to improve their effectiveness and to examine whether particular jurisdictions constitute tax havens in light of the factors identified ...

The Forum will be a subsidiary body of the Committee and all the member countries will participate in its work. To enable the Forum to have a truly global perspective on the issues discussed in this Report, it will engage in a dialogue with non-member countries using the well established procedures already available under OECD rules. The Forum will report directly to the Committee which, in turn, will report, when appropriate, to the OECD Council. The mandate of the Forum will be reviewed after five years and thereafter at three year intervals thereby enabling the Committee and the Council to evaluate periodically its role and effectiveness.

The operation of the Forum and the Guidelines would be governed by the normal procedural rules of the Organization. At its first meeting, the Forum would decide upon how the general procedural rules would apply to the Guidelines, in particular for the application of paragraphs 2 and 4 of the Guidelines and for Recommendation 16, and the working of the Forum itself.

The Forum would be responsible for monitoring the implementation of the Guidelines and Recommendations set out in this Report and for taking forward the "Topics For Further Study."[3] The Forum would, when necessary, seek technical opinions or documentation on the economic and revenue impact of preferential tax regimes from the other subsidiary bodies of the Committee. The Forum will be responsible for taking forward work on the wider aspects of the mandate referred to in the Introduction, including engaging in a dialogue with non-member countries. A priority task for the Forum would be to complete the list of tax havens referred to in Recommendation 16. It would also be responsible for improving international co-operation in this area by implementing the Recommendations set

3. Ibid.

out in this section, by encouraging countries to develop mutually reinforcing responses to problems identified and thereby ensuring that no country gains an unfair competitive advantage by failing to comply with the Guidelines referred to above. The Forum will also assess the effectiveness of existing measures taken by countries.

In applying the Guidelines, the Forum would provide a focal point for discussion on harmful preferential tax regimes in specific countries which, where appropriate, would be undertaken on the basis of cross-country reviews of categories of such regimes which may give rise to harmful tax competition. In this respect the Forum would build upon the work already undertaken by the Special Sessions in examining types of preferential tax regimes. These cross-country reviews will provide within the context of the Forum an overview of how different types of preferential tax regimes operate. This, in turn, will enable the Forum to put the reviews of specific preferential tax regimes in a broader context and thereby achieve the level playing field referred to in paragraph 8.

This work on establishing generic descriptions of harmful preferential tax regimes will be carried out in parallel with the review of such regimes in specific countries. In the context of the self reviews referred to in paragraph 2 of the Guidelines, each Member country will be encouraged to describe the operation of generic preferential tax regimes identified by the Forum as having the potential to cause harmful effects, including details on the operation of the regimes, their effects and why they do not in the opinion of that country constitute harmful tax practices. The Forum will elaborate on these procedures at its first meeting. The Committee considers that these cross-country reviews will assist countries in meeting the Guidelines.

The Forum would also encourage countries to examine the structural features of their tax systems which may accentuate harmful competition, including the balance of roles of resident and source countries in countering such behavior.

RECOMMENDATION 15 GUIDELINES FOR DEALING WITH HARMFUL PREFERENTIAL TAX REGIMES IN MEMBER COUNTRIES

While recognizing the positive aspects of the new global environment in which tax systems operate, member countries have concluded that they need to act collectively and individually to curb harmful tax competition and to counter the spread of harmful preferential tax regimes directed at financial and service activities. Harmful preferential tax regimes can distort trade and investment patterns, and are a threat both to domestic tax systems and to the overall structure of international taxation. These regimes undermine the fairness of the tax systems, cause undesired shifts of part of the tax burden from income to consumption, shift part of the tax burden from capital to labor and thereby may have a negative impact on employment. Since it is generally considered that it is difficult for individual countries to combat effectively the spread of harmful preferential tax regimes, a co-ordinated approach, including a dialogue with non-member countries, is required to achieve the "level playing field" which is so essential to the continued expansion of global economic growth. International co-operation must be intensified to avoid an aggressive competitive bidding by countries for geographically mobile activities.

The Guidelines are:

1. To refrain from adopting new measures, or extending the scope of, or strengthening existing measures, in the form of legislative provisions or administrative practices related to taxation, that constitute harmful tax practices as defined in ...
2. To review their existing measures for the purpose of identifying those measures, in the form of legislative provisions or administrative practices related to taxation, that constitute harmful tax practices as defined in ... the Report. These measures will be reported to the Forum on Harmful Tax Practices and will be included in a list within 2 years from the date on which these Guidelines are approved by the OECD Council.
3. To remove, before the end of 5 years starting from the date on which the Guidelines are approved by the OECD Council, the harmful features of their preferential tax regimes identified in the list referred to in paragraph 2. However, in respect of taxpayers who are benefiting from such regimes on December 31, 2000, the benefits that they derive will be removed at the latest on December 31, 2005. This will ensure that such particular tax benefits have been entirely removed after that date. The list referred to in paragraph 2 will be reviewed annually to delete those regimes that no longer constitute harmful preferential tax regimes.
4. Each Member country which believes that an existing measure no already included in the list referred to in paragraph 2, or a proposed or new measure of itself or of another country, constitute a measure, in the form of legislative provision or administrative practice related to taxation, that might constitute a harmful tax practice in light of the factors identified in ... the Report, may request that the measure be examined by the

Member countries, through the Forum on Harmful Tax Practices, for purposes of the application of paragraph 1 or for inclusion in the list referred to in paragraph 2. The Forum may issue a non-binding opinion on that question.

5. To co-ordinate, through the Forum, their national and treaty responses to harmful tax practices adopted by other countries.
6. To use the Forum to encourage actively non-member countries to associate themselves with these Guidelines.

16. *Recommendation to produce a list of tax havens: that the Forum be mandated to establish, within one year of the first meeting of the Forum, a list of tax havens on the basis of the factors identified ...*

The Forum is instructed to prepare within one year from its inception a list of tax havens, taking into account the factors set out ... This initial list would be non-exhaustive and would be subject to review by the Forum.

To develop this list, the Forum would examine jurisdictions that seem, prima facie, to meet the factors identified ... This would enable the Forum to explore by all necessary means whether these jurisdictions should be identified as tax havens.

The list will enable Member countries to coordinate their responses to the problem posed by tax havens and to encourage these jurisdictions to re-examine their policies. This list will not constrain countries in applying anti-abuse measures to counteract harmful tax practices.

17. *Recommendation concerning links with tax havens: that countries that have particular political, economic or other links with tax havens ensure that these links do not contribute to harmful tax competition and, in particular, that countries that have dependencies that are tax havens ensure that the links that they have with these tax havens are not used in a way that increase or promote harmful tax competition.*

Many countries have close legal, economic or political ties with tax havens. This is particularly true in the case of countries that have dependencies that engage in harmful tax competition: these dependencies often have links with and obtain assistance from various regulatory authorities in these countries.

At a minimum, these ties should not be used to assist the relevant countries or dependencies in engaging in harmful tax competition. Also, countries that have such ties should consider using them to reduce the harmful tax competition resulting from the existence of these tax havens.

18. ***Recommendation to develop and actively promote Principles of Good Tax Administration: that the Committee be responsible for developing and actively promoting a set of principles that should guide tax administrations in the enforcement of the Recommendations included in this report.***

The effectiveness of many of the Recommendations set out in this Report will depend upon the ways in which they are administered in practice. it is proposed that the OECD, by means of its newly created Strategic Management Forum, should develop best practices in the enforcement of these measures. This approach would intensify co-operation between tax administrations, facilitate the co-ordination of enforcement measures and identify and counter harmful tax competition resulting from tax administration practices. Such an approach would emphasize the positive actions that tax administrations can take.

These practices should address the various aspects of the application of tax laws. They could include, for example, the suggestion that countries should not issue administrative decisions on planned transactions that are primarily aimed at taking advantage of tax conventions.

19. ***Recommendation on associating non-member countries with the Recommendation: That the new Forum engage in a dialogue with non-member countries using, where appropriate, the fora offered by other international tax organisations, with the aim of promoting the Recommendations set out in this Chapter, including the Guidelines.***

To restrain the spread of harmful tax practices, non-member countries should be associated with the Recommendations set out in this Chapter. Whilst the Recommendations in relation to tax havens should reduce the amount of displacement to non-member countries, it will not eliminate it since it would still be possible to relocate to a non-member country with a harmful preferential tax regime. In order to minimize the scope for such displacement, non-member countries should be encouraged to dismantle harmful preferential tax regimes by promoting a broader acceptance of the principles set out in this Report and by engaging in a dialogue with the Member countries on how they could apply the Guidelines. Work on this Recommendation will continue in tandem with the Forum's work on the implementation of the Guidelines in Member countries.

FINANCIAL ACTION TASK FORCE 1998–1999 REPORT ON MONEY LAUNDERING TYPOLOGIES

I. INTRODUCTION

1. The group of experts met on November 17–18, 1998 under the chairmanship of Mr. Simon Goddard, Head of Intelligence, Strategic and Specialist Intelligence Branch, National Criminal Intelligence Service (NCIS). The meeting took place in the conference room of the European Bank for Reconstruction and Development (EBRD) in London. The group comprised representatives of the following FATF members: Australia, Austria, Belgium, Canada, Denmark, European Commission, Finland, France, Germany, Ireland, Italy, Japan, Luxembourg, the Netherlands, Norway, Portugal, Spain, Sweden, Switzerland, Turkey, the United Kingdom, and the United States. Experts from non-member international organizations with observer status, namely the Council of Europe, Interpol, the International Organization of Securities Commissions (IOSCO), and the World Customs Organization (WCO), also attended the meeting. The Council of Europe Select Committee of Experts on the Evaluation of Anti–money laundering Measures (PC-R-EV) was represented by Slovenia.
2. The purpose of the 1998–1999 typologies exercise was, as in previous years, to provide a forum for law enforcement and regulatory experts to discuss recent trends in the laundering of criminal proceeds, emerging threats, and effective countermeasures. While discussions of this exercise generally focus on money laundering developments within FATF member nations, the experts also attempt to examine available information on current money laundering patterns in non-member countries and other regions of the world. Prior to the meeting, delegations were invited to provide written submissions to serve as the starting point for discussions. In a departure from the format of earlier typologies exercises, this year's meeting was led off with in-depth presentations on a series of major money laundering issues that had been agreed upon during the FATF plenary meeting in September 1998.

3. The present report, therefore, focuses first of all on these major issues: the euro currency unit and large denomination banknotes, problems associated with offshore financial centers of non-cooperative countries or jurisdictions, challenges posed by new payment technologies, and the potential use of the gold market in money laundering operations. The report then continues with an examination of other money laundering trends in FATF countries followed by the overview of trends in non-member jurisdictions.

II. MAJOR MONEY LAUNDERING ISSUES

(i) The single European currency and large denomination banknotes

4. The euro currency unit became the single currency of eleven European Union member states[1] on January 1, 1999. At that time, existing national currencies of the participating members became simply an expression of the euro. During the "transitional" period that started on January 1, the euro will not be issued in physical form; the participating members will continue to use their existing coins and notes. On January 1, 2002, euro coins and banknotes will be introduced, and, the existing national currencies of the participating members will then be withdrawn as legal currency by June 30, 2002 at the latest. The exact time for this final "changeover" period (to occur between January 1, and June 30, 2002) will vary according to the implementing legislation of the individual participating member states.

a. Impact on Money Laundering

5. The primary period of potential risk is the six-month window during which the national currencies in paper and coin form will be exchanged for the euro. Some experts expressed the fear that money launderers might use this window to try to introduce illegally derived funds by hiding them among the expected higher volume of operations involving "exchanges" of national currency for the euro. Other experts believed that there might be a rise in laundering in the time before the changeover—by using traditional methods, by exchanging these funds for currency from outside the euro zone, or by increased use of professional services providers—all to avoid detection during the actual changeover period.
6. With the elimination of 11 national currencies, it was agreed that the role of bureaux de change in the countries of the euro zone would diminish

1. The eleven EU members involved in the introduction of the new currency include Austria, Belgium, Finland, France, Germany, Ireland, Italy, Luxembourg, Netherlands, Portugal, and Spain

with regard to money laundering and its detection. Nevertheless, there could be an increase in exchange activities in those European countries outside the euro zone, especially involving traditional currencies such as US dollars, UK pounds, and Swiss francs. Moreover, once money has been converted to euros, the movement of these funds over national borders within the countries of the euro zone will cause less notice. One northern European country stated in its written submission that it might see an overall increase in the volume of cash in circulation prior to January 1, 2002 (with, for example, a possible influx of non-EU money—specifically Russian held US dollars—exchanged for euros).

7. The experts believed that there was little likelihood that international money launderers would convert national currencies to the currencies of non-participating countries (Danish or Swedish kroner, Greek drachma). The only exception, as mentioned above, is the UK pound, which will likely continue to be important in laundering related to certain types of narcotics activity. As for FATF countries in other areas of the world, the experts were of the opinion that the changeover to the euro would have little effect on laundering in North America, Asia or Australia, where the US dollar will probably continue to be the primary currency used in such activity. They recognized, however, that the euro used in wire or electronic transactions may turn up in money laundering operations anywhere in the world after January 1, 1999.

b. Impact on Anti–Money Laundering Measures

8. Almost all of the FATF member countries who are taking part in the changeover to the euro have started to pay attention to the specific money laundering concerns surrounding the introduction of the euro. The Netherlands, for example, has had a working group since 1996 to examine the problem and provide recommendations on necessary countermeasures. In Germany, the Federal Criminal Police produced a study in early 1998, which addresses the issue of the euro introduction as related to potential criminal activity. Italy has also set up a euro implementation coordinating committee of relevant ministries and authorities that will issue detailed implementation rules that take in to account the money laundering risks.

9. Many delegations felt that current anti–money laundering (preventive) systems should be adequate for detecting potential money laundering in this area. Since the changeover to the euro in banknote and coin form will require that national currency be physically presented at a financial institution, there was also felt to be a greater risk of detection for the launderer involved in such cash transactions. It was stressed that all member countries should continue to promote vigilance at financial institutions with regard to suspicious transaction reporting both prior to and during the changeover period.

10. The experts considered the possibility that the increased volume of all activity during the changeover period might overwhelm financial institutions personnel and might make them therefore more likely to miss or disregard potential indicators of money laundering. Another concern was related to which institutions actually perform the currency conversions. One FATF member country feared that non-bank financial institutions involved in the changeover might not have adequate guidance on what constitutes suspicious activity regarding euro conversions.

11. A number of FATF members mentioned that they would increase awareness of the issue and reinforce anti–money laundering measures during the transition period. In the Netherlands, the potential problem with non-bank financial institutions is being dealt with by permitting only banks to carry out exchanges of national currency for euros. Germany will permit other financial services to perform these exchanges, however, only when these institutions are licensed to do so by the Federal Banking Supervisory Office (as is also required for operating a retail foreign exchange business). Additionally, the Federal Banking Supervisory Office issued new guidelines in March 1998 that lowers the threshold (whereby customer identification is required) to DM5,000 (US$3,018) for conversion transactions.

12. Other issues brought up by the experts related to cross-border implications of the introduction of the euro both within and outside the countries of the euro zone. Italy mentioned that conversions of large amounts of national currency in other than its country of origin should be an indicator of suspicious activity. Similarly, conversions of large amounts of national currency to euros by individuals domiciled in other countries might also be a suspicious indicator. The United States raised the question of how existing national currencies (of the euro zone countries) held abroad will be exchanged for euros. These concerns highlight the fact that an internationally coordinated approach—relative to the introduction of the euro—still must be articulated for developing common money laundering indicators, specific sector guidelines, and sharing the information procedures among relevant national anti–money laundering services.

c. Introduction of the Large Denomination Euro Banknote

13. With the introduction of the euro in banknote and coin form (after January 1, 2002), the highest denomination banknotes will be EUR500. This note will be roughly comparable in value to the highest denomination banknotes issued by Germany and the Netherlands. A number of FATF members have expressed concern that the issue of the high denomination euro banknote might make the currency more attractive to money launderers.

14. Several of the delegations saw the introduction of the large denomination euro as not only relating to the euro currency but also a potential problem in all countries having high denomination banknotes. Some of the countries of the euro zone already have high denomination notes (Austria, Belgium, Germany, the Netherlands), and the EUR500 note was designed, according to the European Commission, to fulfil a similar role to that of the original national currency. Moreover, there are large denomination banknotes in other FATF member countries as well (Canada, Singapore, Switzerland), which may continue to exist after the introduction of the euro.

15. The legal use of large denomination notes is currently may often be concentrated in certain economic sectors (used automobiles, livestock, etc.) although this use could not account for all of the large denomination notes issued. Most delegations, including those from countries with large denomination banknotes, recognized that incomplete information is available on the legitimate use of these notes.

16. A number of FATF member countries have observed that large denomination notes tend to be used in the hoarding of money related to tax evasion or avoidance and in criminal activity. US cases illustrated how the bulk of small denomination currency and the difficulties involved in transporting it are still the primary obstacle for money launderers (and one of the easiest ways to detect them). As a further example of criminals preferring large denomination notes, Germany stated that kidnappers routinely demand that ransom money be provided in DM1,000 notes. In Canada, the C$1,000 bill was originally introduced to facilitate bank to bank transfers. This licit use has become outmoded with the ability of banks to transfer funds more rapidly and safely by electronic means. Criminal money movements with these banknotes now show up almost exclusively as related to casino winnings. A case was cited in which C$70 million (nearly US$45.7 million) in C$1,000 bills were alleged to have transited or still to be located in safety deposit boxes of a bank in central Europe.

17. Despite the fact that there is an incomplete understanding of the uses of large denomination banknotes in the legitimate economy, some of the experts felt strongly that the introduction of the EUR500 banknote after January 1, 2002 may facilitate laundering. Other experts believed that large denominations may only facilitate movement of cash (whether legitimate or not) and not money laundering. Large denomination banknotes draw too much attention at financial institutions, thus presenting a potential launderer with increased risk of detection; therefore, "middle-sized" denominations might be more suitable for the purpose of money laundering. Criminal proceeds denominated in EUR500 banknotes would be considerably less bulky than the equivalent value of funds denominated in

US$100 bills. Current anti–money laundering measures within FATF members should be adequate for detecting suspicious cash transactions (including large denomination banknotes). However, with the expanded geographic region that comprises the euro area, there will be fewer internal points at which to detect suspicious currency shipments. It was therefore suggested that study of the subject should continue with a view toward clarifying the legal and illegal uses of large denominations.

18. In discussing the use of large denomination banknotes for laundering, and in particular the potential use of the EUR500 note after January 1, 2002, the experts drew attention to the fact that the money laundering implications of the EUR500 note do not appear to have been considered in planning for this large denomination banknote. The reason that the EUR500 banknote was developed was to offer a denomination that would correspond with already existing high denomination banknotes in the countries of the euro zone. It was also noted by some of the experts that the use of high denomination notes in potential illegal activities, such as money laundering or tax evasion, was not taken into account. One delegation indicated that this issue had indeed been considered. Although experts mentioned a few economic activities in which the use of large denomination banknotes is especially common, the role of these denominations in legitimate commerce has apparently not been examined either. The majority of the FATF experts considered that the potential legitimate and illicit uses of large denomination banknotes ought to be thoroughly examined by the European Central Bank Furthermore, a number of the experts called for the FATF member countries to continue to study the subject with a view toward augmenting any other examination at the international level.

(ii) Offshore financial centers of non-cooperative countries or territories

19. During the past ten years, FATF member countries have made significant progress in adopting anti–money laundering regimes based on the standards set forth in the FATF Forty Recommendations. This progress has also been reflected in the increasing cooperation among members on anti–money laundering investigations. In non-member countries and jurisdictions, there have been signs more recently of an increased willingness to follow the FATF Forty Recommendations and cooperate on anti–money laundering investigations. This increased acceptance of FATF standards contrasts, however, with the unwillingness or outright refusal of certain important financial centers to cooperate in this area. The issue of non-cooperation was therefore identified by FATF members as one that should be addressed during the annual typologies exercise. The typologies discussions on the subject would then serve as a starting point for broader discussions on the issues of international cooperation. Prior to the experts meeting, FATF members were asked to examine the specific operational problems or difficulties that they had encountered with offshore financial centers in such areas as banking secrecy, shell companies, identification of beneficial owners, exchange of information, and other forms of international cooperation.

a. Impact on money laundering

20. Past typologies exercises began the task of identifying how "offshore financial centers" facilitate money laundering. The experts at this meeting agreed that schemes involving these jurisdictions still appear to share common characteristics: a series of multiple financial transactions through the center, use of nominees or other middlemen to manage these transactions, and an international network of shell companies (including a specialized "off-the-shelf" variety that immediately go dormant upon completion of the series of transactions). Often an individual money laundering scheme will include more than one of these centers. An investigating agency can usually see the path that questionable funds follow into or out of such a scheme; however, the exact links between the funds and the illegal act that generated them are lost. Investigations of this type are often therefore unable to be fully exploited to a successful conviction or confiscation.

21. The oft-stated reason for creating an offshore financial center has been to provide certain fiscal advantages to natural or legal persons that use its services. Since tax evasion schemes and money laundering operations often appear to use similar techniques, many money laundering experts believe that the quest for optimal "fiscal advantages" is frequently used as a cover for moving to or through such locations what are in reality criminally derived moneys. One expert pointed out during this exercise, however, that there appears to be one significant difference between the techniques used for taking fiscal advantage of an offshore location and laundering criminal funds. In the former case, the funds usually move to a single offshore location where they are sheltered from the home country's fiscal oversight. In the latter case, that is, involving criminally generated funds, the tendency is for the funds to move rapidly through several offshore locations.

b. Impact on anti–money laundering measures: Role of the foreign legal entity

22. Virtually every FATF member represented at the experts meeting reported having experienced problems in pursuing anti–money laundering investigations with links to offshore financial centers. However, it was also pointed out that some offshore centers of non-cooperative countries were attempting to improve the level of judicial or investigative cooperation within the current framework of their national laws or by making selected changes to their legislation. The experts agreed, therefore, that the problem was most acute with those jurisdictions that are slow or unwilling to assist in international anti–money laundering investigations, particularly in regard to identifying the beneficial owners of legal entities.

23. FATF written submissions and a certain amount of discussion by the experts focused on the major problem posed by foreign legal entities to successful conduct of anti–money laundering investigations. Obtaining information from some offshore jurisdictions on the true owners or beneficiaries of foreign registered business entities—shell companies, international business companies, offshore trusts, etc.—appears to be the primary obstacle in investigating transnational laundering activity.

24. A number of FATF member countries mentioned that they regularly attempt to request information on foreign legal entities using mutual legal assistance treaties or other agreements with the offshore jurisdiction. Often non-cooperative jurisdictions refuse to respond to a foreign request for investigative or judicial assistance because there is no bilateral agreement that would permit such cooperation. The jurisdictions might also refuse the foreign request because the information requested is not maintained in any official registry. In some cases, information on legal entities may be protected from disclosure to foreign investigative agencies because of strict banking secrecy (with a variation related to non-release of fiscal information, including criminal or civil liability for disclosure) that is impenetrable even to domestic judicial or regulatory authorities. Some delegations also mentioned the increasing use of the Internet for the marketing and provision of such services.

25. The experts also highlighted the role of professional services providers in ensuring the good functioning of money laundering operations through non-cooperative jurisdictions. These solicitors, accountants, financial consultants, and company formation agents facilitate the creation of appropriate business entities that serve as the pipeline for moving funds of legal, as well as illegal, origin. Typically, such services are provided to non-residents of the jurisdiction and often at a higher level of confidentiality than that available to residents.

c. Potential solutions

26. In this regard, the experts hoped that the FATF ad hoc group on non-cooperative countries and territories, which was established in September 1998, would be able to develop strategies for addressing the issue. Several members pointed out that they are able to rely, in some cases, on existing international mechanisms for the exchange of information relating to money laundering investigations: mutual legal assistance treaties, memoranda of understanding, and Interpol. Nevertheless, these mechanisms do not work when the jurisdiction receiving the request for assistance refuses to honour it or does not maintain the desired information. The consensus of the experts was that every country or jurisdiction should have a mechanism in place for establishing the beneficial owners of legal entities registered within it and should have the authority to share this information with foreign counterpart investigative agencies. The development of internationally recognized minimum registration requirements would be welcome in this regard. Some of the written submissions also suggested that the so-called "fiscal exemption" should no longer be valid grounds for refusing a foreign request. The work of the Egmont Group of Financial Intelligence Units (FIUs) was also mentioned as a potential channel for resolving this issue, given its work at the operational level to facilitate information sharing and the fact that many offshore financial centers already take part in its activities.

(iii) New payment technologies

27. All delegations continue to report that there have not been as of yet any investigated money laundering cases involving the new payment technologies identified in previous typologies reports. However, there have been several instances of other types of crimes—generally fraud schemes against unsuspecting members of the public that have used the Internet as a means for committing the underlying offence. Law enforcement in FATF member countries remains concerned about the potential for use of these new technologies in money laundering schemes. Specifically, some of these risks include:

- inability to identify and authenticate parties that use the new technologies;
- level of transparency of the transaction;
- lack or inadequacy of audit trails, record keeping, or suspicious transaction reporting by the technology provider;
- use of higher levels of encryption (thus blocking out law enforcement access); and
- transactions that fall outside current legislative or regulatory definition.

a. Status of new payment technology systems

(1) Smartcards

28. Smartcards or electronic purses have been developed as an alternative to currency in paper and coin form. The electronic chip in the card can then store monetary value in electronic form which may then be spent as currency. Because the value on the card has already been debited from the financial institution, if the card is lost, there is no loss to the institution. There is thus no inherent reason for the financial institution to restrict the amount that may be held on an individual card.

29. Smartcard systems in FATF member countries are mostly still in the prototype or early testing phases. Among these systems, there are many variants in terms of specific operating characteristics. Some of the systems are designed to provide transactional anonymity, while others capture data which may be used to construct an audit trail. In this regard, FATF members expressed some concern over the development of smartcard distribution through automated vending machines, which would allow virtually anonymous transfer of value to these cards. Within FATF member countries, the issuers/operators of many smartcard systems have placed limits on the amount of money that may be loaded onto the cards (for example, UK institutions have set the limits at GBP50–500 [US$82–820]); however, it was noted that this is not always the case. In one example, an institution in a non-FATF member country reportedly markets a smartcard with an upper limit of US$92,000. Furthermore, while most smartcard systems do not permit so-called "peer-to-peer" (direct "card-to-card") transactions, others are developing the capability to move funds among cardholders without recourse to a financial intermediary. In any case, it should be noted that, where there are limitations on card functions, these have been set by the card issuers and not by the respective national regulatory authorities.

(2) On-line Banking

30. On-line banking has increasingly come to mean the method whereby certain types of financial transactions may be performed through the Internet website of those banks that offer this service. FATF members reported that there is a great deal of growth in this area. In the United States, nearly 85% of financial institutions have or are planning to establish such services. A significant number of financial institutions in other countries have also set up on-line facilities. In its most basic form, the service provided includes verification of cheque account balances and transfers among accounts at the same institution. In those systems that allow payments or transfers to be made, the customer is often restricted in the amount of transaction or the identity of the beneficiary. All of the systems require that on-line operations be tied to an already existing account at the institution; therefore, there is a continuous record of account activity.

31. The concerns mentioned in this area refer, again, primarily a lack of uniform regulation from supervisory authorities. Thus, although the customer's activity is tied to a particular account set up in his name, there is no way to verify the identity of the Internet transactor once the account has been opened. Indeed, if the on-line financial institution is located in an area known for high levels of banking secrecy and requires little or no proof of identity for opening an account, the money launderer could theoretically move funds from the convenience of his computer terminal. Although there were no reported cases of this type of laundering taking place at this time, the experts believed that technology was developing rapidly and thus worthy of further vigilance.

(3) E-Cash

32. Electronic cash (or "e-cash") seeks to provide a way of paying for goods and services across the Internet. In concept, e-cash would replace notes and coins for normal Internet transactions; however, it has the added advantage of being able to be split into fractions of the lowest denomination coins to allow what are termed "micropayments." These small payments could be made for reading specified sections of on-line newspapers, for example. Under most existing payment systems, these micropayment transactions would not be economical. With e-cash, the customer buys value from an authorized provider—as with the smart card—however, the value is then stored either in customer's home computer or a safe repository on-line. When the funds are spent, the e-cash value is credited to a retailer's e-cash account that then must be later "up-loaded" to the retailer's regular bank account. Security of e-cash systems is concerned primarily with ensuring that value cannot be created except by authorized institutions or that the same value cannot be spent more than one time.

33. Concerns with regard to e-cash are generally the same as those mentioned for smart cards. Since only the initial purchase and the final settlement stages take place through banks, the risk exists that there will be no way to track e-cash in transactions taking place after the initial purchase and before final crediting of the value to a retailer's account. Some systems currently being tested have set limits to the amount that an e-cash "purse" may hold; however, there is at present no uniform regulatory standard, and it is not certain that such regulations would do much to limit the use of e-cash by the consumer. The anonymity of e-cash, similar to coin and banknotes, may also hinder the financial institution with reporting obligations from positively identifying the ultimate source of an e-cash transaction. A further concern is that currently available computer encryption systems may further shield e-cash transactions from the scrutiny of investigative authorities.

b. Countermeasures

34. Smart cards appear to be able to replicate all of the functions of e-cash while allowing portability and use in the real world, as well as over the Internet. There was some uncertainty expressed, therefore, over the ultimate success of e-cash systems. Nevertheless, the experts agreed that the field of new payment technologies is changing very rapidly, and that developments in e-cash systems, along with those of the other proposed systems, should continue to be monitored. The experts discussed a number of possible measures that might limit the vulnerability to money laundering on the new payment technologies. These measures included the following:

- limiting the functions and capacity of smart cards (including maximum value and turnover limits, as well as number of smart cards per customer);
- linking new payment technology to financial institutions and bank accounts;
- requiring standard record keeping procedures for these systems to enable the examination, documentation, and seizure of relevant records by investigating authorities; and
- establishing international standards for these measures.

(iv) Potential use of the gold market in money laundering operations

a. General

35. Following last year's introduction to the issue of money laundering through the gold market, the FATF experts were asked to provide specific examples of such cases from their national experience. A number of members did provide example of cases in which gold transactions were an integral aspect of the investigated money laundering scheme. These cases involved the purchase of gold with illegally obtained funds. The gold was then exported to other locations where it was sold, these funds thus being legitimized as the proceeds of gold sales. Existing reporting requirements for gold purchases were circumvented by structuring the purchases to amounts below the reporting threshold.

36. Several members reported that the vulnerability to money laundering within their countries has increasingly centered on specialized gold bullion sellers. This is due in part to the fact that anti–money laundering legislation targeting traditional financial institutions has generally caused those customers desiring to purchase bullion anonymously to turn to other sources. In many FATF member countries, there is no suspicious transaction-reporting requirement directed toward bullion dealers or other non-financial banking institutions dealing in gold. Additionally, even though the import or export of gold bullion seems to be a key part of money laundering schemes involving the material, members reported that the lack of import/export reporting requirements appears to hamper detection of illegal operations.

37. Members were in some cases able to identify cities or regions within their jurisdictions that specialize in legitimate gold business (for example, Cordobá in Spain and Arezzo and Vicenza in Italy) or in which significant business takes place (Paris region and Marseilles in France). Gold purchases in these areas are often conducted in cash and frequently in non-indigenous currency (especially US dollars). Gold serves as both a commodity and, to a lesser extent, a medium of exchange in money laundering conducted between Latin America, the United States and Europe. In this cycle, gold bullion makes its way to Italy via Swiss brokers. There, it is made into jewelry, much of which is then shipped to Latin America. In Latin America, this jewelry (or the raw gold from which it was made) then becomes one of, if not the most important commodities (others include various consumer goods and electronic equipment) in the black market peso exchange money laundering scheme.

38. Several FATF members also mentioned having received suspicious transaction reports involving gold transactions. In some instances, these transactions appeared to reflect attempts to avoid high VAT rates by making large purchases of gold in countries with low VAT rates and then exporting the bullion back to the country of origin where it could then be resold at a profit.

b. Hawala/Hundi alternative remittance system and gold

39. The question of laundering through the use of gold as a commodity and as a medium of exchange was discussed by the experts in the context of the hawala/hundi alternative remittance system. The word "hawala" means "trust" or "exchange"; "hundi" means "bill of exchange." It is an alternative remittance system that enables the transfer of funds without their actual physical movement (often without the use of a traditional financial institution). Very often, using hawala is more cost effective and less bureaucratic than moving funds through officially recognized banking systems. Built on a system of trust and close business contacts, hawala originated in South Asia; however, it is now used as an alternate remittance system throughout the world.

40. In the laundering associated with this system, gold often plays the role of the primary medium of exchange in certain transactions. Although many hawala transactions may take place without gold, many of these transactions involving the movement of money to South Asia often do involve the metal. There are two reasons for this: the first is the combined historical, religious and cultural importance that gold enjoys in the region, and the second is the increasing distrust in the value of local currencies (many South Asian nations prohibit speculation on their currencies, and exchange rates are fixed by the central banks). Worldwide, gold is often used as a hedge against inflation; in South Asia, gold is often the primary means of preserving and protecting wealth.

41. In one scenario, a gold dealer operating in one country also operates as the "banker" for various jewelry shops in his region. These jewelry shops give him the checks and cash they receive for purchases; he processes these through his own bank accounts. In return, he furnishes them with scrap gold and gold jewelry for use in their businesses. He retains a few percentage points of the money he receives from them for his "services" (as well as for the legal risk he is incurring). The owners of the jewelry shops do not have to deal with the bureaucracy of banking, and, since there is almost no paper trail of their sales, they enjoy a greatly reduced tax liability.

42. In another scenario, money may be moved from one country to another through the hawala system. A "hawaladar" (hawala broker) based in one country facilitates this movement by receiving payments in the local currency. He then makes contact with a hawaladar in South Asia and instructs him to make the necessary payment to a specified beneficiary in that local currency. In order to settle his accounts with the South Asian hawaladars, the hawaladar in the first country might send postal money orders or some other financial instruments to a precious metals house in the Persian Gulf. This precious metals house then effects payment to the South Asian hawaladar in gold (either into a safe-keeping account under his name or by direct export of the gold to the South Asian location).

III. MONEY LAUNDERING TRENDS IN FATF COUNTRIES

(i) Sources of illegal funds

43. Narcotics trafficking appears still to be the primary single source of criminal proceeds among the majority of FATF members. The various types of fraud (fiscal, EU funds, value added tax, insurance, bankruptcy, etc.) are the next major source of illegal funds, if not, in some jurisdictions, the primary source. Organized crime activity generates a considerable amount of illegal proceeds that are laundered in or through FATF member countries. Some members have noted with concern the increasing trend for these crime groups to operate in loose alliances (Russian and Latin American groups, for example). Written submissions from some of the members also mentioned an increase in the number of cases in which laundering was related to official corruption or the funding of international terrorism.

44. The United States has recently substantially elevated the priority assigned to combating terrorist financing (which can constitute the crime of money laundering in the United States). In October 1997, the US government designated 30 foreign organizations as foreign terrorist organizations. In June 1998, US federal authorities seized US$1.4 million in cash and property held by individuals and an organization whose funds were reportedly part of a scheme to support Middle Eastern terrorism. The funds were transferred by wire from Europe and the Middle East to financial institutions in the United States and, through various means, were then used to facilitate recruitment, training, and operations of the terrorist group Hamas. This case marks the first time that civil asset forfeiture laws were used in the United States to seize assets suspected of being involved in money laundering violations related to foreign terrorism. These terrorist operations included a conspiracy to commit extortion, kidnapping, and murder against the citizens and the government of Israel.

(ii) New or significant trends

a. General

45. Many of the submissions of FATF member countries noted an increase in suspicious transaction reporting, both for certain individual money laundering methods and in overall numbers of reports. As for new methods, however, with the exception of new payment technologies described above, the submissions appear to indicate that launderers are using the same practices that they have done in the past. Money laundering within FATF members is characterized, therefore, by a finite number of techniques that can be combined into an almost infinite variety of laundering schemes. Laundering activity is also characterized by its ability to change quickly when faced with new countermeasures by shifting to other techniques or mechanisms, combining these methods into new schemes, or by moving to sectors or regions where government oversight represents less of a threat.

46. Indeed, this last point was cited by virtually all members as a fundamental truth of money laundering today: the lack of comprehensive preventive measures in a particular sector or region will inevitably attract money laundering activity. Members continue to mention bureaux de change, money remittance businesses, and casinos as particularly vulnerable to laundering in some locations. Often these are combined with cash smuggling, alternate remittance systems, or the use of offshore registered businesses, all of which generally operate beyond the framework of traditional financial oversight systems.

47. Another particularly evident trend in the money laundering schemes described by the FATF experts is the growing role played by professional services providers. Accountants, solicitors, and company formation agents turn up ever more frequently in anti–money laundering investigations. In establishing and administering the foreign legal entities which conceal money laundering schemes, it is these professionals that increasingly provide the apparent sophistication and extra layer of respectability to some laundering operations. These services are offered not only at offshore locations (as described above) but also within FATF member countries. One delegation described a money laundering scheme in which a criminal group selected a firm of solicitors to act on their behalf in the purchase of a company. The funds for the purchase were delivered to the solicitors in cash and placed in a client account. When the purchase later fell through, the funds were returned—less fees—to the criminal group in form of a cheque. In fact, the group already owned the company they were attempting to "buy" and had arranged for the failure of the sale since they only wished to convert their criminal proceeds into a cheque from a respectable law firm. This scheme was revealed in a suspicious transaction report from the law firm concerned. More often than not, however, professional services providers are still not subject to suspicious transaction reporting requirements in FATF members. Even when they are subject to such a requirement, the numbers of disclosures made to authorities are frequently disappointing.

48. Even in instances where preventive measures have been implemented, laundering activity still occurs, according to the FATF experts. When faced with suspicious transaction reporting at both banks and other financial services, launderers frequently resort to structured transactions to avoid the reporting threshold. Despite border controls designed to detect smuggling of cash criminal proceeds, bulk shipments of cash continue to be observed by FATF members. The use of legitimate appearing business transactions—claiming that proceeds are generated by a legal currency exchange business, the profit from bona fide commodity sales, the result of factoring operations, for example—is a standard cover used by launderers to hide the criminal origin of those funds. Members mentioned that the only indicator of money laundering in these cases is often the disproportionate size of the transactions (either individually or in aggregate) when compared to the expected economic activity of the business.

49. Several FATF members reported an increase in the appearance of insurance products in laundering schemes. Various products have been noted, including life and property insurance and long term capitalization bonds. Launderers generally pay for the insurance using the cash criminal proceeds. They then request early pay out of the policy (in the case of life insurance or capitalization products) or make a claim against the property insurance, thus obtaining a "legitimate" insurance refund or claim payment.

50. Electronic funds transfers continue to be the preferred method for the layering of criminal proceeds once they enter the legitimate financial system. Frequently, these proceeds are smuggled out of the FATF member country, deposited into the financial system at a foreign location, and then wired back to the country of origin. Wire transfers are often associated with foreign registered business entities as described above. If criminal proceeds are transmitted through "transit" accounts set up in offshore financial centers or—as have been found in some FATF member countries according to the written submissions—the beneficial owner of the funds is effectively hidden.

b. Derivatives and securities markets

51. In recent FATF meetings, questions have arisen concerning the perceived vulnerabilities of the derivatives and security markets as a vehicle for money laundering. As part of the written submission of one member, a paper was prepared on this issue and provided to the experts. According to the paper, there is good reason to suspect that money laundering may pose a substantial threat in these markets. Compared to banks, the derivatives markets and associated products represent perhaps a better opportunity for laundering because of the ease with which audit trails can be obscured. Indeed, any product that offers rapid commercial decision-making, high speed transfer, obscurity of control, or complication of audit trail is at risk. Operators in these markets, when compared to banks, tend to be less familiar with anti–money laundering efforts. There is also evidence—a good example is the BCCI case—which shows the readiness of criminals to use financial products for laundering.

52. The primary opportunity for laundering is in the complex derivatives market. Derivatives are securities that derive their value from another underlying financial instrument or asset; they have no intrinsic value of their own. There are three primary types of derivative contracts: forward contracts, futures, and options. All of these instruments, in simple terms, are contracts sold as a hedge against the future risk of fluctuations in commodity prices, time differentials, interest rates, tax rates, foreign exchange rates, etc. Because of the flexible nature of these products, the derivatives market is particularly attractive to operators willing to risk heavy losses. A high volume of activity on the market is essential to ensure the high degree of liquidity for which these markets are known. The way in which derivatives are traded and the number of operators in the market mean that there is the potential obscuring of the connection between each new participant and the original trade. No single link in the series of transactions will likely know the identity of the person beyond the one with whom he is directly dealing.

53. The derivatives markets have traditionally not been subject to strict regulatory oversight under the assumption that its operators, as high-risk investors, do not need the same level of protection. The introduction of stricter controls would necessarily cause investors to look elsewhere for these markets. For fear of scaring of investors, there is thus no incentive for traders on the market to ask too many questions. This lack of rigorous government control makes the derivatives market even more attractive from the perspective of a money launderer.

(iii) New countermeasures implemented or significant modifications to existing measures

54. The level or type of money laundering activity can change rapidly in response to countermeasures implemented by a particular jurisdiction. FATF members continue to re-examine their anti–money laundering efforts and refine them where necessary. Faced with difficulties in prosecuting money laundering under provisions dealing with receipt of stolen goods, Sweden and the Netherlands plan to set up separate offences of money laundering under their respective penal codes. Some FATF members have extended the list of predicate offences for laundering or plan to do so.

55. Several FATF member countries are working to extend preventive measure (suspicious transaction reporting) beyond the traditional banking sector. New Belgian legislation this year, for example, extends suspicious transaction reporting (STR) requirements to real estate agents, bailiffs ("huissiers de justice"), money courier services, notaries, accountants, and casinos. Sweden plans to introduce a reporting requirement on money laundering for external auditors.

56. The Netherlands has introduced legislation which requires money transfer businesses to report unusual transactions. Germany has already placed a requirement on such businesses to obtain a license from the Federal Banking Supervisory Office (FBSO), the same authority that oversees banking activity. Additionally, the FBSO requires that all transactions dealing in foreign currency valued at DM5,000 (US$3,018) require customer identification. Finland has extended suspicious transaction reporting to its entire financial sector, includes casinos and other gambling related businesses, and has consolidated reporting to a single financial intelligence unit. Similarly, Switzerland's reinforced money laundering legislation, which also establishes a centralized reporting unit, came into effect in April 1998. This legislation also extends the suspicious transaction-reporting obligation to all financial sectors.

57. Japan plans to enact legislation that will strengthen its measures for combating money laundering and organized crime, and this legislation is currently under deliberation in the Diet. This legislation will extend the number of predicate offences for money laundering, provide for enlargement of the measures for confiscation and freezing the proceeds of crime, and centralization of suspicious transaction reporting under the Financial Supervisory Agency.

58. Canada is working to amend existing legislation to require mandatory reporting of suspicious transactions, as well as cross border movement of currencies. The amendment will clarify the ambiguity surrounding the definition of suspicious transactions and when they are required to be reported. Legislation permitting law enforcement to conduct money laundering sting operations has already been implemented.

59. It has become clear that the analysis and discussion of trends in virtually all FATF member countries now begins with analysis of suspicious transaction reports. Preventive systems involving these reports, implemented and used widely to help detect individual instances of money laundering, are the starting point for examining the money laundering phenomenon from a more strategic point of view. This is reflective of the increase in the number of FATF member states which now have functioning financial intelligence units (FIUs) and mandatory suspicious transaction reporting regimes. The written submissions of the experts, as well as the discussions during the typologies meeting indicated that suspicious transaction reporting systems are becoming more effective in detecting new money laundering methods. The ability of FIUs to share information, even informally, has also dramatically increased.

IV. MONEY LAUNDERING TRENDS OUTSIDE FATF COUNTRIES

60. Money laundering is a problem that is not restricted to FATF members alone. Countermeasures implemented in FATF member countries have facilitated the collection and analysis of information on money laundering activity within their respective national areas. These countermeasures have also, in some cases, pushed certain money laundering activity to jurisdictions having little or no anti–money laundering regime. At the same time, an increasing number of non-FATF countries have established or are in the process of developing effective money laundering countermeasures. Nevertheless, information provided by the FATF experts on non-member countries is far from complete; therefore, the following assessment of money laundering trends outside the FATF member countries does not claim to be exhaustive.

(i) Asia and the Pacific Region

61. Sources of information on money laundering activities in the region have been limited. While few non-FATF members in the area have implemented comprehensive anti–money laundering programs, there have been some signs that individual countries are moving to establish such systems. Some FATF members nevertheless continue to find evidence of significant money laundering activity or serious vulnerabilities to it.

62. As noted in previous typologies exercises, South Asia continues to be one locus in the region for such activity. It serves as home to several major international banks and is a transshipment point for drugs produced in Afghanistan and Iran to the west and in Myanmar, Thailand, and Laos to the east. Money laundering related to the narcotics trade, financial fraud, corruption, and other activities is believed to be carried out through both the traditional banking system and the hawala / hundi alternative remittance system.

63. In the Pacific region, a heavy concentration of financial activity related to Russian organized crime has been observed, specifically in Western Samoa, Nauru, Vanuatu, and the Cook Islands. One delegation mentioned an increasingly common scheme whereby apparently American middlemen are used to open accounts or charter banks in one of the locations. Given the increased suspicion aroused by visible Russian business activity in these jurisdictions, the laundering scheme thus operates under the cover of non-Russian linked business. Internet gambling, which generates nearly $1.5 million a month in this region, represents a major new business trend in Western Samoa, Niue, Vanuatu, Tonga, and Fiji and another potential vulnerability for money laundering and financial crime in those jurisdictions.

64. FATF members greatly welcomed the fact that the Asia/Pacific Group (APG), this region's new anti–money laundering body, held its first typologies workshop in October 1998 in Wellington, New Zealand. Experts from 25 jurisdictions in the area and 4 international organizations met for two days to highlight the most significant money laundering issues of their particular jurisdictions, as well as the Asia/Pacific region as a whole. The Asia/Pacific Group had not yet released its final typologies report by the time of the FATF experts meeting; however, the group provided a short submission to the FATF which described some of the key findings of the APG experts.

65. The primary sources of criminal proceeds in the region were identified as trafficking in human beings and illicit drugs, gambling and the activities of organized crime groups. Some other identified sources include kidnapping, arms smuggling, hijacking, extortion, public corruption, terrorism, and tax evasion. It was also noted that the perpetrators of the predicate offences commonly launder their own proceeds.

66. Among some of the methods employed for laundering, the APG experts cited the abuse of offshore financial centers and the increasing presence of solicitors, accountants, and other professionals both to set up business entities and facilitate the administration of accounts used in money laundering. Structured transactions, purchase of monetary instruments (bank drafts, checks), and physical removal of currency or monetary instruments were also observed in the region. Criminal proceeds have been moved through the Asia/Pacific area by traditional (electronic) means, as well as alternative remittance systems. The APG experts also mentioned that criminal proceeds are often transferred out of the region under the guise of real estate or other investments, legitimate gambling proceeds, and through the use of credit and debit cards. The group expressed similar concerns to those mentioned by the FATF members regarding the development of new payment technologies.

67. FATF members welcomed the APG decision to hold an annual typologies workshop and noted that the second APG workshop will be held in Tokyo, Japan, on March 2–3, 1999. The workshop will concentrate on the use of underground banking and alternative remittance systems for money laundering purposes.

(ii) Central America, South America, and the Caribbean Basin

68. Drug trafficking and the money laundering activity it engenders continue to be major problems in this region. While most of the countries of the Western Hemisphere have moved to enact anti–money laundering legislation, a number of jurisdictions have not fully implemented these countermeasures. Potential alliances between the region's narcotics traffickers and Russian organized crime, already detected by some FATF members, are a cause for concern, as they may further expand money laundering connections with Europe, North America, and the Pacific regions.

69. With regard to the Caribbean area, the Caribbean Financial Action Task Force (CFATF) completed the last phases of its typologies exercise. The exercise comprised four parts conducted over a two-year period. As mentioned in last year's report, the first two phases of its exercise—examining laundering activities in domestic financial institutions and through the gambling industry—took place during 1997. Since then, CFATF has undertaken an assessment of laundering as it occurs in international financial transactions conducted in both domestic and offshore financial institutions, and also the emerging cyberspace technologies. It is most encouraging to see that CFATF will organize a typologies conference on the vulnerabilities of free trade zones to money laundering activity. CFATF plans to use the conference, which will be hosted by Aruba in 1999, to develop a model free zone compliance programme and code of conduct.

70. Money laundering activity in the Caribbean region remains a significant problem due to its location near major narcotics production and consumption areas and its concentration of offshore financial centers. Antigua was again cited as particularly vulnerable due to its failure to implement fully its existing anti–money laundering legislation. Free trade zones were also mentioned as continuing targets for money laundering schemes. In one instance, wire transfers have increasingly replaced cash deposits as the means of moving illegal proceeds through the jurisdiction. St. Kitts was mentioned as being of some concern due to a reported increase in narcotics related laundering activity. Suspicious transactions have been detected within French overseas departments in the Caribbean area relating to structured deposits.

71. The laundering of criminal proceeds continues to affect the many other nations of Latin America. Narcotics trafficking remains the primary source of these proceeds. Despite steps taken by the Mexican government in the past year to address the problem, laundering activity is still of serious concern in that country. Cross-border laundering of drug proceeds between the United States and Mexico continues with currency smuggling, use of payable through accounts, bureaux de change and the black market peso exchange identified as the key laundering methods. Mexican drug cartels remain the primary force in this activity, although the Colombians still play a role. These organizations are able to operate in Mexico by taking advantage of loopholes in existing legislation. Corruption continues to hamper the country's anti–money laundering efforts.

72. Costa Rica was mentioned in connection to laundering activity through financial institutions, casinos, bureaux de change, bulk currency smuggling, and real estate investments. As reported last year, Colombia continues to see the black market peso exchange being used as the primary money laundering system by narcotics traffickers based in that country. The rising cocaine demand in Europe has reportedly resulted in an increase in funds needing to be laundered in the area and the formation of new alliances between Colombian narcotics traffickers and Russian organized crime groups.

73. With its role as a major finance and trading center and its proximity to Colombia, Panama remains attractive to money laundering schemes. The Colón Free Zone is a key target for these laundering activities despite the extension of anti–money laundering measures to the area. Suriname is another country of the region that has an increasingly visible money laundering problem. Methods detected in that country include over-invoicing, gold purchases and account manipulation. Recently, high-level Surinamese officials have been implicated in laundering activity related to international narcotics trafficking.

(iii) Central and Eastern Europe

74. The countries of Central and Eastern Europe remain a significant concern to FATF members. Illegal proceeds are generated by contract and privatization fraud schemes, as well as from the extraction and production of natural resources. In Central Europe, financial institutions continue to be victims of fraud schemes using misrepresented collateral and carried out with the collusion of bank officials. Embezzlement of corporate funds through false contracts is also still a problem.

75. Organized crime activity operating out of the former Soviet Union area was mentioned as being of continuing concern. Many of these organized crime groups bring their criminal proceeds to the nearby FATF members in Europe where they make large real estate investments in such areas as the French and Spanish Mediterranean coast. The groups frequently transfer their funds through various offshore financial centers, such as the Channel Islands, Gibraltar, and the Caribbean area, before using the funds for these investments. The transfers are sometimes made in the name of a legitimate appearing business entity registered in an FATF member country; however, upon further investigation, it is found that the company has no place of business or bank account in the country of registry.

76. FATF members also noted their concern over potential connections of financial institutions to Eastern European organized crime. It is difficult to determine the exact role that Russian financial institutions may wittingly or unwittlingly play with regard to organized crime activity. This difficulty extends to Russian business entities, as well. One member noted that banks operating in Europe seem to be less critical when dealing with other banks even if the counterpart is Russian.

77. A number of members noted an increase in the number of couriers of Central or Eastern European origin involved in reports of unusual or suspicious transactions. These transactions seem especially prevalent with regard to operations at bureaux de change located in FATF member countries. The couriers have no known business or residence connections in the country where they attempt to conduct single transactions with relatively large amounts of cash (individual transactions range from US$50,000 to US$100,000). The large sums and the manner in which the transactions occur seem to indicate that these individuals are not simple tourists.

78. Central and Eastern Europe countries have made a certain amount of progress in developing, adopting and implementing countermeasures during past year. Some examples of this progress include the following: Bulgaria, Estonia, Latvia, Lithuania, and Romania have all enacted anti-money legislation. Latvia and Lithuania have operational financial intelligence units, and Poland hopes to have an operational unit in the first part of 1999. Despite its many internal problems, Russia has enacted a new criminal code that includes money laundering as a crime. The Russian anti–money laundering legislation is scheduled to be approved by the country's parliament in early 1999. Ukraine has effectively abolished anonymous accounts, and its Ministry of Justice is in the process of drafting its first comprehensive anti–money laundering laws. Nevertheless, some FATF members noted that it is still often difficult to obtain information relating to anti–money laundering investigations from certain of the countries of the region. One member mentioned that many of the Central and Eastern European countries have experienced similar frustrations in attempting to obtain information on foreign registered business entities from offshore financial centers in support of their anti–money laundering investigations.

79. FATF welcomed the further development of the Council of Europe initiative to evaluate anti–money laundering systems. The select committee set up for this purpose has adopted an evaluation process based on the one used by the FATF. Its goal is to evaluate the countermeasures in place in each of the 21 members of the committee (the non-FATF members of the Council of Europe). During the past year, the committee conducted seven mutual evaluations. The committee also held its first typologies exercise in December 1998, and it is hoped that this will become a recurring event. Indeed, the Council of Europe typologies exercise, along with those of APG, CFATF, and the FATF, should become the basis for a much clearer picture of money laundering activities throughout the world.

(iv) Middle East and Africa

80. Information on laundering activities in this area of the world is extremely limited. A number of factors favorable to money laundering are known to be present throughout both regions. In the Gulf States (particularly in Bahrain), the banking and finance industries are well established on an international scale. Only a few of the jurisdictions of the region have anti–money laundering legislation. Many expatriate laborers working in the region regularly send money home by using the traditional hawala/hundi alternate remittance system, which offers more favorable rates than those of traditional banks. Gold smuggling is also reportedly used—especially by some professional criminal organizations—as a means of moving funds through the Gulf into the South Asian region. Free trade zones of the area are also likely to attract some of this laundering activity.

81. Still less is known about the Mediterranean area. The growing presence of its own financial centers and its role as a drug transit area appear to make the region vulnerable to laundering activity. Such activity involving organized crime and the diamond industry in Israel has been observed by some FATF experts. With only a few exceptions, most jurisdictions of the region are characterized by the total absence of comprehensive anti–money laundering programs.

82. Africa south of the Sahara is also considered by many of the FATF experts to be vulnerable to money laundering, although, again, information on the region is limited. A factor which contributes to this vulnerability is the increasingly widespread activity of indigenous and, to certain extent, non-indigenous organized crime groups. These groups can operate throughout the region due to lack of strong anti–money laundering laws, combined with the endemic corruption, lack of training, and low pay of government authorities. Only South Africa has criminalized money laundering for crimes beyond those related to narcotics trafficking; however, it has yet to enact comprehensive preventive measures. In other countries of the region, it is believed that only about 20% of the population use traditional banks; thus, there is some concern about how preventive measures could be applied there.

83. FATF experts noted again the ubiquity of West African (especially Nigerian) organized crime groups in money laundering schemes that link FATF countries with the region. As noted in previous reports, fraud seems to be one of the most pervasive sources for laundered funds; however, these groups are also involved in narcotics trafficking, arms smuggling, auto theft, gemstone and ivory smuggling, and trafficking in stolen identity documents. One member noted that there were increasingly ties with some of the francophone countries of western Africa, particularly Togo, Benin, and Senegal. In general, there appears to be a growing frequency of using bureaux de change operations as a cover for converting criminal proceeds. Some groups are using bank accounts in FATF member countries as collector accounts for these proceeds. Funds from these accounts are then used for the purchase of goods that are shipped to Africa and sold as "legitimate" imports. The holders of these accounts charge a percentage for their use but otherwise have neither interest in the source of the funds nor any direct link to the transactions.

V. CONCLUSIONS

84. The London meeting of the group of experts on typologies in November 1998 was the second to undertake in-depth discussions on more focused topics. As mentioned last year and as evidenced by the written submissions of the FATF delegations, the basic techniques and mechanisms for money laundering have been well documented. This meeting examined a number of areas that had not been fully developed. It is hoped, therefore, that the purpose of these expert meetings will continue to be the identification of new approaches taken by launderers, along with significant changes in the patterns of their activity. Through this work, the FATF will acquire additional support and, one might hope, new ideas for appropriate laundering countermeasures.

85. With regard to the money laundering implications of the introduction of the euro in the eleven members of the Economic Monetary Union, experts agreed that there was a potential risk of overwhelming of existing preventive measures due to the increased burden of work for financial institution personnel during the transition phase. The experts also agreed that the introduction of the euro would be a possible opportunity to detect laundering activity. The critical time as far as risk is concerned is the period from January to June 2002, when euros in coin and paper form will replace national currencies. Existing preventive countermeasures should be adequate in detecting possible laundering activity, although a number of FATF members are taking extra steps to re-emphasize or reinforce their anti–money laundering programs. Some experts believe that the introduction of the large denomination euro banknote (EUR500) after January 1, 2002 could affect laundering activity by reducing the bulkiness of criminal proceeds when transported.

86. Non-cooperative jurisdictions or territories remain a continuing area of concern to FATF members. The inability to obtain relevant information on the beneficial owners of foreign legal entities—shell companies, international business corporations, offshore trusts, etc.—represents one of the major roadblocks to successfully detecting, investigating and prosecuting suspected international money launderers. There is the need to foster increased awareness of this problem and exert pressure on certain offshore financial centers in international fora where appropriate. The efforts of the FATF ad hoc working group on non-cooperative countries—both FATF and non-FATF members—will be most welcome in this area.

87. Rapid development and growing consumer acceptance of smartcards, on-line banking, and e-cash continue to be the hallmark of these new payment technologies. As recently as two years ago, many of these systems were not yet beyond the prototype stage, and the potential implications on laundering activity were seen as theoretical. Smartcards are beginning to move beyond testing, and on-line banking is already a reality in a few FATF member countries (and potentially available worldwide through the Internet). The abuse of these systems by launderers is no longer a distant possibility. FATF experts noted that certain money laundering countermeasures could be easily added to the systems; however, decisions to do so have been left to the system developers. Without consistent standards and appropriate regulatory oversight, these new payment technologies will remain highly vulnerable to money laundering activity.

88. Awareness of the potential role of the gold market—and, by extension, of other high-value commodities markets—is growing among FATF member countries. Transactions involving gold are increasingly found in money laundering schemes and are often an integral part of money movements through various parallel banking systems, such as the hawala / hundi system discussed during this typologies meeting. It was emphasized that these money laundering schemes are not limited to any single region of the world. Nevertheless, the particular focal point of gold dealers in the Gulf States for hawala / hundi money movements to and from the South Asia region should be noted.

89. The experts noted the apparent increasing trend for professional services providers—accountants, solicitors, company formation agents, and other similar professions—to be associated with more complex laundering operations. These professionals set up and often run the legal entities that lend the high degree of sophistication and additional layers of respectability to such money laundering schemes. Operating not only in certain offshore locations where they are protected behind a wall of strict confidentiality, these professionals sometimes also provide similar services within FATF member countries themselves. Currently, only a few FATF members impose an obligation on professional services providers to report suspicious transactions. Those members that do have this requirement are not always satisfied with the amount of reporting that takes place from this sector, although the quality of individual reports in some cases appears to justify the need for such reporting.

90. Lastly, this meeting of experts on money laundering typologies has shown in another way the utility of the preventive measures put in place to counter money laundering. The analysis and discussion of methods and trends in virtually all FATF member countries began with analysis of suspicious transaction reports. These systems, implemented to help detect individual instances of money laundering have now become the starting point for examining the phenomenon from a more strategic point of view. Given the insight that this source of information provides to the state of money laundering in a particular jurisdiction, this use of STRs is an encouraging development.

ANNEX TO THE 1998–1999 FATF REPORT ON MONEY LAUNDERING TYPOLOGIES

Selected cases of money laundering

Case N° 1: Accounting firm

Case N° 2: Structuring scheme

Case Nº 3: Gold smuggling

Case Nº 4: Insurance policies and real estate

Case Nº 5: Front companies

Case Nº 6: Money transfers

Case Nº 7: Offshore financial centers, solicitors, and other financial services providers

Case Nº 8: Front companies, insurance, and bureaux de change

Case Nº 9: The derivatives market: a typology

Case Nº 1

Accounting firm

Facts

Beginning in May 1994, two alleged narcotics traffickers used an accounting firm to launder criminal proceeds generated from amphetamine sales. The "clients" of the firm would on a regular basis hand their accountant cash in brown envelopes or shoeboxes for which no receipt was issued. The funds were then stored in the accountant's office until he decided how they could be introduced into the financial system and laundered. At any one time, there were between US$38,000 and US$63,000 stored in the accountant's office.

The law enforcement agency investigating the matter found that the accountant established company and trust accounts on behalf of his clients and opened personal bank accounts in the names of relatives. He then made structured deposits to those accounts with the funds received from the alleged traffickers. Additionally, he transferred approximately US$114,000 overseas—again, using structured transactions—to purchase truck parts, which were later brought back into the country and sold at a profit, and also used some of the funds to purchase properties. The accountant and three of his colleagues (who were also implicated in the scheme) reportedly laundered approximately US$633,900 and received a 10% commission for his services.

Results

The accountant and his colleagues are believed to have acted from the beginning with the suspicion that the clients were involved in illegal activities. Even after obtaining further specific knowledge of his clients' involvement in narcotics trafficking, he and his associates allegedly continued to facilitate money laundering.

Lessons

This case highlights the key role that financial experts can play in the laundering of criminal proceeds. Many of the services provided (establishment of specialized accounts or business entities, making real estate investments) are potential money laundering mechanisms that may be beyond the abilities of the less sophisticated criminal.

Case Nº 2

Structuring scheme

Facts

This case came to the attention of the police through an informant. An individual residing in a small town deposited the equivalent of US$1,038,354 over a three-year period into three financial institutions. The institutions involved were two of the country's major banks and a credit union. Nearly 95% of the deposits were made in cash. The account holder into whose accounts the deposits were made was the citizen of a neighboring country where there had been an outstanding arrest warrant against him since 1982.

During the investigation, it was determined that the employees of the financial institutions had been suspicious of the account activity. They had noticed, for example, that some deposits were made in brown paper bags through the night deposit drawer, yet they did not disclose this information to authorities. Funds deposited into the accounts were ultimately transferred to the account holder by his writing checks on these accounts.

Results

Whether or not suspicious transactions were reported was unfortunately left to the discretion of the financial institution. In this case, the institution employees could not be found to have violated any rules. Due to a lack of vigilance on the part of financial institution employees, even to very obvious suspicious financial activity, an individual was able to launder a substantial sum of money.

Lessons

This example reinforces the need to ensure that financial institution employees know what sort of financial activities might be suspicious and thus worthy of reporting. This case illustrates the advantage of mandatory suspicious transaction reporting. Having such an obligation provides an additional incentive for financial institutions to ensure that their employees have thorough knowledge of what constitutes suspicious financial activity. Furthermore, once in place, mandatory suspicious transaction reporting serves as a deterrent for some of the relatively unsophisticated laundering schemes as described here.

Case № 3

Gold smuggling

Facts

In 1997, a financial intelligence unit (FIU) in country A received various suspicious transaction reports involving nationals from Scandinavian countries. These individuals were making large purchases of gold in their own names using cash in the currencies of their home countries. The transactions were conducted at various financial institutions in country A.

Initial examination of the disclosures indicated that the Scandinavian nationals had neither an official address nor any known legal activity in country A. Information obtained from police and FIUs in their countries of origin revealed that some of the participants in the scheme had outstanding arrest warrants for serious tax fraud. The individuals were suspected to have purchased gold in country A and elsewhere (where the value added tax rate on gold is lower). They then sold the gold in their home countries via various companies.

The suspicious transactions initially appeared to be separate incidents; however, they were grouped together based on such factors as profile of the participants, financial organizations target, and the dates of the transactions. At one of the bureaux de change where the transactions took place, examination of numerical sequence of exchange statements and gold sales invoices provided further information on the methods used by the Scandinavian nationals. For example, the suspects would sometimes conduct their transactions together, and at other times they split up their funds and conducted identical operations on the same day with a series of targeted financial institutions. The coordination among seemingly separate transactions seems to indicate that participants in the scheme were all likely couriers for the same organization.

Results

Given the suspicious nature of this group transactions, the dossier was passed over to the public prosecutor in country A. The dossier also contributed useful evidence to ongoing investigations on the home countries of the suspects.

Lessons

Criminal organizations that are willing to devote the human resources to spreading their laundering operation over a larger geographic area are thus more likely to go undetected. This scheme would not have been detected if the various suspicious transaction reports could not have been brought together and compared. Likewise, the full picture of the scheme could not have been developed had there not been information sharing with foreign counterpart authorities.

Case Nº 4

Insurance polices and real estate

Facts

An insurance company informed an FIU that it had underwritten two life insurance policies with a total value of US$268,000 in the name of two European nationals. Payment was made by a cheque drawn on the accounts of a brokerage firm in a major EU financial market and a notary in the southeastern region of the country.

The two policies were then put up as collateral for a mortgage valued at US$1,783,000 that was provided by a company specializing in leasing transactions. As the policyholders did not pay in their own name, the issuer contacted the brokerage firm in order to discover the exact origin of the funds deposited in its account. It was informed that the funds had been received in cash and that the parties concerned were merely occasional clients.

The parties—two brothers—were known to a law enforcement agency through a separate investigation into the illegal import and export of classic automobiles. Moreover, two individuals with the same surname were suspected by the same agency of drug trafficking and money laundering.

Results

This case has not yet been passed to the prosecutorial authorities.

Lessons

This example shows the necessity for non-bank financial businesses (in this case insurance companies) to be aware of what constitutes suspicious financial activity. It also demonstrates the critical need for effective coordination between the information contained in suspicious transaction reports and law enforcement information.

Case Nº 5

Front companies

Facts

An FIU in country B received a report of a series of suspicious transactions involving the bank accounts of a West African citizen and his businesses, which specialized in industrial fishing. These accounts were opened in banks located in country B and consisted primarily of money changing operations. The businessman also owned several residences in his home country and in the capital region of country B. The companies that he jointly managed all had the same address in his home country.

The personal account of the West African businessman received a number of transfers from accounts in another European country and in his home country (over US$2 million from 1995 to 1996). The business accounts of the companies received transfers from several business entities based in Europe which were ostensibly linked to fishing related activities (over US$7 million from 1994 to 1997). The transfers out of the account (estimated at nearly US$4 million over the same period) were made to various companies whose business was (according to official records) connected with maritime activity and to other individuals.

The FIU's analysis showed that the income of the West African companies concerned was grossly disproportionate to reported sales. In fact, the account transactions seemed to have little to do with industrial fishing (i.e., foreign currency sales, transfers from the bank accounts of European residents, transfers between the personal account of the West African businessman and his businesses, transfers between these businesses and those of Europe-based partners).

Furthermore, according to additional information received by the FIU, one of the partners of the West African businessman, a co-manager of one of the companies, was suspected of being involved in several financial offenses in Italy. This individual reportedly had close associations with two Italian organized crime figures, and his Italian businesses have become the target of investigation into money laundering in that country. Still another business partner of the West African businessman appears also to be involved in financial and fiscal offences.

Results

This case has not yet been passed to prosecutorial authorities.

Lessons

Given the unusual account transactions and the lack of a clear economic connections for some of the business activities, the operations described in this example very likely constitute a money laundering scheme to conceal the illegal sources of proceeds derived from various criminal activities. This case gives further support to the need for analysis of information from a variety of sources (suspicious transaction reports, financial institutions, company registries, police records, etc.) in order to gain a full picture of a complex laundering scheme.

Case Nº 6

Money transfers

Facts

In July 1997, the police arrested the leader of an Iranian drug trafficking group, suspect A, for possessing stimulants and other kinds of drugs. The subsequent investigation revealed that the suspect had remitted part of his illegal proceeds abroad.

A total of US$450,000 was remitted via three banks to an account on behalf of suspect A's older brother B at the head office of an international bank in Dubai. Transfers were made on five occasions during the two months between April and June 1998 in amounts ranging from US$50,000 to US$150,000).

Another individual, suspect C, actually remitted the funds and later returned to Iran. On each occasion, C took the funds in cash to the bank, exchanged them for dollars, and then had the funds transferred. Each of the transactions took about one hour to conduct, and the stated purpose for the remittances was to cover "living expenses."

Results

Suspect A was initially charged with violating provisions of the anti-narcotics trafficking law. The money transfers revealed during the investigation led to additional charges under the anti–money laundering law. This was the first time that anti–money laundering provisions had been applied to the overseas transfers criminal proceeds. Court proceedings for this case are on going.

Lessons

This case represents a classic example of a simple money laundering scheme and is also a good example of a case derived not just from suspicious transaction reporting but also as a follow-up to traditional investigative activity.

Case Nº 7

Offshore financial centers, solicitors, and other financial services providers

Facts

In December 1997, M-Bank, acting as an international clearing bank, received a wire transfer for US$1.4 million that appeared to originate from a UK law firm. The transfer was to be credited to the account of "AZ Brokerage International, Ltd." in G-Bank.

Due to the initials used in the company's name, M-Bank suspected that AZ Brokerage International, Ltd. might be a controlled by Mr. "AZ", who was known to be involved in dubious financial activities. The bank also knew that Mr. AZ had served two years in a foreign prison for his connections to a false monetary instrument scheme and that his personal assets were subject to bankruptcy proceedings.

M-Bank decided to make a suspicious transaction report to the FIU, and, at the same time, they informed G-Bank of their suspicion. G-Bank subsequently disclosed to the FIU that Mr. AZ was operating a number of accounts opened under the names of various companies, including AZ Brokerage International, Ltd.

Preliminary inquiries made by the FIU revealed, among other things, the following:

- A third financial institution, D-Bank, had submitted a report to the FIU a few weeks earlier. The report stated that D-Bank had concluded its banking relationship with Mr. AZ after having received several "suspicious approaches" from him and from foreign sources.
- Mr. AZ appeared to be the principal of 20 legal entities registered in the national company registry. All of these business entities operated from his home address.
- The names of the businesses indicated involvement in various types of financial activity, such as "AZ Fiduciary & Nominees", "AZ Investment & Finance", "AZ Insurance Guaranty Fund", etc.
- The holding company, AZ Holding, Ltd. was stated to have a fully paid share capital of 20 million US$ confirmed by the company's state authorized accountant.
- None of the companies were licensed to provide any type of financial or brokering services in the country of registry, according to the financial supervisory authority.

The FIU requested that the banks disclose additional information on their banking relationship with Mr. AZ or legal entities controlled by him. G-Bank was further requested to freeze the amount of 1.4 million US$ as soon as it was credited to the account controlled by Mr. AZ. This additional information revealed that a number of deposits had been made to the relevant accounts prior to the FIU disclosures. All deposits were made by international wire transfer, and the largest amounted to US$1.5 million. Most of the funds received had been immediately used to purchase bank drafts that were sent to individuals and companies in the United Kingdom and the United States. It was also noted that the purpose of one wire transfer to a US law firm was stated as being a "legal fee for establishment of AZ Merchant Bank."

The above mentioned information was submitted to a criminal investigation team, and the next day Mr. AZ requested that G-Bank transfer several hundred US dollars to an offshore bank account in the name of an individual. The transaction was stopped, and Mr. AZ was arrested as he was due to depart on holiday to the Caribbean where he had planned to meet with several apparently associated individuals.

Documents subsequently seized provided the following information:

- The stated share capital of AZ Holding, Ltd. was based on a Certificate of Deposit with the face value of US$20 million and issued by a Panamanian financial institution.
- Mr. AZ, in addition to the business entities registered in his country, also held beneficial and formal positions in a number of business entities incorporated in several offshore jurisdictions, including "AZ Private Bank, Ltd." registered in Antigua.
- The name of the above-mentioned "AZ Merchant Bank, Inc." had been changed to "AZ Banque de Commerce, Inc." on the advice of the solicitor that later arranged for US incorporation.
- Mr. AZ claims to provide various types of financial services, including private banking and issue of "proof of funds" for use in various types of high-yield investment programs, etc.
- A large number of foreign clients—mainly from Eastern Europe and the United States—had made the initial payment in amounts between US$5,000 and US$50,000 to get access to his services.

After the arrest of Mr. AZ, the investigation team was contacted and later visited by several individuals who claim to represent the beneficiaries of three of the deposits amounting to nearly US$3.5 million— including US$1.6 million that had been frozen. However, no beneficial party was prepared to make a formal statement or to provide documentary evidence of the source of the funds. No formal claims for the release of the seized funds had been received eleven months after the investigation began.

Results

Mr. AZ was released from custody during the on-going investigation. It appeared, however, that he immediately resumed the same business upon his release. The investigative authority has recently requested the assistance of foreign law enforcement authorities in their investigation regarding US$20 million that had been transferred from an offshore financial center to the account of one of Mr. AZ's companies.

Lessons

This case illustrates how financial services providers operating in one country or through an offshore financial center may facilitate money laundering, as well as legitimate business transactions. With any one jurisdiction having only one part of the picture, it is difficult to determine exactly how the whole scheme works. The fact that, after blocking the transfer of funds for eleven months, there were still no concrete claims from the beneficial owners for their return is also a further indication that the funds may not have been of strictly legal origin. This case is also a good example of how financial institutions can work with each other and anti–money laundering authorities to pull together a picture of the suspected laundering scheme.

Case Nº 8

Front companies, insurance, and bureaux de change

Facts

An FIU received a suspicious transaction report from an insurance company that specialized in life insurance. The report referred to Mr. H, born and resident in a Latin American country, as having recently taken out "two sole premium life insurance policies for a total amount of US$702,800." Subsequent information provided to the FIU indicated that the policies premiums had been paid with two personal checks made out by a third party and drawn against a major bank. The third party, Mr. K, was also a resident in the same Latin American country although not a national of that country. Further checks at Mr. K's bank revealed that both he and Mr. H had signature authority on two business accounts, Sam, Ltd. and Dim, Ltd.

Examination of the accounts showed, especially in Mr. K's account, that transactions were carried out on behalf of Mr. H. Thus, the account had received funds from abroad and had also been used for other financial products besides the life insurance policies. Indeed, ten checks in US dollars drawn against American banks and issued by two bureaux de change operating out of the Latin American country where the two men resided, had been deposited into Mr. K's account. The value of these checks totaled US$1,054,200.

This activity appeared to show that the funds had been used to pay the insurance premium on Mr. H's life and to acquire stakes in investment funds, also for Mr. H, amounting to another US$210,840. There were also other related transactions in the accounts of the two companies and Mr. H's personal account. Cash or cheque transactions for amounts between US$14,000 and US$70,000 were among the related transactions. In one instance, a cheque was drawn of the Sam, Ltd. account for US$63,300 on the day following the deposit of US$70,280 in checks into Mr. K's account.

Checks into the backgrounds of Mr. H and Mr. K revealed that Mr. H was suspected of being involved in cocaine trafficking in Latin America. Mr. K had some minor violations (writing bad checks, etc.); however, he had no serious criminal background. The business activities and backgrounds of Sam, Ltd. and Dim, Ltd. were also looked at. In both instances, the companies had been incorporated with a stock capital of US$36,400 in which Mr. H and Mr. K had a 50% interest and were joint directors. Queries made at the "Balance of Payments Office" as to foreign collection and payment revealed a total absence of operations in the previous two financial years.

Result

It appeared, therefore, that Mr. K was being used as the front man for Mr. H's efforts to move funds out of his country of residence. For greater security of the scheme, firms under their control were established that did not perform any corporate or commercial activity. Mr. H received the funds deposited in Mr. K's account through the sole premium insurance policies and shares in investment funds that had been paid for by that account, as well as through indirect income from the companies mentioned. In this case, the FIU believed there to be sufficient signs of money laundering and therefore passed the matter on to prosecutorial authorities.

Lessons

This operation is interesting because it shows that payment instruments or third party involvement having no apparent economic relationship to the transaction are often a key indicator of suspicious activity. It is worth noting that Mr. K was obviously selected based on his lack of prior criminal record and his nationality so as to minimize suspicion. The activities of the front companies were also conducted in such a way as to give the appearance of transactions from corporate activities. The case also highlights the potential value of suspicious transaction reporting by insurance companies.

Case Nº 9

The derivatives market: a typology

The following typology is provided as an example of how funds could be laundered using the derivatives market.

In this method, the broker must be willing to allocate genuinely losing trades to the account in which criminal proceeds are deposited. Instead of relying on misleading or false documentation, the broker uses the genuine loss making documentation to be allocated to the detriment of the dirty money account holder. As an example, a broker uses two accounts, one called "A" into which the client regularly deposits money which needs laundering, and one called "B" which is intended to receive the laundered funds. The broker enters the trading market and "goes long" (purchases) 100 derivative contracts of a commodity, trading at an offer price of $85.02, with a "tick" size of $25. At the same time he "goes short" (sells) 100 contracts of the same commodity at the bid price of $85.00. At that moment, he has two legitimate contracts which have been cleared through the floor of the exchange.

Later in the trading day, the contract price has altered to $84.72 bid and $84.74 offered. The broker returns to the market, closing both open positions at the prevailing prices. Now, the broker, in his own books assigns the original purchase at $85.02 and the subsequent sale at $84.72 to account A. The percentage difference between the two prices is 30 points or ticks (the difference between $84.72 and $85.02). To calculate the loss on this contract, the tick size which is $25 is multiplied by the number of contracts, 100, multiplied by the price movement, 30. Thus: $25 x 100 x 30 = $75,000 (loss).

The other trades are allocated to the B account, which following the same calculation theory of tick size multiplied by the number of contracts multiplied by the price movement results in a profit as follows: $25 x 100 x 26 = $65,000 (profit). The account containing the money to be laundered has just paid out $75,000 for the privilege of receiving a profit of $65,000 on the other side. In other words, the launderer has paid $10,000 for the privilege of successfully laundering $75,000. Such a sum is well within the amount of premium which professional launderers are prepared to pay for the privilege of cleaning up such money. As a transaction, it is perfectly lawful from the point of view of the broker. He has not taken the risk of creating false documentation, which could conceivably be discovered, and everything has been done in full sight of the market.

APPENDIX VII

WHITE PAPER: LOGGING ON TO CYBERSPACE TAX POLICY

EXECUTIVE SUMMARY

I. Introduction

The purpose of this white paper (hereinafter "the White Paper") entitled "Logging on to Cyberspace Tax Policy," is to initiate discussions with the nation's tax policymakers about state and local transaction tax issues affecting the Internet and online services industry (the "Industry"). The White Paper was prepared on behalf of and in conjunction with a Task Force of Interactive Services Association ("ISA") member companies by Ernst & Young LLP.[1]

The Industry is important to the nation's economic growth and to individual states' economic development in that it promises to grow dramatically in the near future. Utilization of the Internet and proprietary subscriber networks[2] will provide increasingly significant consumer benefits, including improved access to information, lower prices and increased business efficiency. Much uncertainty exists as to the manner in which state and local taxes should be applied to the Industry. The uncertainty results from a lack of understanding of a) Internet and online service technology; b) the nature of the various types of businesses providing Internet and/or online services; c) the nature of the various types of transactions that take place over the Internet and proprietary subscriber networks; d) the applicability, if any, of current state tax laws to this new and rapidly evolving Industry; e) whether and how such laws can be implemented in the Internet and online services environment; and f) what state tax approach would best serve the interests of the states and the Industry.

The White Paper seeks to educate policymakers about the technology upon which the Industry is based and about the unique nature of the Industry, as well as to present practical and equitable recommendations which can serve as a basis for construction of a uniform, consistent and fair tax scheme. The recommendations are summarized in Section V, below.

II. Industry Background

A. Internet and Online Activities

Generally, members of the Industry are engaged in the sale of "access services" and/or "content."

1. Access services are those services that enable a customer to get onto the Internet and/or proprietary subscriber networks easily, for example, by simply dialing a phone number.

   a. According to Industry vernacular, generally

   1) An Internet Service Provider (ISP) is a business providing access to the Internet.

   2) An Online Service Provider (OSP) is a business providing access to a proprietary subscriber network. Many OSPs also provide their customers the ability to access the Internet. ISPs and OSPs generally provide their services in return for the payment of subscription and/or usage fees.

2. Content consists of information and services delivered electronically via the Internet or proprietary subscriber networks to the public.

   a. Content is made available to the public by OSPs, by some ISPs, and via the World Wide Web sites of third-party "Content Providers."

   b. The cost of most content provided by OSPs and ISPs is included in their subscription and/or usage fees.

   c. A limited number of Web site operators provide content for a fee which they bill directly to the consumer.

   d. Some sales of content would be treated as taxable sales of tangible personal property if delivered other than electronically, e.g. downloaded videos, music, books. This market is extremely limited at the moment.

B. Mail-Order Sellers

Retailers selling tangible personal property over the Internet and proprietary subscriber networks are essentially mail order sellers who deliver their goods to an identifiable address. The White Paper assumes that mail-order sellers:

1. are simply major users of the Internet and proprietary subscriber networks in marketing their wares over those electronic facilities,
2. are protected by traditional constitutional restraints upon the states,
3. are subjected to traditional state use tax collection requirements,
4. bill their customers directly for their sales.

C. Nexus (Taxing Jurisdiction) Considerations

The United States Supreme Court has ruled that states have taxing jurisdiction over only those out-of-state sellers of tangible personal property who have nexus (sufficient physical contact) with the state. When a transaction involves a sale that is delivered electronically, the seller's lack of any physical contact whatsoever with the state should insulate it from the state's taxing jurisdiction.[3]

D. Relationship to Telecommunications Carriers

Generally, customers of ISPs and OSPs purchase telecommunications capacity from telecommunications carriers in order to gain access to the Internet and online services. ISPs and OSPs also purchase underlying transmission capacity from telecommunications carriers to operate their businesses. All of these parties pay taxes on such telecommunications services provided by the telecommunications carriers.

E. Locating Sales

Internet and online services, by their nature, are not designed with geographical boundaries in mind. This severely limits the Industry's ability to comply with tax administration requirements based upon locating either the source or the destination of electronic transactions. When a sale is delivered electronically, the ISP, OSP or Content Provider often cannot determine the physical location of the sale's destination. This can be true even if the Provider itself happens to be subject to the taxing jurisdiction of the state of the user.

III. Economic Significance of the Industry

A. Economic Benefits

1. Potential

Internet and online services hold enormous potential for reducing customer costs, improving business productivity, and expanding access to information, for consumers, businesses and students. The growth of Internet and online services will generate significant benefits to business and household users as well as employment opportunities in individual states and localities.

2. Recent Employment Experience

For example, Internet and online services-related employment in five of the seven Task Force member companies grew from approximately 3,500 in 1993 to approximately 9,500 in 1995, an annual growth rate exceeding 60 percent.

B. Sizing the Internet and Online Service Market

Internet and online services are experiencing rapid growth, but it is important to recognize that the industry is still relatively young. The Internet and online service marketplace has enormous potential, but the current level of revenues is quite small both in absolute dollars and relative to non-electronic sales of communication and information services.

1. Estimated revenues from Internet access and consumer online services ranged between $1.6 billion and $2.2 billion in 1995, according to two industry research firms. Despite all the attention the Internet and online services have received, they still represent a very small proportion (less than 0.8 percent) of total communication services revenue (including telephone, television and radio broadcasting, and cable and other pay-television services).
2. Revenues for Internet access services in 1995 totaled approximately $250 million, according to SIMBA Information, Inc. and Jupiter Communications.
3. Revenue estimates for consumer online services in 1995 ranged from $1.2 billion (SIMBA Information, Inc.) to $1.8 billion for online content packaging (Jupiter Communication). Most consumers use online services principally for electronic mail and accessing information.
4. Content, which traditionally was supported by subscription revenues from online services, is increasingly being supported by advertising revenues as more content moves to the World Wide Web. Ad spending on the World Wide Web and online services totaled $131 million during 1995 (SIMBA Information, Inc.), or less than 0.5 percent of spending on television, network radio, and magazine advertising.
5. The Internet and online equivalent of mail-order sales of tangible personal property in 1995 totaled approximately $500 million (SIMBA Information, Inc. and Forrester Research), or less than 0.4 percent of consumer mail-order sales.

C. Growth Potential

Internet and online services are projected to grow rapidly during the next five years, assuming that those services can continue to develop in the unimpeded manner that they have over the past few years.

1. By 2000, revenues from subscriptions and advertising for Internet access and consumer online services are projected to grow to between $7 billion (SIMBA Information, Inc.) and $14 billion (Jupiter Communications). Projections also differ on the mix of subscription and advertising revenues.

2. By 2000, the Internet and online equivalent of mail-order sales of tangible property is projected to reach $6.6 billion by Forrester Research. This would represent less than 5 percent of mail-order sales.
3. The growth of Internet and online services will generate new sources of tax revenues for states from expanded employment, increased profitability from business productivity improvements, and expanded use of telecommunication services.

IV. Industry Observations

A. Distinctions Between Telecommunications Services and the Industry's Services

1. The essence of the Industry's services is not telecommunications services.
2. While telecommunications-like services may be a component of Internet and online services, it is a minor one. Other components, such as file transfers, information access and retrieval, and protocol conversions which allow communication with a variety of users, are the true essence of Internet and online services.
3. Underlying transmission services provided by telecommunications carriers are already subjected to specific taxes by many states.
4. Internet and online services fall within the Federal Communications Commission's definition of enhanced services, rather than that of basic telecommunications services.

B. Irrelevance of Location

The states will often be unable to determine the locations of sellers over the Internet and proprietary subscriber networks. In fact, the nature of the Internet and online technology makes the physical location of the seller irrelevant to the seller's business operations. Such a seller may be able to operate in a state's market effectively from far beyond the state's borders, where it may be immune to the state's taxing jurisdiction. Any government seeking to require tax collection by such a seller faces a formidable challenge.

C. Industry's Potential Role

Only through close cooperation between the Industry and the policymakers can there be hope of designing and implementing an effective tax system that takes into account the unique nature of the Industry.

D. Looking Before Leaping

The Industry is concerned that if the states move too quickly, they will risk creating, rather than resolving, major problems. Since relatively small amounts of tax are currently at stake, there is time to work together to develop a fair and efficient tax system. Such a system should ensure uniform application and consistent administration of any tax while allowing the development and expansion of the Industry. A deliberate and cooperative approach will avoid the dangers that lurk in precipitate and uninformed action on the part of the states, dangers that could hinder the development of the Industry.

E. Tax Elements

The Industry believes that the only type of tax that can be applied effectively to Internet and online transactions will be a transaction tax that is imposed upon the purchaser, not upon the Industry; that, in the absence of better information as to the location of the purchaser, a seller should be allowed to rely upon the billing address to identify the state whose tax will apply; and that the billed charges should be used to determine the amount of the end user's tax liability. New developments, such as the increasing use of electronic cash to pay billed charges, can be expected to produce new tax collection and allocation challenges. The Industry stands ready to work with the states in a cooperative effort to meet those challenges.

F. Consistent Definitions

Inconsistency among the states in defining and applying terms defeats the possibility of achieving uniform, fair and efficient administration of any tax. Cooperative efforts must, therefore, concentrate on creating one set of definitions for states to adopt, and those definitions must be interpreted consistently from state to state.

G. Uniform Rate in Each State

The greatest threat to the type of tax system contemplated here is any requirement that a remote seller must account for a multiplicity of taxes at lower levels of government. Relieving the Industry of such a requirement is the key to obtaining the Industry's cooperation to produce an effective tax administration capability for the states with respect to electronic sales. Such relief is a vital prerequisite to achieving the purposes set forth herein.

V. Recommendations

State tax rules should be uniform, fair, certain, and administratively simple. They should not discriminate against electronic commerce or Internet-based transactions, and they should not hinder economic growth. The development of tax rules applicable to the Industry should be pursued with deliberation to ensure the achievement of these goals. Specifically, it is the position of the ISA White Paper Task Force that, if the states adopt a tax system applicable to the Industry, that system should call for the following:

A. Adoption of uniform definitions among the states;

B. Establishment of a single rate, within each state, of any applicable tax;

C. Recognition of the fact that the only type of tax that can be applied effectively to purchases made over the Internet or proprietary subscriber networks will be a tax on the purchaser with respect to the purchase transaction itself;[4] and

D. Attribution, to the extent possible, of any applicable tax to the state into which the sales are billed. The subject of nexus needs rethinking insofar as it pertains to the complex environment that characterizes the Internet and Internet-based transactions.

VI. Conclusion

The above recommendations are intended to address the concerns of tax policymakers, on the one hand, and the Industry, on the other. Their implementation, however, can be accomplished only through close cooperation between the Industry and the policymakers. Time is of the essence. The line of communication is open.

LOGGING ON TO CYBERSPACE TAX POLICY

AN INTERACTIVE SERVICES ASSOCIATION TASK FORCE WHITE PAPER[5]

I. Introduction: Goals and Purposes

It is almost impossible to pick up a magazine or newspaper or turn on the television or radio anywhere in the Western world without hearing something about the Internet or the World Wide Web. There is no shortage of hype or jargon. Phrases like "information superhighway," "digital convergence," "interactive television," "cyberspace," and "information age" are commonplace. In the United States, policymakers at all levels are taking an interest in the Internet and its potential to do everything from making American industry more competitive to improving the quality of education. The predicted growth in the electronic marketplace is staggering. The business promise is tantalizing. Once the Internet and proprietary subscriber networks[6] are utilized by most Americans, revolutionary changes will occur.

The excitement surrounding the world of electronic commerce has not escaped the attention of state and local tax authorities, whose initial reactions have been mixed. While some states appear not to have addressed the issue at all thus far, others have interpreted existing transaction-tax statutes as not being applicable to the Internet and online services industry (the "Industry"), and still others have decided to study the Industry carefully before leaping to conclusions. The latter states appear to be motivated by a desire to encourage the development and growth of in-state Industry members.

On the other hand, some states are already taxing receipts from such Internet and online services in one way or another. These state's initial reactions appear to be motivated by concern about enforcement and compliance issues, concern about the adequacy of the tax base, and a desire to collect additional tax revenues.

The new electronic marketplace is in a relatively early stage of development. Technology standards are still evolving; pricing methodologies and markets are still being developed and tested. Pioneer sellers who seek to capitalize upon the opportunities that electronic marketing presents cannot be certain of success. But, without a coordinated effort between government and the Industry, there will be a mixed bag of state and local tax consequences that will hamper the development of this emerging Industry.

The state ability to offer guidance as to how, whether, and under what circumstances the Industry will be taxed is hampered by the constantly changing nature of the Industry. It is also difficult to fit into existing statutory molds services that were never contemplated when the tax statutes were enacted. It is time for policymakers and the Industry to work together to achieve rational, uniform and fair taxation.

The Task Force seeks to initiate that process with the White Paper. The focus, recommendations and conclusions of this study pertain only to transaction-type taxes. Such taxes are borne by the ultimate consumer. It is not the intent of this paper to suggest that the Industry itself should be exempted from taxation. The fact is that all members of the Industry are already subjected to a myriad of state and local taxes, including income, franchise, property, payroll, and business license taxes.

The goals of the White Paper are fourfold in nature:

1. To Present a Clear Picture of the Industry

Presenting a clear picture of the rapidly-growing, dynamic Industry is, in some ways, like trying to change a tire while driving down the street. As the technology upon which the Industry is based develops and improves, the number of subscribers continues to grow. As a result, the Industry faces market demands for improved services, such as quicker response times, simpler search techniques, and better security. Industry members are meeting such demands by forming strategic alliances among themselves to expand the range of services available to their subscribers.

Moreover, Internet and online services are unique because they exist outside the scope of the traditional telecommunications industry, which is itself subject, in many instances, to state tax systems that are obsolete in that they were designed when the telecommunications industry was an extensively regulated nationwide monopoly. No such monopoly now exists.

Customers of Internet and online service providers purchase telecommunications capacity from telecommunications carriers in order to gain access to Internet and online services. What's more, Internet and online service providers themselves purchase underlying transmission capacity from the carriers to operate their businesses. Telecommunications carriers also provide the conduit for transmitting information, data, or products from service providers to their subscribers. While the Industry uses this conduit to accomplish its purposes, its business is distinct from that of the telecommunications industry.

2. To Demonstrate the Potential Economic Significance of the Industry to the States

The growth of Internet and online services will be increasingly important to every state's economic development. The Industry itself is investing tremendous sums of money to improve its capabilities. As it does so, derivative benefits will accrue to many other businesses, such as those that provide equipment, personnel and services to the Industry. In addition, in-state businesses that take advantage of the efficiencies made possible by Industry services will grow and prosper. States whose tax policies do not impede the Industry's growth will themselves experience increased prosperity. Technological opportunities will naturally migrate to states that are tax friendly. Recognizing this, some states are considering the possibility of shaping their tax policy to provide tax incentives to the Industry in the form of such things as enterprise zones, tax credits, and exemptions for research and development activities. The growth of Internet and online services will also be important to every state's consumer opportunities and educational programs. States and communities can encourage the use of such services by providing low tax rates and exemptions to the Industry. The services will open new possibilities to residents in rural as well as urban areas, often without increasing the demand for physical infrastructure. Encouraging the use of Internet and online services as part of educational programs will provide students with vitally needed skills. On the other hand, states and communities that inhibit the use of Internet and online services through burdensome taxation and compliance requirements will place their residents and businesses at a competitive disadvantage, ultimately stunting the growth of local economies.

3. To Identify Legal Constraints and Logistical Issues Affecting the States' Abilities to Tax Industry Transactions

A. Nexus

The United States Supreme Court has ruled that, under the Commerce Clause of the United States Constitution, states have taxing jurisdiction over only those out-of-state sellers of tangible personal property who have nexus (sufficient physical contact) with the state.[7] The Court's concern about protecting the free flow of interstate commerce applies equally to all types of sales, whether made electronically or by mail, whether they involve sales of tangible personal property or sales of services. Thus, when a transaction involves a sale that is made and delivered solely by electronic means, the seller's lack of physical contact with the state insulates it from the state's taxing jurisdiction. This is true regardless of whether the sale involves tangible personal property or services.

B. Locating Sales

An Internet or online service provider often does not know the geographical location of its customer. Thus, even if the service provider is subject to the taxing jurisdiction of a state, it may be unable to determine which of its sales over the Internet or proprietary network have a destination in that state. The reason is that Internet and online services, by their nature, are designed and operate without reference to geographical boundaries. This severely limits the Industry's ability to comply with existing state and local tax administration requirements that are based upon locating either the source or the destination of electronic transactions.[8]

Furthermore, once a subscriber has gained access to the Internet through the facilities of an Internet or online service provider, the provider cannot know which sites the subscriber visits on the Internet. This means that any thought of imposing tax collection responsibilities on the service provider with respect to third-party Internet sales should be dismissed.

4. To Propose Optional Approaches to the Taxation of Internet and Online Services, Keeping in Mind the Primary Goals of Achieving Simplicity, Uniformity, and Fairness in the Manner in Which the States Tax the Industry

Any tax system for the Industry should seek to achieve simplicity, uniformity and fairness. Both the states and the Industry need reliable uniform taxation guidelines in order to determine whether, how and/or upon whom any tax should fall and how it is to be collected. Furthermore, both need a simple taxing system that is easy to administer and to comply with, and that does not place an unreasonable burden on the resources of either. In addition, neither wants state and local tax obligations to hinder the growth of the Industry. The system must encourage electronic entrepreneurs to enter the electronic commercial forum, thereby contributing to the development of the electronic marketplace.

II. Industry Background

The development of rational tax policy can be accomplished only if readers of this document understand the nature of the Industry. This section seeks to explain how the Industry operates, the services that it offers, how those services differ from telecommunications services, and why its services should not be subjected to the same taxes as telecommunications services.[9]

It is the hope of the Task Force that policymakers, once equipped with an understanding of the Industry and of the world of electronic commerce of which it is a part, will work with the Industry to achieve a tax system that is simple, uniform and fair.

A. The Underlying Technology

1. The Internet

The Internet is an international network of computer networks that is not, as a whole, owned or operated by any single entity. [10] It is made up of many networks of various sizes. All of the computers on the Internet communicate with one another through one communication protocol commonly known as TCP/IP (Transmission Control Protocol/Internet Protocol).

The Internet began in 1969 as an experimental project of the Advanced Research Project Agency (ARPA), and was called "ARPANET." It linked computers and computer networks owned by the military services, defense contractors, and university laboratories that were conducting defense-related research.

From its inception, the Internet was designed to be a decentralized, self-maintaining series of links between computer networks, capable of rapidly transmitting packets of data without direct human involvement or control, and having the ability to re-route communications automatically if one or more individual links suffered damage or became otherwise unavailable, perhaps as a result of war. These features allowed vital research and communications to continue even if portions of the network were down. As it evolved, the ARPANET came to be called the Defense Advanced Research Project Agency ("DARPA") Internet.

In 1986 the National Science Foundation (NSF) developed its high-speed network to allow researchers access to NSF's new supercomputer sites and provide a faster medium for data transmission between the sites. The sites were located throughout the country to reduce total distance from each participant university to the closest site. Because the sites were then tied together, a professor at any university had the ability to contact any one of the supercomputer sites. Other government agencies, including NASA and the Department of Energy, also developed high-speed networks for the use of their researchers and personnel. NSF's network (the "NSFNET") developed into the technical backbone of the Internet, whereupon, in 1990, the ARPANET was no longer in use.[11]

Having reached far beyond its research origins in the United States to encompass universities, corporations, and people throughout the world, the NSFNET is now called simply the Internet. As increasing numbers of private network companies establish links, called "gateways," to the Internet for their private subscriber online services, there is no limit to the extent to which the Internet can expand.

Data transfer on the Internet occurs primarily between a "client" (e.g., a personal computer) and a "server," or "host" computer. The client computer initiates a request for data and the server computer responds to, or serves, that request. In order to serve the needs of client computers, host computers are typically running and connected to the Internet 24 hours a day, while client computers, particularly home or other individual computers, are connected only intermittently.

The Internet has always been rich in content, but, until recently, not very user-friendly. Because of this constraint, it had limited commercial applications until the development of Web technologies, beginning in mid-1993.

2. The World Wide Web

The World Wide Web ("WWW" or "the Web") was designed at the European Particle Physics Laboratory ("CERN") in Switzerland. In general terms, the Web environment provides a user-friendly graphical interface.[12]

The Web environment allows access, with the click of a mouse, to a vast array of data anywhere in the world. By simply clicking on a word, phrase or image, the user can retrieve this data without knowing where it is located. This type of active text is called HyperText. Clicking on the HyperText activates a link (commonly known as a "marker") that contains instructions pointing to the location of the data anywhere on the Internet. A coding language called HTML (HyperText Markup Language) is used to create these links to different locations on the Internet. The World Wide Web contains a multitude of Web sites which are a collection of Web documents usually consisting of a home page, which may in turn link to other pages.[13]

Every Web site has a unique Internet address, called a URL (Uniform Resource Locator) in the file system of a specific Internet server. Because Web sites are linked together via HyperText markers and share a common appearance, they seem to be joined together seamlessly, even though, in reality, they are scattered all over the world.

The Web was at one time viewed as just another method for arranging or cataloging Internet content. Now, however, the huge and growing population of Web sites itself requires cataloging. This problem has been addressed by the creation of tools known generically as search engines, which pursue information across the Web from a predefined set of objectives (e.g., a keyword search) and browsers, which are software programs resident on the user's computer that allow the user to view information located in databases connected to the Web. Internet and online service providers are increasingly supplying such tools to subscribers.

B. Internet and Online Activities

Generally, members of the Industry are engaged in the sale of "access services" and/or "content."

1. Access Services

Access services are those services that enable a customer to get onto the Internet and/or proprietary subscriber networks easily (for example, by simply dialing a phone number). In general, an Internet service provider ("ISP") is a business providing access to the Internet, while an online service provider ("OSP") is a business providing access to and content available on a proprietary subscriber network. Many OSPs also provide their customers with access to the Internet. ISPs and OSPs generally provide their services in return for the payment of subscription and/or usage fees.

2. Content

While content has been available via proprietary subscriber networks for years, it is becoming more widely accessible via the Internet and WWW. Yet, revenues from sales of content are only modest in comparison with their potential.

Content is made available to the public by OSPs, by some ISPs, and via Web sites of third-party content providers. It consists of information and services delivered to the public electronically via the Internet or proprietary subscriber networks. Such services include travel, data processing, brokerage, sports, and entertainment services; information includes items traditionally delivered in tangible form, but which can now be delivered directly to the user/consumer through his/her computer, e.g. newspapers, books, and music.

The following is an example of the way in which an ISP may operate. It is not meant to be all-inclusive. An OSP may, in many ways, operate in a similar manner.[14]

3. Sample Internet Service Provider Business Model

Internet Access

The ISP's Internet access services are available to subscribers on a nationwide basis by way of a national Point-of-Presence ("POP") network which extends to virtually every major market. A POP typically consists of a leased room with modems and routing equipment that may be either owned or leased by the ISP.[15] There are generally no employees at any POP location. In the event that technical difficulties occur at a POP, the ISP tries to correct the problem via remote access. If this is not successful, it sends a technician to correct the problem. A local POP provides the subscriber with access to the Internet via a local phone number, as described below.

Dial-ups and Direct Connections

The ISP has two types of accounts: "dial-up" accounts, mostly for individuals, who need only intermittent connections; and "direct connection" (or dedicated-line access) accounts, mostly for business organizations, which need continuous connections.

Dial-ups The ISP's dial-up account subscribers initiate access to the Internet on their computers. A program instructs the computer to dial the ISP's POP at the designated local access number. A transmission provider such as a Regional Bell Operating Company ("RBOC"), a local exchange carrier or an interexchange carrier maintains the connection between the subscriber's computer and the ISP's POP. The transmission carrier bills the subscriber for the use of this connection in the same manner that it bills for telephone calls. The subscriber pays applicable state and local taxes on this connection charge.

Once connected to the POP, the subscriber is routed either through one or more telephone company central offices to the ISP's "Hub," which consists of high-speed data transmission equipment or to the ISP's Hub through a dedicated link. Once connected to the Hub, the subscriber may be routed through one or more telephone company central offices to the ISP's main operations center. All communications (i.e., transmission) charges incurred beyond the POP are paid by the ISP. The ISP pays applicable state and local taxes on these charges, which become a cost of doing business and may affect its pricing structure.

The ISP's main operations center verifies the subscriber's identification and password, whereupon the subscriber is routed back to the local POP and assigned an Internet Protocol Address. The subscriber may then be routed from the local POP through the Hub to a Network Access Point ("NAP") for access to the Internet. A NAP, operated by a transmission carrier, consists of an electronic interchange through which traffic is routed to final destinations.

Direct Connections The same steps apply, with some modifications, to a direct connection subscriber, which generally maintains a dedicated connection between its place of business and the ISP's POP. No authentication process is required of such a subscriber, whose dedicated connection can be established on either a "point-to-point" or a "frame-relay" basis.

A point-to-point subscriber leases both the connection from the subscriber's place of business to the telecommunications carrier and the connection from the carrier to the ISP's POP. The carrier bills the subscriber directly for its services plus any applicable state and local taxes, just as would be the case on any telephone bill. A frame-relay subscriber leases only the connection from its place of business to the telecommunications carrier, while the ISP leases the connection from the carrier to the POP. Here, again, the ISP pays applicable state and local taxes to the carrier.

Content Made Available by the ISP

The ISP's core business is that of providing Internet access to subscribers for a fee. In an effort to attract subscribers, ISPs frequently offer various other products and services, such as:

- Electronic mail ("E-mail")—This provides for the exchange of messages among individuals anywhere in the world via the Internet.
- Ability to create a custom Web site—Each of an ISP's subscribers can establish a Web site on the Internet by entering specific data into an electronic "template" provided by the ISP. The ISP's software uses this data to create the Web site. More sophisticated subscribers can use HTML to create Web sites without any ISP processing.
- 1-800 telephone services—These services are offered for two purposes: 1) to enable callers to speak with the ISP's customer service representatives regarding the ISP's products and services, and 2) to make the ISP's Internet access services available to those subscribers who are not located near a POP.
- Various Internet software tools—These are software programs that enhance the value of the ISP's services to the user. They may include e-mail manage-

ment software and filtering software that allows subscribers to control their children's access to inappropriate content on the Internet.

- Access to the WWW via search engines and browsers.

C. Economic Significance of the Industry

Internet and online services are experiencing rapid growth, but it is important to recognize that the Industry is still relatively young. The Internet and online services marketplace has enormous potential, but the current level of revenues is small both in absolute dollars and as compared to non-electronic sales of communication and information services.

1. Current Size of the Market

While potential use of the electronic marketplace is huge, actual usage of the Internet and online services is currently relatively limited. A recent survey of households in the United States and Canada revealed that only 17 percent of individuals over the age of 16 had used the Internet during the previous six months, 13 percent had used the World Wide Web, and only 14 percent of those users, or 1.8 percent of the total population had purchased anything over the Web.[16] Most Internet and online subscribers currently use the Internet principally to obtain e-mail capability and to browse information content.[17]

According to two industry research firms, SIMBA Information, Inc. and Jupiter Communications, estimated domestic revenues from Internet access and consumer online services ranged between $1.6 billion and $2.2 billion in 1995.[18] Revenue estimates for Internet access and consumer online services come from three sources: subscription revenues for Internet access, subscription revenues for consumer online services, and advertising revenues.

Revenues for Internet access services in 1995 totaled approximately $250 million in 1995.[19]

Revenue estimates for "online content packaging" in 1995 ranged from $1.2 to $1.8 billion.[20]

Content, which traditionally has been supported by subscription revenues from online services, is increasingly being supported by advertising revenues as more content moves to the World Wide Web. Ad spending on the World Wide Web and online services totaled $131 million during 1995.[21]

Despite all the attention Internet and online services have received, they still represent a small amount of revenue compared with revenue from communication services. The $1.6 to $2.2 billion of revenues from Internet and online services in 1995 represent only 0.8 percent of the $265 billion total communication revenues (including telephone, television and radio broadcasting, and cable and other pay-television services) in 1994.[22] Advertising revenues from the World Wide Web and online services represented approximately 0.3 percent of total spending on television, network, radio, newspaper and magazine advertising.[23]

The Internet and online equivalent of mail-order sales of tangible personal property in 1995 totaled approximately $500 million.[24] Online sales of tangible personal property involve the sales of such items as computer products, records, books, apparel, and gifts and flowers.[25] As a percent of traditional consumer mail-order sales, the $500 million of Internet and online sales of tangible personal property represent less than 0.4 percent of the $130 billion of consumer mail order sales in 1994.[26]

2. Projected Size of the Market

While today's market for Internet and online services is relatively small, the Industry is projected to grow rapidly during the next few years.

Estimates vary as to the extent to which revenues from Internet access and online services will grow by 2000. One major research company projects a total figure of $7 billion;[27] another projects $14 billion.[28] Projections also differ as to the mix of subscription and advertising revenues.

By 2000, the Internet and online equivalent of mail order sales of tangible personal property is projected to reach $6.6 billion.[29] This would be less than 5 percent of current consumer mail order sales, which constitute only 4 percent of retail sales and only 2 percent of consumer services.[30]

3. Effects on Tax Revenues

The growth of Internet and online services will generate new state tax revenues from expanded employment, higher corporate profits from business productivity improvements, and expanded use of telecommunication services. Internet and online services will become an increasingly important source of employment in individual states and localities. For example, Internet and online services-related employment in five of the seven Task Force members grew from approximately 3,500 employees in 1993 to approximately 9,500 employees in 1995. This represents an annual growth rate exceeding 60 percent. Growth of this type, which will generate both individual income and employment tax revenues, can be expected by states that attract businesses through Industry-friendly tax and business policies.

The growth of Internet and online services will affect other industries that are important to state and local governments and their revenues. For example, the growth of Internet and online services has contributed to a doubling of the growth rate in telephone access lines in recent years. Telephone access lines grew at a 4.6 percent annual growth rate in both 1994 and 1995, compared to only 2.3 percent in 1988 and 1989.[31] Since telephone access and usage is currently heavily taxed at the state and local level, this growth is already producing additional tax revenues for state and local governments.

In addition, the growth of Internet and online services will increase the productivity of many different businesses, making them more competitive in the global economy and expanding U.S. sales of new products and services. Increased profitability and investments as a result of the Internet and online industry will also increase state tax revenues.

States should be careful not to rush to tax the small, but growing, Industry before establishing rational and fair tax rules. The growth of the Industry will depend upon a reasonable tax regime that does not impose higher burdens on Internet and online services than on other types of services. The current usage level of Internet and online services does not justify state concern about lost revenue.

III. True Essence of the Industry

A. Use of Internet and Online Services by Mail-Order Sellers of Tangible Personal Property

Retailers who sell tangible personal property over the Internet and proprietary subscriber networks are similar to mail-order sellers who deliver their goods to identifiable addresses. This activity encompasses sales of mail-order-type items such as clothing and household goods ordered via an electronic catalog but delivered by traditional means such as the postal service or common carriers. For example, once online, a subscriber may purchase a T-shirt from a third-party seller. The T-shirt is then delivered to the subscriber via the United States Postal Service. This paper assumes that mail-order sellers:

- are simply users of the Internet and proprietary subscriber networks in marketing their wares over electronic facilities;
- are protected by traditional constitutional restraints upon the states;
- are subjected to traditional state use tax collection requirements; and
- bill their customers directly for items sold.

Some ISPs and OSPs may also make sales of tangible personal property via the Internet or proprietary subscriber networks. Any sale of tangible personal property by an ISP or OSP is separate and distinct from its sales of access services or content. The ISP or OSP makes a separate additional charge to its subscriber for these sales of tangible personal property.

B. Internet and Online Services Distinguished from Telecommunications Services

Some states are applying existing telecommunications taxes to Internet and online services. This amounts to trying to fit a square peg into a round hole. There are structural differences between the two kinds of services. One critical distinction is that the Internet and online service provider often does not know and cannot determine the point of origin or destination of the service being received by the end user. This makes it virtually impossible to apply a telecommunications tax that distinguishes, as it must, between interstate and intrastate transactions. What's more, Internet and online services are easily distinguished from telecommunication services based simply upon the fact that what most subscribers use the Internet for has nothing to do with telephony. Rather, most Internet subscribers use the Internet as a means of accessing information.

The Industry's position that Internet and online services are not telecommunications services is supported by definitions and determinations included in the federal Telecommunications Act of 1996 (1996 Act).[32] That Act defines the term "telecommunications service" as "the offering of telecommunications for a fee." It defines "telecommunications" as "the transmission [1] between or among points specified by the user, [2] of information of the user's choosing, [3] without change in the form or content of the information as sent and received." A service is a telecommunications service only if it meets all three separate requirements. Neither the Internet nor any online service does so, as we demonstrate below.[33]

1. Online Services

An online service fails all three of these tests for defining a telecommunications service.

An online service does not transmit information between or among points specified by the user. It permits the user to choose the location of the user's terminal or computer, but not the location from which the online service emanates. Online services operate on a client-server model, whereas telecommunication services operate on a peer-to-peer model.

An online service does not enable users to transmit information of their own choosing. Instead, its essence is the interactive storage, retrieval, and processing of information through electronic means. The fact that this is accomplished across a transmission link, usually a telephone line, does not transform the service into a telecommunications service.

Finally, the information provided by an online service is nearly always altered in some way during the delivery to the end user. For example, documents and files are stored in online databases in compressed form to make the best use of available storage space; they are expanded or decompressed when delivered to the user.

2. Internet Services

Internet access services fail to meet two of the three requirements of a telecommunications service. In this case as well, the provider does not deliver information between points of the user's choosing. Internet access services, like an online service, operate on a client-server model. The user may choose the client end of the communications path but has no choice about the server end. The user generally does not know or care about the geographic location of the host computer from which desired information emanates.

In addition, information transmitted between the Internet access provider and the user changes in form and content during the transfer. It is stored in as many different formats as there are kinds of computers.

3. Congressional Intent

The fact that Congress did not intend Internet and online services to be classified as telecommunications services is evidenced by the plain wording of the 1996 Act, which makes it clear that the services offered by Internet and online service providers are not telecommunications services. While the Act gives the Federal Communications Commission (FCC) authority to levy a surcharge on providers of telecommunications services only, the same provision authorizes the Commission to give the proceeds of these surcharges to providers of either telecommunications services or information services. If Congress had intended to authorize the Commission to impose a surcharge on providers of information services as well as on providers of telecommunications services, it would not have differentiated between the two in this manner. Texas has recently recognized the distinction, ruling that Internet access services are information services, not telecommunications services.[34]

The 1996 Act defines information service as the offering of a capability for generating, acquiring, storing, transforming, processing, retrieving, utilizing, or making available information via telecommunications. The protocol conversion capabilities of Internet and online access providers constitute such an information service in that they provide the means to process and transform information via telecommunications for use by the Internet. The other online functions provided by Internet and online service providers (e.g. bulletin boards and e-mail) offer the capability of generating, processing, storing, and retrieving information via telecommunications. Still other functions, such as news retrieval and stock quotations, offer the capability of acquiring, retrieving, utilizing or making available information via telecommunications.

Each state may have its own definition of an "information service," which may bear no relationship to the definition in the 1996 Act. However, Congress has acknowledged a difference between activities conducted by Internet and online service providers and activities which it has defined as telecommunications services. Most importantly, Congress has mandated that the two types of services receive different tax treatment. The states should follow suit.

4. Sound Public Policy

For the following reasons, sound public policy dictates that Internet and online services be outside the definition of telecommunications services.

First, imposing a telecommunications tax on these services would have the unfair effect of taxing them twice. Internet and online service providers use the facilities of telecommunications carriers to deliver their services; these carriers are generally already subject to the state's telecommunications tax and, therefore, will pass the tax along to the Internet and online service providers in some form.

Second, officials at all levels of the federal government, from the FCC Chairman to Members of Congress, to the Vice President and the President himself, have made plain their view that all governmental policy should be designed to facilitate the rapid growth of the Industry. Any unfair or unreasonable tax imposed at any level of the Industry's activities by any level of government would simply impede such growth.

Third, any decision that Internet and online services are telecommunications services would undermine the long-standing distinction made by the FCC between "basic services" (which were to be subject to regulation), and "enhanced services," (which were not to be subject to regulation).

This demarcation has several benefits. Foremost is the fact that it frees the more dynamic enhanced services field from any possible inhibitory effects of regulation, while at the same time it provides for continued public interest regulation of the basic communications services upon which our national telecommunications industry is founded. Internet and online access services are enhanced services under the basic/enhanced dichotomy.[35]

Furthermore, the 1996 Act charged the Federal Communications Commission Federal-State Joint Board on Universal Service to recommend a new set of universal service support mechanisms. Such mechanisms are to be explicit and sufficient to advance the universal service principles enumerated in the 1996 Act (e.g., to ensure quality telecommunications services at affordable rates to consumers, including low-income consumers, in all regions of the nation, including rural, insular, and high-cost areas). The Joint Board was to define the set of telecommunications services that should be supported by those mechanisms. In so doing, the Joint Board (which included 20 representatives from 13 states) determined "that the provision of Internet service does not meet the statutory definition of a 'telecommunications service.'"[36]

IV. Nexus (Taxing Jurisdiction)

A. Electronic Commerce and Nexus Considerations

In general "nexus" means "contact." For state tax purposes, "taxable nexus" means sufficient in-state contact to subject an out-of-state seller to the taxing jurisdiction of a state. In state tax circles, however, "nexus" is often used to mean "taxable nexus," and it will be so used here.

Both businesses and the states need meaningful, uniform nexus standards for the electronic marketplace. A well-structured, rational and uniform approach to nexus issues and state taxation affecting the various participants in electronic commerce is critical to all parties. Establishing such an approach now may well be the key to achieving the full commercial potential of the electronic marketplace.

There is no statutory authority and little case law that specifically addresses Industry nexus matters. There is, however, a well-developed body of nexus standards pertaining to out-of-state sellers of tangible personal property. The "substantial presence" standard recently established by the United States Supreme Court has equal applicability to sellers in the electronic marketplace.

The jurisdictional reach of the states for transaction tax purposes is limited by the Due Process and Commerce Clauses of the United States Constitution.[37] Only those businesses that have sufficient contact with a state may be subjected to such taxes by that state.

B. Constitutional Limitations

The determination of what is "sufficient" in-state contact to establish taxing jurisdiction depends primarily upon interpretation of the Due Process and Commerce Clauses of the United States Constitution. In its 1992 decision in Quill v. North Dakota, 504 U.S. 298, the United States Supreme Court set forth guidelines to be used in making such a determination.

1. Due Process Considerations

For all practical purposes, Quill eliminated the Due Process Clause as a protection against a state's taxing jurisdiction for any out-of-state seller who purposefully seeks to make sales into that state. The Court concluded that such activities, so long as they are more than minimal, afford fair warning that the state may tax the seller.[38] Furthermore, this holding is widely viewed as the Court's invitation to Congress to do something, under the authority of the Commerce Clause, to establish a rational approach to state taxation of interstate commerce. The Quill ruling reduced the Due Process threshold for nexus to such a de minimis level that the Clause now appears to provide little meaningful protection.

2. Commerce Clause Considerations

The Quill decision did provide protection on another basis, however, holding that, under the Commerce Clause, a state is prohibited from requiring an out-of-state seller of tangible personal property to collect and remit use tax applicable to its taxable sales unless it has a "substantial nexus" with the state. It ruled that the sending of mail-order catalogs into a state plus the ownership of four floppy disks of mail-order software there did not constitute such a contact. The Quill Court also rejected the state's arguments that an "economic presence" in the form of mere efforts by a remote seller to extract business from within the state constituted the "substantial nexus" required to subject the seller to the state's taxing jurisdiction.

In defining 'substantial nexus,' the Court adhered to the physical presence bright-line test contemplated in its 1967 decision in National Bellas Hess v. Illinois, 386 US 753, upon which the mail-order industry had been relying. It found such a test in the area of state sales and use taxation to be useful to encourage settled expectations and to protect interstate commerce against undue burdens.

The Quill decision provides absolute protection against a state's taxing jurisdiction for out-of-state sellers of tangible personal property if their in-state activities are limited to the making of sales by means of mail-order catalogs, by telephone, by Internet or by any combination thereof. This means that, if they have no substantial nexus in-state, they are not subject to the state's taxing jurisdiction.

C. A Physical Presence Standard Applied to Providers of Internet and Online Access Services Alone

An ISP's or OSP's physical presence in a state will often consist of nothing more than its POP or POPs, the means by which it provides local access to the Internet or to private networks, and a POP may consist of nothing more than a small computer or other piece of electronic equipment. The in-state presence of a POP or POPs appears to be a fragile basis upon which to assert taxing jurisdiction, as some states do. Such a contact does not constitute a *substantial* contact; rather, it constitutes only a "de minimis" contact, one that is too insubstantial to support taxing jurisdiction.

In any event, state taxing authorities should be wary of treating POPs as substantial contacts because such treatment may compel the Internet and online service provider to move its POPs from one state to another when feasible. The costs of such moves may impede the growth of the Industry. Furthermore, state reliance upon POPs for taxing jurisdiction may be comparable to constructing a tax system on quicksand in that the increasing use of satellite or other wireless technologies may eliminate any need for POPs. State tax policy should take into account the unique nature of the Industry, not only as it exists today but as it is evolving from minute to minute.

D. A Physical Presence Standard Applied to Internet and Online Service Providers Who Also Make Electronic Sales of Content

A seller's in-state selling activities can trigger nexus for all of its sales, even those to which the in-state activities do not pertain.[39] This could mean that any nexus triggered by a service provider's sales of services would extend to its sales of content. For example, a service provider may have an in-state substantial physical presence in the form of in-state sellers of its subscription services, causing it to be required to collect any applicable use tax on its sales of content, e.g., newspapers, books, music. In no event, however, should the nexus of the service provider constitute, in and of itself, nexus for third-party sellers of content from whom its subscribers make purchases and who themselves have no substantial nexus in the state.

E. A Physical Presence Standard Applied to Electronic Sales of Tangible Personal Property

For use tax collection purposes, traditional mail-order sellers of tangible personal property should benefit from the Quill physical presence standard when they sell over the Internet. As long as the vendor does not have a substantial physical presence in the destination state, its sales of goods and services do not trigger nexus there regardless of the mode of delivery.[40]

Under the physical presence standard, a vendor of tangible personal property over the Internet or a private online network has nexus in only those states where it has a substantial physical presence in the form of owned or rented real or tangible personal property and/or in which representatives, agents or employees act on its behalf. State taxing authorities have been applying alternative nexus theories to other types of remote sellers, and appear to be planning to do so to Internet and online sellers of tangible personal property. Thus, the states may present arguments that nexus over an out-of-state Internet/online vendor can be established through (1) the seller's affiliation with an in-state corporation or (2) an agency or representational relationship between the vendor and the Internet and online service provider.

1. Nexus Through Affiliation: Background

Nexus through affiliation is based upon an unsubstantiated belief that it is appropriate to attribute to the out-of-state seller the in-state contacts of its parent, subsidiary or brother-sister affiliate. Though several states have tried, no state has succeeded in establishing taxing jurisdiction over an out-of-state seller on the sole basis of a relationship with affiliates that themselves had a nexus in the state. These failures should reduce the likelihood that states will continue to pursue the affiliated nexus theory. Three typical cases are the following:

1. In SFA Folio Collections, Inc. v. Bannon, 217 Conn. 220, 585 A.2d 666 (1991), Connecticut's revenue department claimed that, primarily because Saks Fifth Avenue Stamford, Inc. (Saks-Stamford) had nexus in the state in the form of the stores that it operated there, its mail-order affiliate, SFA Folio Collections, Inc. (Folio), was required to collect use tax on its taxable sales into the state. The state relied solely upon the relationship rather than upon any proof that Saks Stamford was performing any in-state activities on behalf of Folio. The state's Supreme Court struck the effort down.[41]
2. In Current, Inc. v. [California] State Board of Equalization, (SBE), 29 Cal. Rptr. 2d 407 (1st Dist. 1994), the Board claimed that, because Deluxe Checkprinters, Inc. had a nexus in the state and because its wholly owned mail-order subsidiary, Current, Inc., sold many of the same items as its parent, the subsidiary was required to collect use tax on taxable sales into

the state. The California Court of Appeal ruled against SBE. Here the state relied solely upon the relationship rather than upon any proof that the parent was performing any in-state activities on behalf of the subsidiary.[42]

3. In SFA Folio Collections, Inc. (Folio) v. Tracy, 652 N.E.2d 693 (1995), the Ohio Department of Revenue similarly claimed that the out-of-state mail-order seller, Folio, must collect use tax on its taxable sales into the state solely by virtue of its relationship to an affiliate, Saks Fifth Avenue of Ohio, Inc. (Saks-Ohio) that operated stores in the state. In this case, the Department relied upon a statute specifying that a seller had taxable nexus if it "Maintains a place of business within this state . . . operated by . . . a member of an affiliated group . . . of which the seller is a member . . . ." The state's Supreme Court ruled that the Department's interpretation of the statute was erroneous and that Folio did not have taxable nexus in the state.

2. Nexus Through Agents, Representatives, or Independent Contractors: Background

In general, nexus will be created for an out-of-state vendor by activities engaged in on the vendor's behalf by parties who qualify as agents in the traditional sense, i.e., acting under the direction of, operating on behalf of, and carrying the authority of the "principal"/vendor. In some instances, the U.S. Supreme Court has stretched this agency concept for tax purposes to sweep in "sales representatives" and "independent contractors" whose in-state activities are performed for the benefit of the vendor with its knowledge but not necessarily under its direction and not necessarily with any particular *agency* authority from the vendor in the traditional sense.[43] The law is unclear as to whether such activities must be sales activities in order to trigger nexus.[44] It is certainly clear, however, that the absence of any agents, representatives, independent contractors or other substantial physical presence immunizes a seller against a state's taxing jurisdiction.

F. Possible State Positions and Likely Results Regarding Nexus Based upon Agency and Affiliation

One or more states may present an argument that:

1. Third-party sellers of tangible personal property and/or content into a state via an electronic service will be subject to the use tax collection requirements of the state if the ISP or OSP has a substantial physical presence in the state.

   The states' reasoning will be that the service provider is a representative of the seller. This is a weak argument. It is based upon the contention that the presence of the service provider's POP has a different tax consequence than does the presence of the telecommunications facilities over which mail-order sellers have traditionally enjoyed tax immunity while selling into a state.[45]

As noted earlier, ISPs and OSPs enable subscribers to access the Internet or private network. After gaining access, the subscriber may visit any of a myriad of electronic stores, information services, or vendors. The Internet and online service provider does not control the "online" movements of the subscriber and generally has no way of identifying or tracking the subscriber's online purchases, especially when the subscriber makes such purchases while on the Internet.

Gaining Internet and online access and acquiring content or tangible personal property from a third-party vendor are separate and distinct transactions. Making sales over the facilities of a telephone company that is subject to a state's taxing jurisdiction does not trigger nexus for the out-of-state vendor; making sales over the facilities of a similarly situated Internet and online service provider should not do so either.[46]

2. An ISP or OSP should be liable for collection of use taxes attributable to third-party vendors' sales of content and/or tangible personal property to subscribers.

   This possibility is not based upon the reality of the world of state taxation, and there is no law to support it. The service provider is merely an intermediary between the third-party vendor and the subscriber. Under the current status of the law, the seller is responsible for collecting tax for any state in which it has nexus, and intermediary common carriers (e.g., railroads, trucking companies, or delivery companies, such as United Parcel Service, Federal Express, or the U.S. Postal Service) that deliver the goods for the seller cannot be held responsible for any tax with respect to the transaction of sale between buyer and seller.

G. A Physical Presence Standard Applied to Third-Party Content Providers

States may argue that, for use tax collection purposes, third-party content providers do not qualify for the same protection as sellers of tangible personal property. This position would be based upon the contention that, since the Quill decision deals specifically with sales of tangible personal property, it does not offer a safe harbor for sales of products or services delivered electronically.[47] The states may also argue that Quill affords no Commerce Clause protection against taxes of any type other than sales and use taxes. Indeed, the South Carolina Supreme Court agreed with such a narrow interpretation of Quill. As we shall establish below, however, such arguments rely upon an economic presence theory that has no merit.

H. Nexus Based on Economic Presence

The states can be expected to renew the "economic presence" argument that was made in Quill. The argument is that an out-of-state seller's direction of regular and systematic sales solicitation efforts toward a state constitutes a substantial nexus with the state, thereby subjecting the seller to the use tax collection requirements of the state. The U.S. Supreme Court rejected the argument in Quill, refusing to repudiate its rejection of a substantially similar contention twenty-five years earlier in National Bellas Hess, Inc. v. Department of Revenue of Illinois.[48] Although attempts may be made to limit the purview of Quill to mail-order sales of tangible personal property, its protection should apply equally to sales of services and content over the Internet.

V. Situsing Sales

The Supreme Court has established a practical method of determining the tax situs of telecommunications services for transaction tax purposes. In Goldberg v. Sweet,[49] it approved use of the consumer's service address to situs receipts from a telephone call, assuming that either the origin or destination of the call takes places within the state.[50] One should not jump to the conclusion that such an approach could be applied to the Industry's sales of subscription services or content without significant modification. The reason is that determining the origin or destination of such transactions is generally not possible since the geographical locations of buyer and seller (subscriber and service provider) are irrelevant in the Internet and online service provider's business model. Nevertheless, a practical agreement between the Industry and the states to rely upon the subscriber's billing address as the equivalent of the service address in determining the situs of a sale could solve most problems in this area.

VI. Issues at Hand

A. Industry Expertise

The Task Force believes that success in making tax sense out of the Industry's activities depends upon the policymakers' attainment of a certain level of electronic marketplace expertise. The Industry believes that now is the time for it to help in this regard, since no significant exodus of commerce away from local retailers to the electronic marketplace has yet taken place. There is time, therefore, for policymakers to look before they leap, to become sophisticated about the Industry, and to accomplish state purposes rationally and constructively without hindering the Industry's potential for rapid development.

B. Nexus Limitations

State and local tax authorities worry that existing limitations on their jurisdictional reach will result in a significant reduction in their tax bases as more and more consumers purchase goods and services in the electronic marketplace. Such a concern on the part of the states is misplaced. Electronic commerce will not erode a state's existing tax base; it is similar to mail order commerce in that it simply allows the state to tax only those transactions that they are entitled to tax.

The earlier nexus discussion highlights the fact that remote sellers of tangible personal property into a state via the Internet or private network are beyond the jurisdictional reach of the state. This is as it should be. Tax authorities should accept the fact that remote sellers of tangible personal property selling online are functionally equivalent to remote mail-order vendors. Remote online vendors should be afforded the same nexus protection as offline vendors.

C. Consistent Definitions

Many states are already attempting to impose their existing transaction taxes on the Industry. In doing so, these states are defining Internet and online services inconsistently and are finding that Internet and online services cannot easily be categorized under existing definitions. And the Industry is finding that, as the states continue to try to shoehorn Internet and online services into existing definitions of taxable services, the result is an application of tax that is inconsistent, confusing and unfair.

Inconsistency among the states in defining and applying terms defeats the possibility of achieving uniform, fair and efficient administration of any tax. Cooperative efforts between the Industry and the states must, therefore, concentrate on creating one set of definitions for states to adopt, and those definitions must be interpreted consistently from state to state.

Further, it is imperative that those definitions clearly and accurately describe the Industry and be easily applied to it. A principal concern of the Task Force is that arbitrary or inaccurate tax distinctions will be drawn between the various components of the Industry; for example, that the taxable nature of an Internet or online service will depend upon whether it is purely an access service, or access is *bundled* with other services such as a browser or electronic mail capabilities.

It is not very useful to create definitions for the access versus content provided by an ISP or OSP and then attempt to *carve out* different tax treatment for each. Today, very few, if any, ISPs sell only access to the Internet. Competition in the marketplace has forced most, if not all, ISPs to bundle access services with some amount of content (e.g., a news service). Likewise, access to a proprietary subscriber network, the Internet, and content are all made available by OSPs to their subscribers for a bundled price.

Bundling of access services and content for a single subscription fee also fosters use of Internet and online services in that less sophisticated subscribers are not overwhelmed by being forced to make many decisions from an "a la carte" menu of separately priced services each time the subscriber attempts to access the online service. Absent full exemption from tax for Internet and online services, the Industry and the states must work together to create useful definitions which accurately describe the Industry and which can be applied consistently from state to state.

D. Compliance

Absent a rational, uniform taxing scheme which is appropriate for the Industry, the states will continue to face formidable impediments to identifying and locating providers and receivers of services and content, establishing taxing jurisdiction over these parties, and collecting applicable tax.

E. Local Taxes

The Industry is concerned about the mind-boggling problems presented by local taxation in the form of many different taxes, business licenses and fees[51] imposed by thousands of taxing jurisdictions.[52]

The administrative and compliance burdens associated with local-level taxes are extraordinarily cumbersome for even a well-established, traditional business to manage. Having to comply with a myriad of city, county, transit district, and other local taxes, and cope with inconsistent and disparate rules regarding the taxability of various transactions and the geographic incidence of tax could jeopardize development of the electronic marketplace more than any other requirement. The cost and inconvenience of contending with even the threat of inappropriate local taxation cannot be justified. With input from the Industry, the administration of local taxes must be simplified.

F. Clear Policy

Because the Industry has evolved rapidly in the marketplace, because state legislatures often do not respond quickly to new tax challenges, because state taxing authorities are saddled with trying to fit existing tax laws to changing situations, and because each state faces each challenge within the parameters of its own requirements as opposed to the overall requirements of states as a group, there is no clear or uniform policy as to how the Industry will or should be taxed among the states. Several states have begun to review the issue. The Task Force appreciates the time and effort some states are devoting to identifying and resolving the taxation issues facing the Industry. The Task Force believes that the states and the Industry, working together, will benefit from a review of Industry-related issues and that such cooperation between the parties will result in a rational tax policy for the Industry.

G. Lack of Uniformity among States

As previously noted, several states are currently asserting that Internet and online service providers are subject to various of their state and local transaction taxes. Uniformity among the states imposing such taxes is scarce. This disparity among the states in their treatment of identical or similar services represents a significant impediment to the development of the Industry due to the following:

Pyramiding of Taxes

Pyramiding of taxes, i.e., the charging of *tax on tax* occurs when a purchaser, e.g. an Internet and online service provider, is required to pay one type of tax on a purchase (e.g., of telecommunications carrier services) and another tax (e.g., a sales tax) on a subscription fee that includes the tax paid earlier.

Multiple Taxation

Multiple taxation involves subjecting the same transaction to more than one tax, e.g., a state's application of two different taxes to the same transaction or two states' application of their similar taxes to the same transaction. The absence of established situs rules regarding the taxation of transactions occurring via the Internet or a private network (such as those rules governing the situs of traditional offline sales of tangible personal property) creates such a possibility. This is simply unacceptable to the Industry. It is, therefore, essential that, as suggested above, a practical agreement between the Industry and the states be reached wherein Industry members may rely upon a subscriber's billing address in determining the situs of a sale.

VII. Conclusion and Recommendations

The Industry offers the states an opportunity to establish a tax scheme uniquely fitted to the Industry. That scheme should be characterized by uniformity, clarity, fairness, ease of compliance and ease of administration. It should contemplate appropriate exemptions to preclude multiple taxation and tax pyramiding. It should also provide certainty as to when and whether any tax applies, who should pay it, who must collect it, how it should be collected, and what state is entitled to it.

The nature of the Industry's activities poses serious tax administration problems for the states and comparably difficult compliance problems for the Industry. Only by working together can the entities hope to establish an appropriate atmosphere in which their respective interests are protected. For the states, that interest is to protect revenues; for the Industry, it is to enable the Internet to grow, to flourish and to achieve its full potential as a new medium. Before imposing or determining the rate of any transaction taxes on Internet and online services, states should consider the beneficial impact that the increased productivity spurred by Internet and online usage will have on income tax revenues.

The sponsors of the White Paper want to make their position very clear, to wit: the growth of Internet access and online services should not be impeded either by expansive interpretation of existing tax laws or the imposition of new taxes on the Industry. However, if states do impose taxes on Internet and online services, they should:

- adopt uniform definitions among the states;
- establish a single rate, within each state, of any applicable tax;
- recognize the fact that the only type of tax that can be applied effectively to purchases made over the Internet or proprietary subscriber networks will be a tax on the purchaser with respect to the purchase transaction itself;
- attribute, to the extent possible, receipts from the sale of Internet and online services to the state into which the sales are billed; and
- rethink nexus standards insofar as they apply to the Internet and Internet-based transactions.

The Industry urges policymakers to move quickly to become fully acquainted with the Industry in order to avoid premature actions that could jeopardize its future. Cooperative efforts between the states and the Industry can result in a proper approach to problems associated with the Industry, thereby protecting the best interests of both the states and the Industry. Time is of the essence. The line of communication is open.

Notes

1. This Executive Summary is copyrighted by the Interactive Services Association and its state online taxation white paper taskforce. With proper attribution, it may be quoted or reprinted. Companies having representatives on the Task Force include America Online, Inc., AT&T, CompuServe Inc., GE Information Services, Inc., IBM, Microsoft Corporation, and NETCOM On-Line Communication Services, Inc.
2. For purposes of this paper, the term "proprietary subscriber network" refers to networks that are proprietarily or corporately owned but which make their services available to the public for fees. Private or intracompany networks, sometimes called "intranets," are outside the scope of the White Paper.
3. The White Paper explores the question of whether a Point of Presence (POP) in the form of readily movable equipment (e.g., a computer, modem or router) subjects a remote ISP or OSP to the taxing jurisdiction of a state for transaction tax purposes. The White Paper does not address the question of whether a POP subjects a remote ISP or OSP to the taxing jurisdiction of a state for income tax purposes or a local taxing jurisdiction for property tax purposes.
4. The focus, recommendations and conclusions of the White Paper pertain only to transaction-type taxes. Such taxes are typically viewed as being a cost of doing business that is passed on to the ultimate consumer. It is not the intent of this paper to suggest that the Industry itself should be exempted from taxation. The fact is that all members of the Industry are already subjected to a myriad of state and local taxes, including income, franchise, property, payroll, and business license taxes.

5. This white paper (hereinafter "the White Paper") is copyrighted by the Interactive Services Association ("ISA") and its state online taxation white paper task force. With proper attribution, it may be quoted and reprinted. Companies having representatives on the Task Force include America Online, Inc., AT&T, CompuServe Inc., GE Information Services, Inc., IBM, Microsoft Corporation, and NETCOM On-Line Communication Services, Inc. The White Paper was prepared by Ernst & Young, LLP on behalf of and in conjunction with the Task Force.
6. For purposes of this paper, the term "proprietary subscriber network" refers to networks that are proprietarily or corporately owned but which make their services available to the public for fees. Private or intracompany networks, sometimes called "intranets," are outside the scope of the White Paper.
7. See Quill v. North Dakota, 504 U.S. 298 (1992).
8. Some observers contend that state and local taxation issues faced by the Industry are not unlike those faced by the Cellular telephone industry at its inception. That view is inaccurate for at least two reasons. First, though a new technology was being employed, wireless cellular services were substantially similar to existing wireline telephone services. By way of contrast, Internet and online services utilize both existing and new technologies to provide unique services. Second, although wireless technology presented new challenges to the geographical sourcing of receipts for tax purposes, the fact that the Cellular industry maintained geographical data made it possible for the Cellular industry and the states to agree informally upon a rational attribution method. Internet and online services are designed to operate without regard to geographical boundaries. The Industry seeks to work with the states in identifying an appropriate approach for situsing Industry sales.
9. For excellent reviews of the Industry and of Industry-related activities, see Sections 2 and 3 of "Selected Tax Policy Implications of Global Electronic Commerce," Office of Tax Policy, Department of the Treasury (November 1996), and "The Nature of Cyberspace" in the findings of fact in the decision of the U.S. District Court Eastern District of PA, in ACLU v. Janet Reno, No. 96-963, 6/11/96.
10. A network consists of two or more computers that communicate with each other by means of telephone lines, satellite links or other technologies. The networks that comprise the Internet are themselves owned and operated by individual organizations that "are administratively independent from one another. There is no central, worldwide, technical control point. Yet, working together, these organizations have created what to a user seems to be a virtual network that spans the globe." M. Meeker & C. Depuy, The Internet Report 1-9 (1996).
11. See Wessells, Arnold & Henderson, Industry Report, "Internet Opportunities: Access, Service and Content"; May, 1995.

12. Technically, the WWW is a subset of Internet servers that support the HyperText Transfer Protocol (HTTP), which is the set of rules that is generally adopted by participating networks to control the transfer of most documents traveling over the Web.
13. For example, the ISA's home page (http://www.isa.net) provides information about the organization, as well as links to the home pages of its members and other related information.
14. There are, nevertheless, differences between ISPs and OSPs that are not addressed here.
15. Occasionally, an ISP will rely upon another ISP's POPs in providing its service.
16. See CommerceNet/Nielsen Media Research Recontact Study, published August 13, 1996.
17. See USA Today, October 9, 1996.
18. SIMBA Information, Inc., "Online Services: 1996 Review Trends and Forecast" and additional telephone conversations, and Jupiter Communications, Inc., www.jup.com.
19. Ibid.
20. Ibid.
21. SIMBA Information, Inc., "Online Services: 1996 Review Trends and Forecast" and unpublished information.
22. U.S. Department of Commerce, Bureau of the Census, Annual Survey of Communication Services: 1994.
23. Advertising Age, Sept. 2, 1996.
24. SIMBA Information, Inc. and Forrester Research, Inc.
25. Forrester Research, Inc.
26. Direct Marketing Association, 1996 Statistical Fact Book.
27. SIMBA Information, Inc.
28. Jupiter Communications.
29. Forrester Research, Inc.
30. Direct Marketing Association, 1996 Statistical Fact Book. Consumer services include financial, legal, tax return, etc. services.
31. U.S. Telephone Association's "1996 Statistics of the Local Exchange Carriers."
32. 1996 Act, Pub. L. No. 104-104, 110 Stat. 56. The 1996 Act amends the Communications Act of 1934, 47 U.S.C. §§ 151 et. seq.
33. This section briefly sets forth the ISA's position concerning the distinction between telecommunications services, on the one hand, and Internet and

online services, on the other. For a full discussion of this matter, see Comments of the Interactive Services Association before the Federal Communications Commission Federal-State Joint Board on Universal Service, April 12, 1996; CC Docket No. 96-45.

34. See the September 1996 issue of "Sales Tax Update," by John Sharp, Texas Comptroller of Public Accounts.

35. The FCC adopted a regulatory scheme under the Communications Act of 1934, as amended, that distinguishes between the common carrier offering of basic transmission services and the provision of enhanced services. This scheme is embodied in Section 64.702 of the Commission's Rules, 47 CFR Section 64.702. Specifically, "the term enhanced services shall refer to services, offered over common carrier transmission facilities used in interstate communications, which employ computer processing applications that act on the format, content, code, protocol or similar aspects of the subscriber's transmitted information; provide the subscriber additional, different, or restructured information; or involve subscriber interaction with stored information." Enhanced services are not regulated under Title II of the Act.

    Basic services, on the other hand, are defined as the common carrier offering of transmission capacity for the movement of information. Basic services are regulated under Title II of the Communications Act of 1934.

36. In the Matter of Federal-State Joint Board on Universal Service, CC Docket No. 96-45, FCC 96J-3, (November 8, 1996), Section IV.C.3. paragraph 69.

37. A federal statute, Public Law 86-272, further limits the reach of the states with respect to taxes based upon corporate net income of sellers of tangible personal property. This White Paper does not address matters pertaining to income taxing jurisdiction.

38. In Bensusan Restaurant Corp. v. King, 96 Civ 3992 (S.D.N.Y., 9/9/96), an owner placed an advertisement for his Missouri jazz club, The Blue Note, on an Internet Web site located on a server in Missouri. The owner of a New York establishment that was also called The Blue Note sued in a federal district court in New York to stop the Missouri owner from using the same name. But that court held that the Missouri owner was not subject to the personal jurisdiction of New York. The Court said that the placing of the advertisement on the Web site did not rise to the level of the minimal connection required by the Due Process Clause as a prerequisite to his being subject to New York's jurisdiction, and that this was true even though the advertisement was accessible by residents of New York. Although the case involved personal jurisdiction rather than taxing jurisdiction, the same analysis of the Due Process Clause applies to both. The Court distinguished this case from CompuServe Inc. v. Patterson, 89 F.3d 1257 (6th Cir., 7/22/96; rehrg. denied 9/19/96). There, another federal court held that a Texas attorney's contacts with Ohio,

which were almost entirely electronic in nature, did rise to the level of the minimal connection required by the Due Process Clause to establish personal jurisdiction over him. That court found that the attorney had entered into a written contract with CompuServe under which he marketed his computer software product in other states, sending it regularly to CompuServe's Ohio system and using CompuServe's Ohio facility as his distribution center, thereby purposefully availing himself of the privilege of doing business in Ohio. [The contract provided for the application of Ohio law.] The Court specified that it was not holding that the attorney would, by virtue of his use of CompuServe's services, be subject to suit in any state where his software was purchased or used, that question not being before the Court.

In other cases involving personal jurisdiction, two different federal district courts held that foreign corporations were subject to the jurisdiction of states in which their sole contacts were through the Internet. In Inset Systems, Inc. v. Instruction Set, Inc., 95 Civ 1314 (D.C. Connecticut 4/17/96) and Maritz, Inc. v. Cybergold, Inc., 96 Civ 1340 (S.D.C. Missouri 8/19/96), the Courts concluded that the plaintiffs purposefully directed their advertising efforts toward the states, via the Internet, for the purpose of doing business within the states, thereby subjecting themselves to the states' jurisdiction. The Cybergold Court cited both Inset and CompuServe approvingly.

See National Geographic Society v. California Board of Equalization, 430 U.S. 551 (1977), in which the activity of Society employees operating out of in-state offices to make nontaxable sales of advertising triggered a nexus that resulted in the Society's being required to collect and to remit to the State of California use tax applicable to the Society's mail-order sales of tangible personal property into the state. Nonetheless, a New York State Administrative Law Judge has recently held that the in-state activities of independent advertising agents who had their own offices in the state did not constitute nexus for the seller even though the seller's employees made some 20 non-sales trips into the state during the audit period. Matter of NADA Services Corp., Administrative Law Judge, February 1, 1996. Whether this constitutes a correct interpretation of the National Geographic decision is open to question.

39. An exception to this general statement: Delivery in the vendor's own vehicles has been held to constitute such a physical presence for use tax collection purposes by the supreme courts of several states. See Brown's Furniture, Inc. v. Dir. of Revenue, Supreme Court of Ill., 171 ILL2D 410, cert. denied, U.S. Sup. Ct., Dkt. No. 96-94, 10/7/96; Good's Furniture House, Inc. v. Iowa State Board of Review, Iowa Supreme Court, No. 85-827, 2/19/86; and In the Matter of State Sales Tax Liability of Webber Furniture, South Dakota Supreme Court, 4/9/80. The United States Supreme Court laid the groundwork for such decisions in Miller Brothers Co. v. Maryland, 347 U.S. 340 (1953), when it ruled that the state did not have taxing jurisdiction because,

among other things, in-state deliveries using the seller's vehicles were only occasional in nature.

40. In an earlier decision involving a substantially similar factual situation, Bloomingdale's By Mail, Ltd. v. Commonwealth Department of Revenue, 567 A2d 773 (1989), the Pennsylvania Department of Revenue had based its nexus claim on an agency relationship between the affiliates rather than upon their being members of the same affiliated group. The state's highest court found that the Department had not proven the existence of such a relationship and that nexus did not, therefore, exist on the part of the out-of-state seller.
41. The Board had also relied upon a statutory provision, Revenue & Taxation Code Section 6203(g) that defined "Retailer doing business in this state" to mean and include "Any retailer owned or controlled by the same interests which own or control any retailer engaged in business in the same or a similar line of business in this state." The Court ducked the issue by ruling that the two corporations were engaged in "substantially dissimilar" activities. Nevertheless, the 1995 legislature repealed the provision effective 1/1/96.
42. See Scripto v. Carson, 362 US 207 (1960), in which the activities of independent contractors triggered nexus, and Tyler Pipe Industries, Inc. v. Washington Department of Revenue, 438 US 232 (1987), in which the court agreed with the conclusion that a "showing of sufficient nexus could not be defeated by the argument that the taxpayer's representative was properly characterized as an independent contractor instead of as an agent."
43. See Multistate Tax Commission Nexus Program Bulletin 95-1 and commentary thereon, e.g. COST's statement opposing adoption of the Bulletin (See State Tax Notes, March 25, 1996, p. 973) and "MTC Nexus Bulletin 95-1 Goes Beyond Existing Law," State Tax Notes, April 15, 1996, p. 1168, wherein extensive reference is made to Standard Pressed Steel Co. v. Department of Revenue, 419 U.S. 560 (1975), Tyler Pipe, supra, and Scripto, supra.
44. See Quill, supra.
45. California businesses were so concerned about the danger of such a potential state position that they successfully sought protective legislation in 1994. Section 6203(j) of the California Sales and Use Tax Law now provides that "For purposes of this section, 'engaged in business in this state' does not include the taking of orders from customers in this state through a computer telecommunications network located in this state which is not directly or indirectly owned by the retailer when the orders result from the electronic display of products on that same network. The exclusion provided by this subdivision shall apply only to a computer telecommunications network that consists substantially of on-line communications services other than the displaying and taking of orders for products." This provision became effective January 1, 1995 and will expire December 31, 1999 unless legislatively extended.

46. Their delivery of content over the Internet or a private online network is analogous to delivery via common carriers, such as the United States Post Office, UPS or Federal Express and should not trigger nexus.
47. 386 U.S. 753 (1967).
48. See, for example, Geoffrey v. South Carolina, 437 S.E.2d.13 (9/22/93), in which the South Carolina Supreme Court ruled that an out-of-state subsidiary had nexus in the state in the form of intangible trademarks and trade names that were licensed to its in-state parent as well as in the form of in-state accounts receivable and so was subject to the taxing jurisdiction of the state. That case involved only income tax jurisdiction, however, and is highly suspect even though the U.S. Supreme Court refused to review it. Its rationale was specifically rejected by an Administrative Law Judge in Cerro Copper Products, Inc. v. State of Alabama Department of Revenue, DOR ALJ Div., No. F. 94-444, 12/11/95.
49. 488 US 252 (1989).
50. A credit provision protected the taxpayer, in that case, against multiple taxation. The decision has no value for purposes of determining nexus since nexus was acknowledged by the taxpayer in the case. The discussion here has validity only in instances in which the remote seller is subject to the state's taxing jurisdiction.
51. Business licenses and fees are included here because many of them have the same effect as taxes.
52. According to Taxware International, Inc. there are more than 6,000 taxing locations and 65,000 potential tax jurisdiction combinations in North America. See Taxware International, Inc. www.taxware.com.

INDEX

A

B

C

D

E

G

J

N

O

U

READ THE TERMS AND CONDITIONS OF THIS LICENSE AGREEMENT CAREFULLY BEFORE INSTALLING THE SOFTWARE (THE "PROGRAM") TO ACCOMPANY *INTERNATIONAL TAX HAVENS* (THE "BOOK"). THE PROGRAM IS COPYRIGHTED AND LICENSED (NOT SOLD). BY INSTALLING THE PROGRAM, YOU ARE ACCEPTING AND AGREEING TO THE TERMS OF THIS LICENSE AGREEMENT. IF YOU ARE NOT WILLING TO BE BOUND BY THE TERMS OF THIS LICENSE AGREEMENT, YOU SHOULD PROMPTLY RETURN THE PACKAGE IN RESELLABLE CONDITION AND YOU WILL RECEIVE A REFUND OF YOUR MONEY. THIS LICENSE AGREEMENT REPRESENTS THE ENTIRE AGREEMENT CONCERNING THE PROGRAM BETWEEN YOU AND HARCOURT BRACE & COMPANY (REFERRED TO AS "LICENSOR"), AND IT SUPERSEDES ANY PRIOR PROPOSAL, REPRESENTATION, OR UNDERSTANDING BETWEEN THE PARTIES.

1. License Grant. Licensor hereby grants to you, and you accept, a nonexclusive license to use the Program CD-ROM and the computer programs contained therein in machine-readable, object code form only (collectively referred to as the "Software"), and the accompanying User Documentation, only as authorized in this License Agreement. The Software may be used only on a single computer owned, leased, or otherwise controlled by you; or in the event of the inoperability of that computer, on a backup computer selected by you. Neither concurrent use on two or more computers nor use in a local area network or other network is permitted without separate authorization and the possible payment of other license fees. You agree that you will not assign, sublease, transfer, pledge, lease, rent, or share your rights under the License Agreement. You agree that you may not reverse engineer, decompile dissemble, or otherwise adapt, modify, or translate the Software.

Upon loading the Software into your computer, you may retain the Program CD-ROM for backup purposes. In addition, you may make one copy of the Software on a set of diskettes (or other storage medium) for the purpose of backup in the event the Program Diskettes are damaged or destroyed. You may make one copy of any additional User Documentation (such as the README.TXT file or the "About the CD-ROM" section of the Book) for backup purposes. Any such copies of the Software or the User Documentation shall include Licensor's copyright and other proprietary notices. Except as authorized under this paragraph, no copies of the program or any portions thereof may be made by you or any person under your authority or control.

2. Licensor's Rights. You acknowledge and agree that the Software and the User Documentation are proprietary products of Licensor protected under U.S. copyright law. You further acknowledge and agree that all right, title, and interest in and to the Program, including associated intellectual property rights, are and shall remain with Licensor. This License Agreement does not convey to you an interest in or to the Program, including associated intellectual property rights, are and shall remain with Licensor. This License Agreement does not convey to you an interest in or to the Program, but only a limited right of use revocable in accordance with the terms of the License Agreement.

3. License Fees. The license fees paid by you are paid in consideration of the licenses granted under this License Agreement.

4. Term. This License Agreement is effective upon your installing this software and shall continue until terminated. You may terminate this License Agreement at any time by returning the Program and all copies thereof and extracts therefrom to Licensor. Licensor may terminate this License Agreement upon the breach by you of any term hereof. Upon such termination by Licensor, you agree to return to Licensor the Program and all copies and portions thereof.

5. Limited Warranty. Licensor warrants, for our benefit alone, for a period of 90 days from the date of commencement of this License Agreement (referred to as the "Warranty Period") that the Program CD-ROM in which the Software is contained is free from defects in material and workmanship. If during the Warranty Period, a defect appears in the Program diskettes, you may return the Program to Licensor for either replacement or, at Licensor's option, refund of amounts paid by you under this License Agreement. You agree that the foregoing constitutes your sole and exclusive remedy for breach by Licensor of any warranties made under this Agreement. EXCEPT FOR THE WARRANTIES SET FORTH ABOVE, THE PROGRAM, AND THE SOFTWARE CONTAINED THEREIN, ARE LICENSED "AS IS," AND LICENSOR DISCLAIMS ANY AND ALL OTHER WARRANTIES, WHETHER EXPRESS OR IMPLIED, INCLUDING, WITHOUT LIMITATION, ANY IMPLIED WARRANTIES OF MERCHANTABILITY OR FITNESS FOR A PARTICULAR PURPOSE.

6. Limitation of Liability. Licensor's cumulative liability to you or any other party for any loss or damages resulting from any claims, demands, or actions arising out of or relating to this Agreement shall not exceed the license free paid to Licensor for the use of the Program. IN NO EVENT SHALL LICENSOR BE LIABLE FOR ANY INDIRECT, INCIDENTAL, CONSEQUENTIAL, SPECIAL, OR EXEMPLARY DAMAGES (INCLUDING, BUT NOT LIMITED TO, LOSS OF DATA, BUSINESS INTERRUPTION, OR LOST PROFITS) EVEN IF LICENSOR HAS BEEN ADVISED OF THE POSSIBILITY OF SUCH DAMAGES.

7. Miscellaneous. This License Agreement shall be construed and governed in accordance with the laws of the State of California. Should any term of this License Agreement be declared void or unenforceable by any court of competent jurisdiction, such declaration shall have no effect on the remaining terms hereof. The failure of either party to enforce any rights granted hereunder or to take action against the other party in the event of any breach hereunder shall not be deemed a waiver by that party as to subsequent enforcement of rights or subsequent actions in the event of future breaches.

ISBN 0-15-607007-3
59999
9 780156 070072